Our Lord of The Gospels

Our Lord
of
The Gospels

A HARMONY OF THE GOSPELS

Being a life of Jesus Christ while he dwelt upon the earth in mortality and in the days immediately following his resurrection, as recorded in the Sacred Autographs, as they have come down to us, and in the Book of Mormon—chronologically arranged.

KING JAMES VERSION

(VARIORUM TEXT)

BY

J. REUBEN CLARK, JR.

"Who also hath made us able ministers of the new testament; not of the letter, but of the spirit: for the letter killeth, but the spirit giveth life."—(II Corinthians 3:6.)

DESERET BOOK COMPANY
Salt Lake City, Utah
1974

Fourth Printing
1974

Preface

For this book, I alone am responsible. It is not a Church publication.

Many years ago I became convinced that no life of Jesus the Christ in Palestine had been or could be written that would equal the account contained in the Gospels. Geographical and other like details, more or less accurate, may be added, but beyond that the record must stand as to the incidents and the teachings of the Christ while he was mortal in Palestine, as we find it in the Gospels, supplemented by the other books of the New Testament.

For the record of Christ's works and teachings in America, before and after his birth, and, later after his resurrection, we must look to the Book of Mormon, principally the Book of 3 Nephi, — sometimes by us affectionately and reverently spoken of as the Fifth Gospel.

Years ago I began something of a study of a chronological arrangement of the account of the ministry of Jesus in Palestine,—a *harmony*, as it is called, as recorded in the four Gospels. I have worked at the arrangement off and on, mostly off, since that time, coming back to it at long intervals and then working upon it for short periods.

There have been many such *harmonies* framed by scholars, beginning with Tatian (150-175 A. D.) and coming to the present. Some of them have seemingly been attempts at *doctrinal* harmonies. One of the chronological (not doctrinal) harmonies most esteemed by scholars is that of Edward Robinson, first prepared in Greek and later in English. (It seems to be the basis of the harmony of the Gospels found in the various editions of the Variorum Bible.)

In arranging the harmony printed herein, I have used Edward Robinson (Union Theological Seminary), Samuel J. Andrews (Irvingite), George W. Clark (Baptist), William Arnold Stevens and Ernest DeWitt Burton (Baptists), John A. Broadus (American Baptist), and Archibald T. Robertson (Baptist). There are others to be found in students' and teachers' Bibles.

As will be seen from Division Two,—"A Digest of the Gospel Records, Chronologically Arranged," I have grouped the incidents of the Savior's life into eight periods based primarily upon the different missionary activities of his life, plus his pre-missionary activities. This arrangement assumes that his missionary labors in Palestine covered approximately three years.

I have arranged the incidents in a chronological order that seemed generally to represent the majority view of the harmonists consulted. It is not to be assumed that they necessarily represent the true chronological order of the incidents that made up the Savior's life. It is thought they may approximate that order. It is certain that some would make a different chronological order from the one here used.

But after all, the precise order of events may not be too material. What Jesus said and what he did, his teaching and doctrines, these are the things that are important.

Nor is the place where things were said and done of great importance, though it adds to the interest of the history. It will be observed that in most cases the place where the incident appears to have taken place, has been given, with the name of the scholar fixing it where the Gospel text does not declare it.

The reader will see that, as to some of the incidents, the assumed day of the month, the month itself, and the assumed year of the Christian era of the happening are shown. These are taken from the works of scholars whose names are given. But the time, actual or relative, of the happenings is not of vital importance, either.

Some may sharply disagree with the computations (now accepted by many scholars) that fix the date of the Savior's birth at the end of 5 B.C., or the beginning or early part of 4 B.C. The Church has made no official declaration on the matter, beyond that contained in Verse 1 of Section 20 of the Doctrine and Covenants. In the early editions of the *Doctrine and Covenants Commentary* (by Brothers Hyrum M. Smith and Janne M. Sjodahl) this verse was interpreted as follows:

"The organization of the Church in the year 1830 is hardly to be regarded as giving divine authority to the commonly accepted calendar. There are reasons for believing that those who, a long time after our Savior's birth, tried to ascertain the correct time, erred in their calculations, and that the Nativity occurred four years before our era, or in the year of Rome 750. All that this Revelation means to say is that the Church was organized in the year that is commonly accepted as 1830, A.D." (p. 138.) Rome 750 is equivalent (say the scholars) to 4 B.C.

This statement has been omitted in the latest edition of the *Commentary.*

I am not proposing any date as the true date. But in order to be as helpful to students as I could, I have taken as the date of the Savior's birth the date now accepted by many scholars,—late 5 B.C., or early 4 B.C., because Bible Commentaries and the writings of scholars are frequently keyed upon that chronology and because I believe that so to do will facilitate and make easier the work of those studying the life and works of the Savior from sources using this accepted chronology.

My original plan (which I have not abandoned) was to annotate these Gospel texts by references to our own scriptures on important doctrinal matters. Our own scriptures have for years been annotated with references to the Bible, but no one has yet annotated the Bible with references to our own scriptures. The work on this annotation is progressing. I am aware there are several "Ready References" but these do not meet this problem, any more than these same "References" meet the problem involved in annotating our scriptures to the Bible.

I have used the King James (Authorized Version) text, believing it best.

I feel this book may have this value: It will indicate the fact (which some of our own scholars seem to hesitate to adopt) that the Gospels do contain the life history of Jesus, who had a real personality,—a man part-mortal, part-divine—who was born as ordinary mortals are born, who moved about on the earth as a mortal man moves (with certain supermortal experiences, such as walking on the water), who mingled with fellow mortals, and who lived and died as did they, and that these Gospels contain a record of that man. The book is intended to make clear that Jesus was not, as some schools of the higher critics contend, a half-mythical person who may have had an actual existence with some life experiences but not those recorded in the Gospels, which experiences (say such critics) are myths in their miraculous elements, and that around these myths, hanging as it were as festoons, are (still say the critics) a number of ethical principles, not necessarily taught by him, but partly so, perhaps, with spurious additions made by his followers in the earlier decades following his death.

Believing with all my soul that such an appraisal of Jesus is a re-crucifixion of the Christ, that Jesus was a real personality, that he moved among men as a mortal, that he did the works and taught the doctrines credited to him in the Gospels, that he was in fact the Christ, and that the account of his conception, birth, life, death, and resurrection are as factual as any in all history, I have felt to set out the Gospels' story in such an arrangement as would facilitate a study of his life with this true concept, and in the very language of the Gospels.

I say once more and finally: Many will not agree with the arrangement I have made of the events of his life, nor with such time and place specifications as are given. They may be right. That is not the important thing. The important thing is to give him a real life, for such he had, with the actual teachings and experiences that made up that life, whatever the exact sequence of events at any one time or at any one place may have been.

With these thoughts, I commend this *Harmony* to your kindly consideration and treatment, hopeful that it will help to accomplish the major purpose I have in mind,—increasing the knowledge of his life, works, and teachings, and the testimony that he was indeed the Christ, the First Fruits of the Resurrection, the Atoning Sacrifice which made possible the resurrection of all men of all time.

—J. REUBEN CLARK, JR.

Salt Lake City, Utah
November 24, 1954.

ACKNOWLEDGMENTS

While I assume all and full responsibility for this book and all of its parts, I must acknowledge my deep obligation for helpful suggestions from several of the Brethren who counselled with me concerning the work and who gave me much encouragement regarding its publication. This is especially true as to the plan of the book and as to arrangements for printing the book, where Elder Mark E. Petersen, Elder Alva H. Parry, Manager of the Deseret Book Company, and Bishop Thomas S. Monson of the Deseret News Press, have given unstintedly of their time and counsel. I owe a special debt of gratitude to Sister Rowena Miller, my secretary, for her many, many hours of painstaking investigation in connection with the tables printed, in checking and verifying the hundreds of references and citations, and for virtually "seeing the book through the press."

J. R. C.

ACKNOWLEDGMENTS

[illegible]

Table of Contents

Division One

AIDS FOR USING THE HARMONY

OUTLINE OF THE SAVIOR'S LABORS AND MINISTRATIONS ON EARTH, BY PERIODS

FIRST PERIOD

B.C. 6 to A.D. 26.	FROM THE BEGINNING OF THE GOSPEL RECORD TO JOHN'S MINISTRY. Sections 1-24.

SECOND PERIOD

Summer, A.D. 26 to Mar.-Apr., A.D. 27.	FROM THE BEGINNING OF JOHN'S MINISTRY TO THE FIRST PASSOVER OF THE MINISTRY OF JESUS. Sections 25-33.

THIRD PERIOD

Apr. 11-17, A.D. 27 to Dec., A.D. 27.	THE EARLY JUDEAN MINISTRY, FROM THE FIRST PASSOVER TO HIS RETURN TO GALILEE. Sections 34-41.

FOURTH PERIOD

Winter, A.D. 27-28 to Oct., A.D. 29.	THE GREAT GALILEAN MINISTRY. Sections 42-113.
Winter, A.D. 27-28 to Early Summer, A.D. 28.	I. From the Return to Galilee Until the Choosing of the Twelve. Sections 42-59. (Covering the Second Passover, Sec. 55.)
Early Summer, A.D. 28 to Apr., A.D. 29.	II. From the Choosing of the Twelve to the Tour in Northern Galilee. Sections 60-91. (The time of the Third Passover follows Sec. 91.)
Spring to Oct., A.D. 29.	III. From the Retirement Into Northern Galilee Until the Closing of the Galilean Ministry. Sections 92-113.

FIFTH PERIOD

Oct. 11-18 to Dec. 20-27, A.D. 29.	THE LATER JUDEAN MINISTRY. Sections 114-128.

SIXTH PERIOD

Jan. to Mar.-Apr., A.D. 30.	THE PEREAN MINISTRY. Sections 129-159.

SEVENTH PERIOD

Fri., Mar. 31 to May, A.D. 30.	THE WEEK OF THE ATONING SACRIFICE AND TO THE ASCENSION. Sections 160-171.
Fri., Mar. 31, 8th Nisan, or Sat., Apr. 1, 9th Nisan.	Jesus Comes to Bethany. Section 160.
Sun., Apr. 2, 10th Nisan.	First Day of the Week. From Bethany to Jerusalem and Return to Bethany. Section 161.
Mon., Apr. 3, 11th Nisan.	Second Day of the Week. Bethany to Jerusalem, Cleansing Temple, and Back to Bethany. Section 162.
Tue., Apr. 4, 12th Nisan	Third Day of the Week. Bethany to Jerusalem, in the Temple, and Back to Bethany. Section 163.
Wed., Apr. 5, 13th Nisan.	Fourth Day of the Week. At Bethany (?).
Thurs., Apr. 6, 14th Nisan.	Fifth Day of the Week. Bethany to Jerusalem, the Last Supper, the Mount of Olives, Gethsemane, the Betrayal, the Arrest. Section 164.
Fri., Apr. 7, 15th Nisan.	Sixth Day of the Week. The Trial and Crucifixion. Section 165.
Sat., Apr. 8, 16th Nisan.	Seventh Day of the Week. In the Tomb. Section 166.
Sun., Apr. 9, 17th Nisan.	First Day of the Week. The Resurrection. Section 167.
Apr.-May, A.D. 30.	Appearances Subsequent to Those of the First Day of the Week. Sections 168-171.

EIGHTH PERIOD

125th-126th Year of the Reign of the Judges. 34th year after the birth of Christ.	THE BENEDICTION UPON OUR LORD'S MINISTRY—HIS VISIT TO THE WESTERN HEMISPHERE AFTER HIS ASCENSION IN PALESTINE—BOOK OF MORMON. Sections 172-191.

INDEX

LIST OF RECORDED EVENTS IN THE SAVIOR'S LIFE AND WORKS ON EARTH, CHRONOLOGICALLY ARRANGED

FIRST PERIOD

From the Beginning of the Gospel Record to John's Ministry

SEC. & PG.	EVENT, TIME AND PLACE	MATT.	MARK	LUKE	JOHN	3 NEPHI
§19 p. 179	A new star in Western Hemisphere	....	....	....	....	1:21-22
§20 p. 179	The flight into Egypt	2:13-15	....	....	....	....
§21 p. 180	The slaughter of the babes	2:16-18	....	....	....	....
§22 p. 180	Return from Egypt	2:19-23	....	2:40	....	....
§23 p. 181	Jesus in the Temple	....	....	2:41-50	....	....
§24 p. 182	Jesus goes back to Nazareth and lives there	....	....	2:51-52	....	....

SECOND PERIOD

From the Beginning of John's Ministry to the First Passover of the Ministry of Jesus

SEC. & PG.	EVENT, TIME AND PLACE	MATT.	MARK	LUKE	JOHN	3 NEPHI
§25 p. 183	The early ministry of John the Baptist	....	....	....	....	....
(a) p. 183	The time of the beginning of John's ministry	....	....	3:1-2	....	....
(b) p. 183	The messenger and the message	3:1-6	1:1-6	3:3-6	....	....
(c) p. 184	John's preaching	3:7-10	....	3:7-14	....	....
(d) p. 185	John announces coming of Jesus	3:11-12	1:7-8	3:15-18	....	....
§26 p. 186	John baptizes Jesus	3:13-17	1:9-11	3:21-23a	....	....
§27 p. 187	The temptation	4:1-11	1:12-13	4:1-13	....	....
§28 p. 188	John proclaims he is not the Christ	....	....	....	1:19-28	....
§29 p. 189	John testifies Jesus is Lamb of God	....	....	....	1:29-34	....
§30 p. 190	Andrew and Simon meet Jesus	....	....	....	1:35-42	....
§31 p. 190	Philip and Nathanael found	....	....	....	1:43-51	....
§32 p. 191	The first miracle	....	....	....	2:1-11	....
§33 p. 192	Jesus goes to Capernaum	....	....	....	2:12	....

THIRD PERIOD

The Early Judean Ministry, From the First Passover to His Return to Galilee

Sec. & Pg.	Event, Time and Place	Matt.	Mark	Luke	John	3 Nephi
§34 p. 193	The first Passover	....	....	....	2:13-25	....
§35 p. 194	Nicodemus visits Jesus	....	....	....	3:1-21	....
§36 p. 195	Jesus goes into Judea	....	....	....	3:22	....
§37 p. 195	John's testimony	....	....	....	3:23-36	....
§38 p. 196	Herod imprisons John	14:3-5	6:17-20	3:19-20	....	....
§39 p. 197	Jesus leaves Judea for Galilee	4:12	1:14	4:14	4:1-3	....
§40 p. 198	The woman of Samaria	....	....	....	4:4-42	....
§41 p. 200	He goes into Galilee	....	....	....	4:43-44	....

FOURTH PERIOD

The Great Galilean Ministry

I. From the Return to Galilee Until the Choosing of the Twelve

Sec. & Pg.	Event, Time and Place	Matt.	Mark	Luke	John	3 Nephi
§42 p. 201	Jesus preaches in Galilee ..	4:17	1:14-15	4:14-15	4:45	....
§43 p. 201	Healing nobleman's son	....	....	....	4:46-54	....
§44 p. 202	Jesus rejected at Nazareth	....	....	4:16-30	....	....
§45 p. 203	He goes to Capernaum	4:13-16	....	4:31a	....	....
§46 p. 204	Jesus chooses Peter, Andrew, James, and John	4:18-22	1:16-20	5:1-11	....	....
§47 p. 206	An unclean spirit cast out..	....	1:21-28	4:31-37	....	....
§48 p. 207	Peter's wife's mother healed; a day of miracles	8:14-17	1:29-34	4:38-41	....	....
§49 p. 208	Jesus makes first tour of Galilee, preaching	4:23-25	1:35-39	4:42-44	....	....

SEC. & PG.	EVENT, TIME AND PLACE	MATT.	MARK	LUKE	JOHN	3 NEPHI
§50 p. 209	The Sermon on the Mount	Chaps. 5-7	....	....	....	....
§51 p. 215	The leper healed	8:1-4	1:40-45	5:12-16	....	....
§52 p. 216	One sick with palsy is healed	9:2-8	2:1-12	5:17-26	....	....
§53 p. 218	Jesus chooses Matthew who gives a feast	9:9-13	2:13-17	5:27-32	....	....
§54 p. 220	John's disciples question Jesus about fasting	9:14-17	2:18-22	5:33-39	....	....
§55 p. 221	The second Passover	....	....	....	5:1-47	....
§56 p. 224	Disciples pluck corn on Sabbath	12:1-8	2:23-28	6:1-5	....	....
§57 p. 225	Man with withered hand healed	12:9-14	3:1-6	6:6-11	....	....
§58 p. 226	Jesus withdraws to the sea	12:15-21	3:7-12	....	....	....
§59 p. 227	The Twelve chosen	10:2-4	3:13-21	6:12-16	....	....

II. From the Choosing of the Twelve to the Tour in Northern Galilee

SEC. & PG.	EVENT, TIME AND PLACE	MATT.	MARK	LUKE	JOHN	3 NEPHI
§60 p. 229	The Sermon on the Plain	....	....	6:17-49	....	....
§61 p. 231	The Centurion's servant healed	8:5-13	....	7:1-10	....	....
§62 p. 232	The son of widow of Nain raised	....	....	7:11-17	....	....
§63 p. 233	John sends messengers, questioning, to Jesus	11:2-30	....	7:18-35	....	....
§64 p. 236	Jesus anointed by sinning woman	....	....	7:36-50	....	....
§65 p. 237	Another tour of Galilee	....	....	8:1-3	....	....
§66 p. 238	Blind and dumb man healed	12:22-23	....	....	....	....
§67 p. 238	They charge he is in league with Beelzebub	12:24-37	3:22-30	....	....	....
§68 p. 240	Jesus discourses on signs	12:38-45	....	....	....	....
§69 p. 241	His mother and brethren seek him	12:46-50	3:31-35	8:19-21	....	....

Sec. & Pg.	Event, Time and Place	Matt.	Mark	Luke	John	3 Nephi
§85 p. 265	He goes to Bethsaida	14:13	6:31-32	9:10b-11a	....	....
§86 p. 265	The five thousand fed	14:14-21	6:33-44	9:11b-17	6:1-14	....
§87 p. 268	Jesus prevents their making him king	14:22-23	6:45-46	....	6:15	....
§88 p. 268	Jesus walks on sea	14:24-33	6:47-52	....	6:16-21	....
§89 p. 270	The discourse to the multitude on the bread of life	....	....	....	6:22-71	....
§90 p. 273	People in the land of Gennesaret healed	14:34-36	6:53-56	....	....	....
§91 p. 273	The discourses upon cleanliness	15:1-20	7:1-23	....	....	....

(*This is the time of the third Passover*)

III. From the Retirement into Northern Galilee Until the Closing of the Galilean Ministry

Sec. & Pg.	Event, Time and Place	Matt.	Mark	Luke	John	3 Nephi
§92 p. 276	Jesus goes into northern Galilee	15:21	7:24	....	7:1	....
§93 p. 277	The daughter of the Greek woman healed	15:22-28	7:25-30	....	....	....
§94 p. 278	He returns to Sea of Galilee	15:29a	7:31	....	....	....
§95 p. 278	Jesus heals deaf man	....	7:32-37	....	....	....
§96 p. 279	The four thousand fed	15:29b-38	8:1-9	....	....	....
§97 p. 280	Jesus goes to Magdala	15:39	8:10	....	....	....
§98 p. 280	He again discourses about signs	16:1-12	8:11-21	....	....	....
§99 p. 282	A blind man healed	....	8:22-26	....	....	....
§100 p. 283	Peter's testimony of the Christ	16:13-20	8:27-30	9:18-22	....	....
§101 p. 284	He teaches his disciples concerning his death and resurrection	16:21-28	8:31-38, 9:1	9:23-27	....	....
§102 p. 286	The transfiguration	17:1-13	9:2-13	9:28-36	....	....

FIFTH PERIOD

The Later Judean Ministry

Sec. & Pg.	Event, Time and Place	Matt.	Mark	Luke	John	3 Nephi
§122 p. 312	He casts out a dumb devil and is again accused of being in league with Beelzebub	....	....	11:14-36	....	....
§123 p. 313	Another discourse on cleanliness	....	....	11:37-54	....	....
§124 p. 315	Jesus teaches multitude; parable of the foolish rich man	....	....	12:1-59	....	....
§125 p. 319	The slaughter of the Galileans	....	....	13:1-9	....	....
§126 p. 320	Jesus heals man born blind	....	....	....	9:1-41	....
§127 p. 322	The parable of the good shepherd	....	....	....	10:1-21	....
§128 p. 324	The Feast of Dedication	....	....	....	10:22-39a	....

SIXTH PERIOD

The Perean Ministry

Sec. & Pg.	Event, Time and Place	Matt.	Mark	Luke	John	3 Nephi
§129 p. 327	Jesus goes beyond the Jordan	....	....	....	10:39b-42	....
§130 p. 327	The healing on the Sabbath of woman long ill	....	....	13:10-17	....	....
§131 p. 328	The parable of the mustard seed	....	....	13:18-21	....	....
§132 p. 328	The beginning of journey to Jerusalem	....	....	13:22-30	....	....
§133 p. 329	The warning about Herod Antipas	....	....	13:31-35	....	....
§134 p. 330	The message that Lazarus is sick	....	....	....	11:1-16	....
§135 p. 331	Man with dropsy healed on the Sabbath	....	....	14:1-24	....	....
§136 p. 333	Another discourse on sacrifice	....	....	14:25-35	....	....
§137 p. 334	A group of parables	....	....	15:1-2	....	....
(a) p. 334	Parable of the lost sheep	....	....	15:3-7	....	....
(b) p. 334	Parable of the ten pieces of silver	....	....	15:8-10	....	....

SEC. & PG.	EVENT, TIME AND PLACE	MATT.	MARK	LUKE	JOHN	3 NEPHI
§137	*(Cont'd)*					
(c) p. 335	Parable of the return of the prodigal son	....	....	15:11-32	....	....
(d) p. 336	Parable of the unjust steward	....	....	16:1-13	....	....
§138 p. 337	A discourse on covetousness	....	....	16:14-18	....	....
§139 p. 338	Parable of rich man and Lazarus	....	....	16:19-31	....	....
§140 p. 339	Discourse on those who bring offense and on faith	....	....	17:1-10	....	....
§141 p. 340	The raising of Lazarus	....	....	....	11:17-46	....
§142 p. 342	They plot against Jesus	....	....	....	11:47-53	....
§143 p. 342	He goes to city of Ephraim	....	....	....	11:54	....
§144 p. 343	The beginning of the final journey to Jerusalem	....	....	17:11-19	....	....
§145 p. 343	A discourse on kingdom of God	....	....	17:20-37	....	....
§146 p. 345	Jesus again speaks in parables	....	....	....	....	....
(a) p. 345	Parable of the importunate widow	....	....	18:1-8	....	....
(b) p. 345	Parable of the Pharisee and the publican	....	....	18:9-14	....	....
§147 p. 346	He crosses Jordan into Perea, going towards Jerusalem	19:1-2	10:1	....	....	....
§148 p. 347	Pharisees tempt Jesus	19:3-12	10:2-12	....	....	....
§149 p. 348	He blesses little children	19:13-15	10:13-16	18:15-17	....	....
§150 p. 349	The rich young ruler	19:16-30	10:17-31	18:18-30	....	....
§151 p. 352	The parable of the laborers in the vineyard	20:1-16	....	....	....	....
§152 p. 353	He goes before the Twelve, towards Jerusalem	20:17-19	10:32-34	18:31-34	....	....
§153 p. 354	Ambitions of James and John	20:20-28	10:35-45	....	....	....
§154 p. 355	Bartimaeus healed	20:29-34	10:46-52	18:35-43	....	....

Sec. & Pg.	Event, Time and Place	Matt.	Mark	Luke	John	3 Nephi
§155 p. 357	Zacchaeus, the publican	....	....	19:1-10	....	....
§156 p. 358	The parable of the ten pounds	....	....	19:11-27	....	....
§157 p. 359	Jesus proceeds on his way to Jerusalem	....	....	19:28	....	....
§158 p. 359	Many seek him	....	....	....	11:55-57	....
§159 p. 360	People in Western Hemisphere look for sign	....	....	....	....	8:1-4

SEVENTH PERIOD
The Week of the Atoning Sacrifice and to the Ascension

Sec. & Pg.	Event, Time and Place	Matt.	Mark	Luke	John	3 Nephi
§160 p. 361	Jesus comes to Bethany	....	....	....	12:1, 9-11	....
	First Day of the Week					
§161 p. 361	From Bethany to Jerusalem and return to Bethany	....	....	....	....	....
(a) p. 361	Entry into Jerusalem	21:1-11	11:1-11a	19:29-44	12:12-19	....
(b) p. 364	Return to Bethany	....	11:11b	....	....	....
	Second Day of the Week					
§162 p. 365	Bethany to Jerusalem, cleansing Temple, and back to Bethany	....	....	....	....	....
(a) p. 365	Cursing of the barren fig tree	21:18-19a	11:12-14	....	....	....
(b) p. 365	Jesus cleanses the Temple ..	21:12-16	11:15-18	19:45-48	....	....
(c) p. 366	Return to Bethany	21:17	11:19	21:37	....	....
	Third Day of the Week					
§163 p. 367	Bethany to Jerusalem, in the Temple, and back to Bethany	....	....	....	....	....
(a) p. 367	A discourse on faith	21:19b-22	11:20-26	21:38	....	....
(b) p. 368	The question of his authority	21:23-27	11:27-33	20:1-8	....	....
(c) p. 369	Parable of the two sons	21:28-32	....	....	....	....
(d) p. 369	Parable of the wicked husbandman	21:33-46	12:1-12	20:9-18	....	....

Sec. & Pg.	Event, Time and Place	Matt.	Mark	Luke	John	3 Nephi
§163	*(Cont'd)*					
(e) p. 372	Parable of the king's son	22:1-14	....	....	....	....
(f) p. 373	The question about tribute..	22:15-22	12:13-17	20:19-26	....	....
(g) p. 374	The Sadducees question about marriage after the resurrection	22:23-33	12:18-27	20:27-40	....	....
(h) p. 376	The lawyer questions about the great commandment	22:34-40	12:28-34	....	....	....
(i) p. 377	Jesus asks Pharisees whose son Christ is	22:41-46	12:35-37	20:41-44	....	....
(j) p. 378	The scribes and Pharisees condemned	23:1-36	12:38-40	20:45-47	....	....
(k) p. 380	Jesus' lamentation over Jerusalem	23:37-39	....	....	....	....
(l) p. 381	The widow's mite	....	12:41-44	21:1-4	....	....
(m) p. 381	The Greeks seek him; a voice from heaven	....	....	....	12:20-36	....
(n) p. 382	Timidity of chief rulers who believe	....	....	....	12:37-50	....
(o) p. 383	The Olivet discourse	24:1-51	13:1-37	21:5-36	....	....
(p) p. 390	Parable of the ten virgins..	25:1-13	....	....	....	....
(q) p. 390	Parable of the talents	25:14-30	....	....	....	....
(r) p. 392	The final judgment	25:31-46	....	....	....	....
(s) p. 393	The betrayal foretold	26:1-2	....	....	....	....
(t) p. 393	The plot to take him	26:3-5	14:1-2	22:1-2	....	....
(u) p. 393	At Simon's supper Mary anoints him	26:6-13	14:3-9	....	12:2-8	....
(v) p. 395	Judas arranges betrayal	26:14-16	14:10-11	22:3-6	....	....
	Fourth Day of the Week					
	At Bethany (?)	....	....	....	....	....
	Fifth Day of the Week					
§164 p. 396	The Last Supper, the Mount of Olives, Gethsemane, the betrayal, the arrest	....	....	....	....	....

SEC. & PG.	EVENT, TIME AND PLACE	MATT.	MARK	LUKE	JOHN	3 NEPHI
§164	*(Cont'd)*					
(a) p. 396	Disciples arrange for Passover meal	26:17-19	14:12-16	22:7-13	....	....
(b) p. 397	They sit down in Passover chamber	26:20	14:17	22:14	....	....
(c) p. 397	The strife about precedence	....	....	22:24-30	....	....
(d) p. 398	He washes his disciples' feet	....	....	....	13:1-20	....
(e) p. 399	The Passover meal	....	....	22:15-18	....	....
(f) p. 400	He indicates his betrayer	26:21-25	14:18-21	22:21-23	13:21-26	....
(g) p. 401	Judas leaves the chamber	....	....	....	13:27-30	....
(h) p. 401	Jesus foretells his death	....	....	....	13:31-35	....
(i) p. 402	The sacrament	26:26-29	14:22-25	22:19-20	....	....
(j) p. 402	Peter declares his loyalty	....	....	22:31-38	13:36-38	....
(k) p. 403	The discourse about the Comforter	....	....	....	14:1-31	....
(l) p. 405	They sing a hymn and go out to the Mount of Olives	26:30	14:26	22:39	....	....
(m) p. 405	He explains his relationship to them and theirs to him and the Father	....	....	....	15:1-27	....
(n) p. 407	He again explains his death	....	....	....	16:1-33	....
(o) p. 409	The great prayer	....	....	....	17:1-26	....
(p) p. 411	Peter and rest declare their loyalty	26:31-35	14:27-31	....	....	....
(q) p. 412	He prays in the Garden	26:36-46	14:32-42	22:40-46	18:1-2	....
(r) p. 413	The betrayal	26:47-50a	14:43-45	22:47-48	18:3-9	....
(s) p. 415	The arrest	26:50b-56	14:46-52	22:49-53	18:10-12	....
	Sixth Day of the Week					
§165 p. 416	The trial and crucifixion	....	....	....	....	....

Sec. & Pg.	Event, Time and Place	Matt.	Mark	Luke	John	3 Nephi
§165	*(Cont'd)*					
(a) p. 416	Jesus before Annas	....	....	....	18:13-14, 19-23	....
(b) p. 417	He is sent to Caiaphas	26:57-58	14:53-54	22:54	18:24	....
(c) p. 417	The night examination	26:59-66	14:55-64	....	....	....
(d) p. 419	They maltreat him	26:67-68	14:65	22:63-65	....	....
(e) p. 419	Peter denies him	26:69-75	14:66-72	22:55-62	18:15-18, 25-27	....
(f) p. 421	The formal trial and condemnation	27:1-2	15:1	22:66-71; 23:1	....	....
(g) p. 422	Judas Iscariot commits suicide	27:3-10	....	....	....	....
(h) p. 423	Before Pilate	27:11-14	15:2-5	23:2-5	18:28-38	....
(i) p. 424	Before Herod	....	....	23:6-12	....	....
(j) p. 425	Again before Pilate	27:15-23	15:6-14	23:13-23	18:39-40	....
(k) p. 427	Pilate releases Barabbas	27:26-30	15:15-19	23:24-25	19:1-3	....
(l) p. 428	Pilate pleads for Jesus but finally delivers him for crucifixion	27:24-25	....	....	19:4-16a	....
(m) p. 429	They take him to be crucified	27:31-34, 38	15:20-23, 25, 27-28	23:26-33	19:16b-18	....
(n) p. 431	Pilate places a superscription on the cross	27:37	15:26	23:38	19:19-22	....
(o) p. 431	The first words on the cross	....	....	23:34a	....	....
(p) p. 431	The soldiers divide his clothes	27:35-36	15:24	23:34b	19:23-24	....
(q) p. 432	The mocking and scoffing of the rulers and the multitude	27:39-44	15:29-32	23:35-37	....	....
(r) p. 433	Second words from the cross	....	....	23:39-43	....	....
(s) p. 433	Third words from the cross	....	....	....	19:25-27	....
(t) p. 434	Darkness covers the earth	27:45	15:33	23:44-45a	....	....

Sec. & Pg.	Event, Time and Place	Matt.	Mark	Luke	John	3 Nephi
§165	*(Cont'd)*					
(u) p. 434	Signs in the Western Hemisphere	....	....	....	....	8:5-25
(v) p. 436	Fourth words from the cross	27:46-47	15:34-35	....	....	....
(w) p. 437	Fifth words from the cross	27:48-49	15:36	....	19:28-29	....
(x) p. 437	Sixth words from the cross	....	....	....	19:30a	....
(y) p. 437	Seventh words from the cross	27:50	15:37	23:46	19:30b	....
(z) p. 438	The Centurion's testimony	27:51-56	15:38-41	23:45b, 47-49	....	....
(aa) p. 439	His side pierced	....	....	....	19:31-37	....
(bb) p. 439	His burial	27:57-61	15:42-47	23:50-56	19:38-42	....
	Seventh Day of the Week					
§166 p. 441	The guard placed at the tomb and the voice heard in the Western Hemisphere	....	....	....	....	....
(a) p. 441	The placing of the guard at the tomb	27:62-66	....	....	....	....
(b) p. 442	In Western Hemisphere, a voice from heaven declares the woes of the people	....	....	....	....	9:1-22
(c) p. 444	Silence in the land of Western Hemisphere	....	....	....	....	10:1-2
(d) p. 444	In Western Hemisphere, again a voice from heaven	....	....	....	....	10:3-8
	First Day of the Week					
§167 p. 445	The Resurrection	....	....	....	....	....
(a) p. 445	An angel opens the tomb	28:2-4	....	....	....	....
(b) p. 446	In Western Hemisphere, darkness disappears and earth restored	....	....	....	....	10:9-17
(c) p. 447	Mary Magdalene first to the tomb	....	16:9	....	20:1	....
(d) p. 447	Mary tells Peter and John	....	....	....	20:2-5	....

EIGHTH PERIOD

The Benediction Upon Our Lord's Ministry—His Visit to the Western Hemisphere after His Ascension in Palestine—Book of Mormon

SEC. & PG.	EVENT, TIME AND PLACE	MATT.	MARK	LUKE	JOHN	3 NEPHI
§172 p. 463	The Lord foretells his appearance on Western Hemisphere	....	....	....	....	10:18-19
§173 p. 463	A voice out of heaven	....	....	....	....	....
(a) p. 463	The first voice not understood	....	....	....	....	11:1-3
(b) p. 464	The voice comes the second time, still not understood	....	....	....	....	11:4
(c) p. 464	The voice comes a third time	....	....	....	....	11:5-7
§174 p. 464	The multitude see Jesus descending	....	....	....	....	11:8-9
§175 p. 465	He begins his mission	....	....	....	....	11:10-12
§176 p. 465	The great opening day of Christ's ministry upon the Western Hemisphere	....	....	....	....	....
(a) p. 465	He invites multitude to handle his body	....	....	....	....	11:13-15
(b) p. 466	The people convinced	....	....	....	....	11:16-17
(c) p. 466	Nephi called forth, and others	....	....	....	....	11:18-27
(d) p. 467	The Twelve warned	....	....	....	....	11:28-32
(e) p. 468	Jesus discourses on repentance and baptism and the necessity therefor	....	....	....	....	11:33-41
(f) p. 468	The calling of the Twelve explained	....	....	....	....	12:1-2
(g) p. 469	Jesus repeats the great truths given in the Sermon on the Mount and the Sermon on the Plain	....	....	....	....	12:3-48, 13:1-24
(h) p. 473	The Twelve instructed	....	....	....	....	13:25-34
(i) p. 474	The multitude instructed	....	....	....	....	14:1-27

Sec. & Pg.	Event, Time and Place	Matt.	Mark	Luke	John	3 Nephi
§178	(*Cont'd*)					
(e) p. 490	He again prays	....	....	....	....	19:25-36
(f) p. 491	He tells them to cease their prayers	....	....	....	....	20:1-2
(g) p. 492	He again administers the sacrament	....	....	....	....	20:3-9
§179 p. 492	He gives commandments ..	....	....	....	....	....
(a) p. 492	He quotes Isaiah	....	....	....	....	20:10-22
(b) p. 494	He proclaims his identity ..	....	....	....	....	20:23-29
(c) p. 495	Discourse on glory of Israel	....	....	....	....	20:30-46
(d) p. 496	The signs of the gathering	....	....	....	....	21:1-13
(e) p. 497	The woes of the Gentiles	....	....	....	....	21:14-21
(f) p. 498	How Gentiles may share glories	....	....	....	....	21:22-27
(g) p. 499	The Father will commence work	....	....	....	....	21:28-29
(h) p. 499	He again quotes Isaiah	....	....	....	....	22:1-17
(i) p. 500	The people to search scriptures	....	....	....	....	23:1-6
(j) p. 501	Their records criticized	....	....	....	....	23:7-14
(k) p. 502	Record to be made of Malachi's words	....	....	....	....	24:1-18, 25:1-6
(l) p. 504	The scriptures expounded ..	....	....	....	....	26:1-5
(m) p. 504	Moroni explains records	....	....	....	....	26:6-12
§180 p. 505	He teaches the people	....	....	....	....	26:13
§181 p. 505	Works of Jesus among the people	....	....	....	....	26:14-16
§182 p. 506	Disciples begin work	....	....	....	....	26:17-21

Sec. & Pg.	Event, Time and Place	Matt.	Mark	Luke	John	3 Nephi
§183 p. 507	Another warning	....	....	....	....	27:1-12
§184 p. 508	Jesus again declares himself	....	....	....	....	27:13-15
§185 p. 508	Baptism explained	....	....	....	....	27:16-22
§186 p. 509	The keeping of records recommended	....	....	....	....	27:23-27
§187 p. 510	The final words to the disciples	....	....	....	....	....
(a) p. 510	He must go to the Father	....	....	....	....	27:28
(b) p. 510	None of this generation to be lost	....	....	....	....	27:29-31
(c) p. 510	Fourth generation to be led captive	....	....	....	....	27:32
(d) p. 511	Further instructions	....	....	....	....	27:33
(e) p. 511	Jesus' gifts to nine Disciples	....	....	....	....	28:1-3
(f) p. 511	Jesus' gifts to three Disciples	....	....	....	....	28:4-11
§188 p. 512	Jesus ascends; the Three as if transfigured	....	....	....	....	28:12-15
§189 p. 513	Ministry of the Three	....	....	....	....	28:16-23
§190 p. 514	Moroni finishes record	....	....	....	....	28:24-40
§191 p. 515	Moroni's closing words to the Gentiles	....	....	....	....	Chaps. 29-30

TABLE FOR FINDING IN THE HARMONY ANY PASSAGE IN THE GOSPELS

MATTHEW

Chapter	*Verse*	*Section*
1	1—17	3
	18—25	8
2	1—12	18
	13—15	20
	16—18	21
	19—23	22
3	1—6	25-b
	7—10	25-c
	11—12	25-d
	13—17	26
4	1—11	27
	12	39
	13—16	45
	17	42
	18—22	46
	23—25	49
5	1—48	50
6	1—34	50
7	1—29	50
8	1—4	51
	5—13	61
	14—17	48
	18—27	71
	28—34	72
9	1	73
	2—8	52
	9—13	53
	14—17	54
	18—19	74
	20—22	75
	23—26	74
	27—31	76
	32—34	77
	35—38	79
10	1	80
	2—4	59
	5—42	80
11	1	81
	2—30	63
12	1—8	56
	9—14	57
	15—21	58
	22—23	66
	24—37	67
	38—45	68
	46—50	69
13	1—3a	70
	3b—23	70-a
	24—30	70-c
13	31—35	70-d
	36—43	70-e
	44—53	70-f
	54—58	78
14	1—2	83
	3—5	38
	6—12	82
	13	85
	14—21	86
	22—23	87
	24—33	88
	34—36	90
15	1—20	91
	21	92
	22—28	93
	29a	94
	29b—38	96
	39	97
16	1—12	98
	13—20	100
	21—28	101
17	1—13	102
	14—21	103
	22—23	104
	24—27	105
18	1—14	106
	15—20	107
	21—35	108
19	1—2	147
	3—12	148
	13—15	149
	16—30	150
20	1—16	151
	17—19	152
	20—28	153
	29—34	154
21	1—11	161-a
	12—16	162-b
	17	162-c
	18—19a	162-a
	19b—22	163-a
	23—27	163-b
	28—32	163-c
	33—46	163-d
22	1—14	163-e
	15—22	163-f
	23—33	163-g
	34—40	163-h
	41—46	163-i
23	1—36	163-j
	37—39	163-k
24	1—51	163-o
25	1—13	163-p
	14—30	163-q
	31—46	163-r
26	1—2	163-s
	3—5	163-t
	6—13	163-u
	14—16	163-v
	17—19	164-a
	20	164-b
	21—25	164-f
	26—29	164-i
	30	164-l
	31—35	164-p
	36—46	164-q
	47—50a	164-r
	50b—56	164-s
	57—58	165-b
	59—66	165-c
	67—68	165-d
	69—75	165-e
27	1—2	165-f
	3—10	165-g
	11—14	165-h
	15—23	165-j
	24—25	165-l
	26—30	165-k
	31—34	165-m
	35—36	165-p
	37	165-n
	38	165-m
	39—44	165-q
	45	165-t
	46—47	165-v
	48—49	165-w
	50	165-y
	51—56	165-z
	57—61	165-bb
	62—66	166-a
28	1	167-h
	2—4	167-a
	5—7	167-h
	8	167-j
	9—10	167-i
	11—15	167-k
	16—20	168-g

MARK

Chapter	*Verse*	*Section*	*Chapter*	*Verse*	*Section*	*Chapter*	*Verse*	*Section*
1	1—6	25-b	6	53—56	90	14	1—2	163-t
	7—8	25-d	7	1—23	91		3—9	163-u
	9—11	26		24	92		10—11	163-v
	12—13	27		25—30	93		12—16	164-a
	14	39		31	94		17	164-b
	14—15	42		32—37	95		18—21	164-f
	16—20	46	8	1—9	96		22—25	164-i
	21—28	47		10	97		26	164-l
	29—34	48		11—21	98		27—31	164-p
	35—39	49		22—26	99		32—42	164-q
	40—45	51		27—30	100		43—45	164-r
2	1—12	52		31—38	101		46—52	164-s
	13—17	53	9	1	101		53—54	165-b
	18—22	54		2—13	102		55—64	165-c
	23—28	56		14—29	103		65	165-d
3	1—6	57		30—32	104		66—72	165-e
	7—12	58		33—37	106	15	1	165-f
	13—21	59		38—42	109		2—5	165-h
	22—30	67		43—50	106		6—14	165-j
	31—35	69	10	1	147		15—19	165-k
4	1—2	70		2—12	148		20—23	165-m
	3—25	70-a		13—16	149		24	165-p
	26—29	70-b		17—31	150		25	165-m
	30—34	70-d		32—34	152		26	165-n
	35—41	71		35—45	153		27—28	165-m
5	1—20	72		46—52	154		29—32	165-q
	21	73	11	1—11a	161-a		33	165-t
	22—24	74		11b	161-b		34—35	165-v
	25—34	75		12—14	162-a		36	165-w
	35—43	74		15—18	162-b		37	165-y
6	1—6a	78		19	162-c		38—41	165-z
	6b	79		20—26	163-a		42—47	165-bb
	7—13	80		27—33	163-b	16	1—7	167-h
	14—16	83	12	1—12	163-d		8	167-j
	17—20	38		13—17	163-f		9	167-c
	21—29	82		18—27	163-g		10—11	167-g
	30	84		28—34	163-h		12—13	167-l
	31—32	85		35—37	163-i		14	167-n
	33—44	86		38—40	163-j		15—18	168-g
	45—46	87		41—44	163-l		19	169
	47—52	88	13	1—37	163-o		20	170

LUKE

Chapter	Verse	Section
1	1 — 4	2
	5 —23	4
	24 —25	5
	26 —38	6
	39 —56	7
	57 —80	9
2	1 — 5	10
	6 — 7	12
	8 —20	13
	21	15
	22 —38	16
	39	17
	40	22
	41 —50	23
	51 —52	24
3	1 — 2	25-a
	3 — 6	25-b
	7 —14	25-c
	15 —18	25-d
	19 —20	38
	21 —23a	26
	23 —38	3
4	1 —13	27
	14	39
	14 —15	42
	16 —30	44
	31a	45
	31 —37	47
	38 —41	48
	42 —44	49
5	1 —11	46
	12 —16	51
	17 —26	52
	27 —32	53
	33 —39	54
6	1 — 5	56
	6 —11	57
	12 —16	59
	17 —49	60
7	1 —10	61
	11 —17	62
	18 —35	63
	36 —50	64
8	1 — 3	65
	4	70
	5 —18	70-a
	19 —21	69
	22 —25	71
	26 —39	72
	40	73
	41 —42	74
	43 —48	75
8	49 —56	74
9	1 — 6	80
	7 — 9	83
	10a	84
	10b—11a	85
	11b—17	86
	18 —22	100
	23 —27	101
	28 —36	102
	37 —43a	103
	43b—45	104
	46 —48	106
	49 —50	109
	51 —56	113
	57 —62	110
10	1 —16	111
	17 —24	118
	25 —37	119
	38 —42	120
11	1 —13	121
	14 —36	122
	37 —54	123
12	1 —59	124
13	1 — 9	125
	10 —17	130
	18 —21	131
	22 —30	132
	31 —35	133
14	1 —24	135
	25 —35	136
15	1 — 2	137
	3 — 7	137-a
	8 —10	137-b
	11 —32	137-c
16	1 —13	137-d
	14 —18	138
	19 —31	139
17	1 —10	140
	11 —19	144
	20 —37	145
18	1 — 8	146-a
	9 —14	146-b
	15 —17	149
	18 —30	150
	31 —34	152
	35 —43	154
19	1 —10	155
	11 —27	156
	28	157
	29 —44	161-a
	45 —48	162-b
20	1 — 8	163-b
	9 —18	163-d
	19 —26	163-f
	27 —40	163-g
	41 —44	163-i
	45 —47	163-j
21	1 — 4	163-l
	5 —36	163-o
	37	162-c
	38	163-a
22	1 — 2	163-t
	3 — 6	163-v
	7 —13	164-a
	14	164-b
	15 —18	164-e
	19 —20	164-i
	21 —23	164-f
	24 —30	164-c
	31 —38	164-j
	39	164-l
	40 —46	164-q
	47 —48	164-r
	49 —53	164-s
	54	165-b
	55 —62	165-e
	63 —65	165-d
	66 —71	165-f
23	1	165-f
	2 — 5	165-h
	6 —12	165-i
	13 —23	165-j
	24 —25	165-k
	26 —33	165-m
	34a	165-o
	34b	165-p
	35 —37	165-q
	38	165-n
	39 —43	165-r
	44 —45a	165-t
	45b	165-z
	46	165-y
	47 —49	165-z
	50 —56	165-bb
24	1 — 8	167-h
	9 —11	167-j
	12	167-e
	13 —32	167-l
	33 —49	167-n
	34	167-m
	50 —51	169
	52 —53	170

JOHN

Chapter	Verse	Section
1	1 —19	1
	19 —28	28
	29 —34	29
	35 —42	30
	43 —51	31
2	1 —11	32
	12	33
	13 —25	34
3	1 —21	35
	22	36
	23 —36	37
4	1 — 3	39
	4 —42	40
	43 —44	41
	45	42
	46 —54	43
5	1 —47	55
6	1 —14	86
	15	87
	16 —21	88
	22 —71	89
7	1	92
	2 — 9	112
	10	113
	11 —53	114
8	1 —11	115
	12 —30	116
	31 —59	117
9	1 —41	126

Chapter	Verse	Section
10	1 —21	127
	22 —39a	128
	39b—42	129
11	1 —16	134
	17 —46	141
	47 —53	142
	54	143
	55 —57	158
12	1	160
	2 — 8	163-u
	9 —11	160
	12 —19	161-a
	20 —36	163-m
	37 —50	163-n
13	1 —20	164-d
	21 —26	164-f
	27 —30	164-g
	31 —35	164-h
	36 —38	164-j
14	1 —31	164-k
15	1 —27	164-m
16	1 —33	164-n
17	1 —26	164-o
18	1 — 2	164-q
	3 — 9	164-r
	10 —12	164-s
	13 —14	165-a
	15 —18	165-e
	19 —23	165-a

Chapter	Verse	Section
18	24	165-b
	25 —27	165-e
	28 —38	165-h
	39 —40	165-j
19	1 — 3	165-k
	4 —16a	165-l
	16b—18	165-m
	19 —22	165-n
	23 —24	165-p
	25 —27	165-s
	28 —29	165-w
	30a	165-x
	30b	165-y
	31 —37	165-aa
	38 —42	165-bb
20	1	167-c
	2 — 5	167-d
	6 —10	167-e
	11 —17	167-f
	18	167-g
	19 —23	167-n
	24 —29	168-a
	30 —31	171
21	1 —14	168-b
	15 —19	168-c
	20 —23	168-d
	24 —25	171

ACTS AND EPISTLES

ACTS

Chapter	Verse	Section
1	1 — 8	168-g
	9 —11	169
	12 —15	170

FIRST CORINTHIANS

Chapter	Verse	Section
15	5a	167-m
	6	168-e
	7a	168-f

THIRD NEPHI

Chapter	Verse	Section	Chapter	Verse	Section	Chapter	Verse	Section
1	4–14	11	15	2–10	176-k	21	22–27	179-f
	15–20	14		11–24	176-l		28–29	179-g
	21–22	19	16	1–5	176-m	22	1–17	179-h
8	1–4	159		6–20	176-n	23	1–6	179-i
	5–25	165-u	17	1–5	176-o		7–14	179-j
9	1–22	166-b		6–10	176-p	24	1–18	179-k
10	1–2	166-c		11–22	176-q	25	1–6	179-k
	3–8	166-d		23–25	176-r	26	1–5	179-l
	9–17	167-b	18	1–4	176-s		6–12	179-m
	18–19	172		5–16	176-t		13	180
11	1–3	173-a		17–25	176-u		14–16	181
	4	173-b		26–34	176-v		17–21	182
	5–7	173-c		35–39	176-w	27	1–12	183
	8–9	174	19	1–3	177		13–15	184
	10–12	175		4–8	178-a		16–22	185
	13–15	176-a		9–14	178-b		23–27	186
	16–17	176-b		15–17	178-c		28	187-a
	18–27	176-c		18–24	178-d		29–31	187-b
	28–32	176-d		25–36	178-e		32	187-c
	33–41	176-e	20	1–2	178-f		33	187-d
12	1–2	176-f		3–9	178-g	28	1–3	187-e
	3–48	176-g		10–22	179-a		4–11	187-f
13	1–24	176-g		23–29	179-b		12–15	188
	25–34	176-h		30–46	179-c		16–23	189
14	1–27	176-i	21	1–13	179-d		24–40	190
15	1	176-j		14–21	179-e	29	1–9	191
						30	1–2	191

Division Two

Our Lord of The Gospels

A Digest of the Gospel Records, Chronologically Arranged

FIRST PERIOD

From the Beginning of the Gospel Record to John's Ministry

Sec. & Pg.	Event, Time and Place	Matt.	Mark	Luke	John	3 Nephi
§1 p. 163	**John's testimony.**				1:1-19	No Record
§2 p. 164	**Luke's preface.**			1:1-4		
§3 p. 164	**The genealogies.**	1:1-17		3:23-38		
§4 p. 166	**The annunciation to Zacharias.** Time: B.C. 6, Oct. (Andrews; Croscup) (See Preface) The angel announces to Zacharias (while he is executing the priest's office) the birth of a son; Zacharias, unbelieving, asks for a sign, and is struck dumb; returning to the people outside the temple, they perceive he has seen a vision; his priestly ministration accomplished, he departs to his own house. JERUSALEM, TEMPLE			1:5-23		
§5 p. 168	**Elisabeth goes into retirement.** Elisabeth conceives and goes into retirement for five months. JUDEA (Andrews); HEBRON OR JUTTAH (Croscup)			1:24-25		
§6 p. 168	**The annunciation to Mary.** Time: B.C. 5, Mar.-Apr. (Andrews) In the sixth month of Elisabeth's conception the angel Gabriel, sent from God, announces to Mary, a virgin of Nazareth betrothed to Joseph of the house of David, that she shall be the mother of the Messiah. NAZARETH			1:26-38		

Sec. & Pg.	Event, Time and Place	Matt.	Mark	Luke	John	3 Nephi
§7 p. 169	**Mary visits Elisabeth.** **Time: B.C. 5, Mar.-Apr.** (Andrews) Mary visits Elisabeth, whose unborn babe leaps for joy at the sound of Mary's voice; Elisabeth declares the blessedness of Mary, who sings her hymn of praise,—the "Magnificat." JUDEA (Andrews), HEBRON OR JUTTAH (Croscup)			1:39-56		No Record
§8 p. 170	**The annunciation to Joseph.** **Time: B.C. 5, Mar.-Apr.** (Andrews) An angel of the Lord appears in a dream to Joseph, to whom Mary was espoused, and, explaining Mary's condition, tells Joseph he need not fear to take Mary to wife, for she is to be the mother of one whose name shall be Emmanuel; Joseph, awakening, does as the Lord had bidden him. NAZARETH (Andrews)	1:18-25				
§9 p. 171	**John is born.** **Time: B.C. 5, June** (Andrews) Elisabeth gives birth to a son; her cousins, at the time of John's circumcision, call babe Zacharias; Elisabeth says his name shall be called John; the cousins appeal to the father Zacharias who writes on a tablet that the babe's name shall be John, whereupon the tongue of Zacharias is loosed and he praises God—the "Benedictus." JUDEA (Andrews)			1:57-80		

SEC. & PG.	EVENT, TIME AND PLACE	MATT.	MARK	LUKE	JOHN	3 NEPHI
§10 p. 172	**Caesar Augustus levies a tax.** **Time: B. C. 5, Dec.** (Andrews) Caesar Augustus declares a tax; Joseph and Mary go from Nazareth to Bethlehem to be taxed. NAZARETH TO BETHLEHEM			2:1-5		
§11 p. 173	**Jesus announces his birth in the Western Hemisphere.** **Time: 92nd year of the Reign of the Judges** Voice of the Lord comes to Nephi, son of Nephi, and announces that on this night the sign of his coming shall be given and that on the morrow he will come into the world. ZARAHEMLA					1:4-14
§12 p. 174	**Jesus born.** **Time: B.C. 5, Dec.** (Andrews) **(Others give B.C. 4, January to April)** Mary gives birth to Jesus, who is laid in a manger, there being no place at the inn. BETHLEHEM			2:6-7		
§13 p. 174	**An angel tells the shepherds.** **Time: B.C. 5, Dec.** (Andrews) (See Sec. 12) The angel of the Lord announces to the shepherds the birth of Christ the Lord; he tells them where they will find the babe; heavenly hosts with the angel sing praises to God; the shepherds go to Bethlehem, find the babe, and make known abroad their heavenly message. BETHLEHEM			2:8-20		
§14 p. 175	**No darkness in Western Hemisphere.** **Time: 92nd year of Reign of the Judges**					

Sec. & Pg.	Event, Time and Place	Matt.	Mark	Luke	John	3 Nephi
§14	*(Cont'd)* Signs in the Western Hemisphere of the Lord's coming; at going down of sun darkness does not come with night, and no darkness comes before the sun comes up again. WESTERN HEMISPHERE					1:15-20
§15 p. 176	**The circumcision.** **Time: B.C. 4, Jan. (Andrews) (See Sec. 12 above)** When eight days old, Jesus is circumcised and named Jesus. BETHLEHEM			2:21		
§16 p. 176	**Jesus presented in the Temple.** **Time: B.C. 4, Feb. (Andrews) (See Sec. 12 above)** When the days of Mary's purification are accomplished, they take Jesus to the Temple to present him to the Lord and to offer the Mosaic sacrifice (two turtle doves or two young pigeons); Simeon, a just and devout man, to whom it had been revealed he should not die till he had seen the Lord's Christ, comes by the Spirit into the Temple, takes Jesus in his arms and praises God, testifying also to Jesus ("Nunc Dimittis"); Anna, a prophetess, daughter of Phanuel, of the tribe of Aser, of great age, coming in at that instant gives thanks also to the Lord. JERUSALEM, TEMPLE			2:22-38		
§17 p. 178	**The return to Nazareth.** **Time: B.C. 4, Feb.-Mar.** Mary, Joseph, and the Babe return to Nazareth. NAZARETH			2:39		

SEC. & PG.	EVENT, TIME AND PLACE	MATT.	MARK	LUKE	JOHN	3 NEPHI
§18 p. 178	**Visit of the Magi.** **Time: B.C. 4 (Andrews); Feb. (Croscup)** Returning to Bethlehem, the babe Jesus is sought for by the Magi from the East who have seen his star; they go first to Herod, who asks where the Christ is to be born and is told in Bethlehem of Judea; Herod tells the Wise Men to return to him when they find the King of the Jews; the Magi find Jesus, worship him and give gifts, then, warned in a dream they do not return to Herod, but go home another way. BETHLEHEM; JERUSALEM	2:1-12				
§19 p. 179	**New star in Western Hemisphere.** **Time: 92nd year of Reign of the Judges** The new star is seen in the Western Hemisphere. WESTERN HEMISPHERE					1:21-22
§20 p. 179	**The flight into Egypt.** **Time: B.C. 4 (Andrews); Feb. (Croscup)** Joseph and Mary, warned in a dream by an angel, flee with the Babe to escape the wrath of Herod. BETHLEHEM TO EGYPT	2:13-15				
§21 p. 180	**The slaughter of the babes.** **Time: B.C. 4 (Andrews); Feb. (Croscup)** Herod, mocked by the Wise Men and angered, slays all the children that are in Bethlehem and in the coasts thereof, from two years old and under. BETHLEHEM	2:16-18				

Sec. & Pg.	Event, Time and Place	Matt.	Mark	Luke	John	3 Nephi
§22 p. 180	**Return from Egypt.** **Time: B.C. 4, May (Andrews); May (?) (Croscup)** An angel tells Joseph in a dream that Herod is dead, and commands him to return into the land of Israel with his wife and Child; again warned by God in a dream, he goes into Galilee to avoid Herod's son Archelaus; the family comes and dwells in Nazareth. FROM EGYPT TO NAZARETH	2:19-23		2:40		No Record
§23 p. 181	**Jesus in the Temple.** **Time: A.D. 8, April 8 (Andrews); A.D. 9, Mar. 29 (Croscup)** When twelve years old, Jesus visits Jerusalem with his parents on one of their annual visits; when the parents start homeward Jesus remains behind and is found by them three days later sitting in the Temple, in the midst of the doctors, both hearing them and asking them questions. Jesus, answering the reproof of his mother, first intimates his Messiahship: "Wist ye not that I must be about my Father's business?" JERUSALEM			2:41-50		
§24 p. 182	**Jesus goes back to Nazareth and lives there.** **Time: A.D. 8 to A.D. 26 (Andrews); A.D. 9 to A.D. 26 (Croscup)** Jesus returns to Nazareth with his parents, and lives there with them; "but his mother kept all these sayings in her heart." NAZARETH			2:51-52		

SECOND PERIOD

From the Beginning of John's Ministry to the First Passover of the Ministry of Jesus

Sec. & Pg.	Event, Time and Place	Matt.	Mark	Luke	John	3 Nephi
§25 p. 183	**The early ministry of John the Baptist.** **Time: A.D. 26, Summer (Andrews)** JUDEA (Andrews)					
(a) p. 183	**The time of the beginning of John's ministry.**			3:1-2		
(b) p. 183	**The messenger and the message.**	3:1-6	1:1-6	3:3-6		
(c) p. 184	**John's preaching.** Attacks Pharisees and Sadducees; publicans and soldiers ask questions; urges his hearers to cast out the bad and to share their substance with those who have none; special teachings to the soldiers	3:7-10		3:7-14		
(d) p. 185	**John announces coming of Jesus.** John announces coming of another who shall baptize with the Holy Ghost; declares his own unworthiness	3:11-12	1:7-8	3:15-18		No Record
§26 p. 186	**John baptizes Jesus.** **Time: A.D. 27, Jan. (Andrews)** Jesus, about thirty years old, comes from Nazareth to the Jordan, where John baptizes him, the Father speaking from Heaven in witness of the Son, the Holy Ghost descending in bodily shape like a dove—the Trinity of the Godhead being manifest all at one time, as three distinct personages. THE JORDAN; BETHABARA (Croscup)	3:13-17	1:9-11	3:21-23a		

Sec. & Pg.	Event, Time and Place	Matt.	Mark	Luke	John	3 Nephi
§27 p. 187	**The temptation.** **Time: A.D. 27, Jan.-Feb. (Andrews); Feb.-Mar. (Croscup)** Jesus is driven into the wilderness by the Spirit, to be tempted of Satan; he is there for forty days; he withstands the temptations; Satan leaves him, and angels come and minister to him. WILDERNESS OF JUDEA	4:1-11	1:12-13	4:1-13		No Record
§28 p. 188	**John proclaims he is not the Christ.** **Time: A.D. 27, Feb. (Andrews); Mar. (Croscup)** John, answering the priests and Levites (who were of the Pharisees) from Jerusalem, denies he is the Christ or Elias, nor "that prophet," and declares he is the voice of one crying in the wilderness; he explains his baptism and announces the Christ as standing among them. BETHANY BEYOND THE JORDAN (Andrews); BETHABARA (Croscup)				1:19-28	
§29 p. 189	**John testifies Jesus is Lamb of God.** **Time: A.D. 27, Feb. (Andrews); Mar. (Croscup)** On the next day, John seeing Jesus coming to him, testifies Jesus is the Lamb of God, declares the atonement, witnesses the descent of the Holy Ghost upon Jesus at the time of baptism, and bears record that Jesus is the Son of God. BETHANY BEYOND THE JORDAN (Andrews); BETHABARA (Croscup)				1:29-34	

Sec. & Pg.	Event, Time and Place	Matt.	Mark	Luke	John	3 Nephi
§30 p. 190	**Andrew and Simon meet Jesus.** Time: A.D. 27, Feb. (Andrews); Mar. (Croscup) Again the next day after, John standing with two of his disciples, declares, "Behold the Lamb of God"; the two disciples follow Jesus, ask where he dwells, and abide with him that day; of the two following, one was Andrew, who finds Simon his brother and fetches him to Jesus, who calls him Cephas, a stone. BETHABARA (?) (Croscup)				1:35-42	No Record
§31 p. 190	**Philip and Nathanael found.** Time: A.D. 27, Feb. (Andrews); Mar. (Croscup) On the day following, Jesus, going forth to Galilee, finds Philip and commands him to follow; Philip finds Nathanael, whom Jesus greets as an Israelite without guile; Nathanael believes when Jesus tells him he was under a fig tree; (this is the first recorded use by Jesus of the divine power he possessed over matter, mind, and space). BETHABARA (?) (Croscup)				1:43-51	
§32 p. 191	**The first miracle.** Time: A.D. 27, Mar. (Croscup) On the third day Jesus also performs his first miracle of turning water into wine at a marriage feast in Cana; his mother shows she has knowledge of his divine powers. CANA OF GALILEE				2:1-11	

SEC. & PG.	EVENT, TIME AND PLACE	MATT.	MARK	LUKE	JOHN	3 NEPHI
§33 p. 192	**Jesus goes to Capernaum.** **Time: A.D. 27, Mar.-Apr.** (Croscup) Jesus now goes to Capernaum with his mother, his brethren, and his disciples, and continues there for a few days. CAPERNAUM				2:12	No Record

THIRD PERIOD

The Early Judean Ministry, From the First Passover to His Return to Galilee

Sec. & Pg.	Event, Time and Place	Matt.	Mark	Luke	John	3 Nephi
§34 p. 193	**The first Passover.** **Time: A.D. 27, April 11-17 (Andrews); April 11-18 (Croscup)** Jesus attends the Passover in Jerusalem; goes to the Temple and drives out the traders; he gives his first parable and so makes his first announcement concerning his death and resurrection, — his Messiahship; he performs miracles and many believe; Jesus knows all men. JERUSALEM, TEMPLE				2:13-25	No Record
§35 p. 194	**Nicodemus visits Jesus.** **Time: A.D. 27, April 11-17 (Andrews)** Nicodemus, a Pharisee, visits Jesus secretly by night; Jesus preaches the first great discourse; declares that except a man be born of the water and of the Spirit he cannot enter into the kingdom of God; the Spirit leadeth where it will; Jesus will testify of what he knows and what he has seen; again refers to his crucifixion by citing Moses' lifting up of the serpent in the wilderness, and by saying that God so loved the world that he gave his only begotten Son to save it; men love darkness more than light; he that doeth truth cometh to light. JERUSALEM				3:1-21	

Sec. & Pg.	Event, Time and Place	Matt.	Mark	Luke	John	3 Nephi
§36 p. 195	**Jesus goes into Judea.** **Time: A.D. 27, April (Andrews); April 11-18 (Croscup)** Jesus with his disciples goes into Judea, where Jesus tarries and baptizes. JUDEA				3:22	No Record
§37 p. 195	**John's testimony.** **Time: A.D. 27, Summer (Croscup)** John baptizes at Ænon, near to Salim; John's disciples report Jesus is baptizing; John, in a great discourse, recalls that he has told them he is not the Christ but is sent before him; from now Jesus must increase but John must decrease; discourses upon testimony; he whom God sends preaches the word of God; the Father loveth the Son and has given all things to him; he that believeth on the Son has everlasting life; he that believeth not on the Son shall not see life but the wrath of God abideth on him. JUDEA; ÆNON near SALIM				3:23-36	
§38 p. 196	**Herod imprisons John.** **Time: A.D. 27 (Andrews); Nov. or Dec. (Croscup)** Herod, angered by John's reproof because he (the Tetrarch) had married his brother Philip's wife, Herodias, casts John into prison. FORTRESS OF MACHAERUS — (EAST OF DEAD SEA)	14:3-5	6:17-20	3:19-20		

Sec. & Pg.	Event, Time and Place	Matt.	Mark	Luke	John	3 Nephi
§39 p. 197	**Jesus leaves Judea for Galilee.** **Time: A.D. 27, Dec. (Andrews; Croscup)** Jesus, hearing that John is put into prison, departs into Galilee; he, through his disciples, is baptizing more than John. JUDEA	4:12	1:14	4:14	4:1-3	No Record
§40 p. 198	**The woman of Samaria.** **Time: A.D. 27, Dec. (Andrews; Croscup)** To the woman of Samaria, at Jacob's Well, Jesus preaches his second great discourse; Jesus asks for a drink, and the woman wonders that a Jew should ask a Samaritan for a drink; Jesus reassures her saying that if she had asked him he would have given her living water; he expounds his meaning; he shows he knows her past life; explaining worship, he declares his Messiahship; the disciples returning seemingly reprove him for talking with her; she returns to the city and the men thereof come out to him; he again speaks in parable about the fields white already to harvest; many Samaritans believe and at their request he remains with them two days. SAMARIA—JACOB'S WELL; SYCHAR				4:4-42	
§41 p. 200	**He goes into Galilee.** **Time: A.D. 27, Dec. (Andrews; Croscup)** After two days, Jesus departs from Samaria and goes on to Galilee. SAMARIA TO GALILEE				4:43-44	

FOURTH PERIOD

The Great Galilean Ministry

Sec. & Pg.	Event, Time and Place	Matt.	Mark	Luke	John	3 Nephi
	I. From the Return to Galilee Until the Choosing of the Twelve.					
§42 p. 201	**Jesus preaches in Galilee.** Time: A.D. 27-28, Winter. Jesus comes into Galilee preaching the kingdom of God is at hand; he teaches in the synagogues, all glorifying him; they have seen his works at the feast in Jerusalem. GALILEE	4:17	1:14-15	4:14-15	4:45	
§43 p. 201	**Healing nobleman's son.** Time: A.D. 27-28, Winter. A nobleman of Capernaum seeks Jesus in Cana, and asks Jesus to come to Capernaum to heal his son; speaking of the need of the people for signs to believe, Jesus tells the nobleman to go his way for his son liveth; the nobleman, returning, meets his servants who tell him his son lives; the nobleman checks the time when the child began to mend and finds it was the same hour when Jesus told him his son lives. CANA AND CAPERNAUM				4:46-54	No Record
§44 p. 202	**Jesus rejected at Nazareth.** Time: A.D. 28, Winter (Croscup). Jesus comes to Nazareth; he goes to the synagogue on the Sabbath day, as was his custom; he reads and expounds the scriptures; all the people are surprised at his "gracious words," he continues preaching and shows how God has blessed others than the Israelites,					

Sec. & Pg.	Event, Time and Place	Matt.	Mark	Luke	John	3 Nephi
§44	(*Cont'd*) he charges them with expecting him to do his works there; and he shows how few have been ministered to in the past, and says no prophet is accepted in his own country; angered, they thrust him out of the synagogue and the city, then take him to the brow of a hill to cast him down headlong, but he passes through their midst and goes his way. NAZARETH			4:16-30		No Record
§45 p. 203	**He goes to Capernaum.** **Time: A.D. 28, Winter (Croscup)** Jesus, leaving Nazareth, comes to Capernaum on the seacoast, in the borders of Zabulon and Nephthalim, that the prophecy of Esaias might be fulfilled. CAPERNAUM	4:13-16		4:31a		
§46 p. 204	**Jesus chooses Peter, Andrew, James, and John.** **Time: A.D. 28, Winter (Croscup)** Jesus, pressed by the people, stands by the Lake of Gennesaret; he sits in Simon's boat, and having it pushed out a little from the shore, he teaches the people; he then takes Simon and his boat into the sea, tells Simon to cast his net; Simon demurs, saying he has toiled all night and taken nothing, but says he will do as told; he casts his net and gets so many fish that the net breaks; he beckons his other partners who come and they fill both ships. Peter falls upon his knees saying, "De-					

Sec. & Pg.	Event, Time and Place	Matt.	Mark	Luke	John	3 Nephi
§46	(*Cont'd*) part from me; for I am a sinful man, O Lord"; all are astonished, and he says to them (Peter, Andrew, James, and John), "Follow me, and I will make you fishers of men"; they leave their boats and follow him. Sea of Galilee	4:18-22	1:16-20	5:1-11		
§47 p. 206	**An unclean spirit cast out.** **Time: A.D. 28, Winter (Croscup)** Jesus comes to Capernaum, goes into the synagogue, where they are astonished at his doctrines, for he teaches as one having authority and not as the scribes; an unclean spirit proclaims him the Holy One of God; Jesus rebukes the spirit and commands it to leave the one possessed; the spirit throws the man to the ground and then leaves him uninjured; the people marvel that even the unclean spirits obey him; his fame spreads. Capernaum		1:21-28	4:31-37		No Record
§48 p. 207	**Peter's wife's mother healed; a day of miracles.** **Time: A.D. 28, Winter (Croscup)** Jesus, coming to Peter's home, takes Peter's mother-in-law by the hand, rebukes the fever with which she is afflicted, and she arises and ministers unto them; afterward he heals the multitude that are brought to him, including those possessed, and silences the evil spirits who cry out, "Thou art Christ the Son of God," because they know him. Capernaum	8:14-17	1:29-34	4:38-41		

SEC. & PG.	EVENT, TIME AND PLACE	MATT.	MARK	LUKE	JOHN	3 NEPHI
§49 p. 208	**Jesus makes first tour of Galilee, preaching.** **Time: A.D. 28, Winter-Spring (Croscup)** Beginning the morning after the day of miracles at Peter's house, Jesus, with Simon, and they that are with him following, makes his first preaching tour of Galilee, healing the sick of all manner of diseases, healing those possessed of devils, those who are lunatick; he preaches in their synagogues; multitudes follow him from Galilee, Decapolis, Jerusalem, and Judea and from beyond the Jordan. GALILEE	4:23-25	1:35-39	4:42-44	....	No Record
§50 p. 209	**The Sermon on the Mount.** **Time: A.D. 28** GALILEE	Chaps. 5-7	....	....	....	No Record
§51 p. 215	**The leper healed.** **Time: A.D. 28, March (Croscup)** Multitudes follow Jesus coming down from the mountain; a leper worshiping Jesus, asks to be cleansed; Jesus touching him says: "Be thou clean"; the leper is instantly healed; Jesus tells him to go to the Temple priest, show himself and offer the Mosaic cleansings, but to tell no man; disobeying this, the healed leper blazes it abroad so that Jesus "could no more openly enter into the city, but was without in desert places: and they came to him from every quarter." GALILEE	8:1-4	1:40-45	5:12-16	....	No Record

Sec. & Pg.	Event, Time and Place	Matt.	Mark	Luke	John	3 Nephi
§52 p. 216	**One sick with palsy is healed.** **Time: A.D. 28, March (Croscup)** Jesus returning to Capernaum after some days, it is noised about that he is in the house; many gather there including Pharisees and doctors of law from every town in Galilee, Judea, and from Jerusalem. Jesus preaches to the multitude, which is so great that no one can get near the door; they bring on his bed a man sick with palsy, and as they can not get in to Jesus through the door, they go upon the housetop and let him down through the tiling into the midst before Jesus; and when Jesus sees his faith, he says: "Man, thy sins are forgiven thee"; the scribes and the Pharisees questioning among themselves declare that this is blasphemy; Jesus perceiving what is in their hearts, says: "Why reason ye these things in your hearts? Whether is it easier to say to the sick of the palsy, Thy sins be forgiven thee; or to say, Arise, and take up thy bed," and then commands the man to "arise, and take up thy couch, and go into thine house." The man obeys, and all glorify God. CAPERNAUM	9:2-8	2:1-12	5:17-26		No Record
§53 p. 218	**Jesus chooses Matthew who gives a feast.** **Time: A.D. 28, March (Croscup)** Passing from thence, Jesus goes forth again by the seaside, and multitudes fol-					

Sec. & Pg.	Event, Time and Place	Matt.	Mark	Luke	John	3 Nephi
§53	*(Cont'd)* low him, he teaches them; seeing Levi — Matthew — son of Alphaeus, sitting at the receipt of custom, he says, "Follow me," and Matthew follows; Matthew makes a great feast for Jesus (in Matthew's house) and a great company of publicans and sinners come and sit down; the Pharisees murmur at this, asking why he eats with publicans and sinners; Jesus answers that the sick, not the well, need a physician, and that he comes not to call the righteous but the sinners to repentance. SEA OF GALILEE	9:9-13	2:13-17	5:27-32	....	No Record
§54 p. 220	**John's disciples question Jesus about fasting.** **Time: A.D. 28, March** The disciples of John come to Jesus and ask why do not the disciples of Jesus fast as do they and the Pharisees; Jesus answers in parables—children of the bridechamber, a piece of new cloth in an old garment, new wine in old bottles, and new wine as against old wine. SEA OF GALILEE	9:14-17	2:18-22	5:33-39	....	
§55 p. 221	**The second Passover.** **Time: A.D. 28, April (Croscup)** Jesus goes to Jerusalem to the Passover (the second of his ministry); goes on the Sabbath to the pool of Bethesda and heals there a man with an infirmity of thirty-eight years' standing; Jesus slips away without before the man can tell who Jesus is; the man tells					

Sec. & Pg.	Event, Time and Place	Matt.	Mark	Luke	John	3 Nephi
§55	(*Cont'd*) those asking who healed him that he does not know; later the man sees Jesus in the Temple and knows him as Jesus warns him to sin no more; the Jews seek to kill Jesus because he has healed on the Sabbath (this is the first record of an effort to kill Jesus); Jesus preaches to them, proclaiming his Sonship, for which they again seek his life; he says he does whatever the Father does; preaches knowing the Father and the Son; he declares his powers, but can do nothing of himself; he tells John's mission; he is greater than John; tells of work the Father has given him to do; explains relationship of the Father and himself; tells how they will be accused. JERUSALEM				5:1-47	No Record
§56 p. 224	**Disciples pluck corn on Sabbath.** **Time: A.D. 28, April (Croscup)** The disciples, hungry and going through a field of corn, pluck the ears of corn and eat them; the Pharisees charge them with violating the Sabbath; in justification Jesus cites David's eating of the shewbread, that the priests in the Temple profane the Sabbath and are blameless; declares that in this place there is one greater than the Temple, and that the "Son of man is Lord even of the sabbath day." GALILEE (Croscup)	12:1-8	2:23-28	6:1-5		

Sec. & Pg.	Event, Time and Place	Matt.	Mark	Luke	John	3 Nephi
§57 p. 225	**Man with withered hand healed.** **Time: A.D. 28, April (Croscup)** Jesus enters a synagogue on the Sabbath in which there was a man who has a withered hand; the Pharisees and scribes watch him to see if he will heal on the Sabbath, that they may find an accusation against him; knowing their thoughts, he asks what man among them would not on the Sabbath save a sheep which had fallen into a pit, and how much better is a man than a sheep; he then heals the hand; the Pharisees take counsel with the Herodians how they may destroy Jesus. GALILEE (Croscup)	12:9-14	3:1-6	6:6-11	....	No Record
§58 p. 226	**Jesus withdraws to the sea.** **Time: A.D. 28, May (?) (Croscup)** Hearing that they plot against him, Jesus withdraws to the sea, multitudes follow him; "he healed them all; and charged them that they should not make him known"; he does this that the prophecy by Esaias might be fulfilled. SEA OF GALILEE	12:15-21	3:7-12	....	....	
§59 p. 227	**The Twelve chosen.** **Time: A.D. 28, Early Summer (?) (Croscup)** Jesus goes up into a mountain, and after a night of prayer, "calleth unto him whom he would: and they came unto him," and he chooses and ordains Twelve whom he names Apostles; they are to be with him that he may send them forth to preach, with					

SEC. & PG.	EVENT, TIME AND PLACE	MATT.	MARK	LUKE	JOHN	3 NEPHI
§59	(*Cont'd*) "power to heal sicknesses, and to cast out devils"; then the multitude come together again "so that they could not so much as eat bread"; his friends hearing of this "went out to lay hold on him: for they said, He is beside himself." MOUNTAINS OF GALILEE (Croscup)	10:2-4	3:13-21	6:12-16	....	
	II. From the Choosing of the Twelve to the Tour in Northern Galilee.					
§60 p. 229	**The Sermon on the Plain.** **Time: A.D. 28, Midsummer (Andrews)** NEAR CAPERNAUM (Andrews)	....	....	6:17-49	....	
§61 p. 231	**The Centurion's servant healed.** **Time: A.D. 28, Summer (Andrews)** Jesus, ending his sermon on the plain, enters Capernaum; a Centurion, friendly to the Jews for whom he had built a synagogue, sends unto Jesus the elders asking that Jesus come and heal his servant; Jesus starts toward the Centurion's place, but is met by friends of the Centurion bearing to Jesus the message that he need not trouble to come, the Centurion saying he himself is unworthy that Jesus should come under his roof, and that all Jesus need do is to say that it shall be done, just as the Centurion orders his soldiers, and it will be done; Jesus marvels at this faith, turns himself about, saying that it shall					No Record

Sec. & Pg.	Event, Time and Place	Matt.	Mark	Luke	John	3 Nephi
§61	*(Cont'd)* be as the Centurion believes; the servant is healed; Jesus shows that salvation is to others than the Jews. CAPERNAUM	8:5-13		7:1-10		No Record
§62 p. 232	**The son of widow of Nain raised.** **Time: A.D. 28, Summer (Andrews)** The day after healing the Centurion's servant, Jesus goes to Nain, with many of his disciples and much people; as he is entering the gate of the city he meets the people with the dead son, the only son, of a widow; having compassion on the woman, he touches the bier, the carriers stand still; he commands the man to rise; he that was dead sits up and begins to speak, and Jesus delivers him to his mother; a fear comes on the people, they glorify God, pronounce Jesus a great prophet; this rumor of him goes throughout Judea and the region round about. NAIN			7:11-17		
§63 p. 233	**John sends messengers, questioning, to Jesus.** **Time: A.D. 28, Summer (Andrews)** John being in prison, his disciples tell him of the works of Jesus; John sends his disciples to ask Jesus, "Art thou he that should come? or look we for another"; Jesus tells them to "go and shew John again those things which ye do hear and see," and he names them; Jesus then discourses to the multitude					

Sec. & Pg.	Event, Time and Place	Matt.	Mark	Luke	John	3 Nephi
§63	(*Cont'd*) about John, his mission, and his place; he refers to John's works and asks three times, "What went ye out into the wilderness to see?"; he compares John and himself; he upbraids Chorazin and Bethsaida; the publicans glorify God, being baptized of John; the Pharisees reject God, and also the lawyers, being not baptized of John. GALILEE..	11:2-30	....	7:18-35	....	No Record
§64 p. 236	**Jesus anointed by sinning woman.** **Time: A.D. 28, Autumn (Andrews)** After his discourse about John, Jesus, being desired of a Pharisee, Simon, goes with him to his house to eat with him; a sinner, a woman, comes with an alabaster box of ointment and while washing his feet with her tears and kissing his feet, she anoints them with ointment; the Pharisee reasons that if Jesus were a prophet, he would know what manner of woman this is; Jesus, reading his thoughts, states the parable of the two debtors, both forgiven, and asks which will love him most; Simon answers the one who owed most; Jesus then reproves Simon for his failure to keep the rules of hospitality, and forgives the woman's sins; those at the table ask who is this that forgives sins; Jesus tells the woman that her faith has saved her and that she may go in peace. GALILEE (Andrews)	....	....	7:36-50	....	

Sec. & Pg.	Event, Time and Place	Matt.	Mark	Luke	John	3 Nephi
§65 p. 237	**Another tour of Galilee.** **Time: A.D. 28, Autumn** (Andrews) Jesus makes a tour throughout Galilee, preaching to the people; he takes with him the Twelve, Mary Magdalene, Joanna the wife of Chuza, Herod's steward, and many others "which ministered unto him of their substance." GALILEE (Andrews)			8:1-3		
§66 p. 238	**Blind and dumb man healed.** **Time: A.D. 28, Autumn** (Andrews) Jesus heals a blind and dumb man, possessed with a devil, so that the man both speaks and sees; the people are amazed, and say, "Is not this the son of David?" CAPERNAUM (Andrews)	12:22-23				No Record
§67 p. 238	**They charge he is in league with Beelzebub.** **Time: A.D. 28, Autumn** (Andrews) The Pharisees and the scribes who came down from Jerusalem, seeing Jesus heal the blind and dumb man possessed with a devil, charge that Jesus is casting out devils by the power of Beelzebub, the prince of devils; Jesus shows, by stating the principle and explaining it (that a house divided against itself cannot stand), that he is not working under the power of the devil but under the power of God; he says that blasphemy against the Holy Ghost will not be forgiven; says that out of the abund-					

SEC. & PG.	EVENT, TIME AND PLACE	MATT.	MARK	LUKE	JOHN	3 NEPHI
§67	(*Cont'd*) ance of the heart the mouth speaketh and that man must give account for every idle word. CAPERNAUM (Andrews)	12:24-37	3:22-30			
§68 p. 240	**Jesus discourses on signs.** **Time: A.D. 28, Autumn (Andrews)** Jesus having denied he was in league with Beelzebub, certain of the scribes and of the Pharisees "answered, saying, Master, we would see a sign from thee"; Jesus answers, "an evil and adulterous generation seeketh after a sign," and states none shall be given, except the sign of Jonas; he predicts his death, burial, and resurrection; compares the people of Nineveh and the queen of the south to "this generation"; and closes with a parable. CAPERNAUM (Andrews)	12:38-45				No Record
§69 p. 241	**His mother and brethren seek him.** **Time: A.D. 28, Autumn (Andrews)** While still speaking with the people, his mother and brethren come to see him, but can not get to him for the press of the people; being told they seek him, he asks, "Who is my mother, or my brethren?" and then states the larger relationship—"Whosoever shall do the will of God, the same is my brother, and my sister, and mother." GALILEE (Andrews)	12:46-50	3:31-35	8:19-21		

SEC. & PG.	EVENT, TIME AND PLACE	MATT.	MARK	LUKE	JOHN	3 NEPHI
§70 p. 242	**The multitudes taught by parables.** Time: A.D. 28, Autumn (Andrews) Jesus, on the same day, leaving the house, goes and sits by the seaside; great multitudes out of every city gather; he takes a seat in a ship, the multitude stand on the shore; he teaches them in parables. SEA OF GALILEE (Andrews)	13:1-3a	4:1-2	8:4		No Record
(a) p. 242	**Parable of the sower.**	13:3b-23	4:3-25	8:5-18		
(b) p. 246	**Parable of the seed growing by itself.**		4:26-29			
(c) p. 246	**Parable of the tares.**	13:24-30				
(d) p. 247	**Parable of the mustard seed and the leaven.**	13:31-35	4:30-34			
(e) p. 247	**Parable of the tares explained.**	13:36-43				
(f) p. 248	**Other parables.**	13:44-53				
§71 p. 249	**The storm stilled.** Time: A.D. 28, Autumn (Andrews) Jesus seeing great multitudes about him, gives commandment to depart to the other side of the lake; a scribe desiring to follow, Jesus says the foxes have holes, but the Son of man has nowhere to lay his head; a disciple asks to bury his father before going, Jesus says let the dead bury their dead; along with the ship in which Jesus is, other little ships go; he falls asleep, a great storm arises, the ship fills with water, the disciples awaken him saying, "Lord, save us: we perish." He rebukes the wind and the raging water,					

Sec. & Pg.	Event, Time and Place	Matt.	Mark	Luke	John	3 Nephi
§71	*(Cont'd)* a calm comes; he reproves them for their lack of faith. SEA OF GALILEE	8:18-27	4:35-41	8:22-25		
§72 p. 250	**The Gadarene demoniacs.** **Time: A.D. 28, Autumn (Andrews)** Crossing to the southerly coast of the Sea of Galilee, Jesus comes to the country of the Gadarenes; as he goes forth he meets two possessed with devils, who hail him as Jesus, Son of God and ask why he torments them before their time, and beseech him not to command them to go out into the deep but let them enter a nearby herd of some two thousand swine; Jesus permits this and the swine rush down into the sea and perish; the herders tell the people of the city who come out to see him, and seeing what has happened, they beseech Jesus to leave their country. GADARA	8:28-34	5:1-20	8:26-39		No Record
§73 p. 253	**Jesus returns to Capernaum.** **Time: A.D. 28, Autumn (Andrews)** Jesus enters into a ship and returns to the coast of Capernaum, much people gladly receive him for they are all waiting for him, and he was nigh unto the sea. SEA OF GALILEE TO CAPERNAUM	9:1	5:21	8:40		
§74 p. 253	**The daughter of Jairus raised.** **Time: A.D. 28, Autumn (Andrews)** Jairus, a ruler of the synagogue, whose daughter					

SEC. & PG.	EVENT, TIME AND PLACE	MATT.	MARK	LUKE	JOHN	3 NEPHI
§74	(*Cont'd*) lies dying, comes and asks Jesus to come and lay his hands on her that she may live; while they are on the way, messengers come saying the daughter is dead; Jesus bids Jairus have faith, saying all will be well; reaching the house Jesus tells the people there that the child is not dead but sleeps; they laugh him to scorn; taking Peter, James, and John, and the father and mother into the room with him, and putting all others out, he takes the daughter by the hand and commands her to rise; she rises straightway and he commands that they give her something to eat and charges them they shall tell no man what was done. CAPERNAUM	9:18-19, 23-26	5:22-24, 35-43	8:41-42, 49-56		No Record
§75 p. 255	**The woman with the issue of blood healed.** **Time: A.D. 28, Autumn (Andrews)** Jesus going through the crowd is touched on the garment by a woman who for twelve years has had an issue of blood and had "suffered many things of many physicians, and had spent all that she had, and was nothing bettered, but rather grew worse"; she has faith that if she touches only the garment of Jesus she will be healed; she touches his garment and is healed immediately; Jesus senses the touch for he says, "I perceive that virtue is gone out of me"; Jesus asks					

Sec. & Pg.	Event, Time and Place	Matt.	Mark	Luke	John	3 Nephi
§75	*(Cont'd)* who touched him; the disciples saw no one, she then comes forward and falling down before him, tells all; he says, "Daughter, be of good comfort: thy faith hath made thee whole; go in peace." CAPERNAUM	9:20-22	5:25-34	8:43-48	....	
§76 p. 257	**Two blind men healed.** **Time: A.D. 28, Autumn (Andrews)** Two blind men follow Jesus, asking to be healed, he asks them if they believe he is able to do this, they say, "Yea, Lord"; he touches their eyes saying, "According to your faith be it unto you," and their eyes are opened; he charges them to tell no one, but they spread his fame abroad. CAPERNAUM	9:27-31	....	....	....	**No Record**
§77 p. 257	**The dumb demoniac healed.** **Time: A.D. 28, Autumn (Andrews)** As the blind men go out, they bring to Jesus a dumb man possessed with a devil; Jesus casts out the devil and the dumb man speaks; the multitude marvel, saying it was never seen in Israel; the Pharisees renew the charge that Jesus is in league with the devils. CAPERNAUM	9:32-34	....	....	....	
§78 p. 258	**The second rejection at Nazareth.** **Time: A.D. 29, Winter (Andrews)** Jesus returns to Nazareth and teaches in the synagogue; the people marvel at him, his preaching, his					

Sec. & Pg.	Event, Time and Place	Matt.	Mark	Luke	John	3 Nephi
§78	*(Cont'd)* works, they refer to the fact that his mother, his brothers, and sisters are still among them; he tells them a prophet is not without honor save in his own country, but he can there do no great works; "he laid his hands upon a few sick folk, and healed them"; he marvels because of their unbelief. NAZARETH	13:54-58	6:1-6a			No Record
§79 p. 259	**Jesus again tours Galilee.** **Time: A.D. 29, Winter (Andrews)** Jesus makes another tour of Galilee, teaching in their synagogues, and "healing every sickness and every disease among the people"; he is moved with compassion because the people are scattered abroad as sheep without a shepherd; he tells his disciples "the harvest truly is plenteous, but the labourers are few"; he tells them to pray the Lord that the labourers will be sent forth to the harvest. GALILEE	9:35-38	6:6b			
§80 p. 259	**The Twelve sent forth.** **Time: A.D. 29, Winter (Andrews)** The Twelve sent forth by Jesus; his charge to them. GALILEE	10:1, 5-42	6:7-13	9:1-6		
§81 p. 262	**Jesus continues tour.** **Time: A.D. 29, Winter (Andrews)** Jesus, having charged the Twelve, continues his tour of preaching. GALILEE	11:1				

Sec. & Pg.	Event, Time and Place	Matt.	Mark	Luke	John	3 Nephi
§82 p. 262	**Herod beheads John.** **Time: A.D. 29, Winter (Andrews)** Herod giving a feast on his birthday, promises the daughter of his wife Herodias (the daughter having danced before him) anything she might ask for; she goes forth and asks her mother what she shall ask for; Herodias tells her to ask for the head of John the Baptist; she asks this of Herod who regretfully grants her request, orders John beheaded, and the head brought on a charger and given to the damsel. FORTRESS OF MACHAERUS (EAST SIDE OF DEAD SEA) (Andrews)	14:6-12	6:21-29			
§83 p. 263	**Herod thinks Jesus is John.** **Time: A.D. 29, Winter (Andrews)** Herod, hearing of the fame of Jesus (seemingly for the first time), thinks Jesus is John the Baptist resurrected, and he desires Jesus brought to him. GALILEE (Andrews)	14:1-2	6:14-16	9:7-9		No Record
§84 p. 264	**The Twelve report.** **Time: A.D. 29, April (Andrews)** The Twelve gather themselves together unto Jesus and tell him what they had done and what they had taught. CAPERNAUM (Andrews)		6:30	9:10a		
§85 p. 265	**He goes to Bethsaida.** **Time: A.D. 29, April (Andrews)** Jesus hearing of Herod's desire to see him, takes his disciples by ship, into a desert place belonging to					

SEC. & PG.	EVENT, TIME AND PLACE	MATT.	MARK	LUKE	JOHN	3 NEPHI
§85	*(Cont'd)* the city called Bethsaida, to rest awhile, "for there were many coming and going, and they had no leisure so much as to eat"; and the people when they knew it, "followed him on foot out of the cities." NEAR BETHSAIDA	14:13	6:31-32	9:10b-11a		No Record
§86 p. 265	**The five thousand fed.** **Time: A.D. 29, April (Andrews)** Jesus, seeing the multitude who were as sheep without a shepherd, has compassion on them; he heals their sick and teaches them concerning the kingdom of God; when evening was come, instead of sending them away to the villages to buy food as the disciples suggested, he has them sit down by fifties in a company; he then takes the five loaves and two fishes which the disciples had, blesses them and passes them around amongst the people; the whole multitude of 5,000 men besides the women and children, are fed, and there are gathered up after all had had enough, twelve baskets of the fragments and of the fishes. NEAR BETHSAIDA	14:14-21	6:33-44	9:11b-17	6:1-14	
§87 p. 268	**Jesus prevents their making him king.** **Time: A.D. 29, April (Andrews)** The 5,000 men, seeing the miracle of the feeding of the multitude, would "come and take him by force, to make him a king," but he departs again "into a mountain himself alone," after					

Sec. & Pg.	Event, Time and Place	Matt.	Mark	Luke	John	3 Nephi
§87	(*Cont'd*) sending his disciples away to the other side while he sends the multitudes away. MOUNTAIN, NEAR SEA OF GALILEE	14:22-23	6:45-46	....	6:15	No Record
§88 p. 268	**Jesus walks on sea.** **Time: A.D. 29, April (Andrews)** The disciples begin crossing the sea towards Capernaum; a great wind blows and the sea arises; the wind being contrary to them, they are forced to row; Jesus seeing this walks to them on the sea; they are frightened, thinking him a spirit, and cry out for fear; Jesus calls to them, "It is I; be not afraid"; Peter says: "Lord, if it be thou, bid me come unto thee on the water"; Jesus says, "Come"; Peter starts, but fearing the waves, begins to sink and calls to Jesus for help; Jesus takes his hand and reproves him for lack of faith; the wind ceases; the disciples worship him saying: "Of a truth thou art the Son of God." SEA OF GALILEE	14:24-33	6:47-52	....	6:16-21	
§89 p. 270	**The discourse to the multitude on the bread of life.** **Time: A.D. 29, April (Andrews)** The people missing Jesus on the eastern shore of the Sea, take shipping and go to Capernaum and finding Jesus, ask why he came there; he answers saying they come to him not because of his miracles but because he feeds them; Jesus then preaches his great sermon on the bread of life;					

Sec. & Pg.	Event, Time and Place	Matt.	Mark	Luke	John	3 Nephi
§89	*(Cont'd)* he tells them to labor not for meat that perisheth, but for the meat which endureth unto eternal life which the Son of man shall give them; they ask what shall they do; then ask for a sign; Jesus compares manna with the bread of God; Jesus announces his Messiahship; Jews murmur because Jesus said he is the bread; Jesus declares his relationship to the Father; he tells them what bread he is; he declares the atonement by his flesh and blood; many of his disciples murmur at the doctrine and "went back, and walked no more with him"; Peter declares, "thou art that Christ, the Son of the living God"; Jesus declares one of the Twelve is a devil. CAPERNAUM				6:22-71	No Record
§90 p. 273	**People in land of Gennesaret healed.** **Time: A.D. 29, April (Andrews)** Jesus coming into the land of Gennesaret, the people know him, and run through the whole region carrying to him in beds those who are sick, who seek only to touch the hem of his garment, and as many as touch are healed; and this is done wheresoever he goes. GENNESARET	14:34-36	6:53-56			
§91 p. 273	**The discourses upon cleanliness.** **Time: A.D. 29, April (Andrews)** The scribes and Pharisees come from Jerusalem, complain that the disciples					

Sec. & Pg.	Event, Time and Place	Matt.	Mark	Luke	John	3 Nephi
§91	*(Cont'd)* eat with unwashen hands, contrary to the traditions of the elders; Jesus first calling attention to their own violation of the law, calls them hypocrites, refers to the prophecy of Esaias about people drawing near God with their lips, while their hearts are far from him; says that man is defiled by what comes out of his mouth, not by what is taken in (he later explains this parable, answering Peter); they tell him the Pharisees are much offended, and Jesus tells his disciples to leave the Pharisees alone, for they are the blind leading the blind. CAPERNAUM	15:1-20	7:1-23	....	....	No Record
	(This is the time of the third Passover)					
	III. From the Retirement into Northern Galilee Until the Closing of the Galilean Ministry.					
§92 p. 276	**Jesus goes into northern Galilee.** **Time: A.D. 29, Spring-Summer (Andrews)** Jesus now goes into northern Galilee, to the coasts of Tyre and Sidon; "he would not walk in Jewry, because the Jews sought to kill him"; he enters into a house, trying not to be known, "but he could not be hid." GALILEE	15:21	7:24	....	7:1	

SEC. & PG.	EVENT, TIME AND PLACE	MATT.	MARK	LUKE	JOHN	3 NEPHI
§93 p. 277	**The daughter of the Greek woman healed.** **Time: A.D. 29, Summer** (Andrews) A Greek woman (Syrophenician by nation) whose daughter is possessed with a devil, seeks Jesus to have him cast it forth; Jesus not answering at first, his disciples ask him to send her away; Jesus replies that he is not sent but to the lost sheep of Israel; she again approaches Jesus and worships, asking again that he heal her daughter; Jesus says it is not meet to take the children's bread and cast it to the dogs; she replies that the dogs may eat the crumbs that fall from the master's table; he replies: "O woman, great is thy faith: be it unto thee even as thou wilt"; her daughter is healed. REGION OF TYRE AND SIDON	15:22-28	7:25-30			No Record
§94 p. 278	**He returns to Sea of Galilee.** **Time: A.D. 29, Summer** (Andrews) Jesus leaves the coasts of Tyre and Sidon and returns to the Sea of Galilee through "the midst of the coasts of Decapolis." GALILEE	15:29a	7:31			
§95 p. 278	**Jesus heals deaf man.** **Time: A.D. 29, Summer** (Andrews) The people bring to Jesus a deaf man with an impediment in his speech and ask Jesus to put his hand upon him; Jesus takes him aside, puts his fingers into his					

Sec. & Pg.	Event, Time and Place	Matt.	Mark	Luke	John	3 Nephi
§95	*(Cont'd)* ears, spits and touches his tongue, and the man hears and speaks; Jesus charges them not to tell of this, but they do, and the more he charges the more they publish. DECAPOLIS (Andrews)		7:32-37			No Record
§96 p. 279	**The four thousand fed.** **Time: A.D. 29, Summer (Andrews)** Jesus goes up into a mountain and sits down; multitudes come to him with their lame, blind, dumb, maimed, and many others and cast them down at Jesus' feet, and he heals them; after three days he tells his disciples the multitude must be fed; the disciples ask, "From whence can a man satisfy these men with bread here in the wilderness?"; he asks how much bread they have, they say seven loaves; he has the people sit down, then he blesses the bread and the disciples set it before the people; they have a few small fishes, and to these he does the same; after all have eaten, they gather up seven baskets; there were four thousand men besides the women and children. DECAPOLIS (Andrews)	15:29b-38	8:1-9			
§97 p. 280	**Jesus goes to Magdala.** **Time: A.D. 29, Summer (Andrews)** Jesus sends away the multitudes, takes ship, and comes to the coasts of Magdala. SEA OF GALILEE (Andrews)	15:39	8:10			

Sec. & Pg.	Event, Time and Place	Matt.	Mark	Luke	John	3 Nephi
§98 p. 280	**He again discourses about signs.** Time: A.D. 29, Summer (Andrews) The Pharisees and Sadducees come tempting him, and asking for a sign; wearied, he says: "Why doth this generation seek after a sign?"; he tells them, "There shall no sign be given unto this generation"; he points out they can read the signs of the weather but can not read the signs of the times; he tells them that a wicked and adulterous generation seeketh after a sign; he enters the ship and goes to the other side; he tells his disciples to beware of the leaven of the Pharisees and of Herod; they had taken no bread with them and think he refers to that fact; he bemoans their lack of understanding. CAPERNAUM (Andrews)	16:1-12	8:11-21			No Record
§99 p. 282	**A blind man healed.** Time: A.D. 29, Summer (Andrews) Jesus comes to Bethsaida; they bring him a blind man to heal and beseech Jesus to touch him; Jesus takes the man by the hand, leads him out of town, spits on his eyes, puts his hands upon him, and asks him if he sees aught; the man says he sees men as trees walking; Jesus puts his hands again upon his eyes, and the man sees clearly; Jesus sends the man away, telling him not to go into the town nor to tell anyone. BETHSAIDA		8:22-26			

Sec. & Pg.	Event, Time and Place	Matt.	Mark	Luke	John	3 Nephi
§100 p. 283	**Peter's testimony of the Christ.** **Time: A.D. 29, Summer or Autumn** Jesus coming into the coasts of Caesarea Philippi asks his disciples: "Whom do men say that I the Son of man am?"; they answer, some say John the Baptist, some Elias, some Jeremias, or one of the prophets; he then asks, "But whom say ye that I am?" Peter answers, "Thou art the Christ, the Son of the living God"; Jesus blesses Peter and promises the keys of the kingdom and the binding and loosing power; Jesus charges them that they shall tell no one he is the Christ. REGION OF CAESAREA PHILIPPI	16:13-20	8:27-30	9:18-22	....	No Record
§101 p. 284	**He teaches his disciples concerning his death and resurrection.** **Time: A.D. 29, Summer or Autumn** From this time forth Jesus begins to teach his disciples that he will be killed and resurrected on the third day; Peter rebukes Jesus for saying this, and Jesus answers, "Get thee behind me, Satan"; Jesus says men following him must take up the cross; that whosoever saves his life shall lose it, and whosoever loses it for his sake shall find it; he asks what is a man profited if he gain the whole world and lose his soul, or what shall a man give in exchange for his soul; the Son of man					

SEC. & PG.	EVENT, TIME AND PLACE	MATT.	MARK	LUKE	JOHN	3 NEPHI
§101	*(Cont'd)* shall come in glory and reward every man according to his works; finally he tells them that some standing there shall not taste death. REGION OF CAESAREA PHILIPPI (G. W. Clark)	16:21-28	8:31-38, 9:1	9:23-27		No Record
§102 p. 286	**The transfiguration.** **Time: A.D. 29, Summer or Autumn** About a week after, Jesus takes Peter, James, and John "up into an high mountain apart," and "was transfigured before them"; the three see Jesus talking with Moses and Elias, and they speak "of his decease which he should accomplish at Jerusalem"; Peter, James, and John "were heavy with sleep" and "when they were awake, they saw his glory, and the two men that stood with him"; Peter proposes to build "three tabernacles," one each for Jesus, Moses, and Elias; then a bright cloud overshadows them, and they hear a voice say, "This is my beloved Son: hear him." They fall to the ground, Jesus touches them and tells them to arise and be not afraid; Jesus charges them to tell no man of this vision till he has risen from the dead; Jesus discourses regarding Elias. MT. HERMON	17:1-13	9:2-13	9:28-36		No Record
§103 p. 288	**A demoniac healed.** **Time: A.D. 29, Summer-Autumn** Coming down from the mountain, they come to the multitude, where his dis-					No Record

SEC. & PG.	EVENT, TIME AND PLACE	MATT.	MARK	LUKE	JOHN	3 NEPHI
§103	*(Cont'd)* ciples are being questioned by the scribes; a man kneels before Jesus and asks that Jesus heal his only son possessed with a spirit that tears and bruises him, he, foaming at the mouth, gnashing his teeth, and pining away; the disciples have been unable to heal the man; asked if he believes, the father cries: "Lord, I believe; help thou mine unbelief"; Jesus has them bring the child to him and he heals him; Jesus reproves his disciples for unbelief, which prevents their performing the miracle; Jesus states, "Howbeit this kind goeth not out but by prayer and fasting." MT. HERMON (Andrews)	17:14-21	9:14-29	9:37-43a	....	No Record
§104 p. 290	**Jesus again tours Galilee.** **Time: A.D. 29, Summer-Autumn** Jesus passes again through Galilee, teaching his disciples his death and resurrection — "but they understood not that saying, and were afraid to ask him." GALILEE (G. W. Clark)	17:22-23	9:30-32	9:43b-45	....	No Record
§105 p. 291	**The tribute money.** **Time: A.D. 29, Summer-Autumn** Tax collectors ask Peter if Jesus pays tribute; Peter says yes; Jesus, upon Peter's coming into the house, questions him and then tells him to go to the sea, cast in a hook, and he shall find the tax money in the mouth of the first fish Peter catches. CAPERNAUM	17:24-27	....	....	....	No Record

Sec. & Pg.	Event, Time and Place	Matt.	Mark	Luke	John	3 Nephi
§106 p. 291	**The discourse on meekness and humility.** **Time: A.D. 29, Summer-Autumn** Jesus asks his disciples what they disputed on the way; they hold their peace; Jesus, perceiving the thoughts of their hearts that they have disputed amongst themselves who shall be greatest, calls to him a little child and sets him in their midst and gives the great discourse on meekness and humility and becoming as little children; he tells them of the place of children in heaven; "if any man desire to be first, the same shall be last of all, and servant of all"; he tells them to purge themselves of things giving offense; saying the Son of man is come to save that which is lost, he gives the parable of the lost sheep and the man leaving the ninety and nine and going in search of the one lost. CAPERNAUM	18:1-14	9:33-37 43-50	9:46-48	....	No Record
§107 p. 293	**The discourse on forgiveness and the sealing power.** **Time: A.D. 29, Summer-Autumn** Jesus discourses further on dealing with an erring brother; first try to make it right with him alone, then in the presence of witnesses, then before the whole Church, that failing, "let him be unto thee as an heathen man and a publican"; tells them, "Whatsoever ye shall bind on earth shall be bound in heaven: and whatsoever ye shall					

Sec. & Pg.	Event, Time and Place	Matt.	Mark	Luke	John	3 Nephi
§107	(*Cont'd*) loose on earth shall be loosed in heaven"; if two agree on earth "as touching any thing that they shall ask, it shall be done for them of my Father which is in heaven. For where two or three are gathered together in my name, there am I in the midst of them." CAPERNAUM (G. W. Clark)	18:15-20				
§108 p. 294	**A further discourse on forgiveness.** **Time: A.D. 29, Summer-Autumn** Peter inquires of Jesus, "How oft shall my brother sin against me, and I forgive him? till seven times? Jesus saith unto him, I say not unto thee, Until seven times: but, Until seventy times seven"; Jesus gives the parable of the king who forgave the debt of his servant, who at once dealt harshly with one who owed him, whereupon the Lord took harsh measures against the servant on account of his debt: "So likewise shall my heavenly Father do also unto you, if ye from your hearts forgive not every one his brother their trespasses." CAPERNAUM (G. W. Clark)	18:21-35				No Record
§109 p. 295	**Place of those acting in name of Christ.** **Time: A.D. 29, Summer-Autumn** John tells Jesus they saw one who did not follow Jesus casting out devils in Jesus' name, and they forbade the man so to do because he was not a follower; Jesus says to forbid					

SEC. & PG.	EVENT, TIME AND PLACE	MATT.	MARK	LUKE	JOHN	3 NEPHI
§109	(*Cont'd*) him not "for there is no man which shall do a miracle in my name that can lightly speak evil of me; who is not against us is on our part"; whoever gives a cup of water to drink, because the one to drink belongs to Christ, shall not lose his reward; who offends "one of these little ones that believe in me, it is better for him that a millstone were hanged about his neck, and he were cast into the sea." CAPERNAUM (Robertson)		9:38-42	9:49-50		No Record
§110 p. 296	**A discourse on sacrifice.** **Time: A.D. 29, Summer-Autumn** A man telling Jesus he would follow whithersoever Jesus went, Jesus tells him the foxes have holes, and the birds of the air have nests, but the Son of man hath nowhere to lay his head; Jesus tells another to follow him; the man asks time to bury his father; Jesus says, "Let the dead bury their dead: but go thou and preach the kingdom of God"; another says he will follow, but asks to go bid farewell at his home, Jesus says, "No man, having put his hand to the plough, and looking back, is fit for the kingdom of God." CAPERNAUM (?)			9:57-62		
§111 p. 297	**The Seventy sent forth.** **Time: A.D. 29, Summer-Autumn** The Seventy are sent forth under a charge. CAPERNAUM (Robinson)			10:1-16		

Sec. & Pg.	Event, Time and Place	Matt.	Mark	Luke	John	3 Nephi
§112 p. 298	**Jesus' brethren urge him to go to Judea.** **Time: A.D. 29, Summer-Autumn** His brethren urge him to go to Judea to show there his works, because no man doeth things in secret, and he should show himself to the world if he do these things (his brethren do not believe in him); he says his time is not come, their time is always ready; the world cannot hate them but it hates him because he testifies of it, "that the works thereof are evil"; he tells them to go to the feast, but he still abides in Galilee. GALILEE				7:2-9	No Record
§113 p. 298	**Jesus starts for Jerusalem.** **Time: A.D. 29, October (Andrews)** Jesus starts for Jerusalem; sends messengers before him, they made ready for him in a Samaritan village which will not receive him because his face is set for Jerusalem; James and John wish to call down fire from heaven, "even as Elias did," to consume them, but Jesus rebukes them: "Ye know not what manner of spirit ye are of. For the Son of man is not come to destroy men's lives, but to save them"; they go to another village. GALILEE TO JUDEA THROUGH SAMARIA			9:51-56	7:10	No Record

FIFTH PERIOD

The Later Judean Ministry

Sec. & Pg.	Event, Time and Place	Matt.	Mark	Luke	John	3 Nephi
§114 p. 301	**At the Feast of the Tabernacles.** **Time: A.D. 29, October 11-18 (Andrews)** Jesus attends the Feast of the Tabernacles in Jerusalem; people not immediately finding Jesus at the feast, they murmur, some saying he is a good man, others saying he deceives the people; no one speaks openly of him for fear of the Jews; in the midst of the feast Jesus goes into the Temple and teaches; the people marvel at his learning; Jesus answers, "My doctrine is not mine, but his that sent me. If any man will do his will, he shall know of the doctrine, whether it be of God, or whether I speak of myself"; Jesus says they seek to kill him, the people say he is possessed with a devil; he defends healing on the Sabbath; people talk of his boldness in teaching and ask if rulers really know he is the Christ; Jesus affirms they know both who he is and whence he came; no man lays hands on him, but later the Pharisees and chief priests send officers to take him; he tells of his death and resurrection, and they think he speaks of going among the Gentiles; some of the people hearing all this say he is the Christ, others speak otherwise; some would take him, but again no man lays hands on					No Record

Sec. & Pg.	Event, Time and Place	Matt.	Mark	Luke	John	3 Nephi
§114	(*Cont'd*) him; the officers return to the Pharisees and chief priests without Jesus, and they excuse themselves for their failure that "never man spake like this man"; Nicodemus asks if their law judges any man before he is heard; they ask if he is a follower of Jesus; all go to their houses. JERUSALEM				7:11-53	No Record
§115 p. 303	**The woman taken in adultery.** **Time: A.D. 29, October 11-18 (Andrews)** Jesus coming to the Temple early in the morning, the scribes and Pharisees bring to him a woman taken in adultery, ask his judgment on her, telling the law of Moses; he writes on the ground as if he hears them not; they continue asking him, so lifting himself up he says, "He that is without sin among you, let him first cast a stone at her"; he again stoops and writes, the accusers slink away one by one, beginning with the eldest until the last; Jesus and the woman are left alone; Jesus lifts himself up again, and seeing no one but the woman there, he asks, "Woman, where are those thine accusers? hath no man condemned thee? She said, No man, Lord. And Jesus said unto her, Neither do I condemn thee: go, and sin no more." JERUSALEM; TEMPLE				8:1-11	

Sec. & Pg.	Event, Time and Place	Matt.	Mark	Luke	John	3 Nephi
§116 p. 304	**The light of the world; his oneness with the Father.** Time: A.D. 29, October 11-18 (Andrews) Jesus speaks to them saying, "I am the light of the world," those following him will walk in light not in darkness; the Pharisees accuse him of bearing untrue record of himself; Jesus affirms his record is true, that he knows whence he came, whither he goes, they do not know; they do judge after the flesh, he judgeth not, but if he judgeth his judgment is true, "for I am not alone, but I and the Father that sent me"; the law says the testimony of two men is true, he and the Father beareth witness of him, they ask where his Father is; Jesus answers they know neither him nor his Father; he tells them they will die in their sins and whither he goes they can not come; they ask if he will kill himself; he says they are from beneath, he is from above; they will die in their sins; they ask who he is and he answers the same one he has declared from the beginning: "I have many things to say and to judge of you: but he that sent me is true; and I speak to the world those things which I have heard of him"; he says they will know him when they lift him up; he repeats that he does nothing of himself but only what his Father taught him, and that the Father					No Record

Sec. & Pg.	Event, Time and Place	Matt.	Mark	Luke	John	3 Nephi
§116	(*Cont'd*) is with him; many believe. JERUSALEM; TEMPLE TREASURY				8:12-30	
§117 p. 306	**The discourse to the Jews.** **Time: A.D. 29, October 11-18** (Andrews) Jesus preaches to those Jews who believe on him, and tells them, "Ye shall know the truth, and the truth shall make you free"; to their reply that they are Abraham's seed and never were in bondage to any man, he replies that "whosoever committeth sin is the servant of sin," that the Son abideth in the house forever but not the servant, and the Son shall make them free; he says they seek his life because his word has no place in them; he again tells them he speaks what he has seen with his Father and they do what they have seen with their father, they say they are Abraham's children, he tells them to do the works of Abraham; they seek to kill him because he speaks truth; "this did not Abraham"; they say they are not born of fornication; he again speaks of his Messiahship; he tells them they are the children of the devil; "he that is of God heareth God's words"; they ask if he is not a Samaritan and hath not a devil; he answers he has not a devil and honors his Father; he tells them that "if a man keep my saying, he shall					No Record

SEC. & PG.	EVENT, TIME AND PLACE	MATT.	MARK	LUKE	JOHN	3 NEPHI
§117	*(Cont'd)* never see death"; they say they now know he has a devil and ask who he is; he says Abraham rejoiced to see his day; they say he is not fifty years old, how could he see Abraham; he answers, "Before Abraham was, I am"; they take up stones to cast at him, but he slips away from the Temple, "going through the midst of them." JERUSALEM; TEMPLE				8:31-59	No Record
§118 p. 308	**The Seventy return.** **Time: A.D. 29, October-November** The Seventy return in joy saying, "Lord, even the devils are subject unto us through thy name"; Jesus says he saw Satan "as lightning fall from heaven"; he gives unto them power over poisonous things, the power of the enemy, and tells them nothing shall hurt them; tells them to rejoice that their names are written in heaven, rather than to rejoice in their powers; Jesus rejoices and thanks the Father; speaks of the Father and Son; he tells his disciples privately how blessed they are for what they see and hear and do not see and hear. JUDEA (Robertson)			10:17-24		
§119 p. 309	**The two great commandments; parable of the good Samaritan.** **Time: A.D. 29, Oct.-Dec.** A lawyer, tempting Jesus, asks what he shall do to inherit eternal life; Je-					

Sec. & Pg.	Event, Time and Place	Matt.	Mark	Luke	John	3 Nephi
§119	(*Cont'd*) sus asks what is written in the law; the lawyer says the two great commandments of loving God with all one's heart, soul, and strength, and thy neighbor as thyself; Jesus tells him he is right and gives the parable of the good Samaritan, then tells the lawyer to do likewise. JUDEA (Robertson)			10:25-37		No Record
§120 p. 310	**Jesus visits Mary and Martha.** **Time: A.D. 29, Oct.-Dec.** Jesus visits Mary and Martha; Martha "cumbered about much serving," complains because Mary sits at Jesus' feet and leaves the work for her; Jesus replies. BETHANY			10:38-42		
§121 p. 310	**He teaches his disciples to pray.** **Time: A.D. 29, Oct.-Dec.** One of the disciples asks Jesus to teach them how to pray even as John taught his disciples how to pray; Jesus gives "The Lord's Prayer"; he urges prayer to the point of importunity; "ask, and it shall be given you; seek, and ye shall find; knock, and it shall be opened unto you"; he points out that fathers do not give a stone to a son asking for bread, nor a serpent to one asking for fish, and that our Heavenly Father, not less kind than our earthly fathers, will "give the Holy Spirit to them that ask him." JUDEA (Robertson)			11:1-13		

Sec. & Pg.	Event, Time and Place	Matt.	Mark	Luke	John	3 Nephi
§122 p. 312	**He casts out a dumb devil and is again accused of being in league with Beelzebub.** **Time: A.D. 29, Oct.-Dec.** Jesus casts out a dumb devil and the man speaks; some again charge that Jesus does his works by the power of Beelzebub, others tempting him seek for a sign; he reasons how he cannot be doing this by the power of Satan, a house divided against a house falleth; if he casts evil spirits by the power of Satan, by what power have their sons worked; if he works by the power of God, is not his kingdom come; a strong man, armed, holds his goods and palace, but a stranger comes upon him, seizes his palace and divideth his spoils; "he that is not with me is against me: and he that gathereth not with me scattereth"; the parable of the unclean spirit; a woman calls out blessings upon his mother; "but he said, Yea rather, blessed are they that hear the word of God, and keep it"; he speaks to a thick multitude about signs, another sign given of his Messiahship; speaks of Jonas, the Queen of Sheba, of a lighted candle under a bushel, of the light of the eye, of light and darkness, and the whole body lighted. Judea (Robertson)			**11:14-36**		No Record

Sec. & Pg.	Event, Time and Place	Matt.	Mark	Luke	John	3 Nephi
§123 p. 313	**Another discourse on cleanliness.** Time: A.D. 29, Oct.-Dec. As he speaks a Pharisee asks Jesus to eat; the Pharisee marvels that Jesus eats with unwashed hands; Jesus speaks of the outward cleanliness and the inward uncleanliness of the Pharisees; he condemns the hypocrisy of the Pharisees and scribes, and their pride; a lawyer saying that Jesus' words include them too, Jesus condemns lawyers also, tells them they load men with burdens grievous to be borne, but touch not the burdens themselves; he charges they approve the killing of the prophets by their fathers, by building sepulchres for them; he tells them "that the blood of all the prophets, which was shed from the foundation of the world, may be required of this generation"; the lawyers "have taken away the key of knowledge: ye entered not in yourselves, and them that were entering in ye hindered"; the scribes and Pharisees then bait him, laying wait for some words for which they might accuse him. JUDEA (Robertson)			11:37-54		No Record
§124 p. 315	**Jesus teaches multitude; parable of the foolish rich man.** Time: A.D. 29, Oct.-Dec. An innumerable multitude, treading one upon another, gather together meantime; Jesus first					

SEC. & PG.	EVENT, TIME AND PLACE	MATT.	MARK	LUKE	JOHN	3 NEPHI
§124	(*Cont'd*) speaks to his disciples, warning them of the leaven of the Pharisees which is hypocrisy; nothing can be hidden, all will be known; fear him who, killing, may cast into hell; God watches the sparrows, much more you; whoso denies Jesus before men shall be denied before the angels of God; speaking against the Son of man shall be forgiven, but whoso blasphemeth against the Holy Ghost shall never be forgiven; when the disciples are brought before the synagogues or magistrates they shall take no thought of what they shall say, for the Holy Ghost shall teach them in that hour; he denies right to pass upon division of inheritance; speaks the parable of the rich man who in his pride said he was beyond want; tells his disciples to give their time to his work; speaking of the lilies of the field, how they grow, he says the Lord will provide; tells them to sell what they have and give alms; parable of the watchful servants, waiting for the return of their lord; Peter asks if this parable is for all or for the disciples, and is answered by a parable; Jesus says he came to send fire to the earth; he has a baptism; he does not bring peace; tells the people of their blindness; urges that disputes be settled before they get to the courts. JUDEA (Robertson)			12:1-59		No Record

Sec. & Pg.	Event, Time and Place	Matt.	Mark	Luke	John	3 Nephi
§125 p. 319	**The slaughter of the Galileans.** **Time: A.D. 29, Oct.-Dec.** Some of those present tell that Pilate has slaughtered some Galileans and mingled their blood with the blood of their sacrifices; Jesus says these Galileans were not sinners above other Galileans, and "except ye repent, ye shall all likewise perish"; speaks of them upon whom the tower of Siloam fell, repeats the question put to them about the Galileans, and gives the same admonition; gives the parable of the unfruitful fig tree. JUDEA (Robertson)			13:1-9		No Record
§126 p. 320	**Jesus heals man born blind.** **Time: A.D. 29, Oct.-Dec.** Jesus passing by sees a man blind from his birth; the disciples ask, "Who did sin, this man, or his parents, that he was born blind?"; Jesus replies neither, but this blindness was "that the works of God should be made manifest in him"; Jesus says he must do the work of him who sent him while it is yet day, for "the night cometh, when no man can work"; "as long as I am in the world, I am the light of the world"; Jesus spits on the ground, moistens clay, anoints the eyes of the blind man and tells him to wash in the pool of Siloam; he goes, washes, and comes away seeing; the neighbors see him seeing, and cannot believe their own eyes; he admits he is					

Sec. & Pg.	Event, Time and Place	Matt.	Mark	Luke	John	3 Nephi
§126	*(Cont'd)* the one born blind, they ask who healed him, he says Jesus; they take the man to the Pharisees who investigate the case, they divide about Jesus; the Jews call the parents who say the man is their son, but they do not know how he came by his sight; they then examine the man himself again; they accuse him of being a disciple of Jesus; the man makes a powerful defense; they cast the man out; Jesus hearing this seeks the man out and asks, "Dost thou believe on the Son of God?"; to the question of the man, "Who is he, Lord, that I might believe on him," the Lord says, "Thou hast both seen him, and it is he that talketh with thee," and the man answers: "Lord, I believe," and worships; the Lord says that he came into the world that those who see not might see, and some Pharisees hearing, ask, "Are we blind also?" Jesus answers them. JUDEA (Robertson says Jerusalem)				9:1-41	No Record
§127 p. 322	**The parable of the good shepherd.** **Time: A.D. 29, Oct.-Dec.** Jesus speaks unto them the parable of the good shepherd, but they understand not; Jesus says: "I am the door of the sheep," "I am the good shepherd," and "know my sheep, and am known of mine"; and "other sheep I have, which are not of this fold: them also I					

Sec. & Pg.	Event, Time and Place	Matt.	Mark	Luke	John	3 Nephi
§127	(*Cont'd*) must bring, and they shall hear my voice; and there shall be one fold, and one shepherd. Therefore doth my Father love me, because I lay down my life, that I might take it again. No man taketh it from me, but I lay it down of myself. I have power to lay it down, and I have power to take it again. This commandment have I received of my Father"; the Jews are still divided on the matter, some saying he has a devil, some otherwise. JERUSALEM (Robertson)				10:1-21	No Record
§128 p. 324	**The Feast of Dedication.** Time: A.D. 29, Dec. 20-27 (Andrews) Jesus at the Feast of the Dedication, walks in Solomon's Porch of the Temple; the Jews demand that he tell them plainly whether he be Christ; he says he has told them and that his works bear witness; "but ye believe not, because ye are not of my sheep. . . . My sheep hear my voice, and I know them, and they follow me: and I give unto them eternal life"; "I and my Father are one"; the Jews take up stones to stone him, he asks why, they say for blasphemy, "because that thou, being a man, makest thyself God"; Jesus points out to them that the law says, "Ye are gods," and asserts his Messiahship; they seek to take him, and he escapes. JERUSALEM: TEMPLE, SOLOMON'S PORCH				10:22-39a	

SIXTH PERIOD

The Perean Ministry

Sec. & Pg.	Event, Time and Place	Matt.	Mark	Luke	John	3 Nephi
§129 p. 327	**Jesus goes beyond the Jordan.** **Time: A.D. 30, Jan. (Andrews)** Jesus escapes those who seek to take him, and goes beyond the Jordan to the place where John at first baptized, and there abides; many come to see him, saying, "John did no miracle: but all things that John spake of this man were true"; many believed. PEREA				10:39b-42	No Record
§130 p. 327	**The healing on the Sabbath of woman long ill.** **Time: A.D. 30** Jesus, teaching in one of the synagogues on the Sabbath, sees a woman afflicted for eighteen years, and calls her to him and says: "Woman, thou art loosed from thine infirmity. And he laid his hands on her"; she is immediately healed; a ruler of the synagogue indignantly complains that with six days to work, Jesus heals on the Sabbath; Jesus replies by showing how they water their cattle on the Sabbath, and ought not this woman to be healed on the Sabbath; the adversaries of Jesus are ashamed and the people rejoice. PEREA (G. W. Clark)			13:10-17		No Record
§131 p. 328	**The parable of the mustard seed.** **Time: A.D. 30** Jesus speaks the parables of the mustard seed and the leaven. PEREA (G. W. Clark)			13:18-21		No Record

Sec. & Pg.	Event, Time and Place	Matt.	Mark	Luke	John	3 Nephi
§132 p. 328	**The beginning of journey to Jerusalem.** **Time: A.D. 30** Jesus begins journeying towards Jerusalem, teaching in the cities and villages on the way; one says to him: "Lord, are there few that be saved?"; he speaks to them, partly in parable, showing how that many who seek salvation shall not secure it; those who seek entry to the door because they ate with the Master or he taught in the streets, shall be shut out; they will see Abraham, Isaac, and Jacob, and all the prophets inside, and "you yourselves thrust out"; many shall come from the east, west, north, and south, and sit down in the kingdom of God; "and, behold, there are last which shall be first, and there are first which shall be last." PEREA (G. W. Clark)			13:22-30		No Record
§133 p. 329	**The warning about Herod Antipas.** **Time: A.D. 30** Pharisees come and warn Jesus that Herod Antipas will kill him; Jesus replies by referring to his death and resurrection; he states he must go to Jerusalem "for it cannot be that a prophet perish out of Jerusalem"; he laments over Jerusalem. PEREA			13:31-35		
§134 p. 330	**The message that Lazarus is sick.** **Time: A.D. 30, Winter (?)** Mary and Martha send word to Jesus to tell him					

Sec. & Pg.	Event, Time and Place	Matt.	Mark	Luke	John	3 Nephi
§134	(*Cont'd*) Lazarus is sick; Jesus loves Martha, Mary, and Lazarus; Jesus abides for two days in the place where he hears the news; he then suggests to his disciples that they go to Judea; but they point out that the Jews sought to stone him; Jesus answers in a parable; he then says Lazarus sleepeth, but he goes to waken him; the disciples say, "if he sleep, he shall do well"; "then said Jesus unto them plainly, Lazarus is dead"; he says he is glad he was not there, so they may believe; Thomas, which is called Didymus, says to his fellow disciples, "Let us also go, that we may die with him." PEREA (G. W. Clark)				11:1-16	No Record
§135 p. 331	**Man with dropsy healed on the Sabbath.** **Time: A.D. 30, Winter (?)** Jesus goes to the house of a Pharisee to eat bread on the Sabbath; they watch him; a man with dropsy comes before Jesus; he asks the Pharisees if it is lawful to heal on the Sabbath; they remaining silent, he heals the man; Jesus puts to the Pharisees the case of the ox in the pit, and they can not answer; he gives the parable of the wedding feast; he tells the Pharisee, his host, to make a feast for the poor, the maimed, and the blind, and his recompense will come in the resurrection of the just; a fellow guest says: "Blessed is he that shall eat bread in					

Sec. & Pg.	Event, Time and Place	Matt.	Mark	Luke	John	3 Nephi
§135	(*Cont'd*) the kingdom of God," and Jesus replying gives the parable of the man inviting his friends who made excuses for not coming and then of the man going out and filling up the table with the poor, the maimed, the halt, and the blind, so that none of those first invited could eat. PEREA (G. W. Clark)			14:1-24		No Record
§136 p. 333	**Another discourse on sacrifice.** **Time: A.D. 30, Winter (?)** Jesus tells the multitude of the sacrifice which must be made by his followers, one not forsaking his family and hating his own life, "cannot be my disciple"; he gives, to show what he means, the example of a man building a tower, and a king making war; "whosoever he be of you that forsaketh not all that he hath, he cannot be my disciple"; he gives a further example of salt losing its savor, and its proper use. PEREA (G. W. Clark)			14:25-35		
§137 p. 334	**A group of parables.** **Time: A.D. 30, Winter (?)** All the publicans and sinners draw near unto Jesus; the Pharisees and scribes murmur: "This man receiveth sinners, and eateth with them." PEREA (G. W. Clark)			15:1-2		
(a) p. 334	**Parable of the lost sheep.** Joy in heaven over one sinner that repenteth			15:3-7		

Sec. & Pg.	Event, Time and Place	Matt.	Mark	Luke	John	3 Nephi
§137	*(Cont'd)*					
(b) p. 334	**Parable of the ten pieces of silver.** There is joy in the presence of the angels of God over one sinner that repenteth			15:8-10		
(c) p. 335	**Parable of the return of the prodigal son.**			15:11-32		
(d) p. 336	**Parable of the unjust steward.** Spoken to his disciples; no steward can serve two masters			16:1-13		
§138 p. 337	**A discourse on covetousness.** **Time: A.D. 30, Winter (?)** Jesus, speaking to the covetous Pharisees who hear all these things, says: "Ye . . . justify yourselves before men; but God knoweth your hearts"; Jesus explains how the law stands, and speaks on adultery. PEREA (G. W. Clark)			16:14-18		No Record
§139 p. 338	**Parable of rich man and Lazarus.** **Time: A.D. 30, Winter (?)** Jesus continuing to speak to the covetous Pharisees, gives the parable of the rich man and Lazarus. PEREA (G. W. Clark)			16:19-31		
§140 p. 339	**Discourse on those who bring offense and on faith.** **Time: A.D. 30, Winter (?)** Jesus, speaking unto his disciples, says that offenses must come but woe unto him through whom they come; plight of one who "should offend one of these little ones"; teaches them					

Sec. & Pg.	Event, Time and Place	Matt.	Mark	Luke	John	3 Nephi
§140	(*Cont'd*) about forgiveness; the Apostles ask, "Lord, Increase our faith"; Jesus speaks of the faith of a grain of mustard seed; place of one who does merely that which it is his duty to do. PEREA (G. W. Clark)	....	....	17:1-10	....	
§141 p. 340	**The raising of Lazarus.** **Time: A.D. 30, Winter (?)** Jesus, reaching Bethany, finds that Lazarus has been dead four days; many friends come to Mary and Martha to comfort them; Martha comes out to meet Jesus but "Mary sat still in the house"; Martha tells Jesus if he had been there Lazarus had not died, and that even now God will give Jesus whatever he asks; Jesus says her brother shall rise again; Martha replies he will rise in the resurrection "at the last day"; Jesus says, "I am the resurrection, and the life" and continues with his great statement of his Messiahship; Martha declares, "I believe that thou art the Christ, the Son of God, which should come into the world"; Martha tells Mary Jesus is come, and she rushes to meet him; the mourning friends follow Mary; when they come to Jesus, Mary also says that if Jesus had been there her brother had not died; Jesus seeing them all weeping, grieves in his spirit and asks where they have lain him; they say come and see, and Jesus weeps; some bystanders say also that if					No Record

SEC. & PG.	EVENT, TIME AND PLACE	MATT.	MARK	LUKE	JOHN	3 NEPHI
§141	(*Cont'd*) Jesus had been there he might have saved Lazarus; coming to the cave where lay Lazarus, Jesus (Martha protesting) orders the stone rolled away, and first praying, "cried with a loud voice, Lazarus, come forth," and Lazarus comes forth bound hand and foot with grave clothes; at Jesus' command these are loosed and Lazarus goes; many Jews believe, some go to tell the Pharisees of the happening. BETHANY				11:17-46	No Record
§142 p. 342	**They plot against Jesus.** **Time: A.D. 30, Feb. (Andrews)** The chief priests and the Pharisees gather in council (Sanhedrin-Andrews), Caiaphas being high priest that year; the doctrine that better one man should perish than a whole nation, is stated by Caiaphas; "and this spake he not of himself: but being high priest that year, he prophesied Jesus should die for that nation; and not for that nation only, but that also he should gather together in one the children of God that were scattered abroad"; then after they take counsel, how they can put him to death. JERUSALEM				11:47-53	
§143 p. 342	**He goes to city of Ephraim.** **Time: A.D. 30, Feb. (Andrews)** Jesus walks "no more openly among the Jews," but goes thence near the wilderness to a city called Ephraim where his disci-					

SEC. & PG.	EVENT, TIME AND PLACE	MATT.	MARK	LUKE	JOHN	3 NEPHI
§143	(*Cont'd*) ples come also. BETHANY TO EPHRAIM				11:54	No Record
§144 p. 343	**The beginning of the final journey to Jerusalem.** **Time: A.D. 30, Feb.-Mar.** (Andrews) Finishing his residence in Ephraim, he starts for Jerusalem through the midst of Samaria and Galilee; ten lepers seeing him, stand afar off and cry: "Jesus, Master, have mercy on us"; when he sees them he tells them to go show themselves to the priests, which they doing, are cleansed; one, a Samaritan, seeing he is healed, turns back and glorifies God, falling on his face and giving thanks; Jesus asks if there are not ten, and where are the other nine; continuing he says only this stranger returns to give glory to God. EPHRAIM, GALILEE, SAMARIA			17:11-19		
§145 p. 343	**A discourse on kingdom of God.** **Time: A.D. 30, Feb.-Mar.** (Andrews) Jesus answering the question put by the Pharisees, "When the kingdom of God should come," replies that it does not come by observation; neither shall they say lo, here! or lo, there! "for, behold, the kingdom of God is within you"; he tells his disciples that the day will come when they shall wish to see one of the days of the Son of man, and they shall not see it; then some will say,					

Sec. & Pg.	Event, Time and Place	Matt.	Mark	Luke	John	3 Nephi
§145	*(Cont'd)* see here, others, see there, but "go not after them, nor follow them"; the light of the lightning compared to the Son of man; forecasts his crucifixion; compares the days of Noah and of Lot to the day when the Son of man is revealed; tells them not to do as did Lot's wife, and points out how one will be taken and the other left. GALILEE (G. W. Clark)			17:20-37		No Record
§146 p. 345	**Jesus again speaks in parables.** Time: A.D. 30, Feb.-Mar. (Andrews) Jesus speaks two parables. GALILEE (G.W. Clark)					
(a) p. 345	**Parable of the importunate widow.** Jesus says: "Shall not God avenge his own elect, which cry day and night unto him, that he bear long with them? I tell you that he will avenge them speedily"; he then asks if "when the Son of man cometh, shall he find faith on the earth"			18:1-8		
(b) p. 345	**Parable of the Pharisee and the publican.** Jesus says the publican rather than the Pharisee is justified, "for every one that exalteth himself shall be abased; and he that humbleth himself shall be exalted."			18:9-14		
§147 p. 346	**He crosses Jordan into Perea, going towards Jerusalem.** Time: A.D. 30, Feb.-Mar. (Andrews)					

SEC. & PG.	EVENT, TIME AND PLACE	MATT.	MARK	LUKE	JOHN	3 NEPHI
§147	*(Cont'd)* Jesus travels on towards Jerusalem, leaving Galilee, crossing the Jordan into Perea; great multitudes follow him, whom he teaches and heals. GALILEE-PEREA	19:1-2	10:1	....	....	No Record
§148 p. 347	**Pharisees tempt Jesus.** Time: A.D. 30, Feb.-Mar. (Andrews) The Pharisees come unto Jesus tempting him, saying: "Is it lawful for a man to put away his wife for every cause?" Jesus preaches his great discourse on marriage and divorce. PEREA	19:3-12	10:2-12	....	....	
§149 p. 348	**He blesses little children.** Time: A.D. 30, Feb.-Mar. (Andrews) Then they bring to him little children that he shall put his hands on them and pray; the disciples rebuke them; Jesus seeing this is much displeased, and bids them let the children come, for of such is the kingdom of heaven, saying, "Whosoever shall not receive the kingdom of God as a little child, he shall not enter therein"; he takes them in his arms, puts his hands upon them and blesses them; he then departs. PEREA	19:13-15	10:13-16	18:15-17	....	
§150 p. 349	**The rich young ruler.** Time: A.D. 30, Feb.-Mar. (Andrews) A rich young ruler comes running to Jesus, and kneeling, asks, "Good Master, what shall I do to inherit eternal life?"; Jesus answers, "Thou knowest the					

Sec. & Pg.	Event, Time and Place	Matt.	Mark	Luke	John	3 Nephi
§150	(*Cont'd*) commandments"; the young ruler replies, "all these have I kept from my youth up"; Jesus answers by telling the ruler to sell all he has, if he would be perfect, give it to the poor, and to follow Jesus; the ruler goes away sorrowful for he has great riches; Jesus discourses upon riches; they say among themselves, who then can be saved, and Jesus answers that with God all things are possible; Peter saying they have given up all for Jesus, he points out the rewards of the faithful. PEREA	19:16-30	10:17-31	18:18-30	....	No Record
§151 p. 352	**The parable of the laborers in the vineyard.** Time: A.D. 30, Feb.-Mar. (Andrews) PEREA	20:1-16	....	....	....	
§152 p. 353	**He goes before the Twelve, towards Jerusalem.** Time: A.D. 30, Mar. (Andrews) Jesus, continuing towards Jerusalem, goes before the Twelve (who were with him), to their amazement; they follow, afraid; he takes them unto him, and again carefully tells them of the trial, the death, and resurrection; "and they understood none of these things: and this saying was hid from them, neither knew they the things which were spoken." PEREA	20:17-19	10:32-34	18:31-34	....	
§153 p. 354	**Ambitions of James and John.** Time: A.D. 30, Mar. (Andrews) James and John, either through their mother or by themselves, ask Jesus that					

Sec. & Pg.	Event, Time and Place	Matt.	Mark	Luke	John	3 Nephi
§153	(*Cont'd*) they may sit, one on the right hand and the other on the left hand, of Jesus in his kingdom and glory; Jesus tells them they do not know what they ask, and he asks them if they can drink the cup he drinks and be baptized with the baptism he is baptized with; they say they can; he says they will indeed drink his cup and be baptized with his baptism, but to sit on his right hand and on his left is not his to give; the ten hearing it are moved to indignation; he tells them that while among the Gentiles the princes exercise dominion over the others, yet among them, "whosoever will be great among you, shall be your minister"; and Jesus adds: "For even the Son of man came not to be ministered unto, but to minister, and to give his life a ransom for many." PEREA: JERICHO (?)	20:20-28	10:35-45			No Record
§154 p. 355	**Bartimaeus healed.** **Time: A.D. 30, Mar. (Andrews)** Bartimaeus, the blind son of Timaeus (and another blind man, says Matthew), are sitting by the wayside, as Jesus and a multitude go by; the blind men, hearing Jesus is passing, cry out to him, the multitude rebuke them, but they cry out again, and Jesus has him (them) called to him; the man casts away his garment and comes to Jesus who asks what he wishes; the man answers: "Lord, that I may receive my					

Sec. & Pg.	Event, Time and Place	Matt.	Mark	Luke	John	3 Nephi
§154	*(Cont'd)* sight"; Jesus touches his eyes and he immediately sees and then follows along with the multitude; those who see it praise God. NEAR JERICHO	20:29-34	10:46-52	18:35-43	....	No Record
§155 p. 357	**Zacchaeus, the publican.** Time: A.D. 30, Mar. (Andrews) Zacchaeus, a rich chief among the publicans, being of little stature, can not see Jesus for the press of people, so he climbs a sycamore tree to see Jesus as he passes by; Jesus looking up sees him, and bids him come down, saying he must abide in the house of the publican; Zacchaeus comes down and receives Jesus joyfully; the multitude, seeing this, murmur that he has gone to be guest of a sinner; Zacchaeus tells the Lord he has given half his goods to the poor, that if he has taken anything from a man by false accusation, he restores it fourfold; Jesus tells him that this day salvation has come to his house for he also is a son of Abraham, "for the Son of man is come to seek and to save that which was lost." NEAR OR IN JERICHO	....	....	19:1-10	....	
§156 p. 358	**The parable of the ten pounds.** Time: A.D. 30, Mar. (Andrews) IN OR NEAR JERICHO	....	....	19:11-27	....	
§157 p. 359	**Jesus proceeds on his way to Jerusalem.** Time: A.D. 30, Mar.-Apr. BETWEEN JERICHO AND JERUSALEM	....	....	19:28	....	

Sec. & Pg.	Event, Time and Place	Matt.	Mark	Luke	John	3 Nephi
§158 p. 359	**Many seek him.** **Time: A.D. 30, Mar. (Andrews)** The Passover drawing nigh, and many coming from the country beforehand to purify themselves, they seek for Jesus, and ask one another in the Temple whether they think he might come; the chief priests and the Pharisees give a commandment that if any man knows where he is, he shall tell that they may take him. JERUSALEM				11:55-57	
§159 p. 360	**People in Western Hemisphere look for sign.** **Time: A.D. 30, Mar.-Apr.** The people begin to look with great earnestness for the sign which should be given, as proclaimed by Samuel, the Lamanite, at the death of the Messiah. WESTERN HEMISPHERE					8:1-4

SEVENTH PERIOD

The Week of the Atoning Sacrifice and to the Ascension

Sec. & Pg.	Event, Time and Place	Matt.	Mark	Luke	John	3 Nephi
§160 p. 361	**Jesus comes to Bethany.** Time: A.D. 30, Fri., Mar. 31, 8th Nisan (Andrews); Sat., Apr. 1, 9th Nisan (Robinson) Jesus comes to Bethany; the Jews, knowing Jesus is there, come out to see both Jesus and Lazarus; the chief priests consult how they may also put Lazarus to death, since because of him, many Jews go away believing on Jesus. BETHANY				12:1, 9-11	No Record
	First Day of the Week					
§161 p. 361	**From Bethany to Jerusalem and return to Bethany.** Time: A.D. 30, Sun., Apr. 2, 10th Nisan (Andrews)					
(a) p. 361	**Entry into Jerusalem.** Going from Bethany to Jerusalem, Jesus comes to Bethphage, unto the Mount of Olives; he tells two disciples to go to a nearby village where they will find tied an ass with a colt, whereon man never sat, these they will bring to Jesus and if any man questions, they are to say the Lord hath need of them and straightway he will send them; the disciples go to the village, they find the colt, they loose it, the owners ask the question, they reply as the Lord told them, and the owner lets them take the colt to Jesus; they put their coats on the colt, and set Jesus thereon; the multitude spread in the way their garments and palm branches cut from the trees; descending the Mount of					

SEC. & PG.	EVENT, TIME AND PLACE	MATT.	MARK	LUKE	JOHN	3 NEPHI
§161	*(Cont'd)*					
(a)	Olives, the whole multitude break out in cries of joy, telling the mighty works of Jesus; shouting hosannas and saying, "Blessed be the King that cometh in the name of the Lord"; some of the Pharisees from the multitude ask Jesus to rebuke his disciples, and Jesus answers: "I tell you that, if these should hold their peace, the stones would immediately cry out"; coming near to the city he weeps and laments over it; the people who saw Jesus raise Lazarus bare record, the people who had heard of the miracle follow, in Jerusalem all the city is moved; the Pharisees say among themselves: "Perceive ye how ye prevail nothing? behold, the world is gone after him." Jesus enters the Temple.	21:1-11	11:1-11a	19:29-44	12:12-19	No Record
(b) p. 364	**Return to Bethany.**		11:11b			
	Second Day of the Week					
§162 p. 365	**Bethany to Jerusalem, cleansing Temple, and back to Bethany.**					
	Time: A.D. 30, Mon., Apr. 3, 11th Nisan (Andrews)					
(a) p. 365	**Cursing of the barren fig tree.**					
	In the morning returning unto the city Jesus is hungry; seeing a fig tree afar off, he comes to it, hoping he may find something thereon; finding nothing but leaves, he says, "let no fruit grow on thee henceforward for ever"	21:18-19a	11:12-14			

Sec. & Pg.	Event, Time and Place	Matt.	Mark	Luke	John	3 Nephi
§162	*(Cont'd)*					
(b) p. 365	**Jesus cleanses the Temple.** The blind and the lame come to him in the Temple and he heals them; the children call, "Hosanna to the son of David"; the chief priests and scribes, hearing this and seeing Jesus' works, are displeased; they seek to destroy Jesus; Jesus cleanses the Temple of them that bought and sold and of the money changers.	21:12-16	11:15-18	19:45-48	....	
(c) p. 366	**Return to Bethany.**	21:17	11:19	21:37	....	
	Third Day of the Week					
§163 p. 367	**Bethany to Jerusalem, in the Temple, and back to Bethany.** Time: A.D. 30, Tues., Apr. 4, 12th Nisan (Andrews)	....	....	....	....	No Record
(a) p. 367	**A discourse on faith.** The barren fig tree has withered away. Jesus and his disciples journeying towards Jerusalem in the morning see the fig tree withered away; Jesus makes this the text for a discourse on faith that has power even to the moving of mountains; he again teaches them about prayer and faith in prayer	21:19b-22	11:20-26	21:38	....	
(b) p. 368	**The question of his authority.** Jesus coming into the Temple, the chief priests, the scribes and the elders of the people come to him and ask by what authority does he do these things and who gave the authority;					

Sec. & Pg.	Event, Time and Place	Matt.	Mark	Luke	John	3 Nephi
§163	*(Cont'd)*					
(b)	Jesus answers by a question—was the baptism of John from heaven or of men; they refuse to answer, perceiving they lose whichever way they answer; Jesus thereupon refuses to answer their question	21:23-27	11:27-33	20:1-8	....	No Record
(c) p. 369	**Parable of the two sons.**	21:28-32	....	....	....	No Record
(d) p. 369	**Parable of the wicked husbandman.** When Jesus explains the parable the Pharisees see it has to do with themselves; they seek to lay hands on Jesus, but fear the people, who believe Jesus to be a prophet	21:33-46	12:1-12	20:9-18	....	No Record
(e) p. 372	**Parable of the king's son**	22:1-14	....	....	....	No Record
(f) p. 373	**The question about tribute.** The Pharisees taking counsel how they might entangle Jesus in his talk, send certain of their own with some of the Herodians, who ask Jesus whether it be lawful to pay tribute to Caesar; Jesus, perceiving their wickedness, says to them, "Why tempt ye me, ye hypocrites?"; he asks them to show him the tribute money; they bring him a penny; he asks, "Whose image and superscription hath it?" They answer Caesar's. Jesus says, "Render therefore unto Caesar the things which are Caesar's; and unto God the things that are God's"; they marvel at him, hold their peace, and go their way	22:15-22	12:13-17	20:19-26	....	No Record

Sec. & Pg.	Event, Time and Place	Matt.	Mark	Luke	John	3 Nephi
§163	*(Cont'd)*					
(g) p. 374	**The Sadducees question about marriage after the resurrection.** There come next to tempt Jesus and try him the Sadducees who believe not in the resurrection; they put the case of a woman who, under the Mosaic law which provided for the raising of seed unto the dead husband by a brother, married seven brothers in succession and died childless; they ask whose wife she shall be in the resurrection; Jesus answers	22:23-33	12:18-27	20:27-40		No Record
(h) p. 376	**The lawyer questions about the great commandment.** The Pharisees, hearing the Sadducees have been silenced, gather together, and one of them, a lawyer, to try Jesus, asks: "Master, which is the great commandment in the law?" Jesus replies quoting the two great laws; the lawyer tells Jesus he said the truth, and gives a short discourse on the commandments; Jesus tells him he is not far from the kingdom of God; "and no man after that durst ask him any question"	22:34-40	12:28-34			
(i) p. 377	**Jesus asks Pharisees whose son Christ is.** While the Pharisees are still gathered together Jesus asks, "What think ye of Christ? whose son is he?" They reply: "The son of David"; Jesus asks how is it then that David calls him Lord, for "if David then call him Lord, how is he his son?"; the common peo-					

Sec. & Pg.	Event, Time and Place	Matt.	Mark	Luke	John	3 Nephi
§163	*(Cont'd)*					
(i)	ple hear Jesus gladly; no man thereafter durst ask him any question	22:41-46	12:35-37	20:41-44		
(j) p. 378	**The scribes and Pharisees condemned.** Jesus, speaking to the multitude and to his disciples, condemns the scribes and the Pharisees, and lists their sins, discourses thereon, and tells of the punishments for the sins	23:1-36	12:38-40	20:45-47		
(k) p. 380	**Jesus' lamentation over Jerusalem.**	23:37-39				
(l) p. 381	**The widow's mite.** Jesus, sitting against the treasury, sees the people casting in their money, the poor and the rich who often cast in much; a widow comes casting in two mites, one farthing; Jesus calls his disciples and tells them, "this poor widow hath cast more in, than all they which have cast into the treasury: for all they did cast in of their abundance; but she of her want did cast in all that she had, even all her living"		12:41-44	21:1-4		No Record
(m) p. 381	**The Greeks seek him; a voice from heaven.** Certain Greeks come to worship at the feast, ask Philip (of Bethsaida) who speaks to Andrew, to get them to see Jesus; Philip and Andrew tell Jesus of the wish of the Greeks; Jesus tells them of his approaching death and resurrection, and makes a discourse; during his discourse					

Sec. & Pg.	Event, Time and Place	Matt.	Mark	Luke	John	3 Nephi
§163	*(Cont'd)*					
(m)	a voice comes from heaven; some of the people hearing it think it thunders; others think an angel speaks to him; speaking of the kind of death he should die, the people say they have heard out of the law that Christ abideth forever, yet Jesus speaks of the Son of man being lifted up; they ask who the Son of man is; he answers in parable; then goes and hides himself from them				12:20-36	No Record
(n) p. 382	**Timidity of chief rulers who believe.** Notwithstanding the many miracles of Jesus, they do not believe in him, this in fulfillment of prophecy; yet many among the chief rulers believe on him, but do not confess him, lest they shall be put out of the synagogue, loving the praise of men more than the praise of God; Jesus, declaring, "I am come a light into the world," discourses on his Messiahship and gives the punishment of those rejecting him; he declares what the Father told him to speak				12:37-50	
(o) p. 383	**The Olivet discourse.** Jesus departing from the Temple, the disciples offer to show him the buildings; he prophesies the destruction of the Temple; he then gives the signs of his second coming, of the day and the hour thereof no man knoweth, not even the angels in heaven; he warns and urges to faithfulness	24:1-51	13:1-37	21:5-36		

Sec. & Pg.	Event, Time and Place	Matt.	Mark	Luke	John	3 Nephi
§163	*(Cont'd)*					
(p) p. 390	**Parable of the ten virgins.**	25:1-13	....	....	....	No Record
(q) p. 390	**Parable of the talents.**	25:14-30	....	....	....	
(r) p. 392	**The final judgment.** Jesus discourses upon and pictures the final judgment; the King shall set the sheep on his right hand and the goats on his left hand; he pronounces blessings upon those on his right hand, telling why he does so; he tells those on his left hand to depart, and tells them why	25:31-46	....	....	....	
(s) p. 393	**The betrayal foretold.** Jesus having finished his sayings, tells his disciples that after two days is the feast of the Passover "and the Son of man is betrayed to be crucified"	26:1-2	....	....	....	
(t) p. 393	**The plot to take him.** Two days before the Passover, the chief priests and the scribes and the elders of the people assemble at the palace of the high priest Caiaphas to plot how they may take Jesus by subtilty and kill him, but not on the feast day lest there be an uproar among the people	26:3-5	14:1-2	22:1-2	....	
(u) p. 393	**At Simon's supper Mary anoints him.** They make a supper at the house of Simon the leper, Martha serves, and Lazarus sits at the table with Jesus; Mary takes a pound of very costly ointment of spikenard, anoints the feet of Jesus and wipes					

SEC. & PG.	EVENT, TIME AND PLACE	MATT.	MARK	LUKE	JOHN	3 NEPHI
§163	(*Cont'd*)					
(u)	them with her hair; the odor of the ointment fills the whole house; Judas Iscariot asks why this ointment was not sold and the price given to the poor; Jesus rebukes him and the other disciples who found fault, and says, "For in that she hath poured this ointment on my body, she did it for my burial"; he says the woman's act should be known wherever the Gospel is preached	26:6-13	14:3-9	....	12:2-8	
(v) p. 395	**Judas arranges betrayal.** Then Satan enters into Judas Iscariot and he goes unto the chief priests and captains; he asks them what they will give him to deliver Jesus; they fix the price at thirty pieces of silver; Judas seeks thereafter how he may conveniently betray Jesus in the absence of the multitude	26:14-16	14:10-11	22:3-6	....	No Record
	Fourth Day of the Week					
p. 395	**Bethany.** **Time: A.D. 30, Wed., Apr. 5, 13th Nisan (Andrews)** Apparently this day is spent with his disciples and it is believed at Bethany	....	....	....	....	
	Fifth Day of the Week					
§164 p. 396	**The Last Supper, the Mount of Olives, Gethsemane, the betrayal, the arrest.** **Time: A.D. 30, Thurs., Apr. 6, 14th Nisan (Andrews)** BETHANY, JERUSALEM	....	....	....	....	

Sec. & Pg.	Event, Time and Place	Matt.	Mark	Luke	John	3 Nephi
§164	*(Cont'd)*					
(a) p. 396	**Disciples arrange for Passover meal.** The disciples on the first day of unleavened bread, ask Jesus where they shall prepare to eat the Passover; Jesus tells them to go into the city where they will meet a man carrying a pitcher of water; they shall follow this man and enter the house where he goes and shall tell the good man of the house that the Master wishes to know where is the guest chamber where he shall eat the Passover; the husbandman will show them a large upper room furnished; here they shall prepare; they find all as Jesus had said and make ready the Passover	26:17-19	14:12-16	22:7-13		No Record
(b) p. 397	**They sit down in Passover chamber.** When evening comes, Jesus and the Twelve come and sit down	26:20	14:17	22:14		
(c) p. 397	**The strife about precedence.** There is strife among the Twelve as to who shall be greatest; he contrasts the measure of greatness and how it is shown among the kings of the Gentiles, with how it must be shown among them,—"he that is greatest among you, let him be as the younger; and he that is chief, as he that doth serve." "I am among you as he that serveth"; he tells them he has appointed unto them a kingdom, they may					

SEC. & PG.	EVENT, TIME AND PLACE	MATT.	MARK	LUKE	JOHN	3 NEPHI
§154	(*Cont'd*)					
(c)	eat and drink at his table in his kingdom, "and sit on thrones judging the twelve tribes of Israel"			22:24-30		No Record
(d) p. 398	**He washes his disciples' feet.** Before the feast of the Passover, Jesus (knowing the part Judas Iscariot was to play) rises from the table and laying aside his garments, takes a towel, girds himself and pouring water into a basin begins to wash the disciples' feet; when Peter is come to, he objects strongly to the Lord's washing his feet, but the Lord explains and Peter allows it; having washed their feet, Jesus puts on his garments, sits down again at the table, and gives them a discourse on the meaning of this ceremony; he speaks of his betrayal, and tells the effect of receiving him				13:1-20	
(e) p. 399	**The Passover meal.** Jesus tells them how much he has desired to eat this Passover with them before he suffers, and that he will not eat it again "until it be fulfilled in the kingdom of God"; he takes the cup and gives thanks, telling them to divide it among themselves, "For I say unto you, I will not drink of the fruit of the vine, until the kingdom of God shall come"			22:15-18		
(f) p. 400	**He indicates his betrayer.** As they eat Jesus says one of them shall betray					

Sec. & Pg.	Event, Time and Place	Matt.	Mark	Luke	John	3 Nephi
§164	*(Cont'd)*					
(f)	him; sorrowful, they say among themselves and to him, "Is it I?"; Peter beckons to John, who is leaning on Jesus' bosom, to ask Jesus who it is; Jesus answers: "He it is, to whom I shall give a sop, when I have dipped it"; Jesus dips the sop, and gives it to Judas Iscariot, to whom Jesus said, when Judas asked if he was the betrayer: "Thou hast said"; Jesus speaks of the fate of his betrayer	26:21-25	14:18-21	22:21-23	13:21-26	
(g) p. 401	**Judas leaves the chamber.** After the sop Satan enters Judas and Jesus says unto him, "That thou doest, do quickly"; none of the disciples know the intent of these words, thinking it either, as he has the purse, that he goes to buy something, or to give something to the poor; Judas leaves immediately and it is night				13:27-30	No Record
(h) p. 401	**Jesus foretells his death.** Jesus, after Judas goes out, says, "Now is the Son of man glorified, and God is glorified in him"; he tells the disciples he will be with them but a short time, that where he goes they cannot come, and commands them to love one another as he has loved them, and by that all men shall know they are his disciples				13:31-35	
(i) p. 402	**The sacrament.** Jesus institutes the Lord's Supper—the sacrament; he again says, "I will drink no more of the fruit					

SEC. & PG.	EVENT, TIME AND PLACE	MATT.	MARK	LUKE	JOHN	3 NEPHI
§164	*(Cont'd)*					
(i)	of the vine, until that day that I drink it new in the kingdom of God"	26:26-29	14:22-25	22:19-20		No Record
(j) p. 402	**Peter declares his loyalty.** Peter asks Jesus where he is going; Jesus tells Peter that Satan hath desired to have him that he may sift him as wheat; Peter says he is ready to go with Jesus both to prison and to death; Jesus answers that where he goes Peter cannot follow; Peter asks why he cannot follow, adding, "I will lay down my life for thy sake"; Jesus answers that before the cock crows Peter shall deny him thrice; Jesus speaks of when he sent them out before, and of their going out again, referring to their work after his death; he directs them "now" to travel with purse and scrip and a sword			22:31-38	13:36-38	
(k) p. 403	**The discourse about the Comforter.** Jesus speaks of his going from them and preparing a place for them; Thomas and Philip ask questions; Jesus discourses on the relationship between him and the Father; tells them to keep his commandments; says he will send them the Comforter, which the world cannot receive, and he himself will come; the Father will love them who love him; Judas (not Iscariot) asks him a question, and Jesus says any man who loves him will keep his commandments; again he speaks of					

Sec. & Pg.	Event, Time and Place	Matt.	Mark	Luke	John	3 Nephi
§164	*(Cont'd)*					
(k)	the Comforter which the Father shall send; he leaves peace with them; he says they shall rejoice that he goes to the Father; and ends by saying he has told them all so that they may know when it comes to pass				14:1-31	No Record
(l) p. 405	**They sing a hymn and go out to the Mount of Olives.**	26:30	14:26	22:39		
(m) p. 405	**He explains his relationship to them and theirs to him and the Father.** Jesus further explains his relationship to the Father, their relationship to him, and the relationship between the Father, himself, and them; again commands them to love one another; he calls them his friends, not his servants; he has chosen them, not they him; tells them they are not of the world, which will persecute them; his coming and speaking to the world robs them of their cloak for sin; they have now "both seen and hated both me and my Father"; when the Comforter comes he will testify of Jesus; "and ye also shall bear witness, because ye have been with me from the beginning"				15:1-27	
(n) p. 407	**He again explains his death.** Jesus tells them more of what shall befall them, that they may remember when the things happen; he says he goes his way to him that sent him; it is expedient that he should go, for if he does not go, the Comforter					

Sec. & Pg.	Event, Time and Place	Matt.	Mark	Luke	John	3 Nephi
§164	*(Cont'd)*					
(n)	will not come unto them; tells what the Comforter will do when he comes; Comforter will guide them into all truth; again foretells his death; the disciples say among themselves that they cannot understand, and Jesus discerning this, again explains, foretelling their grief which shall be turned into joy; they shall receive what they ask in the Father's name; further explanation of relationship between him and the Father, his disciples say he now speaks plainly and they understand and believe; he predicts their scattering; have peace; "I have overcome the world"				16:1-33	No Record
(o) p. 409	**The great prayer.** The Prayer of the Great High Priest, or the Intercessory Prayer,—"the hour is come; glorify thy Son, that thy Son also may glorify thee"; "this is life eternal"; he prays for the disciples, whom he has kept all but one, "the son of perdition"; he has given them the word of the Father, and the world hates them; "I pray not that thou shouldest take them out of the world, but that thou shouldest keep them from the evil"; prays not only for the disciples, but for all who believe on him in the world; again speaks of relationship of himself, the Father, and the disciples; asks that those whom the Father has					

Sec. & Pg.	Event, Time and Place	Matt.	Mark	Luke	John	3 Nephi
§164	*(Cont'd)*					
(o)	given him should be with him; asks that the Father's love for him shall be in them and he in them				17:1-26	
(p) p. 411	**Peter and rest declare their loyalty.** Jesus tells them, "All ye shall be offended because of me this night"; says that after he is risen he will go before them to Galilee; Peter says though all others are offended he will never be offended; and Jesus again foretells Peter's denial; thereafter Peter speaks more vehemently, denying he will deny Jesus. "Likewise also said they all"	26:31-35	14:27-31			
(q) p. 412	**He prays in the Garden.** Jesus takes them all to the Garden of Gethsemane; leaving all but Peter, James, and John, whom he takes with him, he goes on into the Garden; saying his soul is sorrowful, he goes still farther on alone and prays; he returns and finds them sleeping; he awakens and mildly rebukes them; he goes the second and the third time, with the same result; whereupon Jesus says: "Rise, let us be going: behold, he is at hand that doth betray me"	26:36-46	14:32-42	22:40-46	18:1-2	No Record
(r) p. 413	**The betrayal.** While Jesus yet speaks, a multitude comes with Judas, of men and officers from the chief priests and Pharisees, armed with swords, staves, and wea-					

Sec. & Pg.	Event, Time and Place	Matt.	Mark	Luke	John	3 Nephi
§164	*(Cont'd)*					
(r)	pons, and carrying lanterns and torches; by a sign arranged beforehand, Judas comes forth and kisses Jesus, saying, "Hail, master"; Jesus says to him, "Judas, betrayest thou the Son of man with a kiss?"; Jesus goes forth and says, "Whom seek ye?"; they answer, "Jesus of Nazareth," and Jesus replies, "I am he"; the multitude go backward and fall to the ground; Jesus again asks the question, and they make the same reply; he says: "I am he: if therefore ye seek me, let these go their way"	26:47-50a	14:43-45	22:47-48	18:3-9	No Record
(s) p. 415	**The arrest.** They then lay hands on Jesus; his disciples ask, "Lord, shall we smite with the sword?" Peter draws his sword and cuts off the right ear of Malchus, the high priest's servant; Jesus answers, "Suffer ye thus far," and touches Malchus' ear and heals it; he tells Peter to put up his sword, "for all they that take the sword shall perish with the sword"; he asks if they do not think that if he were to ask it, the Father would give him more than twelve legions of angels; he asks the multitude why they come with swords and staves to take him as if he were a thief, since he sat with them daily in the Temple teaching, and they laid no hold on him; a young man following along with a linen cloth cast about his					

Sec. & Pg.	Event, Time and Place	Matt.	Mark	Luke	John	3 Nephi
§164	(*Cont'd*)					
(s)	body loses the cloth to some other young men, and he flees from them naked	26:50b-56	14:46-52	22:49-53	18:10-12	
	Sixth Day of the Week					
§165 p. 416	**The trial and crucifixion.** **Time: A.D. 30, Midnight, Thurs., Fri., Apr. 7, 15th Nisan (Andrews)** JERUSALEM					
(a) p. 416	**Jesus before Annas.** Jesus is first taken to Annas, father-in-law to Caiaphas (the titular high priest); the high priest asks Jesus of his doctrine and his disciples; Jesus answers he has taught openly, and in secret said nothing; therefore Annas should ask those who had heard him; one of the officers strikes him for so answering the high priest; Jesus says if he has spoken evil the officer should bear witness thereof, but if well, why is he smitten?				18:13-14, 19-23	No Record
(b) p. 417	**He is sent to Caiaphas.** Annas sends Jesus bound to Caiaphas, where the scribes and elders are assembled; Peter follows afar off	26:57-58	14:53-54	22:54	18:24	
(c) p. 417	**The night examination.** The chief priests, the elders, and all the Council (the Sanhedrin), seek false witness against Jesus to put him to death; many witnesses are called, but no evidence is secured; at last two come who testify concerning Jesus' statement about the destruction and rebuild-					

Sec. & Pg.	Event, Time and Place	Matt.	Mark	Luke	John	3 Nephi
§165	*(Cont'd)*					
(c)	ing of the Temple; Jesus answers nothing; finally the high priest says, "I adjure thee by the living God, that thou tell us whether thou be the Christ, the Son of God"; Jesus says, "Thou hast said: nevertheless I say unto you, Hereafter shall ye see the Son of man sitting on the right hand of power, and coming in the clouds of heaven"; the high priest rends his clothes, and says Jesus has blasphemed; he calls for a verdict, and they pronounce him worthy of death	26:59-66	14:55-64			No Record
(d) p. 419	**They maltreat him.** The men holding Jesus, then smite him, spit in his face and buffet him; they blindfold him, and then striking him, ask him to prophesy who struck him; "and many other things blasphemously spake they against him"	26:67-68	14:65	22:63-65		
(e) p. 419	**Peter denies him.** Peter, with another disciple known to the high priest, goes along to the house of the high priest; the other disciple goes in with Jesus while Peter stands at the door; the other disciple comes to the door and speaking to the maid takes Peter inside; the damsel who keeps the door asks Peter if he was not with Jesus, and Peter makes his first denial; a fire has been kindled in the hall, Peter sits down with them who sit around it; another maid					

Sec. & Pg.	Event, Time and Place	Matt.	Mark	Luke	John	3 Nephi
§165	(*Cont'd*)					
(e)	comes and says Peter is a follower; Peter denies this time also; then those who stand about with him charge him with being a follower; and he again denies; immediately the cock crows; Peter, remembering Christ's words, goes out and weeps bitterly	26:69-75	14:66-72	22:55-62	18:15-18, 25-27	No Record
(f) p. 421	**The formal trial and condemnation.** So soon as it is day, the elders of the people, the chief priests, and the scribes, come together and lead him into their council; they ask if he is the Christ; he answers that if he tells them, they will not believe; that if he questions them, they will not let him go, and again says what he has said to Caiaphas; they then say, "Art thou then the Son of God"; Jesus answers, "Ye say that I am"; the council say they have themselves heard him and need no further witness; they bind him and the whole multitude lead him away to Pontius Pilate	27:1-2	15:1	22:66-71, 23:1	....	
(g) p. 422	**Judas Iscariot commits suicide.** Judas Iscariot, seeing Jesus condemned, repents and offers back the thirty pieces of silver; they say, "What is that to us"; he casts down the silver in the Temple and goes and hangs himself; the chief priests, saying it is unlawful to put blood money in the treas-					

Sec. & Pg.	Event, Time and Place	Matt.	Mark	Luke	John	3 Nephi
§165	(*Cont'd*)					
(g)	ury, take counsel and buy a potters' field to bury strangers in; the words of Jeremy the prophet on this	27:3-10	....	....	....	
(h) p. 423	**Before Pilate.** They lead Jesus to the judgment hall of Pilate, but they go not in that they may not be defiled against eating the Passover; Pilate comes out to them; they accuse Jesus of perverting the nation, forbidding tribute to Caesar, and saying he is king; Jesus does not answer his accusers; Pilate marvels and asks, "Art thou the King of the Jews?"; Jesus answers, "Thou sayest"; Pilate tells them to take Jesus and judge him; they reply that it is unlawful for them to put any one to death; Pilate takes Jesus into the judgment hall and questions him, again asking if Jesus is king of the Jews; Jesus asks if Pilate sayest this of himself, or did others tell him; Pilate says, "Am I a Jew?"; Jesus then explains that his kingdom is not of this world, and explains he came into the world to witness the truth; Pilate says, "What is truth?"; he then goes out and says he finds no fault in Jesus; in the outcry which follows, some one mentions Galilee	27:11-14	15:2-5	23:2-5	18:28-38	No Record
(i) p. 424	**Before Herod.** Pilate hearing of Galilee, asks if Jesus is a Galilean, and finding Jesus belongs unto Herod's jurisdiction,					

Sec. & Pg.	Event, Time and Place	Matt.	Mark	Luke	John	3 Nephi
§165	*(Cont'd)*					
(i)	sends him to Herod who is in the city; Herod, having long heard of Jesus, is desirous of seeing him, hoping Jesus will perform a miracle for him (Herod); Herod "questioned with him in many words"; but Jesus answers nothing; the chief priests and scribes vehemently accuse Jesus; Herod and his soldiers mock Jesus, array him in a gorgeous robe, and send him again to Pilate; formerly at enmity between themselves, Herod and Pilate become friends			23:6-12		
(j) p. 425	**Again before Pilate.** Pilate calls together the chief priests, the rulers, and the people, and speaking of the custom of releasing to them a prisoner on this feast day, tells them he finds no fault in Jesus, neither does Herod, and therefore he (Pilate) will chastise Jesus and release him; the multitude, persuaded by the chief priests and elders, calls for the release of Barabbas, a murderer; Pilate's wife sends word of a dream she has had and asks Pilate to do nothing against Jesus; Pilate again proposes to release Jesus; again the multitude refuse, and cry out that Jesus be crucified	27:15-23	15:6-14	23:13-23	18:39-40	No Record
(k) p. 427	**Pilate releases Barabbas.** Pilate releases Barabbas, then scourges Jesus, and delivers him to the soldiers; they take him into the hall,					

SEC. & PG.	EVENT, TIME AND PLACE	MATT.	MARK	LUKE	JOHN	3 NEPHI
§165	(*Cont'd*)					
(k)	strip him, put on him a scarlet robe, plait a crown of thorns and put on his head, put a reed in his hand, and then bow before him, mocking him, saying, "Hail, King of the Jews," then they spit upon him, take the reed from him, and smite him on the head	27:26-30	15:15-19	23:24-25	19:1-3	
(l) p. 428	**Pilate pleads for Jesus but finally delivers him for crucifixion.** Pilate then takes Jesus out again, wearing the crown of thorns and the purple robe, saying he finds no fault in him, "Behold the man"; the chief priests and officers cry, "Crucify him"; Pilate again says he finds no fault in him; Pilate takes Jesus again into the judgment hall, and asks who he is, but Jesus is silent; Pilate points out his power over him; Jesus says Pilate has no power except what he is given from above; Pilate again seeks to release Jesus, until the multitude say that if Pilate lets this man go he is no friend of Caesar; Pilate washes his hands publicly saying he is guiltless of this man's blood; the people cry to let his blood be upon them and their children; Pilate then brings Jesus forth, sits down in the judgment seat in a place called the Pavement; it is about the sixth hour; he says to the Jews, "Behold your King"; the people cry, "Crucify him"; Pilate says, "Shall I crucify your					No Record

Sec. & Pg.	Event, Time and Place	Matt.	Mark	Luke	John	3 Nephi
§165	(*Cont'd*)					
(l)	King?"; the priests answer they have no king but Caesar; Pilate then delivers Jesus to them	27:24-25			19:4-16a	
(m) p. 429	**They take him to be crucified.** After they mock Jesus, they take off the purple from him, put on his own clothes, and lead him away to be crucified, he bearing his own cross, but as they come out they find a man from Cyrene, Simon by name (the father of Alexander and Rufus), and him they compel to bear the cross to Golgotha (Luke calls it Calvary), the place of execution; a great company follow, and they bewail and lament him; Jesus tells them to weep not for him, but for themselves and their children, and he prophesies concerning the ills that are to come; arriving at the place of crucifixion, they offer him a drink of wine mingled with myrrh (Matthew says vinegar and gall), but he refuses it; they crucify him at the third hour, with a thief on each side	27:31-34, 38	15:20-23, 25,27,28	23:26-33	19:16b-18	No Record
(n) p. 431	**Pilate places a superscription on the cross.** Pilate prepares a superscription—in Greek, Latin, and Hebrew — "Jesus of Nazareth the King of the Jews," which is placed on the cross above Jesus' head; the chief priests of the Jews come to Pilate and say: "Write not, The King of					

SEC. & PG.	EVENT, TIME AND PLACE	MATT.	MARK	LUKE	JOHN	3 NEPHI
§165	*(Cont'd)*					
(n)	the Jews; but that he said, I am King of the Jews. Pilate answered, What I have written I have written"	27:37	15:26	23:38	19:19-22	
(o) p. 431	**The first words on the cross.** The first words on the cross: "Father, forgive them; for they know not what they do"	....	....	23:34a	....	
(p) p. 431	**The soldiers divide his clothes.** When the soldiers have crucified him, they take his garments and divide them into four parts and also his coat (woven without a seam) and cast lots for them, what every man shall take; for the coat they cast a special lot so as not to rend it; having done these things, they sit down and watch him there	27:35-36	15:24	23:34b	19:23-24	No Record
(q) p. 432	**The mocking and scoffing of the rulers and the multitude.** The chief priests and scribes mock among themselves, and call upon Jesus to save himself if he be king of the Jews, if he will descend from the cross they will believe, he has saved others, now let him save himself; those who pass also mock, wagging their heads and taunting him about the destruction of the Temple, the thieves also rail at him in the same way	27:39-44	15:29-32	23:35-37	....	
(r) p. 433	**Second words from the cross.** Second words from the cross: But one of the					

Sec. & Pg.	Event, Time and Place	Matt.	Mark	Luke	John	3 Nephi
§165	*(Cont'd)*					
(r)	thieves, when his fellow cries, "If thou be Christ, save thyself and us," rebukes the railer, pointing out that they receive the just reward of their deeds, while Jesus has done nothing amiss; he then says to Jesus, "Lord, remember me when thou comest into thy kingdom," and to him Jesus says, "Verily I say unto thee, To day shalt thou be with me in paradise"			23:39-43		No Record
(s) p. 433	**Third words from the cross.** Third words from the cross: By the cross stand the mother of Jesus, her sister Mary, wife of Cleophas, and Mary Magdalene; John stands there also and to his mother Jesus says, "Woman, behold thy son," to his disciple he says, "Behold thy mother," and "from that hour that disciple took her unto his own home"				19:25-27	
(t) p. 434	**Darkness covers the earth.** A darkness comes over "all the earth," from the sixth to the ninth hour	27:45	15:33	23:44-45a		
(u) p. 434	**Signs in the Western Hemisphere.** Great convulsions of nature on the Western Hemisphere; the greatest storm ever known, tempests, thunder, lightning, one city is set on fire, another is sunk in the sea, another is buried under a mountain; in some places the whole face of the land is changed by tempests, storms, and earth-					

Sec. & Pg.	Event, Time and Place	Matt.	Mark	Luke	John	3 Nephi
§165	(*Cont'd*)					
(u)	quakes; other cities are sunk and buried, others carried away by the whirlwinds; the earth is torn and cracked; the storm lasts for about three hours; then thick darkness comes, so thick its vapors can be felt, and no light will burn; this lasts for the space of three days; the people weep, wail, and howl because of the darkness and great destruction that have come upon them; they vainly cry because they have not repented and listened to the prophets					8:5-25
(v) p. 436	**Fourth words from the cross.** Fourth words from the cross: At the ninth hour Jesus cries: "My God, my God, why hast thou forsaken me?"; some of the bystanders hearing this say, "Behold, he calleth Elias"	27:46-47	15:34-35			
(w) p. 437	**Fifth words from the cross.** Fifth words from the cross: Jesus, "knowing that all things were now accomplished, that the scripture might be fulfilled, saith, I thirst"; they straightway then take a sponge, fill it with vinegar, put it on a reed and give it to him to drink; the rest say: "Let be, let us see whether Elias will come to save him"	27:48-49	15:36		19:28-29	
(x) p. 437	**Sixth words from the cross.** Sixth words from the cross: When Jesus receives the vinegar he says: "It is finished"				19:30a	

Sec. & Pg.	Event, Time and Place	Matt.	Mark	Luke	John	3 Nephi
§165	*(Cont'd)*					
(y) p. 437	**Seventh words from the cross.** Seventh words from the cross: Jesus then cries in a loud voice: "Father, into thy hands I commend my spirit," and having said this, "he gave up the ghost"	27:50	15:37	23:46	19:30b	No Record
(z) p. 438	**The Centurion's testimony.** The veil of the Temple is rent in twain, the earth quakes, and rocks are rent; the centurion seeing all these things, glorifies God saying, "Certainly this was a righteous man"; many stand afar off, among them Mary Magdalene, Mary the mother of James the less and of Joses, and Salome, and the mother of Zebedee's children, as also many women who, beholding from afar, had followed from Galilee and had come with him to Jerusalem.	27:51-56	15:38-41	23:45b, 47-49	....	
(aa) p. 439	**His side pierced.** The Jews beseech Pilate (in order that the bodies might not be left on the cross on the Sabbath) that the legs of those crucified be broken; the legs of the thieves are broken, but Jesus being already dead, they do not break his legs; but one of the soldiers pierces his side with a spear and there come out blood and water	....	....	....	19:31-37	
(bb) p. 439	**His burial.** When the even was come, Joseph of Arimathaea, an honorable counselor (who					

SEC. & PG.	EVENT, TIME AND PLACE	MATT.	MARK	LUKE	JOHN	3 NEPHI
§165	*(Cont'd)*					
(bb)	had not consented "to the counsel and deed of them"), a secret disciple of Jesus, goes boldly to Pilate and asks for the body of Jesus; Pilate marvels that Jesus is so soon dead, and asks the centurion if Jesus is dead; the centurion saying he is, Pilate gives the body to Joseph, who with Nicodemus, takes the body down, wraps it in fine linen, with an hundred weight of myrrh mixed with aloes, and buries it in his own new tomb, which is in a garden near to the place of crucifixion; a great stone is rolled before the door; Mary Magdalene and Mary the mother of Jesus sit near the sepulchre; the women from Galilee follow, behold the sepulchre, and how the body is laid; then "they returned, and prepared spices and ointments; and rested the sabbath day according to the commandment"	27:57-61	15:42-47	23:50-56	19:38-42	No Record
	Seventh Day of the Week					
§166 p. 441	**The guard placed at the tomb and the voice heard in the Western Hemisphere.**					
	Time: A.D. 30, Sat., Apr. 8; 16th Nisan (Andrews)					
	JERUSALEM AND THE WESTERN HEMISPHERE	....	....	....	....	
(a) p. 441	**The placing of the guard at the tomb.**					
	The chief priests and the Pharisees go to Pilate, and saying that "that deceiver" said while yet alive that he					

SEC. & PG.	EVENT, TIME AND PLACE	MATT.	MARK	LUKE	JOHN	3 NEPHI
§166	*(Cont'd)*					
(a)	would rise again, asks that the sepulchre be made sure against the third day, lest his disciples come by night and steal him away and then say he is risen from the dead, so that "the last error shall be worse than the first"; Pilate says: "Ye have a watch: go your way, make it as sure as ye can"; so they make the sepulchre sure, sealing the stone, and setting a watch	27:62-66				
(b) p. 442	**In Western Hemisphere, a voice from heaven declares the woes of the people.** A voice comes from heaven, crying wo unto the people, calling them to repentance from their sins; it tells them of the destruction that has come to them because of their iniquities; it names many cities which have been destroyed, because of the wickedness of their people and their abominations; the voice then tells of the mercy and blessings that will be theirs who come to him, and proclaims himself Jesus Christ, the Son of God; the voice tells of the relationship between himself and the Father, gives a discourse upon the peace of those who come unto him; tells his own place, and that the law of Moses is gone, and gives the new sacrifice, and baptism, again speaking of the atonement					9:1-22

Sec. & Pg.	Event, Time and Place	Matt.	Mark	Luke	John	3 Nephi
§166	*(Cont'd)*					
(c) p. 444	**Silence in the land of Western Hemisphere.** After the voice ceases, there is a silence in the land for many hours, the astonishment of the people being so great that they cease their lamentations					10:1-2
(d) p. 444	**In Western Hemisphere, again a voice from heaven.** Then a voice from heaven comes again to the people, speaking to them as descendants of Jacob, and so of the house of Israel; the voice tells how often the speaker would have gathered and blessed Israel if they had listened and declared their desolation, "until the time of the fulfilling of the covenant to your fathers"; after they heard these words, they begin anew their lamentations for the loss of their kindred and friends					10:3-8
	First Day of the Week					
§167 p. 445	**The Resurrection.** Time: A.D. 30, Sun., Apr. 9; 17th Nisan. JERUSALEM AND VICINITY, AND WESTERN HEMISPHERE					
(a) p. 445	**An angel opens the tomb.** There is a great earthquake; an angel of the Lord comes down and rolls back the stone from the door and sits upon it; "his countenance was like lightning, and his raiment white as snow"; the keepers of the tomb are smitten and become as dead men	28:2-4				

Sec. & Pg.	Event, Time and Place	Matt.	Mark	Luke	John	3 Nephi
§167	*(Cont'd)*					
(b) p. 446	**In Western Hemisphere, darkness disappears and earth restored.** On the morning of the third day darkness disperses off the face of the land, "the earth did cleave together again, that it stood"; the people cease their mournings and become joyful, and give thanks unto Jesus Christ, their Redeemer; the more righteous part of the people have been saved during the great convulsions; the prophets had declared it all beforehand — Zenos and Jacob					10:9-17
(c) p. 447	**Mary Magdalene first to the tomb.** On Sunday morning, while it is yet dark, Mary Magdalene comes to the sepulchre and sees the stone taken away		16:9		20:1	
(d) p. 447	**Mary tells Peter and John.** She at once runs to Peter and John, says they have taken the Lord away, "and we know not where they have laid him"; Peter and John run to the sepulchre, John outrunning Peter and arriving first, stoops down and looking in sees the linen clothes lying, but does not go in				20:2-5	
(e) p. 448	**Peter and John visit tomb.** Peter arriving, he goes into the sepulchre and sees the grave clothes lying about; John then goes in, who "saw, and believed.					

Sec. & Pg.	Event, Time and Place	Matt.	Mark	Luke	John	3 Nephi
§167	*(Cont'd)*					
(e)	For as yet they knew not the scripture, that he must rise again from the dead"; they come out of the sepulchre and go away again to their own home, wondering			24:12	20:6-10	No Record
(f) p. 448	**Jesus appears to Mary.** Mary standing outside the sepulchre, stoops down, looks into the sepulchre, and sees two angels, one sitting at the head and the other at the foot; they ask why she weeps, she says they have taken her Lord away and she does not know where they have laid him; turning back she sees Jesus standing beside her; she does not know him; he asks why she weeps and whom she seeks; she, thinking it is the gardener, says if he has borne her Lord away, tell her where he has laid him and she will take him away; Jesus says, "Mary," she then knows who he is, and would have touched him; but he forbids her, for he has not yet ascended				20:11-17	
(g) p. 449	**Mary tells disciples.** Mary Magdalene goes and tells the disciples of seeing the Lord and of his words; and they believe her not		16:10-11		20:18	
(h) p. 449	**Other women come to the tomb.** Mary the mother of James, and Salome, and Mary Magdalene, and other					

Sec. & Pg.	Event, Time and Place	Matt.	Mark	Luke	John	3 Nephi
§167	*(Cont'd)*					
(h)	women come early to the tomb, bringing sweet spices that they may anoint Jesus; they say among themselves who shall roll the stone away from the door of the sepulchre; they find the stone rolled away; they enter but the body of Jesus is not there; as they stand perplexed, two angels are before them; one tells them not to fear, that Jesus whom they seek has risen, as he said, and he asks them to look where the Lord had lain; he tells them to go quickly and tell the disciples, and that Jesus will go before them to Galilee, where they shall see him	28:1, 5-7	16:1-7	24:1-8	....	No Record
(i) p. 451	**Christ appears to the women.** The women go on their way to tell the disciples; Jesus meets them; they come and hold him by the feet and worship him; he tells them not to fear, but to tell "my brethren" that they shall go unto Galilee where he will see them	28:9-10	....	....	....	
(j) p. 451	**The other women tell disciples.** The women depart from the sepulchre and having seen Jesus on their way "with fear and great joy" they run to the Eleven and tell all these things; "and their words seemed to them as idle tales, and they believed them not"	28:8	16:8	24:9-11	....	

SEC. & PG.	EVENT, TIME AND PLACE	MATT.	MARK	LUKE	JOHN	3 NEPHI
§167	*(Cont'd)*					
(k) p. 451	**Chief priests told of resurrection.** While the women were going to tell the disciples of the resurrection, some of the watch go to the city and tell the chief priests all the things that are done; when the elders assemble they give large sums of money to the watch to say that the disciples came by night and stole Jesus; the elders promise that if it comes to the governor's ears "we will persuade him, and secure you"; the soldiers take the money and do as they are taught; "and this saying is commonly reported among the Jews until this day"	28:11-15				No Record
(l) p. 452	**He appears to two disciples on the road to Emmaus.** Two disciples on their way to Emmaus, talking together about events, are overtaken by Jesus, but "their eyes were holden" and they know him not; he asks what they were talking about; one of them, Cleopas, tells Jesus about the happenings; Jesus then upbraids them for not understanding, and, beginning at Moses, goes over the prophecies concerning himself; coming near the village where they are to stop, they urge him to stay with them; when he sits at meat he takes bread and blesses it and breaks and gives to them; their eyes are opened; he vanishes from their sight; they then remember how their hearts burned					

Sec. & Pg.	Event, Time and Place	Matt.	Mark	Luke	John	3 Nephi
§167	(*Cont'd*)					
(l)	while he talked with them on the way	....	16:12-13	24:13-32	....	No Record
(m) p. 453	**Jesus appears unto Peter.** 1 Cor. 15:5a	....	....	24:34	....	
(n) p. 454	**He appears to all disciples except Thomas.** The two return from Emmaus, and meet with the Eleven (Thomas absent), gathered together, the doors shut for fear of the Jews; the two from Emmaus are telling their experience when Jesus stands in their midst, saying: "Peace be unto you"; they are terrified, thinking he is a spirit, he shows his hands and feet; he breathes on them and says, "Receive ye the Holy Ghost"; then asks for something to eat, and he eats fish and honeycomb; he then again goes over the scriptures, and their understandings are opened; he explains somewhat the atonement; tells them what they must preach, and directs them to tarry in Jerusalem till "ye be endued with power from on high"	....	16:14	24:33-49	20:19-23	
§168 p. 455	**Appearances subsequent to those of the first day of the week.** **Time: A.D. 30, Apr.-May** Jerusalem, Galilee	....	....	....	....	
(a) p. 455	**He appears to disciples, including Thomas.** Thomas, called Didymus, not with the Apostles on the Sunday when Jesus appeared, refuses to believe their testimony and says					

Sec. & Pg.	Event, Time and Place	Matt.	Mark	Luke	John	3 Nephi
§168	*(Cont'd)*					
(a)	he must himself see and feel the body of Jesus; eight days later the disciples are all together again; again the doors are shut; Jesus again stands in their midst, saying, "Peace be unto you"; he asks Thomas to verify his identity by touching him; Thomas answers, "My Lord and my God"; Jesus says, "Thomas, because thou hast seen me, thou hast believed: blessed are they that have not seen, and yet have believed"				20:24-29	
(b) p. 456	**He appears to disciples at Sea of Tiberias.** Seven disciples are at the Sea of Tiberias; Peter takes them fishing; they fish all night and catch nothing; the next morning Jesus (unknown to them) stands on the shore and asks if they have any meat; they answer no; he tells them to cast their net on the right side of the ship; they do so, and are not able to draw for the multitude of fishes; John says to Peter, "It is the Lord"; Peter throws himself into the sea, and the others come in the little ship; when they come to land, they see a fire of coals with fish laid thereon and bread; Jesus tells them to bring of the fish they have caught; Peter draws the net to land full of great fishes, yet the net is not broken; Jesus asks them to come and eat; none durst ask him, "Who art thou? knowing that it was the Lord"; this is the third					No Record

Sec. & Pg.	Event, Time and Place	Matt.	Mark	Luke	John	3 Nephi
§168	(*Cont'd*)					
(b)	time he has shown himself to his disciples after he was risen from the dead				21:1-14	No Record
(c) p. 457	**Jesus asks if Peter loves him.** Jesus questions Peter—whether Peter loves him; the thrice repeated question and thrice repeated command, "Feed my sheep"; Jesus foretells the manner of Peter's death				21:15-19	
(d) p. 458	**Peter asks about John.** Peter sees John following and asks, "Lord, and what shall this man do?" Jesus saith, "If I will that he tarry till I come, what is that to thee? follow thou me"; from which comes the saying abroad that John should not die; but Jesus did not say this but only, "If I will that he tarry till I come, what is that to thee?"				21:20-23	
(e) p. 458	**Jesus appears to a great multitude, "above five hundred."** 1 Cor. 15:6					
(f) p. 458	**Jesus appears to James.** 1 Cor. 15:7a					
(g) p. 459	**He appears to disciples in Galilee.** The eleven disciples go into Galilee, into a mountain where Jesus had appointed them. Here Jesus gives them their final charge. (Luke records in Acts 1:1-8 some matters covered by this charge.)	28:16-20	16:15-18			

SEC. & PG.	EVENT, TIME AND PLACE	MATT.	MARK	LUKE	JOHN	3 NEPHI
§169 p. 460	**The ascension.** **Time: A.D. 30, Thurs., May 18** (Andrews) Taking his disciples to Bethany, he lifts his hands and blesses them, and while he yet blesses them, he is parted from them, and ascends into heaven, a cloud receiving him out of their sight, to be received and sit on the right hand of God; Luke records in Acts that while the disciples stood looking towards heaven, two men stood by them in white apparel, asked why they so looked, and said that Jesus would return as he had gone. (Acts 1:9-11) BETHANY	....	16:19	24:50-51	....	No Record
§170 p. 460	**The disciples return to Jerusalem.** **Time: A.D. 30** They worship and return to Jerusalem, where in an upper room the Eleven with "Mary the mother of Jesus, and with his brethren," continue prayer and supplication, worshipping; they are in the Temple continually, praising and blessing God; they go forth preaching everywhere, the Lord working with them, and confirming the word with signs following; "the number of names together were about an hundred and twenty." (Acts 1:12-15) BETHANY TO JERUSALEM	....	16:20	24:52-53	....	
§171 p. 461	**John's concluding words.**	....	....	....	20:30-31, 21:24-25	

EIGHTH PERIOD

The Benediction Upon Our Lord's Ministry—His Visit to the Western Hemisphere after His Ascension in Palestine — Book of Mormon

Sec. & Pg.	Event, Time and Place	Matt.	Mark	Luke	John	3 Nephi
§172 p. 463	**The Lord foretells his appearance on Western Hemisphere.** **Time: 125th-126th year of the Reign of the Judges** Through his prophets (Zenos, Jacob, and others) of the Western Hemisphere, the Lord foretold his appearance on the Western Hemisphere after his life in Palestine and his ascension at Bethany					10:18-19
§173 p. 463	**A voice out of heaven.** A small piercing voice comes out of heaven to the great multitude gathered round about the Temple in the land Bountiful, "and they were marveling and wondering one with another, and were showing one to another the great and marvelous change which had taken place"; they are conversing about Jesus, when they hear a voice as if coming out of heaven, not a harsh voice, nor a loud one, but a small voice that pierces them to their centers and causes their frames to quake					
(a) p. 463	**The first voice not understood.**					11:1-3
(b) p. 464	**The voice comes the second time, still not understood.**					11:4
(c) p. 464	**The voice comes a third time.**					

SEC. & PG.	EVENT, TIME AND PLACE	MATT.	MARK	LUKE	JOHN	3 NEPHI
§173	*(Cont'd)*					
(c)	The voice is now understood—it is the Father introducing the Son					11:5-7
§174 p. 464	**The multitude see Jesus descending.**					
	The multitude looking towards heaven, see Jesus descending; they watch in silence; they think him an angel; he comes down and stands in their midst					11:8-9
§175 p. 465	**He begins his mission.**					
	Jesus beginning his mission, declares who he is, and speaks of his atonement; the multitude fall to the ground, remembering what had been prophesied of the coming of the Christ among them					11:10-12
§176 p. 465	**The great opening day of Christ's ministry upon the Western Hemisphere.**					
(a) p. 465	**He invites multitude to handle his body.**					
	Jesus asks the multitude to come forward and handle his body that they may know he is who he claims to be					11:13-15
(b) p. 466	**The people convinced.**					
	The people come forth and test Jesus by their hands, and break forth into hosannas					11:16-17
(c) p. 466	**Nephi called forth, and others.**					
	Jesus first calls forth Nephi, charges him and gives him power; he calls others and makes a like bestowal; instructs them in					

Sec. & Pg.	Event, Time and Place	Matt.	Mark	Luke	John	3 Nephi
§176	*(Cont'd)*					
(c)	the manner of baptism; tells them of the relationship of the Trinity					11:18-27
(d) p. 467	**The Twelve warned.** Jesus warns the Twelve against disputations among themselves, and contentions, especially about doctrine					11:28-32
(e) p. 468	**Jesus discourses on repentance and baptism and the necessity therefor.**					11:33-41
(f) p. 468	**The calling of the Twelve explained.** Jesus explains the choosing of the Twelve and their mission to baptize, Jesus saying he would baptize them with the Holy Ghost, after which the testimony of Christ would come to them; tells the multitude how blessed they will be who believe in Jesus because of the testimony of the multitude					12:1-2
(g) p. 469	**Jesus repeats the great truths given in the Sermon on the Mount and the Sermon on the Plain.** (For Sermon on the Mount, see Sec. 50 above, and for the Sermon on the Plain, see Sec. 60 above)					12:3-48, 13:1-24
(h) p. 473	**The Twelve instructed.** Jesus gives special instructions to the Twelve regarding their work; tells them to look after the spiritual things and shows the weakness of the material things; tells them to put their faith and confidence in God					13:25-34

SEC. & PG.	EVENT, TIME AND PLACE	MATT.	MARK	LUKE	JOHN	3 NEPHI
§176	*(Cont'd)*					
(i) p. 474	**The multitude instructed.** Jesus again instructs the multitude on the truths and principles of the Sermons on the Mount and on the Plain					14:1-27
(j) p. 475	**Further instructions.** Jesus tells the multitude that they have heard things which he taught before he ascended to his Father; the blessings of those who remember and do his words					15:1
(k) p. 475	**Jesus explains his relationship to the law of Moses.**					15:2-10
(l) p. 476	**Special instructions to Twelve.** Jesus speaks again to his disciples — the Twelve — tells them he is giving them instructions and information which the Father did not have him give the people in Palestine; explains how the Gentiles are to know him; tells them they are numbered among those whom the Father has given him					15:11-24
(m) p. 477	**He tells of other sheep.** Jesus tells them he has still other sheep that are not here nor in Jerusalem to whom he has not manifested himself, and who have not heard his voice; that the Father has commanded him to go to them, that all shall be of one fold, and that he goes to show himself to them; they are to write these things so that if those in Jerusalem are not faithful, they may know of					

Sec. & Pg.	Event, Time and Place	Matt.	Mark	Luke	John	3 Nephi
§176	(*Cont'd*)					
(m)	him through the Holy Ghost, and that the Gentiles may know of him through these writings, and to the remnant of the seed of the others to whom he goes, all of whom he will gather from the four corners of the earth					16:1-5
(n) p. 478	**The Gentiles blessed and warned.** Jesus blesses the Gentiles, and says because of Israel's unbelief the truth in the latter days shall come through the Gentiles; but wo unto the unbelieving Gentiles who have scattered his people; foretells how he will bring his Gospel forth among the Gentiles, notwithstanding their wickedness; he will then remember his covenants to his people; tells what will happen if the Gentiles do not serve him; repeats a prophecy of Isaiah					16:6-20
(o) p. 480	**He tells multitude to ponder his words.** Jesus, looking round upon the multitude, says his time is at hand; he tells them he sees they are not understanding his words; he sends them to ponder upon the things he has told them, saying he will come again on the morrow; he says he will go to the Father and to the lost tribes, for they are not lost to the Father; the multitude is in tears and look steadfastly upon him as if they wish him to tarry longer with them					17:1-5

Sec. & Pg.	Event, Time and Place	Matt.	Mark	Luke	John	3 Nephi
§176	*(Cont'd)*					
(p) p. 480	**A feast of miracles.** Jesus tells them he is filled with compassion for them; he asks them to bring to him the lame, blind, halt or maimed, or leprous, or they that are withered, or deaf, or afflicted in any manner; he will heal them and show them what he has done in Jerusalem; then the multitude bring their sick and afflicted, and he heals every one as they are brought to him; all bow down and worship at his feet, kissing his feet and bathing them with tears					17:6-10
(q) p. 481	**He blesses the little children.** Jesus tells them to bring their little children to him; when they have all been brought to him, he has the multitude kneel; he groans within himself over the wickedness of Israel; then kneeling upon the earth he prays a prayer which may not be written, because language cannot express what they saw and heard; when Jesus finishes he arises, but the multitude remain kneeling, overcome; Jesus commands them to arise and he blesses them; he weeps, then takes the children one by one and blesses them; then prays and weeps again					17-11-22
(r) p. 482	**Angels minister to the little ones.** Jesus says to the multitude, "Behold your little ones," they look and behold angels descending from					

Sec. & Pg.	Event, Time and Place	Matt.	Mark	Luke	John	3 Nephi
§176	(*Cont'd*)					
(r)	heaven as if in the midst of fire; the angels encircle the little ones, who are encircled by fire; the angels minister unto the children; the multitude, about two thousand five hundred souls, bear record of this					17:23-25
(s) p. 483	**The multitude fed.** Jesus commands his disciples that they shall get bread and wine; they bring it. Jesus blesses it; at his command the disciples first eat, then feed the multitude					18:1-4
(t) p. 483	**He institutes the sacrament.** Jesus tells the multitude that he will ordain one among them who shall break bread and bless it, and give to them in remembrance of his body, which he has shown to them, and remembering him, his spirit shall be with them; he then gives his disciples wine to drink, and tells them to give to the multitude; they and the multitude both drink and are filled; when the disciples have done this he blesses them; he tells them this witnesses unto the Father that they are willing to keep his commandments, and that they do this in remembrance of his blood that was shed for them; those who do these things are built upon a rock, but those who do less are built upon a sandy foundation; blessed are they who keep his commandments; watch					

Sec. & Pg.	Event, Time and Place	Matt.	Mark	Luke	John	3 Nephi
§176	(*Cont'd*)					
(t)	and pray as he has prayed; he is the light					18:5-16
(u) p. 485	**He teaches prayer.** Jesus teaches the multitude that they must pray, he teaches them how to pray, the efficacy of prayer, to pray in their families, and to pray for the wayward; he is the light, they must do as he has done					18:17-25
(v) p. 485	**Instructions regarding the sacrament.** Jesus then turns to his disciples, saying he must give them one further commandment and then go unto his Father; this commandment is that they shall permit no one to partake of the sacrament unworthily, for the unworthy "eateth and drinketh damnation to his soul"; the unworthy are to be forbidden to take of the sacrament, but he shall not be cast out but labored with to bring him back; he gives these commandments because of their disputations					18:26-34
(w) p. 486	**The disciples given power to bestow Holy Ghost; he ascends into heaven.** Jesus touches his disciples one by one and speaks unto them; the multitude do not hear but the disciples bear record that he gave them power to give the Holy Ghost; this done, a cloud overshadows them all, so that they can not see Jesus, and while they are overshadowed, he ascends					

Sec. & Pg.	Event, Time and Place	Matt.	Mark	Luke	John	3 Nephi
§176	(*Cont'd*)					
(w)	into heaven as the disciples bear record					18:35-39
§177 p. 487	**The people return home.** After the ascension of Jesus, the people return to their homes, and begin to spread the news of the visit of Jesus and his ministrations, and that he will come on the morrow; great multitudes labor that they may be at the meeting-place on the morrow					19:1-3
§178 p. 488	**The succeeding two days of Christ's ministry on the Western Hemisphere.**					
(a) p. 488	**The multitude gather and pray.** On the morrow when the multitude gather together, the Twelve (named here), go and stand in the midst of them; the Twelve divide the multitude into twelve bodies, and having them kneel, they teach them how to pray; after prayer the Twelve rise and minister unto the people; repeating the words of Jesus, they pray again					19:4-8
(b) p. 488	**The Twelve receive the Holy Ghost.** They pray for that which they wish for most — that the Holy Ghost shall be given unto them; Nephi being baptized first, baptizes all the Twelve; and the Holy Ghost falls upon them, so that they are filled with it and with fire; they are encircled about with fire as it were, which comes down					

SEC. & PG.	EVENT, TIME AND PLACE	MATT.	MARK	LUKE	JOHN	3 NEPHI
§178	*(Cont'd)*					
(b)	from heaven; the multitude witness this, and see angels come down from heaven and minister unto the Twelve					19:9-14
(c) p. 489	**He comes again.** While the angels minister to the disciples, Jesus comes and stands in their midst and ministers to them; he speaks to the multitude and commands them and his disciples to kneel down; all kneeling, he commands his disciples that they pray					19:15-17
(d) p. 489	**He prays.** As they pray, Jesus moves a little way off and prays; he thanks the Father for the Holy Ghost given unto them; he prays the Father to give the Holy Ghost to all who believe in him; Jesus finishing his prayer returns and finds the disciples still praying; "for it was given unto them what they should pray, and they were filled with desire"					19:18-24
(e) p. 490	**He again prays.** Jesus smiles upon the disciples praying, and their countenances shine as white as Jesus'; telling them to pray on, he again draws aside and bowing to the earth, again prays to the Father whom he thanks for purifying the disciples, and prays that all who believe on him shall be likewise purified; he prays not for the world, but for those whom the Father has given					

Sec. & Pg.	Event, Time and Place	Matt.	Mark	Luke	John	3 Nephi
§178	*(Cont'd)*					
(e)	him out of the world; Jesus again returns and finding the disciples still praying, he again retires and prays what cannot be written, but the multitude understand for their hearts are open; coming back to the disciples, he says he has not seen such great faith among the Jews, and therefore he could not show unto them such great miracles; the Jews had not seen nor heard the things they have seen and heard					19:25-36
(f) p. 491	**He tells them to cease their prayers.** Jesus commands the disciples and the multitude to cease praying — though always praying in their hearts — and to arise and stand upon their feet, and they obey					20:1-2
(g) p. 492	**He again administers the sacrament.** Jesus administers the sacrament to the multitude, through the disciples, the bread and wine being miraculously provided; he explains the meaning of the sacrament; when the multitude have partaken of the sacrament they cry with one voice and give glory to Jesus, whom they both see and hear					20:3-9
§179 p. 492	**He gives commandments.** Jesus says he must now give them the commandments which the Father has commanded him concerning his people, who are a remnant of the house of Israel					

SEC. & PG.	EVENT, TIME AND PLACE	MATT.	MARK	LUKE	JOHN	3 NEPHI
§179	*(Cont'd)*					
(a) p. 492	**He quotes Isaiah.** Jesus quotes Isaiah regarding the gathering of the remnants of Israel; declares this land is for the remnant of the house of Jacob; warns the Gentiles; tells of their fate if they do not repent and tells how the remnant will punish them; this shall be a New Jerusalem, and the powers of heaven and Jesus will be in the midst of them					20:10-22
(b) p. 494	**He proclaims his identity.** Jesus again declares his identity and refers to the prophecy of Moses and of the prophets since; again tells them who they are, the children of Abraham, the children of the covenant; calls upon them to forsake sin; foretells the curse of the Gentiles, the scattering of the house of Israel, and the returning of their iniquities upon their own heads; he will remember his covenants with his people, their gathering together, the giving to them of the land, which is promised unto them forever					20:23-29
(c) p. 495	**Discourse on glory of Israel.** Jesus discourses on the future glory of Israel, quoting from the prophets, and telling when these covenants shall be fulfilled					20:30-46
(d) p. 496	**The signs of the gathering.** Jesus discourses upon the signs which shall tell when all these shall "be about to					

SEC. & PG.	EVENT, TIME AND PLACE	MATT.	MARK	LUKE	JOHN	3 NEPHI
§179	(*Cont'd*)					
(d)	take place," tells of the great work which the Father shall do for his sake; they who do not receive the word of his servant shall be cut off; the remnant of his people shall be among the Gentiles as a lion among the beasts of the field or a young lion among the sheep, treading down and tearing apart, and "their hand shall be lifted up upon their adversaries, and all their enemies shall be cut off"					21:1-13
(e) p. 497	**The woes of the Gentiles.** Jesus discourses upon the woes which shall come to the Gentiles in those days					21:14-21
(f) p. 498	**How Gentiles may share glories.** Jesus promises that if the Gentiles will repent and assist his people, they shall share in the glories which come to his people; the work shall then commence among all his dispersed peoples, even the tribes which are lost, that they may come unto him and call upon the Father in his name					21:22-27
(g) p. 499	**The Father will commence work.** The Father will then commence his work among all the nations for the gathering of his people to the land of their inheritance; they shall go out from all nations, not in haste and not in fright, "and I will be their rearward"					21:28-29

SEC. & PG.	EVENT, TIME AND PLACE	MATT.	MARK	LUKE	JOHN	3 NEPHI
§179	*(Cont'd)*					
(h) p. 499	**He again quotes Isaiah.** Jesus again repeats from the words of the prophet Isaiah — the rejoicings of God's people, and his rejoicings over his people					22:1-17
(i) p. 500	**The people to search scriptures.** Jesus commands that they search the words of Isaiah, that they write the things which he has told them and to search the scriptures; he states there are other scriptures they should write which they do not have					23:1-6
(j) p. 501	**Their records criticized.** Jesus tells Nephi to bring forth the records, and when Nephi brings them, Jesus points out they contain no record of the prophecies of Samuel regarding the resurrection of the Saints, and he tells them to make record of these things; he commands that they shall teach the things he has expounded					23:7-14
(k) p. 502	**Record to be made of Malachi's words.** Jesus commands them to make a record of the words of Malachi, which he gives unto them					24:1-18, 25:1-6
(l) p. 504	**The scriptures expounded.** Jesus expounds these scriptures at the direction of the Father, and all things he expounds from the beginning until the end when					

SEC. & PG.	EVENT, TIME AND PLACE	MATT.	MARK	LUKE	JOHN	3 NEPHI
§179	(*Cont'd*)					
(l)	the heavens and earth should pass away, and the great last day of judgment which shall be given according "to the mercy, and the justice, and the holiness which is in Christ, who was before the world began"					26:1-5
(m) p. 504	**Moroni explains records.** Moroni explains the omissions from these records, and gives the commandment of the Lord touching the matter					26:6-12
§180 p. 505	**He teaches the people.** Jesus "truly did teach the people, for the space of three days; and after that he did show himself unto them oft, and did break bread oft, and bless it, and give it unto them"					26:13
§181 p. 505	**Works of Jesus among the people.**					26:14-16
§182 p. 506	**Disciples begin work.** The disciples begin their work from that time forth, baptizing; those who are baptized are filled with the Holy Ghost and see many unspeakable things not lawful to be written; they teach one another, have all things in common, deal justly one with another, and do all things as Jesus commanded, and those baptized are called the Church of Christ					26:17-21
§183 p. 507	**Another warning.** The disciples, being gathered together and engaged in mighty prayer and fast-					

SEC. & PG.	EVENT, TIME AND PLACE	MATT.	MARK	LUKE	JOHN	3 NEPHI
§183	*(Cont'd)* ing, Jesus comes to them and asks what they wish him to give them; he gives them instruction about the name of the Church and why					27:1-12
§184 p. 508	**Jesus again declares himself.** Jesus again declares himself and discourses upon his mission and atonement					27:13-15
§185 p. 508	**Baptism explained.** Jesus explains the effect of baptism upon them who endure to the end, and upon them who do not endure; no unclean thing can enter into his kingdom, only they who wash their garments in his blood, and, because of their faith, repent and hold their faithfulness to the end; declares what his Gospel is; the Church must do his works; and if they do these things they are blessed and "shall be lifted up at the last day"					27:16-22
§186 p. 509	**The keeping of records recommended.** Jesus instructs the disciples to keep record of all things; "out of the books which shall be written shall the world be judged"; all his disciples shall be judged of this people, according to the judgment he shall give them, which shall be just; his disciples ought to be even as Jesus is					27:23-27
§187 p. 510	**The final words to the disciples.**					

SEC. & PG.	EVENT, TIME AND PLACE	MATT.	MARK	LUKE	JOHN	3 NEPHI
§187	*(Cont'd)*					
(a) p. 510	**He must go to the Father.** Jesus tells the disciples he must go unto the Father; tells what they ask the Father in his name shall be given					27:28
(b) p. 510	**None of this generation to be lost.** Jesus directs them to ask and they shall receive, declares his joy because of this generation, and the Father rejoiceth also, for none of that generation shall be lost, that is, none of those now alive and in them he has a fulness of joy					27:29-31
(c) p. 510	**Fourth generation to be led captive.** Jesus foretells that the fourth generation from this shall be led away captive, following the son of perdition, and selling Jesus for silver and gold; in that day he will visit them, "turning their works upon their own heads"					27:32
(d) p. 511	**Further instructions.** Telling his disciples to enter into the strait gate and narrow way leading to eternal life, he also tells them that wide is the gate and broad the way that leads to death; many travel it; "the night cometh, wherein no man can work"					27:33
(e) p. 511	**Jesus' gifts to nine Disciples.** Having finished the instructions, Jesus asks them, "What is it that ye desire					

SEC. & PG.	EVENT, TIME AND PLACE	MATT.	MARK	LUKE	JOHN	3 NEPHI
§187	*(Cont'd)*					
(e)	of me, after that I am gone to the Father"; all speak but three, the others said that when they had finished their normal course they wished they might "speedily come unto thee in thy kingdom"; Jesus said they were blessed because of this desire, and when they were seventy-two years old they should come to him "and with me ye shall find rest"					28:1-3
(f) p. 511	**Jesus' gifts to three Disciples.**					
	Jesus then asks the three what they wish; they dare not tell their wish; he tells them he knows their thoughts — that they wish what he gave to John; he promises them they shall never taste death, but shall live to behold all of God's dealings with the children of men; when he comes they shall be changed in the twinkling of an eye, never tasting death, nor have pain or sorrow while in the flesh, because they have desired that they might bring the souls of men unto him; he promises them their reward					28:4-11
§188 p. 512	**Jesus ascends; the Three as if transfigured.**					
	Having finished his instructions, he touches all but the three with his finger, and then he departs. The heavens are opened and the three are caught up into heaven and hear unspeakable things, and whether they were in the body or out, they knew not, but it					

Sec. & Pg.	Event, Time and Place	Matt.	Mark	Luke	John	3 Nephi
§188	*(Cont'd)* seemed like a transfiguration, that they were changed from a body of flesh into an immortal state that they could behold the things of God					28:12-15
§189 p. 513	**Ministry of the Three.** The ministry of the Three Nephites among the people, their mighty works and miracles, and miraculous deliveries; they teach and convert the people					28:16-23
§190 p. 514	**Moroni finishes record.** Moroni finishes his record of the Three Nephites, he does not tell their names; they will work among the Jews and Gentiles, and go unto the scattered tribes of Israel; they are the angels of God, and will do a mighty and marvelous work; Moroni tells of the woes of those who do not listen to their message and speaks more of the condition of the bodies of the Three Nephites and their final reward					28:24-40
§191 p. 515	**Moroni's closing words to the Gentiles.**					Chaps. 29-30

Division Three

Our Lord of The Gospels

A Harmony

NOTE: Already in the Preface (to which the reader is referred), mention has been made and brief explanation given of the dates shown in the texts herein. It was noted there that after all, the exact date on which some event took place or some sermon was preached, was not the important thing; it was the happening of the event or the giving of the sermon and its content that really mattered. It was also noted that the date of the birth of the Savior herein used (late 5 B.C. or early 4 B.C.) seemed now to be accepted by many scholars, and was generally the basis of the chronologies they use. It was pointed out that this date was used herein to facilitate the work of students, who might use the commentaries and other critical books making use of this chronology. Again it should be said, it is not intended to contend for any date, but merely to attempt to facilitate study.

In order to show the considerable difference among the scholars on this question of the year of the birth of Jesus, I quote below one paragraph from Samuel J. Andrews (*The Life of Our Lord Upon the Earth*, p. 12). In reading this it should be noted that the year of Rome 747 equals 7 B.C.; 748, 6 B.C.; 749, 5 B.C.; 750, 4 B.C.; 751, 3 B.C.; 752, 2 B.C.; 753, 1 B.C. The paragraph reads:

"We give the opinions of some of the older and of the more modern chronologists and commentators:

"For the year 747, Sanclemente, Wurm, Ideler, Munter, Sepp, Jarvis, Alford, Patritius, Ebrard, Zumpt, Keim; 748, Kepler, Lewin; 749, Petavius, Usher, Norris, Tillemont, Lichtenstein, Ammer, Friedlieb, Bucher, Browne, Godet, McClellan; 750, Bengel, Wieseler, Greswell, Ellicott, Pressense, Thomson; for 751, Keil, Quandt; 752, Caspari, Reiss; Lardner hesitates between 748 and 749; so Robinson, 'not later than the autumn of 749, perhaps a year earlier'; so Beyschlag, Schenkel; Pound, 'August 749—August 750.' Clinton finds the earliest possible date the autumn of 748, the latest that of 750; Woolsey, undecided."

The pivotal point in the discussions of the scholars seems to be the death of Herod. Andrews, after discussing the evidence, says: "His [Herod's] death must therefore be placed between the 13th March and 4th April, 750. We may take the 1st of April as an approximate date. [i.e. 4 B.C.] . . . This would bring His birth into January, or February at latest, 750." (id. pp. 1-2.)

I say again I am not proposing any particular date.

One of the difficult minor matters of chronology concerns the visit of the Magi. Scholars disagree in their conclusions, some placing it before Mary's purification, some after. The arrangement herein (which puts the visit of the Magi after the purification) takes Luke's account to its end, and then follows Matthew, neither of them covering in his narrative of the Nativity the incidents narrated by the other. There is authority for this. The exact order seems unimporant.

FIRST PERIOD

FROM THE BEGINNING OF THE GOSPEL RECORD TO JOHN'S MINISTRY

Section 1

JOHN'S TESTIMONY

Matt.: No record; Mark: No record; Luke: No record; John 1:1-19.

Matthew: No record.

Mark: No record.

Luke: No record.

JOHN 1:1. In the beginning was the Word, and the Word was with God, and the Word was God.

2. The same was in the beginning with God.

3. All things were made by him; and without him was not any thing made that was made.

4. In him was life; and the life was the light of men.

5. And the light shineth in darkness; and the darkness comprehended it not.

6. ¶ There was a man sent from God, whose name *was* John.

7. The same came for a witness, to bear witness of the Light, that all *men* through him might believe.

8. He was not that Light, but *was sent* to bear witness of that Light.

9. *That* was the true Light, which lighteth every man that cometh into the world.

10. He was in the world, and the world was made by him, and the world knew him not.

11. He came unto his own, and his own received him not.

12. But as many as received him, to them gave he power to become the sons of God, *even* to them that believe on his name:

13. Which were born, not of blood, nor of the will of the flesh, nor of the will of man, but of God.

14. And the Word was made flesh, and dwelt among us, (and we beheld his glory, the glory as of the only begotten of the Father,) full of grace and truth.

15. ¶ John bare witness of him, and cried, saying, This was he of whom I spake, He that cometh after me is preferred before me: for he was before me.

16. And of his fulness have all we received, and grace for grace.

17. For the law was given by Moses, *but* grace and truth came by Jesus Christ.

18. No man hath seen God at any time; the only begotten

Son, which is in the bosom of the Father, he hath declared *him*.

19. ¶ And this is the record of John, when the Jews sent priests and Levites from Jerusalem to ask him, Who art thou?

Section 2

LUKE'S PREFACE

Matt.: No record; Mark: No record; Luke 1:1-4; John: No record.

Matthew: No record.

Mark: No record.

LUKE 1:1. Forasmuch as many have taken in hand to set forth in order a declaration of those things which are most surely believed among us,

2. Even as they delivered them unto us, which from the beginning were eyewitnesses, and ministers of the word;

3. It seemed good to me also, having had perfect understanding of all things from the very first, to write unto thee in order, most excellent Theophilus,

4. That thou mightest know the certainty of those things, wherein thou hast been instructed.

John: No record.

Section 3

THE GENEALOGIES

Matt. 1:1-17; Mark: No record; Luke 3:23-38; John: No record.

MATTHEW 1:1. The book of the generation of Jesus Christ, the son of David, the son of Abraham.

2. Abraham begat Isaac; and Isaac begat Jacob; and Jacob begat Judas and his brethren;

3. And Judas begat Phares and Zara of Thamar; and Phares begat Esrom; and Esrom begat Aram;

4. And Aram begat Aminadab; and Aminadab begat Naasson; and Naasson begat Salmon;

5. And Salmon begat Booz of Rachab; and Booz begat Obed of Ruth; and Obed begat Jesse;

6. And Jesse begat David the king; and David the king begat Solomon of her *that had been the wife* of Urias;

7. And Solomon begat Roboam; and Roboam begat Abia; and Abia begat Asa;

8. And Asa begat Josaphat; and Josaphat begat Joram; and Joram begat Ozias;

9. And Ozias begat Joatham; and Joatham begat Achaz; and Achaz begat Ezekias;

10. And Ezekias begat Ma-

nasses; and Manasses begat Amon; and Amon begat Josias;
11. And Josias begat Jechonias and his brethren, about the time they were carried away to Babylon:
12. And after they were brought to Babylon, Jechonias begat Salathiel; and Salathiel begat Zorobabel;
13. And Zorobabel begat Abiud; and Abiud begat Eliakim; and Eliakim begat Azor;
14. And Azor begat Sadoc; and Sadoc begat Achim; and Achim begat Eliud;
15. And Eliud begat Eleazar; and Eleazar begat Matthan; and Matthan begat Jacob;
16. And Jacob begat Joseph the husband of Mary, of whom was born Jesus, who is called Christ.
17. So all the generations from Abraham to David *are* fourteen generations; and from David until the carrying away into Babylon *are* fourteen generations; and from the carrying away into Babylon unto Christ *are* fourteen generations.

Mark: No record.

LUKE 3:23. And Jesus himself began to be about thirty years of age, being (as was supposed) the son of Joseph, which was *the son* of Heli,
24. Which was *the son* of Matthat, which was *the son* of Levi, which was *the son* of Melchi, which was *the son* of Janna, which was *the son* of Joseph,
25. Which was *the son* of Mattathias, which was *the son* of Amos, which was *the son* of Naum, which was *the son* of Esli, which was *the son* of Nagge,
26. Which was *the son* of Maath, which was *the son* of Mattathias, which was *the son* of Semei, which was *the son* of Joseph, which was *the son* of Juda,
27. Which was *the son* of Joanna, which was *the son* of Rhesa, which was *the son* of Zorobabel, which was *the son* of Salathiel, which was *the son* of Neri,
28. Which was *the son* of Melchi, which was *the son* of Addi, which was *the son* of Cosam, which was *the son* of Elmodam, which was *the son* of Er,
29. Which was *the son* of Jose, which was *the son* of Eliezer, which was *the son* of Jorim, which was *the son* of Matthat, which was *the son* of Levi,
30. Which was *the son* of Simeon, which was *the son* of Juda, which was *the son* of Joseph, which was *the son* of Jonan, which was *the son* of Eliakim,
31. Which was *the son* of Melea, which was *the son* of Menan, which was *the son* of Mattatha, which was *the son* of Nathan, which was *the son* of David,

32. Which was *the son* of Jesse, which was *the son* of Obed, which was *the son* of Booz, which was *the son* of Salmon, which was *the son* of Naasson,

33. Which was *the son* of Aminadab, which was *the son* of Aram, which was *the son* of Esrom, which was *the son* of Phares, which was *the son* of Juda,

34. Which was *the son* of Jacob, which was *the son* of Isaac, which was *the son* of Abraham, which was *the son* of Thara, which was *the son* of Nachor,

35. Which was *the son* of Saruch, which was *the son* of Ragau, which was *the son* of Phalec, which was *the son* of Heber, which was *the son* of Sala,

36. Which was *the son* of Cainan, which was *the son* of Arphaxad, which was *the son* of Sem, which was *the son* of Noe, which was *the son* of Lamech,

37. Which was *the son* of Mathusala, which was *the son* of Enoch, which was *the son* of Jared, which was *the son* of Maleleel, which was *the son* of Cainan,

38. Which was *the son* of Enos, which was *the son* of Seth, which was *the son* of Adam, which was *the son* of God.

John: No record.

Section 4

THE ANNUNCIATION TO ZACHARIAS

The angel announces to Zacharias (while he is executing the priest's office) the birth of a son; Zacharias, unbelieving, asks for a sign, and is struck dumb; returning to the people outside the temple, they perceive he has seen a vision; his priestly ministration accomplished, he departs to his own house.

Matt.: No record; Mark: No record; Luke 1:5-23; John: No record.

Time: B.C. 6, October (ANDREWS, CROSCUP).

Place: Jerusalem, Temple.

Matthew: No record.

Mark: No record.

LUKE 1:5. ¶There was in the days of Herod, the king of Judæa, a certain priest named Zacharias, of the course of Abia: and his wife *was* of the daughters of Aaron, and her name *was* Elisabeth.

6. And they were both righteous before God, walking in all the commandments and ordinances of the Lord blameless.

7. And they had no child, because that Elisabeth was barren, and they both were *now* well stricken in years.

8. And it came to pass, that while he executed the priest's office before God in the order of his course,

9. According to the custom of the priest's office, his lot was to burn incense when he went into the temple of the Lord.

10.And the whole multitude of the people were praying without at the time of incense.

11. And there appeared unto him an angel of the Lord standing on the right side of the altar of incense.

12. And when Zacharias saw *him*, he was troubled, and fear fell upon him.

13. But the angel said unto him, Fear not, Zacharias: for thy prayer is heard; and thy wife Elisabeth shall bear thee a son, and thou shalt call his name John.

14. And thou shalt have joy and gladness; and many shall rejoice at his birth.

15. For he shall be great in the sight of the Lord, and shall drink neither wine nor strong drink; and he shall be filled with the Holy Ghost, even from his mother's womb.

16. And many of the children of Israel shall he turn to the Lord their God.

17. And he shall go before him in the spirit and power of Elias, to turn the hearts of the fathers to the children, and the disobedient to the wisdom of the just; to make ready a people prepared for the Lord.

18. And Zacharias said unto the angel, Whereby shall I know this? for I am an old man, and my wife well stricken in years.

19. And the angel answering said unto him, I am Gabriel, that stand in the presence of God; and am sent to speak unto thee, and to shew thee these glad tidings.

20. And, behold, thou shalt be dumb, and not able to speak, until the day that these things shall be performed, because thou believest not my words, which shall be fulfilled in their season.

21. And the people waited for Zacharias, and marvelled that he tarried so long in the temple.

22. And when he came out, he could not speak unto them: and they perceived that he had seen a vision in the temple: for he beckoned unto them, and remained speechless.

23. And it came to pass, that, as soon as the days of his ministration were accomplished, he departed to his own house.

John: No record.

Section 5

ELISABETH GOES INTO RETIREMENT

Elisabeth conceives and goes into retirement for five months.

Matt.: No record; Mark: No record; Luke 1:24-25; John: No record.
Place: Judea (ANDREWS); Hebron or Juttah (CROSCUP).

Matthew: No record.

Mark: No record.

LUKE 1:24. And after those days his wife Elisabeth conceived, and hid herself five months, saying,

25. Thus hath the Lord dealt with me in the days wherein he looked on *me*, to take away my reproach among men.

John: No record.

Section 6

THE ANNUNCIATION TO MARY

In the sixth month of Elisabeth's conception the angel Gabriel, sent from God, announces to Mary, a virgin of Nazareth betrothed to Joseph of the house of David, that she shall be the mother of the Messiah.

Matt.: No record; Mark: No record; Luke 1:26-38; John: No record.
Time: B.C. 5, March-April (ANDREWS).
Place: Nazareth.

Matthew: No record.

Mark: No record.

LUKE 1:26. And in the sixth month the angel Gabriel was sent from God unto a city of Galilee, named Nazareth,

27. To a virgin espoused to a man whose name was Joseph, of the house of David; and the virgin's name *was* Mary.

28. And the angel came in unto her, and said, Hail, *thou that art* highly favoured, the Lord *is* with thee: blessed *art* thou among women.

29. And when she saw *him*, she was troubled at his saying, and cast in her mind what manner of salutation this should be.

30. And the angel said unto her, Fear not, Mary: for thou hast found favour with God.

31. And, behold, thou shalt conceive in thy womb, and bring forth a son, and shalt call his name JESUS.

32. He shall be great, and shall be called the Son of the Highest: and the Lord God shall give unto him the throne of his father David:

33. And he shall reign over the house of Jacob for ever; and of his kingdom there shall be no end.

34. Then said Mary unto the angel, How shall this be, seeing I know not a man?

35. And the angel answered and said unto her, The Holy

Ghost shall come upon thee, and the power of the Highest shall overshadow thee: therefore also that holy thing which shall be born of thee shall be called the Son of God.

36. And, behold, thy cousin Elisabeth, she hath also conceived a son in her old age: and this is the sixth month with her, who was called barren.

37. For with God nothing shall be impossible.

38. And Mary said, Behold the handmaid of the Lord; be it unto me according to thy word. And the angel departed from her.

John: No record.

Section 7

MARY VISITS ELISABETH

Mary visits Elisabeth, whose unborn babe leaps for joy at the sound of Mary's voice; Elisabeth declares the blessedness of Mary, who sings her hymn of praise,—the "Magnificat."

Matt.: No record; Mark: No record; Luke 1:39-56; John: No record.

Time: B.C. 5, March-April (ANDREWS).

Place: Judea (ANDREWS), Hebron or Juttah (CROSCUP).

Matthew: No record.

Mark: No record.

LUKE 1:39. And Mary arose in those days, and went into the hill country with haste, into a city of Juda;

40. And entered into the house of Zacharias, and saluted Elisabeth.

41. And it came to pass, that, when Elisabeth heard the salutation of Mary, the babe leaped in her womb; and Elisabeth was filled with the Holy Ghost:

42. And she spake out with a loud voice, and said, Blessed *art* thou among women, and blessed *is* the fruit of thy womb.

43. And whence *is* this to me, that the mother of my Lord should come to me?

44. For, lo, as soon as the voice of thy salutation sounded in mine ears, the babe leaped in my womb for joy.

45. And blessed *is* she that believed: for there shall be a performance of those things which were told her from the Lord.

46. And Mary said, My soul doth magnify the Lord,

47. And my spirit hath rejoiced in God my Saviour.

48. For he hath regarded the low estate of his handmaiden: for, behold, from henceforth all generations shall call me blessed.

49. For he that is mighty hath done to me great things; and holy *is* his name.

50. And his mercy *is* on them that fear him from generation to generation.

51. He hath shewed strength with his arm; he hath scattered the proud in the imagination of their hearts.

52. He hath put down the mighty from *their* seats, and exalted them of low degree.

53. He hath filled the hungry with good things; and the rich he hath sent empty away.

54. He hath holpen his servant Israel, in remembrance of *his* mercy;

55. As he spake to our fathers, to Abraham, and to his seed for ever.

56. And Mary abode with her about three months, and returned to her own house.

John: No record.

Section 8

THE ANNUNCIATION TO JOSEPH

An angel of the Lord appears in a dream to Joseph, to whom Mary was espoused, and, explaining Mary's condition, tells Joseph he need not fear to take Mary to wife, for she is to be the mother of one whose name shall be Emmanuel; Joseph, awakening, does as the Lord had bidden him.

Matt. 1:18-25; Mark: No record; Luke: No record; John: No record.
Time: B.C. 5, March-April (ANDREWS).
Place: Nazareth (ANDREWS).

MATTHEW 1:18. ¶Now the birth of Jesus Christ was on this wise: When as his mother Mary was espoused to Joseph, before they came together, she was found with child of the Holy Ghost.

19. Then Joseph her husband, being a just *man*, and not willing to make her a publick example, was minded to put her away privily.

20. But while he thought on these things, behold, the angel of the Lord appeared unto him in a dream, saying, Joseph, thou son of David, fear not to take unto thee Mary thy wife: for that which is conceived in her is of the Holy Ghost.

21. And she shall bring forth a son, and thou shalt call his name JESUS: for he shall save his people from their sins.

22. Now all this was done, that it might be fulfilled which was spoken of the Lord by the prophet, saying,

23. Behold, a virgin shall be with child, and shall bring forth a son, and they shall call his name Emmanuel, which being interpreted is, God with us.

24. Then Joseph being raised from sleep did as the angel of the Lord had bidden him, and took unto him his wife:

25. And knew her not till she had brought forth her firstborn son: and he called his name JESUS.

Mark: No record.

Luke: No record.

John: No record.

Section 9

JOHN IS BORN

Elisabeth gives birth to a son; her cousins, at the time of John's circumcision, call babe Zacharias; Elisabeth says his name shall be called John; the cousins appeal to the father Zacharias who writes on a tablet that the babe's name shall be John, whereupon the tongue of Zacharias is loosed and he praises God,—the "Benedictus."

Matt.: No record; Mark: No record; Luke 1:57-80; John: No record.

Time: B.C. 5, June (ANDREWS).

Place: Judea (ANDREWS).

Matthew: No record.

Mark: No record.

LUKE 1:57. Now Elisabeth's full time came that she should be delivered; and she brought forth a son.

58. And her neighbours and her cousins heard how the Lord had shewed great mercy upon her; and they rejoiced with her.

59. And it came to pass, that on the eighth day they came to circumcise the child; and they called him Zacharias, after the name of his father.

60. And his mother answered and said, Not *so;* but he shall be called John.

61. And they said unto her, There is none of thy kindred that is called by this name.

62. And they made signs to his father, how he would have him called.

63. And he asked for a writing table, and wrote, saying, His name is John. And they marvelled all.

64. And his mouth was opened immediately, and his tongue *loosed,* and he spake, and praised God.

65. And fear came on all that dwelt round about them: and all these sayings were noised abroad throughout all the hill country of Judæa.

66. And all they that heard *them* laid *them* up in their hearts, saying, What manner of child shall this be! And the hand of the Lord was with him.

67. And his father Zacharias was filled with the Holy Ghost, and prophesied, saying,

68. Blessed *be* the Lord God of Israel; for he hath visited and redeemed his people,

69. And hath raised up an horn of salvation for us in the house of his servant David;

70. As he spake by the

mouth of his holy prophets, which have been since the world began:

71. That we should be saved from our enemies, and from the hand of all that hate us;

72. To perform the mercy *promised* to our fathers, and to remember his holy covenant;

73. The oath which he sware to our father Abraham,

74. That he would grant unto us, that we being delivered out of the hand of our enemies might serve him without fear,

75. In holiness and righteousness before him, all the days of our life.

76. And thou, child, shalt be called the prophet of the Highest: for thou shalt go before the face of the Lord to prepare his ways;

77. To give knowledge of salvation unto his people by the remission of their sins,

78. Through the tender mercy of our God; whereby the dayspring from on high hath visited us,

79. To give light to them that sit in darkness and *in* the shadow of death, to guide our feet into the way of peace.

80. And the child grew, and waxed strong in spirit, and was in the deserts till the day of his shewing unto Israel.

John: No record.

Section 10

CAESAR AUGUSTUS LEVIES A TAX

Caesar Augustus declares a tax; Joseph and Mary go from Nazareth to Bethlehem to be taxed.

Matt.: No record; Mark: No record; Luke 2:1-5; John: No record.
Time: B.C. 5, December (ANDREWS).
Place: Nazareth to Bethlehem.

Matthew: No record.

Mark: No record.

LUKE 2:1. And it came to pass in those days, that there went out a decree from Cæsar Augustus, that all the world should be taxed.

2. (*And* this taxing was first made when Cyrenius was governor of Syria.)

3. And all went to be taxed, every one into his own city.

4. And Joseph also went up from Galilee, out of the city of Nazareth, into Judæa, unto the city of David, which is called Bethlehem; (because he was of the house and lineage of David:)

5. To be taxed with Mary his espoused wife, being great with child.

John: No record.

Section 11

JESUS ANNOUNCES HIS BIRTH IN THE WESTERN HEMISPHERE

Voice of the Lord comes to Nephi, son of Nephi, and announces that on this night the sign of his coming shall be given and that on the morrow he will come into the world.

3 Nephi 1:4-14.

Time: 92nd year of the Reign of the Judges.

Place: Zarahemla.

3 NEPHI 1:4. And it came to pass that in the commencement of the ninety and second year, behold, the prophecies of the prophets began to be fulfilled more fully; for there began to be greater signs and greater miracles wrought among the people.

5. But there were some who began to say that the time was past for the words to be fulfilled, which were spoken by Samuel, the Lamanite.

6. And they began to rejoice over their brethren, saying: Behold the time is past, and the words of Samuel are not fulfilled; therefore, your joy and your faith concerning this thing hath been vain.

7. And it came to pass that they did make a great uproar throughout the land; and the people who believed began to be very sorrowful, lest by any means those things which had been spoken might not come to pass.

8. But behold, they did watch steadfastly for that day and that night and that day which should be as one day as if there were no night, that they might know that their faith had not been vain.

9. Now it came to pass that there was a day set apart by the unbelievers, that all those who believed in those traditions should be put to death except the sign should come to pass, which had been given by Samuel the prophet.

10. Now it came to pass that when Nephi, the son of Nephi, saw this wickedness of his people, his heart was exceedingly sorrowful.

11. And it came to pass that he went out and bowed himself down upon the earth, and cried mightily to his God in behalf of his people, yea, those who were about to be destroyed because of their faith in the tradition of their fathers.

12. And it came to pass that he cried mightily unto the Lord, all the day; and behold, the voice of the Lord came unto him, saying:

13. Lift up your head and be of good cheer; for behold, the time is at hand, and on this night shall the sign be given, and on the morrow come I into the world, to show unto the

world that I will fulfill all that which I have caused to be spoken by the mouth of my holy prophets.

14. Behold, I come unto my own, to fulfill all things which I have made known unto the children of men from the foundation of the world, and to do the will, both of the Father and of the Son—of the Father because of me, and of the Son because of my flesh. And behold, the time is at hand, and this night shall the sign be given.

Section 12

JESUS BORN

Mary gives birth to Jesus, who is laid in a manger, there being no place at the inn.

Matt.: No record; Mark: No record; Luke 2:6-7; John: No record.

Time: B.C. 5, December (ANDREWS); others give B.C. 4, January to April.

Place: Bethlehem.

Matthew: No record.

Mark: No record.

LUKE 2:6. And so it was, that, while they were there, the days were accomplished that she should be delivered.

7. And she brought forth her firstborn son, and wrapped him in swaddling clothes, and laid him in a manger; because there was no room for them in the inn.

John: No record.

Section 13

AN ANGEL TELLS THE SHEPHERDS

The angel of the Lord announces to the shepherds the birth of Christ the Lord; he tells them where they will find the babe; heavenly hosts with the angel sing praises to God; the shepherds go to Bethlehem, find the babe, and make known abroad their heavenly message.

Matt.: No record; Mark: No record; Luke 2:8-20; John: No record.

Time: B.C. 5, December (ANDREWS); (see Sec. 12).

Place: Bethlehem.

Matthew: No record.

Mark: No record.

LUKE 2:8. And there were in the same country shepherds abiding in the field, keeping watch over their flock by night.

9. And, lo, the angel of the Lord came upon them, and the glory of the Lord shone round about them: and they were sore afraid.

10. And the angel said unto them, Fear not: for, behold,

I bring you good tidings of great joy, which shall be to all people.

11. For unto you is born this day in the city of David a Saviour, which is Christ the Lord.

12. And this *shall be* a sign unto you; Ye shall find the babe wrapped in swaddling clothes, lying in a manger.

13. And suddenly there was with the angel a multitude of the heavenly host praising God, and saying,

14. Glory to God in the highest, and on earth peace, good will toward men.

15. And it came to pass, as the angels were gone away from them into heaven, the shepherds said one to another, Let us now go even unto Bethlehem, and see this thing which is come to pass, which the Lord hath made known unto us.

16. And they came with haste, and found Mary, and Joseph, and the babe lying in a manger.

17. And when they had seen *it*, they made known abroad the saying which was told them concerning this child.

18. And all they that heard *it* wondered at those things which were told them by the shepherds.

19. But Mary kept all these things, and pondered *them* in her heart.

20. And the shepherds returned, glorifying and praising God for all the things that they had heard and seen, as it was told unto them.

John: No record.

Section 14

NO DARKNESS IN WESTERN HEMISPHERE

Signs in the Western Hemisphere of the Lord's coming; at going down of sun darkness does not come with night, and no darkness comes before the sun comes up again.

3 Nephi 1:15-20.

Time: 92nd year of Reign of the Judges.

Place: Western Hemisphere.

3 NEPHI 1:15. And it came to pass that the words which came unto Nephi were fulfilled, according as they had been spoken; for behold, at the going down of the sun there was no darkness; and the people began to be astonished because there was no darkness when the night came.

16. And there were many, who had not believed the words of the prophets, who fell to the earth and became as if they were dead, for they knew that the great plan of destruction which they had laid for those who believed in the words of the prophets had been frustrated; for the signal which

had been given was already at hand.

17. And they began to know that the Son of God must shortly appear; yea, in fine, all the people upon the face of the whole earth from the west to the east, both in the land north and in the land south, were so exceedingly astonished that they fell to the earth.

18. For they knew that the prophets had testified of these things for many years, and that the sign which had been given was already at hand; and they began to fear because of their iniquity and their unbelief.

19. And it came to pass that there was no darkness in all that night, but it was as light as though it was mid-day. And it came to pass that the sun did rise in the morning again, according to its proper order; and they knew that it was the day that the Lord should be born, because of the sign which had been given.

20. And it had come to pass, yea, all things, every whit, according to the words of the prophets.

Section 15

THE CIRCUMCISION

When eight days old, Jesus is circumcised and named Jesus.

Matt.: No record; Mark: No record; Luke 2:21; John: No record.
Time: B.C. 4, January (ANDREWS); (see Sec. 12, above).
Place: Bethlehem.

Matthew: No record.

Mark: No record.

LUKE 2:21. And when eight days were accomplished for the circumcising of the child, his name was called JESUS, which was so named of the angel before he was conceived in the womb.

John: No record.

Section 16

JESUS PRESENTED IN THE TEMPLE

When the days of Mary's purification are accomplished, they take Jesus to the Temple to present him to the Lord and to offer the Mosaic sacrifice (two turtledoves or two young pigeons); Simeon, a just and devout man, to whom it had been revealed he should not die till he had seen the Lord's Christ, comes by the Spirit into the Temple, takes Jesus in his arms and praises God, testifying also to Jesus ("Nunc Dimittis"); Anna, a prophetess, daughter of Phanuel, of the tribe of Aser, of great age, coming in at that instant gives thanks also to the Lord.

Matt: No record; Mark: No record; Luke 2:22-38; John: No record.
Time: B.C. 4, February (ANDREWS); (see Sec. 12, above).
Place: Jerusalem, Temple.

Matthew: No record.

Mark: No record.

LUKE 2:22. And when the days of her purification according to the law of Moses were accomplished, they brought him to Jerusalem, to present *him* to the Lord;

23. (As it is written in the law of the Lord, Every male that openeth the womb shall be called holy to the Lord;)

24. And to offer a sacrifice according to that which is said in the law of the Lord, A pair of turtledoves, or two young pigeons.

25. And, behold, there was a man in Jerusalem, whose name *was* Simeon; and the same man *was* just and devout, waiting for the consolation of Israel: and the Holy Ghost was upon him.

26. And it was revealed unto him by the Holy Ghost, that he should not see death, before he had seen the Lord's Christ.

27. And he came by the Spirit into the temple: and when the parents brought in the child Jesus, to do for him after the custom of the law,

28. Then took he him up in his arms, and blessed God, and said,

29. Lord, now lettest thou thy servant depart in peace, according to thy word:

30. For mine eyes have seen thy salvation,

31. Which thou hast prepared before the face of all people;

32. A light to lighten the Gentiles, and the glory of thy people Israel.

33. And Joseph and his mother marvelled at those things which were spoken of him.

34. And Simeon blessed them, and said unto Mary his mother, Behold, this *child* is set for the fall and rising again of many in Israel; and for a sign which shall be spoken against;

35. (Yea, a sword shall pierce through thy own soul also,) that the thoughts of many hearts may be revealed.

36. And there was one Anna, a prophetess, the daughter of Phanuel, of the tribe of Aser: she was of a great age, and had lived with an husband seven years from her virginity;

37. And she *was* a widow of about fourscore and four years, which departed not from the temple, but served *God* with fastings and prayers night and day.

38. And she coming in that instant gave thanks likewise unto the Lord, and spake of him to all them that looked for redemption in Jerusalem.

John: No record.

Section 17

THE RETURN TO NAZARETH

Mary, Joseph, and the Babe return to Nazareth.

Matt.: No record; Mark: No record; Luke 2:39; John: No record.
Time: B.C. 4, February-March.
Place: Nazareth.

Matthew: No record.

Mark: No record.

LUKE 2:39. And when they had performed all things according to the law of the Lord, they returned into Galilee, to their own city Nazareth.

John: No record.

Section 18

VISIT OF THE MAGI

Returning to Bethlehem, the babe Jesus is sought for by the Magi from the East who have seen his star; they go first to Herod, who asks where the Christ is to be born and is told in Bethlehem of Judea; Herod tells the Wise Men to return to him when they find the King of the Jews; the Magi find Jesus, worship him and give gifts, then, warned in a dream they do not return to Herod, but go home another way.

Matt. 2:1-12; Mark: No record; Luke: No record; John: No record.
Time: B.C. 4 (ANDREWS); February (CROSCUP).
Place: Bethlehem; Jerusalem.

MATTHEW 2:1. Now when Jesus was born in Bethlehem of Judæa in the days of Herod the king, behold, there came wise men from the east to Jerusalem,

2. Saying, Where is he that is born King of the Jews? for we have seen his star in the east, and are come to worship him.

3. When Herod the king had heard *these things*, he was troubled, and all Jerusalem with him.

4. And when he had gathered all the chief priests and scribes of the people together, he demanded of them where Christ should be born.

5. And they said unto him, In Bethlehem of Judæa: for thus it is written by the prophet,

6. And thou Bethlehem, *in* the land of Juda, art not the least among the princes of Juda: for out of thee shall come a Governor, that shall rule my people Israel.

7. Then Herod, when he had privily called the wise men, enquired of them diligently what time the star appeared.

8. And he sent them to Bethlehem, and said, Go and search diligently for the young child; and when ye have found *him*, bring me word again, that I

may come and worship him also.

9. When they had heard the king, they departed; and, lo, the star, which they saw in the east, went before them, till it came and stood over where the young child was.

10. When they saw the star, they rejoiced with exceeding great joy.

11. ¶ And when they were come into the house, they saw the young child with Mary his mother, and fell down, and worshipped him: and when they had opened their treasures, they presented unto him gifts; gold, and frankincense, and myrrh.

12. And being warned of God in a dream that they should not return to Herod, they departed into their own country another way.

Mark: No record.

Luke: No record.

John: No record.

Section 19

A NEW STAR IN WESTERN HEMISPHERE

The new star is seen in the Western Hemisphere.

3 Nephi 1:21-22.

Time: 92nd year of Reign of the Judges.

Place: Western Hemisphere.

3 NEPHI 1:21. And it came to pass also that a new star did appear, according to the word.

22. And it came to pass that from this time forth there began to be lyings sent forth among the people, by Satan, to harden their hearts, to the intent that they might not believe in those signs and wonders which they had seen; but notwithstanding these lyings and deceivings the more part of the people did believe, and were converted unto the Lord.

Section 20

THE FLIGHT INTO EGYPT

Joseph and Mary, warned in a dream by an angel, flee with the Babe to escape the wrath of Herod.

Matt. 2:13-15; Mark: No record; Luke: No record; John: No record.

Time: B.C. 4 (ANDREWS); February (CROSCUP).

Place: Bethlehem to Egypt.

MATTHEW 2:13. And when they were departed, behold, the angel of the Lord appeareth to Joseph in a dream, saying, Arise, and take the young child and his mother, and flee into Egypt, and be thou there until I bring thee word: for

Herod will seek the young child to destroy him.

14. When he arose, he took the young child and his mother by night, and departed into Egypt:

15. And was there until the death of Herod: that it might be fulfilled which was spoken of the Lord by the prophet, saying, Out of Egypt have I called my son.

Mark: No record.

Luke: No record.

John: No record.

Section 21

THE SLAUGHTER OF THE BABES

Herod, mocked by the Wise Men and angered, slays all the children that are in Bethlehem and in the coasts thereof, from two years old and under.

Matt. 2:16-18; Mark: No record; Luke: No record; John: No record.

Time: B.C. 4 (ANDREWS); February (CROSCUP).

Place: Bethlehem.

MATTHEW 2:16. ¶Then Herod, when he saw that he was mocked of the wise men, was exceeding wroth, and sent forth, and slew all the children that were in Bethlehem, and in all the coasts thereof, from two years old and under, according to the time which he had diligently enquired of the wise men.

17. Then was fulfilled that which was spoken by Jeremy the prophet, saying,

18. In Rama was there a voice heard, lamentation, and weeping, and great mourning, Rachel weeping *for* her children, and would not be comforted, because they are not.

Mark: No record.

Luke: No record.

John: No record.

Section 22

RETURN FROM EGYPT

An angel tells Joseph in a dream that Herod is dead, and commands him to return into the land of Israel with his wife and Child; again warned by God in a dream, he goes into Galilee to avoid Herod's son Archelaus; the family comes and dwells in Nazareth.

Matt. 2:19-23; Mark: No record; Luke 2:40; John: No record.

Time: B.C. 4, May (ANDREWS); May (?) (CROSCUP).

Place: From Egypt to Nazareth.

MATTHEW 2:19. ¶But when Herod was dead, behold, an angel of the Lord appeareth in a dream to Joseph in Egypt,

20. Saying, Arise, and take the young child and his mother, and go into the land of Israel: for they are dead which sought the young child's life.

21. And he arose, and took the young child and his mother, and came into the land of Israel.

22. But when he heard that Archelaus did reign in Judæa in the room of his father Herod, he was afraid to go thither: notwithstanding, being warned of God in a dream, he turned aside into the parts of Galilee:

23. And he came and dwelt in a city called Nazareth: that it might be fulfilled which was spoken by the prophets, He shall be called a Nazarene.

Mark: No record.

LUKE 2:40. And the child grew, and waxed strong in spirit, filled with wisdom: and the grace of God was upon him.

John: No record.

Section 23

JESUS IN THE TEMPLE

When twelve years old, Jesus visits Jerusalem with his parents on one of their annual visits; when the parents start homeward Jesus remains behind and is found by them three days later sitting in the Temple, in the midst of the doctors, both hearing them and asking them questions. Jesus, answering the reproof of his mother, first intimates his Messiahship: "Wist ye not that I must be about my Father's business?"

Matt.: No record; Mark: No record; Luke 2:41-50; John: No record.

Time: A.D. 8, April 8 (ANDREWS); A.D. 9, March 29 (CROSCUP).

Place: Jerusalem.

Matthew: No record.

Mark: No record.

LUKE 2:41. Now his parents went to Jerusalem every year at the feast of the passover.

42. And when he was twelve years old, they went up to Jerusalem after the custom of the feast.

43. And when they had fulfilled the days, as they returned, the child Jesus tarried behind in Jerusalem; and Joseph and his mother knew not *of it.*

44. But they, supposing him to have been in the company, went a day's journey; and they sought him among *their* kinsfolk and acquaintance.

45. And when they found him not, they turned back again to Jerusalem, seeking him.

46. And it came to pass, that after three days they found him in the temple, sitting in the midst of the doctors, both hearing them, and asking them questions.

47. And all that heard him

were astonished at his understanding and answers.

48. And when they saw him, they were amazed: and his mother said unto him, Son, why hast thou thus dealt with us? behold, thy father and I have sought thee sorrowing.

49. And he said unto them, How is it that ye sought me? wist ye not that I must be about my Father's business?

50. And they understood not the saying which he spake unto them.

John: No record.

Section 24

JESUS GOES BACK TO NAZARETH AND LIVES THERE

Jesus returns to Nazareth with his parents, and lives there with them; "but his mother kept all these sayings in her heart."

Matt.: No record; Mark: No record; Luke 2:51-52; John: No record.
Time: A.D. 8 to A.D. 26 (ANDREWS); A.D. 9 to A.D. 26 (CROSCUP).
Place: Nazareth.

Matthew: No record.

Mark: No record.

LUKE 2:51. And he went down with them, and came to Nazareth, and was subject unto them: but his mother kept all these sayings in her heart.

52. And Jesus increased in wisdom and stature, and in favour with God and man.

John: No record.

SECOND PERIOD

FROM THE BEGINNING OF JOHN'S MINISTRY TO THE FIRST PASSOVER OF THE MINISTRY OF JESUS

Section 25

THE EARLY MINISTRY OF JOHN THE BAPTIST

Time: A.D. 26, Summer (ANDREWS).
Place: Judea (ANDREWS).

(a) The Time of the Beginning of John's Ministry

Matt.: No record; Mark: No record; Luke 3:1-2; John: No record.

Matthew: No record.

Mark: No record.

LUKE 3:1. Now in the fifteenth year of the reign of Tiberius Cæsar, Pontius Pilate being governor of Judæa, and Herod being tetrarch of Galilee, and his brother Philip tetrarch of Ituræa and of the region of Trachonitis, and Lysanias the tetrarch of Abilene,

2. Annas and Caiaphas being the high priests, the word of God came unto John the son of Zacharias in the wilderness.

John: No record.

(b) The Messenger and the Message

Matt. 3:1-6; Mark 1:1-6; Luke 3:3-6; John: No record.

MATTHEW 3:1. In those days came John the Baptist, preaching in the wilderness of Judæa,

2. And saying, Repent ye: for the kingdom of heaven is at hand.

3. For this is he that was spoken of by the prophet Esaias, saying, The voice of one crying in the wilderness, Prepare ye the way of the Lord, make his paths straight.

4. And the same John had his raiment of camel's hair, and a leathern girdle about his loins; and his meat was locusts and wild honey.

5. Then went out to him Jerusalem, and all Judæa, and all the region round about Jordan,

6. And were baptized of him in Jordan, confessing their sins.

MARK 1:1. The beginning of the gospel of Jesus Christ, the Son of God;

2. As it is written in the prophets, Behold, I sent my

messenger before thy face, which shall prepare thy way before thee.

3. The voice of one crying in the wilderness, Prepare ye the way of the Lord, make his paths straight.

4. John did baptize in the wilderness, and preach the baptism of repentance for the remission of sins.

5. And there went out unto him all the land of Judæa, and they of Jerusalem, and were all baptized of him in the river of Jordan, confessing their sins.

6. And John was clothed with camel's hair, and with a girdle of a skin about his loins; and he did eat locusts and wild honey; . . . .

LUKE 3:3. And he came into all the country about Jordan, preaching the baptism of repentance for the remission of sins;

4. As it is written in the book of the words of Esaias the prophet, saying, The voice of one crying in the wilderness, Prepare ye the way of the Lord, make his paths straight.

5. Every valley shall be filled, and every mountain and hill shall be brought low; and the crooked shall be made straight, and the rough ways *shall be* made smooth;

6. And all flesh shall see the salvation of God.

John: No record.

(c) John's Preaching

Attacks Pharisees and Sadducees; publicans and soldiers ask questions; urges his hearers to cast out the bad and to share their substance with those who have none; special teachings to the soldiers.

Matt. 3:7-10; Mark: No record; Luke 3:7-14; John: No record.

MATTHEW 3:7. ¶But when he saw many of the Pharisees and Sadducees come to his baptism, he said unto them, O generation of vipers, who hath warned you to flee from the wrath to come?

8. Bring forth therefore fruits meet for repentance:

9. And think not to say within yourselves, We have Abraham to *our* father: for I say unto you, that God is able of these stones to raise up children unto Abraham.

10. And now also the axe is laid unto the root of the trees: therefore every tree which bringeth not forth good fruit is hewn down, and cast into the fire.

Mark: No record.

LUKE 3:7. Then said he to the multitude that came forth to be baptized of him, O generation of vipers, who hath warned you to flee from the wrath to come?

8. Bring forth therefore fruits worthy of repentance,

and begin not to say within yourselves, We have Abraham to *our* father: for I say unto you, That God is able of these stones to raise up children unto Abraham.

9. And now also the axe is laid unto the root of the trees: every tree therefore which bringeth not forth good fruit is hewn down, and cast into the fire.

10. And the people asked him, saying, What shall we do then?

11. He answereth and saith unto them, He that hath two coats, let him impart to him that hath none; and he that hath meat, let him do likewise.

12. Then came also publicans to be baptized, and said unto him, Master, what shall we do?

13. And he said unto them, Exact no more than that which is appointed you.

14. And the soldiers likewise demanded of him, saying, And what shall we do? And he said unto them, Do violence to no man, neither accuse *any* falsely; and be content with your wages.

John: No record.

(d) John Announces Coming of Jesus

John announces coming of another who shall baptize with the Holy Ghost; declares his own unworthiness.

Matt. 3:11-12; Mark 1:7-8; Luke 3:15-18; John: No record.

MATTHEW 3:11. I indeed baptize you with water unto repentance: but he that cometh after me is mightier than I, whose shoes I am not worthy to bear: he shall baptize you with the Holy Ghost, and *with* fire:

12. Whose fan *is* in his hand, and he will throughly purge his floor, and gather his wheat into the garner; but he will burn up the chaff with unquenchable fire.

MARK 1:7. And preached, saying, There cometh one mightier than I after me, the latchet of whose shoes I am not worthy to stoop down and unloose.

8. I indeed have baptized you with water: but he shall baptize you with the Holy Ghost.

LUKE 3:15. And as the people were in expectation, and all men mused in their hearts of John, whether he were the Christ, or not;

16. John answered, saying unto *them* all, I indeed baptize you with water; but one mightier than I cometh, the latchet of whose shoes I am not worthy to unloose: he shall baptize you with the Holy Ghost and with fire:

17. Whose fan *is* in his hand, and he will throughly

purge his floor, and will gather the wheat into his garner; but the chaff he will burn with fire unquenchable.

18. And many other things in his exhortation preached he unto the people.

John: No record.

Section 26

JOHN BAPTIZES JESUS

Jesus, about thirty years old, comes from Nazareth to the Jordan, where John baptizes him, the Father speaking from Heaven in witness of the Son, the Holy Ghost descending in bodily shape like a dove—the Trinity of the Godhead being manifest all at one time, as three distinct personages.

Matt. 3:13-17; Mark 1:9-11; Luke 3:21-23a; John: No record.

Time: A.D. 27, January (ANDREWS).

Place: The Jordan; Bethabara (CROSCUP).

MATTHEW 3:13. ¶ Then cometh Jesus from Galilee to Jordan unto John, to be baptized of him.

14. But John forbad him, saying, I have need to be baptized of thee, and comest thou to me?

15. And Jesus answering said unto him, Suffer *it to be so* now: for thus it becometh us to fulfil all righteousness. Then he suffered him.

16. And Jesus, when he was baptized, went up straightway out of the water: and, lo, the heavens were opened unto him, and he saw the Spirit of God descending like a dove, and lighting upon him:

17. And lo a voice from heaven, saying, This is my beloved Son, in whom I am well pleased.

MARK 1:9. And it came to pass in those days, that Jesus came from Nazareth of Galilee, and was baptized of John in Jordan.

10. And straightway coming up out of the water, he saw the heavens opened, and the Spirit like a dove descending upon him:

11. And there came a voice from heaven, *saying*, Thou art my beloved Son, in whom I am well pleased.

LUKE 3:21. Now when all the people were baptized, it came to pass, that Jesus also being baptized, and praying, the heaven was opened,

22. And the Holy Ghost descended in a bodily shape like a dove upon him, and a voice came from heaven, which said, Thou art my beloved Son; in thee I am well pleased.

23. And Jesus himself began to be about thirty years of age. . . .

John: No record.

Section 27

THE TEMPTATION

Jesus is driven into the wilderness by the Spirit, to be tempted of Satan; he is there for forty days; he withstands the temptations; Satan leaves him, and angels come and minister to him.

Matt. 4:1-11; Mark 1:12-13; Luke 4:1-13; John: No record.

Time: A.D. 27, January - February (ANDREWS); February - March (CROSCUP).

Place: Wilderness of Judea.

MATTHEW 4:1. Then was Jesus led up of the spirit into the wilderness to be tempted of the devil.

2. And when he had fasted forty days and forty nights, he was afterward an hungred.

3. And when the tempter came to him, he said, If thou be the Son of God, command that these stones be made bread.

4. But he answered and said, It is written, Man shall not live by bread alone, but by every word that proceedeth out of the mouth of God.

5. Then the devil taketh him up into the holy city, and setteth him on a pinnacle of the temple,

6. And saith unto him, If thou be the Son of God, cast thyself down: for it is written, He shall give his angels charge concerning thee: and in *their* hands they shall bear thee up, lest at any time thou dash thy foot against a stone.

7. Jesus said unto him, It is written again, Thou shalt not tempt the Lord thy God.

8. Again, the devil taketh him up into an exceeding high mountain, and sheweth him all the kingdoms of the world, and the glory of them;

9. And saith unto him, All these things will I give thee, if thou wilt fall down and worship me.

10. Then saith Jesus unto him, Get thee hence, Satan: for it is written, Thou shalt worship the Lord thy God, and him only shalt thou serve.

11. Then the devil leaveth him, and, behold, angels came and ministered unto him.

MARK 1:12. And immediately the spirit driveth him into the wilderness.

13. And he was there in the wilderness forty days, tempted of Satan; and was with the wild beasts; and the angels ministered unto him.

LUKE 4:1. And Jesus being full of the Holy Ghost returned from Jordan, and was led by the Spirit into the wilderness,

2. Being forty days tempted of the devil. And in those days he did eat nothing: and when they were ended, he afterward hungered.

3. And the devil said unto him, If thou be the Son of God, command this stone that it be made bread.

4. And Jesus answered him, saying, It is written, That man shall not live by bread alone, but by every word of God.

5. And the devil, taking him up into an high mountain, shewed unto him all the kingdoms of the world in a moment of time.

6. And the devil said unto him, All this power will I give thee, and the glory of them: for that is delivered unto me; and to whomsoever I will I give it.

7. If thou therefore wilt worship me, all shall be thine.

8. And Jesus answered and said unto him, Get thee behind me, Satan: for it is written, Thou shalt worship the Lord thy God, and him only shalt thou serve.

9. And he brought him to Jerusalem, and set him on a pinnacle of the temple, and said unto him, If thou be the Son of God, cast thyself down from hence:

10. For it is written, He shall give his angels charge over thee, to keep thee:

11. And in *their* hands they shall bear thee up, lest at any time thou dash thy foot against a stone.

12. And Jesus answering said unto him, It is said, Thou shalt not tempt the Lord thy God.

13. And when the devil had ended all the temptation, he departed from him for a season.

John: No record.

Section 28

JOHN PROCLAIMS HE IS NOT THE CHRIST

John, answering the priests and Levites (who were of the Pharisees) from Jerusalem, denies he is the Christ or Elias, nor "that prophet," and declares he is the voice of one crying in the wilderness; he explains his baptism and announces the Christ as standing among them.

Matt.: No record; Mark: No record; Luke: No record; John 1:19-28.

Time: A.D. 27, February (ANDREWS); March (CROSCUP).

Place: Bethany Beyond the Jordan (ANDREWS); Bethabara (CROSCUP).

Matthew: No record.

Mark: No record.

Luke: No record.

JOHN 1:19. ¶ And this is the record of John, when the Jews sent priests and Levites from Jerusalem to ask him, Who art thou?

20. And he confessed, and denied not; but confessed, I am not the Christ.

21. And they asked him, What then? Art thou Elias?

And he saith, I am not. Art thou that prophet? And he answered, No.

22. Then said they unto him, Who art thou? that we may give an answer to them that sent us. What sayest thou of thyself?

23. He said, I *am* the voice of one crying in the wilderness, Make straight the way of the Lord, as said the prophet Esaias.

24. And they which were sent were of the Pharisees.

25. And they asked him, and said unto him, Why baptizest thou then, if thou be not that Christ, nor Elias, neither that prophet?

26. John answered them, saying, I baptize with water: but there standeth one among you, whom ye know not;

27. He it is, who coming after me is preferred before me, whose shoe's latchet I am not worthy to unloose.

28. These things were done in Bethabara beyond Jordan, where John was baptizing.

Section 29

JOHN TESTIFIES JESUS IS LAMB OF GOD

On the next day, John seeing Jesus coming to him, testifies Jesus is the Lamb of God, declares the atonement, witnesses the descent of the Holy Ghost upon Jesus at the time of baptism, and bears record that Jesus is the Son of God.

Matt.: No record; Mark: No record; Luke: No record; John 1:29-34.
Time: A.D. 27, February (ANDREWS); March (CROSCUP).
Place: Bethany Beyond the Jordan (ANDREWS); Bethabara (CROSCUP).

Matthew: No record.

Mark: No record.

Luke: No record.

JOHN 1:29. ¶The next day John seeth Jesus coming unto him, and saith, Behold the Lamb of God, which taketh away the sin of the world.

30. This is he of whom I said, After me cometh a man which is preferred before me: for he was before me.

31. And I knew him not: but that he should be made manifest to Israel, therefore am I come baptizing with water.

32. And John bare record, saying, I saw the Spirit descending from heaven like a dove, and it abode upon him.

33. And I knew him not: but he that sent me to baptize with water, the same said unto me, Upon whom thou shalt see the Spirit descending, and remaining on him, the same is he which baptizeth with the Holy Ghost.

34. And I saw, and bare record that this is the Son of God.

Section 30

ANDREW AND SIMON MEET JESUS

Again the next day after, John standing with two of his disciples, declares, "Behold the Lamb of God"; the two disciples follow Jesus, ask where he dwells, and abide with him that day; of the two following, one was Andrew, who finds Simon his brother and fetches him to Jesus, who calls him Cephas, a stone.

Matt.: No record; Mark: No record; Luke: No record; John 1:35-42.
Time: A.D. 27, February (ANDREWS); March (CROSCUP).
Place: Bethabara (?) (CROSCUP).

Matthew: No record.

Mark: No record.

Luke: No record.

JOHN 1:35. ¶Again the next day after John stood, and two of his disciples;

36. And looking upon Jesus as he walked, he saith, Behold the Lamb of God!

37. And the two disciples heard him speak, and they followed Jesus.

38. Then Jesus turned, and saw them following, and saith unto them, What seek ye? They said unto him, Rabbi, (which is to say, being interpreted, Master,) where dwellest thou?

39. He saith unto them, Come and see. They came and saw where he dwelt, and abode with him that day: for it was about the tenth hour.

40. One of the two which heard John *speak*, and followed him, was Andrew, Simon Peter's brother.

41. He first findeth his own brother Simon, and saith unto him, We have found the Messias, which is, being interpreted, the Christ.

42. And he brought him to Jesus. And when Jesus beheld him, he said, Thou art Simon the son of Jona: thou shalt be called Cephas, which is by interpretation, A stone.

Section 31

PHILIP AND NATHANAEL FOUND

On the day following, Jesus, going forth to Galilee, finds Philip and commands him to follow; Philip finds Nathanael, whom Jesus greets as an Israelite without guile; Nathanael believes when Jesus tells him he was under a fig tree; (this is the first recorded use by Jesus of the divine power he possessed over matter, mind, and space).

Matt.: No record; Mark: No record; Luke: No record; John 1:43-51.
Time: A.D. 27, February (ANDREWS); March (CROSCUP).
Place: Bethabara (?) (CROSCUP).

Matthew: No record.

Mark: No record.

Luke: No record.

JOHN 1:43. ¶The day following Jesus would go forth into Galilee, and findeth Philip, and saith unto him, Follow me.

44. Now Philip was of Bethsaida, the city of Andrew and Peter.

45. Philip findeth Nathanael, and saith unto him, We have found him, of whom Moses in the law, and the prophets, did write, Jesus of Nazareth, the son of Joseph.

46. And Nathanael said unto him, Can there any good thing come out of Nazareth? Philip saith unto him, Come and see.

47. Jesus saw Nathanael coming to him, and saith of him, Behold an Israelite indeed, in whom is no guile!

48. Nathanael saith unto him, Whence knowest thou me? Jesus answered and said unto him, Before that Philip called thee, when thou wast under the fig tree, I saw thee.

49. Nathanael answered and saith unto him, Rabbi, thou art the Son of God; thou art the King of Israel.

50. Jesus answered and said unto him, Because I said unto thee, I saw thee under the fig tree, believest thou? thou shalt see greater things than these.

51. And he saith unto him, Verily, verily, I say unto you, Hereafter ye shall see heaven open, and the angels of God ascending and descending upon the Son of man.

Section 32

THE FIRST MIRACLE

On the third day Jesus also performs his first miracle of turning water into wine at a marriage feast in Cana; his mother shows she has knowledge of his divine powers.

Matt.: No record; Mark: No record; Luke: No record; John 2:1-11.
Time: A.D. 27, March (CROSCUP).
Place: Cana of Galilee.

Matthew: No record.

Mark: No record.

Luke: No record.

JOHN 2:1. And the third day there was a marriage in Cana of Galilee; and the mother of Jesus was there:

2. And both Jesus was called, and his disciples, to the marriage.

3. And when they wanted wine, the mother of Jesus saith unto him, They have no wine.

4. Jesus saith unto her, Woman, what have I to do with thee? mine hour is not yet come.

5. His mother saith unto the servants, Whatsoever he saith unto you, do *it*.

6. And there were set there six waterpots of stone, after the manner of the purifying

of the Jews, containing two or three firkins apiece.

7. Jesus saith unto them, Fill the waterpots with water. And they filled them up to the brim.

8. And he saith unto them, Draw out now, and bear unto the governor of the feast. And they bare *it*.

9. When the ruler of the feast had tasted the water that was made wine, and knew not whence it was: (but the servants which drew the water knew;) the governor of the feast called the bridegroom,

10. And saith unto him, Every man at the beginning doth set forth good wine; and when men have well drunk, then that which is worse: *but* thou hast kept the good wine until now.

11. This beginning of miracles did Jesus in Cana of Galilee, and manifested forth his glory; and his disciples believed on him.

Section 33

JESUS GOES TO CAPERNAUM

Jesus now goes to Capernaum with his mother, his brethren, and his disciples, and continues there for a few days.

Matt.: No record; Mark: No record; Luke: No record; John 2:12.

Time: A.D. 27, March-April (CROSCUP).

Place: Capernaum.

Matthew: No record.

Mark: No record.

Luke: No record.

JOHN 2:12. ¶ After this he went down to Capernaum, he, and his mother, and his brethren, and his disciples: and they continued there not many days.

THIRD PERIOD

THE EARLY JUDEAN MINISTRY, FROM THE FIRST PASSOVER TO HIS RETURN TO GALILEE

Section 34

THE FIRST PASSOVER

Jesus attends the Passover in Jerusalem; goes to the Temple and drives out the traders; he gives his first parable and so makes his first announcement concerning his death and resurrection,—his Messiahship; he performs miracles and many believe; Jesus knows all men.

Matt.: No record; Mark: No record; Luke: No record; John 2:13-25.
Time: A.D. 27, April 11-17 (ANDREWS); April 11-18 (CROSCUP).
Place: Jerusalem, Temple.

Matthew: No record.

Mark: No record.

Luke: No record.

JOHN 2:13. ¶ And the Jews' passover was at hand, and Jesus went up to Jerusalem,

14. And found in the temple those that sold oxen and sheep and doves, and the changers of money sitting:

15. And when he had made a scourge of small cords, he drove them all out of the temple, and the sheep, and the oxen; and poured out the changers' money, and overthrew the tables;

16. And said unto them that sold doves, Take these things hence; make not my Father's house an house of merchandise.

17. And his disciples remembered that it was written, The zeal of thine house hath eaten me up.

18. ¶Then answered the Jews and said unto him, What sign shewest thou unto us, seeing that thou doest these things?

19. Jesus answered and said unto them, Destroy this temple, and in three days I will raise it up.

20. Then said the Jews, Forty and six years was this temple in building, and wilt thou rear it up in three days?

21. But he spake of the temple of his body.

22. When therefore he was risen from the dead, his disciples remembered that he had said this unto them; and they believed the scripture, and the word which Jesus had said.

23. ¶Now when he was in Jerusalem at the passover, in the feast *day*, many believed in his name, when they saw the miracles which he did.

24. But Jesus did not commit himself unto them, because he knew all *men*,

25. And needed not that any should testify of man: for he knew what was in man.

Section 35

NICODEMUS VISITS JESUS

Nicodemus, a Pharisee, visits Jesus secretly by night; Jesus preaches the first great discourse; declares that except a man be born of the water and of the Spirit he cannot enter into the kingdom of God; the Spirit leadeth where it will; Jesus will testify of what he knows and what he has seen; again refers to his crucifixion by citing Moses' lifting up of the serpent in the wilderness, and by saying that God so loved the world that he gave his only begotten Son to save it; men love darkness more than light; he that doeth truth cometh to light.

Matt.: No record; Mark: No record; Luke: No record; John 3:1-21.

Time: A.D. 27, April 11-17 (ANDREWS).

Place: Jerusalem.

Matthew: No record.

Mark: No record.

Luke: No record.

JOHN 3:1. There was a man of the Pharisees, named Nicodemus, a ruler of the Jews:

2. The same came to Jesus by night, and said unto him, Rabbi, we know that thou art a teacher come from God: for no man can do these miracles that thou doest, except God be with him.

3. Jesus answered and said unto him, Verily, verily, I say unto thee, Except a man be born again, he cannot see the kingdom of God.

4. Nicodemus saith unto him, How can a man be born when he is old? can he enter the second time into his mother's womb, and be born?

5. Jesus answered, Verily, verily, I say unto thee, Except a man be born of water and *of* the Spirit, he cannot enter into the kingdom of God.

6. That which is born of the flesh is flesh; and that which is born of the Spirit is spirit.

7. Marvel not that I said unto thee, Ye must be born again.

8. The wind bloweth where it listeth, and thou hearest the sound thereof, but canst not tell whence it cometh, and whither it goeth: so is every one that is born of the Spirit.

9. Nicodemus answered and said unto him, How can these things be?

10. Jesus answered and said unto him, Art thou a master of Israel, and knowest not these things?

11. Verily, verily, I say unto thee, We speak that we do know, and testify that we have seen; and ye receive not our witness.

12. If I have told you earthly things, and ye believe not, how shall ye believe, if I tell you *of* heavenly things?

13. And no man hath ascended up to heaven, but he that came down from heaven,

even the Son of man which is in heaven.

14. ¶ And as Moses lifted up the serpent in the wilderness, even so must the Son of man be lifted up:

15. That whosoever believeth in him should not perish, but have eternal life.

16. ¶ For God so loved the world, that he gave his only begotten Son, that whosoever believeth in him should not perish, but have everlasting life.

17. For God sent not his Son into the world to condemn the world; but that the world through him might be saved.

18. ¶ He that believeth on him is not condemned: but he that believeth not is condemned already, because he hath not believed in the name of the only begotten Son of God.

19. And this is the condemnation, that light is come into the world, and men loved darkness rather than light, because their deeds were evil.

20. For every one that doeth evil hateth the light, neither cometh to the light, lest his deeds should be reproved.

21. But he that doeth truth cometh to the light, that his deeds may be made manifest, that they are wrought in God.

Section 36

JESUS GOES INTO JUDEA

Jesus with his disciples goes into Judea, where Jesus tarries and baptizes.

Matt.: No record; Mark: No record; Luke: No record; John 3:22.

Time: A.D. 27, April (ANDREWS); April 11-18 (CROSCUP).

Place: Judea.

Matthew: No record.

Mark: No record.

Luke: No record.

JOHN 3:22. ¶After these things came Jesus and his disciples into the land of Judæa; and there he tarried with them, and baptized.

Section 37

JOHN'S TESTIMONY

John baptizes at Ænon, near to Salim; John's disciples report Jesus is baptizing; John, in a great discourse, recalls that he has told them he is not the Christ but is sent before him; from now Jesus must increase but John must decrease; discourses upon testimony; he whom God sends preaches the word of God; the Father loveth the Son and has given all things to him; he that believeth on the Son has everlasting life; he that believeth not on the Son shall not see life but the wrath of God abideth on him.

Matt.: No record; Mark: No record; Luke: No record; John 3:23-36.
Time: A.D. 27, Summer (CROSCUP).
Place: Judea; Ænon near Salim.

Matthew: No record.

Mark: No record.

Luke: No record.

JOHN 3:23. ¶ And John also was baptizing in Ænon near to Salim, because there was much water there: and they came, and were baptized.

24. For John was not yet cast into prison.

25. ¶Then there arose a question between *some* of John's disciples and the Jews about purifying.

26. And they came unto John, and said unto him, Rabbi, he that was with thee beyond Jordan, to whom thou barest witness, behold, the same baptizeth, and all *men* come to him.

27. John answered and said, A man can receive nothing, except it be given him from heaven.

28. Ye yourselves bear me witness, that I said, I am not the Christ, but that I am sent before him.

29. He that hath the bride is the bridegroom: but the friend of the bridegroom, which standeth and heareth him, rejoiceth greatly because of the bridegroom's voice: this my joy therefore is fulfilled.

30. He must increase, but I *must* decrease.

31. He that cometh from above is above all: he that is of the earth is earthly, and speaketh of the earth: he that cometh from heaven is above all.

32. And what he hath seen and heard, that he testifieth; and no man receiveth his testimony.

33. He that hath received his testimony hath set to his seal that God is true.

34. For he whom God hath sent speaketh the words of God: for God giveth not the Spirit by measure *unto him.*

35. The Father loveth the Son, and hath given all things into his hand.

36. He that believeth on the Son hath everlasting life: and he that believeth not the Son shall not see life; but the wrath of God abideth on him.

Section 38

HEROD IMPRISONS JOHN

Herod, angered by John's reproof because he (the Tetrarch) had married his brother Philip's wife, Herodias, casts John into prison.

Matt. 14:3-5; Mark 6:17-20; Luke 3:19-20; John: No record.
Time: A.D. 27 (ANDREWS); November or December (CROSCUP).
Place: Fortress of Machaerus—(East of Dead Sea).

MATTHEW 14:3. ¶ For Herod had laid hold on John, and bound him, and put *him* in prison for Herodias' sake, his brother Philip's wife.

4. For John said unto him, It is not lawful for thee to have her.

5. And when he would have put him to death, he feared the multitude, because they counted him as a prophet.

MARK 6:17. For Herod himself had sent forth and laid hold upon John, and bound him in prison for Herodias' sake, his brother Philip's wife: for he had married her.

18. For John had said unto Herod, It is not lawful for thee to have thy brother's wife.

19. Therefore Herodias had a quarrel against him, and would have killed him; but she could not:

20. For Herod feared John, knowing that he was a just man and an holy, and observed him; and when he heard him, he did many things, and heard him gladly.

LUKE 3:19. But Herod the tetrarch, being reproved by him for Herodias his brother Philip's wife, and for all the evils which Herod had done,

20. Added yet this above all, that he shut up John in prison.

John: No record.

Section 39

JESUS LEAVES JUDEA FOR GALILEE

Jesus, hearing that John is put into prison, departs into Galilee; he, through his disciples, is baptizing more than John.

Matt. 4:12; Mark 1:14; Luke 4:14; John 4:1-3.

Time: A.D. 27, December (ANDREWS; CROSCUP).

Place: Judea.

MATTHEW 4:12. ¶ Now when Jesus had heard that John was cast into prison, he departed into Galilee; . . .

MARK 1:14. Now after that John was put in prison, Jesus came into Galilee, preaching the gospel of the kingdom of God, . . .

LUKE 4:14. ¶ And Jesus returned in the power of the Spirit into Galilee: and there went out a fame of him through all the region round about.

JOHN 4:1. When therefore the Lord knew how the Pharisees had heard that Jesus made and baptized more disciples than John,

2. (Though Jesus himself baptized not, but his disciples,)

3. He left Judæa, and departed again into Galilee.

Section 40

THE WOMAN OF SAMARIA

To the woman of Samaria, at Jacob's Well, Jesus preaches his second great discourse; Jesus asks for a drink, and the woman wonders that a Jew should ask a Samaritan for a drink; Jesus reassures her saying that if she had asked him he would have given her living water; he expounds his meaning; he shows he knows her past life; explaining worship, he declares his Messiahship; the disciples returning seemingly reprove him for talking with her; she returns to the city and the men thereof come out to him; he again speaks in parable about the fields white already to harvest; many Samaritans believe and at their request he remains with them two days.

Matt.: No record; Mark: No record; Luke: No record; John 4:4-42.
Time: A.D. 27, December (ANDREWS; CROSCUP).
Place: Samaria—Jacob's Well; Sychar.

Matthew: No record.

Mark: No record.

Luke: No record.

JOHN 4:4. And he must needs go through Samaria.

5. Then cometh he to a city of Samaria, which is called Sychar, near to the parcel of ground that Jacob gave to his son Joseph.

6. Now Jacob's well was there. Jesus therefore, being wearied with *his* journey, sat thus on the well: *and* it was about the sixth hour.

7. There cometh a woman of Samaria to draw water: Jesus saith unto her, Give me to drink.

8. (For his disciples were gone away unto the city to buy meat.)

9. Then saith the woman of Samaria unto him, How is it that thou, being a Jew, askest drink of me, which am a woman of Samaria? for the Jews have no dealings with the Samaritans.

10. Jesus answered and said unto her, If thou knewest the gift of God, and who it is that saith to thee, Give me to drink; thou wouldest have asked of him, and he would have given thee living water.

11. The woman saith unto him, Sir, thou hast nothing to draw with, and the well is deep: from whence then hast thou that living water?

12. Art thou greater than our father Jacob, which gave us the well, and drank thereof himself, and his children, and his cattle?

13. Jesus answered and said unto her, Whosoever drinketh of this water shall thirst again:

14. But whosoever drinketh of the water that I shall give him shall never thirst; but the water that I shall give him shall be in him a well of water springing up into everlasting life.

15. The woman saith unto

him, Sir, give me this water, that I thirst not, neither come hither to draw.

16. Jesus saith unto her, Go, call thy husband, and come hither.

17. The woman answered and said, I have no husband. Jesus said unto her, Thou hast well said, I have no husband:

18. For thou hast had five husbands; and he whom thou now hast is not thy husband: in that saidst thou truly.

19. The woman saith unto him, Sir, I perceive that thou art a prophet.

20. Our fathers worshipped in this mountain; and ye say, that in Jerusalem is the place where men ought to worship.

21. Jesus saith unto her, Woman, believe me, the hour cometh, when ye shall neither in this mountain, nor yet at Jerusalem, worship the Father.

22. Ye worship ye know not what: we know what we worship: for salvation is of the Jews.

23. But the hour cometh, and now is, when the true worshippers shall worship the Father in spirit and in truth: for the Father seeketh such to worship him.

24. God *is* a Spirit: and they that worship him must worship *him* in spirit and in truth.

25. The woman saith unto him, I know that Messias cometh, which is called Christ: when he is come, he will tell us all things.

26. Jesus saith unto her, I that speak unto thee am *he*.

27. ¶ And upon this came his disciples, and marvelled that he talked with the woman: yet no man said, What seekest thou? or, Why talkest thou with her?

28. The woman then left her waterpot, and went her way into the city, and saith to the men,

29. Come, see a man, which told me all things that ever I did: is not this the Christ?

30. Then they went out of the city, and came unto him.

31. ¶ In the mean while his disciples prayed him, saying, Master, eat.

32. But he said unto them, I have meat to eat that ye know not of.

33. Therefore said the disciples one to another, Hath any man brought him *ought* to eat?

34. Jesus saith unto them, My meat is to do the will of him that sent me, and to finish his work.

35. Say not ye, There are yet four months, and *then* cometh harvest? behold, I say unto you, Lift up your eyes, and look on the fields; for they are white already to harvest.

36. And he that reapeth receiveth wages, and gathereth fruit unto life eternal: that both he that soweth and he that reapeth may rejoice together.

37. And herein is that saying true, One soweth, and another reapeth.

38. I sent you to reap that whereon ye bestowed no labour: other men laboured, and ye are entered into their labours.

39. ¶ And many of the Samaritans of that city believed on him for the saying of the woman, which testified, He told me all that ever I did.

40. So when the Samaritans were come unto him, they besought him that he would tarry with them: and he abode there two days.

41. And many more believed because of his own word;

42. And said unto the woman, Now we believe, not because of thy saying: for we have heard *him* ourselves, and know that this is indeed the Christ, the Saviour of the world.

Section 41

HE GOES INTO GALILEE

After two days, Jesus departs from Samaria and goes on to Galilee.

Matt.: No record; Mark: No record; Luke: No record; John 4:43-44.
Time: A.D. 27, December (ANDREWS; CROSCUP).
Place: Samaria to Galilee.

Matthew: No record.

Mark: No record.

Luke: No record.

JOHN 4:43. ¶ Now after two days he departed thence, and went into Galilee.

44. For Jesus himself testified, that a prophet hath no honour in his own country.

FOURTH PERIOD

THE GREAT GALILEAN MINISTRY

I. From the Return to Galilee Until the Choosing of the Twelve

Section 42

JESUS PREACHES IN GALILEE

Jesus comes into Galilee preaching the kingdom of God is at hand; he teaches in the synagogues, all glorifying him; they have seen his works at the feast in Jerusalem.

Matt. 4:17; Mark 1:14-15; Luke 4:14-15; John 4:45.

Time: A.D. 27-28, Winter.

Place: Galilee.

MATTHEW 4:17. ¶ From that time Jesus began to preach, and to say, Repent: for the kingdom of heaven is at hand.

MARK 1:14. Now after that John was put in prison, Jesus came into Galilee, preaching the gospel of the kingdom of God,

15. And saying, The time is fulfilled, and the kingdom of God is at hand: repent ye, and believe the gospel.

LUKE 4:14. ¶And Jesus returned in the power of the Spirit into Galilee: and there went out a fame of him through all the region round about.

15. And he taught in their synagogues, being glorified of all.

JOHN 4:45. Then when he was come into Galilee, the Galilæans received him, having seen all the things that he did at Jerusalem at the feast: for they also went unto the feast.

Section 43

HEALING NOBLEMAN'S SON

A nobleman of Capernaum seeks Jesus in Cana, and asks Jesus to come to Capernaum to heal his son; speaking of the need of the people for signs to believe, Jesus tells the nobleman to go his way for his son liveth; the nobleman, returning, meets his servants who tell him his son lives; the nobleman checks the time when the child began to mend and finds it was the same hour when Jesus told him his son lives.

Matt.: No record; Mark: No record; Luke: No record; John 4:46-54.

Time: A.D. 27-28, Winter.

Place: Cana and Capernaum.

Matthew: No record.

Mark: No record.

Luke: No record.

JOHN 4:46. So Jesus came again into Cana of Galilee, where he made the water wine. And there was a certain nobleman, whose son was sick at Capernaum.

47. When he heard that Jesus was come out of Judæa into Galilee, he went unto him, and besought him that he would come down, and heal his son: for he was at the point of death.

48. Then said Jesus unto him, Except ye see signs and wonders, ye will not believe.

49. The nobleman saith unto him, Sir, come down ere my child die.

50. Jesus saith unto him, Go thy way; thy son liveth. And the man believed the word that Jesus had spoken unto him, and he went his way.

51. And as he was now going down, his servants met him, and told *him*, saying, Thy son liveth.

52. Then enquired he of them the hour when he began to amend. And they said unto him, Yesterday at the seventh hour the fever left him.

53. So the father knew that *it was* at the same hour, in the which Jesus said unto him, Thy son liveth: and himself believed, and his whole house.

54. This *is* again the second miracle *that* Jesus did, when he was come out of Judæa into Galilee.

Section 44

JESUS REJECTED AT NAZARETH

Jesus comes to Nazareth; he goes to the synagogue on the Sabbath day, as was his custom; he reads and expounds the scriptures; all the people are surprised at his "gracious words," he continues preaching and shows how God has blessed others than the Israelites, he charges them with expecting him to do his works there; and he shows how few have been ministered to in the past, and says no prophet is accepted in his own country; angered, they thrust him out of the synagogue and the city, then take him to the brow of a hill to cast him down headlong, but he passes through their midst and goes his way.

Matt.: No record; **Mark:** No record; **Luke** 4:16-30; **John:** No record.
Time: A.D. 28, Winter (CROSCUP).
Place: Nazareth.

Matthew: No record.

Mark: No record.

LUKE 4:16. ¶And he came to Nazareth, where he had been brought up: and, as his custom was, he went into the synagogue on the sabbath day, and stood up for to read.

17. And there was delivered unto him the book of the prophet Esaias. And when he had opened the book, he found the place where it was written,

18. The Spirit of the Lord *is* upon me, because he hath anointed me to preach the gospel to the poor; he hath sent me to heal the brokenhearted, to preach deliverance to the captives, and recovering of sight to the blind, to set at liberty them that are bruised,

19. To preach the acceptable year of the Lord.

20. And he closed the book, and he gave *it* again to the minister, and sat down. And the eyes of all them that were in the synagogue were fastened on him.

21. And he began to say unto them, This day is this scripture fulfilled in your ears.

22. And all bare him witness, and wondered at the gracious words which proceeded out of his mouth. And they said, Is not this Joseph's son?

23. And he said unto them, Ye will surely say unto me this proverb, Physician, heal thyself: whatsoever we have heard done in Capernaum, do also here in thy country.

24. And he said, Verily I say unto you, No prophet is accepted in his own country.

25. But I tell you of a truth, many widows were in Israel in the days of Elias, when the heaven was shut up three years and six months, when great famine was throughout all the land;

26. But unto none of them was Elias sent, save unto Sarepta, *a city* of Sidon, unto a woman *that was* a widow.

27. And many lepers were in Israel in the time of Eliseus the prophet; and none of them was cleansed, saving Naaman the Syrian.

28. And all they in the synagogue, when they heard these things, were filled with wrath,

29. And rose up, and thrust him out of the city, and led him unto the brow of the hill whereon their city was built, that they might cast him down headlong.

30. But he passing through the midst of them went his way, . . .

John: No record.

Section 45

HE GOES TO CAPERNAUM

Jesus, leaving Nazareth, comes to Capernaum on the seacoast, in the borders of Zabulon and Nephthalim, that the prophecy of Esaias might be fulfilled.

Matt. 4:13-16; Mark: No record; Luke 4:31a; John: No record.
Time: A.D. 28, Winter (Croscup).
Place: Capernaum.

MATTHEW 4:13. And leaving Nazareth, he came and dwelt in Capernaum, which is upon the sea coast, in the borders of Zabulon and Nephthalim:

14. That it might be fulfilled which was spoken by Esaias the prophet, saying,

15. The land of Zabulon, and the land of Nephthalim, *by* the way of the sea, beyond Jordan, Galilee of the Gentiles;

16. The people which sat in darkness saw great light; and to them which sat in the region and shadow of death light is sprung up.

Mark: No record.

LUKE 4:31. And came down to Capernaum, a city of Galilee . . . .

John: No record.

Section 46

JESUS CHOOSES PETER, ANDREW, JAMES, AND JOHN

Jesus, pressed by the people, stands by the Lake of Gennesaret; he sits in Simon's boat, and having it pushed out a little from the shore, he teaches the people; he then takes Simon and his boat into the sea, tells Simon to cast his net; Simon demurs, saying he has toiled all night and taken nothing, but says he will do as told; he casts his net and gets so many fish that the net breaks; he beckons his other partners who come and they fill both ships. Peter falls upon his knees saying, "Depart from me; for I am a sinful man, O Lord"; all are astonished, and he says to them (Peter, Andrew, James, and John), "Follow me, and I will make you fishers of men"; they leave their boats and follow him.

Matt. 4:18-22; Mark 1:16-20; Luke 5:1-11; John: No record.
Time: A.D. 28, Winter (CROSCUP).
Place: Sea of Galilee.

MATTHEW 4:18. ¶And Jesus, walking by the sea of Galilee, saw two brethren, Simon called Peter, and Andrew his brother, casting a net into the sea: for they were fishers.

19. And he saith unto them, Follow me, and I will make you fishers of men.

20. And they straightway left *their* nets, and followed him.

21. And going on from thence, he saw other two brethren, James *the son* of Zebedee, and John his brother, in a ship with Zebedee their father, mending their nets; and he called them.

22. And they immediately left the ship and their father, and followed him.

MARK 1:16. Now as he walked by the sea of Galilee, he saw Simon and Andrew his brother casting a net into the sea: for they were fishers.

17. And Jesus said unto

them, Come ye after me, and I will make you to become fishers of men.

18. And straightway they forsook their nets, and followed him.

19. And when he had gone a little farther thence, he saw James the *son* of Zebedee, and John his brother, who also were in the ship mending their nets.

20. And straightway he called them: and they left their father Zebedee in the ship with the hired servants, and went after him.

LUKE 5:1. And it came to pass, that, as the people pressed upon him to hear the word of God, he stood by the lake of Gennesaret,

2. And saw two ships standing by the lake: but the fishermen were gone out of them, and were washing *their* nets.

3. And he entered into one of the ships, which was Simon's, and prayed him that he would thrust out a little from the land. And he sat down, and taught the people out of the ship.

4. Now when he had left speaking, he said unto Simon, Launch out into the deep, and let down your nets for a draught.

5. And Simon answering said unto him, Master, we have toiled all the night, and have taken nothing: nevertheless at thy word I will let down the net.

6. And when they had this done, they inclosed a great multitude of fishes: and their net brake.

7. And they beckoned unto *their* partners, which were in the other ship, that they should come and help them. And they came, and filled both the ships, so that they began to sink.

8. When Simon Peter saw *it*, he fell down at Jesus' knees, saying, Depart from me; for I am a sinful man, O Lord.

9. For he was astonished, and all that were with him, at the draught of the fishes which they had taken:

10. And so *was* also James, and John, the sons of Zebedee, which were partners with Simon. And Jesus said unto Simon, Fear not; from henceforth thou shalt catch men.

11. And when they had brought their ships to land, they forsook all, and followed him.

John: No record.

Section 47

AN UNCLEAN SPIRIT CAST OUT

Jesus comes to Capernaum, goes into the synagogue, where they are astonished at his doctrines, for he teaches as one having authority and not as the scribes; an unclean spirit proclaims him the Holy One of God; Jesus rebukes the spirit and commands it to leave the one possessed; the spirit throws the man to the ground and then leaves him uninjured; the people marvel that even the unclean spirits obey him; his fame spreads.

Matt.: No record; Mark 1:21-28; Luke 4:31-37; John: No record.

Time: A.D. 28, Winter (CROSCUP).

Place: Capernaum.

Matthew: No record.

MARK 1:21. And they went into Capernaum; and straightway on the sabbath day he entered into the synagogue, and taught.

22. And they were astonished at his doctrine: for he taught them as one that had authority, and not as the scribes.

23. And there was in their synagogue a man with an unclean spirit; and he cried out,

24. Saying, Let *us* alone; what have we to do with thee, thou Jesus of Nazareth? art thou come to destroy us? I know thee who thou art, the Holy One of God.

25. And Jesus rebuked him, saying, Hold thy peace, and come out of him.

26. And when the unclean spirit had torn him, and cried with a loud voice, he came out of him.

27. And they were all amazed, insomuch that they questioned among themselves, saying, What thing is this? what new doctrine *is* this? for with authority commandeth he even the unclean spirits, and they do obey him.

28. And immediately his fame spread abroad throughout all the region round about Galilee.

LUKE 4:31. And came down to Capernaum, a city of Galilee, and taught them on the sabbath days.

32. And they were astonished at his doctrine: for his word was with power.

33. ¶ And in the synagogue there was a man, which had a spirit of an unclean devil, and cried out with a loud voice,

34. Saying, Let *us* alone; what have we to do with thee, *thou* Jesus of Nazareth? art thou come to destroy us? I know thee who thou art; the Holy One of God.

35. And Jesus rebuked him, saying, Hold thy peace, and come out of him. And when the devil had thrown him in

the midst, he came out of him, and hurt him not.

36. And they were all amazed, and spake among themselves, saying, What a word *is* this! for with authority and power he commandeth the unclean spirits, and they come out.

37. And the fame of him went out into every place of the country round about.

John: No record.

Section 48

PETER'S WIFE'S MOTHER HEALED; A DAY OF MIRACLES

Jesus, coming to Peter's home, takes Peter's mother-in-law by the hand, rebukes the fever with which she is afflicted, and she arises and ministers unto them; afterward he heals the multitude that are brought to him, including those possessed, and silences the evil spirits who cry out, "Thou art Christ the Son of God," because they know him.

Matt. 8:14-17; Mark 1:29-34; Luke 4:38-41; John: No record.

Time: A.D. 28, Winter (CROSCUP).

Place: Capernaum.

MATTHEW 8:14. ¶ And when Jesus was come into Peter's house, he saw his wife's mother laid, and sick of a fever.

15. And he touched her hand, and the fever left her: and she arose, and ministered unto them.

16. ¶When the even was come, they brought unto him many that were possessed with devils: and he cast out the spirits with *his* word, and healed all that were sick:

17. That it might be fulfilled which was spoken by Esaias the prophet, saying, Himself took our infirmities, and bare *our* sicknesses.

MARK 1:29. And forthwith, when they were come out of the synagogue, they entered into the house of Simon and Andrew, with James and John.

30. But Simon's wife's mother lay sick of a fever, and anon they tell him of her.

31. And he came and took her by the hand, and lifted her up; and immediately the fever left her, and she ministered unto them.

32. And at even, when the sun did set, they brought unto him all that were diseased, and them that were possessed with devils.

33. And all the city was gathered together at the door.

34. And he healed many that were sick of divers diseases, and cast out many devils; and suffered not the devils to speak, because they knew him.

LUKE 4:38. ¶ And he arose out of the synagogue, and entered into Simon's house. And Simon's wife's mother was taken with a great fever; and they besought him for her.

39. And he stood over her, and rebuked the fever; and it left her: and immediately she arose and ministered unto them.

40. ¶ Now when the sun was setting, all they that had any sick with divers diseases brought them unto him; and he laid his hands on every one of them, and healed them.

41. And devils also came out of many, crying out, and saying, Thou art Christ the Son of God. And he rebuking *them* suffered them not to speak: for they knew that he was Christ.

John: No record.

Section 49

JESUS MAKES FIRST TOUR OF GALILEE, PREACHING

Beginning the morning after the day of miracles at Peter's house, Jesus, with Simon, and they that are with him following, makes his first preaching tour of Galilee, healing the sick of all manner of diseases, healing those possessed of devils, those who are lunatick; he preaches in their synagogues; multitudes follow him from Galilee, Decapolis, Jerusalem, and Judea and from beyond the Jordan.

Matt. 4:23-25; Mark 1:35-39; Luke 4:42-44; John: No record.
Time: A.D. 28, Winter-Spring (CROSCUP).
Place: Galilee.

MATTHEW 4:23. ¶ And Jesus went about all Galilee, teaching in their synagogues, and preaching the gospel of the kingdom, and healing all manner of sickness and all manner of disease among the people.

24. And his fame went throughout all Syria: and they brought unto him all sick people that were taken with divers diseases and torments, and those which were possessed with devils, and those which were lunatick, and those that had the palsy; and he healed them.

25. And there followed him great multitudes of people from Galilee, and *from* Decapolis, and *from* Jerusalem, and *from* Judæa, and *from* beyond Jordan.

MARK 1:35. And in the morning, rising up a great while before day, he went out, and departed into a solitary place, and there prayed.

36. And Simon and they that were with him followed after him.

37. And when they had found him, they said unto him, All *men* seek for thee.

38. And he said unto them, Let us go into the next towns, that I may preach there also: for therefore came I forth.

39. And he preached in their synagogues throughout all Galilee, and cast out devils.

LUKE 4:42. And when it was day, he departed and went into a desert place: and the people sought him, and came unto him, and stayed him, that he should not depart from them.

43. And he said unto them, I must preach the kingdom of God to other cities also: for therefore am I sent.

44. And he preached in the synagogues of Galilee.

John: No record.

Section 50

THE SERMON ON THE MOUNT

Matt. Chaps. 5-7; Mark: No record; Luke: No record; John: No record.
Time: A.D. 28.
Place: Galilee.

MATTHEW 5:1. And seeing the multitudes, he went up into a mountain: and when he was set, his disciples came unto him:

2. And he opened his mouth, and taught them, saying,

3. Blessed *are* the poor in spirit: for their's is the kingdom of heaven.

4. Blessed *are* they that mourn: for they shall be comforted.

5. Blessed *are* the meek: for they shall inherit the earth.

6. Blessed *are* they which do hunger and thirst after righteousness: for they shall be filled.

7. Blessed *are* the merciful: for they shall obtain mercy.

8. Blessed *are* the pure in heart: for they shall see God.

9. Blessed *are* the peacemakers: for they shall be called the children of God.

10. Blessed *are* they which are persecuted for righteousness' sake: for their's is the kingdom of heaven.

11. Blessed are ye, when *men* shall revile you, and persecute *you*, and shall say all manner of evil against you falsely, for my sake.

12. Rejoice, and be exceeding glad: for great *is* your reward in heaven: for so persecuted they the prophets which were before you.

13. ¶ Ye are the salt of the earth: but if the salt have lost his savour, wherewith shall it be salted? it is thenceforth good for nothing, but to be cast out, and to be trodden under foot of men.

14. Ye are the light of the world. A city that is set on an hill cannot be hid.

15. Neither do men light a candle, and put it under a bushel, but on a candlestick;

and it giveth light unto all that are in the house.

16. Let your light so shine before men, that they may see your good works, and glorify your Father which is in heaven.

17. ¶ Think not that I am come to destroy the law, or the prophets: I am not come to destroy, but to fulfil.

18. For verily I say unto you, Till heaven and earth pass, one jot or one tittle shall in no wise pass from the law, till all be fulfilled.

19. Whosoever therefore shall break one of these least commandments, and shall teach men so, he shall be called the least in the kingdom of heaven: but whosoever shall do and teach *them*, the same shall be called great in the kingdom of heaven.

20. For I say unto you, That except your righteousness shall exceed *the righteousness* of the scribes and Pharisees, ye shall in no case enter into the kingdom of heaven.

21. ¶ Ye have heard that it was said by them of old time, Thou shalt not kill; and whosoever shall kill shall be in danger of the judgment:

22. But I say unto you, That whosoever is angry with his brother without a cause shall be in danger of the judgment: and whosoever shall say to his brother, Raca, shall be in danger of the council: but whosoever shall say, Thou fool, shall be in danger of hell fire.

23. Therefore if thou bring thy gift to the altar, and there rememberest that thy brother hath ought against thee;

24. Leave there thy gift before the altar, and go thy way; first be reconciled to thy brother, and then come and offer thy gift.

25. Agree with thine adversary quickly, whiles thou art in the way with him; lest at any time the adversary deliver thee to the judge, and the judge deliver thee to the officer, and thou be cast into prison.

26. Verily I say unto thee, Thou shalt by no means come out thence, till thou hast paid the uttermost farthing.

27. ¶ Ye have heard that it was said by them of old time, Thou shalt not commit adultery:

28. But I say unto you, That whosoever looketh on a woman to lust after her hath committed adultery with her already in his heart.

29. And if thy right eye offend thee, pluck it out, and cast *it* from thee: for it is profitable for thee that one of thy members should perish, and not *that* thy whole body should be cast into hell.

30. And if thy right hand offend thee, cut it off, and cast *it* from thee: for it is profitable for thee that one of thy members should perish, and

not *that* thy whole body should be cast into hell.

31. It hath been said, Whosoever shall put away his wife, let him give her a writing of divorcement:

32. But I say unto you, That whosoever shall put away his wife, saving for the cause of fornication, causeth her to commit adultery: and whosoever shall marry her that is divorced committeth adultery.

33. ¶ Again, ye have heard that it hath been said by them of old time, Thou shalt not forswear thyself, but shalt perform unto the Lord thine oaths:

34. But I say unto you, Swear not at all; neither by heaven; for it is God's throne:

35. Nor by the earth; for it is his footstool: neither by Jerusalem; for it is the city of the great King.

36. Neither shalt thou swear by thy head, because thou canst not make one hair white or black.

37. But let your communication be, Yea, yea; Nay, nay: for whatsoever is more than these cometh of evil.

38. ¶ Ye have heard that it hath been said, An eye for an eye, and a tooth for a tooth:

39. But I say unto you, That ye resist not evil: but whosoever shall smite thee on thy right cheek, turn to him the other also.

40. And if any man will sue thee at the law, and take away thy coat, let him have *thy* cloke also.

41. And whosoever shall compel thee to go a mile, go with him twain.

42. Give to him that asketh thee, and from him that would borrow of thee turn not thou away.

43. ¶ Ye have heard that it hath been said, Thou shalt love thy neighbour, and hate thine enemy.

44. But I say unto you, Love your enemies, bless them that curse you, do good to them that hate you, and pray for them which despitefully use you, and persecute you;

45. That ye may be the children of your Father which is in heaven: for he maketh his sun to rise on the evil and on the good, and sendeth rain on the just and on the unjust.

46. For if ye love them which love you, what reward have ye? do not even the publicans the same?

47. And if ye salute your brethren only, what do ye more *than others?* do not even the publicans so?

48. Be ye therefore perfect, even as your Father which is in heaven is perfect.

CHAPTER 6

1. Take heed that ye do not your alms before men, to be seen of them: otherwise ye have no reward of your Father which is in heaven.

2. Therefore when thou doest *thine* alms, do not sound a trumpet before thee, as the hypocrites do in the synagogues and in the streets, that they may have glory of men. Verily I say unto you, They have their reward.

3. But when thou doest alms, let not thy left hand know what thy right hand doeth:

4. That thine alms may be in secret: and thy Father which seeth in secret himself shall reward thee openly.

5. ¶ And when thou prayest, thou shalt not be as the hypocrites *are*: for they love to pray standing in the synagogues and in the corners of the streets, that they may be seen of men. Verily I say unto you, They have their reward.

6. But thou, when thou prayest, enter into thy closet, and when thou hast shut thy door, pray to thy Father which is in secret; and thy Father which seeth in secret shall reward thee openly.

7. But when ye pray, use not vain repetitions, as the heathen *do*: for they think that they shall be heard for their much speaking.

8. Be not ye therefore like unto them: for your Father knoweth what things ye have need of, before ye ask him.

9. After this manner therefore pray ye: Our Father which art in heaven, Hallowed be thy name.

10. Thy kingdom come. Thy will be done in earth, as *it is* in heaven.

11. Give us this day our daily bread.

12. And forgive us our debts, as we forgive our debtors.

13. And lead us not into temptation, but deliver us from evil: For thine is the kingdom, and the power, and the glory, for ever. Amen.

14. For if ye forgive men their trespasses, your heavenly Father will also forgive you:

15. But if ye forgive not men their trespasses, neither will your Father forgive your trespasses.

16. ¶Moreover when ye fast, be not, as the hypocrites, of a sad countenance: for they disfigure their faces, that they may appear unto men to fast. Verily I say unto you, They have their reward.

17. But thou, when thou fastest, anoint thine head, and wash thy face;

18. That thou appear not unto men to fast, but unto thy Father which is in secret: and thy Father, which seeth in secret, shall reward thee openly.

19. ¶Lay not up for yourselves treasures upon earth, where moth and rust doth corrupt, and where thieves break through and steal:

20. But lay up for yourselves treasures in heaven, where neither moth nor rust doth corrupt, and where thieves do not break through nor steal:

21. For where your treasure is, there will your heart be also.

22. The light of the body is the eye: if therefore thine eye be single, thy whole body shall be full of light.

23. But if thine eye be evil, thy whole body shall be full of darkness. If therefore the light that is in thee be darkness, how great *is* that darkness!

24. ¶ No man can serve two masters: for either he will hate the one, and love the other; or else he will hold to the one, and despise the other. Ye cannot serve God and mammon.

25. Therefore I say unto you, Take no thought for your life, what ye shall eat, or what ye shall drink; nor yet for your body, what ye shall put on. Is not the life more than meat, and the body than raiment?

26. Behold the fowls of the air: for they sow not, neither do they reap, nor gather into barns; yet your heavenly Father feedeth them. Are ye not much better than they?

27. Which of you by taking thought can add one cubit unto his stature?

28. And why take ye thought for raiment? Consider the lilies of the field, how they grow; they toil not, neither do they spin:

29. And yet I say unto you, That even Solomon in all his glory was not arrayed like one of these.

30. Wherefore, if God so clothe the grass of the field, which to day is, and to morrow is cast into the oven, *shall he* not much more *clothe* you, O ye of little faith?

31. Therefore take no thought, saying, What shall we eat? or, What shall we drink? or, Wherewithal shall we be clothed?

32. (For after all these things do the Gentiles seek:) for your heavenly Father knoweth that ye have need of all these things.

33. But seek ye first the kingdom of God, and his righteousness; and all these things shall be added unto you.

34. Take therefore no thought for the morrow: for the morrow shall take thought for the things of itself. Sufficient unto the day *is* the evil thereof.

CHAPTER 7

1. Judge not, that ye be not judged.

2. For with what judgment ye judge, ye shall be judged: and with what measure ye mete, it shall be measured to you again.

3. And why beholdest thou the mote that is in thy brother's eye, but considerest not the beam that is in thine own eye?

4. Or how wilt thou say to thy brother, Let me pull out the mote out of thine eye; and, behold, a beam *is* in thine own eye?

5. Thou hypocrite, first cast out the beam out of thine own eye; and then shalt thou see clearly to cast out the mote out of thy brother's eye.

6. ¶ Give not that which is holy unto the dogs, neither cast ye your pearls before swine, lest they trample them under their feet, and turn again and rend you.

7. ¶ Ask, and it shall be given you; seek, and ye shall find; knock, and it shall be opened unto you:

8. For every one that asketh receiveth; and he that seeketh findeth; and to him that knocketh it shall be opened.

9. Or what man is there of you, whom if his son ask bread, will he give him a stone?

10. Or if he ask a fish, will he give him a serpent?

11. If ye then, being evil, know how to give good gifts unto your children, how much more shall your Father which is in heaven give good things to them that ask him?

12. Therefore all things whatsoever ye would that men should do to you, do ye even so to them: for this is the law and the prophets.

13. ¶Enter ye in at the strait gate: for wide *is* the gate, and broad *is* the way, that leadeth to destruction, and many there be which go in thereat:

14. Because strait *is* the gate, and narrow *is* the way, which leadeth unto life, and few there be that find it.

15. ¶Beware of false prophets, which come to you in sheep's clothing, but inwardly they are ravening wolves.

16. Ye shall know them by their fruits. Do men gather grapes of thorns, or figs of thistles?

17. Even so every good tree bringeth forth good fruit; but a corrupt tree bringeth forth evil fruit.

18. A good tree cannot bring forth evil fruit, neither *can* a corrupt tree bring forth good fruit.

19. Every tree that bringeth not forth good fruit is hewn down, and cast into the fire.

20. Wherefore by their fruits ye shall know them.

21. ¶ Not every one that saith unto me, Lord, Lord, shall enter into the kingdom of heaven; but he that doeth the will of my Father which is in heaven.

22. Many will say to me in that day, Lord, Lord, have we not prophesied in thy name? and in thy name have cast out devils? and in thy name done many wonderful works?

23. And then will I profess unto them, I never knew you: depart from me, ye that work iniquity.

24. ¶ Therefore whosoever heareth these sayings of mine, and doeth them, I will liken him unto a wise man, which built his house upon a rock:

25. And the rain descended, and the floods came, and the

winds blew, and beat upon that house; and it fell not: for it was founded upon a rock.

26. And every one that heareth these sayings of mine, and doeth them not, shall be likened unto a foolish man, which built his house upon the sand:

27. And the rain descended, and the floods came, and the winds blew, and beat upon that house; and it fell: and great was the fall of it.

28. And it came to pass, when Jesus had ended these sayings, the people were astonished at his doctrine:

29. For he taught them as *one* having authority, and not as the scribes.

Mark: No record.
Luke: No record.
John: No record.

Section 51

THE LEPER HEALED

Multitudes follow Jesus coming down from the mountain; a leper worshiping Jesus, asks to be cleansed; Jesus touching him says: "Be thou clean"; the leper is instantly healed; Jesus tells him to go to the Temple priest, show himself and offer the Mosaic cleansings, but to tell no man; disobeying this, the healed leper blazes it abroad so that Jesus "could no more openly enter into the city, but was without in desert places: and they came to him from every quarter."

Matt. 8:1-4; Mark 1:40-45; Luke 5:12-16; John: No record.
Time: A.D. 28, March (CROSCUP).
Place: Galilee.

MATTHEW 8:1. When he was come down from the mountain, great multitudes followed him.

2. And, behold, there came a leper and worshipped him, saying, Lord, if thou wilt, thou canst make me clean.

3. And Jesus put forth *his* hand, and touched him, saying, I will; be thou clean. And immediately his leprosy was cleansed.

4. And Jesus saith unto him, See thou tell no man; but go thy way, shew thyself to the priest, and offer the gift that Moses commanded, for a testimony unto them.

MARK 1:40. And there came a leper to him, beseeching him, and kneeling down to him, and saying unto him, If thou wilt, thou canst make me clean.

41. And Jesus, moved with compassion, put forth *his* hand, and touched him, and saith unto him, I will; be thou clean.

42. And as soon as he had spoken, immediately the leprosy departed from him, and he was cleansed.

43. And he straitly charged him, and forthwith sent him away;

44. And saith unto him, See thou say nothing to any man: but go thy way, shew thyself

to the priest, and offer for thy cleansing those things which Moses commanded, for a testimony unto them.

45. But he went out, and began to publish *it* much, and to blaze abroad the matter, insomuch that Jesus could no more openly enter into the city, but was without in desert places: and they came to him from every quarter.

LUKE 5:12. ¶And it came to pass, when he was in a certain city, behold a man full of leprosy: who seeing Jesus fell on *his* face, and besought him, saying, Lord, if thou wilt, thou canst make me clean.

13. And he put forth *his* hand, and touched him, saying, I will: be thou clean. And immediately the leprosy departed from him.

14. And he charged him to tell no man: but go, and shew thyself to the priest, and offer for thy cleansing, according as Moses commanded, for a testimony unto them.

15. But so much the more went there a fame abroad of him: and great multitudes came together to hear, and to be healed by him of their infirmities.

16. ¶ And he withdrew himself into the wilderness, and prayed.

John: No record.

Section 52

ONE SICK WITH PALSY IS HEALED

Jesus returning to Capernaum after some days, it is noised about that he is in the house; many gather there including Pharisees and doctors of law from every town in Galilee, Judea, and from Jerusalem. Jesus preaches to the multitude, which is so great that no one can get near the door; they bring on his bed a man sick with palsy, and as they can not get in to Jesus through the door, they go upon the housetop and let him down through the tiling into the midst before Jesus; and when Jesus sees his faith, he says: "Man, thy sins are forgiven thee"; the scribes and the Pharisees questioning among themselves declare that this is blasphemy; Jesus perceiving what is in their hearts, says: "Why reason ye these things in your hearts? Whether is it easier to say to the sick of the palsy, Thy sins be forgiven thee; or to say, Arise, and take up thy bed," and then commands the man to "arise, and take up thy couch, and go into thine house." The man obeys, and all glorify God.

Matt. 9:2-8; Mark 2:1-12; Luke 5:17-26; John: No record.
Time: A.D. 28, March (CROSCUP).
Place: Capernaum.

MATTHEW 9:2. And, behold, they brought to him a man sick of the palsy, lying on a bed: and Jesus seeing their faith said unto the sick of the palsy; Son, be of good cheer; thy sins be forgiven thee.

3. And, behold, certain of the

scribes said within themselves, This *man* blasphemeth.

4. And Jesus knowing their thoughts said, Wherefore think ye evil in your hearts?

5. For whether is easier, to say, *Thy* sins be forgiven thee; or to say, Arise, and walk?

6. But that ye may know that the Son of man hath power on earth to forgive sins, (then saith he to the sick of the palsy,) Arise, take up thy bed, and go unto thine house.

7. And he arose, and departed to his house.

8. But when the multitudes saw *it*, they marvelled, and glorified God, which had given such power unto men.

MARK 2:1. And again he entered into Capernaum after *some* days; and it was noised that he was in the house.

2. And straightway many were gathered together, insomuch that there was no room to receive *them*, no, not so much as about the door: and he preached the word unto them.

3. And they come unto him, bringing one sick of the palsy, which was borne of four.

4. And when they could not come nigh unto him for the press, they uncovered the roof where he was: and when they had broken *it* up, they let down the bed wherein the sick of the palsy lay.

5. When Jesus saw their faith, he said unto the sick of the palsy, Son, thy sins be forgiven thee.

6. But there were certain of the scribes sitting there, and reasoning in their hearts,

7. Why doth this *man* thus speak blasphemies? who can forgive sins but God only?

8. And immediately when Jesus perceived in his spirit that they so reasoned within themselves, he said unto them, Why reason ye these things in your hearts?

9. Whether is it easier to say to the sick of the palsy, *Thy* sins be forgiven thee; or to say, Arise, and take up thy bed, and walk?

10. But that ye may know that the Son of man hath power on earth to forgive sins, (he saith to the sick of the palsy,)

11. I say unto thee, Arise, and take up thy bed, and go thy way into thine house.

12. And immediately he arose, took up the bed, and went forth before them all; insomuch that they were all amazed, and glorified God, saying, We never saw it on this fashion.

LUKE 5:17. And it came to pass on a certain day, as he was teaching, that there were Pharisees and doctors of the law sitting by, which were come out of every town of Galilee, and Judæa, and Jerusalem: and the power of the Lord was *present* to heal them.

18. ¶ And, behold, men

brought in a bed a man which was taken with a palsy: and they sought *means* to bring him in, and to lay *him* before him.

19. And when they could not find by what *way* they might bring him in because of the multitude, they went upon the housetop, and let him down through the tiling with *his* couch into the midst before Jesus.

20. And when he saw their faith, he said unto him, Man, thy sins are forgiven thee.

21. And the scribes and the Pharisees began to reason, saying, Who is this which speaketh blasphemies? Who can forgive sins, but God alone?

22. But when Jesus perceived their thoughts, he answering said unto them, What reason ye in your hearts?

23. Whether is easier, to say, Thy sins be forgiven thee; or to say, Rise up and walk?

24. But that ye may know that the Son of man hath power upon earth to forgive sins, (he said unto the sick of the palsy,) I say unto thee, Arise, and take up thy couch, and go into thine house.

25. And immediately he rose up before them, and took up that whereon he lay, and departed to his own house, glorifying God.

26. And they were all amazed, and they glorified God, and were filled with fear, saying, We have seen strange things to day.

John: No record.

Section 53

JESUS CHOOSES MATTHEW WHO GIVES A FEAST

Passing from thence, Jesus goes forth again by the seaside, and multitudes follow him, he teaches them; seeing Levi—Matthew—son of Alphaeus, sitting at the receipt of custom, he says, "Follow me," and Matthew follows; Matthew makes a great feast for Jesus (in Matthew's house) and a great company of publicans and sinners come and sit down; the Pharisees murmur at this, asking why he eats with publicans and sinners; Jesus answers that the sick, not the well, need a physician, and that he comes not to call the righteous but the sinners to repentance.

Matt. 9:9-13; Mark 2:13-17; Luke 5:27-32; John: No record.
Time: A.D. 28, March (CROSCUP).
Place: Sea of Galilee.

MATTHEW 9:9. ¶And as Jesus passed forth from thence, he saw a man, named Matthew, sitting at the receipt of custom: and he saith unto him, Follow me. And he arose, and followed him.

10. ¶ And it came to pass, as Jesus sat at meat in the house, behold, many publicans and

sinners came and sat down with him and his disciples.

11. And when the Pharisees saw *it*, they said unto his disciples, Why eateth your Master with publicans and sinners?

12. But when Jesus heard *that*, he said unto them, They that be whole need not a physician, but they that are sick.

13. But go ye and learn what *that* meaneth, I will have mercy, and not sacrifice: for I am not come to call the righteous, but sinners to repentance.

MARK 2:13. And he went forth again by the sea side; and all the multitude resorted unto him, and he taught them.

14. And as he passed by, he saw Levi the *son* of Alphæus sitting at the receipt of custom, and said unto him, Follow me. And he arose and followed him.

15. And it came to pass, that, as Jesus sat at meat in his house, many publicans and sinners sat also together with Jesus and his disciples: for there were many, and they followed him.

16. And when the scribes and Pharisees saw him eat with publicans and sinners, they said unto his disciples, How is it that he eateth and drinketh with publicans and sinners?

17. When Jesus heard *it*, he saith unto them, They that are whole have no need of the physician, but they that are sick: I came not to call the righteous, but sinners to repentance.

LUKE 5:27. ¶ And after these things he went forth, and saw a publican, named Levi, sitting at the receipt of custom: and he said unto him, Follow me.

28. And he left all, rose up, and followed him.

29. And Levi made him a great feast in his own house: and there was a great company of publicans and of others that sat down with them.

30. But their scribes and Pharisees murmured against his disciples, saying, Why do ye eat and drink with publicans and sinners?

31. And Jesus answering said unto them, They that are whole need not a physician; but they that are sick.

32. I came not to call the righteous, but sinners to repentance.

John: No record.

Section 54

JOHN'S DISCIPLES QUESTION JESUS ABOUT FASTING

The disciples of John come to Jesus and ask why do not the disciples of Jesus fast as do they and the Pharisees; Jesus answers in parables—children of the bridechamber, a piece of new cloth in an old garment, new wine in old bottles, and new wine as against old wine.

Matt. 9:14-17; Mark 2:18-22; Luke 5:33-39; John: No record.
Time: A.D. 28, March.
Place: Sea of Galilee.

MATTHEW 9:14. ¶Then came to him the disciples of John, saying, Why do we and the Pharisees fast oft, but thy disciples fast not?

15. And Jesus said unto them, Can the children of the bridechamber mourn, as long as the bridegroom is with them? but the days will come, when the bridegroom shall be taken from them, and then shall they fast.

16. No man putteth a piece of new cloth unto an old garment, for that which is put in to fill it up taketh from the garment, and the rent is made worse.

17. Neither do men put new wine into old bottles: else the bottles break, and the wine runneth out, and the bottles perish: but they put new wine into new bottles, and both are preserved.

MARK 2:18. And the disciples of John and of the Pharisees used to fast: and they come and say unto him, Why do the disciples of John and of the Pharisees fast, but thy disciples fast not?

19. And Jesus said unto them, Can the children of the bridechamber fast, while the bridegroom is with them? as long as they have the bridegroom with them, they cannot fast.

20. But the days will come, when the bridegroom shall be taken away from them, and then shall they fast in those days.

21. No man also seweth a piece of new cloth on an old garment: else the new piece that filled it up taketh away from the old, and the rent is made worse.

22. And no man putteth new wine into old bottles: else the new wine doth burst the bottles, and the wine is spilled, and the bottles will be marred: but new wine must be put into new bottles.

LUKE 5:33. ¶ And they said unto him, Why do the disciples of John fast often, and make prayers, and likewise *the disciples* of the Pharisees; but thine eat and drink?

34. And he said unto them, Can ye make the children of

the bridechamber fast, while the bridegroom is with them?

35. But the days will come, when the bridegroom shall be taken away from them, and then shall they fast in those days.

36. ¶And he spake also a parable unto them; No man putteth a piece of a new garment upon an old; if otherwise, then both the new maketh a rent, and the piece that was *taken* out of the new agreeth not with the old.

37. And no man putteth new wine into old bottles; else the new wine will burst the bottles, and be spilled, and the bottles shall perish.

38. But new wine must be put into new bottles; and both are preserved.

39. No man also having drunk old *wine* straightway desireth new: for he saith, The old is better.

John: No record.

Section 55

THE SECOND PASSOVER

Jesus goes to Jerusalem to the Passover (the second of his ministry); goes on the Sabbath to the pool of Bethesda and heals there a man with an infirmity of thirty-eight years' standing; Jesus slips away without before the man can tell who Jesus is; the man tells those asking who healed him that he does not know; later the man sees Jesus in the Temple and knows him as Jesus warns him to sin no more; the Jews seek to kill Jesus because he has healed on the Sabbath (this is the first record of an effort to kill Jesus); Jesus preaches to them, proclaiming his Sonship, for which they again seek his life; he says he does whatever the Father does; preaches knowing the Father and the Son; he declares his powers, but can do nothing of himself; he tells John's mission; he is greater than John; tells of work the Father has given him to do; explains relationship of the Father and himself; tells how they will be accused.

Matt.: No record; Mark: No record; Luke: No record; John 5:1-47.
Time: A.D. 28, April (CROSCUP).
Place: Jerusalem.

Matthew: No record.

Mark: No record.

Luke: No record.

JOHN 5:1. After this there was a feast of the Jews; and Jesus went up to Jerusalem.

2. Now there is at Jerusalem by the sheep *market* a pool, which is called in the Hebrew tongue Bethesda, having five porches.

3. In these lay a great multitude of impotent folk, of blind, halt, withered, waiting for the moving of the water.

4. For an angel went down at a certain season into the pool, and troubled the water: whosoever then first after the

troubling of the water stepped in was made whole of whatsoever disease he had.

5. And a certain man was there, which had an infirmity thirty and eight years.

6. When Jesus saw him lie, and knew that he had been now a long time *in that case*, he saith unto him, Wilt thou be made whole?

7. The impotent man answered him, Sir, I have no man, when the water is troubled, to put me into the pool: but while I am coming, another steppeth down before me.

8. Jesus saith unto him, Rise, take up thy bed, and walk.

9. And immediately the man was made whole, and took up his bed, and walked: and on the same day was the sabbath.

10. ¶The Jews therefore said unto him that was cured, It is the sabbath day: it is not lawful for thee to carry *thy* bed.

11. He answered them, He that made me whole, the same said unto me, Take up thy bed, and walk.

12. Then asked they him, What man is that which said unto thee, Take up thy bed, and walk?

13. And he that was healed wist not who it was: for Jesus had conveyed himself away, a multitude being in *that* place.

14. Afterward Jesus findeth him in the temple, and said unto him, Behold, thou art made whole: sin no more, lest a worse thing come unto thee.

15. The man departed, and told the Jews that it was Jesus, which had made him whole.

16. And therefore did the Jews persecute Jesus, and sought to slay him, because he had done these things on the sabbath day.

17. ¶ But Jesus answered them, My Father worketh hitherto, and I work.

18. Therefore the Jews sought the more to kill him, because he not only had broken the sabbath, but said also that God was his Father, making himself equal with God.

19. Then answered Jesus and said unto them, Verily, verily, I say unto you, The Son can do nothing of himself, but what he seeth the Father do: for what things soever he doeth, these also doeth the Son likewise.

20. For the Father loveth the Son, and sheweth him all things that himself doeth: and he will shew him greater works than these, that ye may marvel.

21. For as the Father raiseth up the dead, and quickeneth *them;* even so the Son quickeneth whom he will.

22. For the Father judgeth no man, but hath committed all judgment unto the Son:

23. That all *men* should honour the Son, even as they honour the Father. He that honoureth not the Son honoureth not the Father which hath sent him.

24. Verily, verily, I say unto you, He that heareth my word, and believeth on him that sent me, hath everlasting life, and shall not come into condemnation; but is passed from death unto life.

25. Verily, verily, I say unto you, The hour is coming, and now is, when the dead shall hear the voice of the Son of God: and they that hear shall live.

26. For as the Father hath life in himself; so hath he given to the Son to have life in himself;

27. And hath given him authority to execute judgment also, because he is the Son of man.

28. Marvel not at this: for the hour is coming, in the which all that are in the graves shall hear his voice,

29. And shall come forth; they that have done good, unto the resurrection of life; and they that have done evil, unto the resurrection of damnation.

30. I can of mine own self do nothing: as I hear, I judge: and my judgment is just; because I seek not mine own will, but the will of the Father which hath sent me.

31. If I bear witness of myself, my witness is not true.

32. ¶ There is another that beareth witness of me; and I know that the witness which he witnesseth of me is true.

33. Ye sent unto John, and he bare witness unto the truth.

34. But I receive not testimony from man: but these things I say, that ye might be saved.

35. He was a burning and a shining light: and ye were willing for a season to rejoice in his light.

36. ¶But I have greater witness than *that* of John: for the works which the Father hath given me to finish, the same works that I do, bear witness of me, that the Father hath sent me.

37. And the Father himself, which hath sent me, hath borne witness of me. Ye have neither heard his voice at any time, nor seen his shape.

38. And ye have not his word abiding in you: for whom he hath sent, him ye believe not.

39. ¶ Search the scriptures; for in them ye think ye have eternal life: and they are they which testify of me.

40. And ye will not come to me, that ye might have life.

41. I receive not honour from men.

42. But I know you, that ye have not the love of God in you.

43. I am come in my Father's name, and ye receive me not: if another shall come in his own name, him ye will receive.

44. How can ye believe, which receive honour one of another, and seek not the honour that *cometh* from God only?

45. Do not think that I will accuse you to the Father: there is *one* that accuseth you, *even* Moses, in whom ye trust.

46. For had ye believed Moses, ye would have believed me: for he wrote of me.

47. But if ye believe not his writings, how shall ye believe my words?

Section 56

DISCIPLES PLUCK CORN ON SABBATH

The disciples, hungry and going through a field of corn, pluck the ears of corn and eat them; the Pharisees charge them with violating the Sabbath; in justification Jesus cites David's eating of the shewbread, that the priests in the Temple profane the Sabbath and are blameless; declares that in this place there is one greater than the Temple, and that the "Son of man is Lord even of the sabbath day."

Matt. 12:1-8; Mark 2:23-28; Luke 6:1-5; John: No record.

Time: A.D. 28, April (CROSCUP).

Place: Galilee (CROSCUP).

MATTHEW 12:1. At that time Jesus went on the sabbath day through the corn; and his disciples were an hungred, and began to pluck the ears of corn, and to eat.

2. But when the Pharisees saw *it*, they said unto him, Behold, thy disciples do that which is not lawful to do upon the sabbath day.

3. But he said unto them, Have ye not read what David did, when he was an hungred, and they that were with him;

4. How he entered into the house of God, and did eat the shewbread, which was not lawful for him to eat, neither for them which were with him, but only for the priests?

5. Or have ye not read in the law, how that on the sabbath days the priests in the temple profane the sabbath, and are blameless?

6. But I say unto you, That in this place is *one* greater than the temple.

7. But if ye had known what *this* meaneth, I will have mercy, and not sacrifice, ye would not have condemned the guiltless.

8. For the Son of man is Lord even of the sabbath day.

MARK 2:23. And it came to pass, that he went through the corn fields on the sabbath day; and his disciples began, as they went, to pluck the ears of corn.

24. And the Pharisees said unto him, Behold, why do they on the sabbath day that which is not lawful?

25. And he said unto them, Have ye never read what David did, when he had need, and was an hungred, he, and they that were with him?

26. How he went into the

house of God in the days of Abiathar the high priest, and did eat the shewbread, which is not lawful to eat but for the priests, and gave also to them which were with him?

27. And he said unto them, The sabbath was made for man, and not man for the sabbath:

28. Therefore the Son of man is Lord also of the sabbath.

LUKE 6:1. And it came to pass on the second sabbath after the first, that he went through the corn fields; and his disciples plucked the ears of corn, and did eat, rubbing *them* in *their* hands.

2. And certain of the Pharisees said unto them, Why do ye that which is not lawful to do on the sabbath days?

3. And Jesus answering them said, Have ye not read so much as this, what David did, when himself was an hungred, and they which were with him;

4. How he went into the house of God, and did take and eat the shrewbread, and gave also to them that were with him; which it is not lawful to eat but for the priests alone?

5. And he said unto them, That the Son of man is Lord also of the sabbath.

John: No record.

Section 57

MAN WITH WITHERED HAND HEALED

Jesus enters a synagogue on the Sabbath in which there was a man who has a withered hand; the Pharisees and scribes watch him to see if he will heal on the Sabbath, that they may find an accusation against him; knowing their thoughts, he asks what man among them would not on the Sabbath save a sheep which had fallen into a pit, and how much better is a man than a sheep; he then heals the hand; the Pharisees take counsel with the Herodians how they may destroy Jesus.

Matt. 12:9-14; Mark 3:1-6; Luke 6:6-11; John: No record.
Time: A.D. 28, April (CROSCUP).
Place: Galilee (CROSCUP).

MATTHEW 12:9. And when he was departed thence, he went into their synagogue:

10. ¶ And, behold, there was a man which had *his* hand withered. And they asked him, saying, Is it lawful to heal on the sabbath days? that they might accuse him.

11. And he said unto them, What man shall there be among you, that shall have one sheep, and if it fall into a pit on the sabbath day, will he not lay hold on it, and lift *it* out?

12. How much then is a man better than a sheep? Wherefore it is lawful to do well on the sabbath days.

13. Then saith he to the man,

Stretch forth thine hand. And he stretched *it* forth; and it was restored whole, like as the other.

14. ¶ Then the Pharisees went out, and held a council against him, how they might destroy him.

MARK 3:1. And he entered again into the synagogue; and there was a man there which had a withered hand.

2. And they watched him, whether he would heal him on the sabbath day; that they might accuse him.

3. And he saith unto the man which had the withered hand, Stand forth.

4. And he saith unto them, Is it lawful to do good on the sabbath days, or to do evil? to save life, or to kill? But they held their peace.

5. And when he had looked round about on them with anger, being grieved for the hardness of their hearts, he saith unto the man, Stretch forth thine hand. And he stretched *it* out: and his hand was restored whole as the other.

6. And the Pharisees went forth, and straightway took counsel with the Herodians against him, how they might destroy him.

LUKE 6:6. And it came to pass also on another sabbath, that he entered into the synagogue and taught: and there was a man whose right hand was withered.

7. And the scribes and Pharisees watched him, whether he would heal on the sabbath day; that they might find an accusation against him.

8. But he knew their thoughts, and said to the man which had the withered hand, Rise up, and stand forth in the midst. And he arose and stood forth.

9. Then said Jesus unto them, I will ask you one thing; Is it lawful on the sabbath days to do good, or to do evil? to save life, or to destroy *it?*

10. And looking round about upon them all, he said unto the man, Stretch forth thy hand. And he did so: and his hand was restored whole as the other.

11. And they were filled with madness; and communed one with another what they might do to Jesus.

John: No record.

Section 58

JESUS WITHDRAWS TO THE SEA

Hearing that they plot against him, Jesus withdraws to the sea, multitudes follow him; "he healed them all; and charged them that they should not make him known"; he does this that the prophecy by Esaias might be fulfilled.

Matt. 12:15-21; Mark 3:7-12; Luke: No record; John: No record.
Time: A.D. 28, May (?) (CROSCUP).
Place: Sea of Galilee.

MATTHEW 12:15. But when Jesus knew *it*, he withdrew himself from thence: and great multitudes followed him, and he healed them all;

16. And charged them that they should not make him known:

17. That it might be fulfilled which was spoken by Esaias the prophet, saying,

18. Behold my servant, whom I have chosen; my beloved, in whom my soul is well pleased: I will put my spirit upon him, and he shall shew judgment to the Gentiles.

19. He shall not strive, nor cry; neither shall any man hear his voice in the streets.

20. A bruised reed shall he not break, and smoking flax shall he not quench, till he send forth judgment unto victory.

21. And in his name shall the Gentiles trust.

MARK 3:7. But Jesus withdrew himself with his disciples to the sea: and a great multitude from Galilee followed him, and from Judæa,

8. And from Jerusalem, and from Idumæa, and *from* beyond Jordan; and they about Tyre and Sidon, a great multitude, when they had heard what great things he did, came unto him.

9. And he spake to his disciples, that a small ship should wait on him because of the multitude, lest they should throng him.

10. For he had healed many; insomuch that they pressed upon him for to touch him, as many as had plagues.

11. And unclean spirits, when they saw him, fell down before him, and cried, saying, Thou art the Son of God.

12. And he straitly charged them that they should not make him known.

Luke: No record.

John: No record.

Section 59

THE TWELVE CHOSEN

Jesus goes up into a mountain, and after a night of prayer, "calleth unto him whom he would: and they came unto him," and he chooses and ordains Twelve whom he names Apostles; they are to be with him that he may send them forth to preach, with "power to heal sicknesses, and to cast out devils"; then the multitude come together again "so that they could not so much as eat bread"; his friends hearing of this "went out to lay hold on him: for they said, He is beside himself."

Matt. 10:2-4; Mark 3:13-21; Luke 6:12-16; John: No record.
Time: A.D. 28, Early Summer (?) (CROSCUP).
Place: Mountains of Galilee (CROSCUP).

MATTHEW 10:2. Now the names of the twelve apostles are these; The first, Simon, who is called Peter, and Andrew his brother; James *the son* of Zebedee, and John his brother;

3. Philip, and Bartholomew; Thomas, and Matthew the publican; James *the son* of Alphæus, and Lebbæus, whose surname was Thaddæus;

4. Simon the Canaanite, and Judas Iscariot, who also betrayed him.

MARK 3:13. And he goeth up into a mountain, and calleth *unto him* whom he would: and they came unto him.

14. And he ordained twelve, that they should be with him, and that he might send them forth to preach,

15. And to have power to heal sicknesses, and to cast out devils:

16. And Simon he surnamed Peter;

17. And James the *son* of Zebedee, and John the brother of James; and he surnamed them Boanerges, which is, The sons of thunder:

18. And Andrew, and Philip, and Bartholomew, and Matthew, and Thomas, and James the *son* of Alphæus, and Thaddæus, and Simon the Canaanite,

19. And Judas Iscariot, which also betrayed him: and they went into an house.

20. And the multitude cometh together again, so that they could not so much as eat bread.

21. And when his friends heard *of it*, they went out to lay hold on him: for they said, He is beside himself.

LUKE 6:12. And it came to pass in those days, that he went out into a mountain to pray, and continued all night in prayer to God.

13. ¶And when it was day, he called *unto him* his disciples: and of them he chose twelve, whom also he named apostles;

14. Simon, (whom he also named Peter,) and Andrew his brother, James and John, Philip and Bartholomew,

15. Matthew and Thomas, James the *son* of Alphæus, and Simon called Zelotes,

16. And Judas *the brother* of James, and Judas Iscariot, which also was the traitor.

John: No record.

II. From the Choosing of the Twelve to the Tour In Northern Galilee

Section 60

THE SERMON ON THE PLAIN

Matt.: No record; Mark: No record; Luke 6:17-49; John: No record.
Time: A.D. 28, Midsummer (ANDREWS).
Place: Near Capernaum (ANDREWS).

Matthew: No record.

Mark: No record.

LUKE 6:17. ¶ And he came down with them, and stood in the plain, and the company of his disciples, and a great multitude of people out of all Judæa and Jerusalem, and from the sea coast of Tyre and Sidon, which came to hear him, and to be healed of their diseases;

18. And they that were vexed with unclean spirits: and they were healed.

19. And the whole multitude sought to touch him: for there went virtue out of him, and healed *them* all.

20. ¶And he lifted up his eyes on his disciples, and said, Blessed *be ye* poor: for your's is the kingdom of God.

21. Blessed *are ye* that hunger now: for ye shall be filled. Blessed *are ye* that weep now: for ye shall laugh.

22. Blessed are ye, when men shall hate you, and when they shall separate you *from their company*, and shall reproach *you*, and cast out your name as evil, for the Son of man's sake.

23. Rejoice ye in that day, and leap for joy: for, behold, your reward *is* great in heaven: for in the like manner did their fathers unto the prophets.

24. But woe unto you that are rich! for ye have received your consolation.

25. Woe unto you that are full! for ye shall hunger. Woe unto you that laugh now! for ye shall mourn and weep.

26. Woe unto you, when all men shall speak well of you! for so did their fathers to the false prophets.

27. ¶But I say unto you which hear, Love your enemies, do good to them which hate you,

28. Bless them that curse you, and pray for them which despitefully use you.

29. And unto him that smiteth thee on the *one* cheek offer also the other; and him that taketh away thy cloke forbid not *to take thy* coat also.

30. Give to every man that asketh of thee; and of him that taketh away thy goods ask *them* not again.

31. And as ye would that

men should do to you, do ye also to them likewise.

32. For if ye love them which love you, what thank have ye? for sinners also love those that love them.

33. And if ye do good to them which do good to you, what thank have ye? for sinners also do even the same.

34. And if ye lend *to them* of whom ye hope to receive, what thank have ye? for sinners also lend to sinners, to receive as much again.

35. But love ye your enemies, and do good, and lend, hoping for nothing again; and your reward shall be great, and ye shall be the children of the Highest: for he is kind unto the unthankful and *to* the evil.

36. Be ye therefore merciful, as your Father also is merciful.

37. Judge not, and ye shall not be judged: condemn not, and ye shall not be condemned: forgive, and ye shall be forgiven:

38. Give, and it shall be given unto you; good measure, pressed down, and shaken together, and running over, shall men give into your bosom. For with the same measure that ye mete withal it shall be measured to you again.

39. And he spake a parable unto them, Can the blind lead the blind? shall they not both fall into the ditch?

40. The disciple is not above his master: but every one that is perfect shall be as his master.

41. And why beholdest thou the mote that is in thy brother's eye, but perceivest not the beam that is in thine own eye?

42. Either how canst thou say to thy brother, Brother, let me pull out the mote that is in thine eye, when thou thyself beholdest not the beam that is in thine own eye? Thou hypocrite, cast out first the beam out of thine own eye, and then shalt thou see clearly to pull out the mote that is in thy brother's eye.

43. For a good tree bringeth not forth corrupt fruit; neither doth a corrupt tree bring forth good fruit.

44. For every tree is known by his own fruit. For of thorns men do not gather figs, nor of a bramble bush gather they grapes.

45. A good man out of the good treasure of his heart bringeth forth that which is good; and an evil man out of the evil treasure of his heart bringeth forth that which is evil: for of the abundance of the heart his mouth speaketh.

46. ¶And why call ye me, Lord, Lord, and do not the things which I say?

47. Whosoever cometh to me, and heareth my sayings, and doeth them, I will shew you to whom he is like:

48. He is like a man which

built an house, and digged deep, and laid the foundation on a rock: and when the flood arose, the stream beat vehemently upon that house, and could not shake it: for it was founded upon a rock.

49. But he that heareth, and doeth not, is like a man that without a foundation built an house upon the earth; against which the stream did beat vehemently, and immediately it fell; and the ruin of that house was great.

John: No record.

Section 61

THE CENTURION'S SERVANT HEALED

Jesus, ending his sermon on the plain, enters Capernaum; a Centurion, friendly to the Jews for whom he had built a synagogue, sends unto Jesus the elders asking that Jesus come and heal his servant; Jesus starts toward the Centurion's place, but is met by friends of the Centurion bearing to Jesus the message that he need not trouble to come, the Centurion saying he himself is unworthy that Jesus should come under his roof, and that all Jesus need do is to say that it shall be done, just as the Centurion orders his soldiers, and it will be done; Jesus marvels at this faith, turns himself about, saying that it shall be as the Centurion believes; the servant is healed; Jesus shows that salvation is to others than the Jews.

Matt. 8:5-13; Mark: No record; Luke 7:1-10; John: No record.
Time: A.D. 28, Summer (ANDREWS).
Place: Capernaum.

MATTHEW 8:5. ¶And when Jesus was entered into Capernaum, there came unto him a centurion, beseeching him,

6. And saying, Lord, my servant lieth at home sick of the palsy, grievously tormented.

7. And Jesus saith unto him, I will come and heal him.

8. The centurion answered and said, Lord, I am not worthy that thou shouldest come under my roof: but speak the word only, and my servant shall be healed.

9. For I am a man under authority, having soldiers under me: and I say to this *man*, Go, and he goeth; and to another, Come, and he cometh; and to my servant, Do this, and he doeth *it*.

10. When Jesus heard *it*, he marvelled, and said to them that followed, Verily I say unto you, I have not found so great faith, no, not in Israel.

11. And I say unto you, That many shall come from the east and west, and shall sit down with Abraham, and Isaac, and Jacob, in the kingdom of heaven.

12. But the children of the kingdom shall be cast out into

outer darkness: there shall be weeping and gnashing of teeth.

13. And Jesus said unto the centurion, Go thy way; and as thou hast believed, *so* be it done unto thee. And his servant was healed in the selfsame hour.

Mark: No record.

LUKE 7:1. Now when he had ended all his sayings in the audience of the people, he entered into Capernaum.

2. And a certain centurion's servant, who was dear unto him, was sick, and ready to die.

3. And when he heard of Jesus, he sent unto him the elders of the Jews, beseeching him that he would come and heal his servant.

4. And when they came to Jesus, they besought him instantly, saying, That he was worthy for whom he should do this:

5. For he loveth our nation, and he hath built us a synagogue.

6. Then Jesus went with them. And when he was now not far from the house, the centurion sent friends to him, saying unto him, Lord, trouble not thyself: for I am not worthy that thou shouldest enter under my roof:

7. Wherefore neither thought I myself worthy to come unto thee: but say in a word, and my servant shall be healed.

8. For I also am a man set under authority, having under me soldiers, and I say unto one, Go, and he goeth; and to another, Come, and he cometh; and to my servant, Do this, and he doeth *it*.

9. When Jesus heard these things, he marvelled at him, and turned him about, and said unto the people that followed him, I say unto you, I have not found so great faith, no, not in Israel.

10. And they that were sent, returning to the house, found the servant whole that had been sick.

John: No record.

Section 62

THE SON OF WIDOW OF NAIN RAISED

The day after healing the Centurion's servant, Jesus goes to Nain, with many of his disciples and much people; as he is entering the gate of the city he meets the people with the dead son, the only son, of a widow; having compassion on the woman, he touches the bier, the carriers stand still; he commands the man to rise; he that was dead sits up and begins to speak, and Jesus delivers him to his mother; a fear comes on the people, they glorify God, pronounce Jesus a great prophet; this rumor of him goes throughout Judea and the region round about.

Matt.: No record; Mark: No record; Luke 7:11-17; John: No record.
Time: A.D. 28, Summer (ANDREWS).
Place: Nain.

Matthew: No record.

Mark: No record.

LUKE 7:11. ¶ And it came to pass the day after, that he went into a city called Nain; and many of his disciples went with him, and much people.

12. Now when he came nigh to the gate of the city, behold, there was a dead man carried out, the only son of his mother, and she was a widow: and much people of the city was with her.

13. And when the Lord saw her, he had compassion on her, and said unto her, Weep not.

14. And he came and touched the bier: and they that bare *him* stood still. And he said, Young man, I say unto thee, Arise.

15. And he that was dead sat up, and began to speak. And he delivered him to his mother.

16. And there came a fear on all: and they glorified God, saying, That a great prophet is risen up among us; and, That God hath visited his people.

17. And this rumour of him went forth throughout all Judæa, and throughout all the region round about.

John: No record.

Section 63

JOHN SENDS MESSENGERS, QUESTIONING, TO JESUS

John being in prison, his disciples tell him of the works of Jesus; John sends his disciples to ask Jesus, "Art thou he that should come? or look we for another"; Jesus tells them to "go and shew John again those things which ye do hear and see," and he names them; Jesus then discourses to the multitude about John, his mission, and his place; he refers to John's works and asks three times, "What went ye out into the wilderness to see?"; he compares John and himself; he upbraids Chorazin and Bethsaida; the publicans glorify God, being baptized of John; the Pharisees reject God, and also the lawyers, being not baptized of John.

Matt. 11:2-30; Mark: No record; Luke 7:18-35; John: No record.
Time: A.D. 28, Summer (ANDREWS).
Place: Galilee.

MATTHEW 11:2. Now when John had heard in the prison the works of Christ, he sent two of his disciples,

3. And said unto him, Art thou he that should come, or do we look for another?

4. Jesus answered and said

unto them, Go and shew John again those things which ye do hear and see:

5. The blind receive their sight, and the lame walk, the lepers are cleansed, and the deaf hear, the dead are raised up, and the poor have the gospel preached to them.

6. And blessed is *he*, whosoever shall not be offended in me.

7. ¶ And as they departed, Jesus began to say unto the multitudes concerning John, What went ye out into the wilderness to see? A reed shaken with the wind?

8. But what went ye out for to see? A man clothed in soft raiment? behold, they that wear soft *clothing* are in kings' houses.

9. But what went ye out for to see? A prophet? yea, I say unto you, and more than a prophet.

10. For this is *he*, of whom it is written, Behold, I send my messenger before thy face, which shall prepare thy way before thee.

11. Verily I say unto you, Among them that are born of women there hath not risen a greater than John the Baptist: notwithstanding he that is least in the kingdom of heaven is greater than he.

12. And from the days of John the Baptist until now the kingdom of heaven suffereth violence, and the violent take it by force.

13. For all the prophets and the law prophesied until John.

14. And if ye will receive *it*, this is Elias, which was for to come.

15. He that hath ears to hear, let him hear.

16. ¶ But whereunto shall I liken this generation? It is like unto children sitting in the markets, and calling unto their fellows,

17. And saying, We have piped unto you, and ye have not danced; we have mourned unto you, and ye have not lamented.

18. For John came neither eating nor drinking, and they say, He hath a devil.

19. The Son of man came eating and drinking, and they say, Behold a man gluttonous, and a winebibber, a friend of publicans and sinners. But wisdom is justified of her children.

20. ¶ Then began he to upbraid the cities wherein most of his mighty works were done, because they repented not:

21. Woe unto thee, Chorazin! woe unto thee, Bethsaida! for if the mighty works, which were done in you, had been done in Tyre and Sidon, they would have repented long ago in sackcloth and ashes.

22. But I say unto you, It shall be more tolerable for Tyre and Sidon at the day of judgment, than for you.

23. And thou, Capernaum, which art exalted unto heaven,

shalt be brought down to hell: for if the mighty works, which have been done in thee, had been done in Sodom, it would have remained until this day.

24. But I say unto you, That it shall be more tolerable for the land of Sodom in the day of judgment, than for thee.

25. ¶ At that time Jesus answered and said, I thank thee, O Father, Lord of heaven and earth, because thou hast hid these things from the wise and prudent, and hast revealed them unto babes.

26. Even so, Father: for so it seemed good in thy sight.

27. All things are delivered unto me of my Father: and no man knoweth the Son, but the Father; neither knoweth any man the Father, save the Son, and *he* to whomsoever the Son will reveal *him*.

28. ¶ Come unto me, all *ye* that labour and are heavy laden, and I will give you rest.

29. Take my yoke upon you, and learn of me; for I am meek and lowly in heart: and ye shall find rest unto your souls.

30. For my yoke *is* easy, and my burden is light.

Mark: No record.

LUKE 7:18. And the disciples of John shewed him of all these things.

19. ¶ And John calling *unto him* two of his disciples sent *them* to Jesus, saying, Art thou he that should come? or look we for another?

20. When the men were come unto him, they said, John Baptist hath sent us unto thee, saying, Art thou he that should come? or look we for another?

21. And in that same hour he cured many of *their* infirmities and plagues, and of evil spirits; and unto many *that were* blind he gave sight.

22. Then Jesus answering said unto them, Go your way, and tell John what things ye have seen and heard; how that the blind see, the lame walk, the lepers are cleansed, the deaf hear, the dead are raised, to the poor the gospel is preached.

23. And blessed is *he*, whosoever shall not be offended in me.

24. ¶ And when the messengers of John were departed, he began to speak unto the people concerning John, What went ye out into the wilderness for to see? A reed shaken with the wind?

25. But what went ye out for to see? A man clothed in soft raiment? Behold, they which are gorgeously apparelled, and live delicately, are in kings' courts.

26. But what went ye out for to see? A prophet? Yea, I say unto you, and much more than a prophet.

27. This is *he*, of whom it is written, Behold, I send my messenger before thy face, which shall prepare thy way before thee.

28. For I say unto you, Among those that are born of women there is not a greater prophet than John the Baptist: but he that is least in the kingdom of God is greater than he.

29. And all the people that heard *him*, and the publicans, justified God, being baptized with the baptism of John.

30. But the Pharisees and lawyers rejected the counsel of God against themselves, being not baptized of him.

31. ¶ And the Lord said, Whereunto then shall I liken the men of this generation? and to what are they like?

32. They are like unto children sitting in the marketplace, and calling one to another, and saying, We have piped unto you, and ye have not danced; we have mourned to you, and ye have not wept.

33. For John the Baptist came neither eating bread nor drinking wine; and ye say, He hath a devil.

34. The Son of man is come eating and drinking; and ye say, Behold a gluttonous man, and a winebibber, a friend of publicans and sinners!

35. But wisdom is justified of all her children.

John: No record.

Section 64

JESUS ANOINTED BY SINNING WOMAN

After his discourse about John, Jesus, being desired of a Pharisee, Simon, goes with him to his house to eat with him; a sinner, a woman, comes with an alabaster box of ointment and while washing his feet with her tears and kissing his feet, she anoints them with ointment; the Pharisee reasons that if Jesus were a prophet, he would know what manner of woman this is; Jesus, reading his thoughts, states the parable of the two debtors, both forgiven, and asks which will love him most; Simon answers the one who owed most; Jesus then reproves Simon for his failure to keep the rules of hospitality, and forgives the woman's sins; those at the table ask who is this that forgives sins; Jesus tells the woman that her faith has saved her and that she may go in peace.

Matt.: No record; Mark: No record; Luke 7:36-50; John: No record.
Time: A.D. 28, Autumn (ANDREWS).
Place: Galilee (ANDREWS).

Matthew: No record.

Mark: No record.

LUKE 7:36. ¶ And one of the Pharisees desired him that he would eat with him. And he went into the Pharisee's house, and sat down to meat.

37. And, behold, a woman in the city, which was a sinner, when she knew that *Jesus* sat at meat in the Pharisee's house, brought an alabaster box of ointment,

38. And stood at his feet be-

hind *him* weeping, and began to wash his feet with tears, and did wipe *them* with the hairs of her head, and kissed his feet, and anointed *them* with the ointment.

39. Now when the Pharisee which had bidden him saw *it*, he spake within himself, saying, This man, if he were a prophet, would have known who and what manner of woman *this is* that toucheth him: for she is a sinner.

40. And Jesus answering said unto him, Simon, I have somewhat to say unto thee. And he saith, Master, say on.

41. There was a certain creditor which had two debtors: the one owed five hundred pence, and the other fifty.

42. And when they had nothing to pay, he frankly forgave them both. Tell me therefore, which of them will love him most?

43. Simon answered and said, I suppose that *he*, to whom he forgave most. And he said unto him, Thou hast rightly judged.

44. And he turned to the woman, and said unto Simon, Seest thou this woman? I entered into thine house, thou gavest me no water for my feet: but she hath washed my feet with tears, and wiped *them* with the hairs of her head.

45. Thou gavest me no kiss: but this woman since the time I came in hath not ceased to kiss my feet.

46. My head with oil thou didst not anoint: but this woman hath anointed my feet with ointment.

47. Wherefore I say unto thee, Her sins, which are many, are forgiven; for she loved much: but to whom little is forgiven, *the same* loveth little.

48. And he said unto her, Thy sins are forgiven.

49. And they that sat at meat with him began to say within themselves, Who is this that forgiveth sins also?

50. And he said to the woman, Thy faith hath saved thee; go in peace.

John: No record.

Section 65

ANOTHER TOUR OF GALILEE

Jesus makes a tour throughout Galilee, preaching to the people; he takes with him the Twelve, Mary Magdalene, Joanna the wife of Chuza, Herod's steward, and many others "which ministered unto him of their substance."

Matt.: No record; Mark: No record; Luke 8:1-3; John: No record.
Time: A.D. 28, Autumn (ANDREWS).
Place: Galilee (ANDREWS).

Matthew: No record.

Mark: No record.

LUKE 8:1. And it came to pass afterward, that he went throughout every city and village, preaching and shewing the glad tidings of the kingdom of God: and the twelve *were* with him,

2. And certain women, which had been healed of evil spirits and infirmities, Mary called Magdalene, out of whom went seven devils,

3. And Joanna the wife of Chuza Herod's steward, and Susanna, and many others, which ministered unto him of their substance.

John: No record.

Section 66

BLIND AND DUMB MAN HEALED

Jesus heals a blind and dumb man, possessed with a devil, so that the man both speaks and sees; the people are amazed, and say, "Is not this the son of David?"

Matt. 12:22-23; Mark: No record; Luke: No record; John: No record.
Time: A.D. 28, Autumn (ANDREWS).
Place: Capernaum (ANDREWS).

MATTHEW 12:22. ¶ Then was brought unto him one possessed with a devil, blind, and dumb: and he healed him, insomuch that the blind and dumb both spake and saw.

23. And all the people were amazed, and said, Is not this the son of David?

Mark: No record.

Luke: No record.

John: No record.

Section 67

THEY CHARGE HE IS IN LEAGUE WITH BEELZEBUB

The Pharisees and the scribes who came down from Jerusalem, seeing Jesus heal the blind and dumb man possessed with a devil, charge that Jesus is casting out devils by the power of Beelzebub, the prince of devils; Jesus shows, by stating the principle and explaining it (that a house divided against itself cannot stand), that he is not working under the power of the devil but under the power of God; he says that blasphemy against the Holy Ghost will not be forgiven; says that out of the abundance of the heart the mouth speaketh and that man must give account for every idle word.

Matt. 12:24-37; Mark 3:22-30; Luke: No record; John: No record.
Time: A.D. 28, Autumn (ANDREWS).
Place: Capernaum (ANDREWS).

MATTHEW 12:24. But when the Pharisees heard *it*, they said, This *fellow* doth not cast out devils, but by Beelzebub the prince of the devils.

25. And Jesus knew their thoughts, and said unto them, Every kingdom divided against itself is brought to desolation; and every city or house divided against itself shall not stand:

26. And if Satan cast out Satan, he is divided against himself; how shall then his kingdom stand?

27. And if I by Beelzebub cast out devils, by whom do your children cast *them* out? therefore they shall be your judges.

28. But if I cast out devils by the Spirit of God, then the kingdom of God is come unto you.

29. Or else how can one enter into a strong man's house, and spoil his goods, except he first bind the strong man? and then he will spoil his house.

30. He that is not with me is against me; and he that gathereth not with me scattereth abroad.

31. ¶ Wherefore I say unto you, All manner of sin and blasphemy shall be forgiven unto men: but the blasphemy *against* the *Holy* Ghost shall not be forgiven unto men.

32. And whosoever speaketh a word against the Son of man, it shall be forgiven him: but whosoever speaketh against the Holy Ghost, it shall not be forgiven him, neither in this world, neither in the *world* to come.

33. Either make the tree good, and his fruit good; or else make the tree corrupt, and his fruit corrupt: for the tree is known by *his* fruit.

34. O generation of vipers, how can ye, being evil, speak good things? for out of the abundance of the heart the mouth speaketh.

35. A good man out of the good treasure of the heart bringeth forth good things: and an evil man out of the evil treasure bringeth forth evil things.

36. But I say unto you, That every idle word that men shall speak, they shall give account thereof in the day of judgment.

37. For by thy words thou shalt be justified, and by thy words thou shalt be condemned.

MARK 3:22. ¶ And the scribes which came down from Jerusalem said, He hath Beelzebub, and by the prince of the devils casteth he out devils.

23. And he called them *unto him*, and said unto them in parables, How can Satan cast out Satan?

24. And if a kingdom be divided against itself, that kingdom cannot stand.

25. And if a house be divided

against itself, that house cannot stand.

26. And if Satan rise up against himself, and be divided, he cannot stand, but hath an end.

27. No man can enter into a strong man's house, and spoil his goods, except he will first bind the strong man; and then he will spoil his house.

28. Verily I say unto you, All sins shall be forgiven unto the sons of men, and blasphemies wherewith soever they shall blaspheme:

29. But he that shall blaspheme against the Holy Ghost hath never forgiveness, but is in danger of eternal damnation:

30. Because they said, He hath an unclean spirit.

Luke: No record.

John: No record.

Section 68

JESUS DISCOURSES ON SIGNS

Jesus having denied he was in league with Beelzebub, certain of the scribes and of the Pharisees "answered, saying, Master, we would see a sign from thee"; Jesus answers, "an evil and adulterous generation seeketh after a sign," and states none shall be given, except the sign of Jonas; he predicts his death, burial, and resurrection; compares the people of Nineveh and the queen of the south to "this generation"; and closes with a parable.

Matt. 12:38-45; Mark: No record; Luke: No record; John: No record.
Time: A.D. 28, Autumn (ANDREWS).
Place: Capernaum (ANDREWS).

MATTHEW 12:38. ¶ Then certain of the scribes and of the Pharisees answered, saying, Master, we would see a sign from thee.

39. But he answered and said unto them, An evil and adulterous generation seeketh after a sign; and there shall no sign be given to it, but the sign of the prophet Jonas:

40. For as Jonas was three days and three nights in the whale's belly; so shall the Son of man be three days and three nights in the heart of the earth.

41. The men of Nineveh shall rise in judgment with this generation, and shall condemn it: because they repented at the preaching of Jonas; and, behold, a greater than Jonas *is* here.

42. The queen of the south shall rise up in the judgment with this generation, and shall condemn it: for she came from the uttermost parts of the earth to hear the wisdom of Solomon; and, behold, a greater than Solomon *is* here.

43. When the unclean spirit is gone out of a man, he walk-

eth through dry places, seeking rest, and findeth none.

44. Then he saith, I will return into my house from whence I came out; and when he is come, he findeth *it* empty, swept, and garnished.

45. Then goeth he, and taketh with himself seven other spirits more wicked than himself, and they enter in and dwell there: and the last *state* of that man is worse than the first. Even so shall it be also unto this wicked generation.

Mark: No record.

Luke: No record.

John: No record.

Section 69

HIS MOTHER AND BRETHREN SEEK HIM

While still speaking with the people, his mother and brethren come to see him, but can not get to him for the press of the poeple; being told they seek him, he asks, "Who is my mother, or my brethren?" and then states the larger relationship—"Whosoever shall do the will of God, the same is my brother, and my sister, and mother."

Matt. 12:46-50; Mark 3:31-35; Luke 8:19-21; John: No record.
Time: A.D. 28, Autumn (ANDREWS).
Place: Galilee (ANDREWS).

MATTHEW 12:46. ¶ While he yet talked to the people, behold, *his* mother and his brethren stood without, desiring to speak with him.

47. Then one said unto him, Behold, thy mother and thy brethren stand without, desiring to speak with thee.

48. But he answered and said unto him that told him, Who is my mother? and who are my brethren?

49. And he stretched forth his hand toward his disciples, and said, Behold my mother and my brethren!

50. For whosoever shall do the will of my Father which is in heaven, the same is my brother, and sister, and mother.

MARK 3:31. ¶ There came then his brethren and his mother, and, standing without, sent unto him, calling him.

32. And the multitude sat about him, and they said unto him, Behold, thy mother and thy brethren without seek for thee.

33. And he answered them, saying, Who is my mother, or my brethren?

34. And he looked round about on them which sat about him, and said, Behold my mother and my brethren!

35. For whosoever shall do the will of God, the same is my brother, and my sister, and mother.

LUKE 8:19. ¶ Then came to him *his* mother and his brethren, and could not come at him for the press.

20. And it was told him *by certain* which said, Thy mother and thy brethren stand without, desiring to see thee.

21. And he answered and said unto them, My mother and my brethren are these which hear the word of God, and do it.

John: No record.

Section 70

THE MULTITUDES TAUGHT BY PARABLES

Jesus, on the same day, leaving the house, goes and sits by the seaside; great multitudes out of every city gather; he takes a seat in a ship, the multitude stand on the shore; he teaches them in parables.

Matt. 13:1-3a; Mark 4:1-2; Luke 8:4; John: No record.

Time: A.D. 28, Autumn (ANDREWS).

Place: Sea of Galilee (ANDREWS).

MATTHEW 13:1. The same day went Jesus out of the house, and sat by the sea side.

2. And great multitudes were gathered together unto him, so that he went into a ship, and sat; and the whole multitude stood on the shore.

3. And he spake many things unto them in parables, saying....

MARK 4:1. And he began again to teach by the sea side: and there was gathered unto him a great multitude, so that he entered into a ship, and sat in the sea; and the whole multitude was by the sea on the land.

2. And he taught them many things by parables, and said unto them in his doctrine, . . .

LUKE 8:4. ¶ And when much people were gathered together, and were come to him out of every city, he spake by a parable: . . .

John: No record.

(a) Parable of the Sower

Matt. 13:3b-23; Mark 4:3-25; Luke 8:5-18; John: No record.

MATTHEW 13:3 . . . . Behold, a sower went forth to sow;

4. And when he sowed, some *seeds* fell by the way side, and the fowls came and devoured them up:

5. Some fell upon stony places, where they had not much earth: and forthwith they sprung up, because they had no deepness of earth:

6. And when the sun was up, they were scorched; and because they had no root, they withered away.

7. And some fell among thorns; and the thorns sprung up, and choked them:

8. But other fell into good ground, and brought forth fruit, some an hundredfold, some sixtyfold, some thirty-fold.

9. Who hath ears to hear, let him hear.

10. And the disciples came, and said unto him, Why speakest thou unto them in parables?

11. He answered and said unto them, Because it is given unto you to know the mysteries of the kingdom of heaven, but to them it is not given.

12. For whosoever hath, to him shall be given, and he shall have more abundance: but whosoever hath not, from him shall be taken away even that he hath.

13. Therefore speak I to them in parables: because they seeing see not; and hearing they hear not, neither do they understand.

14. And in them is fulfilled the prophecy of Esaias, which saith, By hearing ye shall hear, and shall not understand; and seeing ye shall see, and shall not perceive:

15. For this people's heart is waxed gross, and *their* ears are dull of hearing, and their eyes they have closed; lest at any time they should see with *their* eyes, and hear with *their* ears, and should understand with *their* heart, and should be converted, and I should heal them.

16. But blessed *are* your eyes, for they see: and your ears, for they hear.

17. For verily I say unto you, That many prophets and righteous *men* have desired to see *those things* which ye see, and have not seen *them;* and to hear *those things* which ye hear, and have not heard *them.*

18. ¶ Hear ye therefore the parable of the sower.

19. When any one heareth the word of the kingdom, and understandeth *it* not, then cometh the wicked *one*, and catcheth away that which was sown in his heart. This is he which received seed by the way side.

20. But he that received the seed into stony places, the same is he that heareth the word, and anon with joy receiveth it;

21. Yet hath he not root in himself, but dureth for a while: for when tribulation or persecution ariseth because of the word, by and by he is offended.

22. He also that received seed among the thorns is he that heareth the word; and the care of this world, and the deceitfulness of riches, choke the word, and he becometh unfruitful.

23. But he that received seed into the good ground is he that heareth the word, and understandeth *it;* which also beareth fruit, and bringeth forth, some

an hundredfold, some sixty, some thirty.

MARK 4:3. Hearken; Behold, there went out a sower to sow:

4. And it came to pass, as he sowed, some fell by the way side, and the fowls of the air came and devoured it up.

5. And some fell on stony ground, where it had not much earth; and immediately it sprang up, because it had no depth of earth:

6. But when the sun was up, it was scorched; and because it had no root, it withered away.

7. And some fell among thorns, and the thorns grew up, and choked it, and it yielded no fruit.

8. And other fell on good ground, and did yield fruit that sprang up and increased; and brought forth, some thirty, and some sixty, and some an hundred.

9. And he said unto them, He that hath ears to hear, let him hear.

10. And when he was alone, they that were about him with the twelve asked of him the parable.

11. And he said unto them, Unto you it is given to know the mystery of the kingdom of God: but unto them that are without, all *these* things are done in parables:

12. That seeing they may see, and not perceive; and hearing they may hear, and not understand; lest at any time they should be converted, and *their* sins should be forgiven them.

13. And he said unto them, Know ye not this parable? and how then will ye know all parables?

14. ¶ The sower soweth the word.

15. And these are they by the way side, where the word is sown; but when they have heard, Satan cometh immediately, and taketh away the word that was sown in their hearts.

16. And these are they likewise which are sown on stony ground; who, when they have heard the word, immediately receive it with gladness;

17. And have no root in themselves, and so endure but for a time: afterward, when affliction or persecution ariseth for the word's sake, immediately they are offended.

18. And these are they which are sown among thorns; such as hear the word,

19. And the cares of this world, and the deceitfulness of riches, and the lusts of other things entering in, choke the word, and it becometh unfruitful.

20. And these are they which are sown on good ground; such as hear the word, and receive *it*, and bring forth fruit, some thirtyfold, some sixty, and some an hundred.

21. ¶ And he said unto them, Is a candle brought to be put under a bushel, or under a bed? and not to be set on a candlestick?

22. For there is nothing hid, which shall not be manifested; neither was any thing kept secret, but that it should come abroad.

23. If any man have ears to hear, let him hear.

24. And he said unto them, Take heed what ye hear: with what measure ye mete, it shall be measured to you: and unto you that hear shall more be given.

25. For he that hath, to him shall be given: and he that hath not, from him shall be taken even that which he hath.

LUKE 8:5. A sower went out to sow his seed: and as he sowed, some fell by the way side; and it was trodden down, and the fowls of the air devoured it.

6. And some fell upon a rock; and as soon as it was sprung up, it withered away, because it lacked moisture.

7. And some fell among thorns; and the thorns sprang up with it, and choked it.

8. And other fell on good ground, and sprang up, and bare fruit an hundredfold. And when he had said these things, he cried, He that hath ears to hear, let him hear.

9. And his disciples asked him, saying, What might this parable be?

10. And he said, Unto you it is given to know the mysteries of the kingdom of God: but to others in parables; that seeing they might not see, and hearing they might not understand.

11. Now the parable is this: The seed is the word of God.

12. Those by the way side are they that hear; then cometh the devil, and taketh away the word out of their hearts, lest they should believe and be saved.

13. They on the rock *are they*, which, when they hear, receive the word with joy; and these have no root, which for a while believe, and in time of temptation fall away.

14. And that which fell among thorns are they, which, when they have heard, go forth, and are choked with cares and riches and pleasures of *this* life, and bring no fruit to perfection.

15. But that on the good ground are they, which in an honest and good heart, having heard the word, keep *it*, and bring forth fruit with patience.

16. ¶ No man, when he hath lighted a candle, covereth it with a vessel, or putteth *it* under a bed; but setteth *it* on a candlestick, that they which enter in may see the light.

17. For nothing is secret, that shall not be made mani-

fest; neither *any thing* hid, that shall not be known and come abroad.

18. Take heed therefore how ye hear: for whosoever hath, to him shall be given; and whosoever hath not, from him shall be taken even that which he seemeth to have.

John: No record.

(b) Parable of the Seed Growing by Itself

Matt.: No record; Mark 4:26-29; Luke: No record; John: No record.

Matthew: No record.

MARK 4:26. ¶ And he said, So is the kingdom of God, as if a man should cast seed into the ground;

27. And should sleep, and rise night and day, and the seed should spring and grow up, he knoweth not how.

28. For the earth bringeth forth fruit of herself; first the blade, then the ear, after that the full corn in the ear.

29. But when the fruit is brought forth, immediately he putteth in the sickle, because the harvest is come.

Luke: No record.

John: No record.

(c) Parable of the Tares

Matt. 13:24-30; Mark: No record; Luke: No record; John: No record.

MATTHEW 13:24. ¶Another parable put he forth unto them, saying, The kingdom of heaven is likened unto a man which sowed good seed in his field:

25. But while men slept, his enemy came and sowed tares among the wheat, and went his way.

26. But when the blade was sprung up, and brought forth fruit, then appeared the tares also.

27. So the servants of the householder came and said unto him, Sir, didst not thou sow good seed in thy field? from whence then hath it tares?

28. He said unto them, An enemy hath done this. The servants said unto him, Wilt thou then that we go and gather them up?

29. But he said, Nay; lest while ye gather up the tares, ye root up also the wheat with them.

30. Let both grow together until the harvest: and in the time of harvest I will say to the reapers, Gather ye together first the tares, and bind them in bundles to burn them: but gather the wheat into my barn.

Mark: No record.

Luke: No record.

John: No record.

(d) Parable of the Mustard Seed and the Leaven

Matt. 13:31-35; Mark 4:30-34; Luke: No record; John: No record.

MATTHEW 13:31. ¶ Another parable put he forth unto them, saying, The kingdom of heaven is like to a grain of mustard seed, which a man took, and sowed in his field:

32. Which indeed is the least of all seeds: but when it is grown, it is the greatest among herbs, and becometh a tree, so that the birds of the air come and lodge in the branches thereof.

33. ¶Another parable spake he unto them; The kingdom of heaven is like unto leaven, which a woman took, and hid in three measures of meal, till the whole was leavened.

34. All these things spake Jesus unto the multitude in parables; and without a parable spake he not unto them:

35. That it might be fulfilled which was spoken by the prophet, saying, I will open my mouth in parables; I will utter things which have been kept secret from the foundation of the world.

MARK 4:30. ¶ And he said, Whereunto shall we liken the kingdom of God? or with what comparison shall we compare it?

31. *It is* like a grain of mustard seed, which, when it is sown in the earth, is less than all the seeds that be in the earth:

32. But when it is sown, it groweth up, and becometh greater than all herbs, and shooteth out great branches; so that the fowls of the air may lodge under the shadow of it.

33. And with many such parables spake he the word unto them, as they were able to hear *it*.

34. But without a parable spake he not unto them: and when they were alone, he expounded all things to his disciples.

Luke: No record.

John: No record.

(e) Parable of the Tares Explained

Matt. 13:36-43; Mark: No record; Luke: No record; John: No record.

MATTHEW 13:36. Then Jesus sent the multitude away, and went into the house: and his disciples came unto him, saying, Declare unto us the parable of the tares of the field.

37. He answered and said unto them, He that soweth the good seed is the Son of man;

38. The field is the world; the good seed are the children of the kingdom; but the tares

are the children of the wicked *one;*

39. The enemy that sowed them is the devil; the harvest is the end of the world; and the reapers are the angels.

40. As therefore the tares are gathered and burned in the fire; so shall it be in the end of this world.

41. The Son of man shall send forth his angels, and they shall gather out of his kingdom all things that offend, and them which do iniquity;

42. And shall cast them into a furnace of fire: there shall be wailing and gnashing of teeth.

43. Then shall the righteous shine forth as the sun in the kingdom of their Father. Who hath ears to hear, let him hear.

Mark: No record.

Luke: No record.

John: No record.

(f) Other Parables

Matt. 13:44-53; Mark: No record; Luke: No record; John: No record.

MATTHEW 13:44. ¶ Again, the kingdom of heaven is like unto treasure hid in a field; the which when a man hath found, he hideth, and for joy thereof goeth and selleth all that he hath, and buyeth that field.

45. ¶ Again, the kingdom of heaven is like unto a merchant man, seeking goodly pearls:

46. Who, when he had found one pearl of great price, went and sold all that he had, and bought it.

47. ¶ Again, the kingdom of heaven is like unto a net, that was cast into the sea, and gathered of every kind:

48. Which, when it was full, they drew to shore, and sat down, and gathered the good into vessels, but cast the bad away.

49. So shall it be at the end of the world: the angels shall come forth, and sever the wicked from among the just,

50. And shall cast them into the furnace of fire: there shall be wailing and gnashing of teeth.

51. Jesus saith unto them, Have ye understood all these things? They say unto him, Yea, Lord.

52. Then said he unto them, Therefore every scribe *which is* instructed unto the kingdom of heaven is like unto a man *that is* an householder, which bringeth forth out of his treasure *things* new and old.

53. ¶And it came to pass, *that* when Jesus had finished these parables, he departed thence.

Mark: No record.

Luke: No record.

John: No record.

Section 71

THE STORM STILLED

Jesus seeing great multitudes about him, gives commandment to depart to the other side of the lake; a scribe desiring to follow, Jesus says the foxes have holes, but the Son of man has nowhere to lay his head; a disciple asks to bury his father before going, Jesus says let the dead bury their dead; along with the ship in which Jesus is, other little ships go; he falls asleep, a great storm arises, the ship fills with water, the disciples awaken him saying, "Lord, save us: we perish." He rebukes the wind and the raging water, a calm comes; he reproves them for their lack of faith.

Matt. 8:18-27; **Mark** 4:35-41; **Luke** 8:22-25; **John: No record.**
Time: A.D. 28, Autumn (ANDREWS).
Place: Sea of Galilee.

MATTHEW 8:18. ¶ Now when Jesus saw great multitudes about him, he gave commandment to depart unto the other side.

19. And a certain scribe came, and said unto him, Master, I will follow thee whithersoever thou goest.

20. And Jesus saith unto him, The foxes have holes, and the birds of the air *have* nests; but the Son of man hath not where to lay *his* head.

21. And another of his disciples said unto him, Lord, suffer me first to go and bury my father.

22. But Jesus said unto him, Follow me; and let the dead bury their dead.

23. ¶ And when he was entered into a ship, his disciples followed him.

24. And, behold, there arose a great tempest in the sea, insomuch that the ship was covered with the waves: but he was asleep.

25. And his disciples came to *him*, and awoke him, saying, Lord, save us: we perish.

26. And he saith unto them, Why are ye fearful, O ye of little faith? Then he arose, and rebuked the winds and the sea; and there was a great calm.

27. But the men marvelled, saying, What manner of man is this, that even the winds and the sea obey him!

MARK 4:35. And the same day, when the even was come, he saith unto them, Let us pass over unto the other side.

36. And when they had sent away the multitude, they took him even as he was in the ship. And there were also with him other little ships.

37. And there arose a great storm of wind, and the waves beat into the ship, so that it was now full.

38. And he was in the hinder part of the ship, asleep on a pillow: and they awake him,

and say unto him, Master, carest thou not that we perish?

39. And he arose, and rebuked the wind, and said unto the sea, Peace, be still. And the wind ceased, and there was a great calm.

40. And he said unto them, Why are ye so fearful? how is it that ye have no faith?

41. And they feared exceedingly, and said one to another, What manner of man is this, that even the wind and the sea obey him?

LUKE 8:22. ¶ Now it came to pass on a certain day, that he went into a ship with his disciples: and he said unto them, Let us go over unto the other side of the lake. And they launched forth.

23. But as they sailed he fell asleep: and there came down a storm of wind on the lake; and they were filled *with water*, and were in jeopardy.

24. And they came to him, and awoke him, saying, Master, master, we perish. Then he arose, and rebuked the wind and the raging of the water: and they ceased, and there was a calm.

25. And he said unto them, Where is your faith? And they being afraid wondered, saying one to another, What manner of man in this! for he commandeth even the winds and water, and they obey him.

John: No record.

Section 72

THE GADARENE DEMONIACS

Crossing to the southerly coast of the Sea of Galilee, Jesus comes to the country of the Gadarenes; as he goes forth he meets two possessed with devils, who hail him as Jesus, Son of God and ask why he torments them before their time, and beseech him not to command them to go out into the deep but let them enter a nearby herd of some two thousand swine; Jesus permits this and the swine rush down into the sea and perish; the herders tell the people of the city who come out to see him, and seeing what has happened, they beseech Jesus to leave their country.

Matt. 8:28-34; Mark 5:1-20; Luke 8:26-39; John: No record.

Time: A.D. 28, Autumn (ANDREWS).

Place: Gadara.

MATTHEW 8:28. ¶And when he was come to the other side into the country of the Gergesenes, there met him two possessed with devils, coming out of the tombs, exceeding fierce, so that no man might pass by that way.

29. And, behold, they cried out, saying, What have we to

do with thee, Jesus, thou Son of God? art thou come hither to torment us before the time?

30. And there was a good way off from them an herd of many swine feeding.

31. So the devils besought him, saying, If thou cast us out, suffer us to go away into the herd of swine.

32. And he said unto them, Go. And when they were come out, they went into the herd of swine: and, behold, the whole herd of swine ran violently down a steep place into the sea, and perished in the waters.

33. And they that kept them fled, and went their ways into the city, and told every thing, and what was befallen to the possessed of the devils.

34. And, behold, the whole city came out to meet Jesus: and when they saw him, they besought *him* that he would depart out of their coasts.

MARK 5:1. And they came over unto the other side of the sea, into the country of the Gadarenes.

2. And when he was come out of the ship, immediately there met him out of the tombs a man with an unclean spirit,

3. Who had *his* dwelling among the tombs; and no man could bind him, no, not with chains:

4. Because that he had been often bound with fetters and chains, and the chains had been plucked asunder by him, and the fetters broken in pieces: neither could any *man* tame him.

5. And always, night and day, he was in the mountains, and in the tombs, crying, and cutting himself with stones.

6. But when he saw Jesus afar off, he ran and worshipped him,

7. And cried with a loud voice, and said, What have I to do with thee, Jesus, *thou* Son of the most high God? I adjure thee by God, that thou torment me not.

8. For he said unto him, Come out of the man, *thou* unclean spirit.

9. And he asked him, What *is* thy name? And he answered, saying, My name *is* Legion: for we are many.

10. And he besought him much that he would not send them away out of the country.

11. Now there was there nigh unto the mountains a great herd of swine feeding.

12. And all the devils besought him, saying, Send us into the swine, that we may enter into them.

13. And forthwith Jesus gave them leave. And the unclean spirits went out, and entered into the swine: and the herd ran violently down a steep place into the sea, (they were about two thousand;) and were choked in the sea.

14. And they that fed the

swine fled, and told *it* in the city, and in the country. And they went out to see what it was that was done.

15. And they come to Jesus, and see him that was possessed with the devil, and had the legion, sitting, and clothed, and in his right mind: and they were afraid.

16. And they that saw *it* told them how it befell to him that was possessed with the devil, and *also* concerning the swine.

17. And they began to pray him to depart out of their coasts.

18. And when he was come into the ship, he that had been possessed with the devil prayed him that he might be with him.

19. Howbeit Jesus suffered him not, but saith unto him, Go home to thy friends, and tell them how great things the Lord hath done for thee, and hath had compassion on thee.

20. And he departed, and began to publish in Decapolis how great things Jesus had done for him: and all *men* did marvel.

LUKE 8:26. ¶ And they arrived at the country of the Gadarenes, which is over against Galilee.

27. And when he went forth to land, there met him out of the city a certain man, which had devils long time, and ware no clothes, neither abode in *any* house, but in the tombs.

28. When he saw Jesus, he cried out, and fell down before him, and with a loud voice said, What have I to do with thee, Jesus, *thou* Son of God most high? I beseech thee, torment me not.

29. (For he had commanded the unclean spirit to come out of the man. For oftentimes it had caught him: and he was kept bound with chains and in fetters; and he brake the bands, and was driven of the devil into the wilderness.)

30. And Jesus asked him, saying, What is thy name? And he said, Legion: because many devils were entered into him.

31. And they besought him that he would not command them to go out into the deep.

32. And there was there an herd of many swine feeding on the mountain: and they besought him that he would suffer them to enter into them. And he suffered them.

33. Then went the devils out of the man, and entered into the swine: and the herd ran violently down a steep place into the lake, and were choked.

34. When they that fed *them* saw what was done, they fled, and went and told *it* in the city and in the country.

35. Then they went out to see what was done; and came to Jesus, and found the man, out of whom the devils were departed, sitting at the feet of

Jesus, clothed, and in his right mind: and they were afraid.

36. They also which saw *it* told them by what means he that was possessed of the devils was healed.

37. ¶ Then the whole multitude of the country of the Gadarenes round about besought him to depart from them; for they were taken with great fear: and he went up into the ship, and returned back again.

38. Now the man out of whom the devils were departed besought him that he might be with him: but Jesus sent him away, saying,

39. Return to thine own house, and shew how great things God hath done unto thee. And he went his way, and published throughout the whole city how great things Jesus had done unto him.

John: No record.

Section 73

JESUS RETURNS TO CAPERNAUM

Jesus enters into a ship and returns to the coast of Capernaum, much people gladly receive him for they are all waiting for him, and he was nigh unto the sea.

Matt. 9:1; **Mark** 5:21; **Luke** 8:40; **John: No record.**
Time: A.D. 28, Autumn (ANDREWS).
Place: Sea of Galilee to Capernaum.

MATTHEW 9:1. And he entered into a ship, and passed over, and came into his own city.

MARK 5:21. And when Jesus was passed over again by ship unto the other side, much people gathered unto him: and he was nigh unto the sea.

LUKE 8:40. And it came to pass, that, when Jesus was returned, the people *gladly* received him: for they were all waiting for him.

John: No record.

Section 74

THE DAUGHTER OF JAIRUS RAISED

Jairus, a ruler of the synagogue, whose daughter lies dying, comes and asks Jesus to come and lay his hands on her that she may live; while they are on the way, messengers come saying the daughter is dead; Jesus bids Jairus have faith, saying all will be well; reaching the house Jesus tells the people there that the child is not dead but sleeps; they laugh him to scorn; taking Peter, James, and John, and the father and mother into the room with him, and putting all others out, he takes the daughter by the hand and commands her to rise; she rises straightway and he commands that they give her something to eat and charges them they shall tell no man what was done.

Matt. 9:18-19, 23-26; Mark 5:22-24, 35-43; Luke 8:41-42, 49-56; John: No record.
Time: A.D. 28, Autumn (ANDREWS).
Place: Capernaum.

MATTHEW 9:18. ¶While he spake these things unto them, behold, there came a certain ruler, and worshipped him, saying, My daughter is even now dead: but come and lay thy hand upon her, and she shall live.

19. And Jesus arose, and followed him, and *so did* his disciples . . . .

23. And when Jesus came into the ruler's house, and saw the minstrels and the people making a noise,

24. He said unto them, Give place: for the maid is not dead, but sleepeth. And they laughed him to scorn.

25. But when the people were put forth, he went in, and took her by the hand, and the maid arose.

26. And the fame hereof went abroad into all that land.

MARK 5:22. And, behold, there cometh one of the rulers of the synagogue, Jairus by name; and when he saw him, he fell at his feet,

23. And besought him greatly, saying, My little daughter lieth at the point of death: *I pray thee,* come and lay thy hands on her, that she may be healed; and she shall live.

24. And *Jesus* went with him; and much people followed him, and thronged him . . . .

35. While he yet spake, there came from the ruler of the synagogue's *house certain* which said, Thy daughter is dead: why troublest thou the Master any further?

36. As soon as Jesus heard the word that was spoken, he saith unto the ruler of the synagogue, Be not afraid, only believe.

37. And he suffered no man to follow him, save Peter, and James, and John the brother of James.

38. And he cometh to the house of the ruler of the synagogue, and seeth the tumult, and them that wept and wailed greatly.

39. And when he was come in, he saith unto them, Why make ye this ado, and weep? the damsel is not dead, but sleepeth.

40. And they laughed him to scorn. But when he had put them all out, he taketh the father and the mother of the damsel, and them that were with him, and entereth in where the damsel was lying.

41. And he took the damsel by the hand, and said unto her, Talitha cumi; which is, being interpreted, Damsel, I say unto thee, arise.

42. And straightway the damsel arose, and walked; for

she was *of the age* of twelve years. And they were astonished with a great astonishment.

43. And he charged them straitly that no man should know it; and commanded that something should be given her to eat.

LUKE 8:41. ¶ And, behold, there came a man named Jairus, and he was a ruler of the synagogue: and he fell down at Jesus' feet, and besought him that he would come into his house:

42. For he had one only daughter, about twelve years of age, and she lay a dying. But as he went the people thronged him . . . .

49. ¶While he yet spake, there cometh one from the ruler of the synagogue's *house*, saying to him, Thy daughter is dead; trouble not the Master.

50. But when Jesus heard *it*, he answered him, saying, Fear not: believe only, and she shall be made whole.

51. And when he came into the house, he suffered no man to go in, save Peter, and James, and John, and the father and the mother of the maiden.

52. And all wept, and bewailed her: but he said, Weep not; she is not dead, but sleepeth.

53. And they laughed him to scorn, knowing that she was dead.

54. And he put them all out, and took her by the hand, and called, saying, Maid, arise.

55. And her spirit came again, and she arose straightway: and he commanded to give her meat.

56. And her parents were astonished: but he charged them that they should tell no man what was done.

John: No record.

Section 75

THE WOMAN WITH THE ISSUE OF BLOOD HEALED

Jesus going through the crowd is touched on the garment by a woman who for twelve years has had an issue of blood and had "suffered many things of many physicians, and had spent all that she had, and was nothing bettered, but rather grew worse"; she has faith that if she touches only the garment of Jesus she will be healed; she touches his garment and is healed immediately; Jesus senses the touch for he says, "I perceive that virtue is gone out of me"; Jesus asks who touched him; the disciples saw no one, she then comes forward and falling down before him, tells all; he says, "Daughter, be of good comfort: thy faith hath made thee whole; go in peace."

Matt. 9:20-22; Mark 5:25-34; Luke 8:43-48; John: No record.
Time: A.D. 28, Autumn (ANDREWS).
Place: Capernaum.

MATTHEW 9:20. ¶And, behold, a woman, which was diseased with an issue of blood twelve years, came behind *him*, and touched the hem of his garment:

21. For she said within herself, If I may but touch his garment, I shall be whole.

22. But Jesus turned him about, and when he saw her, he said, Daughter, be of good comfort; thy faith hath made thee whole. And the woman was made whole from that hour.

MARK 5:25. And a certain woman, which had an issue of blood twelve years,

26. And had suffered many things of many physicians, and had spent all that she had, and was nothing bettered, but rather grew worse,

27. When she had heard of Jesus, came in the press behind, and touched his garment.

28. For she said, If I may touch but his clothes, I shall be whole.

29. And straightway the fountain of her blood was dried up; and she felt in *her* body that she was healed of that plague.

30. And Jesus, immediately knowing in himself that virtue had gone out of him, turned him about in the press, and said, Who touched my clothes?

31. And his disciples said unto him, Thou seest the multitude thronging thee, and sayest thou, Who touched me?

32. And he looked round about to see her that had done this thing.

33. But the woman fearing and trembling, knowing what was done in her, came and fell down before him, and told him all the truth.

34. And he said unto her, Daughter, thy faith hath made thee whole; go in peace, and be whole of thy plague.

LUKE 8:43. ¶ And a woman having an issue of blood twelve years, which had spent all her living upon physicians, neither could be healed of any,

44. Came behind *him*, and touched the border of his garment: and immediately her issue of blood stanched.

45. And Jesus said, Who touched me? When all denied, Peter and they that were with him said, Master, the multitude throng thee and press *thee*, and sayest thou, Who touched me?

46. And Jesus said, Somebody hath touched me: for I perceive that virtue is gone out of me.

47. And when the woman saw that she was not hid, she came trembling, and falling down before him, she declared unto him before all the people for what cause she had touched him, and how she was healed immediately.

48. And he said unto her, Daughter, be of good comfort: thy faith hath made thee whole; go in peace.

John: No record.

Section 76

TWO BLIND MEN HEALED

Two blind men follow Jesus, asking to be healed, he asks them if they believe he is able to do this, they say, "Yea, Lord"; he touches their eyes saying, "According to your faith be it unto you," and their eyes are opened; he charges them to tell no one, but they spread his fame abroad.

Matt. 9:27-31; Mark: No record; Luke: No record; John: No record.
Time: A.D. 28, Autumn (ANDREWS).
Place: Capernaum.

MATTHEW 9:27 ¶ And when Jesus departed thence, two blind men followed him, crying, and saying, *Thou* son of David, have mercy on us.

28. And when he was come into the house, the blind men came to him: and Jesus saith unto them, Believe ye that I am able to do this? They said unto him, Yea, Lord.

29. Then touched he their eyes, saying, According to your faith be it unto you.

30. And their eyes were opened; and Jesus straitly charged them, saying, See *that* no man know *it*.

31. But they, when they were departed, spread abroad his fame in all that country.

Mark: No record.

Luke: No record.

John: No record.

Section 77

THE DUMB DEMONIAC HEALED

As the blind men go out, they bring to Jesus a dumb man possessed with a devil; Jesus casts out the devil and the dumb man speaks; the multitude marvel, saying it was never seen in Israel; the Pharisees renew the charge that Jesus is in league with the devils.

Matt. 9:32-34; Mark: No record; Luke: No record; John: No record.
Time: A.D. 28, Autumn (ANDREWS).
Place: Capernaum.

MATTHEW 9:32. ¶As they went out, behold, they brought to him a dumb man possessed with a devil.

33. And when the devil was cast out, the dumb spake: and the multitudes marvelled, saying, It was never so seen in Israel.

34. But the Pharisees said, He casteth out devils through the prince of the devils.

Mark: No record.
Luke: No record.
John: No record.

Section 78

THE SECOND REJECTION AT NAZARETH

Jesus returns to Nazareth and teaches in the synagogue; the people marvel at him, his preaching, his works, they refer to the fact that his mother, his brothers, and sisters are still among them; he tells them a prophet is not without honor save in his own country, but he can there do no great works; "he laid his hands upon a few sick folk, and healed them"; he marvels because of their unbelief.

Matt. 13:54-58; Mark 6:1-6a; Luke: No record; John: No record.

Time: A.D. 29, Winter (ANDREWS).

Place: Nazareth.

MATTHEW 13:54. And when he was come into his own country, he taught them in their synagogue, insomuch that they were astonished, and said, Whence hath this *man* this wisdom, and *these* mighty works?

55. Is not this the carpenter's son? is not his mother called Mary? and his brethren, James, and Joses, and Simon, and Judas?

56. And his sisters, are they not all with us? Whence then hath this *man* all these things?

57. And they were offended in him. But Jesus said unto them, A prophet is not without honour, save in his own country, and in his own house.

58. And he did not many mighty works there because of their unbelief.

MARK 6:1. And he went out from thence, and came into his own country; and his disciples follow him.

2. And when the sabbath day was come, he began to teach in the synagogue: and many hearing *him* were astonished, saying, From whence hath this *man* these things? and what wisdom *is* this which is given unto him, that even such mighty works are wrought by his hands?

3. Is not this the carpenter, the son of Mary, the brother of James, and Joses, and of Juda, and Simon? and are not his sisters here with us? And they were offended at him.

4. But Jesus said unto them, A prophet is not without honour, but in his own country, and among his own kin, and in his own house.

5. And he could there do no mighty work, save that he laid his hands upon a few sick folk, and healed *them*.

6. And he marvelled because of their unbelief. . . .

Luke: No record.

John: No record.

Section 79

JESUS AGAIN TOURS GALILEE

Jesus makes another tour of Galilee, teaching in their synagogues, and "healing every sickness and every disease among the people"; he is moved with compassion because the people are scattered abroad as sheep without a shepherd; he tells his disciples "the harvest truly is plenteous, but the labourers are few"; he tells them to pray the Lord that the labourers will be sent forth to the harvest.

Matt. 9:35-38; Mark 6:6b; Luke: No record; John: No record.
Time: A.D. 29, Winter (ANDREWS).
Place: Galilee.

MATTHEW 9:35. And Jesus went about all the cities and villages, teaching in their synagogues, and preaching the gospel of the kingdom, and healing every sickness and every disease among the people.

36. ¶ But when he saw the multitudes, he was moved with compassion on them, because they fainted, and were scattered abroad, as sheep having no shepherd.

37. Then saith he unto his disciples, The harvest truly *is* plenteous, but the labourers *are* few;

38. Pray ye therefore the Lord of the harvest, that he will send forth labourers into his harvest.

MARK 6:6. . . . And he went round about the villages, teaching.

Luke: No record.

John: No record.

Section 80

THE TWELVE SENT FORTH

The Twelve sent forth by Jesus; his charge to them.

Matt. 10:1, 5-42; Mark 6:7-13; Luke 9:1-6; John: No record.
Time: A.D. 29, Winter (ANDREWS).
Place: Galilee.

MATTHEW 10:1. And when he had called unto *him* his twelve disciples, he gave them power *against* unclean spirits, to cast them out, and to heal all manner of sickness and all manner of disease . . . .

5. These twelve Jesus sent forth, and commanded them, saying, Go not into the way of the Gentiles, and into *any* city of the Samaritans enter ye not:

6. But go rather to the lost sheep of the house of Israel.

7. And as ye go, preach, saying, The kingdom of heaven is at hand.

8. Heal the sick, cleanse the lepers, raise the dead, cast out

devils: freely ye have received, freely give.

9. Provide neither gold, nor silver, nor brass in your purses,

10. Nor scrip for *your* journey, neither two coats, neither shoes, nor yet staves: for the workman is worthy of his meat.

11. And into whatsoever city or town ye shall enter, enquire who in it is worthy; and there abide till ye go thence.

12. And when ye come into an house, salute it.

13. And if the house be worthy, let your peace come upon it: but if it be not worthy, let your peace return to you.

14. And whosoever shall not receive you, nor hear your words, when ye depart out of that house or city, shake off the dust of your feet.

15. Verily I say unto you, It shall be more tolerable for the land of Sodom and Gomorrha in the day of judgment, than for that city.

16. ¶ Behold, I send you forth as sheep in the midst of wolves: be ye therefore wise as serpents, and harmless as doves.

17. But beware of men: for they will deliver you up to the councils, and they will scourge you in their synagogues;

18. And ye shall be brought before governors and kings for my sake, for a testimony against them and the Gentiles.

19. But when they deliver you up, take no thought how or what ye shall speak: for it shall be given you in that same hour what ye shall speak.

20. For it is not ye that speak, but the Spirit of your Father which speaketh in you.

21. And the brother shall deliver up the brother to death, and the father the child: and the children shall rise up against *their* parents, and cause them to be put to death.

22. And ye shall be hated of all *men* for my name's sake: but he that endureth to the end shall be saved.

23. But when they persecute you in this city, flee ye into another: for verily I say unto you, Ye shall not have gone over the cities of Israel, till the Son of man be come.

24. The disciple is not above *his* master, nor the servant above his lord.

25. It is enough for the disciple that he be as his master, and the servant as his lord. If they have called the master of the house Beelzebub, how much more *shall they call* them of his household?

26. Fear them not therefore: for there is nothing covered, that shall not be revealed; and hid, that shall not be known.

27. What I tell you in darkness, *that* speak ye in light: and what ye hear in the ear, *that* preach ye upon the housetops.

28. And fear not them which kill the body, but are not able

to kill the soul: but rather fear him which is able to destroy both soul and body in hell.

29. Are not two sparrows sold for a farthing? and one of them shall not fall on the ground without your Father.

30. But the very hairs of your head are all numbered.

31. Fear ye not therefore, ye are of more value than many sparrows.

32. Whosoever therefore shall confess me before men, him will I confess also before my Father which is in heaven.

33. But whosoever shall deny me before men, him will I also deny before my Father which is in heaven.

34. Think not that I am come to send peace on earth: I came not to send peace, but a sword.

35. For I am come to set a man at variance against his father, and the daughter against her mother, and the daughter in law against her mother in law.

36. And a man's foes *shall be* they of his own household.

37. He that loveth father or mother more than me is not worthy of me: and he that loveth son or daughter more than me is not worthy of me.

38. And he that taketh not his cross, and followeth after me, is not worthy of me.

39. He that findeth his life shall lose it: and he that loseth his life for my sake shall find it.

40. ¶ He that receiveth you receiveth me, and he that receiveth me receiveth him that sent me.

41. He that receiveth a prophet in the name of a prophet shall receive a prophet's reward; and he that receiveth a righteous man in the name of a righteous man shall receive a righteous man's reward.

42. And whosoever shall give to drink unto one of these little ones a cup of cold *water* only in the name of a disciple, verily I say unto you, he shall in no wise lose his reward.

MARK 6:7. ¶ And he called *unto him* the twelve, and began to send them forth by two and two; and gave them power over unclean spirits;

8. And commanded them that they should take nothing for *their* journey, save a staff only; no scrip, no bread, no money in *their* purse:

9. But *be* shod with sandals; and not put on two coats.

10. And he said unto them, In what place soever ye enter into an house, there abide till ye depart from that place.

11. And whosoever shall not receive you, nor hear you, when ye depart thence, shake off the dust under your feet for a testimony against them. Verily I say unto you, It shall be more tolerable for Sodom and Gomorrha in the day of judgment, than for that city.

12. And they went out, and

preached that men should repent.

13. And they cast out many devils, and anointed with oil many that were sick, and healed *them.*

LUKE 9:1. Then he called his twelve disciples together, and gave them power and authority over all devils, and to cure diseases.

2. And he sent them to preach the kingdom of God, and to heal the sick.

3. And he said unto them, Take nothing for *your* journey, neither staves, nor scrip, neither bread, neither money; neither have two coats apiece.

4. And whatsoever house ye enter into, there abide, and thence depart.

5. And whosoever will not receive you, when ye go out of that city, shake off the very dust from your feet for a testimony against them.

6. And they departed, and went through the towns, preaching the gospel, and healing every where.

John: No record.

Section 81

JESUS CONTINUES TOUR

Jesus, having charged the Twelve, continues his tour of preaching.

Matt. 11:1; Mark: No record; Luke: No record; John: No record.

Time: A.D. 29, Winter (ANDREWS).

Place: Galilee.

MATTHEW 11:1. And it came to pass, when Jesus had made an end of commanding his twelve disciples, he departed thence to teach and to preach in their cities.

Mark: No record.

Luke: No record.

John: No record.

Section 82

HEROD BEHEADS JOHN

Herod giving a feast on his birthday, promises the daughter of his wife Herodias (the daughter having danced before him) anything she might ask for; she goes forth and asks her mother what she shall ask for; Herodias tells her to ask for the head of John the Baptist; she asks this of Herod who regretfully grants her request, orders John beheaded, and the head brought on a charger and given to the damsel.

Matt. 14:6-12; Mark 6:21-29; Luke: No record; John: No record.

Time: A.D. 29, Winter (ANDREWS).

Place: Fortress of Machaerus (East side of Dead Sea) (ANDREWS).

MATTHEW 14:6. But when Herod's birthday was kept, the daughter of Herodias danced before them, and pleased Herod.

7. Whereupon he promised with an oath to give her whatsoever she would ask.

8. And she, being before instructed of her mother, said, Give me here John Baptist's head in a charger.

9. And the king was sorry: nevertheless for the oath's sake, and them which sat with him at meat, he commanded *it* to be given *her*.

10. And he sent, and beheaded John in the prison.

11. And his head was brought in a charger, and given to the damsel: and she brought *it* to her mother.

12. And his disciples came, and took up the body, and buried it, and went and told Jesus.

MARK 6:21. And when a convenient day was come, that Herod on his birthday made a supper to his lords, high captains, and chief *estates* of Galilee;

22. And when the daughter of the said Herodias came in, and danced, and pleased Herod and them that sat with him, the king said unto the damsel, Ask of me whatsoever thou wilt, and I will give *it* thee.

23. And he sware unto her, Whatsoever thou shalt ask of me, I will give *it* thee, unto the half of my kingdom.

24. And she went forth, and said unto her mother, What shall I ask? And she said, The head of John the Baptist.

25. And she came in straightway with haste unto the king, and asked, saying, I will that thou give me by and by in a charger the head of John the Baptist.

26. And the king was exceeding sorry; *yet* for his oath's sake, and for their sakes which sat with him, he would not reject her.

27. And immediately the king sent an executioner, and commanded his head to be brought: and he went and beheaded him in the prison,

28. And brought his head in a charger, and gave it to the damsel: and the damsel gave it to her mother.

29. And when his disciples heard *of it*, they came and took up his corpse, and laid it in a tomb.

Luke: No record.

John: No record.

Section 83

HEROD THINKS JESUS IS JOHN

Herod, hearing of the fame of Jesus (seemingly for the first time), thinks Jesus is John the Baptist resurrected, and he desires Jesus brought to him.

Matt. 14:1-2; Mark 6:14-16; Luke 9:7-9; John: No record.
Time: A.D. 29, Winter (ANDREWS).
Place: Galilee (ANDREWS).

MATTHEW 14:1. At that time Herod the tetrarch heard of the fame of Jesus,

2. And said unto his servants, This is John the Baptist; he is risen from the dead; and therefore mighty works do shew forth themselves in him.

MARK 6:14. And king Herod heard *of him*; (for his name was spread abroad:) and he said, That John the Baptist was risen from the dead, and therefore mighty works do shew forth themselves in him.

15. Others said, That it is Elias. And others said, That it is a prophet, or as one of the prophets.

16. But when Herod heard *thereof*, he said, It is John, whom I beheaded: he is risen from the dead.

LUKE 9:7. ¶ Now Herod the tetrarch heard of all that was done by him: and he was perplexed, because that it was said of some, that John was risen from the dead;

8. And of some, that Elias had appeared; and of others, that one of the old prophets was risen again.

9. And Herod said, John have I beheaded: but who is this, of whom I hear such things? And he desired to see him.

John: No record.

Section 84

THE TWELVE REPORT

The Twelve gather themselves together unto Jesus and tell him what they had done and what they had taught.

Matt.: No record; Mark 6:30; Luke 9:10a; John: No record.
Time: A.D. 29, April (ANDREWS).
Place: Capernaum (ANDREWS).

Matthew: No record.

MARK 6:30. And the apostles gathered themselves together unto Jesus, and told him all things, both what they had done, and what they had taught.

LUKE 9:10. ¶ And the apostles, when they were returned, told him all that they had done . . . .

John: No record.

Section 85

HE GOES TO BETHSAIDA

Jesus hearing of Herod's desire to see him, takes his disciples by ship, into a desert place belonging to the city called Bethsaida, to rest awhile, "for there were many coming and going, and they had no leisure so much as to eat"; and the people when they knew it, "followed him on foot out of the cities."

Matt. 14:13; Mark 6:31-32; Luke 9:10b-11a; John: No record.

Time: A.D. 29, April (ANDREWS).

Place: Near Bethsaida.

MATTHEW 14:13. ¶ When Jesus heard *of it*, he departed thence by ship into a desert place apart: and when the people had heard *thereof*, they followed him on foot out of the cities.

MARK 6:31. And he said unto them, Come ye yourselves apart into a desert place, and rest a while: for there were many coming and going, and they had no leisure so much as to eat.

32. And they departed into a desert place by ship privately.

LUKE 9:10 .... And he took them, and went aside privately into a desert place belonging to the city called Bethsaida.

11. And the people, when they knew *it*, followed him:....

John: No record.

Section 86

THE FIVE THOUSAND FED

Jesus, seeing the multitude who were as sheep without a shepherd, has compassion on them; he heals their sick and teaches them concerning the kingdom of God; when evening was come, instead of sending them away to the villages to buy food as the disciples suggested, he has them sit down by fifties in a company; he then takes the five loaves and two fishes which the disciples had, blesses them and passes them around amongst the people; the whole multitude of 5,000 men besides the women and children, are fed, and there are gathered up after all had had enough, twelve baskets of the fragments and of the fishes.

Matt. 14:14-21; Mark 6:33-44; Luke 9:11b-17; John 6:1-14.

Time: A.D. 29, April (ANDREWS).

Place: Near Bethsaida.

MATTHEW 14:14. And Jesus went forth, and saw a great multitude, and was moved with compassion toward them, and he healed their sick.

15. ¶And when it was evening, his disciples came to him, saying, This is a desert place, and the time is now past; send the multitude away, that they

may go into the villages, and buy themselves victuals.

16. But Jesus said unto them, They need not depart; give ye them to eat.

17. And they say unto him, We have here but five loaves, and two fishes.

18. He said, Bring them hither to me.

19. And he commanded the multitude to sit down on the grass, and took the five loaves, and the two fishes, and looking up to heaven, he blessed, and brake, and gave the loaves to *his* disciples, and the disciples to the multitude.

20. And they did all eat, and were filled: and they took up of the fragments that remained twelve baskets full.

21. And they that had eaten were about five thousand men, beside women and children.

MARK 6:33. And the people saw them departing, and many knew him, and ran afoot thither out of all cities, and outwent them, and came together unto him.

34. And Jesus, when he came out, saw much people, and was moved with compassion toward them, because they were as sheep not having a shepherd: and he began to teach them many things.

35. And when the day was now far spent, his disciples came unto him, and said, This is a desert place, and now the time *is* far passed:

36. Send them away, that they may go into the country round about, and into the villages, and buy themselves bread: for they have nothing to eat.

37. He answered and said unto them, Give ye them to eat. And they say unto him, Shall we go and buy two hundred pennyworth of bread, and give them to eat?

38. He saith unto them, How many loaves have ye? go and see. And when they knew, they say, Five, and two fishes.

39. And he commanded them to make all sit down by companies upon the green grass.

40. And they sat down in ranks, by hundreds, and by fifties.

41. And when he had taken the five loaves and the two fishes, he looked up to heaven, and blessed, and brake the loaves, and gave *them* to his disciples to set before them; and the two fishes divided he among them all.

42. And they did all eat, and were filled.

43. And they took up twelve baskets full of the fragments, and of the fishes.

44. And they that did eat of the loaves were about five thousand men.

LUKE 9:11. . . . and he received them, and spake unto them of the kingdom of God, and healed them that had need of healing.

12. And when the day began to wear away, then came the twelve, and said unto him, Send the multitude away, that they may go into the towns and country round about, and lodge, and get victuals: for we are here in a desert place.

13. But he said unto them, Give ye them to eat. And they said, We have no more but five loaves and two fishes; except we should go and buy meat for all this people.

14. For they were about five thousand men. And he said to his disciples, Make them sit down by fifties in a company.

15. And they did so, and made them all sit down.

16. Then he took the five loaves and the two fishes, and looking up to heaven, he blessed them, and brake, and gave to the disciples to set before the multitude.

17. And they did eat, and were all filled: and there was taken up of fragments that remained to them twelve baskets.

JOHN 6:1. After these things Jesus went over the sea of Galilee, which is *the sea* of Tiberias.

2. And a great multitude followed him, because they saw his miracles which he did on them that were diseased.

3. And Jesus went up into a mountain, and there he sat with his disciples.

4. And the passover, a feast of the Jews, was nigh.

5. ¶When Jesus then lifted up *his* eyes, and saw a great company come unto him, he saith unto Philip, Whence shall we buy bread, that these may eat?

6. And this he said to prove him: for he himself knew what he would do.

7. Philip answered him, Two hundred pennyworth of bread is not sufficient for them, that every one of them may take a little.

8. One of his disciples, Andrew, Simon Peter's brother, saith unto him,

9. There is a lad here, which hath five barley loaves, and two small fishes: but what are they among so many?

10. And Jesus said, Make the men sit down. Now there was much grass in the place. So the men sat down, in number about five thousand.

11. And Jesus took the loaves; and when he had given thanks, he distributed to the disciples, and the disciples to them that were set down; and likewise of the fishes as much as they would.

12. When they were filled, he said unto his disciples, Gather up the fragments that remain, that nothing be lost.

13. Therefore they gathered *them* together, and filled twelve baskets with the fragments of the five barley loaves, which remained over and above unto them that had eaten.

14. Then those men, when they had seen the miracle that Jesus did, said, This is of a truth that prophet that should come into the world.

Section 87

JESUS PREVENTS THEIR MAKING HIM KING

The 5,000 men, seeing the miracle of the feeding of the multitude, would "come and take him by force, to make him a king," but he departs again "into a mountain himself alone," after sending his disciples away to the other side while he sends the multitudes away.

Matt. 14:22-23; Mark 6:45-46; Luke: No record; John 6:15.

Time: A.D. 29, April (ANDREWS).

Place: Mountain, near Sea of Galilee.

MATTHEW 14:22 ¶ And straightway Jesus constrained his disciples to get into a ship, and to go before him unto the other side, while he sent the multitudes away.

23. And when he had sent the multitudes away, he went up into a mountain apart to pray: and when the evening was come, he was there alone.

MARK 6:45. And straightway he constrained his disciples to get into the ship, and to go to the other side before unto Bethsaida, while he sent away the people.

46. And when he had sent them away, he departed into a mountain to pray.

Luke: No record.

JOHN 6:15. ¶ When Jesus therefore perceived that they would come and take him by force, to make him a king, he departed again into a mountain himself alone.

Section 88

JESUS WALKS ON SEA

The disciples begin crossing the sea towards Capernaum; a great wind blows and the sea arises; the wind being contrary to them, they are forced to row; Jesus seeing this walks to them on the sea; they are frightened, thinking him a spirit, and cry out for fear; Jesus calls to them, "It is I; be not afraid"; Peter says: "Lord, if it be thou, bid me come unto thee on the water"; Jesus says, "Come"; Peter starts, but fearing the waves, begins to sink and calls to Jesus for help; Jesus takes his hand and reproves him for lack of faith; the wind ceases; the disciples worship him saying: "Of a truth thou art the Son of God."

Matt. 14:24-33; Mark 6:47-52; Luke: No record; John 6:16-21.

Time: A.D. 29, April (ANDREWS).

Place: Sea of Galilee.

MATTHEW 14:24. But the ship was now in the midst of the sea, tossed with waves: for the wind was contrary.

25. And in the fourth watch of the night Jesus went unto them, walking on the sea.

26. And when the disciples saw him walking on the sea, they were troubled, saying, It is a spirit; and they cried out for fear.

27. But straightway Jesus spake unto them, saying, Be of good cheer; it is I; be not afraid.

28. And Peter answered him and said, Lord, if it be thou, bid me come unto thee on the water.

29. And he said, Come. And when Peter was come down out of the ship, he walked on the water, to go to Jesus.

30. But when he saw the wind boisterous, he was afraid; and beginning to sink, he cried, saying, Lord, save me.

31. And immediately Jesus stretched forth *his* hand, and caught him, and said unto him, O thou of little faith, wherefore didst thou doubt?

32. And when they were come into the ship, the wind ceased.

33. Then they that were in the ship came and worshipped him, saying, Of a truth thou art the Son of God.

MARK 6:47. And when even was come, the ship was in the midst of the sea, and he alone on the land.

48. And he saw them toiling in rowing; for the wind was contrary unto them: and about the fourth watch of the night he cometh unto them, walking upon the sea, and would have passed by them.

49. But when they saw him walking upon the sea, they supposed it had been a spirit, and cried out:

50. For they all saw him, and were troubled. And immediately he talked with them, and saith unto them, Be of good cheer: it is I; be not afraid.

51. And he went up unto them into the ship; and the wind ceased: and they were sore amazed in themselves beyond measure, and wondered.

52. For they considered not *the miracle* of the loaves: for their heart was hardened.

Luke: No record.

JOHN 6:16. And when even was *now* come, his disciples went down unto the sea,

17. And entered into a ship, and went over the sea toward Capernaum. And it was now dark, and Jesus was not come to them.

18. And the sea arose by reason of a great wind that blew.

19. So when they had rowed about five and twenty or thirty furlongs, they see Jesus walking on the sea, and drawing

nigh unto the ship: and they were afraid.

20. But he saith unto them, It is I; be not afraid.

21. Then they willingly received him into the ship: and immediately the ship was at the land whither they went.

Section 89

THE DISCOURSE TO THE MULTITUDE ON THE BREAD OF LIFE

The people missing Jesus on the eastern shore of the Sea, take shipping and go to Capernaum and finding Jesus, ask why he came there; he answers saying they come to him not because of his miracles but because he feeds them; Jesus then preaches his great sermon on the bread of life; he tells them to labor not for meat that perisheth, but for the meat which endureth unto eternal life which the Son of man shall give them; they ask what shall they do; then ask for a sign; Jesus compares manna with the bread of God; Jesus announces his Messiahship; Jews murmur because Jesus said he is the bread; Jesus declares his relationship to the Father; he tells them what bread he is; he declares the atonement by his flesh and blood; many of his disciples murmur at the doctrine and "went back, and walked no more with him"; Peter declares, "thou art that Christ, the Son of the living God"; Jesus declares one of the Twelve is a devil.

Matt. No record; **Mark:** No record; **Luke:** No record; **John** 6:22-71.
Time: A.D. 29, April (ANDREWS).
Place: Capernaum.

Matthew: No record.

Mark: No record.

Luke: No record.

JOHN 6:22. ¶ The day following, when the people which stood on the other side of the sea saw that there was none other boat there, save that one whereinto his disciples were entered, and that Jesus went not with his disciples into the boat, but *that* his disciples were gone away alone;

23. (Howbeit there came other boats from Tiberias nigh unto the place where they did eat bread, after that the Lord had given thanks:)

24. When the people therefore saw that Jesus was not there, neither his disciples, they also took shipping, and came to Capernaum, seeking for Jesus.

25. And when they had found him on the other side of the sea, they said unto him, Rabbi, when camest thou hither?

26. Jesus answered them and said, Verily, verily, I say unto you, Ye seek me, not because ye saw the miracles, but because ye did eat of the loaves, and were filled.

27. Labour not for the meat which perisheth, but for that meat which endureth unto

everlasting life, which the Son of man shall give unto you: for him hath God the Father sealed.

28. Then said they unto him, What shall we do, that we might work the works of God?

29. Jesus answered and said unto them, This is the work of God, that ye believe on him whom he hath sent.

30. They said therefore unto him, What sign shewest thou then, that we may see, and believe thee? what dost thou work?

31. Our fathers did eat manna in the desert; as it is written, He gave them bread from heaven to eat.

32. Then Jesus said unto them, Verily, verily, I say unto you, Moses gave you not that bread from heaven; but my Father giveth you the true bread from heaven.

33. For the bread of God is he which cometh down from heaven, and giveth life unto the world.

34. Then said they unto him, Lord, evermore give us this bread.

35. And Jesus said unto them, I am the bread of life: he that cometh to me shall never hunger; and he that believeth on me shall never thirst.

36. But I said unto you, That ye also have seen me, and believe not.

37. All that the Father giveth me shall come to me; and him that cometh to me I will in no wise cast out.

38. For I came down from heaven, not to do mine own will, but the will of him that sent me.

39. And this is the Father's will which hath sent me, that of all which he hath given me I should lose nothing, but should raise it up again at the last day.

40. And this is the will of him that sent me, that every one which seeth the Son, and believeth on him, may have everlasting life: and I will raise him up at the last day.

41. The Jews then murmured at him, because he said, I am the bread which came down from heaven.

42. And they said, Is not this Jesus, the son of Joseph, whose father and mother we know? how is it then that he saith, I came down from heaven?

43. Jesus therefore answered and said unto them, Murmur not among yourselves.

44. No man can come to me, except the Father which hath sent me draw him: and I will raise him up at the last day.

45. It is written in the prophets, And they shall be all taught of God. Every man therefore that hath heard, and hath learned of the Father, cometh unto me.

46. Not that any man hath seen the Father, save he which

is of God, he hath seen the Father.

47. Verily, verily, I say unto you, He that believeth on me hath everlasting life.

48. I am that bread of life.

49. Your fathers did eat manna in the wilderness, and are dead.

50. This is the bread which cometh down from heaven, that a man may eat thereof, and not die.

51. I am the living bread which came down from heaven: if any man eat of this bread, he shall live for ever: and the bread that I will give is my flesh, which I will give for the life of the world.

52. The Jews therefore strove among themselves, saying, How can this man give us *his* flesh to eat?

53. Then Jesus said unto them, Verily, verily, I say unto you, Except ye eat the flesh of the Son of man, and drink his blood, ye have no life in you.

54. Whoso eateth my flesh, and drinketh my blood, hath eternal life; and I will raise him up at the last day.

55. For my flesh is meat indeed, and my blood is drink indeed.

56. He that eateth my flesh, and drinketh my blood, dwelleth in me, and I in him.

57. As the living Father hath sent me, and I live by the Father: so he that eateth me, even he shall live by me.

58. This is that bread which came down from heaven: not as your fathers did eat manna, and are dead: he that eateth of this bread shall live for ever.

59. These things said he in the synagogue, as he taught in Capernaum.

60. Many therefore of his disciples, when they had heard *this*, said, This is an hard saying; who can hear it?

61. When Jesus knew in himself that his disciples murmured at it, he said unto them, Doth this offend you?

62. *What* and if ye shall see the Son of man ascend up where he was before?

63. It is the spirit that quickeneth; the flesh profiteth nothing: the words that I speak unto you, *they* are spirit, and *they* are life.

64. But there are some of you that believe not. For Jesus knew from the beginning who they were that believed not, and who should betray him.

65. And he said, Therefore said I unto you, that no man can come unto me, except it were given unto him of my Father.

66. ¶ From that *time* many of his disciples went back, and walked no more with him.

67. Then said Jesus unto the twelve, Will ye also go away?

68. Then Simon Peter answered him, Lord, to whom

shall we go? thou hast the words of eternal life.

69. And we believe and are sure that thou art that Christ, the Son of the living God.

70. Jesus answered them, Have not I chosen you twelve, and one of you is a devil?

71. He spake of Judas Iscariot *the son* of Simon: for he it was that should betray him, being one of the twelve.

Section 90

PEOPLE IN THE LAND OF GENNESARET HEALED

Jesus coming into the land of Gennesaret, the people know him, and run through the whole region carrying to him in beds those who are sick, who seek only to touch the hem of his garment, and as many as touch are healed; and this is done wheresoever he goes.

Matt. 14:34-36; Mark 6:53-56; Luke: No record; John: No record.
Time: A.D. 29, April (ANDREWS).
Place: Gennesaret.

MATTHEW 14:34. ¶ And when they were gone over, they came into the land of Gennesaret.

35. And when the men of that place had knowledge of him, they sent out into all that country round about, and brought unto him all that were diseased;

36. And besought him that they might only touch the hem of his garment: and as many as touched were made perfectly whole.

MARK 6:53. And when they had passed over, they came into the land of Gennesaret, and drew to the shore.

54. And when they were come out of the ship, straightway they knew him,

55. And ran through that whole region round about, and began to carry about in beds those that were sick, where they heard he was.

56. And whithersoever he entered, into villages, or cities, or country, they laid the sick in the streets, and besought him that they might touch if it were but the border of his garment: and as many as touched him were made whole.

Luke: No record.

John: No record.

Section 91

THE DISCOURSES UPON CLEANLINESS

The scribes and Pharisees come from Jerusalem, complain that the disciples eat with unwashen hands, contrary to the traditions of the elders; Jesus first calling attention to their own violation of the law, calls them hypocrites, refers to the prophecy of Esaias about people

drawing near God with their lips, while their hearts are far from him; says that man is defiled by what comes out of his mouth, not by what is taken in (he later explains this parable, answering Peter); they tell him the Pharisees are much offended, and Jesus tells his disciples to leave the Pharisees alone, for they are the blind leading the blind.

Matt. 15:1-20; Mark 7:1-23; Luke: No record; John: No record.
Time: A.D. 29, April (ANDREWS).
Place: Capernaum.

MATTHEW 15:1. Then came to Jesus scribes and Pharisees, which were of Jerusalem, saying,

2. Why do thy disciples transgress the tradition of the elders? for they wash not their hands when they eat bread.

3. But he answered and said unto them, Why do ye also transgress the commandment of God by your tradition?

4. For God commanded, saying, Honour thy father and mother: and, He that curseth father or mother, let him die the death.

5. But ye say, Whosoever shall say to *his* father or *his* mother, *It is* a gift, by whatsoever thou mightest be profited by me;

6. And honour not his father or his mother, *he shall be free.* Thus have ye made the commandment of God of none effect by your tradition.

7. *Ye* hypocrites, well did Esaias prophesy of you, saying,

8. This people draweth nigh unto me with their mouth, and honoureth me with *their* lips; but their heart is far from me.

9. But in vain they do worship me, teaching *for* doctrines the commandments of men.

10. ¶ And he called the multitude, and said unto them, Hear, and understand:

11. Not that which goeth into the mouth defileth a man; but that which cometh out of the mouth, this defileth a man.

12. Then came his disciples, and said unto him, Knowest thou that the Pharisees were offended, after they heard this saying?

13. But he answered and said, Every plant, which my heavenly Father hath not planted, shall be rooted up.

14. Let them alone: they be blind leaders of the blind. And if the blind lead the blind, both shall fall into the ditch.

15. Then answered Peter and said unto him, Declare unto us this parable.

16. And Jesus said, Are ye also yet without understanding?

17. Do not ye yet understand, that whatsoever entereth in at the mouth goeth into the belly, and is cast out into the draught?

18. But those things which

proceed out of the mouth come forth from the heart; and they defile the man.

19. For out of the heart proceed evil thoughts, murders, adulteries, fornications, thefts, false witness, blasphemies:

20. These are *the things* which defile a man: but to eat with unwashen hands defileth not a man.

MARK 7:1. Then came together unto him the Pharisees, and certain of the scribes, which came from Jerusalem.

2. And when they saw some of his disciples eat bread with defiled, that is to say, with unwashen, hands, they found fault.

3. For the Pharisees, and all the Jews, except they wash *their* hands oft, eat not, holding the tradition of the elders.

4. And *when they come* from the market, except they wash, they eat not. And many other things there be, which they have received to hold, *as* the washing of cups, and pots, brasen vessels, and of tables.

5. Then the Pharisees and scribes asked him, Why walk not thy disciples according to the tradition of the elders, but eat bread with unwashen hands?

6. He answered and said unto them, Well hath Esaias prophesied of you hypocrites, as it is written, This people honoureth me with *their* lips, but their heart is far from me.

7. Howbeit in vain do they worship me, teaching *for* doctrines the commandments of men.

8. For laying aside the commandment of God, ye hold the tradition of men, *as* the washing of pots and cups: and many other such like things ye do.

9. And he said unto them, Full well ye reject the commandment of God, that ye may keep your own tradition.

10. For Moses said, Honour thy father and thy mother; and, Whoso curseth father or mother, let him die the death:

11. But ye say, If a man shall say to his father or mother, *It is* Corban, that is to say, a gift, by whatsoever thou mightest be profited by me; *he shall be free.*

12. And ye suffer him no more to do ought for his father or his mother;

13. Making the word of God of none effect through your tradition, which ye have delivered: and many such like things do ye.

14. ¶ And when he had called all the people *unto him,* he said unto them, Hearken unto me every one *of you,* and understand:

15. There is nothing from without a man, that entering into him can defile him: but the things which come out of him, those are they that defile the man.

16. If any man have ears to hear, let him hear.

17. And when he was entered into the house from the people, his disciples asked him concerning the parable.

18. And he saith unto them, Are ye so without understanding also? Do ye not perceive, that whatsoever thing from without entereth into the man, *it* cannot defile him;

19. Because it entereth not into his heart, but into the belly, and goeth out into the draught, purging all meats?

20. And he said, That which cometh out of the man, that defileth the man.

21. For from within, out of the heart of men, proceed evil thoughts, adulteries, fornications, murders,

22. Thefts, covetousness, wickedness, deceit, lasciviousness, an evil eye, blasphemy, pride, foolishness:

23. All these evil things come from within, and defile the man.

Luke: No record.

John: No record.

(*This is the time of the third Passover.*)

III. From the Retirement Into Northern Galilee Until the Closing of the Galilean Ministry

Section 92

JESUS GOES INTO NORTHERN GALILEE

Jesus now goes into northern Galilee, to the coasts of Tyre and Sidon; "he would not walk in Jewry, because the Jews sought to kill him"; he enters into a house, trying not to be known, "but he could not be hid."

Matt. 15:21; Mark 7:24; Luke: No record; John 7:1.
Time: A.D. 29, Spring-Summer (ANDREWS).
Place: Galilee.

MATTHEW 15:21. ¶ Then Jesus went thence, and departed into the coasts of Tyre and Sidon.

MARK 7:24. ¶ And from thence he arose, and went into the borders of Tyre and Sidon, and entered into an house, and would have no man know *it*: but he could not be hid.

Luke: No record.

JOHN 7:1. After these things Jesus walked in Galilee: for he would not walk in Jewry, because the Jews sought to kill him.

Section 93

THE DAUGHTER OF THE GREEK WOMAN HEALED

A Greek woman (Syrophenician by nation) whose daughter is possessed with a devil, seeks Jesus to have him cast it forth; Jesus not answering at first, his disciples ask him to send her away; Jesus replies that he is not sent but to the lost sheep of Israel; she again approaches Jesus and worships, asking again that he heal her daughter; Jesus says it is not meet to take the children's bread and cast it to the dogs; she replies that the dogs may eat the crumbs that fall from the master's table; he replies: "O woman, great is thy faith: be it unto thee even as thou wilt"; her daughter is healed.

Matt. 15:22-28; Mark 7:25-30; Luke: No record; John: No record.

Time: A.D. 29, Summer (ANDREWS).

Place: Region of Tyre and Sidon.

MATTHEW 15:22. And, behold, a woman of Canaan came out of the same coasts, and cried unto him, saying, Have mercy on me, O Lord, *thou* son of David; my daughter is grievously vexed with a devil.

23. But he answered her not a word. And his disciples came and besought him, saying, Send her away; for she crieth after us.

24. But he answered and said, I am not sent but unto the lost sheep of the house of Israel.

25. Then came she and worshipped him, saying, Lord, help me.

26. But he answered and said, It is not meet to take the children's bread, and to cast *it* to dogs.

27. And she said, Truth, Lord: yet the dogs eat of the crumbs which fall from their masters' table.

28. Then Jesus answered and said unto her, O woman, great *is* thy faith: be it unto thee even as thou wilt. And her daughter was made whole from that very hour.

MARK 7:25. For a *certain* woman, whose young daughter had an unclean spirit, heard of him, and came and fell at his feet:

26. The woman was a Greek, a Syrophenician by nation; and she besought him that he would cast forth the devil out of her daughter.

27. But Jesus said unto her, Let the children first be filled: for it is not meet to take the children's bread, and to cast *it* unto the dogs.

28. And she answered and said unto him, Yes, Lord: yet the dogs under the table eat of the children's crumbs.

29. And he said unto her, For this saying go thy way; the devil is gone out of thy daughter.

30. And when she was come to her house, she found the

devil gone out, and her daughter laid upon the bed.

Luke: No record.
John: No record.

Section 94

HE RETURNS TO SEA OF GALILEE

Jesus leaves the coasts of Tyre and Sidon and returns to the Sea of Galilee through "the midst of the coasts of Decapolis."

Matt. 15:29a; Mark 7:31; Luke: No record; John: No record.
Time: A.D. 29, Summer (ANDREWS).
Place: Galilee.

MATTHEW 15:29. And Jesus departed from thence, and came nigh unto the sea of Galilee . . . .

MARK 7:31. ¶And again, departing from the coasts of Tyre and Sidon, he came unto the sea of Galilee, through the midst of the coasts of Decapolis.

Luke: No record.
John: No record.

Section 95

JESUS HEALS DEAF MAN

The people bring to Jesus a deaf man with an impediment in his speech and ask Jesus to put his hand upon him; Jesus takes him aside, puts his fingers into his ears, spits and touches his tongue, and the man hears and speaks; Jesus charges them not to tell of this, but they do, and the more he charges the more they publish.

Matt.: No record; Mark 7:32-37; Luke: No record; John: No record.
Time: A.D. 29, Summer (ANDREWS).
Place: Decapolis (ANDREWS).

Matthew: No record.

MARK 7:32. And they bring unto him one that was deaf, and had an impediment in his speech; and they beseech him to put his hand upon him.

33. And he took him aside from the multitude, and put his fingers into his ears, and he spit, and touched his tongue;

34. And looking up to heaven, he sighed, and saith unto him, Ephphatha, that is, Be opened.

35. And straightway his ears were opened, and the string of his tongue was loosed, and he spake plain.

36. And he charged them that they should tell no man: but the more he charged them, so much the more a great deal they published *it;*

37. And were beyond measure astonished, saying, He

hath done all things well: he maketh both the deaf to hear, and the dumb to speak.

Luke: No record.

John: No record.

Section 96

THE FOUR THOUSAND FED

Jesus goes up into a mountain and sits down; multitudes come to him with their lame, blind, dumb, maimed, and many others and cast them down at Jesus' feet, and he heals them; after three days he tells his disciples the multitude must be fed; the disciples ask, "From whence can a man satisfy these men with bread here in the wilderness?"; he asks how much bread they have, they say seven loaves; he has the people sit down, then he blesses the bread and the disciples set it before the people; they have a few small fishes, and to these he does the same; after all have eaten, they gather up seven baskets; there were four thousand men besides the women and children.

Matt. 15:29b-38; Mark 8:1-9; Luke: No record; John: No record.
Time: A.D. 29, Summer (ANDREWS).
Place: Decapolis (ANDREWS).

MATTHEW 15:29 . . . and went up into a mountain, and sat down there.

30. And great multitudes came unto him, having with them *those that were* lame, blind, dumb, maimed, and many others, and cast them down at Jesus' feet; and he healed them:

31. Insomuch that the multitude wondered, when they saw the dumb to speak, the maimed to be whole, the lame to walk, and the blind to see: and they glorified the God of Israel.

32. ¶ Then Jesus called his disciples *unto him*, and said, I have compassion on the multitude, because they continue with me now three days, and have nothing to eat: and I will not send them away fasting, lest they faint in the way.

33. And his disciples say unto him, Whence should we have so much bread in the wilderness, as to fill so great a multitude?

34. And Jesus saith unto them, How many loaves have ye? And they said, Seven, and a few little fishes.

35. And he commanded the multitude to sit down on the ground.

36. And he took the seven loaves and the fishes, and gave thanks, and brake *them*, and gave to his disciples, and the disciples to the multitude.

37. And they did all eat, and were filled: and they took up of the broken *meat* that was left seven baskets full.

38. And they that did eat were four thousand men, beside women and children.

MARK 8:1. In those days the multitude being very great, and having nothing to eat, Jesus called his disciples *unto him*, and saith unto them,

2. I have compassion on the multitude, because they have now been with me three days, and have nothing to eat:

3. And if I send them away fasting to their own houses, they will faint by the way: for divers of them came from far.

4. And his disciples answered him, From whence can a man satisfy these *men* with bread here in the wilderness?

5. And he asked them, How many loaves have ye? And they said, Seven.

6. And he commanded the people to sit down on the ground: and he took the seven loaves, and gave thanks, and brake, and gave to his disciples to set before *them;* and they did set *them* before the people.

7. And they had a few small fishes: and he blessed, and commanded to set them also before *them.*

8. So they did eat, and were filled: and they took up of the broken *meat* that was left seven baskets.

9. And they that had eaten were about four thousand: and he sent them away.

Luke: No record.

John: No record.

Section 97

JESUS GOES TO MAGDALA

Jesus sends away the multitudes, takes ship, and comes to the coasts of Magdala.

Matt. 15:39; Mark 8:10; Luke: No record; John: No record.

Time: A.D. 29, Summer (ANDREWS).

Place: Sea of Galilee (ANDREWS).

MATTHEW 15:39. And he sent away the multitude, and took ship, and came into the coasts of Magdala.

MARK 8:10. ¶ And straightway he entered into a ship with his disciples, and came into the parts of Dalmanutha.

Luke: No record.

John: No record.

Section 98

HE AGAIN DISCOURSES ABOUT SIGNS

The Pharisees and Sadducees come tempting him, and asking for a sign; wearied, he says: "Why doth this generation seek after a sign?"; he tells them, "There shall no sign be given unto this generation"; he points out they can read the signs of the weather but can not read the signs of the times; he tells them that a wicked and adulterous generation

seeketh after a sign; he enters the ship and goes to the other side; he tells his disciples to beware of the leaven of the Pharisees and of Herod; they had taken no bread with them and think he refers to that fact; he bemoans their lack of understanding.

Matt. 16:1-12; Mark 8:11-21; Luke: No record; John: No record.
Time: A.D. 29, Summer (ANDREWS).
Place: Capernaum (ANDREWS).

MATTHEW 16:1. The Pharisees also with the Sadducees came, and tempting desired him that he would shew them a sign from heaven.

2. He answered and said unto them, When it is evening, ye say, *It will be* fair weather: for the sky is red.

3. And in the morning, *It will be* foul weather to day: for the sky is red and lowring. O *ye* hypocrites, ye can discern the face of the sky; but can ye not *discern* the signs of the times?

4. A wicked and adulterous generation seeketh after a sign; and there shall no sign be given unto it, but the sign of the prophet Jonas. And he left them, and departed.

5. And when his disciples were come to the other side, they had forgotten to take bread.

6. ¶ Then Jesus said unto them, Take heed and beware of the leaven of the Pharisees and of the Sadducees.

7. And they reasoned among themselves, saying, *It is* because we have taken no bread.

8. *Which* when Jesus perceived, he said unto them, O ye of little faith, why reason ye among yourselves, because ye have brought no bread?

9. Do ye not yet understand, neither remember the five loaves of the five thousand, and how many baskets ye took up?

10. Neither the seven loaves of the four thousand, and how many baskets ye took up?

11. How is it that ye do not understand that I spake *it* not to you concerning bread, that ye should beware of the leaven of the Pharisees and of the Sadducees?

12. Then understood they how that he bade *them* not beware of the leaven of bread, but of the doctrine of the Pharisees and of the Sadducees.

MARK 8:11. And the Pharisees came forth, and began to question with him, seeking of him a sign from heaven, tempting him.

12. And he sighed deeply in his spirit, and saith, Why doth this generation seek after a sign? verily I say unto you, There shall no sign be given unto this generation.

13. And he left them, and entering into the ship again departed to the other side.

14. ¶ Now *the disciples* had

forgotten to take bread, neither had they in the ship with them more than one loaf.

15. And he charged them, saying, Take heed, beware of the leaven of the Pharisees, and *of* the leaven of Herod.

16. And they reasoned among themselves, saying, *It is* because we have no bread.

17. And when Jesus knew *it*, he saith unto them, Why reason ye, because ye have no bread? perceive ye not yet, neither understand? have ye your heart yet hardened?

18. Having eyes, see ye not? and having ears, hear ye not? and do ye not remember?

19. When I brake the five loaves among five thousand, how many baskets full of fragments took ye up? They say unto him, Twelve.

20. And when the seven among four thousand, how many baskets full of fragments took ye up? And they said, Seven.

21. And he said unto them, How is it that ye do not understand?

Luke: No record.

John: No record.

Section 99

A BLIND MAN HEALED

Jesus comes to Bethsaida; they bring him a blind man to heal and beseech Jesus to touch him; Jesus takes the man by the hand, leads him out of town, spits on his eyes, puts his hands upon him, and asks him if he sees aught; the man says he sees men as trees walking; Jesus puts his hands again upon his eyes, and the man sees clearly; Jesus sends the man away, telling him not to go into the town nor to tell anyone.

Matt.: No record; Mark 8:22-26; Luke: No record; John: No record.
Time: A.D. 29, Summer (ANDREWS).
Place: Bethsaida.

Matthew: No record.

MARK 8:22. ¶ And he cometh to Bethsaida; and they bring a blind man unto him, and besought him to touch him.

23. And he took the blind man by the hand, and led him out of the town; and when he had spit on his eyes, and put his hands upon him, he asked him if he saw ought.

24. And he looked up, and said, I see men as trees, walking.

25. After that he put *his* hands again upon his eyes, and made him look up: and he was restored, and saw every man clearly.

26. And he sent him away to his house, saying, Neither go into the town, nor tell *it* to any in the town.

Luke: No record.

John: No record.

Section 100

PETER'S TESTIMONY OF THE CHRIST

Jesus coming into the coasts of Caesarea Philippi asks his disciples: "Whom do men say that I the Son of man am?"; they answer, some say John the Baptist, some Elias, some Jeremias, or one of the prophets; he then asks, "But whom say ye that I am?" Peter answers, "Thou art the Christ, the Son of the living God"; Jesus blesses Peter and promises the keys of the kingdom and the binding and loosing power; Jesus charges them that they shall tell no one he is the Christ.

Matt. 16:13-20; Mark 8:27-30; Luke 9:18-22; John: No record.
Time: A.D. 29, Summer or Autumn.
Place: Region of Caesarea Philippi.

MATTHEW 16:13. ¶ When Jesus came into the coasts of Cæsarea Philippi, he asked his disciples, saying, Whom do men say that I the Son of man am?

14. And they said, Some *say that thou art* John the Baptist: some, Elias; and others, Jeremias, or one of the prophets.

15. He saith unto them, But whom say ye that I am?

16. And Simon Peter answered and said, Thou art the Christ, the Son of the living God.

17. And Jesus answered and said unto him, Blessed art thou, Simon Bar-jona: for flesh and blood hath not revealed *it* unto thee, but my Father which is in heaven.

18. And I say also unto thee, That thou art Peter, and upon this rock I will build my church; and the gates of hell shall not prevail against it.

19. And I will give unto thee the keys of the kingdom of heaven: and whatsoever thou shalt bind on earth shall be bound in heaven: and whatsoever thou shalt loose on earth shall be loosed in heaven.

20. Then charged he his disciples that they should tell no man that he was Jesus the Christ.

MARK 8:27. ¶ And Jesus went out, and his disciples, into the towns of Cæsarea Philippi: and by the way he asked his disciples, saying unto them, Whom do men say that I am?

28. And they answered, John the Baptist: but some *say*, Elias; and others, One of the prophets.

29. And he saith unto them, But whom say ye that I am? And Peter answereth and saith unto him, Thou art the Christ.

30. And he charged them that they should tell no man of him.

LUKE 9:18. ¶ And it came to pass, as he was alone praying, his disciples were with him: and he asked them, saying, Whom say the people that I am?

19. They answering said,

John the Baptist; but some *say*, Elias; and others *say*, that one of the old prophets is risen again.

20. He said unto them, But whom say ye that I am? Peter answering said, The Christ of God.

21. And he straitly charged them, and commanded *them* to tell no man that thing;

22. Saying, The Son of man must suffer many things, and be rejected of the elders and chief priests and scribes, and be slain, and be raised the third day.

John: No record.

Section 101

HE TEACHES HIS DISCIPLES CONCERNING HIS DEATH AND RESURRECTION

From this time forth Jesus begins to teach his disciples that he will be killed and resurrected on the third day; Peter rebukes Jesus for saying this, and Jesus answers, "Get thee behind me, Satan"; Jesus says men following him must take up the cross; that whosoever saves his life shall lose it, and whosoever loses it for his sake shall find it; he asks what is a man profited if he gain the whole world and lose his soul, or what shall a man give in exchange for his soul; the Son of man shall come in glory and reward every man according to his works; finally he tells them that some standing there shall not taste death.

Matt. 16:21-28; Mark 8:31-38, 9:1; Luke 9:23-27; John: No record.
Time: A.D. 29, Summer or Autumn.
Place: Region of Caesarea Philippi (G. W. Clark).

MATTHEW 16:21. ¶ From that time forth began Jesus to shew unto his disciples, how that he must go unto Jerusalem, and suffer many things of the elders and chief priests and scribes, and be killed, and be raised again the third day.

22. Then Peter took him, and began to rebuke him, saying, Be it far from thee, Lord: this shall not be unto thee.

23. But he turned, and said unto Peter, Get thee behind me, Satan: thou art an offence unto me: for thou savourest not the things that be of God, but those that be of men.

24. ¶ Then said Jesus unto his disciples, If any *man* will come after me, let him deny himself, and take up his cross, and follow me.

25. For whosoever will save his life shall lose it: and whosoever will lose his life for my sake shall find it.

26. For what is a man profited if he shall gain the whole world, and lose his own soul? or what shall a man give in exchange for his soul?

27. For the Son of man shall come in the glory of his Father with his angels; and then he shall reward every man according to his works.

28. Verily I say unto you,

There be some standing here, which shall not taste of death, till they see the Son of man coming in his kingdom.

MARK 8:31. And he began to teach them, that the Son of man must suffer many things, and be rejected of the elders, and *of* the chief priests, and scribes, and be killed, and after three days rise again.

32. And he spake that saying openly. And Peter took him, and began to rebuke him.

33. But when he had turned about and looked on his disciples, he rebuked Peter, saying, Get thee behind me, Satan: for thou savourest not the things that be of God, but the things that be of men.

34. ¶And when he had called the people *unto him* with his disciples also, he said unto them, Whosoever will come after me, let him deny himself, and take up his cross, and follow me.

35. For whosoever will save his life shall lose it; but whosoever shall lose his life for my sake and the gospel's, the same shall save it.

36. For what shall it profit a man, if he shall gain the whole world, and lose his own soul?

37. Or what shall a man give in exchange for his soul?

38. Whosoever therefore shall be ashamed of me and of my words in this adulterous and sinful generation; of him also shall the Son of man be ashamed, when he cometh in the glory of his Father with the holy angels.

9:1. And he said unto them, Verily I say unto you, That there be some of them that stand here, which shall not taste of death, till they have seen the kingdom of God come with power.

LUKE 9:23. ¶And he said to *them* all, If any *man* will come after me, let him deny himself, and take up his cross daily, and follow me.

24. For whosoever will save his life shall lose it: but whosoever will lose his life for my sake, the same shall save it.

25. For what is a man advantaged, if he gain the whole world, and lose himself, or be cast away?

26. For whosoever shall be ashamed of me and of my words, of him shall the Son of man be ashamed, when he shall come in his own glory, and *in his* Father's, and of the holy angels.

27. But I tell you of a truth, there be some standing here, which shall not taste of death, till they see the kingdom of God.

John: No record.

Section 102

THE TRANSFIGURATION

About a week after, Jesus takes Peter, James, and John "up into an high mountain apart," and "was transfigured before them"; the three see Jesus talking with Moses and Elias, and they speak "of his decease which he should accomplish at Jerusalem"; Peter, James, and John "were heavy with sleep" and "when they were awake, they saw his glory, and the two men that stood with him"; Peter proposes to build "three tabernacles," one each for Jesus, Moses, and Elias; then a bright cloud overshadows them, and they hear a voice say, "This is my beloved Son: hear him." They fall to the ground, Jesus touches them and tells them to arise and be not afraid; Jesus charges them to tell no man of this vision till he has risen from the dead; Jesus discourses regarding Elias.

Matt. 17:1-13; Mark 9:2-13; Luke 9:28-36; John: No record.

Time: A.D. 29, Summer or Autumn.

Place: Mt. Hermon.

MATTHEW 17:1. And after six days Jesus taketh Peter, James, and John his brother, and bringeth them up into an high mountain apart,

2. And was transfigured before them: and his face did shine as the sun, and his raiment was white as the light.

3. And, behold, there appeared unto them Moses and Elias talking with him.

4. Then answered Peter, and said unto Jesus, Lord, it is good for us to be here: if thou wilt, let us make here three tabernacles; one for thee, and one for Moses, and one for Elias.

5. While he yet spake, behold, a bright cloud overshadowed them: and behold a voice out of the cloud, which said, This is my beloved Son, in whom I am well pleased; hear ye him.

6. And when the disciples heard *it*, they fell on their face, and were sore afraid.

7. And Jesus came and touched them, and said, Arise, and be not afraid.

8. And when they had lifted up their eyes, they saw no man, save Jesus only.

9. And as they came down from the mountain, Jesus charged them, saying, Tell the vision to no man, until the Son of man be risen again from the dead.

10. And his disciples asked him, saying, Why then say the scribes that Elias must first come?

11. And Jesus answered and said unto them, Elias truly shall first come, and restore all things.

12. But I say unto you, That Elias is come already, and they knew him not, but have done unto him whatsoever they listed. Likewise shall also the Son of man suffer of them.

13. Then the disciples understood that he spake unto them of John the Baptist.

MARK 9:2. ¶And after six days Jesus taketh *with him* Peter, and James, and John, and leadeth them up into an high mountain apart by themselves: and he was transfigured before them.

3. And his raiment became shining, exceeding white as snow; so as no fuller on earth can white them.

4. And there appeared unto them Elias with Moses: and they were talking with Jesus.

5. And Peter answered and said to Jesus, Master, it is good for us to be here: and let us make three tabernacles; one for thee, and one for Moses, and one for Elias.

6. For he wist not what to say; for they were sore afraid.

7. And there was a cloud that overshadowed them: and a voice came out of the cloud, saying, This is my beloved Son: hear him.

8. And suddenly, when they had looked round about, they saw no man any more, save Jesus only with themselves.

9. And as they came down from the mountain, he charged them that they should tell no man what things they had seen, till the Son of man were risen from the dead.

10. And they kept that saying with themselves, questioning one with another what the rising from the dead should mean.

11. ¶And they asked him, saying, Why say the scribes that Elias must first come?

12. And he answered and told them, Elias verily cometh first, and restoreth all things; and how it is written of the Son of man, that he must suffer many things, and be set at nought.

13. But I say unto you, That Elias is indeed come, and they have done unto him whatsoever they listed, as it is written of him.

LUKE 9:28. ¶And it came to pass about an eight days after these sayings, he took Peter and John and James, and went up into a mountain to pray.

29. And as he prayed, the fashion of his countenance was altered, and his raiment *was* white *and* glistering.

30. And, behold, there talked with him two men, which were Moses and Elias:

31. Who appeared in glory, and spake of his decease which he should accomplish at Jerusalem.

32. But Peter and they that were with him were heavy with sleep: and when they were awake, they saw his glory, and the two men that stood with him.

33. And it came to pass, as they departed from him, Peter said unto Jesus, Master, it is good for us to be here: and let us make three tabernacles; one for thee, and one for Moses, and one for Elias: not knowing what he said.

34. While he thus spake,

there came a cloud, and overshadowed them: and they feared as they entered into the cloud.

35. And there came a voice out of the cloud, saying, This is my beloved Son: hear him.

36. And when the voice was past, Jesus was found alone. And they kept *it* close, and told no man in those days any of those things which they had seen.

John: No record.

Section 103

A DEMONIAC HEALED

Coming down from the mountain, they come to the multitude, where his disciples are being questioned by the scribes; a man kneels before Jesus and asks that Jesus heal his only son possessed with a spirit that tears and bruises him, he, foaming at the mouth, gnashing his teeth, and pining away; the disciples have been unable to heal the man; asked if he believes, the father cries: "Lord, I believe; help thou mine unbelief"; Jesus has them bring the child to him and he heals him; Jesus reproves his disciples for unbelief, which prevents their performing the miracle; Jesus states, "Howbeit this kind goeth not out but by prayer and fasting."

Matt. 17:14-21; Mark 9:14-29; Luke 9:37-43a; John: No record.
Time: A.D. 29, Summer-Autumn.
Place: Mt. Hermon (ANDREWS).

MATTHEW 17:14. ¶ And when they were come to the multitude, there came to him a *certain* man, kneeling down to him, and saying,

15. Lord, have mercy on my son: for he is lunatick, and sore vexed: for ofttimes he falleth into the fire, and oft into the water.

16. And I brought him to thy disciples, and they could not cure him.

17. Then Jesus answered and said, O faithless and perverse generation, how long shall I be with you? how long shall I suffer you? bring him hither to me.

18. And Jesus rebuked the devil; and he departed out of him: and the child was cured from that very hour.

19. Then came the disciples to Jesus apart, and said, Why could not we cast him out?

20. And Jesus said unto them, Because of your unbelief: for verily I say unto you, If ye have faith as a grain of mustard seed, ye shall say unto this mountain, Remove hence to yonder place; and it shall remove; and nothing shall be impossible unto you.

21. Howbeit this kind goeth not out but by prayer and fasting.

MARK 9:14. ¶ And when he came to *his* disciples, he saw a great multitude about them, and the scribes questioning with them.

15. And straightway all the people, when they beheld him, were greatly amazed, and running to *him* saluted him.

16. And he asked the scribes, What question ye with them?

17. And one of the multitude answered and said, Master, I have brought unto thee my son, which hath a dumb spirit;

18. And wheresoever he taketh him, he teareth him: and he foameth and gnasheth with his teeth, and pineth away: and I spake to thy disciples that they should cast him out; and they could not.

19. He answereth him, and saith, O faithless generation, how long shall I be with you? how long shall I suffer you? bring him unto me.

20. And they brought him unto him: and when he saw him, straightway the spirit tare him; and he fell on the ground, and wallowed foaming.

21. And he asked his father, How long is it ago since this came unto him? And he said, Of a child.

22. And ofttimes it hath cast him into the fire, and into the waters, to destroy him: but if thou canst do any thing, have compassion on us, and help us.

23. Jesus said unto him, If thou canst believe, all things *are* possible to him that believeth.

24. And straightway the father of the child cried out, and said with tears, Lord, I believe; help thou mine unbelief.

25. When Jesus saw that the people came running together, he rebuked the foul spirit, saying unto him, *Thou* dumb and deaf spirit, I charge thee, come out of him, and enter no more into him.

26. And *the spirit* cried, and rent him sore, and came out of him: and he was as one dead; insomuch that many said, He is dead.

27. But Jesus took him by the hand, and lifted him up; and he arose.

28. And when he was come into the house, his disciples asked him privately, Why could not we cast him out?

29. And he said unto them, This kind can come forth by nothing, but by prayer and fasting.

LUKE 9:37. ¶ And it came to pass, that on the next day, when they were come down from the hill, much people met him.

38. And, behold, a man of the company cried out, saying, Master, I beseech thee, look upon my son: for he is mine only child.

39. And, lo, a spirit taketh him, and he suddenly crieth out; and it teareth him that he foameth again, and bruising him hardly departeth from him.

40. And I besought thy disciples to cast him out; and they could not.

41. And Jesus answering said, O faithless and perverse generation, how long shall I be with you, and suffer you? Bring thy son hither.

42. And as he was yet a coming, the devil threw him down, and tare *him*. And Jesus rebuked the unclean spirit, and healed the child, and delivered him again to his father.

43. ¶And they were all amazed at the mighty power of God. . . .

John: No record.

Section 104

JESUS AGAIN TOURS GALILEE

Jesus passes again through Galilee, teaching his disciples his death and resurrection—"but they understood not that saying, and were afraid to ask him."

Matt. 17:22-23; Mark 9:30-32; Luke 9:43b-45; John: No record.
Time: A.D. 29, Summer-Autumn.
Place: Galilee (G. W. CLARK).

MATTHEW 17:22. ¶And while they abode in Galilee, Jesus said unto them, The Son of man shall be betrayed into the hands of men:

23. And they shall kill him, and the third day he shall be raised again. And they were exceeding sorry.

MARK 9:30. ¶And they departed thence, and passed through Galilee; and he would not that any man should know *it*.

31. For he taught his disciples, and said unto them, The Son of man is delivered into the hands of men, and they shall kill him; and after that he is killed, he shall rise the third day.

32. But they understood not that saying, and were afraid to ask him.

LUKE 9:43. . . . But while they wondered every one at all things which Jesus did, he said unto his disciples,

44. Let these sayings sink down into your ears: for the Son of man shall be delivered into the hands of men.

45. But they understood not this saying, and it was hid from them, that they perceived it not: and they feared to ask him of that saying.

John: No record.

Section 105
THE TRIBUTE MONEY

Tax collectors ask Peter if Jesus pays tribute; Peter says yes; Jesus, upon Peter's coming into the house, questions him and then tells him to go to the sea, cast in a hook, and he shall find the tax money in the mouth of the first fish Peter catches.

Matt. 17:24-27; Mark: No record; Luke: No record; John: No record.
Time: A.D. 29, Summer-Autumn.
Place: Capernaum.

MATTHEW 17:24. ¶ And when they were come to Capernaum, they that received tribute *money* came to Peter, and said, Doth not your master pay tribute?

25. He saith, Yes. And when he was come into the house, Jesus prevented him, saying, What thinkest thou, Simon? of whom do the kings of the earth take custom or tribute? of their own children, or of strangers?

26. Peter saith unto him, Of strangers. Jesus saith unto him, Then are the children free.

27. Notwithstanding, lest we should offend them, go thou to the sea, and cast an hook, and take up the fish that first cometh up; and when thou hast opened his mouth, thou shalt find a piece of money: that take, and give unto them for me and thee.

Mark: No record.
Luke: No record.
John: No record.

Section 106
THE DISCOURSE ON MEEKNESS AND HUMILITY

Jesus asks his disciples what they disputed on the way; they hold their peace; Jesus, perceiving the thoughts of their hearts that they have disputed amongst themselves who shall be greatest, calls to him a little child and sets him in their midst and gives the great discourse on meekness and humility and becoming as little children; he tells them of the place of children in heaven; "if any man desire to be first, the same shall be last of all, and servant of all"; he tells them to purge themselves of things giving offense; saying the Son of man is come to save that which is lost, he gives the parable of the lost sheep and the man leaving the ninety and nine and going in search of the one lost.

Matt. 18:1-14; Mark 9:33-37, 43-50; Luke 9:46-48; John: No record.
Time: A.D. 29, Summer-Autumn.
Place: Capernaum.

MATTHEW 18:1. At the same time came the disciples unto Jesus, saying, Who is the greatest in the kingdom of heaven?

2. And Jesus called a little child unto him, and set him in the midst of them,

3. And said, Verily I say unto you, Except ye be convert-

ed, and become as little children, ye shall not enter into the kingdom of heaven.

4. Whosoever therefore shall humble himself as this little child, the same is greatest in the kingdom of heaven.

5. And whoso shall receive one such little child in my name receiveth me.

6. But whoso shall offend one of these little ones which believe in me, it were better for him that a millstone were hanged about his neck, and *that* he were drowned in the depth of the sea.

7. ¶ Woe unto the world because of offences! for it must needs be that offences come; but woe to that man by whom the offence cometh!

8. Wherefore if thy hand or thy foot offend thee, cut them off, and cast *them* from thee: it is better for thee to enter into life halt or maimed, rather than having two hands or two feet to be cast into everlasting fire.

9. And if thine eye offend thee, pluck it out, and cast *it* from thee: it is better for thee to enter into life with one eye, rather than having two eyes to be cast into hell fire.

10. Take heed that ye despise not one of these little ones; for I say unto you, That in heaven their angels do always behold the face of my Father which is in heaven.

11. For the Son of man is come to save that which was lost.

12. How think ye? if a man have an hundred sheep, and one of them be gone astray, doth he not leave the ninety and nine, and goeth into the mountains, and seeketh that which is gone astray?

13. And if so be that he find it, verily I say unto you, he rejoiceth more of that *sheep*, than of the ninety and nine which went not astray.

14. Even so it is not the will of your Father which is in heaven, that one of these little ones should perish.

MARK 9:33. ¶And he came to Capernaum: and being in the house he asked them, What was it that ye disputed among yourselves by the way?

34. But they held their peace: for by the way they had disputed among themselves, who *should be* the greatest.

35. And he sat down, and called the twelve, and saith unto them, If any man desire to be first, *the same* shall be last of all, and servant of all.

36. And he took a child, and set him in the midst of them: and when he had taken him in his arms, he said unto them,

37. Whosoever shall receive one of such children in my name, receiveth me: and whosoever shall receive me, receiveth not me, but him that sent me. . . .

43. And if thy hand offend thee, cut it off: it is better for thee to enter into life maimed, than having two hands to go

into hell, into the fire that never shall be quenched:

44. Where their worm dieth not, and the fire is not quenched.

45. And if thy foot offend thee, cut it off: it is better for thee to enter halt into life, than having two feet to be cast into hell, into the fire that never shall be quenched:

46. Where their worm dieth not, and the fire is not quenched.

47. And if thine eye offend thee, pluck it out: it is better for thee to enter into the kingdom of God with one eye, than having two eyes to be cast into hell fire:

48. Where their worm dieth not, and the fire is not quenched.

49. For every one shall be salted with fire, and every sacrifice shall be salted with salt.

50. Salt *is* good: but if the salt have lost his saltness, wherewith will ye season it? Have salt in yourselves, and have peace one with another.

LUKE 9:46. ¶ Then there arose a reasoning among them, which of them should be greatest.

47. And Jesus, perceiving the thought of their heart, took a child, and set him by him,

48. And said unto them, Whosoever shall receive this child in my name receiveth me: and whosoever shall receive me receiveth him that sent me: for he that is least among you all, the same shall be great.

John: No record.

Section 107

THE DISCOURSE ON FORGIVENESS AND THE SEALING POWER

Jesus discourses further on dealing with an erring brother; first try to make it right with him alone, then in the presence of witnesses, then before the whole Church, that failing, "let him be unto thee as an heathen man and a publican"; tells them, "Whatsoever ye shall bind on earth shall be bound in heaven: and whatsoever ye shall loose on earth shall be loosed in heaven"; if two agree on earth "as touching any thing that they shall ask, it shall be done for them of my Father which is in heaven. For where two or three are gathered together in my name, there am I in the midst of them."

Matt. 18:15-20; Mark: No record; Luke: No record; John: No record.
Time: A.D. 29, Summer-Autumn.
Place: Capernaum (G. W. CLARK).

MATTHEW 18:15. ¶ Moreover if thy brother shall trespass against thee, go and tell him his fault between thee and him alone: if he shall hear thee, thou hast gained thy brother.

16. But if he will not hear *thee, then* take with thee one or two more, that in the mouth of two or three witnesses every word may be established.

17. And if he shall neglect to

hear them, tell *it* unto the church: but if he neglect to hear the church, let him be unto thee as an heathen man and a publican.

18. Verily I say unto you, Whatsoever ye shall bind on earth shall be bound in heaven: and whatsoever ye shall loose on earth shall be loosed in heaven.

19. Again I say unto you, That if two of you shall agree on earth as touching any thing that they shall ask, it shall be done for them of my Father which is in heaven.

20. For where two or three are gathered together in my name, there am I in the midst of them.

Mark: No record.

Luke: No record.

John: No record.

Section 108

A FURTHER DISCOURSE ON FORGIVENESS

Peter inquires of Jesus, "How oft shall my brother sin against me, and I forgive him? till seven times? Jesus saith unto him, I say not unto thee, Until seven times: but, Until seventy times seven"; Jesus gives the parable of the king who forgave the debt of his servant, who at once dealt harshly with one who owed him, whereupon the Lord took harsh measures against the servant on account of his debt: "So likewise shall my heavenly Father do also unto you, if ye from your hearts forgive not every one his brother their trespasses."

Matt. 18:21-35; Mark: No record; Luke: No record; John: No record.
Time: A.D. 29, Summer-Autumn.
Place: Capernaum (G. W. CLARK).

MATTHEW 18:21. ¶ Then came Peter to him, and said, Lord, how oft shall my brother sin against me, and I forgive him? till seven times?

22. Jesus saith unto him, I say not unto thee, Until seven times: but, Until seventy times seven.

23. ¶Therefore is the kingdom of heaven likened unto a certain king, which would take account of his servants.

24. And when he had begun to reckon, one was brought unto him, which owed him ten thousand talents.

25. But forasmuch as he had not to pay, his lord commanded him to be sold, and his wife, and children, and all that he had, and payment to be made.

26. The servant therefore fell down, and worshipped him, saying, Lord, have patience with me, and I will pay thee all.

27. Then the lord of that servant was moved with compassion, and loosed him, and forgave him the debt.

28. But the same servant went out, and found one of his fellowservants, which owed him an hundred pence: and he laid hands on him, and took *him* by the throat, saying, Pay me that thou owest.

29. And his fellowservant fell down at his feet, and besought him, saying, Have patience with me, and I will pay thee all.

30. And he would not: but went and cast him into prison, till he should pay the debt.

31. So when his fellowservants saw what was done, they were very sorry, and came and told unto their lord all that was done.

32. Then his lord, after that he had called him, said unto him, O thou wicked servant, I forgave thee all that debt, because thou desiredst me:

33. Shouldest not thou also have had compassion on thy fellowservant, even as I had pity on thee?

34. And his lord was wroth, and delivered him to the tormentors, till he should pay all that was due unto him.

35. So likewise shall my heavenly Father do also unto you, if ye from your hearts forgive not every one his brother their trespasses.

Mark: No record.

Luke: No record.

John: No record.

Section 109

PLACE OF THOSE ACTING IN NAME OF CHRIST

John tells Jesus they saw one who did not follow Jesus casting out devils in Jesus' name, and they forbade the man so to do because he was not a follower; Jesus says to forbid him not "for there is no man which shall do a miracle in my name that can lightly speak evil of me; who is not against us is on our part"; whoever gives a cup of water to drink, because the one to drink belongs to Christ, shall not lose his reward; who offends "one of these little ones that believe in me, it is better for him that a millstone were hanged about his neck, and he were cast into the sea."

Matt.: No record; Mark 9:38-42; Luke 9:49-50; John: No record.
Time: A.D. 29, Summer-Autumn.
Place: Capernaum (ROBERTSON).

Matthew: No record.

MARK 9:38. ¶And John answered him, saying, Master, we saw one casting out devils in thy name, and he followeth not us: and we forbad him, because he followeth not us.

39. But Jesus said, Forbid him not: for there is no man which shall do a miracle in my name, that can lightly speak evil of me.

40. For he that is not against us is on our part.

41. For whosoever shall give you a cup of water to drink in my name, because ye belong to Christ, verily I say unto you, he shall not lose his reward.

42. And whosoever shall offend one of *these* little ones

that believe in me, it is better for him that a millstone were hanged about his neck, and he were cast into the sea.

LUKE 9:49. ¶And John answered and said, Master, we saw one casting out devils in thy name; and we forbad him, because he followeth not with us.

50. And Jesus said unto him, Forbid *him* not: for he that is not against us is for us.

John: No record.

Section 110

A DISCOURSE ON SACRIFICE

A man telling Jesus he would follow whithersoever Jesus went, Jesus tells him the foxes have holes, and the birds of the air have nests, but the Son of man hath nowhere to lay his head; Jesus tells another to follow him; the man asks time to bury his father; Jesus says, "Let the dead bury their dead: but go thou and preach the kingdom of God"; another says he will follow, but asks to go bid farewell at his home, Jesus says, "No man, having put his hand to the plough, and looking back, is fit for the kingdom of God."

Matt.: No record; Mark: No record; Luke 9:57-62; John: No record.
Time: A.D. 29, Summer-Autumn.
Place: Capernaum (?).

Matthew: No record.

Mark: No record.

LUKE 9:57. ¶And it came to pass, that, as they went in the way, a certain *man* said unto him, Lord, I will follow thee whithersoever thou goest.

58. And Jesus said unto him, Foxes have holes, and birds of the air *have* nests; but the Son of man hath not where to lay *his* head.

59. And he said unto another, Follow me. But he said, Lord, suffer me first to go and bury my father.

60. Jesus said unto him, Let the dead bury their dead: but go thou and preach the kingdom of God.

61. And another also said, Lord, I will follow thee; but let me first go bid them farewell, which are at home at my house.

62. And Jesus said unto him, No man, having put his hand to the plough, and looking back, is fit for the kingdom of God.

John: No record.

Section 111
THE SEVENTY SENT FORTH

The Seventy are sent forth under a charge.

Matt.: No record; Mark: No record; Luke 10:1-16; John: No record.
Time: A.D. 29, Summer-Autumn.
Place: Capernaum (ROBINSON).

Matthew: No record.

Mark: No record.

LUKE 10:1. After these things the Lord appointed other seventy also, and sent them two and two before his face into every city and place, whither he himself would come.

2. Therefore said he unto them, The harvest truly *is* great, but the labourers *are* few: pray ye therefore the Lord of the harvest, that he would send forth labourers into his harvest.

3. Go your ways: behold, I send you forth as lambs among wolves.

4. Carry neither purse, nor scrip, nor shoes: and salute no man by the way.

5. And into whatsoever house ye enter, first say, Peace *be* to this house.

6. And if the son of peace be there, your peace shall rest upon it: if not, it shall turn to you again.

7. And in the same house remain, eating and drinking such things as they give: for the labourer is worthy of his hire. Go not from house to house.

8. And into whatsoever city ye enter, and they receive you, eat such things as are set before you:

9. And heal the sick that are therein, and say unto them, The kingdom of God is come nigh unto you.

10. But into whatsoever city ye enter, and they receive you not, go your ways out into the streets of the same, and say,

11. Even the very dust of your city, which cleaveth on us, we do wipe off against you: notwithstanding be ye sure of this, that the kingdom of God is come nigh unto you.

12. But I say unto you, that it shall be more tolerable in that day for Sodom, than for that city.

13. Woe unto thee, Chorazin! woe unto thee, Bethsaida! for if the mighty works had been done in Tyre and Sidon, which have been done in you, they had a great while ago repented, sitting in sackcloth and ashes.

14. But it shall be more tolerable for Tyre and Sidon at the judgment, than for you.

15. And thou, Capernaum, which art exalted to heaven, shalt be thrust down to hell.

16. He that heareth you heareth me; and he that despiseth you despiseth me; and he that despiseth me despiseth him that sent me.

John: No record.

Section 112

JESUS' BRETHREN URGE HIM TO GO TO JUDEA

His brethren urge him to go to Judea to show there his works, because no man doeth things in secret, and he should show himself to the world if he do these things (his brethren do not believe in him); he says his time is not come, their time is always ready; the world cannot hate them but it hates him because he testifies of it, "that the works thereof are evil"; he tells them to go to the feast, but he still abides in Galilee.

Matt.: No record; Mark: No record; Luke: No record; John 7:2-9.
Time: A.D. 29, Summer-Autumn.
Place: Galilee.

Matthew: No record.

Mark: No record.

Luke: No record.

JOHN 7:2. Now the Jews' feast of tabernacles was at hand.

3. His brethren therefore said unto him, Depart hence, and go into Judæa, that thy disciples also may see the works that thou doest.

4. For *there is* no man *that* doeth any thing in secret, and he himself seeketh to be known openly. If thou do these things, shew thyself to the world.

5. For neither did his brethren believe in him.

6. Then Jesus said unto them, My time is not yet come: but your time is alway ready.

7. The world cannot hate you; but me it hateth, because I testify of it, that the works thereof are evil.

8. Go ye up unto this feast: I go not up yet unto this feast; for my time is not yet full come.

9. When he had said these words unto them, he abode *still* in Galilee.

Section 113

JESUS STARTS FOR JERUSALEM

Jesus starts for Jerusalem; sends messengers before him, they made ready for him in a Samaritan village which will not receive him because his face is set for Jerusalem; James and John wish to call down fire from heaven, "even as Elias did," to consume them, but Jesus rebukes them: "Ye know not what manner of spirit ye are of. For the Son of man is not come to destroy men's lives, but to save them"; they go to another village.

Matt.: No record; Mark: No record; Luke 9:51-56; John 7:10.
Time: A.D. 29, October (ANDREWS).
Place: Galilee to Judea through Samaria.

Matthew: No record.

Mark: No record.

LUKE 9:51. ¶And it came to pass, when the time was come that he should be received up, he stedfastly set his face to go to Jerusalem,

52. And sent messengers before his face: and they went, and entered into a village of the Samaritans, to make ready for him.

53. And they did not receive him, because his face was as though he would go to Jerusalem.

54. And when his disciples James and John saw *this*, they said, Lord, wilt thou that we command fire to come down from heaven, and consume them, even as Elias did?

55. But he turned, and rebuked them, and said, Ye know not what manner of spirit ye are of.

56. For the Son of man is not come to destroy men's lives, but to save *them*. And they went to another village.

JOHN 7:10. ¶ But when his brethren were gone up, then went he also up unto the feast, not openly, but as it were in secret.

FIFTH PERIOD

THE LATER JUDEAN MINISTRY

Section 114

AT THE FEAST OF THE TABERNACLES

Jesus attends the Feast of the Tabernacles in Jerusalem; people not immediately finding Jesus at the feast, they murmur, some saying he is a good man, others saying he deceives the people; no one speaks openly of him for fear of the Jews; in the midst of the feast Jesus goes into the Temple and teaches; the people marvel at his learning; Jesus answers, "My doctrine is not mine, but his that sent me. If any man will do his will, he shall know of the doctrine, whether it be of God, or whether I speak of myself"; Jesus says they seek to kill him, the people say he is possessed with a devil; he defends healing on the Sabbath; people talk of his boldness in teaching and ask if rulers really know he is the Christ; Jesus affirms they know both who he is and whence he came; no man lays hands on him, but later the Pharisees and chief priests send officers to take him; he tells of his death and resurrection, and they think he speaks of going among the Gentiles; some of the people hearing all this say he is the Christ, others speak otherwise; some would take him, but again no man lays hands on him; the officers return to the Pharisees and chief priests without Jesus, and they excuse themselves for their failure that "never man spake like this man"; Nicodemus asks if their law judges any man before he is heard; they ask if he is a follower of Jesus; all go to their houses.

Matt.: No record; Mark: No record; Luke: No record; John 7:11-53.
Time: A.D. 29, October 11-18 (ANDREWS).
Place: Jerusalem.

Matthew: No record.

Mark: No record.

Luke: No record.

JOHN 7:11. Then the Jews sought him at the feast, and said, Where is he?

12. And there was much murmuring among the people concerning him: for some said, He is a good man: others said, Nay; but he deceiveth the people.

13. Howbeit no man spake openly of him for fear of the Jews.

14. ¶Now about the midst of the feast Jesus went up into the temple, and taught.

15. And the Jews marvelled, saying, How knoweth this man letters, having never learned?

16. Jesus answered them, and said, My doctrine is not mine, but his that sent me.

17. If any man will do his will, he shall know of the doctrine, whether it be of God, or *whether* I speak of myself.

18. He that speaketh of himself seeketh his own glory: but he that seeketh his glory that

sent him, the same is true, and no unrighteousness is in him.

19. Did not Moses give you the law, and *yet* none of you keepeth the law? Why go ye about to kill me?

20. The people answered and said, Thou hast a devil: who goeth about to kill thee?

21. Jesus answered and said unto them, I have done one work, and ye all marvel.

22. Moses therefore gave unto you circumcision; (not because it is of Moses, but of the fathers;) and ye on the sabbath day circumcise a man.

23. If a man on the sabbath day receive circumcision, that the law of Moses should not be broken; are ye angry at me, because I have made a man every whit whole on the sabbath day?

24. Judge not according to the appearance, but judge righteous judgment.

25. Then said some of them of Jerusalem, Is not this he, whom they seek to kill?

26. But, lo, he speaketh boldly, and they say nothing unto him. Do the rulers know indeed that this is the very Christ?

27. Howbeit we know this man whence he is: but when Christ cometh, no man knoweth whence he is.

28. Then cried Jesus in the temple as he taught, saying, Ye both know me, and ye know whence I am: and I am not come of myself, but he that sent me is true, whom ye know not.

29. But I know him: for I am from him, and he hath sent me.

30. Then they sought to take him: but no man laid hands on him, because his hour was not yet come.

31. And many of the people believed on him, and said, When Christ cometh, will he do more miracles than these which this *man* hath done?

32. ¶ The Pharisees heard that the people murmured such things concerning him; and the Pharisees and the chief priests sent officers to take him.

33. Then said Jesus unto them, Yet a little while am I with you, and *then* I go unto him that sent me.

34. Ye shall seek me, and shall not find *me*: and where I am, *thither* ye cannot come.

35. Then said the Jews among themselves, Whither will he go, that we shall not find him? will he go unto the dispersed among the Gentiles, and teach the Gentiles?

36. What *manner of* saying is this that he said, Ye shall seek me, and shall not find *me*: and where I am, *thither* ye cannot come?

37. In the last day, that great *day* of the feast, Jesus stood and cried, saying, If any man thirst, let him come unto me, and drink.

38. He that believeth on me, as the scripture hath said, out

of his belly shall flow rivers of living water.

39. (But this spake he of the Spirit, which they that believe on him should receive: for the Holy Ghost was not yet *given;* because that Jesus was not yet glorified.)

40. ¶ Many of the people therefore, when they heard this saying, said, Of a truth this is the Prophet.

41. Others said, This is the Christ. But some said, Shall Christ come out of Galilee?

42. Hath not the scripture said, That Christ cometh of the seed of David, and out of the town of Bethlehem, where David was?

43. So there was a division among the people because of him.

44. And some of them would have taken him; but no man laid hands on him.

45. ¶ Then came the officers to the chief priests and Pharisees; and they said unto them, Why have ye not brought him?

46. The officers answered, Never man spake like this man.

47. Then answered them the Pharisees, Are ye also deceived?

48. Have any of the rulers or of the Pharisees believed on him?

49. But this people who knoweth not the law are cursed.

50. Nicodemus saith unto them, (he that came to Jesus by night, being one of them,)

51. Doth our law judge *any* man, before it hear him, and know what he doeth?

52. They answered and said unto him, Art thou also of Galilee? Search, and look: for out of Galilee ariseth no prophet.

53. And every man went unto his own house.

Section 115

THE WOMAN TAKEN IN ADULTERY

Jesus coming to the Temple early in the morning, the scribes and Pharisees bring to him a woman taken in adultery, ask his judgment on her, telling the law of Moses; he writes on the ground as if he hears them not; they continue asking him, so lifting himself up he says, "He that is without sin among you, let him first cast a stone at her"; he again stoops and writes, the accusers slink away one by one, beginning with the eldest until the last; Jesus and the woman are left alone; Jesus lifts himself up again, and seeing no one but the woman there, he asks, "Woman, where are those thine accusers? hath no man condemned thee? She said, No man, Lord. And Jesus said unto her, Neither do I condemn thee: go, and sin no more."

Matt.: No record; Mark: No record; Luke: No record; John 8:1-11.
Time: A.D. 29, October 11-18 (ANDREWS).
Place: Jerusalem; Temple.

Matthew: No record.

Mark: No record.

Luke: No record.

JOHN 8:1. Jesus went unto the mount of Olives.

2. And early in the morning he came again into the temple, and all the people came unto him; and he sat down, and taught them.

3. And the scribes and Pharisees brought unto him a woman taken in adultery; and when they had set her in the midst,

4. They say unto him, Master, this woman was taken in adultery, in the very act.

5. Now Moses in the law commanded us, that such should be stoned: but what sayest thou?

6. This they said, tempting him, that they might have to accuse him. But Jesus stooped down, and with *his* finger wrote on the ground, *as though he heard them not.*

7. So when they continued asking him, he lifted up himself, and said unto them, He that is without sin among you, let him first cast a stone at her.

8. And again he stooped down, and wrote on the ground.

9. And they which heard *it,* being convicted by *their own* conscience, went out one by one, beginning at the eldest, *even* unto the last: and Jesus was left alone, and the woman standing in the midst.

10. When Jesus had lifted up himself, and saw none but the woman, he said unto her, Woman, where are those thine accusers? hath no man condemned thee?

11. She said, No man, Lord. And Jesus said unto her, Neither do I condemn thee: go, and sin no more.

Section 116

THE LIGHT OF THE WORLD; HIS ONENESS WITH THE FATHER

Jesus speaks to them saying, "I am the light of the world," those following him will walk in light not in darkness; the Pharisees accuse him of bearing untrue record of himself; Jesus affirms his record is true, that he knows whence he came, whither he goes, they do not know; they do judge after the flesh, he judgeth not, but if he judgeth his judgment is true, "for I am not alone, but I and the Father that sent me"; the law says the testimony of two men is true, he and the Father beareth witness of him, they ask where his Father is; Jesus answers they know neither him nor his Father; he tells them they will die in their sins and whither he goes they can not come; they ask if he will kill himself; he says they are from beneath, he is from above; they will die in their sins; they ask who he is and he answers the same one he has declared from the beginning: "I have many things to say and to judge of you: but he that sent me is true; and I speak to the world those

things which I have heard of him"; he says they will know him when they lift him up; he repeats that he does nothing of himself but only what his Father taught him, and that the Father is with him; many believe.

Matt.: No record; Mark: No record; Luke: No record; John 8:12-30.
Time: A.D. 29, October 11-18 (ANDREWS).
Place: Jerusalem; Temple Treasury.

Matthew: No record.

Mark: No record.

Luke: No record.

JOHN 8:12. ¶Then spake Jesus again unto them, saying, I am the light of the world: he that followeth me shall not walk in darkness, but shall have the light of life.

13. The Pharisees therefore said unto him, Thou bearest record of thyself; thy record is not true.

14. Jesus answered and said unto them, Though I bear record of myself, *yet* my record is true: for I know whence I came, and whither I go; but ye cannot tell whence I come, and whither I go.

15. Ye judge after the flesh; I judge no man.

16. And yet if I judge, my judgment is true: for I am not alone, but I and the Father that sent me.

17. It is also written in your law, that the testimony of two men is true.

18. I am one that bear witness of myself, and the Father that sent me beareth witness of me.

19. Then said they unto him, Where is thy Father? Jesus answered, Ye neither know me, nor my Father: if ye had known me, ye should have known my Father also.

20. These words spake Jesus in the treasury, as he taught in the temple: and no man laid hands on him; for his hour was not yet come.

21. Then said Jesus again unto them, I go my way, and ye shall seek me, and shall die in your sins: whither I go, ye cannot come.

22. Then said the Jews, Will he kill himself? because he saith, Whither I go, ye cannot come.

23. And he said unto them, Ye are from beneath; I am from above: ye are of this world; I am not of this world.

24. I said therefore unto you, that ye shall die in your sins: for if ye believe not that I am *he*, ye shall die in your sins.

25. Then said they unto him, Who art thou? And Jesus saith unto them, Even *the same* that I said unto you from the beginning.

26. I have many things to say and to judge of you: but he that sent me is true; and I speak to the world those things which I have heard of him.

27. They understood not that he spake to them of the Father.

28. Then said Jesus unto them, When ye have lifted up the Son of man, then shall ye know that I am *he*, and *that* I do nothing of myself; but as my Father hath taught me, I speak these things.

29. And he that sent me is with me: the Father hath not left me alone; for I do always those things that please him.

30. As he spake these words, many believed on him.

Section 117

THE DISCOURSE TO THE JEWS

Jesus preaches to those Jews who believe on him, and tells them, "Ye shall know the truth, and the truth shall make you free"; to their reply that they are Abraham's seed and never were in bondage to any man, he replies that "whosoever committeth sin is the servant of sin," that the Son abideth in the house forever but not the servant, and the Son shall make them free; he says they seek his life because his word has no place in them; he again tells them he speaks what he has seen with his Father and they do what they have seen with their father, they say they are Abraham's children, he tells them to do the works of Abraham; they seek to kill him because he speaks truth; "this did not Abraham"; they say they are not born of fornication; he again speaks of his Messiahship; he tells them they are the children of the devil; "he that is of God heareth God's words"; they ask if he is not a Samaritan and hath not a devil; he answers he has not a devil and honors his Father; he tells them that "if a man keep my saying, he shall never see death"; they say they now know he has a devil and ask who he is; he says Abraham rejoiced to see his day; they say he is not fifty years old, how could he see Abraham; he answers, "Before Abraham was, I am"; they take up stones to cast at him, but he slips away from the Temple, "going through the midst of them."

Matt.: No record; Mark: No record; Luke: No record; John 8:31-59.
Time: A.D. 29, October 11-18 (ANDREWS).
Place: Jerusalem; Temple.

Matthew: No record.

Mark: No record.

Luke: No record.

JOHN 8:31. Then said Jesus to those Jews which believed on him, If ye continue in my word, *then* are ye my disciples indeed;

32. And ye shall know the truth, and the truth shall make you free.

33. ¶They answered him, We be Abraham's seed, and were never in bondage to any man: how sayest thou, Ye shall be made free?

34. Jesus answered them, Verily, verily, I say unto you, Whosoever committeth sin is the servant of sin.

35. And the servant abideth not in the house for ever: *but* the Son abideth ever.

36. If the Son therefore shall make you free, ye shall be free indeed.

37. I know that ye are Abraham's seed; but ye seek to kill me, because my word hath no place in you.

38. I speak that which I have seen with my Father: and ye do that which ye have seen with your father.

39. They answered and said unto him, Abraham is our father. Jesus saith unto them, If ye were Abraham's children, ye would do the works of Abraham.

40. But now ye seek to kill me, a man that hath told you the truth, which I have heard of God: this did not Abraham.

41. Ye do the deeds of your father. Then said they to him, We be not born of fornication; we have one Father, *even* God.

42. Jesus said unto them, If God were your Father, ye would love me: for I proceeded forth and came from God; neither came I of myself, but he sent me.

43. Why do ye not understand my speech? *even* because ye cannot hear my word.

44. Ye are of *your* father the devil, and the lusts of your father ye will do. He was a murderer from the beginning, and abode not in the truth, because there is no truth in him. When he speaketh a lie, he speaketh of his own: for he is a liar, and the father of it.

45. And because I tell *you* the truth, ye believe me not.

46. Which of you convinceth me of sin? And if I say the truth, why do ye not believe me?

47. He that is of God heareth God's words: ye therefore hear *them* not, because ye are not of God.

48. Then answered the Jews, and said unto him, Say we not well that thou art a Samaritan, and hast a devil?

49. Jesus answered, I have not a devil; but I honour my Father, and ye do dishonour me.

50. And I seek not mine own glory: there is one that seeketh and judgeth.

51. Verily, verily, I say unto you, If a man keep my saying, he shall never see death.

52. Then said the Jews unto him, Now we know that thou hast a devil. Abraham is dead, and the prophets; and thou sayest, If a man keep my saying, he shall never taste of death.

53. Art thou greater than our father Abraham, which is dead? and the prophets are dead: whom makest thou thyself?

54. Jesus answered, If I honour myself, my honour is nothing: it is my Father that honoureth me; of whom ye say, that he is your God:

55. Yet ye have not known him; but I know him: and if I should say, I know him not,

I shall be a liar like unto you: but I know him, and keep his saying.

56. Your father Abraham rejoiced to see my day: and he saw *it*, and was glad.

57. Then said the Jews unto him, Thou art not yet fifty years old, and hast thou seen Abraham?

58. Jesus said unto them, Verily, verily, I say unto you, Before Abraham was, I am.

59. Then took they up stones to cast at him: but Jesus hid himself, and went out of the temple, going through the midst of them, and so passed by.

Section 118

THE SEVENTY RETURN

The Seventy return in joy saying, "Lord, even the devils are subject unto us through thy name"; Jesus says he saw Satan "as lightning fall from heaven"; he gives unto them power over poisonous things, the power of the enemy, and tells them nothing shall hurt them; tells them to rejoice that their names are written in heaven, rather than to rejoice in their powers; Jesus rejoices and thanks the Father; speaks of the Father and Son; he tells his disciples privately how blessed they are for what they see and hear and do not see and hear.

Matt.: No record; Mark: No record; Luke 10:17-24; John: No record.
Time: A.D. 29, October-November.
Place: Judea (ROBERTSON).

Matthew: No record.

Mark: No record.

LUKE 10:17. ¶ And the seventy returned again with joy, saying, Lord, even the devils are subject unto us through thy name.

18. And he said unto them, I beheld Satan as lightning fall from heaven.

19. Behold, I give unto you power to tread on serpents and scorpions, and over all the power of the enemy: and nothing shall by any means hurt you.

20. Notwithstanding in this rejoice not, that the spirits are subject unto you; but rather rejoice, because your names are written in heaven.

21. ¶In that hour Jesus rejoiced in spirit, and said, I thank thee, O Father, Lord of heaven and earth, that thou hast hid these things from the wise and prudent, and hast revealed them unto babes: even so, Father; for so it seemed good in thy sight.

22. All things are delivered to me of my Father: and no man knoweth who the Son is, but the Father; and who the Father is, but the Son, and *he* to whom the son will reveal *him*.

23. ¶ And he turned him unto *his* disciples, and said privately, Blessed *are* the eyes which see the things that ye see:

24. For I tell you, that many prophets and kings have desired to see those things which ye see, and have not seen *them;* and to hear those things which ye hear, and have not heard *them.*

John: No record.

Section 119

THE TWO GREAT COMMANDMENTS; PARABLE OF THE GOOD SAMARITAN

A lawyer, tempting Jesus, asks what he shall do to inherit eternal life; Jesus asks what is written in the law; the lawyer says the two great commandments of loving God with all one's heart, soul, and strength, and thy neighbor as thyself; Jesus tells him he is right and gives the parable of the good Samaritan, then tells the lawyer to do likewise.

Matt.: No record; Mark: No record; Luke 10:25-37; John: No record.
Time: A.D. 29, October-December.
Place: Judea (ROBERTSON).

Matthew: No record.

Mark: No record.

LUKE 10:25. ¶And, behold, a certain lawyer stood up, and tempted him, saying, Master, what shall I do to inherit eternal life?

26. He said unto him, What is written in the law? how readest thou?

27. And he answering said, Thou shalt love the Lord thy God with all thy heart, and with all thy soul, and with all thy strength, and with all thy mind; and thy neighbour as thyself.

28. And he said unto him, Thou hast answered right: this do, and thou shalt live.

29. But he, willing to justify himself, said unto Jesus, And who is my neighbour?

30. And Jesus answering said, A certain *man* went down from Jerusalem to Jericho, and fell among thieves, which stripped him of his raiment, and wounded *him,* and departed, leaving *him* half dead.

31. And by chance there came down a certain priest that way: and when he saw him, he passed by on the other side.

32. And likewise a Levite, when he was at the place, came and looked *on him,* and passed by on the other side.

33. But a certain Samaritan, as he journeyed, came where he was: and when he saw him, he had compassion *on him,*

34. And went to *him,* and bound up his wounds, pouring

in oil and wine, and set him on his own beast, and brought him to an inn, and took care of him.

35. And on the morrow when he departed, he took out two pence, and gave *them* to the host, and said unto him, Take care of him; and whatsoever thou spendest more, when I come again, I will repay thee.

36. Which now of these three, thinkest thou, was neighbour unto him that fell among the thieves?

37. And he said, He that shewed mercy on him. Then said Jesus unto him, Go, and do thou likewise.

John: No record.

Section 120

JESUS VISITS MARY AND MARTHA

Jesus visits Mary and Martha; Martha "cumbered about much serving," complains because Mary sits at Jesus' feet and leaves the work for her; Jesus replies.

Matt.: No record; Mark: No record; Luke 10:38-42; John: No record.
Time: A.D. 29, October-December.
Place: Bethany.

Matthew: No record.

Mark: No record.

LUKE 10:38. ¶ Now it came to pass, as they went, that he entered into a certain village: and a certain woman named Martha received him into her house.

39. And she had a sister called Mary, which also sat at Jesus' feet, and heard his word.

40. But Martha was cumbered about much serving, and came to him, and said, Lord, dost thou not care that my sister hath left me to serve alone? bid her therefore that she help me.

41. And Jesus answered and said unto her, Martha, Martha, thou art careful and troubled about many things:

42. But one thing is needful: and Mary hath chosen that good part, which shall not be taken away from her.

John: No record.

Section 121

HE TEACHES HIS DISCIPLES TO PRAY

One of the disciples asks Jesus to teach them how to pray even as John taught his disciples how to pray; Jesus gives "The Lord's Prayer"; he urges prayer to the point of importunity; "ask, and it shall be given you; seek, and ye shall find; knock, and it shall be opened unto you";

he points out that fathers do not give a stone to a son asking for bread, nor a serpent to one asking for fish, and that our Heavenly Father, not less kind than our earthly fathers, will "give the Holy Spirit to them that ask him."

Matt.: No record; Mark: No record; Luke 11:1-13; John: No record.
Time: A.D. 29, October-December.
Place: Judea (ROBERTSON).

Matthew: No record.

Mark: No record.

LUKE 11:1. And it came to pass, that, as he was praying in a certain place, when he ceased, one of his disciples said unto him, Lord, teach us to pray, as John also taught his disciples.

2. And he said unto them, When ye pray, say, Our Father which art in heaven, Hallowed be thy name. Thy kingdom come. Thy will be done, as in heaven, so in earth.

3. Give us day by day our daily bread.

4. And forgive us our sins; for we also forgive every one that is indebted to us. And lead us not into temptation; but deliver us from evil.

5. And he said unto them, Which of you shall have a friend, and shall go unto him at midnight, and say unto him, Friend, lend me three loaves;

6. For a friend of mine in his journey is come to me, and I have nothing to set before him?

7. And he from within shall answer and say, Trouble me not: the door is now shut, and my children are with me in bed; I cannot rise and give thee.

8. I say unto you, Though he will not rise and give him, because he is his friend, yet because of his importunity he will rise and give him as many as he needeth.

9. And I say unto you, Ask, and it shall be given you; seek, and ye shall find; knock, and it shall be opened unto you.

10. For every one that asketh receiveth; and he that seeketh findeth; and to him that knocketh it shall be opened.

11. If a son shall ask bread of any of you that is a father, will he give him a stone? or if *he ask* a fish, will he for a fish give him a serpent?

12. Or if he shall ask an egg, will he offer him a scorpion?

13. If ye then, being evil, know how to give good gifts unto your children: how much more shall *your* heavenly Father give the Holy Spirit to them that ask him?

John: No record.

Section 122

HE CASTS OUT A DUMB DEVIL AND IS AGAIN ACCUSED OF BEING IN LEAGUE WITH BEELZEBUB

Jesus casts out a dumb devil and the man speaks; some again charge that Jesus does his works by the power of Beelzebub, others tempting him seek for a sign; he reasons how he cannot be doing this by the power of Satan, a house divided against a house falleth; if he casts evil spirits by the power of Satan, by what power have their sons worked; if he works by the power of God, is not his kingdom come; a strong man, armed, holds his goods and palace, but a stranger comes upon him, seizes his palace and divideth his spoils; "he that is not with me is against me: and he that gathereth not with me scattereth"; the parable of the unclean spirit; a woman calls out blessings upon his mother; "but he said, Yea rather, blessed are they that hear the word of God, and keep it"; he speaks to a thick multitude about signs, another sign given of his Messiahship; speaks of Jonas, the Queen of Sheba, of a lighted candle under a bushel, of the light of the eye, of light and darkness, and the whole body lighted.

Matt.: No record; Mark: No record; Luke 11:14-36; John: No record.
Time: A.D. 29, October-December.
Place: Judea (ROBERTSON).

Matthew: No record.

Mark: No record.

LUKE 11:14. ¶ And he was casting out a devil, and it was dumb. And it came to pass, when the devil was gone out, the dumb spake; and the people wondered.

15. But some of them said, He casteth out devils through Beelzebub the chief of the devils.

16. And others, tempting *him*, sought of him a sign from heaven.

17. But he, knowing their thoughts, said unto them, Every kingdom divided against itself is brought to desolation; and a house *divided* against a house falleth.

18. If Satan also be divided against himself, how shall his kingdom stand? because ye say that I cast out devils through Beelzebub.

19. And if I by Beelzebub cast out devils, by whom do your sons cast *them* out? therefore shall they be your judges.

20. But if I with the finger of God cast out devils, no doubt the kingdom of God is come upon you.

21. When a strong man armed keepeth his palace, his goods are in peace:

22. But when a stronger than he shall come upon him, and overcome him, he taketh from him all his armour wherein he trusted, and divideth his spoils.

23. He that is not with me is against me: and he that gathereth not with me scattereth.

24. When the unclean spirit is gone out of a man, he walketh through dry places, seeking rest; and finding none, he saith, I will return unto my house whence I came out.

25. And when he cometh, he findeth *it* swept and garnished.

26. Then goeth he, and taketh *to him* seven other spirits more wicked than himself; and they enter in, and dwell there: and the last *state* of that man is worse than the first.

27. ¶ And it came to pass, as he spake these things, a certain woman of the company lifted up her voice, and said unto him, Blessed *is* the womb that bare thee, and the paps which thou hast sucked.

28. But he said, Yea rather, blessed *are* they that hear the word of God, and keep it.

29. ¶And when the people were gathered thick together, he began to say, This is an evil generation: they seek a sign; and there shall no sign be given it, but the sign of Jonas the prophet.

30. For as Jonas was a sign unto the Ninevites, so shall also the Son of man be to this generation.

31. The queen of the south shall rise up in the judgment with the men of this generation, and condemn them: for she came from the utmost parts of the earth to hear the wisdom of Solomon; and, behold, a greater than Solomon *is* here.

32. The men of Nineve shall rise up in the judgment with this generation, and shall condemn it: for they repented at the preaching of Jonas; and, behold, a greater than Jonas *is* here.

33. No man, when he hath lighted a candle, putteth *it* in a secret place, neither under a bushel, but on a candlestick, that they which come in may see the light.

34. The light of the body is the eye: therefore when thine eye is single, thy whole body also is full of light; but when *thine eye* is evil, thy body also *is* full of darkness.

35. Take heed therefore that the light which is in thee be not darkness.

36. If thy whole body therefor *be* full of light, having no part dark, the whole shall be full of light, as when the bright shining of a candle doth give thee light.

John: No record.

Section 123

ANOTHER DISCOURSE ON CLEANLINESS

As he speaks a Pharisee asks Jesus to eat; the Pharisee marvels that Jesus eats with unwashed hands; Jesus speaks of the outward cleanliness and the inward uncleanliness of the Pharisees; he condemns the

hypocrisy of the Pharisees and scribes, and their pride; a lawyer saying that Jesus' words include them too, Jesus condemns lawyers also, tells them they load men with burdens grievous to be borne, but touch not the burdens themselves; he charges they approve the killing of the prophets by their fathers, by building sepulchres for them; he tells them "that the blood of all the prophets, which was shed from the foundation of the world, may be required of this generation"; the lawyers "have taken away the key of knowledge: ye entered not in yourselves, and them that were entering in ye hindered"; the scribes and Pharisees then bait him, laying wait for some words for which they might accuse him.

Matt.: No record; Mark: No record; Luke 11:37-54; John: No record.
Time: A.D. 29, October-December.
Place: Judea (ROBERTSON).

Matthew: No record.

Mark: No record.

LUKE 11:37. ¶ And as he spake, a certain Pharisee besought him to dine with him: and he went in, and sat down to meat.

38. And when the Pharisee saw *it*, he marvelled that he had not first washed before dinner.

39. And the Lord said unto him, Now do ye Pharisees make clean the outside of the cup and the platter; but your inward part is full of ravening and wickedness.

40. *Ye* fools, did not he that made that which is without make that which is within also?

41. But rather give alms of such things as ye have; and, behold, all things are clean unto you.

42. But woe unto you, Pharisees! for ye tithe mint and rue and all manner of herbs, and pass over judgment and the love of God: these ought ye to have done, and not to leave the other undone.

43. Woe unto you, Pharisees! for ye love the uppermost seats in the synagogues, and greetings in the markets.

44. Woe unto you, scribes and Pharisees, hypocrites! for ye are as graves which appear not, and the men that walk over *them* are not aware *of them*.

45. ¶ Then answered one of the lawyers, and said unto him, Master, thus saying thou reproachest us also.

46. And he said, Woe unto you also, *ye* lawyers! for ye lade men with burdens grievous to be borne, and ye yourselves touch not the burdens with one of your fingers.

47. Woe unto you! for ye build the sepulchres of the prophets, and your fathers killed them.

48. Truly ye bear witness that ye allow the deeds of your fathers: for they indeed killed them, and ye build their sepulchres.

49. Therefore also said the wisdom of God, I will send them prophets and apostles, and *some* of them they shall slay and persecute:

50. That the blood of all the prophets, which was shed from the foundation of the world, may be required of this generation;

51. From the blood of Abel unto the blood of Zacharias, which perished between the altar and the temple: verily I say unto you, It shall be required of this generation.

52. Woe unto you, lawyers! for ye have taken away the key of knowledge: ye entered not in yourselves, and them that were entering in ye hindered.

53. And as he said these things unto them, the scribes and the Pharisees began to urge *him* vehemently, and to provoke him to speak of many things:

54. Laying wait for him, and seeking to catch something out of his mouth, that they might accuse him.

John: No record.

Section 124

JESUS TEACHES MULTITUDE; PARABLE OF THE FOOLISH RICH MAN

An innumerable multitude, treading one upon another, gather together meantime; Jesus first speaks to his disciples, warning them of the leaven of the Pharisees which is hypocrisy; nothing can be hidden, all will be known; fear him who, killing, may cast into hell; God watches the sparrows, much more you; whoso denies Jesus before men shall be denied before the angels of God; speaking against the Son of man shall be forgiven, but whoso blasphemeth against the Holy Ghost shall never be forgiven; when the disciples are brought before the synagogues or magistrates they shall take no thought of what they shall say, for the Holy Ghost shall teach them in that hour; he denies right to pass upon division of inheritance; speaks the parable of the rich man who in his pride said he was beyond want; tells his disciples to give their time to his work; speaking of the lilies of the field, how they grow, he says the Lord will provide; tells them to sell what they have and give alms; parable of the watchful servants, waiting for the return of their lord; Peter asks if this parable is for all or for the disciples, and is answered by a parable; Jesus says he came to send fire to the earth; he has a baptism; he does not bring peace; tells the people of their blindness; urges that disputes be settled before they get to the courts.

Matt.: No record; Mark: No record; Luke 12:1-59; John: No record.
Time: A.D. 29, October-December.
Place: Judea (ROBERTSON).

Matthew: No record.

Mark: No record.

LUKE 12:1. In the mean time, when there were gathered together an innumerable multitude of people, insomuch that they trode one upon another, he began to say unto his disciples first of all, Beware ye of the leaven of the Pharisees, which is hypocrisy.

2. For there is nothing covered, that shall not be revealed; neither hid, that shall not be known.

3. Therefore whatsoever ye have spoken in darkness shall be heard in the light; and that which ye have spoken in the ear in closets shall be proclaimed upon the housetops.

4. And I say unto you my friends, Be not afraid of them that kill the body, and after that have no more that they can do.

5. But I will forewarn you whom ye shall fear: Fear him, which after he hath killed hath power to cast into hell; yea, I say unto you, Fear him.

6. Are not five sparrows sold for two farthings, and not one of them is forgotten before God?

7. But even the very hairs of your head are all numbered. Fear not therefore: ye are of more value than many sparrows.

8. Also I say unto you, Whosoever shall confess me before men, him shall the Son of man also confess before the angels of God:

9. But he that denieth me before men shall be denied before the angels of God.

10. And whosoever shall speak a word against the Son of man, it shall be forgiven him: but unto him that blasphemeth against the Holy Ghost it shall not be forgiven.

11. And when they bring you unto the synagogues, and *unto* magistrates, and powers, take ye no thought how or what thing ye shall answer, or what ye shall say:

12. For the Holy Ghost shall teach you in the same hour what ye ought to say.

13. ¶And one of the company said unto him, Master, speak to my brother, that he divide the inheritance with me.

14. And he said unto him, Man, who made me a judge or a divider over you?

15. And he said unto them, Take heed, and beware of covetousness: for a man's life consisteth not in the abundance of the things which he possesseth.

16. And he spake a parable unto them, saying, The ground of a certain rich man brought forth plentifully:

17. And he thought within himself, saying, What shall I do, because I have no room where to bestow my fruits?

18. And he said, This will I do: I will pull down my barns, and build greater; and there will I bestow all my fruits and my goods.

19. And I will say to my soul, Soul, thou hast much goods laid up for many years; take thine ease, eat, drink, *and* be merry.

20. But God said unto him, *Thou* fool, this night thy soul shall be required of thee: then

whose shall those things be, which thou hast provided?

21. So *is* he that layeth up treasure for himself, and is not rich toward God.

22. ¶And he said unto his disciples, Therefore I say unto you; Take no thought for your life, what ye shall eat; neither for the body, what ye shall put on.

23. The life is more than meat, and the body *is more* than raiment.

24. Consider the ravens: for they neither sow nor reap; which neither have storehouse nor barn; and God feedeth them: how much more are ye better than the fowls?

25. And which of you with taking thought can add to his stature one cubit?

26. If ye then be not able to do that thing which is least, why take ye thought for the rest?

27. Consider the lilies how they grow: they toil not, they spin not; and yet I say unto you, that Solomon in all his glory was not arrayed like one of these.

28. If then God so clothe the grass, which is to day in the field, and to morrow is cast into the oven; how much more *will he clothe* you, O ye of little faith?

29. And seek not ye what ye shall eat, or what ye shall drink, neither be ye of doubtful mind.

30. For all these things do the nations of the world seek after: and your Father knoweth that ye have need of these things.

31. ¶But rather seek ye the kingdom of God; and all these things shall be added unto you.

32. Fear not, little flock; for it is your Father's good pleasure to give you the kingdom.

33. Sell that ye have, and give alms; provide yourselves bags which wax not old, a treasure in the heavens that faileth not, where no thief approacheth, neither moth corrupteth.

34. For where your treasure is, there will your heart be also.

35. Let your loins be girded about, and *your* lights burning;

36. And ye yourselves like unto men that wait for their lord, when he will return from the wedding; that when he cometh and knocketh, they may open unto him immediately.

37. Blessed *are* those servants, whom the lord when he cometh shall find watching: verily I say unto you, that he shall gird himself, and make them to sit down to meat, and will come forth and serve them.

38. And if he shall come in the second watch, or come in the third watch, and find *them* so, blessed are those servants.

39. And this know, that if the goodman of the house had known what hour the thief would come, he would have watched, and not have suffered his house to be broken through.

40. Be ye therefore ready also: for the Son of man cometh at an hour when ye think not.

41. ¶ Then Peter said unto him, Lord, speakest thou this parable unto us, or even to all?

42. And the Lord said, Who then is that faithful and wise steward, whom *his* lord shall make ruler over his household, to give *them their* portion of meat in due season?

43. Blessed *is* that servant, whom his lord when he cometh shall find so doing.

44. Of a truth I say unto you, that he will make him ruler over all that he hath.

45. But and if that servant say in his heart, My lord delayeth his coming; and shall begin to beat the menservants and maidens, and to eat and drink, and to be drunken;

46. The lord of that servant will come in a day when he looketh not for *him*, and at an hour when he is not aware, and will cut him in sunder, and will appoint him his portion with the unbelievers.

47. And that servant, which knew his lord's will, and prepared not *himself*, neither did according to his will, shall be beaten with many *stripes*.

48. But he that knew not, and did commit things worthy of stripes, shall be beaten with few *stripes*. For unto whomsoever much is given, of him shall be much required: and to whom men have committed much, of him they will ask the more.

49. ¶ I am come to send fire on the earth; and what will I, if it be already kindled?

50. But I have a baptism to be baptized with; and how am I straitened till it be accomplished!

51. Suppose ye that I am come to give peace on earth? I tell you, Nay; but rather division:

52. For from henceforth there shall be five in one house divided, three against two, and two against three.

53. The father shall be divided against the son, and the son against the father; the mother against the daughter, and the daughter against the mother; the mother in law against her daughter in law, and the daughter in law against her mother in law.

54. ¶And he said also to the people, When ye see a cloud rise out of the west, straightway ye say, There cometh a shower; and so it is.

55. And when *ye see* the south wind blow, ye say, There will be heat; and it cometh to pass.

56. *Ye* hypocrites, ye can discern the face of the sky and of the earth; but how is it that ye do not discern this time?

57. Yea, and why even of yourselves judge ye not what is right?

58. ¶When thou goest with

thine adversary to the magistrate, *as thou art* in the way, give diligence that thou mayest be delivered from him; lest he hale thee to the judge, and the judge deliver thee to the officer, and the officer cast thee into prison.

59. I tell thee, thou shalt not depart thence, till thou hast paid the very last mite.

John: No record.

Section 125

THE SLAUGHTER OF THE GALILEANS

Some of those present tell that Pilate has slaughtered some Galileans and mingled their blood with the blood of their sacrifices; Jesus says these Galileans were not sinners above other Galileans, and "except ye repent, ye shall all likewise perish"; speaks of them upon whom the tower of Siloam fell, repeats the question put to them about the Galileans, and gives the same admonition; gives the parable of the unfruitful fig tree.

Matt.: No record; Mark: No record; Luke 13:1-9; John: No record.

Time: A.D. 29, October-December.

Place: Judea (ROBERTSON).

Matthew: No record.

Mark: No record.

LUKE 13:1. There were present at that season some that told him of the Galilæans, whose blood Pilate had mingled with their sacrifices.

2. And Jesus answering said unto them, Suppose ye that these Galilæans were sinners above all the Galilæans, because they suffered such things?

3. I tell you, Nay: but, except ye repent, ye shall all likewise perish.

4. Or those eighteen, upon whom the tower in Siloam fell, and slew them, think ye that they were sinners above all men that dwelt in Jerusalem?

5. I tell you, Nay: but, except ye repent, ye shall all likewise perish.

6. ¶He spake also this parable; A certain *man* had a fig tree planted in his vineyard; and he came and sought fruit thereon, and found none.

7. Then said he unto the dresser of his vineyard, Behold, these three years I come seeking fruit on this fig tree, and find none: cut it down; why cumbereth it the ground?

8. And he answering said unto him, Lord, let it alone this year also, till I shall dig about it, and dung *it*:

9. And if it bear fruit, *well*: and if not, *then* after that thou shalt cut it down.

John: No record.

Section 126

JESUS HEALS MAN BORN BLIND

Jesus passing by sees a man blind from his birth; the disciples ask, "Who did sin, this man, or his parents, that he was born blind?"; Jesus replies neither, but this blindness was "that the works of God should be made manifest in him"; Jesus says he must do the work of him who sent him while it is yet day, for "the night cometh, when no man can work"; "as long as I am in the world, I am the light of the world"; Jesus spits on the ground, moistens clay, anoints the eyes of the blind man and tells him to wash in the pool of Siloam; he goes, washes, and comes away seeing; the neighbors see him seeing, and cannot believe their own eyes; he admits he is the one born blind, they ask who healed him, he says Jesus; they take the man to the Pharisees who investigate the case, they divide about Jesus; the Jews call the parents who say the man is their son, but they do not know how he came by his sight; they then examine the man himself again; they accuse him of being a disciple of Jesus; the man makes a powerful defense; they cast the man out; Jesus hearing this seeks the man out and asks, "Dost thou believe on the Son of God?"; to the question of the man, "Who is he, Lord, that I might believe on him," the Lord says, "Thou hast both seen him, and it is he that talketh with thee," and the man answers: "Lord, I believe," and worships; the Lord says that he came into the world that those who see not might see, and some Pharisees hearing, ask, "Are we blind also?" Jesus answers them.

Matt.: No record; Mark: No record; Luke: No record; John 9:1-41.

Time: A.D. 29, October-December.

Place: Judea (ROBERTSON says Jerusalem).

Matthew: No record.

Mark: No record.

Luke: No record.

JOHN 9:1. And as *Jesus* passed by, he saw a man which was blind from *his* birth.

2. And his disciples asked him, saying, Master, who did sin, this man, or his parents, that he was born blind?

3. Jesus answered, Neither hath this man sinned, nor his parents: but that the works of God should be made manifest in him.

4. I must work the works of him that sent me, while it is day: the night cometh, when no man can work.

5. As long as I am in the world, I am the light of the world.

6. When he had thus spoken, he spat on the ground, and made clay of the spittle, and he anointed the eyes of the blind man with the clay,

7. And said unto him, Go, wash in the pool of Siloam, (which is by interpretation, Sent.) He went his way therefore, and washed, and came seeing.

8. ¶ The neighbours therefore, and they which before had seen him that he was blind, said, Is not this he that sat and begged?

9. Some said, This is he:

others *said*, He is like him: *but* he said, I am *he*.

10. Therefore said they unto him, How were thine eyes opened?

11. He answered and said, A man that is called Jesus made clay, and anointed mine eyes, and said unto me, Go to the pool of Siloam, and wash: and I went and washed, and I received sight.

12. Then said they unto him, Where is he? He said, I know not.

13. ¶They brought to the Pharisees him that aforetime was blind.

14. And it was the sabbath day when Jesus made the clay, and opened his eyes.

15. Then again the Pharisees also asked him how he had received his sight. He said unto them, He put clay upon mine eyes, and I washed, and do see.

16. Therefore said some of the Pharisees, This man is not of God, because he keepeth not the sabbath day. Others said, How can a man that is a sinner do such miracles? And there was a division among them.

17. They say unto the blind man again, What sayest thou of him, that he hath opened thine eyes? He said, He is a prophet.

18. But the Jews did not believe concerning him, that he had been blind, and received his sight, until they called the parents of him that had received his sight.

19. And they asked them, saying, Is this your son, who ye say was born blind? how then doth he now see?

20. His parents answered them and said, We know that this is our son, and that he was born blind:

21. But by what means he now seeth, we know not; or who hath opened his eyes, we know not: he is of age; ask him: he shall speak for himself.

22. These *words* spake his parents, because they feared the Jews: for the Jews had agreed already, that if any man did confess that he was Christ, he should be put out of the synagogue.

23. Therefore said his parents, He is of age; ask him.

24. Then again called they the man that was blind, and said unto him, Give God the praise: we know that this man is a sinner.

25. He answered and said, Whether he be a sinner *or no*, I know not: one thing I know, that, whereas I was blind, now I see.

26. Then said they to him again, What did he to thee? how opened he thine eyes?

27. He answered them, I have told you already, and ye did not hear: wherefore would ye hear *it* again? will ye also be his disciples?

28. Then they reviled him, and said, Thou art his disciple; but we are Moses' disciples.

29. We know that God spake

unto Moses: *as for* this *fellow*, we know not from whence he is.

30. The man answered and said unto them, Why herein is a marvellous thing, that ye know not from whence he is, and *yet* he hath opened mine eyes.

31. Now we know that God heareth not sinners: but if any man be a worshipper of God, and doeth his will, him he heareth.

32. Since the world began was it not heard that any man opened the eyes of one that was born blind.

33. If this man were not of God, he could do nothing.

34. They answered and said unto him, Thou wast altogether born in sins, and dost thou teach us? And they cast him out.

35. Jesus heard that they had cast him out; and when he had found him, he said unto him, Dost thou believe on the Son of God?

36. He answered and said, Who is he, Lord, that I might believe on him?

37. And Jesus said unto him, Thou hast both seen him, and it is he that talketh with thee.

38. And he said, Lord, I believe. And he worshipped him.

39. ¶ And Jesus said, For judgment I am come into this world, that they which see not might see; and that they which see might be made blind.

40. And *some* of the Pharisees which were with him heard these words, and said unto him, Are we blind also?

41. Jesus said unto them, If ye were blind, ye should have no sin: but now ye say, We see; therefore your sin remaineth.

Section 127

THE PARABLE OF THE GOOD SHEPHERD

Jesus speaks unto them the parable of the good shepherd, but they understand not; Jesus says: "I am the door of the sheep," "I am the good shepherd," and "know my sheep, and am known of mine"; and "other sheep I have, which are not of this fold: them also I must bring, and they shall hear my voice; and there shall be one fold, and one shepherd. Therefore doth my Father love me, because I lay down my life, that I might take it again. No man taketh it from me, but I lay it down of myself. I have power to lay it down, and I have power to take it again. This commandment have I received of my Father"; the Jews are still divided on the matter, some saying he has a devil, some otherwise.

Matt.: No record; Mark: No record; Luke: No record; John 10:1-21.
Time: A.D. 29, October-December.
Place: Jerusalem (ROBERTSON).

Matthew: No record.
Mark: No record.
Luke: No record.

JOHN 10:1. Verily, verily, I say unto you, He that entereth not by the door into the sheepfold, but climbeth up some other way, the same is a thief and a robber.

2. But he that entereth in by the door is the shepherd of the sheep.

3. To him the porter openeth; and the sheep hear his voice: and he calleth his own sheep by name, and leadeth them out.

4. And when he putteth forth his own sheep, he goeth before them, and the sheep follow him: for they know his voice.

5. And a stranger will they not follow, but will flee from him: for they know not the voice of strangers.

6. This parable spake Jesus unto them: but they understood not what things they were which he spake unto them.

7. Then said Jesus unto them again, Verily, verily, I say unto you, I am the door of the sheep.

8. All that ever came before me are thieves and robbers: but the sheep did not hear them.

9. I am the door: by me if any man enter in, he shall be saved, and shall go in and out, and find pasture.

10. The thief cometh not, but for to steal, and to kill, and to destroy: I am come that they might have life, and that they might have *it* more abundantly.

11. I am the good shepherd: the good shepherd giveth his life for the sheep.

12. But he that is an hireling, and not the shepherd, whose own the sheep are not, seeth the wolf coming, and leaveth the sheep, and fleeth: and the wolf catcheth them, and scattereth the sheep.

13. The hireling fleeth, because he is an hireling, and careth not for the sheep.

14. I am the good shepherd, and know my *sheep*, and am known of mine.

15. As the Father knoweth me, even so know I the Father: and I lay down my life for the sheep.

16. And other sheep I have, which are not of this fold: them also I must bring, and they shall hear my voice; and there shall be one fold, *and* one shepherd.

17. Therefore doth my Father love me, because I lay down my life, that I might take it again.

18. No man taketh it from me, but I lay it down of myself. I have power to lay it down, and I have power to take it again. This commandment have I received of my Father.

19. ¶ There was a division therefore again among the Jews for these sayings.

20. And many of them said,

He hath a devil, and is mad; why hear ye him?

21. Others said, These are not the words of him that hath a devil. Can a devil open the eyes of the blind?

Section 128

THE FEAST OF DEDICATION

Jesus at the Feast of the Dedication, walks in Solomon's Porch of the Temple; the Jews demand that he tell them plainly whether he be Christ; he says he has told them and that his works bear witness; "but ye believe not, because ye are not of my sheep. . . . My sheep hear my voice, and I know them, and they follow me: and I give unto them eternal life"; "I and my Father are one"; the Jews take up stones to stone him, he asks why, they say for blasphemy, "because that thou, being a man, makest thyself God"; Jesus points out to them that the law says, "Ye are gods," and asserts his Messiahship; they seek to take him, and he escapes.

Matt.: No record; Mark: No record; Luke: No record; John 10:22-39a.
Time: A.D. 29, December 20-27 (ANDREWS).
Place: Jerusalem: Temple, Solomon's Porch.

Matthew: No record.

Mark: No record.

Luke: No record.

JOHN 10:22. ¶And it was at Jerusalem the feast of the dedication, and it was winter.

23. And Jesus walked in the temple in Solomon's porch.

24. Then came the Jews round about him, and said unto him, How long dost thou make us to doubt? If thou be the Christ, tell us plainly.

25. Jesus answered them, I told you, and ye believed not: the works that I do in my Father's name, they bear witness of me.

26. But ye believe not, because ye are not of my sheep, as I said unto you.

27. My sheep hear my voice, and I know them, and they follow me:

28. And I give unto them eternal life; and they shall never perish, neither shall any *man* pluck them out of my hand.

29. My Father, which gave *them* me, is greater than all; and no *man* is able to pluck *them* out of my Father's hand.

30. I and *my* Father are one.

31. Then the Jews took up stones again to stone him.

32. Jesus answered them, Many good works have I shewed you from my Father; for which of those works do ye stone me?

33. The Jews answered him, saying, For a good work we stone thee not; but for blasphemy; and because that thou, being a man, makest thyself God.

34. Jesus answered them, Is

it not written in your law, I said, Ye are gods?

35. If he called them gods, unto whom the word of God came, and the scripture cannot be broken;

36. Say ye of him, whom the Father hath sanctified, and sent into the world, Thou blasphemest; because I said, I am the Son of God?

37. If I do not the works of my Father, believe me not.

38. But if I do, though ye believe not me, believe the works: that ye may know, and believe, that the Father *is* in me, and I in him.

39. Therefore they sought again to take him. . . .

SIXTH PERIOD

THE PEREAN MINISTRY

Section 129

JESUS GOES BEYOND THE JORDAN

Jesus escapes those who seek to take him, and goes beyond the Jordan to the place where John at first baptized, and there abides; many come to see him, saying, "John did no miracle: but all things that John spake of this man were true"; many believed.

Matt.: No record; Mark: No record; Luke: No record; John 10:39b-42.
Time: A.D. 30, January (ANDREWS).
Place: Perea.

Matthew: No record.

Mark: No record.

Luke: No record.

JOHN 10:39 . . . . but he escaped out of their hand,

40. And went away again beyond Jordan into the place where John at first baptized; and there he abode.

41. And many resorted unto him, and said, John did no miracle: but all things that John spake of this man were true.

42. And many believed on him there.

Section 130

THE HEALING ON THE SABBATH OF WOMAN LONG ILL

Jesus, teaching in one of the synagogues on the Sabbath, sees a woman afflicted for eighteen years, and calls her to him and says: "Woman, thou art loosed from thine infirmity. And he laid his hands on her"; she is immediately healed; a ruler of the synagogue indignantly complains that with six days to work, Jesus heals on the Sabbath; Jesus replies by showing how they water their cattle on the Sabbath, and ought not this woman to be healed on the Sabbath; the adversaries of Jesus are ashamed and the people rejoice.

Matt.: No record; Mark: No record; Luke 13:10-17; John: No record.
Time: A.D. 30 .
Place: Perea (G. W. CLARK).

Matthew: No record.
Mark: No record.
LUKE 13:10. And he was teaching in one of the synagogues on the sabbath.

11. ¶And, behold, there was a woman which had a spirit of infirmity eighteen years, and was bowed together, and could in no wise lift up *herself*.

12. And when Jesus saw her, he called *her to him*, and said unto her, Woman, thou art loosed from thine infirmity.

13. And he laid *his* hands on her: and immediately she was made straight, and glorified God.

14. And the ruler of the synagogue answered with indignation, because that Jesus had healed on the sabbath day, and said unto the people, There are six days in which men ought to work: in them therefore come and be healed, and not on the sabbath day.

15. The Lord then answered him, and said, *Thou* hypocrite, doth not each one of you on the sabbath loose his ox or *his* ass from the stall, and lead *him* away to watering?

16. And ought not this woman, being a daughter of Abraham, whom Satan hath bound, lo, these eighteen years, be loosed from this bond on the sabbath day?

17. And when he had said these things, all his adversaries were ashamed: and all the people rejoiced for all the glorious things that were done by him.

John: No record.

Section 131

THE PARABLE OF THE MUSTARD SEED

Jesus speaks the parables of the mustard seed and the leaven.

Matt.: No record; Mark: No record; Luke 13:18-21; John: No record.
Time: A.D. 30.
Place: Perea (G. W. CLARK).

Matthew: No record.

Mark: No record.

LUKE 13:18. ¶Then said he, Unto what is the kingdom of God like? and whereunto shall I resemble it?

19. It is like a grain of mustard seed, which a man took, and cast into his garden; and it grew, and waxed a great tree; and the fowls of the air lodged in the branches of it.

20. And again he said, Whereunto shall I liken the kingdom of God?

21. It is like leaven, which a woman took and hid in three measures of meal, till the whole was leavened.

John: No record.

Section 132

THE BEGINNING OF JOURNEY TO JERUSALEM

Jesus begins journeying towards Jerusalem, teaching in the cities and villages on the way; one says to him: "Lord, are there few that be saved?"; he speaks to them, partly in parable, showing how that many

who seek salvation shall not secure it; those who seek entry to the door because they ate with the Master or he taught in the streets, shall be shut out; they will see Abraham, Isaac, and Jacob, and all the prophets inside, and "you yourselves thrust out"; many shall come from the east, west, north, and south, and sit down in the kingdom of God; "and, behold, there are last which shall be first, and there are first which shall be last."

Matt.: No record; Mark: No record; Luke 13:22-30; John: No record.
Time: A.D. 30.
Place: Perea (G. W. CLARK).

Matthew: No record.

Mark: No record.

LUKE 13:22. And he went through the cities and villages, teaching, and journeying toward Jerusalem.

23. Then said one unto him, Lord, are there few that be saved? And he said unto them,

24. ¶ Strive to enter in at the strait gate: for many, I say unto you, will seek to enter in, and shall not be able.

25. When once the master of the house is risen up, and hath shut to the door, and ye begin to stand without, and to knock at the door, saying, Lord, Lord, open unto us; and he shall answer and say unto you, I know you not whence ye are:

26. Then shall ye begin to say, We have eaten and drunk in thy presence, and thou hast taught in our streets.

27. But he shall say, I tell you, I know you not whence ye are; depart from me, all *ye* workers of iniquity.

28. There shall be weeping and gnashing of teeth, when ye shall see Abraham, and Isaac, and Jacob, and all the prophets, in the kingdom of God, and you *yourselves* thrust out.

29. And they shall come from the east, and *from* the west, and from the north, and *from* the south, and shall sit down in the kingdom of God.

30. And, behold, there are last which shall be first, and there are first which shall be last.

John: No record.

Section 133

THE WARNING ABOUT HEROD ANTIPAS

Pharisees come and warn Jesus that Herod Antipas will kill him; Jesus replies by referring to his death and resurrection; he states he must go to Jerusalem "for it cannot be that a prophet perish out of Jerusalem"; he laments over Jerusalem.

Matt.: No record; Mark: No record; Luke 13:31-35; John: No record.
Time: A.D. 30.
Place: Perea.

Matthew: No record.

Mark: No record.

LUKE 13:31. ¶The same day there came certain of the Pharisees, saying unto him, Get thee out, and depart hence: for Herod will kill thee.

32. And he said unto them, Go ye, and tell that fox, Behold, I cast out devils, and I do cures to day and to morrow, and the third *day* I shall be perfected.

33. Nevertheless I must walk to day, and to morrow, and the *day* following: for it cannot be that a prophet perish out of Jerusalem.

34. O Jerusalem, Jerusalem, which killest the prophets, and stonest them that are sent unto thee; how often would I have gathered thy children together, as a hen *doth gather* her brood under *her* wings, and ye would not!

35. Behold, your house is left unto you desolate: and verily I say unto you, Ye shall not see me, until *the time* come when ye shall say, Blessed *is* he that cometh in the name of the Lord.

John: No record.

Section 134

THE MESSAGE THAT LAZARUS IS SICK

Mary and Martha send word to Jesus to tell him Lazarus is sick; Jesus loves Martha, Mary, and Lazarus; Jesus abides for two days in the place where he hears the news; he then suggests to his disciples that they go to Judea; but they point out that the Jews sought to stone him; Jesus answers in a parable; he then says Lazarus sleepeth, but he goes to waken him; the disciples say, "if he sleep, he shall do well"; "then said Jesus unto them plainly, Lazarus is dead"; he says he is glad he was not there, so they may believe; Thomas, which is called Didymus, says to his fellow disciples, "Let us also go, that we may die with him."

Matt.: No record; Mark: No record; Luke: No record; John 11:1-16.

Time: A.D. 30, Winter (?).

Place: Perea (G. W. CLARK).

Matthew: No record.

Mark: No record.

Luke: No record.

JOHN 11:1. Now a certain *man* was sick, *named* Lazarus, of Bethany, the town of Mary and her sister Martha.

2. (It was *that* Mary which anointed the Lord with ointment, and wiped his feet with her hair, whose brother Lazarus was sick.)

3. Therefore his sisters sent unto him, saying, Lord, behold, he whom thou lovest is sick.

4. When Jesus heard *that*, he said, This sickness is not unto death, but for the glory of God, that the Son of God might be glorified thereby.

5. Now Jesus loved Martha, and her sister, and Lazarus.

6. When he had heard therefore that he was sick, he abode two days still in the same place where he was.

7. Then after that saith he to *his* disciples, Let us go into Judæa again.

8. *His* disciples say unto him, Master, the Jews of late sought to stone thee; and goest thou thither again?

9. Jesus answered, Are there not twelve hours in the day? If any man walk in the day, he stumbleth not, because he seeth the light of this world.

10. But if a man walk in the night, he stumbleth, because there is no light in him.

11. These things said he: and after that he saith unto them, Our friend Lazarus sleepeth; but I go, that I may awake him out of sleep.

12. Then said his disciples, Lord, if he sleep, he shall do well.

13. Howbeit Jesus spake of his death: but they thought that he had spoken of taking of rest in sleep.

14. Then said Jesus unto them plainly, Lazarus is dead.

15. And I am glad for your sakes that I was not there, to the intent ye may believe; nevertheless let us go unto him.

16. Then said Thomas, which is called Didymus, unto his fellow disciples, Let us also go, that we may die with him.

Section 135

MAN WITH DROPSY HEALED ON THE SABBATH

Jesus goes to the house of a Pharisee to eat bread on the Sabbath; they watch him; a man with dropsy comes before Jesus; he asks the Pharisees if it is lawful to heal on the Sabbath; they remaining silent, he heals the man; Jesus puts to the Pharisees the case of the ox in the pit, and they can not answer; he gives the parable of the wedding feast; he tells the Pharisee, his host, to make a feast for the poor, the maimed, and the blind, and his recompense will come in the resurrection of the just; a fellow guest says: "Blessed is he that shall eat bread in the kingdom of God," and Jesus replying gives the parable of the man inviting his friends who made excuses for not coming and then of the man going out and filling up the table with the poor, the maimed, the halt, and the blind, so that none of those first invited could eat.

Matt.: No record; Mark: No record; Luke 14:1-24; John: No record.
Time: A.D. 30, Winter (?).
Place: Perea (G. W. CLARK).

Matthew: No record.

Mark: No record.

LUKE 14:1. And it came to pass, as he went into the house of one of the chief Pharisees to eat bread on the sabbath day, that they watched him.

2. And, behold, there was a

certain man before him which had the dropsy.

3. And Jesus answering spake unto the lawyers and Pharisees, saying, Is it lawful to heal on the sabbath day?

4. And they held their peace. And he took *him*, and healed him, and let him go;

5. And answered them, saying, Which of you shall have an ass or an ox fallen into a pit, and will not straightway pull him out on the sabbath day?

6. And they could not answer him again to these things.

7. ¶ And he put forth a parable to those which were bidden, when he marked how they chose out the chief rooms; saying unto them,

8. When thou art bidden of any *man* to a wedding, sit not down in the highest room; lest a more honourable man than thou be bidden of him;

9. And he that bade thee and him come and say to thee, Give this man place; and thou begin with shame to take the lowest room.

10. But when thou art bidden, go and sit down in the lowest room; that when he that bade thee cometh, he may say unto thee, Friend, go up higher: then shalt thou have worship in the presence of them that sit at meat with thee.

11. For whosoever exalteth himself shall be abased; and he that humbleth himself shall be exalted.

12. ¶ Then said he also to him that bade him, When thou makest a dinner or a supper, call not thy friends, nor thy brethren, neither thy kinsmen, nor *thy* rich neighbours; lest they also bid thee again, and a recompence be made thee.

13. But when thou makest a feast, call the poor, the maimed, the lame, the blind:

14. And thou shalt be blessed; for they cannot recompense thee: for thou shalt be recompensed at the resurrection of the just.

15. ¶ And when one of them that sat at meat with him heard these things, he said unto him, Blessed *is* he that shall eat bread in the kingdom of God.

16. Then said he unto him, A certain man made a great supper, and bade many:

17. And sent his servant at supper time to say to them that were bidden, Come; for all things are now ready.

18. And they all with one *consent* began to make excuse. The first said unto him, I have bought a piece of ground, and I must needs go and see it: I pray thee have me excused.

19. And another said, I have bought five yoke of oxen, and I go to prove them: I pray thee have me excused.

20. And another said, I have married a wife, and therefore I cannot come.

21. So that servant came, and shewed his lord these things. Then the master of the

house being angry said to his servant, Go out quickly into the streets and lanes of the city, and bring in hither the poor, and the maimed, and the halt, and the blind.

22. And the servant said, Lord, it is done as thou hast commanded, and yet there is room.

23. And the lord said unto the servant, Go out into the highways and hedges, and compel *them* to come in, that my house may be filled.

24. For I say unto you, That none of those men which were bidden shall taste of my supper.

John: No record.

Section 136

ANOTHER DISCOURSE ON SACRIFICE

Jesus tells the multitude of the sacrifice which must be made by his followers, one not forsaking his family and hating his own life, "cannot be my disciple"; he gives, to show what he means, the example of a man building a tower, and a king making war; "whosoever he be of you that forsaketh not all that he hath, he cannot be my disciple"; he gives a further example of salt losing its savor, and its proper use.

Matt.: No record; Mark: No record; Luke 14:25-35; John: No record.
Time: A.D. 30, Winter (?).
Place: Perea (G. W. CLARK).

Matthew: No record.

Mark: No record.

LUKE 14:25. ¶ And there went great multitudes with him: and he turned, and said unto them,

26. If any *man* come to me, and hate not his father, and mother, and wife, and children, and brethren, and sisters, yea, and his own life also, he cannot be my disciple.

27. And whosoever doth not bear his cross, and come after me, cannot be my disciple.

28. For which of you, intending to build a tower, sitteth not down first, and counteth the cost, whether he have *sufficient* to finish *it?*

29. Lest haply, after he hath laid the foundation, and is not able to finish *it*, all that behold *it* begin to mock him,

30. Saying, This man began to build, and was not able to finish.

31. Or what king, going to make war against another king, sitteth not down first, and consulteth whether he be able with ten thousand to meet him that cometh against him with twenty thousand?

32. Or else, while the other is yet a great way off, he sendeth an ambassage, and desireth conditions of peace.

33. So likewise, whosoever he be of you that forsaketh not all that he hath, he cannot be my disciple.

34. ¶ Salt *is* good: but if the salt have lost his savour, wherewith shall it be seasoned?

35. It is neither fit for the land, nor yet for the dunghill; *but* men cast it out. He that hath ears to hear, let him hear.

John: No record.

Section 137

A GROUP OF PARABLES

All the publicans and sinners draw near unto Jesus; the Pharisees and scribes murmur: "This man receiveth sinners, and eateth with them."

Matt.: No record; Mark: No record; Luke 15:1-2; John: No record.

Time: A.D. 30, Winter (?).

Place: Perea (G. W. Clark).

Matthew: No record.

Mark: No record.

LUKE 15:1. Then drew near unto him all the publicans and sinners for to hear him.

2. And the Pharisees and scribes murmured, saying, This man receiveth sinners, and eateth with them.

John: No record.

(a) Parable of the Lost Sheep

Joy in heaven over one sinner that repenteth.

Matt.: No record; Mark: No record; Luke 15:3-7; John: No record.

Matthew: No record.

Mark: No record.

LUKE 15:3. ¶ And he spake this parable unto them, saying,

4. What man of you, having an hundred sheep, if he lose one of them, doth not leave the ninety and nine in the wilderness, and go after that which is lost, until he find it?

5. And when he hath found *it*, he layeth *it* on his shoulders, rejoicing.

6. And when he cometh home, he calleth together *his* friends and neighbours, saying unto them, Rejoice with me; for I have found my sheep which was lost.

7. I say unto you, that likewise joy shall be in heaven over one sinner that repenteth, more than over ninety and nine just persons, which need no repentance.

John: No record.

(b) Parable of the Ten Pieces of Silver

There is joy in the presence of the angels of God over one sinner that repenteth.

Matt.: No record; Mark: No record; Luke 15:8-10; John: No record.

Matthew: No record.

Mark: No record.

LUKE 15:8. ¶ Either what woman having ten pieces of silver, if she lose one piece, doth not light a candle, and sweep the house, and seek diligently till she find *it?*

9. And when she hath found *it*, she calleth *her* friends and *her* neighbours together, saying, Rejoice with me; for I have found the piece which I had lost.

10. Likewise, I say unto you, there is joy in the presence of the angels of God over one sinner that repenteth.

John: No record.

(c) Parable of the Return of the Prodigal Son

Matt.: No record; Mark: No record; Luke 15:11-32; John: No record.

Matthew: No record.

Mark: No record.

LUKE 15:11. ¶ And he said, A certain man had two sons:

12. And the younger of them said to *his* father, Father, give me the portion of goods that falleth *to me.* And he divided unto them *his* living.

13. And not many days after the younger son gathered all together, and took his journey into a far country, and there wasted his substance with riotous living.

14. And when he had spent all, there arose a mighty famine in that land; and he began to be in want.

15. And he went and joined himself to a citizen of that country; and he sent him into his fields to feed swine.

16. And he would fain have filled his belly with the husks that the swine did eat: and no man gave unto him.

17. And when he came to himself, he said, How many hired servants of my father's have bread enough and to spare, and I perish with hunger!

18. I will arise and go to my father, and will say unto him, Father, I have sinned against heaven, and before thee,

19. And am no more worthy to be called thy son: make me as one of thy hired servants.

20. And he arose, and came to his father. But when he was yet a great way off, his father saw him, and had compassion, and ran, and fell on his neck, and kissed him.

21. And the son said unto him, Father, I have sinned against heaven, and in thy sight, and am no more worthy to be called thy son.

22. But the father said to his servants, Bring forth the best robe, and put *it* on him; and put a ring on his hand, and shoes on *his* feet:

23. And bring hither the fatted calf, and kill *it;* and let us eat, and be merry:

24. For this my son was dead, and is alive again; he was lost, and is found. And they began to be merry.

25. Now his elder son was in the field: and as he came and drew nigh to the house, he heard musick and dancing.

26. And he called one of the servants, and asked what these things meant.

27. And he said unto him, Thy brother is come; and thy father hath killed the fatted calf, because he hath received him safe and sound.

28. And he was angry, and would not go in: therefore came his father out, and intreated him.

29. And he answering said to *his* father, Lo, these many years do I serve thee, neither transgressed I at any time thy commandment: and yet thou never gavest me a kid, that I might make merry with my friends:

30. But as soon as this thy son was come, which hath devoured thy living with harlots, thou hast killed for him the fatted calf.

31. And he said unto him, Son, thou art ever with me, and all that I have is thine.

32. It was meet that we should make merry, and be glad: for this thy brother was dead, and is alive again; and was lost, and is found.

John: No record.

(d) Parable of the Unjust Steward

Spoken to his disciples; no steward can serve two masters.

Matt.: No record; Mark: No record; Luke 16:1-13; John; No record.

Matthew: No record.

Mark: No record.

LUKE 16:1. And he said also unto his disciples, There was a certain rich man, which had a steward; and the same was accused unto him that he had wasted his goods.

2. And he called him, and said unto him, How is it that I hear this of thee? give an account of thy stewardship; for thou mayest be no longer steward.

3. Then the steward said within himself, What shall I do? for my lord taketh away from me the stewardship: I cannot dig; to beg I am ashamed.

4. I am resolved what to do, that, when I am put out of the stewardship, they may receive me into their houses.

5. So he called every one of his lord's debtors *unto him*, and said unto the first, How much owest thou unto my lord?

6. And he said, An hundred measures of oil. And he said unto him, Take thy bill, and sit down quickly, and write fifty.

7. Then said he to another, And how much owest thou? And he said, An hundred meas-

ures of wheat. And he said unto him, Take thy bill, and write fourscore.

8. And the lord commended the unjust steward, because he had done wisely: for the children of this world are in their generation wiser than the children of light.

9. And I say unto you, Make to yourselves friends of the mammon of unrighteousness; that, when ye fail, they may receive you into everlasting habitations.

10. He that is faithful in that which is least is faithful also in much: and he that is unjust in the least is unjust also in much.

11. If therefore ye have not been faithful in the unrighteous mammon, who will commit to your trust the true *riches?*

12. And if ye have not been faithful in that which is another man's, who shall give you that which is your own?

13. ¶ No servant can serve two masters: for either he will hate the one, and love the other; or else he will hold to the one, and despise the other. Ye cannot serve God and mammon.

John: No record.

Section 138

A DISCOURSE ON COVETOUSNESS

Jesus, speaking to the covetous Pharisees who hear all these things, says: "Ye . . . justify yourselves before men; but God knoweth your hearts"; Jesus explains how the law stands, and speaks on adultery.

Matt.: No record; Mark: No record; Luke 16:14-18; John: No record.
Time: A.D. 30, Winter (?).
Place: Perea (G. W. CLARK).

Matthew: No record.

Mark: No record.

LUKE 16:14. And the Pharisees also, who were covetous, heard all these things: and they derided him.

15. And he said unto them, Ye are they which justify yourselves before men; but God knoweth your hearts: for that which is highly esteemed among men is abomination in the sight of God.

16. The law and the prophets *were* until John: since that time the kingdom of God is preached, and every man presseth into it.

17. And it is easier for heaven and earth to pass, than one tittle of the law to fail.

18. Whosoever putteth away his wife, and marrieth another, committeth adultery: and whosoever marrieth her that is put away from *her* husband committeth adultery.

John: No record.

Section 139

PARABLE OF RICH MAN AND LAZARUS

Jesus continuing to speak to the covetous Pharisees, gives the parable of the rich man and Lazarus.

Matt.: No record; Mark: No record; Luke 16:19-31; John: No record.
Time: A.D. 30, Winter (?).
Place: Perea (G. W. CLARK).

Matthew: No record.

Mark: No record.

LUKE 16:19. ¶There was a certain rich man, which was clothed in purple and fine linen, and fared sumptuously every day:

20. And there was a certain beggar named Lazarus, which was laid at his gate, full of sores,

21. And desiring to be fed with the crumbs which fell from the rich man's table: moreover the dogs came and licked his sores.

22. And it came to pass, that the beggar died, and was carried by the angels into Abraham's bosom: the rich man also died, and was buried;

23. And in hell he lift up his eyes, being in torments, and seeth Abraham afar off, and Lazarus in his bosom.

24. And he cried and said, Father Abraham, have mercy on me, and send Lazarus, that he may dip the tip of his finger in water, and cool my tongue; for I am tormented in this flame.

25. But Abraham said, Son, remember that thou in thy lifetime receivedst thy good things, and likewise Lazarus evil things: but now he is comforted, and thou art tormented.

26. And beside all this, between us and you there is a great gulf fixed: so that they which would pass from hence to you cannot; neither can they pass to us, that *would come* from thence.

27. Then he said, I pray thee therefore, father, that thou wouldest send him to my father's house:

28. For I have five brethren; that he may testify unto them, lest they also come into this place of torment.

29. Abraham saith unto him, They have Moses and the prophets; let them hear them.

30. And he said, Nay, father Abraham: but if one went unto them from the dead, they will repent.

31. And he said unto him, If they hear not Moses and the prophets, neither will they be persuaded, though one rose from the dead.

John: No record.

Section 140

DISCOURSE ON THOSE WHO BRING OFFENSE AND ON FAITH

Jesus, speaking unto his disciples, says that offenses must come but woe unto him through whom they come; plight of one who "should offend one of these little ones"; teaches them about forgiveness; the Apostles ask, "Lord, Increase our faith"; Jesus speaks of the faith of a grain of mustard seed; place of one who does merely that which it is his duty to do.

Matt.: No record; Mark: No record; Luke 17:1-10; John: No record.
Time: A.D. 30, Winter (?).
Place: Perea (G. W. CLARK).

Matthew: No record.

Mark: No record.

LUKE 17:1. Then said he unto the disciples, It is impossible but that offences will come: but woe *unto him*, through whom they come!

2. It were better for him that a millstone were hanged about his neck, and he cast into the sea, than that he should offend one of these little ones.

3. ¶Take heed to yourselves: If thy brother trespass against thee, rebuke him; and if he repent, forgive him.

4. And if he trespass against thee seven times in a day, and seven times in a day turn again to thee, saying, I repent; thou shalt forgive him.

5. And the apostles said unto the Lord, Increase our faith.

6. And the Lord said, if ye had faith as a grain of mustard seed, ye might say unto this sycamine tree, Be thou plucked up by the root, and be thou planted in the sea; and it should obey you.

7. But which of you, having a servant plowing or feeding cattle, will say unto him by and by, when he is come from the field, Go and sit down to meat?

8. And will not rather say unto him, Make ready wherewith I may sup, and gird thyself, and serve me, till I have eaten and drunken; and afterward thou shalt eat and drink?

9. Doth he thank that servant because he did the things that were commanded him? I trow not.

10. So likewise ye, when ye shall have done all those things which are commanded you, say, We are unprofitable servants: we have done that which was our duty to do.

John: No record.

Section 141

THE RAISING OF LAZARUS

Jesus, reaching Bethany, finds that Lazarus has been dead four days; many friends come to Mary and Martha to comfort them; Martha comes out to meet Jesus but "Mary sat still in the house"; Martha tells Jesus if he had been there Lazarus had not died, and that even now God will give Jesus whatever he asks; Jesus says her brother shall rise again; Martha replies he will rise in the resurrection "at the last day"; Jesus says, "I am the resurrection, and the life" and continues with his great statement of his Messiahship; Martha declares, "I believe that thou art the Christ, the Son of God, which should come into the world"; Martha tells Mary Jesus is come, and she rushes to meet him; the mourning friends follow Mary; when they come to Jesus, Mary also says that if Jesus had been there her brother had not died; Jesus seeing them all weeping, grieves in his spirit and asks where they have lain him; they say come and see, and Jesus weeps; some bystanders say also that if Jesus had been there he might have saved Lazarus; coming to the cave where lay Lazarus, Jesus (Martha protesting) orders the stone rolled away, and first praying, "cried with a loud voice, Lazarus, come forth," and Lazarus comes forth bound hand and foot with grave clothes; at Jesus' command these are loosed and Lazarus goes; many Jews believe, some go to tell the Pharisees of the happening.

Matt.: No record; Mark: No record; Luke: No record; John 11:17-46.
Time: A.D. 30, Winter (?).
Place: Bethany.

Matthew: No record.

Mark: No record.

Luke: No record.

JOHN 11:17. Then when Jesus came, he found that he had *lain* in the grave four days already.

18. Now Bethany was nigh unto Jerusalem, about fifteen furlongs off:

19. And many of the Jews came to Martha and Mary, to comfort them concerning their brother.

20. Then Martha, as soon as she heard that Jesus was coming, went and met him: but Mary sat *still* in the house.

21. Then said Martha unto Jesus, Lord, if thou hadst been here, my brother had not died.

22. But I know, that even now, whatsoever thou wilt ask of God, God will give *it* thee.

23. Jesus saith unto her, Thy brother shall rise again.

24. Martha saith unto him, I know that he shall rise again in the resurrection at the last day.

25. Jesus said unto her, I am the resurrection, and the life: he that believeth in me, though he were dead, yet shall he live:

26. And whosoever liveth and believeth in me shall never die. Believest thou this?

27. She saith unto him, Yea, Lord: I believe that thou art the Christ, the Son of God,

which should come into the world.

28. And when she had so said, she went her way, and called Mary her sister secretly, saying, The Master is come, and calleth for thee.

29. As soon as she heard *that*, she arose quickly, and came unto him.

30. Now Jesus was not yet come into the town, but was in that place where Martha met him.

31. The Jews then which were with her in the house, and comforted her, when they saw Mary, that she rose up hastily and went out, followed her, saying, She goeth unto the grave to weep there.

32. Then when Mary was come where Jesus was, and saw him, she fell down at his feet, saying unto him, Lord, if thou hadst been here, my brother had not died.

33. When Jesus therefore saw her weeping, and the Jews also weeping which came with her, he groaned in the spirit, and was troubled,

34. And said, Where have ye laid him? They said unto him, Lord, come and see.

35. Jesus wept.

36. Then said the Jews, Behold how he loved him!

37. And some of them said, Could not this man, which opened the eyes of the blind, have caused that even this man should not have died?

38. Jesus therefore again groaning in himself cometh to the grave. It was a cave, and a stone lay upon it.

39. Jesus said, Take ye away the stone. Martha, the sister of him that was dead, saith unto him, Lord, by this time he stinketh: for he hath been *dead* four days.

40. Jesus saith unto her, Said I not unto thee, that, if thou wouldest believe, thou shouldest see the glory of God?

41. Then they took away the stone *from the place* where the dead was laid. And Jesus lifted up *his* eyes, and said, Father, I thank thee that thou hast heard me.

42. And I knew that thou hearest me always: but because of the people which stand by I said *it*, that they may believe that thou hast sent me.

43. And when he thus had spoken, he cried with a loud voice, Lazarus, come forth.

44. And he that was dead came forth, bound hand and foot with graveclothes: and his face was bound about with a napkin. Jesus saith unto them, Loose him, and let him go.

45. Then many of the Jews which came to Mary, and had seen the things which Jesus did, believed on him.

46. But some of them went their ways to the Pharisees, and told them what things Jesus had done.

Section 142

THEY PLOT AGAINST JESUS

The chief priests and the Pharisees gather in council (Sanhedrin-Andrews), Caiaphas being high priest that year; the doctrine that better one man should perish than a whole nation, is stated by Caiaphas; "and this spake he not of himself: but being high priest that year, he prophesied that Jesus should die for that nation; and not for that nation only, but that also he should gather together in one the children of God that were scattered abroad"; then after they take counsel, how they can put him to death.

Matt.: No record; Mark: No record; Luke: No record; John 11:47-53.
Time: A.D. 30, February (ANDREWS).
Place: Jerusalem.

Matthew: No record.

Mark: No record.

Luke: No record.

JOHN 11:47. ¶ Then gathered the chief priests and the Pharisees a council, and said, What do we? for this man doeth many miracles.

48. If we let him thus alone, all *men* will believe on him: and the Romans shall come and take away both our place and nation.

49. And one of them, *named* Caiaphas, being the high priest that same year, said unto them, Ye know nothing at all,

50. Nor consider that it is expedient for us, that one man should die for the people, and that the whole nation perish not.

51. And this spake he not of himself: but being high priest that year, he prophesied that Jesus should die for that nation;

52. And not for that nation only, but that also he should gather together in one the children of God that were scattered abroad.

53. Then from that day forth they took counsel together for to put him to death.

Section 143

HE GOES TO CITY OF EPHRAIM

Jesus walks "no more openly among the Jews," but goes thence near the wilderness to a city called Ephraim where his disciples come also.

Matt.: No record; Mark: No record; Luke: No record; John 11:54.
Time: A.D. 30, February (ANDREWS).
Place: Bethany to Ephraim.

Matthew: No record.

Mark: No record.

Luke: No record.

JOHN 11:54. Jesus therefore walked no more openly among the Jews; but went thence unto a country near to the wilderness, into a city called Ephraim, and there continued with his disciples.

Section 144

THE BEGINNING OF THE FINAL JOURNEY TO JERUSALEM

Finishing his residence in Ephraim, he starts for Jerusalem through the midst of Samaria and Galilee; ten lepers seeing him, stand afar off and cry: "Jesus, Master, have mercy on us"; when he sees them he tells them to go show themselves to the priests, which they doing, are cleansed; one, a Samaritan, seeing he is healed, turns back and glorifies God, falling on his face and giving thanks; Jesus asks if there are not ten, and where are the other nine; continuing he says only this stranger returns to give glory to God.

Matt.: No record; Mark: No record; Luke 17:11-19; John: No record.

Time: A.D. 30, February-March (ANDREWS).

Place: Ephraim, Galilee, Samaria.

Matthew: No record.

Mark: No record.

LUKE 17:11. ¶And it came to pass, as he went to Jerusalem, that he passed through the midst of Samaria and Galilee.

12. And as he entered into a certain village, there met him ten men that were lepers, which stood afar off:

13. And they lifted up *their* voices, and said, Jesus, Master, have mercy on us.

14. And when he saw *them*, he said unto them, Go shew yourselves unto the priests. And it came to pass, that, as they went, they were cleansed.

15. And one of them, when he saw that he was healed, turned back, and with a loud voice glorified God,

16. And fell down on *his* face at his feet, giving him thanks: and he was a Samaritan.

17. And Jesus answering said, Were there not ten cleansed? but where *are* the nine?

18. There are not found that returned to give glory to God, save this stranger.

19. And he said unto him, Arise, go thy way: thy faith hath made thee whole.

John: No record.

Section 145

A DISCOURSE ON KINGDOM OF GOD

Jesus answering the question put by the Pharisees, "When the kingdom of God should come," replies that it does not come by observation; neither shall they say lo, here! or lo, there! "for, behold, the kingdom of God is within you"; he tells his disciples that the day will come

when they shall wish to see one of the days of the Son of man, and they shall not see it; then some will say, see here, others, see there, but "go not after them, nor follow them"; the light of the lightning compared to the Son of man; forecasts his crucifixion; compares the days of Noah and of Lot to the day when the Son of man is revealed; tells them not to do as did Lot's wife, and points out how one will be taken and the other left.

Matt.: No record; Mark: No record; Luke 17:20-37; John: No record.
Time: A.D. 30, February-March (ANDREWS).
Place: Galilee (G. W. CLARK).

Matthew: No record.

Mark: No record.

LUKE 17:20. ¶And when he was demanded of the Pharisees, when the kingdom of God should come, he answered them and said, The kingdom of God cometh not with observation:

21. Neither shall they say, Lo here! or, lo there! for, behold, the kingdom of God is within you.

22. And he said unto the disciples, The days will come, when ye shall desire to see one of the days of the Son of man, and ye shall not see *it*.

23. And they shall say to you, See here; or, see there: go not after *them*, nor follow *them*.

24. For as the lightning, that lighteneth out of the one *part* under heaven, shineth unto the other *part* under heaven; so shall also the Son of man be in his day.

25. But first must he suffer many things, and be rejected of this generation.

26. And as it was in the days of Noe, so shall it be also in the days of the Son of man.

27. They did eat, they drank, they married wives, they were given in marriage, until the day that Noe entered into the ark, and the flood came, and destroyed them all.

28. Likewise also as it was in the days of Lot; they did eat, they drank, they bought, they sold, they planted, they builded;

29. But the same day that Lot went out of Sodom it rained fire and brimstone from heaven, and destroyed *them* all.

30. Even thus shall it be in the day when the Son of man is revealed.

31. In that day, he which shall be upon the housetop, and his stuff in the house, let him not come down to take it away: and he that is in the field, let him likewise not return back.

32. Remember Lot's wife.

33. Whosoever shall seek to save his life shall lose it; and whosoever shall lose his life shall preserve it.

34. I tell you, in that night there shall be two *men* in one bed; the one shall be taken, and the other shall be left.

35. Two *women* shall be grinding together; the one shall be taken, and the other left.

36. Two *men* shall be in the field; the one shall be taken, and the other left.

37. And they answered and said unto him, Where, Lord? And he said unto them, Wheresoever the body *is*, thither will the eagles be gathered together.

John: No record.

Section 146

JESUS AGAIN SPEAKS IN PARABLES

Jesus speaks two parables.

Time: A.D. 30, February-March (ANDREWS).

Place: Galilee (G. W. CLARK).

(a) Parable of the Importunate Widow

Jesus says: "Shall not God avenge his own elect, which cry day and night unto him, that he bear long with them? I tell you that he will avenge them speedily"; he then asks if "when the Son of man cometh, shall he find faith on the earth?"

Matt.: No record; Mark: No record; Luke 18:1-8; John: No record.

Matthew: No record.

Mark: No record.

LUKE 18:1. And he spake a parable unto them *to this end*, that men ought always to pray, and not to faint;

2. Saying, There was in a city a judge, which feared not God, neither regarded man:

3. And there was a widow in that city; and she came unto him, saying, Avenge me of mine adversary.

4. And he would not for a while: but afterward he said within himself, Though I fear not God, nor regard man;

5. Yet because this widow troubleth me, I will avenge her, lest by her continual coming she weary me.

6. And the Lord said, Hear what the unjust judge saith.

7. And shall not God avenge his own elect, which cry day and night unto him, though he bear long with them?

8. I tell you that he will avenge them speedily. Nevertheless when the Son of man cometh, shall he find faith on the earth?

John: No record.

(b) Parable of the Pharisee and the Publican

Jesus says the publican rather than the Pharisee is justified, "for every one that exalteth himself shall be abased; and he that humbleth himself shall be exalted."

Matt.: No record; Mark: No record; Luke 18:9-14; John: No record.

Matthew: No record.

Mark: No record.

LUKE 18:9. And he spake this parable unto certain which trusted in themselves that they were righteous, and despised others:

10. Two men went up into the temple to pray; the one a Pharisee, and the other a publican.

11. The Pharisee stood and prayed thus with himself, God, I thank thee, that I am not as other men *are*, extortioners, unjust, adulterers, or even as this publican.

12. I fast twice in the week, I give tithes of all that I possess.

13. And the publican, standing afar off, would not lift up so much as *his* eyes unto heaven, but smote upon his breast, saying, God be merciful to me a sinner.

14. I tell you, this man went down to his house justified *rather* than the other: for every one that exalteth himself shall be abased; and he that humbleth himself shall be exalted.

John: No record.

Section 147

HE CROSSES JORDAN INTO PEREA, GOING TOWARDS JERUSALEM

Jesus travels on towards Jerusalem, leaving Galilee, crossing the Jordan into Perea; great multitudes follow him, whom he teaches and heals.

Matt. 19:1-2; Mark 10:1; Luke: No record; John: No record.
Time: A.D. 30, February-March (ANDREWS).
Place: Galilee-Perea.

MATTHEW 19:1. And it came to pass, *that* when Jesus had finished these sayings, he departed from Galilee, and came into the coasts of Judæa beyond Jordan;

2. And great multitudes followed him; and he healed them there.

MARK 10:1. And he arose from thence, and cometh into the coasts of Judæa by the farther side of Jordan: and the people resort unto him again; and, as he was wont, he taught them again.

Luke: No record.

John: No record.

Section 148

PHARISEES TEMPT JESUS

The Pharisees come unto Jesus tempting him, saying: "Is it lawful for a man to put away his wife for every cause?" Jesus preaches his great discourse on marriage and divorce.

Matt. 19:3-12; Mark 10:2-12; Luke: No record; John: No record.
Time: A.D. 30, February-March (ANDREWS).
Place: Perea.

MATTHEW 19:3. ¶The Pharisees also came unto him, tempting him, and saying unto him, Is it lawful for a man to put away his wife for every cause?

4. And he answered and said unto them, Have ye not read, that he which made *them* at the beginning made them male and female,

5. And said, For this cause shall a man leave father and mother, and shall cleave to his wife: and they twain shall be one flesh?

6. Wherefore they are no more twain, but one flesh. What therefore God hath joined together, let not man put asunder.

7. They say unto him, Why did Moses then command to give a writing of divorcement, and to put her away?

8. He saith unto them, Moses because of the hardness of your hearts suffered you to put away your wives: but from the beginning it was not so.

9. And I say unto you, Whosoever shall put away his wife, except *it be* for fornication, and shall marry another, committeth adultery: and whoso marrieth her which is put away doth commit adultery.

10. ¶His disciples say unto him, If the case of the man be so with *his* wife, it is not good to marry.

11. But he said unto them, All *men* cannot receive this saying, save *they* to whom it is given.

12. For there are some eunuchs, which were so born from *their* mother's womb: and there are some eunuchs, which were made eunuchs of men: and there be eunuchs, which have made themselves eunuchs for the kingdom of heaven's sake. He that is able to receive *it*, let him receive *it*.

MARK 10:2. ¶And the Pharisees came to him, and asked him, Is it lawful for a man to put away *his* wife? tempting him.

3. And he answered and said unto them, What did Moses command you?

4. And they said, Moses suffered to write a bill of divorcement, and to put *her* away.

5. And Jesus answered and said unto them, For the hardness of your heart he wrote you this precept.

6. But from the beginning of the creation God made them male and female.
7. For this cause shall a man leave his father and mother, and cleave to his wife;
8. And they twain shall be one flesh: so then they are no more twain, but one flesh.
9. What therefore God hath joined together, let not man put asunder.
10. And in the house his disciples asked him again of the same *matter*.
11. And he saith unto them, Whosoever shall put away his wife, and marry another, committeth adultery against her.
12. And if a woman shall put away her husband, and be married to another, she committeth adultery.

Luke: No record.

John: No record.

Section 149

HE BLESSES LITTLE CHILDREN

Then they bring to him little children that he shall put his hands on them and pray; the disciples rebuke them; Jesus seeing this is much displeased, and bids them let the children come, for of such is the kingdom of heaven, saying, "Whosoever shall not receive the kingdom of God as a little child, he shall not enter therein"; he takes them in his arms, puts his hands upon them and blesses them; he then departs.

Matt. 19:13-15; Mark 10:13-16; Luke 18:15-17; John: No record.
Time: A.D. 30, February-March (ANDREWS).
Place: Perea.

MATTHEW 19:13. ¶ Then were there brought unto him little children, that he should put *his* hands on them, and pray: and the disciples rebuked them.
14. But Jesus said, Suffer little children, and forbid them not, to come unto me: for of such is the kingdom of heaven.
15. And he laid *his* hands on them, and departed thence.

MARK 10:13. ¶ And they brought young children to him, that he should touch them: and *his* disciples rebuked those that brought *them*.
14. But when Jesus saw *it*, he was much displeased, and said unto them, Suffer the little children to come unto me, and forbid them not: for of such is the kingdom of God.
15. Verily I say unto you, Whosoever shall not receive the kingdom of God as a little child, he shall not enter therein.
16. And he took them up in his arms, put *his* hands upon them, and blessed them.

LUKE 18:15. And they brought unto him also infants, that he would touch them: but when *his* disciples saw *it*, they rebuked them.

16. But Jesus called them *unto him*, and said, Suffer little children to come unto me, and forbid them not: for of such is the kingdom of God.

17. Verily I say unto you, Whosoever shall not receive the kingdom of God as a little child shall in no wise enter therein.

John: No record.

Section 150

THE RICH YOUNG RULER

A rich young ruler comes running to Jesus, and kneeling, asks, "Good Master, what shall I do to inherit eternal life?"; Jesus answers, "Thou knowest the commandments"; the young ruler replies, "all these have I kept from my youth up"; Jesus answers by telling the ruler to sell all he has, if he would be perfect, give it to the poor, and to follow Jesus; the ruler goes away sorrowful for he has great riches; Jesus discourses upon riches; they say among themselves, who then can be saved, and Jesus answers that with God all things are possible; Peter saying they have given up all for Jesus, he points out the rewards of the faithful.

Matt. 19:16-30; Mark 10:17-31; Luke 18:18-30; John: No record.
Time: A.D. 30, February-March (ANDREWS).
Place: Perea.

MATTHEW 19:16. ¶And, behold, one came and said unto him, Good Master, what good thing shall I do, that I may have eternal life?

17. And he said unto him, Why callest thou me good? *there is* none good but one, *that is*, God: but if thou wilt enter into life, keep the commandments.

18. He saith unto him, Which? Jesus said, Thou shalt do no murder, Thou shalt not commit adultery, Thou shalt not steal, Thou shalt not bear false witness,

19. Honour thy father and *thy* mother: and, Thou shalt love thy neighbour as thyself.

20. The young man saith unto him, All these things have I kept from my youth up: what lack I yet?

21. Jesus said unto him, If thou wilt be perfect, go *and* sell that thou hast, and give to the poor, and thou shalt have treasure in heaven: and come *and* follow me.

22. But when the young man heard that saying, he went away sorrowful: for he had great possessions.

23. ¶ Then said Jesus unto his disciples, Verily I say unto you, That a rich man shall hardly enter into the kingdom of heaven.

24. And again I say unto you, It is easier for a camel to go through the eye of a needle, than for a rich man to enter into the kingdom of God.

25. When his disciples heard *it*, they were exceedingly amazed, saying, Who then can be saved?

26. But Jesus beheld *them*, and said unto them, With men this is impossible; but with God all things are possible.

27. ¶ Then answered Peter and said unto him, Behold, we have forsaken all, and followed thee; what shall we have therefore?

28. And Jesus said unto them, Verily I say unto you, That ye which have followed me, in the regeneration when the Son of man shall sit in the throne of his glory, ye also shall sit upon twelve thrones, judging the twelve tribes of Israel.

29. And every one that hath forsaken houses, or brethren, or sisters, or father, or mother, or wife, or children, or lands, for my name's sake, shall receive an hundredfold, and shall inherit everlasting life.

30. But many *that are* first shall be last; and the last *shall be* first.

MARK 10:17. ¶And when he was gone forth into the way, there came one running, and kneeled to him, and asked him, Good Master, what shall I do that I may inherit eternal life?

18. And Jesus said unto him, Why callest thou me good? *there is* none good but one, *that is*, God.

19. Thou knowest the commandments, Do not commit adultery, Do not kill, Do not steal, Do not bear false witness, Defraud not, Honour thy father and mother.

20. And he answered and said unto him, Master, all these have I observed from my youth.

21. Then Jesus beholding him loved him, and said unto him, One thing thou lackest: go thy way, sell whatsoever thou hast, and give to the poor, and thou shalt have treasure in heaven: and come, take up the cross, and follow me.

22. And he was sad at that saying, and went away grieved: for he had great possessions.

23. ¶And Jesus looked round about, and saith unto his disciples, How hardly shall they that have riches enter into the kingdom of God!

24. And the disciples were astonished at his words. But Jesus answereth again, and saith unto them, Children, how hard is it for them that trust in riches to enter into the kingdom of God!

25. It is easier for a camel to go through the eye of a needle, than for a rich man to enter into the kingdom of God.

26. And they were astonished out of measure, saying among themselves, Who then can be saved?

27. And Jesus looking upon

them saith, With men *it is* impossible, but not with God: for with God all things are possible.

28. ¶Then Peter began to say unto him, Lo, we have left all, and have followed thee.

29. And Jesus answered and said, Verily I say unto you, There is no man that hath left house, or brethren, or sisters, or father, or mother, or wife, or children, or lands, for my sake, and the gospel's,

30. But he shall receive an hundredfold now in this time, houses, and brethren, and sisters, and mothers, and children, and lands, with persecutions; and in the world to come eternal life.

31. But many *that are* first shall be last; and the last first.

LUKE 18:18. And a certain ruler asked him, saying, Good Master, what shall I do to inherit eternal life?

19. And Jesus said unto him, Why callest thou me good? none *is* good, save one, *that is*, God.

20. Thou knowest the commandments, Do not commit adultery, Do not kill, Do not steal, Do not bear false witness, Honour thy father and thy mother.

21. And he said, All these have I kept from my youth up.

22. Now when Jesus heard these things, he said unto him, Yet lackest thou one thing: sell all that thou hast, and distribute unto the poor, and thou shalt have treasure in heaven: and come, follow me.

23. And when he heard this, he was very sorrowful: for he was very rich.

24. And when Jesus saw that he was very sorrowful, he said, How hardly shall they that have riches enter into the kingdom of God!

25. For it is easier for a camel to go through a needle's eye, than for a rich man to enter into the kingdom of God.

26. And they that heard *it* said, Who then can be saved?

27. And he said, The things which are impossible with men are possible with God.

28. ¶Then Peter said, Lo, we have left all, and followed thee.

29. And he said unto them, Verily I say unto you, There is no man that hath left house, or parents, or brethren, or wife, or children, for the kingdom of God's sake,

30. Who shall not receive manifold more in this present time, and in the world to come life everlasting.

John: No record.

Section 151

THE PARABLE OF THE LABORERS IN THE VINEYARD

Matt. 20:1-16; **Mark: No record; Luke: No record; John: No record.**
Time: A.D. 30, February-March (ANDREWS).
Place: Perea.

MATTHEW 20:1. For the kingdom of heaven is like unto a man *that is* an householder, which went out early in the morning to hire labourers into his vineyard.

2. And when he had agreed with the labourers for a penny a day, he sent them into his vineyard.

3. And he went out about the third hour, and saw others standing idle in the marketplace,

4. And said unto them; Go ye also into the vineyard, and whatsoever is right I will give you. And they went their way.

5. Again he went out about the sixth and ninth hour, and did likewise.

6. And about the eleventh hour he went out, and found others standing idle, and saith unto them, Why stand ye here all the day idle?

7. They say unto him, Because no man hath hired us. He saith unto them, Go ye also into the vineyard; and whatsoever is right, *that* shall ye receive.

8. So when even was come, the lord of the vineyard saith unto his steward, Call the labourers, and give them *their* hire, beginning from the last unto the first.

9. And when they came that *were hired* about the eleventh hour, they received every man a penny.

10. But when the first came, they supposed that they should have received more; and they likewise received every man a penny.

11. And when they had received *it*, they murmured against the goodman of the house,

12. Saying, These last have wrought *but* one hour, and thou hast made them equal unto us, which have borne the burden and heat of the day.

13. But he answered one of them, and said, Friend, I do thee no wrong: didst not thou agree with me for a penny?

14. Take *that* thine *is*, and go thy way: I will give unto this last, even as unto thee.

15. Is it not lawful for me to do what I will with mine own? Is thine eye evil, because I am good?

16. So the last shall be first, and the first last: for many be called, but few chosen.

Mark: No record.
Luke: No record.
John: No record.

Section 152

HE GOES BEFORE THE TWELVE, TOWARDS JERUSALEM

Jesus, continuing towards Jerusalem, goes before the Twelve (who were with him), to their amazement; they follow, afraid; he takes them unto him, and again carefully tells them of the trial, the death, and resurrection; "and they understood none of these things: and this saying was hid from them, neither knew they the things which were spoken."

Matt. 20:17-19; Mark 10:32-34; Luke 18:31-34; John: No record.
Time: A.D. 30, March (ANDREWS).
Place: Perea.

MATTHEW 20:17. ¶And Jesus going up to Jerusalem took the twelve disciples apart in the way, and said unto them,

18. Behold, we go up to Jerusalem; and the Son of man shall be betrayed unto the chief priests and unto the scribes, and they shall condemn him to death,

19. And shall deliver him to the Gentiles to mock, and to scourge, and to crucify *him*: and the third day he shall rise again.

MARK 10:32. ¶And they were in the way going up to Jerusalem; and Jesus went before them: and they were amazed; and as they followed, they were afraid. And he took again the twelve, and began to tell them what things should happen unto him,

33. *Saying*, Behold, we go up to Jerusalem; and the Son of man shall be delivered unto the chief priests, and unto the scribes; and they shall condemn him to death, and shall deliver him to the Gentiles:

34. And they shall mock him, and shall scourge him, and shall spit upon him, and shall kill him: and the third day he shall rise again.

LUKE 18:31. ¶Then he took *unto him* the twelve, and said unto them, Behold, we go up to Jerusalem, and all things that are written by the prophets concerning the Son of man shall be accomplished.

32. For he shall be delivered unto the Gentiles, and shall be mocked, and spitefully entreated, and spitted on:

33. And they shall scourge *him*, and put him to death: and the third day he shall rise again.

34. And they understood none of these things: and this saying was hid from them, neither knew they the things which were spoken.

John: No record.

Section 153

AMBITIONS OF JAMES AND JOHN

James and John, either through their mother or by themselves, ask Jesus that they may sit, one on the right hand and the other on the left hand, of Jesus in his kingdom and glory; Jesus tells them they do not know what they ask, and he asks them if they can drink the cup he drinks and be baptized with the baptism he is baptized with; they say they can; he says they will indeed drink his cup and be baptized with his baptism, but to sit on his right hand and on his left is not his to give; the ten hearing it are moved to indignation; he tells them that while among the Gentiles the princes exercise dominion over the others, yet among them, "whosoever will be great among you, shall be your minister"; and Jesus adds: "For even the Son of man came not to be ministered unto, but to minister, and to give his life a ransom for many."

Matt. 20:20-28; Mark 10:35-45; Luke: No record; John: No record.
Time: A.D. 30, March (ANDREWS).
Place: Perea: Jericho (?).

MATTHEW 20:20. ¶ Then came to him the mother of Zebedee's children with her sons, worshipping *him*, and desiring a certain thing of him.

21. And he said unto her, What wilt thou? She saith unto him, Grant that these my two sons may sit, the one on thy right hand, and the other on the left, in thy kingdom.

22. But Jesus answered and said, Ye know not what ye ask. Are ye able to drink of the cup that I shall drink of, and to be baptized with the baptism that I am baptized with? They say unto him, We are able.

23. And he saith unto them, Ye shall drink indeed of my cup, and be baptized with the baptism that I am baptized with: but to sit on my right hand, and on my left, is not mine to give, but *it shall be given to them* for whom it is prepared of my Father.

24. And when the ten heard *it*, they were moved with indignation against the two brethren.

25. But Jesus called them *unto him*, and said, Ye know that the princes of the Gentiles exercise dominion over them, and they that are great exercise authority upon them.

26. But it shall not be so among you: but whosoever will be great among you, let him be your minister;

27. And whosoever will be chief among you, let him be your servant:

28. Even as the Son of man came not to be ministered unto, but to minister, and to give his life a ransom for many.

MARK 10:35. ¶ And James and John, the sons of Zebedee,

come unto him, saying, Master, we would that thou shouldest do for us whatsoever we shall desire.

36. And he said unto them, What would ye that I should do for you?

37. They said unto him, Grant unto us that we may sit, one on thy right hand, and the other on thy left hand, in thy glory.

38. But Jesus said unto them, Ye know not what ye ask: can ye drink of the cup that I drink of? and be baptized with the baptism that I am baptized with?

39. And they said unto him, We can. And Jesus said unto them, Ye shall indeed drink of the cup that I drink of; and with the baptism that I am baptized withal shall ye be baptized:

40. But to sit on my right hand and on my left hand is not mine to give; but *it shall be given to them* for whom it is prepared.

41. And when the ten heard *it*, they began to be much displeased with James and John.

42. But Jesus called them *to him*, and saith unto them, Ye know that they which are accounted to rule over the Gentiles exercise lordship over them; and their great ones exercise authority upon them.

43. But so shall it not be among you: but whosoever will be great among you, shall be your minister:

44. And whosoever of you will be the chiefest, shall be servant of all.

45. For even the Son of man came not to be ministered unto, but to minister, and to give his life a ransom for many.

Luke: No record.

John: No record.

Section 154

BARTIMAEUS HEALED

Bartimaeus, the blind son of Timaeus (and another blind man, says Matthew), are sitting by the wayside, as Jesus and a multitude go by; the blind men, hearing Jesus is passing, cry out to him, the multitude rebuke them, but they cry out again, and Jesus has him (them) called to him; the man casts away his garment and comes to Jesus who asks what he wishes; the man answers: "Lord, that I may receive my sight"; Jesus touches his eyes and he immediately sees and then follows along with the multitude; those who see it praise God.

Matt. 20:29-34; Mark 10:46-52; Luke 18:35-43; John: No record.
Time: A.D. 30, March (ANDREWS).
Place: Near Jericho.

MATTHEW 20:29. And as they departed from Jericho, a great multitude followed him.

30. ¶ And, behold, two blind men sitting by the way side, when they heard that Jesus

passed by, cried out, saying, Have mercy on us, O Lord, *thou* son of David.

31. And the multitude rebuked them, because they should hold their peace: but they cried the more, saying, Have mercy on us, O Lord, *thou* son of David.

32. And Jesus stood still, and called them, and said, What will ye that I shall do unto you?

33. They say unto him, Lord, that our eyes may be opened.

34. So Jesus had compassion *on them,* and touched their eyes: and immediately their eyes received sight, and they followed him.

MARK 10:46. ¶ And they came to Jericho: and as he went out of Jericho with his disciples and a great number of people, blind Bartimæus, the son of Timæus, sat by the highway side begging.

47. And when he heard that it was Jesus of Nazareth, he began to cry out, and say, Jesus, *thou* son of David, have mercy on me.

48. And many charged him that he should hold his peace: but he cried the more a great deal, *Thou* son of David, have mercy on me.

49. And Jesus stood still, and commanded him to be called. And they call the blind man, saying unto him, Be of good comfort, rise; he calleth thee.

50. And he, casting away his garment, rose, and came to Jesus.

51. And Jesus answered and said unto him, What wilt thou that I should do unto thee? The blind man said unto him, Lord, that I might receive my sight.

52. And Jesus said unto him, Go thy way; thy faith hath made thee whole. And immediately he received his sight, and followed Jesus in the way.

LUKE 18:35. ¶ And it came to pass, that as he was come nigh unto Jericho, a certain blind man sat by the way side begging:

36. And hearing the multitude pass by, he asked what it meant.

37. And they told him, that Jesus of Nazareth passeth by.

38. And he cried, saying, Jesus, *thou* son of David, have mercy on me.

39. And they which went before rebuked him, that he should hold his peace: but he cried so much the more, *Thou* son of David, have mercy on me.

40. And Jesus stood, and commanded him to be brought unto him: and when he was come near, he asked him,

41. Saying, What wilt thou that I shall do unto thee? And he said, Lord, that I may receive my sight.

42. And Jesus said unto him, Receive thy sight: thy faith hath saved thee.

43. And immediately he received his sight, and followed him, glorifying God: and all the people, when they saw *it*, gave praise unto God.

John: No record.

Section 155

ZACCHAEUS, THE PUBLICAN

Zacchaeus, a rich chief among the publicans, being of little stature, can not see Jesus for the press of people, so he climbs a sycamore tree to see Jesus as he passes by; Jesus looking up sees him, and bids him come down, saying he must abide in the house of the publican; Zacchaeus comes down and receives Jesus joyfully; the multitude, seeing this, murmur that he has gone to be guest of a sinner; Zacchaeus tells the Lord he has given half his goods to the poor, that if he has taken anything from a man by false accusation, he restores it fourfold; Jesus tells him that this day salvation has come to his house for he also is a son of Abraham, "for the Son of man is come to seek and to save that which was lost."

Matt.: No record; Mark: No record; Luke 19:1-10; John: No record.
Time: A.D. 30, March (ANDREWS).
Place: Near or in Jericho.

Matthew: No record.

Mark: No record.

LUKE 19:1. And *Jesus* entered and passed through Jericho.

2. And, behold, *there was* a man named Zacchæus, which was the chief among the publicans, and he was rich.

3. And he sought to see Jesus who he was; and could not for the press, because he was little of stature.

4. And he ran before, and climbed up into a sycomore tree to see him: for he was to pass that *way*.

5. And when Jesus came to the place, he looked up, and saw him, and said unto him, Zacchæus, make haste, and come down; for to day I must abide at thy house.

6. And he made haste, and came down, and received him joyfully.

7. And when they saw *it*, they all murmured, saying, That he was gone to be guest with a man that is a sinner.

8. And Zacchæus stood, and said unto the Lord; Behold, Lord, the half of my goods I give to the poor; and if I have taken any thing from any man by false accusation, I restore *him* fourfold.

9. And Jesus said unto him, This day is salvation come to this house, forsomuch as he also is a son of Abraham.

10. For the Son of man is come to seek and to save that which was lost.

John: No record.

Section 156

THE PARABLE OF THE TEN POUNDS

Matt.: No record; Mark: No record; Luke 19:11-27; John: No record.
Time: A.D. 30, March (ANDREWS).
Place: In or near Jericho.

Matthew: No record.

Mark: No record.

LUKE 19:11. And as they heard these things, he added and spake a parable, because he was nigh to Jerusalem, and because they thought that the kingdom of God should immediately appear.

12. He said therefore, A certain nobleman went into a far country to receive for himself a kingdom, and to return.

13. And he called his ten servants, and delivered them ten pounds, and said unto them, Occupy till I come.

14. But his citizens hated him, and sent a message after him, saying, We will not have this *man* to reign over us.

15. And it came to pass, that when he was returned, having received the kingdom, then he commanded these servants to be called unto him, to whom he had given the money, that he might know how much every man had gained by trading.

16. Then came the first, saying, Lord, thy pound hath gained ten pounds.

17. And he said unto him, Well, thou good servant: because thou hast been faithful in a very little, have thou authority over ten cities.

18. And the second came, saying, Lord, thy pound hath gained five pounds.

19. And he said likewise to him, Be thou also over five cities.

20. And another came, saying, Lord, behold, *here is* thy pound, which I have kept laid up in a napkin:

21. For I feared thee, because thou art an austere man: thou takest up that thou layedst not down, and reapest that thou didst not sow.

22. And he saith unto him, Out of thine own mouth will I judge thee, *thou* wicked servant. Thou knewest that I was an austere man, taking up that I laid not down, and reaping that I did not sow:

23. Wherefore then gavest not thou my money into the bank, that at my coming I might have required mine own with usury?

24. And he said unto them that stood by, Take from him the pound, and give *it* to him that hath ten pounds.

25. (And they said unto him, Lord, he hath ten pounds.)

26. For I say unto you, That unto every one which hath shall be given; and from him

that hath not, even that he hath shall be taken away from him.

27. But those mine enemies, which would not that I should reign over them, bring hither, and slay *them* before me.

John: No record.

Section 157

JESUS PROCEEDS ON HIS WAY TO JERUSALEM

Matt.: No record; **Mark:** No record; **Luke** 19:28; **John:** No record.
Time: A.D. 30, March-April.
Place: Between Jericho and Jerusalem.

Matthew: No record.

Mark: No record.

LUKE 19:28. ¶ And when he had thus spoken, he went before, ascending up to Jerusalem.

John: No record.

Section 158

MANY SEEK HIM

The Passover drawing nigh, and many coming from the country beforehand to purify themselves, they seek for Jesus, and ask one another in the Temple whether they think he might come; the chief priests and the Pharisees give a commandment that if any man knows where he is, he shall tell that they may take him.

Matt.: No record; **Mark:** No record; **Luke:** No record; **John** 11:55-57.
Time: A.D. 30, March (ANDREWS).
Place: Jerusalem.

Matthew: No record.

Mark: No record.

Luke: No record.

JOHN 11:55. ¶And the Jews' passover was nigh at hand: and many went out of the country up to Jerusalem before the passover, to purify themselves.

56. Then sought they for Jesus, and spake among themselves, as they stood in the temple, What think ye, that he will not come to the feast?

57. Now both the chief priests and the Pharisees had given a commandment, that, if any man knew where he were, he should shew *it*, that they might take him.

Section 159

PEOPLE IN WESTERN HEMISPHERE LOOK FOR SIGN

The people begin to look with great earnestness for the sign which should be given, as proclaimed by Samuel, the Lamanite, at the death of the Messiah.

3 Nephi 8:1-4.

Time: A.D. 30, March-April.

Place: Western Hemisphere.

3 NEPHI 8:1. And now it came to pass that according to our record, and we know our record to be true, for behold, it was a just man who did keep the record—for he truly did many miracles in the name of Jesus; and there was not any man who could do a miracle in the name of Jesus save he were cleansed every whit from his iniquity—

2. And now it came to pass, if there was no mistake made by this man in the reckoning of our time, the thirty and third year had passed away;

3. And the people began to look with great earnestness for the sign which had been given by the prophet Samuel, the Lamanite, yea, for the time that there should be darkness for the space of three days over the face of the land.

4. And there began to be great doubtings and disputations among the people, notwithstanding so many signs had been given.

SEVENTH PERIOD

THE WEEK OF THE ATONING SACRIFICE AND TO THE ASCENSION

Section 160

JESUS COMES TO BETHANY

Jesus comes to Bethany; the Jews, knowing Jesus is there, come out to see both Jesus and Lazarus; the chief priests consult how they may also put Lazarus to death, since because of him, many Jews go away believing on Jesus.

Matt.: No record; Mark: No record; Luke: No record; John 12:1, 9-11.
Time: A.D. 30, Friday, March 31, 8th Nisan (ANDREWS); Saturday, April 1, 9th Nisan (ROBINSON).
Place: Bethany.

Matthew: No record.

Mark: No record.

Luke: No record.

JOHN 12:1. Then Jesus six days before the passover came to Bethany, where Lazarus was which had been dead, whom he raised from the dead . . . .

9. Much people of the Jews therefore knew that he was there: and they came not for Jesus' sake only, but that they might see Lazarus also, whom he had raised from the dead.

10. ¶ But the chief priests consulted that they might put Lazarus also to death;

11. Because that by reason of him many of the Jews went away, and believed on Jesus.

First Day of the Week

Section 161

FROM BETHANY TO JERUSALEM AND RETURN TO BETHANY

Time: A.D. 30, Sunday, April 2, 10th Nisan (ANDREWS).
Place: Bethany to Jerusalem and back.

(a) Entry into Jerusalem

Going from Bethany to Jerusalem, Jesus comes to Bethphage, unto the Mount of Olives; he tells two disciples to go to a nearby village where they will find tied an ass with a colt, whereon man never sat, these they will bring to Jesus and if any man questions, they are to say the Lord hath need of them and straightway he will send them; the disciples go to the village, they find the colt, they loose it, the owners ask the question, they reply as the Lord told them, and the owner lets them take the colt to Jesus; they put their coats on the colt, and set Jesus thereon; the multitude spread in the way their garments and palm branches cut from the trees; descending the Mount of Olives, the whole multitude break out in cries of joy, telling the mighty works of Jesus; shouting hosannas and saying, "Blessed be the King that cometh in the name of the Lord"; some of the Pharisees from the multitude ask Jesus to rebuke his disciples, and Jesus answers: "I tell you that, if these should hold their peace, the stones would immediately cry out"; coming near to the city he weeps and laments over it; the people who saw Jesus raise Lazarus bare record, the people who had heard of the miracle follow, in Jerusalem all the city is moved; the Pharisees say among themselves: "Perceive ye how ye prevail nothing? behold, the world is gone after him." Jesus enters the Temple.

Matt. 21:1-11; Mark 11:1-11a; Luke 19:29-44; John 12:12-19.

MATTHEW 21:1. And when they drew nigh unto Jerusalem, and were come to Bethphage, unto the mount of Olives, then sent Jesus two disciples,

2. Saying unto them, Go into the village over against you, and straightway ye shall find an ass tied, and a colt with her: loose *them*, and bring *them* unto me.

3. And if any *man* say ought unto you, ye shall say, The Lord hath need of them; and straightway he will send them.

4. All this was done, that it might be fulfilled which was spoken by the prophet, saying,

5. Tell ye the daughter of Sion, Behold, thy King cometh unto thee, meek, and sitting upon an ass, and a colt the foal of an ass.

6. And the disciples went, and did as Jesus commanded them,

7. And brought the ass, and the colt, and put on them their clothes, and they set *him* thereon.

8. And a very great multitude spread their garments in the way; others cut down branches from the trees, and strawed *them* in the way.

9. And the multitudes that went before, and that followed, cried, saying, Hosanna to the son of David: Blessed *is* he that cometh in the name of the Lord; Hosanna in the highest.

10. And when he was come into Jerusalem, all the city was moved, saying, Who is this?

11. And the multitude said, This is Jesus the prophet of Nazareth of Galilee.

MARK 11:1. And when they came nigh to Jerusalem, unto Bethphage and Bethany, at the mount of Olives, he sendeth forth two of his disciples,

2. And saith unto them, Go your way into the village over against you: and as soon as ye be entered into it, ye shall find a colt tied, whereon never man sat; loose him, and bring *him*.

3. And if any man say unto

you, Why do ye this? say ye that the Lord hath need of him; and straightway he will send him hither.

4. And they went their way, and found the colt tied by the door without in a place where two ways met; and they loose him.

5. And certain of them that stood there said unto them, What do ye, loosing the colt?

6. And they said unto them even as Jesus had commanded: and they let them go.

7. And they brought the colt to Jesus, and cast their garments on him; and he sat upon him.

8. And many spread their garments in the way: and others cut down branches off the trees, and strawed *them* in the way.

9. And they that went before, and they that followed, cried, saying, Hosanna; Blessed *is* he that cometh in the name of the Lord:

10. Blessed *be* the kingdom of our father David, that cometh in the name of the Lord: Hosanna in the highest.

11. And Jesus entered into Jerusalem, and into the temple: . . . .

LUKE 19:29. And it came to pass, when he was come nigh to Bethphage and Bethany, at the mount called *the mount* of Olives, he sent two of his disciples,

30. Saying, Go ye into the village over against *you*: in the which at your entering ye shall find a colt tied, whereon yet never man sat: loose him, and bring *him hither*.

31. And if any man ask you, Why do ye loose *him?* thus shall ye say unto him, Because the Lord hath need of him.

32. And they that were sent went their way, and found even as he had said unto them.

33. And as they were loosing the colt, the owners thereof said unto them, Why loose ye the colt?

34. And they said, The Lord hath need of him.

35. And they brought him to Jesus: and they cast their garments upon the colt, and they set Jesus thereon.

36. And as he went, they spread their clothes in the way.

37. And when he was come nigh, even now at the descent of the mount of Olives, the whole multitude of the disciples began to rejoice and praise God with a loud voice for all the mighty works that they had seen;

38. Saying, Blessed *be* the King that cometh in the name of the Lord: peace in heaven, and glory in the highest.

39. And some of the Pharisees from among the multitude said unto him, Master, rebuke thy disciples.

40. And he answered and said unto them, I tell you that, if these should hold their

peace, the stones would immediately cry out.

41. ¶ And when he was come near, he beheld the city, and wept over it,

42. Saying, If thou hadst known, even thou, at least in this thy day, the things *which belong* unto thy peace! but now they are hid from thine eyes.

43. For the days shall come upon thee, that thine enemies shall cast a trench about thee, and compass thee round, and keep thee in on every side,

44. And shall lay thee even with the ground, and thy children within thee; and they shall not leave in thee one stone upon another; because thou knewest not the time of thy visitation.

JOHN 12:12. ¶ On the next day much people that were come to the feast, when they heard that Jesus was coming to Jerusalem,

13. Took branches of palm trees, and went forth to meet him, and cried, Hosanna: Blessed *is* the King of Israel that cometh in the name of the Lord.

14. And Jesus, when he had found a young ass, sat thereon; as it is written,

15. Fear not, daughter of Sion: behold, thy King cometh, sitting on an ass's colt.

16. These things understood not his disciples at the first: but when Jesus was glorified, then remembered they that these things were written of him, and *that* they had done these things unto him.

17. The people therefore that was with him when he called Lazarus out of his grave, and raised him from the dead, bare record.

18. For this cause the people also met him, for that they heard that he had done this miracle.

19. The Pharisees therefore said among themselves, Perceive ye how ye prevail nothing? behold, the world is gone after him.

(b) Return to Bethany

Matt.: No record; Mark 11:11b; Luke: No record; John: No record.

Matthew: No record.

MARK 11:11. . . . and when he had looked round about upon all things, and now the eventide was come, he went out unto Bethany with the twelve.

Luke: No record.

John: No record.

Second Day of the Week

Section 162

BETHANY TO JERUSALEM, CLEANSING TEMPLE, AND BACK TO BETHANY

Time: A.D. 30, Monday, April 3, 11th Nisan (ANDREWS).
Place: Bethany to Jerusalem and back.

(a) Cursing of the Barren Fig Tree

In the morning returning unto the city Jesus is hungry; seeing a fig tree afar off, he comes to it, hoping he may find something thereon; finding nothing but leaves, he says, "let no fruit grow on thee henceforward for ever."

Matt. 21:18-19a; Mark 11:12-14; Luke: No record; John: No record.

MATTHEW 21:18. Now in the morning as he returned into the city, he hungered.

19. And when he saw a fig tree in the way, he came to it, and found nothing thereon, but leaves only, and said unto it, Let no fruit grow on thee henceforward for ever . . . .

MARK 11:12. ¶ And on the morrow, when they were come from Bethany, he was hungry:

13. And seeing a fig tree afar off having leaves, he came, if haply he might find any thing thereon: and when he came to it, he found nothing but leaves; for the time of figs was not *yet.*

14. And Jesus answered and said unto it, No man eat fruit of thee hereafter for ever. And his disciples heard *it.*

Luke: No record.

John: No record.

(b) Jesus Cleanses the Temple

The blind and the lame come to him in the Temple and he heals them; the children call, "Hosanna to the son of David"; the chief priests and scribes, hearing this and seeing Jesus' works, are displeased; they seek to destroy Jesus; Jesus cleanses the Temple of them that bought and sold and of the money changers.

Matt. 21:12-16; Mark 11:15-18; Luke 19:45-48; John: No record.

MATTHEW 21:12. ¶ And Jesus went into the temple of God, and cast out all them that sold and bought in the temple, and overthrew the tables of the moneychangers, and the seats of them that sold doves,

13. And said unto them, It is written, My house shall be called the house of prayer; but

ye have made it a den of thieves.

14. And the blind and the lame came to him in the temple; and he healed them.

15. And when the chief priests and scribes saw the wonderful things that he did, and the children crying in the temple, and saying, Hosanna to the son of David; they were sore displeased,

16. And said unto him, Hearest thou what these say? And Jesus saith unto them, Yea; have ye never read, Out of the mouth of babes and sucklings thou hast perfected praise?

MARK 11:15. ¶ And they come to Jerusalem: and Jesus went into the temple, and began to cast out them that sold and bought in the temple, and overthrew the tables of the moneychangers, and the seats of them that sold doves;

16. And would not suffer that any man should carry *any* vessel through the temple.

17. And he taught, saying unto them, Is it not written, My house shall be called of all nations the house of prayer? but ye have made it a den of thieves.

18. And the scribes and chief priests heard *it*, and sought how they might destroy him: for they feared him, because all the people was astonished at his doctrine.

LUKE 19:45. And he went into the temple, and began to cast out them that sold therein, and them that bought;

46. Saying unto them, It is written, My house is the house of prayer: but ye have made it a den of thieves.

47. And he taught daily in the temple. But the chief priests and the scribes and the chief of the people sought to destroy him,

48. And could not find what they might do: for all the people were very attentive to hear him.

John: No record.

(c) Return to Bethany

Matt. 21:17; Mark 11:19; Luke 21:37; John: No record.

MATTHEW 21:17. ¶ And he left them, and went out of the city into Bethany; and he lodged there.

MARK 11:19. And when even was come, he went out of the city.

LUKE 21:37. And in the day time he was teaching in the temple; and at night he went out, and abode in the mount that is called *the mount* of Olives.

John: No record.

Third Day of the Week

Section 163

BETHANY TO JERUSALEM, IN THE TEMPLE, AND BACK TO BETHANY

Time: A.D. 30, Tuesday, April 4, 12th Nisan (ANDREWS).
Place: Bethany to Jerusalem, in the Temple, and back to Bethany.

(a) A Discourse on Faith

The barren fig tree has withered away. Jesus and his disciples journeying towards Jerusalem in the morning see the fig tree withered away; Jesus makes this the text for a discourse on faith that has power even to the moving of mountains; he again teaches them about prayer and faith in prayer.

Matt. 21:19b-22; Mark 11:20-26; Luke 21:38; John: No record.

MATTHEW 21:19 .... And presently the fig tree withered away.

20. And when the disciples saw *it*, they marvelled, saying, How soon is the fig tree withered away!

21. Jesus answered and said unto them, Verily I say unto you, If ye have faith, and doubt not, ye shall not only do this *which is done* to the fig tree, but also if ye shall say unto this mountain, Be thou removed, and be thou cast into the sea; it shall be done.

22. And all things, whatsoever ye shall ask in prayer, believing, ye shall receive.

MARK 11:20. ¶ And in the morning, as they passed by, they saw the fig tree dried up from the roots.

21. And Peter calling to remembrance saith unto him, Master, behold, the fig tree which thou cursedst is withered away.

22. And Jesus answering saith unto them, Have faith in God.

23. For verily I say unto you, That whosoever shall say unto this mountain, Be thou removed, and be thou cast into the sea; and shall not doubt in his heart, but shall believe that those things which he saith shall come to pass; he shall have whatsoever he saith.

24. Therefore I say unto you, What things soever ye desire, when ye pray, believe that ye receive *them*, and ye shall have *them*.

25. And when ye stand praying, forgive, if ye have ought against any: that your Father also which is in heaven may forgive you your trespasses.

26. But if ye do not forgive,

neither will your Father which is in heaven forgive your trespasses.

LUKE 21:38. And all the people came early in the morning to him in the temple, for to hear him.

John: No record.

(b) The Question of His Authority

Jesus coming into the Temple, the chief priests, the scribes and the elders of the people come to him and ask by what authority does he do these things and who gave the authority; Jesus answers by a question—was the baptism of John from heaven or of men; they refuse to answer, perceiving they lose whichever way they answer; Jesus thereupon refuses to answer their question.

Matt. 21:23-27; Mark 11:27-33; Luke 20:1-8; John: No record.

MATTHEW 21:23. ¶ And when he was come into the temple, the chief priests and the elders of the people came unto him as he was teaching, and said, By what authority doest thou these things? and who gave thee this authority?

24. And Jesus answered and said unto them, I also will ask you one thing, which if ye tell me, I in like wise will tell you by what authority I do these things.

25. The baptism of John, whence was it? from heaven, or of men? And they reasoned with themselves, saying, If we shall say, From heaven; he will say unto us, Why did ye not then believe him?

26. But if we shall say, Of men; we fear the people; for all hold John as a prophet.

27. And they answered Jesus, and said, We cannot tell. And he said unto them, Neither tell I you by what authority I do these things.

MARK 11:27. ¶ And they come again to Jerusalem: and as he was walking in the temple, there come to him the chief priests, and the scribes, and the elders,

28. And say unto him, By what authority doest thou these things? and who gave thee this authority to do these things?

29. And Jesus answered and said unto them, I will also ask of you one question, and answer me, and I will tell you by what authority I do these things.

30. The baptism of John, was *it* from heaven, or of men? answer me.

31. And they reasoned with themselves, saying, If we shall say, From heaven; he will say, Why then did ye not believe him?

32. But if we shall say, Of men; they feared the people: for all *men* counted John, that he was a prophet indeed.

33. And they answered and said unto Jesus, We cannot

tell. And Jesus answering saith unto them, Neither do I tell you by what authority I do these things.

LUKE 20:1. And it came to pass, *that* on one of those days, as he taught the people in the temple, and preached the gospel, the chief priests and the scribes came upon *him* with the elders,

2. And spake unto him, saying, Tell us, by what authority dost thou these things? or who is he that gave thee this authority?

3. And he answered and said unto them, I will also ask you one thing; and answer me:

4. The baptism of John, was it from heaven, or of men?

5. And they reasoned with themselves, saying, If we shall say, From heaven; he will say, Why then believed ye him not?

6. But and if we say, Of men; all the people will stone us: for they be persuaded that John was a prophet.

7. And they answered, that they could not tell whence *it was*:

8. And Jesus said unto them, Neither tell I you by what authority I do these things.

John: No record.

(c) Parable of the Two Sons

Matt. 21:28-32; Mark: No record; Luke: No record; John: No record.

MATTHEW 21:28. ¶ But what think ye? A *certain* man had two sons; and he came to the first, and said, Son, go work to day in my vineyard.

29. He answered and said, I will not: but afterward he repented, and went.

30. And he came to the second, and said likewise. And he answered and said, I *go*, sir: and went not.

31. Whether of them twain did the will of *his* father? They say unto him, The first. Jesus saith unto them, Verily I say unto you, That the publicans and the harlots go into the kingdom of God before you.

32. For John came unto you in the way of righteousness, and ye believed him not: but the publicans and the harlots believed him: and ye, when ye have seen *it*, repented not afterward, that ye might believe him.

Mark: No record.
Luke: No record.
John: No record.

(d) Parable of the Wicked Husbandman

When Jesus explains the parable the Pharisees see it has to do with themselves; they seek to lay hands on Jesus, but fear the people, who believe Jesus to be a prophet.

Matt. 21:33-46; Mark 12:1-12; Luke 20:9-18; John: No record.

MATTHEW 21:33. ¶ Hear another parable: There was a certain householder, which planted a vineyard, and hedged it round about, and digged a wine-press in it, and built a tower, and let it out to husbandmen, and went into a far country:

34. And when the time of the fruit drew near, he sent his servants to the husbandmen, that they might receive the fruits of it.

35. And the husbandmen took his servants, and beat one, and killed another, and stoned another.

36. Again, he sent other servants more than the first: and they did unto them likewise.

37. But last of all he sent unto them his son, saying, They will reverence my son.

38. But when the husbandmen saw the son, they said among themselves, This is the heir; come, let us kill him, and let us seize on his inheritance.

39. And they caught him, and cast *him* out of the vineyard, and slew *him*.

40. When the lord therefore of the vineyard cometh, what will he do unto those husbandmen?

41. They say unto him, He will miserably destroy those wicked men, and will let out *his* vineyard unto other husbandmen, which shall render him the fruits in their seasons.

42. Jesus saith unto them, Did ye never read in the scriptures, The stone which the builders rejected, the same is become the head of the corner: this is the Lord's doing, and it is marvellous in our eyes?

43. Therefore say I unto you, The kingdom of God shall be taken from you, and given to a nation bringing forth the fruits thereof.

44. And whosoever shall fall on this stone shall be broken: but on whomsoever it shall fall, it will grind him to powder.

45. And when the chief priests and Pharisees had heard his parables, they perceived that he spake of them.

46. But when they sought to lay hands on him, they feared the multitude, because they took him for a prophet.

MARK 12:1. And he began to speak unto them by parables. A *certain* man planted a vineyard, and set an hedge about *it*, and digged *a place for* the winefat, and built a tower, and let it out to husbandmen, and went into a far country.

2. And at the season he sent to the husbandmen a servant, that he might receive from the husbandmen of the fruit of the vineyard.

3. And they caught *him*, and beat him, and sent *him* away empty.

4. And again he sent unto them another servant; and at him they cast stones, and wounded *him* in the head, and sent *him* away shamefully handled.

5. And again he sent another; and him they killed, and many others; beating some, and killing some.

6. Having yet therefore one son, his wellbeloved, he sent him also last unto them, saying, They will reverence my son.

7. But those husbandmen said among themselves, This is the heir; come, let us kill him, and the inheritance shall be our's.

8. And they took him, and killed *him*, and cast *him* out of the vineyard.

9. What shall therefore the lord of the vineyard do? he will come and destroy the husbandmen, and will give the vineyard unto others.

10. And have ye not read this scripture; The stone which the builders rejected is become the head of the corner:

11. This was the Lord's doing, and it is marvellous in our eyes?

12. And they sought to lay hold on him, but feared the people: for they knew that he had spoken the parable against them: and they left him, and went their way.

LUKE 20:9. Then began he to speak to the people this parable; A certain man planted a vineyard, and let it forth to husbandmen, and went into a far country for a long time.

10. And at the season he sent a servant to the husbandmen, that they should give him of the fruit of the vineyard: but the husbandmen beat him, and sent *him* away empty.

11. And again he sent another servant: and they beat him also, and entreated *him* shamefully, and sent *him* away empty.

12. And again he sent a third: and they wounded him also, and cast *him* out.

13. Then said the lord of the vineyard, What shall I do? I will send my beloved son: it may be they will reverence *him* when they see him.

14. But when the husbandmen saw him, they reasoned among themselves, saying, This is the heir: come, let us kill him, that the inheritance may be our's.

15. So they cast him out of the vineyard, and killed *him*. What therefore shall the lord of the vineyard do unto them?

16. He shall come and destroy these husbandmen, and shall give the vineyard to others. And when they heard *it*, they said, God forbid.

17. And he beheld them, and said, What is this then that is written, The stone which the

builders rejected, the same is become the head of the corner?

18. Whosoever shall fall upon that stone shall be broken; but on whomsoever it shall fall, it will grind him to powder.

John: No record.

(e) Parable of the King's Son

Matt. 22:1-14; Mark: No record; Luke: No record; John: No record.

MATTHEW 22:1. And Jesus answered and spake unto them again by parables, and said,

2. The kingdom of heaven is like unto a certain king, which made a marriage for his son,

3. And sent forth his servants to call them that were bidden to the wedding: and they would not come.

4. Again, he sent forth other servants, saying, Tell them which are bidden, Behold, I have prepared my dinner: my oxen and *my* fatlings *are* killed, and all things *are* ready: come unto the marriage.

5. But they made light of *it,* and went their ways, one to his farm, another to his merchandise:

6. And the remnant took his servants, and entreated *them* spitefully, and slew *them.*

7. But when the king heard *thereof,* he was wroth: and he sent forth his armies, and destroyed those murderers, and burned up their city.

8. Then saith he to his servants, The wedding is ready, but they which were bidden were not worthy.

9. Go ye therefore into the highways, and as many as ye shall find bid to the marriage.

10. So those servants went out into the highways, and gathered together all as many as they found, both bad and good: and the wedding was furnished with guests.

11. ¶ And when the king came in to see the guests, he saw there a man which had not on a wedding garment:

12. And he saith unto him, Friend, how camest thou in hither not having a wedding garment? And he was speechless.

13. Then said the king to the servants, Bind him hand and foot, and take him away, and cast *him* into outer darkness; there shall be weeping and gnashing of teeth.

14. For many are called, but few *are* chosen.

Mark: No record.

Luke: No record.

John: No record.

(f) The Question About Tribute

The Pharisees taking counsel how they might entangle Jesus in his talk, send certain of their own with some of the Herodians, who ask Jesus whether it be lawful to pay tribute to Caesar; Jesus, perceiving their wickedness, says to them, "Why tempt ye me, ye hypocrites?"; he asks them to show him the tribute money; they bring him a penny; he asks, "Whose image and superscription hath it?" They answer Caesar's. Jesus says, "Render therefore unto Caesar the things which are Caesar's; and unto God the things that are God's"; they marvel at him, hold their peace, and go their way.

Matt. 22:15-22; Mark 12:13-17; Luke 20:19-26; John: No record.

MATTHEW 22:15. ¶ Then went the Pharisees, and took counsel how they might entangle him in *his* talk.

16. And they sent out unto him their disciples with the Herodians, saying, Master, we know that thou art true, and teachest the way of God in truth, neither carest thou for any *man*: for thou regardest not the person of men.

17. Tell us therefore, What thinkest thou? Is it lawful to give tribute unto Cæsar, or not?

18. But Jesus perceived their wickedness, and said, Why tempt ye me, *ye* hypocrites?

19. Shew me the tribute money. And they brought unto him a penny.

20. And he saith unto them, Whose *is* this image and superscription?

21. They say unto him, Cæsar's. Then saith he unto them, Render therefore unto Cæsar the things which are Cæsar's; and unto God the things that are God's.

22. When they had heard *these words*, they marvelled, and left him, and went their way.

MARK 12:13. ¶ And they send unto him certain of the Pharisees and of the Herodians, to catch him in *his* words.

14. And when they were come, they say unto him, Master, we know that thou art true, and carest for no man: for thou regardest not the person of men, but teachest the way of God in truth: Is it lawful to give tribute to Cæsar, or not?

15. Shall we give, or shall we not give? But he, knowing their hypocrisy, said unto them, Why tempt ye me? bring me a penny, that I may see *it*.

16. And they brought *it*. And he saith unto them, Whose *is* this image and superscription? And they said unto him, Cæsar's.

17. And Jesus answering said unto them, Render to Cæsar the things that are Cæsar's, and to God the things that are God's. And they marvelled at him.

LUKE 20:19. ¶ And the chief priests and the scribes the same hour sought to lay hands on him; and they feared the people: for they perceived that he had spoken this parable against them.

20. And they watched *him*, and sent forth spies, which should feign themselves just men, that they might take hold of his words, that so they might deliver him unto the power and authority of the governor.

21. And they asked him, saying, Master, we know that thou sayest and teachest rightly, neither acceptest thou the person *of any*, but teachest the way of God truly:

22. Is it lawful for us to give tribute unto Cæsar, or no?

23. But he perceived their craftiness, and said unto them, Why tempt ye me?

24. Shew me a penny. Whose image and superscription hath it? They answered and said, Cæsar's.

25. And he said unto them, Render therefore unto Cæsar the things which be Cæsar's, and unto God the things which be God's.

26. And they could not take hold of his words before the people: and they marvelled at his answer, and held their peace.

John: No record.

(g) The Sadducees Question About Marriage After the Resurrection

There come next to tempt Jesus and try him the Sadducees who believe not in the resurrection; they put the case of a woman who, under the Mosaic law which provided for the raising of seed unto the dead husband by a brother, married seven brothers in succession and died childless; they ask whose wife she shall be in the resurrection; Jesus answers.

Matt. 22:23-33; Mark 12:18-27; Luke 20:27-40; John: No record.

MATTHEW 22:23. ¶ The same day came to him the Sadducees, which say that there is no resurrection, and asked him,

24. Saying, Master, Moses said, If a man die, having no children, his brother shall marry his wife, and raise up seed unto his brother.

25. Now there were with us seven brethren: and the first, when he had married a wife, deceased, and, having no issue, left his wife unto his brother:

26. Likewise the second also, and the third, unto the seventh.

27. And last of all the woman died also.

28. Therefore in the resurrection whose wife shall she be of the seven? for they all had her.

29. Jesus answered and said unto them, Ye do err, not

knowing the scriptures, nor the power of God.

30. For in the resurrection they neither marry, nor are given in marriage, but are as the angels of God in heaven.

31. But as touching the resurrection of the dead, have ye not read that which was spoken unto you by God, saying,

32. I am the God of Abraham, and the God of Isaac, and the God of Jacob? God is not the God of the dead, but of the living.

33. And when the multitude heard *this*, they were astonished at his doctrine.

MARK 12:18. ¶ Then come unto him the Sadducees, which say there is no resurrection; and they asked him, saying,

19. Master, Moses wrote unto us, If a man's brother die, and leave *his* wife *behind him*, and leave no children, that his brother should take his wife, and raise up seed unto his brother.

20. Now there were seven brethren: and the first took a wife, and dying left no seed.

21. And the second took her, and died, neither left he any seed: and the third likewise.

22. And the seven had her, and left no seed: last of all the woman died also.

23. In the resurrection therefore, when they shall rise, whose wife shall she be of them? for the seven had her to wife.

24. And Jesus answering said unto them, Do ye not therefore err, because ye know not the scriptures, neither the power of God?

25. For when they shall rise from the dead, they neither marry, nor are given in marriage; but are as the angels which are in heaven.

26. And as touching the dead, that they rise: have ye not read in the book of Moses, how in the bush God spake unto him, saying, I *am* the God of Abraham, and the God of Isaac, and the God of Jacob?

27. He is not the God of the dead, but the God of the living: ye therefore do greatly err.

LUKE 20:27. ¶ Then came to *him* certain of the Sadducees, which deny that there is any resurrection; and they asked him,

28. Saying, Master, Moses wrote unto us, If any man's brother die, having a wife, and he die without children, that his brother should take his wife, and raise up seed unto his brother.

29. There were therefore seven brethren: and the first took a wife, and died without children.

30. And the second took her to wife, and he died childless.

31. And the third took her; and in like manner the seven also: and they left no children, and died.

32. Last of all the woman died also.

33. Therefore in the resurrection whose wife of them is she? for seven had her to wife.

34. And Jesus answering said unto them, The children of this world marry, and are given in marriage:

35. But they which shall be accounted worthy to obtain that world, and the resurrection from the dead, neither marry, nor are given in marriage:

36. Neither can they die any more: for they are equal unto the angels; and are the children of God, being the children of the resurrection.

37. Now that the dead are raised, even Moses shewed at the bush, when he calleth the Lord the God of Abraham, and the God of Isaac, and the God of Jacob.

38. For he is not a God of the dead, but of the living: for all live unto him.

39. ¶ Then certain of the scribes answering said, Master, thou hast well said.

40. And after that they durst not ask him any *question at all.*

John: No record.

(h) The Lawyer Questions About the Great Commandment

The Pharisees, hearing the Sadducees have been silenced, gather together, and one of them, a lawyer, to try Jesus, asks: "Master, which is the great commandment in the law?" Jesus replies quoting the two great laws; the lawyer tells Jesus he said the truth, and gives a short discourse on the commandments; Jesus tells him he is not far from the kingdom of God; "and no man after that durst ask him any question."

Matt. 22:34-40; Mark 12:28-34; Luke: No record; John: No record.

MATTHEW 22:34. ¶ But when the Pharisees had heard that he had put the Sadducees to silence, they were gathered together.

35. Then one of them, *which was* a lawyer, asked *him a question,* tempting him, and saying,

36. Master, which *is* the great commandment in the law?

37. Jesus said unto him, Thou shalt love the Lord thy God with all thy heart, and with all thy soul, and with all thy mind.

38. This is the first and great commandment.

39. And the second *is* like unto it, Thou shalt love thy neighbour as thyself.

40. On these two commandments hang all the law and the prophets.

MARK 12:28. ¶ And one of the scribes came, and having heard them reasoning together, and perceiving that he had answered them well, asked him, Which is the first commandment of all?

29. And Jesus answered him, The first of all the commandments *is*, Hear, O Israel; The Lord our God is one Lord:

30. And thou shalt love the Lord thy God with all thy heart, and with all thy soul, and with all thy mind, and with all thy strength: this *is* the first commandment.

31. And the second *is* like, *namely* this, Thou shalt love thy neighbour as thyself. There is none other commandment greater than these.

32. And the scribe said unto him, Well, Master, thou hast said the truth: for there is one God; and there is none other but he:

33. And to love him with all the heart, and with all the understanding, and with all the soul, and with all the strength, and to love *his* neighbour as himself, is more than all whole burnt offerings and sacrifices.

34. And when Jesus saw that he answered discreetly, he said unto him, Thou art not far from the kingdom of God. And no man after that durst ask him *any question*.

Luke: No record.

John: No record.

(i) Jesus Asks Pharisees Whose Son Christ Is

While the Pharisees are still gathered together Jesus asks, "What think ye of Christ? whose son is he?" They reply: "The son of David"; Jesus asks how is it then that David calls him Lord, for "if David then call him Lord, how is he his son?"; the common people hear Jesus gladly; no man thereafter durst ask him any question.

Matt. 22:41-46; Mark 12:35-37; Luke 20:41-44; John: No record.

MATTHEW 22:41. ¶ While the Pharisees were gathered together, Jesus asked them,

42. Saying, What think ye of Christ? whose son is he? They say unto him, *The son* of David.

43. He saith unto them, How then doth David in spirit call him Lord, saying,

44. The Lord said unto my Lord, Sit thou on my right hand, till I make thine enemies thy footstool?

45. If David then call him Lord, how is he his son?

46. And no man was able to answer him a word, neither durst any *man* from that day forth ask him any more *questions*.

MARK 12:35. ¶ And Jesus answered and said, while he taught in the temple, How say the scribes that Christ is the son of David?

36. For David himself said by the Holy Ghost, The Lord said to my Lord, Sit thou on my right hand, till I make thine enemies thy footstool.

37. David therefore himself calleth him Lord; and whence is he *then* his son? And the common people heard him gladly.

LUKE 20:41. And he said unto them, How say they that Christ is David's son?

42. And David himself saith in the book of Psalms, The Lord said unto my Lord, Sit thou on my right hand,

43. Till I make thine enemies thy footstool.

44. David therefore calleth him Lord, how is he then his son?

John: No record.

(j) The Scribes and Pharisees Condemned

Jesus, speaking to the multitude and to his disciples, condemns the scribes and the Pharisees, and lists their sins, discourses thereon, and tells of the punishments for the sins.

Matt. 23:1-36; Mark 12:38-40; Luke 20:45-47; John: No record.

MATTHEW 23:1. Then spake Jesus to the multitude, and to his disciples,

2. Saying, The scribes and the Pharisees sit in Moses' seat:

3. All therefore whatsoever they bid you observe, *that* observe and do; but do not ye after their works: for they say, and do not.

4. For they bind heavy burdens and grievous to be borne, and lay *them* on men's shoulders; but they *themselves* will not move them with one of their fingers.

5. But all their works they do for to be seen of men: they make broad their phylacteries, and enlarge the borders of their garments,

6. And love the uppermost rooms at feasts, and the chief seats in the synagogues,

7. And greetings in the markets, and to be called of men, Rabbi, Rabbi.

8. But be not ye called Rabbi: for one is your Master, *even* Christ; and all ye are brethren.

9. And call no *man* your father upon the earth: for one is your Father, which is in heaven.

10. Neither be ye called masters: for one is your Master, *even* Christ.

11. But he that is greatest among you shall be your servant.

12. And whosoever shall exalt himself shall be abased; and he that shall humble himself shall be exalted.

13. ¶ But woe unto you, scribes and Pharisees, hypocrites! for ye shut up the kingdom of heaven against men: for ye neither go in *yourselves*, neither suffer ye them that are entering to go in.

14. Woe unto you, scribes and Pharisees, hypocrites! for ye devour widows' houses, and

for a pretence make long prayer: therefore ye shall receive the greater damnation.

15. Woe unto you, scribes and Pharisees, hypocrites! for ye compass sea and land to make one proselyte, and when he is made, ye make him twofold more the child of hell than yourselves.

16. Woe unto you, *ye* blind guides, which say, Whosoever shall swear by the temple, it is nothing; but whosoever shall swear by the gold of the temple, he is a debtor!

17. *Ye* fools and blind: for whether is greater, the gold, or the temple that sanctifieth the gold?

18. And, Whosoever shall swear by the altar, it is nothing; but whosoever sweareth by the gift that is upon it, he is guilty.

19. *Ye* fools and blind: for whether *is* greater, the gift, or the altar that sanctifieth the gift?

20. Whoso therefore shall swear by the altar, sweareth by it, and by all things thereon.

21. And whoso shall swear by the temple, sweareth by it, and by him that dwelleth therein.

22. And he that shall swear by heaven, sweareth by the throne of God, and by him that sitteth thereon.

23. Woe unto you, scribes and Pharisees, hypocrites! for ye pay tithe of mint and anise and cummin, and have omitted the weightier *matters* of the law, judgment, mercy, and faith: these ought ye to have done, and not to leave the other undone.

24. *Ye* blind guides, which strain at a gnat, and swallow a camel.

25. Woe unto you, scribes and Pharisees, hypocrites! for ye make clean the outside of the cup and of the platter, but within they are full of extortion and excess.

26. *Thou* blind Pharisee, cleanse first that *which is* within the cup and platter, that the outside of them may be clean also.

27. Woe unto you, scribes and Pharisees, hypocrites! for ye are like unto whited sepulchres, which indeed appear beautiful outward, but are within full of dead *men's* bones, and of all uncleanness.

28. Even so ye also outwardly appear righteous unto men, but within ye are full of hypocrisy and iniquity.

29. Woe unto you, scribes and Pharisees, hypocrites! because ye build the tombs of the prophets, and garnish the sepulchres of the righteous,

30. And say, If we had been in the days of our fathers, we would not have been partakers with them in the blood of the prophets.

31. Wherefore ye be witnesses unto yourselves, that ye are the children of them which killed the prophets.

32. Fill ye up then the measure of your fathers.

33. *Ye* serpents, *ye* generation of vipers, how can ye escape the damnation of hell?

34. ¶ Wherefore, behold, I send unto you prophets, and wise men, and scribes: and *some* of them ye shall kill and crucify; and *some* of them shall ye scourge in your synagogues, and persecute *them* from city to city:

35. That upon you may come all the righteous blood shed upon the earth, from the blood of righteous Abel unto the blood of Zacharias son of Barachias, whom ye slew between the temple and the altar.

36. Verily I say unto you, All these things shall come upon this generation.

MARK 12:38. ¶ And he said unto them in his doctrine, Beware of the scribes, which love to go in long clothing, and *love* salutations in the market places,

39. And the chief seats in the synagogues, and the uppermost rooms at feasts:

40. Which devour widows' houses, and for a pretence make long prayers: these shall receive greater damnation.

LUKE 20:45. ¶ Then in the audience of all the people he said unto his disciples,

46. Beware of the scribes, which desire to walk in long robes, and love greetings in the markets, and the highest seats in the synagogues, and the chief rooms at feasts;

47. Which devour widows' houses, and for a shew make long prayers: the same shall receive greater damnation.

John: No record.

(k) Jesus' Lamentation Over Jerusalem

Matt. 23:37-39; Mark: No record; Luke: No record; John: No record.

MATTHEW 23:37. O Jerusalem, Jerusalem, *thou* that killest the prophets, and stonest them which are sent unto thee, how often would I have gathered thy children together, even as a hen gathereth her chickens under *her* wings, and ye would not!

38. Behold, your house is left unto you desolate.

39. For I say unto you, Ye shall not see me henceforth, till ye shall say, Blessed *is* he that cometh in the name of the Lord.

Mark: No record.

Luke: No record.

John: No record.

(l) The Widow's Mite

Jesus, sitting against the treasury, sees the people casting in their money, the poor and the rich who often cast in much; a widow comes casting in two mites, one farthing; Jesus calls his disciples and tells them, "this poor widow hath cast more in, than all they which have cast into the treasury: for all they did cast in of their abundance; but she of her want did cast in all that she had, even all her living."

Matt.: No record; Mark 12:41-44; Luke 21:1-4; John: No record.

Matthew: No record.

MARK 12:41. ¶ And Jesus sat over against the treasury, and beheld how the people cast money into the treasury: and many that were rich cast in much.

42. And there came a certain poor widow, and she threw in two mites, which make a farthing.

43. And he called *unto him* his disciples, and saith unto them, Verily I say unto you, That this poor widow hath cast more in, than all they which have cast into the treasury:

44. For all *they* did cast in of their abundance; but she of her want did cast in all that she had, *even* all her living.

LUKE 21:1. And he looked up, and saw the rich men casting their gifts into the treasury.

2. And he saw also a certain poor widow casting in thither two mites.

3. And he said, Of a truth I say unto you, that this poor widow hath cast in more than they all:

4. For all these have of their abundance cast in unto the offerings of God: but she of her penury hath cast in all the living that she had.

John: No record.

(m) The Greeks Seek Him; a Voice From Heaven

Certain Greeks come to worship at the feast, ask Philip (of Bethsaida) who speaks to Andrew, to get them to see Jesus; Philip and Andrew tell Jesus of the wish of the Greeks; Jesus tells them of his approaching death and resurrection, and makes a discourse; during his discourse a voice comes from heaven; some of the people hearing it think it thunders; others think an angel speaks to him; speaking of the kind of death he should die, the people say they have heard out of the law that Christ abideth forever, yet Jesus speaks of the Son of man being lifted up; they ask who the Son of man is; he answers in parable; then goes and hides himself from them.

Matt.: No record; Mark: No record; Luke: No record; John 12:20-36.

Matthew: No record.

Mark: No record.

Luke: No record.

JOHN 12:20. ¶ And there

were certain Greeks among them that came up to worship at the feast:

21. The same came therefore to Philip, which was of Bethsaida of Galilee, and desired him, saying, Sir, we would see Jesus.

22. Philip cometh and telleth Andrew: and again Andrew and Philip tell Jesus.

23. ¶ And Jesus answered them, saying, The hour is come, that the Son of man should be glorified.

24. Verily, verily, I say unto you, Except a corn of wheat fall into the ground and die, it abideth alone: but if it die, it bringeth forth much fruit.

25. He that loveth his life shall lose it; and he that hateth his life in this world shall keep it unto life eternal.

26. If any man serve me, let him follow me; and where I am, there shall also my servant be: if any man serve me, him will *my* Father honour.

27. Now is my soul troubled; and what shall I say? Father, save me from this hour: but for this cause came I unto this hour.

28. Father, glorify thy name. Then came there a voice from heaven, *saying*, I have both glorified *it*, and will glorify *it* again.

29. The people therefore, that stood by, and heard *it*, said that it thundered: others said, An angel spake to him.

30. Jesus answered and said, This voice came not because of me, but for your sakes.

31. Now is the judgment of this world: now shall the prince of this world be cast out.

32. And I, if I be lifted up from the earth, will draw all *men* unto me.

33. This he said, signifying what death he should die.

34. The people answered him, We have heard out of the law that Christ abideth for ever: and how sayest thou, The Son of man must be lifted up? who is this Son of man?

35. Then Jesus said unto them, Yet a little while is the light with you. Walk while ye have the light, lest darkness come upon you: for he that walketh in darkness knoweth not whither he goeth.

36. While ye have light, believe in the light, that ye may be the children of light. These things spake Jesus, and departed, and did hide himself from them.

(n) Timidity of Chief Rulers Who Believe

Notwithstanding the many miracles of Jesus, they do not believe in him, this in fulfillment of prophecy; yet many among the chief rulers believe on him, but do not confess him, lest they shall be put out of the

synagogue, loving the praise of men more than the praise of God; Jesus, declaring, "I am come a light into the world," discourses on his Messiahship and gives the punishment of those rejecting him; he declares what the Father told him to speak.

Matt.: No record; Mark: No record; Luke: No record; John 12:37-50.

Matthew: No record.

Mark: No record.

Luke: No record.

JOHN 12:37. ¶ But though he had done so many miracles before them, yet they believed not on him:

38. That the saying of Esaias the prophet might be fulfilled, which he spake, Lord, who hath believed our report? and to whom hath the arm of the Lord been revealed?

39. Therefore they could not believe, because that Esaias said again,

40. He hath blinded their eyes, and hardened their heart; that they should not see with *their* eyes, nor understand with *their* heart, and be converted, and I should heal them.

41. These things said Esaias, when he saw his glory, and spake of him.

42. ¶ Nevertheless among the chief rulers also many believed on him; but because of the Pharisees they did not confess *him*, lest they should be put out of the synagogue:

43. For they loved the praise of men more than the praise of God.

44. ¶ Jesus cried and said, He that believeth on me, believeth not on me, but on him that sent me.

45. And he that seeth me seeth him that sent me.

46. I am come a light into the world, that whosoever believeth on me should not abide in darkness.

47. And if any man hear my words, and believe not, I judge him not: for I came not to judge the world, but to save the world.

48. He that rejecteth me, and receiveth not my words, hath one that judgeth him: the word that I have spoken, the same shall judge him in the last day.

49. For I have not spoken of myself; but the Father which sent me, he gave me a commandment, what I should say, and what I should speak.

50. And I know that his commandment is life everlasting: whatsoever I speak therefore, even as the Father said unto me, so I speak.

(o) The Olivet Discourse

Jesus departing from the Temple, the disciples offer to show him the buildings; he prophesies the destruction of the Temple; he then

gives the signs of his second coming, of the day and the hour thereof no man knoweth, not even the angels in heaven; he warns and urges to faithfulness.

Matt. 24:1-51; Mark 13:1-37; Luke 21:5-36; John: No record.

MATTHEW 24:1. And Jesus went out, and departed from the temple: and his disciples came to *him* for to shew him the buildings of the temple.

2. And Jesus said unto them, See ye not all these things? verily I say unto you, There shall not be left here one stone upon another, that shall not be thrown down.

3. ¶ And as he sat upon the mount of Olives, the disciples came unto him privately, saying, Tell us, when shall these things be? and what *shall be* the sign of thy coming, and of the end of the world?

4. And Jesus answered and said unto them, Take heed that no man deceive you.

5. For many shall come in my name, saying, I am Christ; and shall deceive many.

6. And ye shall hear of wars and rumours of wars: see that ye be not troubled: for all *these things* must come to pass, but the end is not yet.

7. For nation shall rise against nation, and kingdom against kingdom: and there shall be famines, and pestilences, and earthquakes, in divers places.

8. All these *are* the beginning of sorrows.

9. Then shall they deliver you up to be afflicted, and shall kill you: and ye shall be hated of all nations for my name's sake.

10. And then shall many be offended, and shall betray one another, and shall hate one another.

11. And many false prophets shall rise, and shall deceive many.

12. And because iniquity shall abound, the love of many shall wax cold.

13. But he that shall endure unto the end, the same shall be saved.

14. And this gospel of the kingdom shall be preached in all the world for a witness unto all nations; and then shall the end come.

15. When ye therefore shall see the abomination of desolation, spoken of by Daniel the prophet, stand in the holy place, (whoso readeth, let him understand:)

16. Then let them which be in Judæa flee into the mountains:

17. Let him which is on the housetop not come down to take any thing out of his house:

18. Neither let him which is in the field return back to take his clothes.

19. And woe unto them that

are with child, and to them that give suck in those days!

20. But pray ye that your flight be not in the winter, neither on the sabbath day:

21. For then shall be great tribulation, such as was not since the beginning of the world to this time, no, nor ever shall be.

22. And except those days should be shortened, there should no flesh be saved: but for the elect's sake those days shall be shortened.

23. Then if any man shall say unto you, Lo, here *is* Christ, or there; believe *it* not.

24. For there shall arise false Christs, and false prophets, and shall shew great signs and wonders; insomuch that, if *it were* possible, they shall deceive the very elect.

25. Behold, I have told you before.

26. Wherefore if they shall say unto you, Behold, he is in the desert; go not forth: behold, *he is* in the secret chambers; believe *it* not.

27. For as the lightning cometh out of the east, and shineth even unto the west; so shall also the coming of the Son of man be.

28. For wheresoever the carcase is, there will the eagles be gathered together.

29. ¶ Immediately after the tribulation of those days shall the sun be darkened, and the moon shall not give her light, and the stars shall fall from heaven, and the powers of the heavens shall be shaken:

30. And then shall appear the sign of the Son of man in heaven: and then shall all the tribes of the earth mourn, and they shall see the Son of man coming in the clouds of heaven with power and great glory.

31. And he shall send his angels with a great sound of a trumpet, and they shall gather together his elect from the four winds, from one end of heaven to the other.

32. Now learn a parable of the fig tree; When his branch is yet tender, and putteth forth leaves, ye know that summer *is* nigh:

33. So likewise ye, when ye shall see all these things, know that it is near, *even* at the doors.

34. Verily I say unto you, This generation shall not pass, till all these things be fulfilled.

35. Heaven and earth shall pass away, but my words shall not pass away.

36. ¶ But of that day and hour knoweth no *man*, no, not the angels of heaven, but my Father only.

37. But as the days of Noe *were*, so shall also the coming of the Son of man be.

38. For as in the days that were before the flood they were eating and drinking, marrying and giving in marriage, until the day that Noe entered into the ark,

39. And knew not until the

flood came, and took them all away; so shall also the coming of the Son of man be.

40. Then shall two be in the field; the one shall be taken, and the other left.

41. Two *women shall be* grinding at the mill; the one shall be taken, and the other left.

42. ¶ Watch therefore: for ye know not what hour your Lord doth come.

43. But know this, that if the goodman of the house had known in what watch the thief would come, he would have watched, and would not have suffered his house to be broken up.

44. Therefore be ye also ready: for in such an hour as ye think not the Son of man cometh.

45. Who then is a faithful and wise servant, whom his lord hath made ruler over his household, to give them meat in due season?

46. Blessed *is* that servant, whom his lord when he cometh shall find so doing.

47. Verily I say unto you, That he shall make him ruler over all his goods.

48. But and if that evil servant shall say in his heart, My lord delayeth his coming;

49. And shall begin to smite *his* fellowservants, and to eat and drink with the drunken;

50. The lord of that servant shall come in a day when he looketh not for *him*, and in an hour that he is not aware of,

51. And shall cut him asunder, and appoint *him* his portion with the hypocrites: there shall be weeping and gnashing of teeth.

MARK 13:1. And as he went out of the temple, one of his disciples saith unto him, Master, see what manner of stones and what buildings *are here!*

2. And Jesus answering said unto him, Seest thou these great buildings? there shall not be left one stone upon another, that shall not be thrown down.

3. And as he sat upon the mount of Olives over against the temple, Peter and James and John and Andrew asked him privately,

4. Tell us, when shall these things be? and what *shall be* the sign when all these things shall be fulfilled?

5. And Jesus answering them began to say, Take heed lest any *man* deceive you:

6. For many shall come in my name, saying, I am *Christ*; and shall deceive many.

7. And when ye shall hear of wars and rumours of wars, be ye not troubled: for *such things* must needs be; but the end *shall* not *be* yet.

8. For nation shall rise against nation, and kingdom against kingdom: and there shall be earthquakes in divers places, and there shall be famines and troubles: these *are* the beginnings of sorrows.

9. ¶ But take heed to yourselves: for they shall deliver you up to councils; and in the synagogues ye shall be beaten: and ye shall be brought before rulers and kings for my sake, for a testimony against them.

10. And the gospel must first be published among all nations.

11. But when they shall lead *you*, and deliver you up, take no thought beforehand what ye shall speak, neither do ye premeditate: but whatsoever shall be given you in that hour, that speak ye: for it is not ye that speak, but the Holy Ghost.

12. Now the brother shall betray the brother to death, and the father the son; and children shall rise up against *their* parents, and shall cause them to be put to death.

13. And ye shall be hated of all *men* for my name's sake: but he that shall endure unto the end, the same shall be saved.

14. ¶ But when ye shall see the abomination of desolation, spoken of by Daniel the prophet, standing where it ought not, (let him that readeth understand,) then let them that be in Judæa flee to the mountains:

15. And let him that is on the housetop not go down into the house, neither enter *therein*, to take any thing out of his house:

16. And let him that is in the field not turn back again for to take up his garment.

17. But woe to them that are with child, and to them that give suck in those days!

18. And pray ye that your flight be not in the winter.

19. For *in* those days shall be affliction, such as was not from the beginning of the creation which God created unto this time, neither shall be.

20. And except that the Lord had shortened those days, no flesh should be saved: but for the elect's sake, whom he hath chosen, he hath shortened the days.

21. And then if any man shall say to you, Lo, here *is* Christ; or, lo, *he is* there; believe *him* not:

22. For false Christs and false prophets shall rise, and shall shew signs and wonders, to seduce, if *it were* possible, even the elect.

23. But take ye heed: behold, I have foretold you all things.

24. ¶ But in those days, after that tribulation, the sun shall be darkened, and the moon shall not give her light,

25. And the stars of heaven shall fall, and the powers that are in heaven shall be shaken.

26. And then shall they see the Son of man coming in the clouds with great power and glory.

27. And then shall he send his angels, and shall gather together his elect from the four

winds, from the uttermost part of the earth to the uttermost part of heaven.

28. Now learn a parable of the fig tree; When her branch is yet tender, and putteth forth leaves, ye know that summer is near:

29. So ye in like manner, when ye shall see these things come to pass, know that it is nigh, *even* at the doors.

30. Verily I say unto you, that this generation shall not pass, till all these things be done.

31. Heaven and earth shall pass away: but my words shall not pass away.

32. ¶ But of that day and *that* hour knoweth no man, no, not the angels which are in heaven, neither the Son, but the Father.

33. Take ye heed, watch and pray: for ye know not when the time is.

34. *For the Son of man is* as a man taking a far journey, who left his house, and gave authority to his servants, and to every man his work, and commanded the porter to watch.

35. Watch ye therefore: for ye know not when the master of the house cometh, at even, or at midnight, or at the cockcrowing, or in the morning:

36. Lest coming suddenly he find you sleeping.

37. And what I say unto you I say unto all, Watch.

LUKE 21:5. ¶ And as some spake of the temple, how it was adorned with goodly stones and gifts, he said,

6. *As for* these things which ye behold, the days will come, in the which there shall not be left one stone upon another, that shall not be thrown down.

7. And they asked him, saying, Master, but when shall these things be? and what sign *will there be* when these things shall come to pass?

8. And he said, Take heed that ye be not deceived: for many shall come in my name, saying, I am *Christ;* and the time draweth near: go ye not therefore after them.

9. But when ye shall hear of wars and commotions, be not terrified: for these things must first come to pass; but the end *is* not by and by.

10. Then said he unto them, Nation shall rise against nation, and kingdom against kingdom:

11. And great earthquakes shall be in divers places, and famines, and pestilences; and fearful sights and great signs shall there be from heaven.

12. But before all these, they shall lay their hands on you, and persecute *you*, delivering *you* up to the synagogues, and into prisons, being brought before kings and rulers for my name's sake.

13. And it shall turn to you for a testimony.

14. Settle *it* therefore in your hearts, not to meditate before what ye shall answer:

15. For I will give you a mouth and wisdom, which all your adversaries shall not be able to gainsay nor resist.

16. And ye shall be betrayed both by parents, and brethren, and kinsfolks, and friends; and *some* of you shall they cause to be put to death.

17. And ye shall be hated of all *men* for my name's sake.

18. But there shall not an hair of your head perish.

19. In your patience possess ye your souls.

20. And when ye shall see Jerusalem compassed with armies, then know that the desolation thereof is nigh.

21. Then let them which are in Judæa flee to the mountains; and let them which are in the midst of it depart out; and let not them that are in the countries enter thereinto.

22. For these be the days of vengeance, that all things which are written may be fulfilled.

23. But woe unto them that are with child, and to them that give suck, in those days! for there shall be great distress in the land, and wrath upon this people.

24. And they shall fall by the edge of the sword, and shall be led away captive into all nations: and Jerusalem shall be trodden down of the Gentiles, until the times of the Gentiles be fulfilled.

25. ¶ And there shall be signs in the sun, and in the moon, and in the stars; and upon the earth distress of nations, with perplexity; the sea and the waves roaring;

26. Men's hearts failing them for fear, and for looking after those things which are coming on the earth: for the powers of heaven shall be shaken.

27. And then shall they see the Son of man coming in a cloud with power and great glory.

28. And when these things begin to come to pass, then look up, and lift up your heads; for your redemption draweth nigh.

29. And he spake to them a parable; Behold the fig tree, and all the trees;

30. When they now shoot forth, ye see and know of your own selves that summer is now nigh at hand.

31. So likewise ye, when ye see these things come to pass, know ye that the kingdom of God is nigh at hand.

32. Verily I say unto you, This generation shall not pass away, till all be fulfilled.

33. Heaven and earth shall pass away: but my words shall not pass away.

34. ¶ And take heed to yourselves, lest at any time your hearts be overcharged with

surfeiting, and drunkenness, and cares of this life, and *so* that day come upon you unawares.

35. For as a snare shall it come on all them that dwell on the face of the whole earth.

36. Watch ye therefore, and pray always, that ye may be accounted worthy to escape all these things that shall come to pass, and to stand before the Son of man.

John: No record.

(p) Parable of the Ten Virgins

Matt. 25:1-13; Mark: No record; Luke: No record; John: No record.

MATTHEW 25:1. Then shall the kingdom of heaven be likened unto ten virgins, which took their lamps, and went forth to meet the bridegroom.

2. And five of them were wise, and five *were* foolish.

3. They that *were* foolish took their lamps, and took no oil with them:

4. But the wise took oil in their vessels with their lamps.

5. While the bridegroom tarried, they all slumbered and slept.

6. And at midnight there was a cry made, Behold, the bridegroom cometh; go ye out to meet him.

7. Then all those virgins arose, and trimmed their lamps.

8. And the foolish said unto the wise, Give us of your oil; for our lamps are gone out.

9. But the wise answered, saying, *Not so;* lest there be not enough for us and you: but go ye rather to them that sell, and buy for yourselves.

10. And while they went to buy, the bridegroom came; and they that were ready went in with him to the marriage: and the door was shut.

11. Afterward came also the other virgins, saying, Lord, Lord, open to us.

12. But he answered and said, Verily I say unto you, I know you not.

13. Watch therefore, for ye know neither the day nor the hour wherein the Son of man cometh.

Mark: No record.

Luke: No record.

John: No record.

(q) Parable of the Talents

Matt. 25:14-30; Mark: No record; Luke: No record; John: No record.

MATTHEW 25:14. ¶For *the kingdom of heaven is* as a man travelling into a far country, *who* called his own servants, and delivered unto them his goods.

15. And unto one he gave five talents, to another two, and to another one; to every man according to his several ability; and straightway took his journey.

16. Then he that had received the five talents went and traded with the same, and made *them* other five talents.

17. And likewise he that *had received* two, he also gained other two.

18. But he that had received one went and digged in the earth, and hid his lord's money.

19. After a long time the lord of those servants cometh, and reckoneth with them.

20. And so he that had received five talents came and brought other five talents, saying, Lord, thou deliveredst unto me five talents: behold, I have gained beside them five talents more.

21. His lord said unto him, Well done, *thou* good and faithful servant: thou hast been faithful over a few things, I will make thee ruler over many things: enter thou into the joy of thy lord.

22. He also that had received two talents came and said, Lord, thou deliveredst unto me two talents: behold, I have gained two other talents beside them.

23. His lord said unto him, Well done, good and faithful servant; thou hast been faithful over a few things, I will make thee ruler over many things: enter thou into the joy of thy lord.

24. Then he which had received the one talent came and said, Lord, I knew thee that thou art an hard man, reaping where thou hast not sown, and gathering where thou hast not strawed:

25. And I was afraid, and went and hid thy talent in the earth: lo, *there* thou hast *that is* thine.

26. His lord answered and said unto him, *Thou* wicked and slothful servant, thou knewest that I reap where I sowed not, and gather where I have not strawed:

27. Thou oughtest therefore to have put my money to the exchangers, and *then* at my coming I should have received mine own with usury.

28. Take therefore the talent from him, and give *it* unto him which hath ten talents.

29. For unto every one that hath shall be given, and he shall have abundance: but from him that hath not shall be taken away even that which he hath.

30. And cast ye the unprofitable servant into outer darkness: there shall be weeping and gnashing of teeth.

Mark: No record.

Luke: No record.

John: No record.

(r) The Final Judgment

Jesus discourses upon and pictures the final judgment; the King shall set the sheep on his right hand and the goats on his left hand; he pronounces blessings upon those on his right hand, telling why he does so; he tells those on his left hand to depart, and tells them why.

Matt. 25:31-46; Mark: No record; Luke: No record; John: No record.

MATTHEW 25:31. ¶ When the Son of man shall come in his glory, and all the holy angels with him, then shall he sit upon the throne of his glory:

32. And before him shall be gathered all nations: and he shall separate them one from another, as a shepherd divideth *his* sheep from the goats:

33. And he shall set the sheep on his right hand, but the goats on the left.

34. Then shall the King say unto them on his right hand, Come, ye blessed of my Father, inherit the kingdom prepared for you from the foundation of the world:

35. For I was an hungred, and ye gave me meat: I was thirsty, and ye gave me drink: I was a stranger, and ye took me in:

36. Naked, and ye clothed me: I was sick, and ye visited me: I was in prison, and ye came unto me.

37. Then shall the righteous answer him, saying, Lord, when saw we thee an hungred, and fed *thee?* or thirsty, and gave *thee* drink?

38. When saw we thee a stranger, and took *thee* in? or naked, and clothed *thee?*

39. Or when saw we thee sick, or in prison, and came unto thee?

40. And the King shall answer and say unto them, Verily I say unto you, Inasmuch as ye have done *it* unto one of the least of these my brethren, ye have done *it* unto me.

41. Then shall he say also unto them on the left hand, Depart from me, ye cursed, into everlasting fire, prepared for the devil and his angels:

42. For I was an hungred, and ye gave me no meat: I was thirsty, and ye gave me no drink:

43. I was a stranger, and ye took me not in: naked, and ye clothed me not: sick, and in prison, and ye visited me not.

44. Then shall they also answer him, saying, Lord, when saw we thee an hungred, or athirst, or a stranger, or naked, or sick, or in prison, and did not minister unto thee?

45. Then shall he answer them, saying, Verily I say unto you, Inasmuch as ye did *it* not to one of the least of these, ye did *it* not to me.

46. And these shall go away

into everlasting punishment: but the righteous into life eternal.

Mark: No record.
Luke: No record.
John: No record.

(s) The Betrayal Foretold

Jesus having finished his sayings, tells his disciples that after two days is the feast of the Passover "and the Son of man is betrayed to be crucified."

Matt. 26:1-2; Mark: No record; Luke: No record; John: No record.

MATTHEW 26:1. And it came to pass, when Jesus had finished all these sayings, he said unto his disciples,

2. Ye know that after two days is *the feast of* the passover, and the Son of man is betrayed to be crucified.

Mark: No record.

Luke: No record.

John: No record.

(t) The Plot to Take Him

Two days before the Passover, the chief priests and the scribes and the elders of the people assemble at the palace of the high priest Caiaphas to plot how they may take Jesus by subtilty and kill him, but not on the feast day lest there be an uproar among the people.

Matt. 26:3-5; Mark 14:1-2; Luke 22:1-2; John: No record.

MATTHEW 26:3. Then assembled together the chief priests, and the scribes, and the elders of the people, unto the palace of the high priest, who was called Caiaphas,

4. And consulted that they might take Jesus by subtilty, and kill *him*.

5. But they said, Not on the feast *day*, lest there be an uproar among the people.

MARK 14:1. After two days was *the feast of* the passover, and of unleavened bread: and the chief priests and the scribes sought how they might take him by craft, and put *him* to death.

2. But they said, Not on the feast *day*, lest there be an uproar of the people.

LUKE 22:1. Now the feast of unleavened bread drew nigh, which is called the Passover.

2. And the chief priests and scribes sought how they might kill him; for they feared the people.

John: No record.

(u) At Simon's Supper Mary Anoints Him

They make a supper at the house of Simon the leper, Martha serves, and Lazarus sits at the table with Jesus; Mary takes a pound of very costly ointment of spikenard, anoints the feet of Jesus and wipes them

with her hair; the odor of the ointment fills the whole house; Judas Iscariot asks why this ointment was not sold and the price given to the poor; Jesus rebukes him and the other disciples who found fault, and says, "For in that she hath poured this ointment on my body, she did it for my burial"; he says the woman's act should be known wherever the Gospel is preached.

Matt. 26:6-13; Mark 14:3-9; Luke: No record; John 12:2-8.

MATTHEW 26:6. ¶ Now when Jesus was in Bethany, in the house of Simon the leper,

7. There came unto him a woman having an alabaster box of very precious ointment, and poured it on his head, as he sat *at meat.*

8. But when his disciples saw *it,* they had indignation, saying, To what purpose *is* this waste?

9. For this ointment might have been sold for much, and given to the poor.

10. When Jesus understood *it,* he said unto them, Why trouble ye the woman? for she hath wrought a good work upon me.

11. For ye have the poor always with you; but me ye have not always.

12. For in that she hath poured this ointment on my body, she did *it* for my burial.

13. Verily I say unto you, Wheresoever this gospel shall be preached in the whole world, *there* shall also this, that this woman hath done, be told for a memorial of her.

MARK 14:3. ¶ And being in Bethany in the house of Simon the leper, as he sat at meat, there came a woman having an alabaster box of ointment of spikenard very precious; and she brake the box, and poured *it* on his head.

4. And there were some that had indignation within themselves, and said, Why was this waste of the ointment made?

5. For it might have been sold for more than three hundred pence, and have been given to the poor. And they murmured against her.

6. And Jesus said, Let her alone; why trouble ye her? she hath wrought a good work on me.

7. For ye have the poor with you always, and whensoever ye will ye may do them good: but me ye have not always.

8. She hath done what she could: she is come aforehand to anoint my body to the burying.

9. Verily I say unto you, Wheresoever this gospel shall be preached throughout the whole world, *this* also that she hath done shall be spoken of for a memorial of her.

Luke: No record.

JOHN 12:2. There they made him a supper; and Martha served: but Lazarus was one of them that sat at the table with him.

3. Then took Mary a pound of ointment of spikenard, very costly, and anointed the feet of Jesus, and wiped his feet with her hair: and the house was filled with the odour of the ointment.

4. Then saith one of his disciples, Judas Iscariot, Simon's *son*, which should betray him,

5. Why was not this ointment sold for three hundred pence, and given to the poor?

6. This he said, not that he cared for the poor; but because he was a thief, and had the bag, and bare what was put therein.

7. Then said Jesus, Let her alone: against the day of my burying hath she kept this.

8. For the poor always ye have with you; but me ye have not always.

(v) Judas Arranges Betrayal

Then Satan enters into Judas Iscariot and he goes unto the chief priests and captains; he asks them what they will give him to deliver Jesus; they fix the price at thirty pieces of silver; Judas seeks thereafter how he may conveniently betray Jesus in the absence of the multitude.

Matt. 26:14-16; Mark 14:10-11; Luke 22:3-6; John: No record.

MATTHEW 26:14. ¶ Then one of the twelve, called Judas Iscariot, went unto the chief priests,

15. And said *unto them*, What will ye give me, and I will deliver him unto you? And they covenanted with him for thirty pieces of silver.

16. And from that time he sought opportunity to betray him.

MARK 14:10. ¶ And Judas Iscariot, one of the twelve, went unto the chief priests, to betray him unto them.

11. And when they heard *it*, they were glad, and promised to give him money. And he sought how he might conveniently betray him.

LUKE 22:3. ¶ Then entered Satan into Judas surnamed Iscariot, being of the number of the twelve.

4. And he went his way, and communed with the chief priests and captains, how he might betray him unto them.

5. And they were glad, and covenanted to give him money.

6. And he promised, and sought opportunity to betray him unto them in the absence of the multitude.

John: No record.

Fourth Day of the Week

Apparently this day is spent with his disciples and it is believed at Bethany.

Time: **A.D. 30, Wednesday, April 5, 13th Nisan (ANDREWS).**
Place: **Bethany.**

Fifth Day of the Week

Section 164

THE LAST SUPPER, THE MOUNT OF OLIVES, GETHSEMANE, THE BETRAYAL, THE ARREST

Time: A.D. 30, Thursday, April 6, 14th Nisan (ANDREWS).
Place: Bethany, Jerusalem.

(a) Disciples Arrange for Passover Meal

The disciples on the first day of unleavened bread, ask Jesus where they shall prepare to eat the Passover; Jesus tells them to go into the city where they will meet a man carrying a pitcher of water; they shall follow this man and enter the house where he goes and shall tell the good man of the house that the Master wishes to know where is the guest chamber where he shall eat the Passover; the husbandman will show them a large upper room furnished; here they shall prepare; they find all as Jesus had said and make ready the Passover.

Matt. 26:17-19; Mark 14:12-16; Luke 22:7-13; John: No record.

MATTHEW 26:17. ¶Now the first *day* of the *feast of* unleavened bread the disciples came to Jesus, saying unto him, Where wilt thou that we prepare for thee to eat the passover?

18. And he said, Go into the city to such a man, and say unto him, The Master saith, My time is at hand; I will keep the passover at thy house with my disciples.

19. And the disciples did as Jesus had appointed them; and they made ready the passover.

MARK 14:12. ¶And the first day of unleavened bread, when they killed the passover, his disciples said unto him, Where wilt thou that we go and prepare that thou mayest eat the passover?

13. And he sendeth forth two of his disciples, and saith unto them, Go ye into the city, and there shall meet you a man bearing a pitcher of water: follow him.

14. And wheresoever he shall go in, say ye to the goodman of the house, The Master saith, Where is the guestchamber, where I shall eat the passover with my disciples?

15. And he will shew you a large upper room furnished *and* prepared: there make ready for us.

16. And his disciples went forth, and came into the city, and found as he had said unto them: and they made ready the passover.

LUKE 22:7. ¶ Then came the day of unleavened bread, when the passover must be killed.

8. And he sent Peter and John, saying, Go and prepare

us the passover, that we may eat.

9. And they said unto him, Where wilt thou that we prepare?

10. And he said unto them, Behold, when ye are entered into the city, there shall a man meet you, bearing a pitcher of water; follow him into the house where he entereth in.

11. And ye shall say unto the goodman of the house, The Master saith unto thee, Where is the guestchamber, where I shall eat the passover with my disciples?

12. And he shall shew you a large upper room furnished: there make ready.

13. And they went, and found as he had said unto them: and they made ready the passover.

John: No record.

(b) They Sit Down in Passover Chamber

When evening comes, Jesus and the Twelve come and sit down.

Matt. 26:20; Mark 14:17; Luke 22:14; John: No record.

MATTHEW 26:20. Now when the even was come, he sat down with the twelve.

MARK 14:17. And in the evening he cometh with the twelve.

LUKE 22:14. And when the hour was come, he sat down, and the twelve apostles with him.

John: No record.

(c) The Strife About Precedence

There is strife among the Twelve as to who shall be greatest; he contrasts the measure of greatness and how it is shown among the kings of the Gentiles, with how it must be shown among them, — "he that is greatest among you, let him be as the younger; and he that is chief, as he that doth serve." "I am among you as he that serveth"; he tells them he has appointed unto them a kingdom, they may eat and drink at his table in his kingdom, "and sit on thrones judging the twelve tribes of Israel."

Matt.: No record; Mark: No record; Luke 22:24-30; John: No record.

Matthew: No record.

Mark: No record.

LUKE 22:24. ¶ And there was also a strife among them, which of them should be accounted the greatest.

25. And he said unto them, The kings of the Gentiles exercise lordship over them; and they that exercise authority upon them are called benefactors.

26. But ye *shall* not *be* so: but he that is greatest among you, let him be as the younger; and he that is chief, as he that doth serve.

27. For whether *is* greater, he that sitteth at meat, or he that serveth? *is* not he that sitteth at meat? but I am among you as he that serveth.

28. Ye are they which have continued with me in my temptations.

29. And I appoint unto you a kingdom, as my Father hath appointed unto me;

30. That ye may eat and drink at my table in my kingdom, and sit on thrones judging the twelve tribes of Israel.

John: No record.

(d) He Washes His Disciples' Feet

Before the feast of the Passover, Jesus (knowing the part Judas Iscariot was to play) rises from the table and laying aside his garments, takes a towel, girds himself and pouring water into a basin begins to wash the disciples' feet; when Peter is come to, he objects strongly to the Lord's washing his feet, but the Lord explains and Peter allows it; having washed their feet, Jesus puts on his garments, sits down again at the table, and gives them a discourse on the meaning of this ceremony; he speaks of his betrayal, and tells the effect of receiving him.

Matt.: No record; Mark: No record; Luke: No record; John 13:1-20.

Matthew: No record.

Mark: No record.

Luke: No record.

JOHN 13:1. Now before the feast of the passover, when Jesus knew that his hour was come that he should depart out of this world unto the Father, having loved his own which were in the world, he loved them unto the end.

2. And supper being ended, the devil having now put into the heart of Judas Iscariot, Simon's *son*, to betray him;

3. Jesus knowing that the Father had given all things into his hands, and that he was come from God, and went to God;

4. He riseth from supper, and laid aside his garments; and took a towel, and girded himself.

5. After that he poureth water into a bason, and began to wash the disciples' feet, and to wipe *them* with the towel wherewith he was girded.

6. Then cometh he to Simon Peter: and Peter saith unto him, Lord, dost thou wash my feet?

7. Jesus answered and said unto him, What I do thou knowest not now; but thou shalt know hereafter.

8. Peter saith unto him, Thou shalt never wash my feet. Jesus answered him, If I wash thee not, thou hast no part with me.

9. Simon Peter saith unto him, Lord, not my feet only, but also *my* hands and *my* head.

10. Jesus saith to him, He that is washed needeth not save to wash *his* feet, but is clean

every whit: and ye are clean, but not all.

11. For he knew who should betray him; therefore said he, Ye are not all clean.

12. So after he had washed their feet, and had taken his garments, and was set down again, he said unto them, Know ye what I have done to you?

13. Ye call me Master and Lord: and ye say well; for *so* I am.

14. If I then, *your* Lord and Master, have washed your feet; ye also ought to wash one another's feet.

15. For I have given you an example, that ye should do as I have done to you.

16. Verily, verily, I say unto you, The servant is not greater than his lord; neither he that is sent greater than he that sent him.

17. If ye know these things, happy are ye if ye do them.

18. ¶ I speak not of you all: I know whom I have chosen: but that the scripture may be fulfilled, He that eateth bread with me hath lifted up his heel against me.

19. Now I tell you before it come, that, when it is come to pass, ye may believe that I am *he*.

20. Verily, verily, I say unto you, He that receiveth whomsoever I send receiveth me; and he that receiveth me receiveth him that sent me.

(e) The Passover Meal

Jesus tells them how much he has desired to eat this Passover with them before he suffers, and that he will not eat it again "until it be fulfilled in the kingdom of God"; he takes the cup and gives thanks, telling them to divide it among themselves, "For I say unto you, I will not drink of the fruit of the vine, until the kingdom of God shall come."

Matt.: No record; Mark: No record; Luke 22:15-18; John: No record.

Matthew: No record.

Mark: No record.

LUKE 22:15. And he said unto them, With desire I have desired to eat this passover with you before I suffer:

16. For I say unto you, I will not any more eat thereof, until it be fulfilled in the kingdom of God.

17. And he took the cup, and gave thanks, and said, Take this, and divide *it* among yourselves:

18. For I say unto you, I will not drink of the fruit of the vine, until the kingdom of God shall come.

John: No record.

(f) He Indicates His Betrayer

As they eat Jesus says one of them shall betray him; sorrowful, they say among themselves and to him, "Is it I?"; Peter beckons to John, who is leaning on Jesus' bosom, to ask Jesus who it is; Jesus answers: "He it is, to whom I shall give a sop, when I have dipped it"; Jesus dips the sop, and gives it to Judas Iscariot, to whom Jesus said, when Judas asked if he was the betrayer: "Thou hast said"; Jesus speaks of the fate of his betrayer.

Matt. 26:21-25; Mark 14:18-21; Luke 22:21-23; John 13:21-26.

MATTHEW 26:21. And as they did eat, he said, Verily I say unto you, that one of you shall betray me.

22. And they were exceeding sorrowful, and began every one of them to say unto him, Lord, is it I?

23. And he answered and said, He that dippeth *his* hand with me in the dish, the same shall betray me.

24. The Son of man goeth as it is written of him: but woe unto that man by whom the Son of man is betrayed! it had been good for that man if he had not been born.

25. Then Judas, which betrayed him, answered and said, Master, is it I? He said unto him, Thou hast said.

MARK 14:18. And as they sat and did eat, Jesus said, Verily I say unto you, One of you which eateth with me shall betray me.

19. And they began to be sorrowful, and to say unto him one by one, *Is* it I? and another *said, Is* it I?

20. And he answered and said unto them, *It is* one of the twelve, that dippeth with me in the dish.

21. The Son of man indeed goeth, as it is written of him: but woe to that man by whom the Son of man is betrayed! good were it for that man if he had never been born.

LUKE 22:21. ¶ But, behold, the hand of him that betrayeth me *is* with me on the table.

22. And truly the Son of man goeth, as it was determined: but woe unto that man by whom he is betrayed!

23. And they began to enquire among themselves, which of them it was that should do this thing.

JOHN 13:21. When Jesus had thus said, he was troubled in spirit, and testified, and said, Verily, verily, I say unto you, that one of you shall betray me.

22. Then the disciples looked one on another, doubting of whom he spake.

23. Now there was leaning on Jesus' bosom one of his disciples, whom Jesus loved.

24. Simon Peter therefore beckoned to him, that he should ask who it should be of whom he spake.

25. He then lying on Jesus'

breast saith unto him, Lord, who is it?

26. Jesus answered, He it is, to whom I shall give a sop, when I have dipped *it*. And when he had dipped the sop, he gave *it* to Judas Iscariot, *the son* of Simon.

(g) Judas Leaves the Chamber

After the sop Satan enters Judas and Jesus says unto him, "That thou doest, do quickly"; none of the disciples know the intent of these words, thinking it either, as he has the purse, that he goes to buy something, or to give something to the poor; Judas leaves immediately and it is night.

Matt.: No record; Mark: No record; Luke: No record; John 13:27-30.

Matthew: No record.

Mark: No record.

Luke: No record.

JOHN 13:27. And after the sop Satan entered into him. Then said Jesus unto him, That thou doest, do quickly.

28. Now no man at the table knew for what intent he spake this unto him.

29. For some *of them* thought, because Judas had the bag, that Jesus had said unto him, Buy *those things* that we have need of against the feast; or, that he should give something to the poor.

30. He then having received the sop went immediately out: and it was night.

(h) Jesus Foretells His Death

Jesus, after Judas goes out, says, "Now is the Son of man glorified, and God is glorified in him"; he tells the disciples he will be with them but a short time, that where he goes they cannot come, and commands them to love one another as he has loved them, and by that all men shall know they are his disciples.

Matt.: No record; Mark: No record; Luke: No record; John 13:31-35.

Matthew: No record.

Mark: No record.

Luke: No record.

JOHN 13:31. ¶ Therefore, when he was gone out, Jesus said, Now is the Son of man glorified, and God is glorified in him.

32. If God be glorified in him, God shall also glorify him in himself, and shall straightway glorify him.

33. Little children, yet a little while I am with you. Ye shall seek me: and as I said unto the Jews, Whither I go, ye cannot come; so now I say to you.

34. A new commandment I give unto you, That ye love one another; as I have loved you, that ye also love one another.

35. By this shall all *men* know that ye are my disciples, if ye have love one to another.

(i) The Sacrament

Jesus institutes the Lord's Supper — the sacrament; he again says, "I will drink no more of the fruit of the vine, until that day that I drink it new in the kingdom of God."

Matt. 26:26-29; Mark 14:22-25; Luke 22:19-20; John: No record.

MATTHEW 26:26. ¶ And as they were eating, Jesus took bread, and blessed *it*, and brake *it*, and gave *it* to the disciples, and said, Take, eat; this is my body.

27. And he took the cup, and gave thanks, and gave *it* to them, saying, Drink ye all of it;

28. For this is my blood of the new testament, which is shed for many for the remission of sins.

29. But I say unto you, I will not drink henceforth of this fruit of the vine, until that day when I drink it new with you in my Father's kingdom.

MARK 14:22. ¶ And as they did eat, Jesus took bread, and blessed, and brake *it*, and gave to them, and said, Take, eat: this is my body.

23. And he took the cup, and when he had given thanks, he gave *it* to them: and they all drank of it.

24. And he said unto them, This is my blood of the new testament, which is shed for many.

25. Verily I say unto you, I will drink no more of the fruit of the vine, until that day that I drink it new in the kingdom of God.

LUKE 22:19. ¶ And he took bread, and gave thanks, and brake *it*, and gave unto them, saying, This is my body which is given for you: this do in remembrance of me.

20. Likewise also the cup after supper, saying, This cup *is* the new testament in my blood, which is shed for you.

John: No record.

(j) Peter Declares His Loyalty

Peter asks Jesus where he is going; Jesus tells Peter that Satan hath desired to have him that he may sift him as wheat; Peter says he is ready to go with Jesus both to prison and to death; Jesus answers that where he goes Peter cannot follow; Peter asks why he cannot follow, adding, "I will lay down my life for thy sake"; Jesus answers that before the cock crows Peter shall deny him thrice; Jesus speaks of when he sent them out before, and of their going out again, referring to their work after his death; he directs them "now" to travel with purse and scrip and a sword.

Matt.: No record; Mark: No record; Luke 22:31-38; John 13:36-38.

Matthew: No record.
Mark: No record.

LUKE 22: 31. ¶ And the Lord said, Simon, Simon, behold, Satan hath desired *to have* you, that he may sift *you* as wheat:

32. But I have prayed for thee, that thy faith fail not: and when thou art converted, strengthen thy brethren.

33. And he said unto him, Lord, I am ready to go with thee, both into prison, and to death.

34. And he said, I tell thee, Peter, the cock shall not crow this day, before that thou shalt thrice deny that thou knowest me.

35. And he said unto them, When I sent you without purse, and scrip, and shoes, lacked ye any thing? And they said, Nothing.

36. Then said he unto them, But now, he that hath a purse, let him take *it*, and likewise *his* scrip: and he that hath no sword, let him sell his garment, and buy one.

37. For I say unto you, that this that is written must yet be accomplished in me, And he was reckoned among the transgressors: for the things concerning me have an end.

38. And they said, Lord, behold, here *are* two swords. And he said unto them, It is enough.

JOHN 13:36. ¶ Simon Peter said unto him, Lord, whither goest thou? Jesus answered him, Whither I go, thou canst not follow me now; but thou shalt follow me afterwards.

37. Peter said unto him, Lord, why cannot I follow thee now? I will lay down my life for thy sake.

38. Jesus answered him, Wilt thou lay down thy life for my sake? Verily, verily, I say unto thee, The cock shall not crow, till thou hast denied me thrice.

(k) The Discourse About the Comforter

Jesus speaks of his going from them and preparing a place for them; Thomas and Philip ask questions; Jesus discourses on the relationship between him and the Father; tells them to keep his commandments; says he will send them the Comforter, which the world cannot receive, and he himself will come; the Father will love them who love him; Judas (not Iscariot) asks him a question, and Jesus says any man who loves him will keep his commandments; again he speaks of the Comforter which the Father shall send; he leaves peace with them; he says they shall rejoice that he goes to the Father; and ends by saying he has told them all so that they may know when it comes to pass.

Matt.: No record; Mark: No record; Luke: No record; John 14:1-31.

Matthew: No record.

Mark: No record.

Luke: No record.

JOHN 14:1. Let not your heart be troubled: ye believe in God, believe also in me.

2. In my Father's house are many mansions: if *it were* not *so*, I would have told you. I go to prepare a place for you.

3. And if I go and prepare a place for you, I will come

again, and receive you unto myself; that where I am, *there* ye may be also.

4. And whither I go ye know, and the way ye know.

5. Thomas saith unto him, Lord, we know not whither thou goest; and how can we know the way?

6. Jesus saith unto him, I am the way, the truth, and the life: no man cometh unto the Father, but by me.

7. If ye had known me, ye should have known my Father also: and from henceforth ye know him, and have seen him.

8. Philip saith unto him, Lord, shew us the Father, and it sufficeth us.

9. Jesus saith unto him, Have I been so long time with you, and yet hast thou not known me, Philip? he that hath seen me hath seen the Father; and how sayest thou *then*, Shew us the Father?

10. Believest thou not that I am in the Father, and the Father in me? the words that I speak unto you I speak not of myself: but the Father that dwelleth in me, he doeth the works.

11. Believe me that I *am* in the Father, and the Father in me: or else believe me for the very works' sake.

12. Verily, verily, I say unto you, He that believeth on me, the works that I do shall he do also; and greater *works* than these shall he do; because I go unto my Father.

13. And whatsoever ye shall ask in my name, that will I do, that the Father may be glorified in the Son.

14. If ye shall ask any thing in my name, I will do *it*.

15. ¶ If ye love me, keep my commandments.

16. And I will pray the Father, and he shall give you another Comforter, that he may abide with you for ever;

17. *Even* the Spirit of truth; whom the world cannot receive, because it seeth him not, neither knoweth him: but ye know him; for he dwelleth with you, and shall be in you.

18. I will not leave you comfortless: I will come to you.

19. Yet a little while, and the world seeth me no more; but ye see me: because I live, ye shall live also.

20. At that day ye shall know that I *am* in my Father, and ye in me, and I in you.

21. He that hath my commandments, and keepeth them, he it is that loveth me: and he that loveth me shall be loved of my Father, and I will love him, and will manifest myself to him.

22. Judas saith unto him, not Iscariot, Lord, how is it that thou wilt manifest thyself unto us, and not unto the world?

23. Jesus answered and said unto him, If a man love me, he will keep my words: and my Father will love him, and we will come unto him, and make our abode with him.

24. He that loveth me not

keepeth not my sayings: and the word which ye hear is not mine, but the Father's which sent me.

25. These things have I spoken unto you, being *yet* present with you.

26. But the Comforter, *which is* the Holy Ghost, whom the Father will send in my name, he shall teach you all things, and bring all things to your remembrance, whatsoever I have said unto you.

27. Peace I leave with you, my peace I give unto you: not as the world giveth, give I unto you. Let not your heart be troubled, neither let it be afraid.

28. Ye have heard how I said unto you, I go away, and come *again* unto you. If ye loved me, ye would rejoice, because I said, I go unto the Father: for my Father is greater than I.

29. And now I have told you before it come to pass, that, when it is come to pass, ye might believe.

30. Hereafter I will not talk much with you: for the prince of this world cometh, and hath nothing in me.

31. But that the world may know that I love the Father; and as the Father gave me commandment, even so I do. Arise, let us go hence.

(l) They Sing a Hymn and Go Out to the Mount of Olives

Matt. 26:30; Mark 14:26; Luke 22:39; John: No record.

MATTHEW 26:30. And when they had sung an hymn, they went out into the mount of Olives.

MARK 14:26. ¶ And when they had sung an hymn, they went out into the mount of Olives.

LUKE 22:39 ¶ And he came out, and went, as he was wont, to the mount of Olives; and his disciples also followed him.

John: No record.

(m) He Explains His Relationship to Them and Theirs to Him and the Father

Jesus further explains his relationship to the Father, their relationship to him, and the relationship between the Father, himself, and them; again commands them to love one another; he calls them his friends, not his servants; he has chosen them, not they him; tells them they are not of the world, which will persecute them; his coming and speaking to the world robs them of their cloak for sin; they have now "both seen and hated both me and my Father"; when the Comforter comes he will testify of Jesus; "and ye also shall bear witness, because ye have been with me from the beginning."

Matt.: No record; Mark: No record; Luke: No record; John 15:1-27.

Matthew: No record.

Mark: No record.

Luke: No record.

JOHN 15:1. I am the true vine, and my Father is the husbandman.

2. Every branch in me that beareth not fruit he taketh away: and every *branch* that beareth fruit, he purgeth it, that it may bring forth more fruit.

3. Now ye are clean through the word which I have spoken unto you.

4. Abide in me, and I in you. As the branch cannot bear fruit of itself, except it abide in the vine; no more can ye, except ye abide in me.

5. I am the vine, ye *are* the branches: He that abideth in me, and I in him, the same bringeth forth much fruit: for without me ye can do nothing.

6. If a man abide not in me, he is cast forth as a branch, and is withered; and men gather them, and cast *them* into the fire, and they are burned.

7. If ye abide in me, and my words abide in you, ye shall ask what ye will, and it shall be done unto you.

8. Herein is my Father glorified, that ye bear much fruit; so shall ye be my disciples.

9. As the Father hath loved me, so have I loved you: continue ye in my love.

10. If ye keep my commandments, ye shall abide in my love; even as I have kept my Father's commandments, and abide in his love.

11. These things have I spoken unto you, that my joy might remain in you, and *that* your joy might be full.

12. This is my commandment, That ye love one another, as I have loved you.

13. Greater love hath no man than this, that a man lay down his life for his friends.

14. Ye are my friends, if ye do whatsoever I command you.

15. Henceforth I call you not servants; for the servant knoweth not what his lord doeth: but I have called you friends; for all things that I have heard of my Father I have made known unto you.

16. Ye have not chosen me, but I have chosen you, and ordained you, that ye should go and bring forth fruit, and *that* your fruit should remain: that whatsoever ye shall ask of the Father in my name, he may give it you.

17. These things I command you, that ye love one another.

18. If the world hate you, ye know that it hated me before *it hated* you.

19. If ye were of the world, the world would love his own: but because ye are not of the world, but I have chosen you out of the world, therefore the world hateth you.

20. Remember the word that I said unto you, The servant is not greater than his lord. If they have persecuted me, they will also persecute you; if they

have kept my saying, they will keep your's also.

21. But all these things will they do unto you for my name's sake, because they know not him that sent me.

22. If I had not come and spoken unto them, they had not had sin: but now they have no cloke for their sin.

23. He that hateth me hateth my Father also.

24. If I had not done among them the works which none other man did, they had not had sin: but now have they both seen and hated both me and my Father.

25. But *this cometh to pass*, that the word might be fulfilled that is written in their law, They hated me without a cause.

26. But when the Comforter is come, whom I will send unto you from the Father, *even* the Spirit of truth, which proceedeth from the Father, he shall testify of me:

27. And ye also shall bear witness, because ye have been with me from the beginning.

(n) He Again Explains His Death

Jesus tells them more of what shall befall them, that they may remember when the things happen; he says he goes his way to him that sent him; it is expedient that he should go, for if he does not go, the Comforter will not come unto them; tells what the Comforter will do when he comes; Comforter will guide them into all truth; again foretells his death; the disciples say among themselves that they cannot understand, and Jesus discerning this, again explains, foretelling their grief which shall be turned into joy; they shall receive what they ask in the Father's name; further explanation of relationship between him and the Father, his disciples say he now speaks plainly and they understand and believe; he predicts their scattering; have peace; "I have overcome the world."

Matt.: No record; Mark: No record; Luke: No record; John 16:1-33.

Matthew: No record.

Mark: No record.

Luke: No record.

JOHN 16:1. These things have I spoken unto you, that ye should not be offended.

2. They shall put you out of the synagogues: yea, the time cometh, that whosoever killeth you will think that he doeth God service.

3. And these things will they do unto you, because they have not known the Father, nor me.

4. But these things have I told you, that when the time shall come, ye may remember that I told you of them. And these things I said not unto you at the beginning, because I was with you.

5. But now I go my way to him that sent me; and none of you asketh me, Whither goest thou?

6. But because I have said

these things unto you, sorrow hath filled your heart.

7. Nevertheless I tell you the truth; It is expedient for you that I go away: for if I go not away, the Comforter will not come unto you; but if I depart, I will send him unto you.

8. And when he is come, he will reprove the world of sin, and of righteousness, and of judgment:

9. Of sin, because they believe not on me;

10. Of righteousness, because I go to my Father, and ye see me no more;

11. Of judgment, because the prince of this world is judged.

12. I have yet many things to say unto you, but ye cannot bear them now.

13. Howbeit when he, the Spirit of truth, is come, he will guide you into all truth: for he shall not speak of himself; but whatsoever he shall hear, *that* shall he speak: and he will shew you things to come.

14. He shall glorify me: for he shall receive of mine, and shall shew *it* unto you.

15. All things that the Father hath are mine: therefore said I, that he shall take of mine, and shall shew *it* unto you.

16. A little while, and ye shall not see me: and again, a little while, and ye shall see me, because I go to the Father.

17. Then said *some* of his disciples among themselves, What is this that he saith unto us, A little while, and ye shall not see me: and again, a little while, and ye shall see me: and, Because I go to the Father?

18. They said therefore, What is this that he saith, A little while? we cannot tell what he saith.

19. Now Jesus knew that they were desirous to ask him, and said unto them, Do ye enquire among yourselves of that I said, A little while, and ye shall not see me: and again, a little while, and ye shall see me?

20. Verily, verily, I say unto you, That ye shall weep and lament, but the world shall rejoice: and ye shall be sorrowful, but your sorrow shall be turned into joy.

21. A woman when she is in travail hath sorrow, because her hour is come: but as soon as she is delivered of the child, she remembereth no more the anguish, for joy that a man is born into the world.

22. And ye now therefore have sorrow: but I will see you again, and your heart shall rejoice, and your joy no man taketh from you.

23. And in that day ye shall ask me nothing. Verily, verily, I say unto you, Whatsoever ye shall ask the Father in my name, he will give *it* you.

24. Hitherto have ye asked nothing in my name: ask, and ye shall receive, that your joy may be full.

25. These things have I spoken unto you in proverbs: but

the time cometh, when I shall no more speak unto you in proverbs, but I shall shew you plainly of the Father.

26. At that day ye shall ask in my name: and I say not unto you, that I will pray the Father for you:

27. For the Father himself loveth you, because ye have loved me, and have believed that I came out from God.

28. I came forth from the Father, and am come into the world: again, I leave the world, and go to the Father.

29. His disciples said unto him, Lo, now speakest thou plainly, and speakest no proverb.

30. Now are we sure that thou knowest all things, and needest not that any man should ask thee: by this we believe that thou camest forth from God.

31. Jesus answered them, Do ye now believe?

32. Behold, the hour cometh, yea, is now come, that ye shall be scattered, every man to his own, and shall leave me alone: and yet I am not alone, because the Father is with me.

33. These things I have spoken unto you, that in me ye might have peace. In the world ye shall have tribulation: but be of good cheer; I have overcome the world.

(a) The Great Prayer

The Prayer of the Great High Priest, or the Intercessory Prayer,—"the hour is come; glorify thy Son, that thy Son also may glorify thee"; "this is life eternal"; he prays for the disciples, whom he has kept all but one, "the son of perdition"; he has given them the word of the Father, and the world hates them; "I pray not that thou shouldest take them out of the world, but that thou shouldest keep them from the evil"; prays not only for the disciples, but for all who believe on him in the world; again speaks of relationship of himself, the Father, and the disciples; asks that those whom the Father has given him should be with him; asks that the Father's love for him shall be in them and he in them.

Matt.: No record; Mark: No record; Luke: No record; John 17:1-26.

Matthew: No record.

Mark: No record.

Luke: No record.

JOHN 17:1. These words spake Jesus, and lifted up his eyes to heaven, and said, Father, the hour is come; glorify thy Son, that thy Son also may glorify thee:

2. As thou hast given him power over all flesh, that he should give eternal life to as many as thou hast given him.

3. And this is life eternal, that they might know thee the only true God, and Jesus Christ, whom thou hast sent.

4. I have glorified thee on the earth: I have finished the work which thou gavest me to do.

5. And now, O Father, glorify thou me with thine own self with the glory which I had with thee before the world was.

6. I have manifested thy name unto the men which thou gavest me out of the world: thine they were, and thou gavest them me; and they have kept thy word.

7. Now they have known that all things whatsoever thou hast given me are of thee.

8. For I have given unto them the words which thou gavest me; and they have received *them*, and have known surely that I came out from thee, and they have believed that thou didst send me.

9. I pray for them: I pray not for the world, but for them which thou hast given me; for they are thine.

10. And all mine are thine, and thine are mine; and I am glorified in them.

11. And now I am no more in the world, but these are in the world, and I come to thee. Holy Father, keep through thine own name those whom thou hast given me, that they may be one, as we *are*.

12. While I was with them in the world, I kept them in thy name: those that thou gavest me I have kept, and none of them is lost, but the son of perdition; that the scripture might be fulfilled.

13. And now come I to thee; and these things I speak in the world, that they might have my joy fulfilled in themselves.

14. I have given them thy word; and the world hath hated them, because they are not of the world, even as I am not of the world.

15. I pray not that thou shouldest take them out of the world, but that thou shouldest keep them from the evil.

16. They are not of the world, even as I am not of the world.

17. Sanctify them through thy truth: thy word is truth.

18. As thou hast sent me into the world, even so have I also sent them into the world.

19. And for their sakes I sanctify myself, that they also might be sanctified through the truth.

20. Neither pray I for these alone, but for them also which shall believe on me through their word;

21. That they all may be one; as thou, Father, *art* in me, and I in thee, that they also may be one in us: that the world may believe that thou hast sent me.

22. And the glory which thou gavest me I have given them; that they may be one, even as we are one:

23. I in them, and thou in me, that they may be made perfect in one; and that the world may know that thou hast sent me, and hast loved them, as thou hast loved me.

24. Father, I will that they also, whom thou hast given me, be with me where I am; that

they may behold my glory, which thou hast given me: for thou lovedst me before the foundation of the world.

25. O righteous Father, the world hath not known thee: but I have known thee, and these have known that thou hast sent me.

26. And I have declared unto them thy name, and will declare *it*: that the love wherewith thou hast loved me may be in them, and I in them.

(p) Peter and Rest Declare Their Loyalty

Jesus tells them, "All ye shall be offended because of me this night"; says that after he is risen he will go before them to Galilee; Peter says though all others are offended he will never be offended; and Jesus again foretells Peter's denial; thereafter Peter speaks more vehemently, denying he will deny Jesus. "Likewise also said they all."

Matt. 26:31-35; Mark 14:27-31; Luke: No record; John: No record.

MATTHEW 26:31. Then saith Jesus unto them, All ye shall be offended because of me this night: for it is written, I will smite the shepherd, and the sheep of the flock shall be scattered abroad.

32. But after I am risen again, I will go before you into Galilee.

33. Peter answered and said unto him, Though all *men* shall be offended because of thee, *yet* will I never be offended.

34. Jesus said unto him, Verily I say unto thee, That this night, before the cock crow, thou shalt deny me thrice.

35. Peter said unto him, Though I should die with thee, yet will I not deny thee. Likewise also said all the disciples.

MARK 14:27. And Jesus saith unto them, All ye shall be offended because of me this night: for it is written, I will smite the shepherd, and the sheep shall be scattered.

28. But after that I am risen, I will go before you into Galilee.

29. But Peter said unto him, Although all shall be offended, yet *will* not I.

30. And Jesus saith unto him, Verily I say unto thee, That this day, *even* in this night, before the cock crow twice, thou shalt deny me thrice.

31. But he spake the more vehemently, If I should die with thee, I will not deny thee in any wise. Likewise also said they all.

Luke: No record.

John: No record.

(q) He Prays in the Garden

Jesus takes them all to the Garden of Gethsemane; leaving all but Peter, James, and John, whom he takes with him, he goes on into the Garden; saying his soul is sorrowful, he goes still farther on alone and prays; he returns and finds them sleeping; he awakens and mildly rebukes them; he goes the second and the third time, with the same result; whereupon Jesus says: "Rise, let us be going: behold, he is at hand that doth betray me."

Matt. 26:36-46; Mark 14:32-42; Luke 22:40-46; John 18:1-2.

MATTHEW 26:36. ¶ Then cometh Jesus with them unto a place called Gethsemane, and saith unto the disciples, Sit ye here, while I go and pray yonder.

37. And he took with him Peter and the two sons of Zebedee, and began to be sorrowful and very heavy.

38. Then saith he unto them, My soul is exceeding sorrowful, even unto death: tarry ye here, and watch with me.

39. And he went a little farther, and fell on his face, and prayed, saying, O my Father, if it be possible, let this cup pass from me: nevertheless not as I will, but as thou *wilt*.

40. And he cometh unto the disciples, and findeth them asleep, and saith unto Peter, What, could ye not watch with me one hour?

41. Watch and pray, that ye enter not into temptation: the spirit indeed *is* willing, but the flesh *is* weak.

42. He went away again the second time, and prayed, saying, O my Father, if this cup may not pass away from me, except I drink it, thy will be done.

43. And he came and found them asleep again: for their eyes were heavy.

44. And he left them, and went away again, and prayed the third time, saying the same words.

45. Then cometh he to his disciples, and saith unto them, Sleep on now, and take *your* rest: behold, the hour is at hand, and the Son of man is betrayed into the hands of sinners.

46. Rise, let us be going: behold, he is at hand that doth betray me.

MARK 14:32. And they came to a place which was named Gethsemane: and he saith to his disciples, Sit ye here, while I shall pray.

33. And he taketh with him Peter and James and John, and began to be sore amazed, and to be very heavy;

34. And saith unto them, My soul is exceeding sorrowful unto death: tarry ye here, and watch.

35. And he went forward a little, and fell on the ground, and prayed that, if it were possible, the hour might pass from him.

36. And he said, Abba, Father, all things *are* possible unto thee; take away this cup from me: nevertheless not what I will, but what thou wilt.

37. And he cometh, and findeth them sleeping, and saith unto Peter, Simon, sleepest thou? couldest not thou watch one hour?

38. Watch ye and pray, lest ye enter into temptation. The spirit truly *is* ready, but the flesh *is* weak.

39. And again he went away, and prayed, and spake the same words.

40. And when he returned, he found them asleep again, (for their eyes were heavy,) neither wist they what to answer him.

41. And he cometh the third time, and saith unto them, Sleep on now, and take *your* rest: it is enough, the hour is come; behold, the Son of man is betrayed into the hands of sinners.

42. Rise up, let us go; lo, he that betrayeth me is at hand.

LUKE 22:40. And when he was at the place, he said unto them, Pray that ye enter not into temptation.

41. And he was withdrawn from them about a stone's cast, and kneeled down, and prayed,

42. Saying, Father, if thou be willing, remove this cup from me: nevertheless not my will, but thine, be done.

43. And there appeared an angel unto him from heaven, strengthening him.

44. And being in an agony he prayed more earnestly: and his sweat was as it were great drops of blood falling down to the ground.

45. And when he rose up from prayer, and was come to his disciples, he found them sleeping for sorrow,

46. And said unto them, Why sleep ye? rise and pray, lest ye enter into temptation.

JOHN 18:1. When Jesus had spoken these words, he went forth with his disciples over the brook Cedron, where was a garden, into the which he entered, and his disciples.

2. And Judas also, which betrayed him, knew the place: for Jesus ofttimes resorted thither with his disciples.

(r) The Betrayal

While Jesus yet speaks, a multitude comes with Judas, of men and officers from the chief priests and Pharisees, armed with swords, staves, and weapons, and carrying lanterns and torches; by a sign arranged beforehand, Judas comes forth and kisses Jesus, saying, "Hail, master"; Jesus says to him, "Judas, betrayest thou the Son of man with a kiss?"; Jesus goes forth and says, "Whom seek ye?"; they answer, "Jesus of Nazareth," and Jesus replies, "I am he"; the multitude go backward and

fall to the ground; Jesus again asks the question, and they make the same reply; he says: "I am he: if therefore ye seek me, let these go their way."

Matt. 26:47-50a; Mark 14:43-45; Luke 22:47-48; John 18:3-9.

MATTHEW 26:47. ¶ And while he yet spake, lo, Judas, one of the twelve, came, and with him a great multitude with swords and staves, from the chief priests and elders of the people.

48. Now he that betrayed him gave them a sign, saying, Whomsoever I shall kiss, that same is he: hold him fast.

49. And forthwith he came to Jesus, and said, Hail, master; and kissed him.

50. And Jesus said unto him, Friend, wherefore art thou come? . . .

MARK 14:43. ¶ And immediately, while he yet spake, cometh Judas, one of the twelve, and with him a great multitude with swords and staves, from the chief priests and the scribes and the elders.

44. And he that betrayed him had given them a token, saying, Whomsoever I shall kiss, that same is he; take him, and lead *him* away safely.

45. And as soon as he was come, he goeth straightway to him, and saith, Master, master; and kissed him.

LUKE 22:47. ¶ And while he yet spake, behold a multitude, and he that was called Judas, one of the twelve, went before them, and drew near unto Jesus to kiss him.

48. But Jesus said unto him, Judas, betrayest thou the Son of man with a kiss?

JOHN 18:3. Judas then, having received a band *of men* and officers from the chief priests and Pharisees, cometh thither with lanterns and torches and weapons.

4. Jesus therefore, knowing all things that should come upon him, went forth, and said unto them, Whom seek ye?

5. They answered him, Jesus of Nazareth. Jesus saith unto them, I am *he*. And Judas also, which betrayed him, stood with them.

6. As soon then as he had said unto them, I am *he*, they went backward, and fell to the ground.

7. Then asked he them again, Whom seek ye? And they said, Jesus of Nazareth.

8. Jesus answered, I have told you that I am *he*: if therefore ye seek me, let these go their way:

9. That the saying might be fulfilled, which he spake, Of them which thou gavest me have I lost none.

(s) The Arrest

They then lay hands on Jesus; his disciples ask, "Lord, shall we smite with the sword?" Peter draws his sword and cuts off the right ear of Malchus, the high priest's servant; Jesus answers, "Suffer ye thus far," and touches Malchus' ear and heals it; he tells Peter to put up his sword, "for all they that take the sword shall perish with the sword"; he asks if they do not think that if he were to ask it, the Father would give him more than twelve legions of angels; he asks the multitude why they come with swords and staves to take him as if he were a thief, since he sat with them daily in the Temple teaching, and they laid no hold on him; a young man following along with a linen cloth cast about his body loses the cloth to some other young men, and he flees from them naked.

Matt. 26:50b-56; Mark 14:46-52; Luke 22:49-53; John 18:10-12.

MATTHEW 26:50. . . . Then came they, and laid hands on Jesus, and took him.

51. And, behold, one of them which were with Jesus stretched out *his* hand, and drew his sword, and struck a servant of the high priest's, and smote off his ear.

52. Then said Jesus unto him, Put up again thy sword into his place: for all they that take the sword shall perish with the sword.

53. Thinkest thou that I cannot now pray to my Father, and he shall presently give me more than twelve legions of angels?

54. But how then shall the scriptures be fulfilled, that thus it must be?

55. In that same hour said Jesus to the multitudes, Are ye come out as against a thief with swords and staves for to take me? I sat daily with you teaching in the temple, and ye laid no hold on me.

56. But all this was done, that the scriptures of the prophets might be fulfilled. Then all the disciples forsook him, and fled.

MARK 14:46. ¶ And they laid their hands on him, and took him.

47. And one of them that stood by drew a sword, and smote a servant of the high priest, and cut off his ear.

48. And Jesus answered and said unto them, Are ye come out, as against a thief, with swords and *with* staves to take me?

49. I was daily with you in the temple teaching, and ye took me not: but the scriptures must be fulfilled.

50. And they all forsook him, and fled.

51. And there followed him a certain young man, having a linen cloth cast about *his* naked *body;* and the young men laid hold on him:

52. And he left the linen cloth, and fled from them naked.

LUKE 22:49. When they which were about him saw

what would follow, they said unto him, Lord, shall we smite with the sword?

50. ¶ And one of them smote the servant of the high priest, and cut off his right ear.

51. And Jesus answered and said, Suffer ye thus far. And he touched his ear, and healed him.

52. Then Jesus said unto the chief priests, and captains of the temple, and the elders, which were come to him, Be ye come out, as against a thief, with swords and staves?

53. When I was daily with you in the temple, ye stretched forth no hands against me: but this is your hour, and the power of darkness.

JOHN 18:10. Then Simon Peter having a sword drew it, and smote the high priest's servant, and cut off his right ear. The servant's name was Malchus.

11. Then said Jesus unto Peter, Put up thy sword into the sheath: the cup which my Father hath given me, shall I not drink it?

12. Then the band and the captain and officers of the Jews took Jesus, and bound him, . . .

Sixth Day of the Week

Section 165

THE TRIAL AND CRUCIFIXION

Time: A. D. 30, Midnight, Thursday-Friday, April 7, 15th Nisan (ANDREWS).

Place: Jerusalem.

(a) Jesus Before Annas

Jesus is first taken to Annas, father-in-law to Caiaphas (the titular high priest); the high priest asks Jesus of his doctrine and his disciples; Jesus answers he has taught openly, and in secret said nothing; therefore Annas should ask those who had heard him; one of the officers strikes him for so answering the high priest; Jesus says if he has spoken evil the officer should bear witness thereof, but if well, why is he smitten?

Matt.: No record; Mark: No record; Luke: No record; John 18:13-14, 19-23.

Matthew: No record.

Mark: No record.

Luke: No record.

JOHN 18:13. And led him away to Annas first; for he was father in law to Caiaphas, which was the high priest that same year.

14. Now Caiaphas was he, which gave counsel to the Jews, that it was expedient that one man should die for the people. . . .

19. ¶ The high priest then asked Jesus of his disciples, and of his doctrine.

20. Jesus answered him, I spake openly to the world; I ever taught in the synagogue, and in the temple, whither the Jews always resort; and in secret have I said nothing.

21. Why askest thou me? ask them which heard me, what I have said unto them: behold, they know what I said.

22. And when he had thus spoken, one of the officers which stood by struck Jesus with the palm of his hand, saying, Answerest thou the high priests so?

23. Jesus answered him, If I have spoken evil, bear witness of the evil: but if well, why smitest thou me?

(b) He Is Sent to Caiaphas

Annas sends Jesus bound to Caiaphas, where the scribes and elders are assembled; Peter follows afar off.

Matt. 26:57-58; Mark 14:53-54; Luke 22:54; John 18:24.

MATTHEW 26 : 57. ¶ And they that had laid hold on Jesus led *him* away to Caiaphas the high priest, where the scribes and the elders were assembled.

58. But Peter followed him afar off unto the high priest's palace, and went in, and sat with the servants, to see the end.

MARK 14:53. ¶ And they led Jesus away to the high priest: and with him were assembled all the chief priests and the elders and the scribes.

54. And Peter followed him afar off, even into the palace of the high priest: and he sat with the servants, and warmed himself at the fire.

LUKE 22:54. ¶ Then took they him, and led *him*, and brought him into the high priest's house. And Peter followed afar off.

JOHN 18:24. Now Annas had sent him bound unto Caiaphas the high priest.

(c) The Night Examination

The chief priests, the elders, and all the Council (the Sanhedrin), seek false witness against Jesus to put him to death; many witnesses are called, but no evidence is secured; at last two come who testify concerning Jesus' statement about the destruction and rebuilding of the Temple; Jesus answers nothing; finally the high priest says, "I adjure thee by the living God, that thou tell us whether thou be the Christ, the Son of God"; Jesus says, "Thou hast said: nevertheless I say unto you, Hereafter shall ye see the Son of man sitting on the right hand of

power, and coming in the clouds of heaven"; the high priest rends his clothes, and says Jesus has blasphemed; he calls for a verdict, and they pronounce him worthy of death.

Matt. 26:59-66; Mark 14:55-64; Luke: No record; John: No record.

MATTHEW 26:59. Now the chief priests, and elders, and all the council, sought false witness against Jesus, to put him to death;

60. But found none: yea, though many false witnesses came, *yet* found they none. At the last came two false witnesses,

61. And said, This *fellow* said, I am able to destroy the temple of God, and to build it in three days.

62. And the high priest arose, and said unto him, Answerest thou nothing? what *is it which* these witness against thee?

63. But Jesus held his peace. And the high priest answered and said unto him, I adjure thee by the living God, that thou tell us whether thou be the Christ, the Son of God.

64. Jesus saith unto him, Thou hast said: nevertheless I say unto you, Hereafter shall ye see the Son of man sitting on the right hand of power, and coming in the clouds of heaven.

65. Then the high priest rent his clothes, saying, He hath spoken blasphemy; what further need have we of witnesses? behold, now ye have heard his blasphemy.

66. What think ye? They answered and said, He is guilty of death.

MARK 14:55. And the chief priests and all the council sought for witness against Jesus to put him to death; and found none.

56. For many bare false witness against him, but their witness agreed not together.

57. And there arose certain, and bare false witness against him, saying,

58. We heard him say, I will destroy this temple that is made with hands, and within three days I will build another made without hands.

59. But neither so did their witness agree together.

60. And the high priest stood up in the midst, and asked Jesus, saying, Answerest thou nothing? what *is it which* these witness against thee?

61. But he held his peace, and answered nothing. Again the high priest asked him, and said unto him, Art thou the Christ, the Son of the Blessed?

62. And Jesus said, I am: and ye shall see the Son of man sitting on the right hand of power, and coming in the clouds of heaven.

63. Then the high priest rent his clothes, and saith, What

need we any further witnesses?

64. Ye have heard the blasphemy: what think ye? And they all condemned him to be guilty of death.

Luke: No record.

John: No record.

(d) They Maltreat Him

The men holding Jesus, then smite him, spit in his face and buffet him; they blindfold him, and then striking him, ask him to prophesy who struck him; "and many other things blasphemously spake they against him."

Matt. 26:67-68; Mark 14:65; Luke 22:63-65; John: No record.

MATTHEW 26:67. Then did they spit in his face, and buffeted him; and others smote *him* with the palms of their hands,

68. Saying, Prophesy unto us, thou Christ, Who is he that smote thee?

MARK 14:65. And some began to spit on him, and to cover his face, and to buffet him, and to say unto him, Prophesy: and the servants did strike him with the palms of their hands.

LUKE 22:63. ¶ And the men that held Jesus mocked him, and smote *him*.

64. And when they had blindfolded him, they struck him on the face, and asked him, saying, Prophesy, who is it that smote thee?

65. And many other things blasphemously spake they against him.

John: No record.

(e) Peter Denies Him

Peter, with another disciple known to the high priest, goes along to the house of the high priest; the other disciple goes in with Jesus while Peter stands at the door; the other disciple comes to the door and speaking to the maid takes Peter inside; the damsel who keeps the door asks Peter if he was not with Jesus, and Peter makes his first denial; a fire has been kindled in the hall, Peter sits down with them who sit around it; another maid comes and says Peter is a follower; Peter denies this time also; then those who stand about with him charge him with being a follower; and he again denies; immediately the cock crows; Peter, remembering Christ's words, goes out and weeps bitterly.

Matt. 26:69-75; Mark 14:66-72; Luke 22:55-62; John 18:15-18, 25-27.

MATTHEW 26:69. ¶ Now Peter sat without in the palace: and a damsel came unto him, saying, Thou also wast with Jesus of Galilee.

70. But he denied before *them* all, saying, I know not what thou sayest.

71. And when he was gone out into the porch, another

maid saw him, and said unto them that were there, This *fellow* was also with Jesus of Nazareth.

72. And again he denied with an oath, I do not know the man.

73. And after a while came unto *him* they that stood by, and said to Peter, Surely thou also art *one* of them; for thy speech bewrayeth thee.

74. Then began he to curse and to swear, *saying*, I know not the man. And immediately the cock crew.

75. And Peter remembered the word of Jesus, which said unto him, Before the cock crow, thou shalt deny me thrice. And he went out, and wept bitterly.

MARK 14:66. ¶ And as Peter was beneath in the palace, there cometh one of the maids of the high priest:

67. And when she saw Peter warming himself, she looked upon him, and said, And thou also wast with Jesus of Nazareth.

68. But he denied, saying, I know not, neither understand I what thou sayest. And he went out into the porch; and the cock crew.

69. And a maid saw him again, and began to say to them that stood by, This is *one* of them.

70. And he denied it again. And a little after, they that stood by said again to Peter, Surely thou art *one* of them: for thou art a Galilæan, and thy speech agreeth *thereto*.

71. But he began to curse and to swear, *saying*, I know not this man of whom ye speak.

72. And the second time the cock crew. And Peter called to mind the word that Jesus said unto him, Before the cock crow twice, thou shalt deny me thrice. And when he thought thereon, he wept.

LUKE 22:55. And when they had kindled a fire in the midst of the hall, and were set down together, Peter sat down among them.

56. But a certain maid beheld him as he sat by the fire, and earnestly looked upon him, and said, This man was also with him.

57. And he denied him, saying, Woman, I know him not.

58. And after a little while another saw him, and said, Thou art also of them. And Peter said, Man, I am not.

59. And about the space of one hour after another confidently affirmed, saying, Of a truth this *fellow* also was with him: for he is a Galilæan.

60. And Peter said, Man, I know not what thou sayest. And immediately, while he yet spake, the cock crew.

61. And the Lord turned, and looked upon Peter. And Peter remembered the word of the Lord, how he had said unto him, Before the cock crow, thou shalt deny me thrice.

62. And Peter went out, and wept bitterly.

JOHN 18:15. ¶ And Simon Peter followed Jesus, and *so did* another disciple: that disciple was known unto the high priest, and went in with Jesus into the palace of the high priest.

16. But Peter stood at the door without. Then went out that other disciple, which was known unto the high priest, and spake unto her that kept the door, and brought in Peter.

17. Then saith the damsel that kept the door unto Peter, Art not thou also *one* of this man's disciples? He saith, I am not.

18. And the servants and officers stood there, who had made a fire of coals; for it was cold: and they warmed themselves: and Peter stood with them, and warmed himself. . . .

25. And Simon Peter stood and warmed himself. They said therefore unto him, Art not thou also *one* of his disciples? He denied *it*, and said, I am not.

26. One of the servants of the high priest, being *his* kinsman whose ear Peter cut off, saith, Did not I see thee in the garden with him?

27. Peter then denied again: and immediately the cock crew.

(f) The Formal Trial and Condemnation

So soon as it is day, the elders of the people, the chief priests, and the scribes, come together and lead him into their council; they ask if he is the Christ; he answers that if he tells them, they will not believe; that if he questions them, they will not let him go, and again says what he has said to Caiaphas; they then say, "Art thou then the Son of God"; Jesus answers, "Ye say that I am"; the council say they have themselves heard him and need no further witness; they bind him and the whole multitude lead him away to Pontius Pilate.

Matt. 27:1-2; Mark 15:1; Luke 22:66-71, 23:1; John: No record.

MATTHEW 27:1. When the morning was come, all the chief priests and elders of the people took counsel against Jesus to put him to death:

2. And when they had bound him, they led *him* away, and delivered him to Pontius Pilate the governor.

MARK 15:1. And straightway in the morning the chief priests held a consultation with the elders and scribes and the whole council, and bound Jesus, and carried *him* away, and delivered *him* to Pilate.

LUKE 22:66. ¶ And as soon as it was day, the elders of the people and the chief priests and the scribes came together, and led him into their council, saying,

67. Art thou the Christ? tell us. And he said unto them, If I tell you, ye will not believe:

68. And if I also ask *you*, ye will not answer me, nor let *me* go.

69. Hereafter shall the Son of man sit on the right hand of the power of God.

70. Then said they all, Art thou then the Son of God? And he said unto them, Ye say that I am.

71. And they said, What need we any further witness? for we ourselves have heard of his own mouth.

23:1. And the whole multitude of them arose, and led him unto Pilate.

John: No record.

(g) Judas Iscariot Commits Suicide

Judas Iscariot, seeing Jesus condemned, repents and offers back the thirty pieces of silver; they say, "What is that to us"; he casts down the silver in the Temple and goes and hangs himself; the chief priests, saying it is unlawful to put blood money in the treasury, take counsel and buy a potters' field to bury strangers in; the words of Jeremy the prophet on this.

Matt. 27:3-10; Mark: No record; Luke: No record; John: No record.

MATTHEW 27:3. ¶Then Judas, which had betrayed him, when he saw that he was condemned, repented himself, and brought again the thirty pieces of silver to the chief priests and elders,

4. Saying, I have sinned in that I have betrayed the innocent blood. And they said, What *is that* to us? see thou *to that.*

5. And he cast down the pieces of silver in the temple, and departed, and went and hanged himself.

6. And the chief priests took the silver pieces, and said, It is not lawful for to put them into the treasury, because it is the price of blood.

7. And they took counsel, and bought with them the potter's field, to bury strangers in.

8. Wherefore that field was called, The field of blood, unto this day.

9. Then was fulfilled that which was spoken by Jeremy the prophet, saying, And they took the thirty pieces of silver, the price of him that was valued, whom they of the children of Israel did value;

10. And gave them for the potter's field, as the Lord appointed me.

Mark: No record.

Luke: No record.

John: No record.

(h) Before Pilate

They lead Jesus to the judgment hall of Pilate, but they go not in that they may not be defiled against eating the Passover; Pilate comes out to them; they accuse Jesus of perverting the nation, forbidding tribute to Caesar, and saying he is king; Jesus does not answer his accusers; Pilate marvels and asks, "Art thou the King of the Jews?"; Jesus answers, "Thou sayest"; Pilate tells them to take Jesus and judge him; they reply that it is unlawful for them to put any one to death; Pilate takes Jesus into the judgment hall and questions him, again asking if Jesus is king of the Jews; Jesus asks if Pilate sayest this of himself, or did others tell him; Pilate says, "Am I a Jew?"; Jesus then explains that his kingdom is not of this world, and explains he came into the world to witness the truth; Pilate says, "What is truth?"; he then goes out and says he finds no fault in Jesus; in the outcry which follows, some one mentions Galilee.

Matt. 27:11-14; Mark 15:2-5; Luke 23:2-5; John 18:28-38.

MATTHEW 27:11. ¶And Jesus stood before the governor: and the governor asked him, saying, Art thou the King of the Jews? And Jesus said unto him, Thou sayest.

12. And when he was accused of the chief priests and elders, he answered nothing.

13. Then said Pilate unto him, Hearest thou not how many things they witness against thee?

14. And he answered him to never a word; insomuch that the governor marvelled greatly.

MARK 15:2. And Pilate asked him, Art thou the King of the Jews? And he answering said unto him, Thou sayest *it*.

3. And the chief priests accused him of many things: but he answered nothing.

4. And Pilate asked him again, saying, Answerest thou nothing? behold how many things they witness against thee.

5. But Jesus yet answered nothing; so that Pilate marvelled.

LUKE 23:2. And they began to accuse him, saying, We found this *fellow* perverting the nation, and forbidding to give tribute to Cæsar, saying that he himself is Christ a King.

3. And Pilate asked him, saying, Art thou the King of the Jews? And he answered him and said, Thou sayest *it*.

4. Then said Pilate to the chief priests and *to* the people, I find no fault in this man.

5. And they were the more fierce, saying, He stirreth up the people, teaching throughout all Jewry, beginning from Galilee to this place.

JOHN 18:28. ¶ Then led they Jesus from Caiaphas unto the hall of judgment: and it was early; and they themselves went not into the judgment hall, lest they should be defiled; but that they might eat the passover.

29. Pilate then went out unto them, and said, What accusation bring ye against this man?

30. They answered and said unto him, If he were not a malefactor, we would not have delivered him up unto thee.

31. Then said Pilate unto them, Take ye him, and judge him according to your law. The Jews therefore said unto him, It is not lawful for us to put any man to death:

32. That the saying of Jesus might be fulfilled, which he spake, signifying what death he should die.

33. Then Pilate entered into the judgment hall again, and called Jesus, and said unto him, Art thou the King of the Jews?

34. Jesus answered him, Sayest thou this thing of thyself, or did others tell it thee of me?

35. Pilate answered, Am I a Jew? Thine own nation and the chief priests have delivered thee unto me: what hast thou done?

36. Jesus answered, My kingdom is not of this world: if my kingdom were of this world, then would my servants fight, that I should not be delivered to the Jews: but now is my kingdom not from hence.

37. Pilate therefore said unto him, Art thou a king then? Jesus answered, Thou sayest that I am a king. To this end was I born, and for this cause came I into the world, that I should bear witness unto the truth. Every one that is of the truth heareth my voice.

38. Pilate saith unto him, What is truth? And when he had said this, he went out again unto the Jews, and saith unto them, I find in him no fault *at all.*

(i) Before Herod

Pilate hearing of Galilee, asks if Jesus is a Galilean, and finding Jesus belongs unto Herod's jurisdiction, sends him to Herod who is in the city; Herod, having long heard of Jesus, is desirous of seeing him, hoping Jesus will perform a miracle for him (Herod); Herod "questioned with him in many words"; but Jesus answers nothing; the chief priests and scribes vehemently accuse Jesus; Herod and his soldiers mock Jesus, array him in a gorgeous robe, and send him again to Pilate; formerly at enmity between themselves, Herod and Pilate become friends.

Matt.: No record; Mark: No record; Luke 23:6-12; John: No record.

Matthew: No record.

Mark: No record.

LUKE 23:6. When Pilate heard of Galilee, he asked whether the man were a Galilæan.

7. And as soon as he knew that he belonged unto Herod's jurisdiction, he sent him to Herod, who himself also was at Jerusalem at that time.

8. ¶ And when Herod saw Jesus, he was exceeding glad: for he was desirous to see him of a long *season*, because he had heard many things of him; and he hoped to have seen some miracle done by him.

9. Then he questioned with him in many words; but he answered him nothing.

10. And the chief priests and scribes stood and vehemently accused him.

11. And Herod with his men of war set him at nought, and mocked *him*, and arrayed him in a gorgeous robe, and sent him again to Pilate.

12. ¶ And the same day Pilate and Herod were made friends together: for before they were at enmity between themselves.

John: No record.

(j) Again Before Pilate

Pilate calls together the chief priests, the rulers, and the people, and speaking of the custom of releasing to them a prisoner on this feast day, tells them he finds no fault in Jesus, neither does Herod, and therefore he (Pilate) will chastise Jesus and release him; the multitude, persuaded by the chief priests and elders, calls for the release of Barabbas, a murderer; Pilate's wife sends word of a dream she has had and asks Pilate to do nothing against Jesus; Pilate again proposes to release Jesus; again the multitude refuse, and cry out that Jesus be crucified.

Matt. 27:15-23; Mark 15:6-14; Luke 23:13-23; John 18:39-40.

MATTHEW 27:15. Now at *that* feast the governor was wont to release unto the people a prisoner, whom they would.

16. And they had then a notable prisoner, called Barabbas.

17. Therefore when they were gathered together, Pilate said unto them, Whom will ye that I release unto you? Barabbas, or Jesus which is called Christ?

18. For he knew that for envy they had delivered him.

19. ¶ When he was set down on the judgment seat, his wife sent unto him, saying, Have thou nothing to do with that just man: for I have suffered many things this day in a dream because of him.

20. But the chief priests and elders persuaded the multitude that they should ask Barabbas, and destroy Jesus.

21. The governor answered and said unto them, Whether of the twain will ye that I release unto you? They said, Barabbas.

22. Pilate saith unto them, What shall I do then with Jesus which is called Christ? *They* all say unto him, Let him be crucified.

23. And the governor said, Why, what evil hath he done? But they cried out the more, saying, Let him be crucified.

MARK 15:6. Now at *that* feast he released unto them one prisoner, whomsoever they desired.

7. And there was *one* named Barabbas, *which lay* bound with them that had made insurrection with him, who had committed murder in the insurrection.

8. And the multitude crying aloud began to desire *him to do* as he had ever done unto them.

9. But Pilate answered them, saying, Will ye that I release unto you the King of the Jews?

10. For he knew that the chief priests had delivered him for envy.

11. But the chief priests moved the people, that he should rather release Barabbas unto them.

12. And Pilate answered and said again unto them, What will ye then that I shall do *unto him* whom ye call the King of the Jews?

13. And they cried out again, Crucify him.

14. Then Pilate said unto them, Why, what evil hath he done? And they cried out the more exceedingly, Crucify him.

LUKE 23:13. ¶ And Pilate, when he had called together the chief priests and the rulers and the people,

14. Said unto them, Ye have brought this man unto me, as one that perverteth the people: and, behold, I, having examined *him* before you, have found no fault in this man touching those things whereof ye accuse him:

15. No, nor yet Herod: for I sent you to him; and, lo, nothing worthy of death is done unto him.

16. I will therefore chastise him, and release *him.*

17. (For of necessity he must release one unto them at the feast.)

18. And they cried out all at once, saying, Away with this *man*, and release unto us Barabbas:

19. (Who for a certain sedition made in the city, and for murder, was cast into prison.)

20. Pilate therefore, willing to release Jesus, spake again to them.

21. But they cried, saying, Crucify *him*, crucify him.

22. And he said unto them the third time, Why, what evil hath he done? I have found no cause of death in him: I will therefore chastise him, and let *him* go.

23. And they were instant with loud voices, requiring

that he might be crucified. And the voices of them and of the chief priests prevailed.

JOHN 18:39. But ye have a custom, that I should release unto you one at the passover: will ye therefore that I release unto you the King of the Jews?

40. Then cried they all again, saying, Not this man, but Barabbas. Now Barabbas was a robber.

(k) Pilate Releases Barabbas

Pilate releases Barabbas, then scourges Jesus, and delivers him to the soldiers; they take him into the hall, strip him, put on him a scarlet robe, plait a crown of thorns and put on his head, put a reed in his hand, and then bow before him, mocking him, saying, "Hail, King of the Jews," then they spit upon him, take the reed from him, and smite him on the head.

Matt. 27:26-30; Mark 15:15-19; Luke 23:24-25; John 19:1-3.

MATTHEW 27:26. ¶Then released he Barabbas unto them: and when he had scourged Jesus, he delivered *him* to be crucified.

27. Then the soldiers of the governor took Jesus into the common hall, and gathered unto him the whole band *of soldiers*.

28. And they stripped him, and put on him a scarlet robe.

29. ¶ And when they had platted a crown of thorns, they put *it* upon his head, and a reed in his right hand: and they bowed the knee before him, and mocked him, saying, Hail, King of the Jews!

30. And they spit upon him, and took the reed, and smote him on the head.

MARK 15:15. ¶ And *so* Pilate, willing to content the people, released Barabbas unto them, and delivered Jesus, when he had scourged *him*, to be crucified.

16. And the soldiers led him away into the hall, called Prætorium; and they call together the whole band.

17. And they clothed him with purple, and platted a crown of thorns, and put it about his *head*,

18. And began to salute him, Hail, King of the Jews!

19. And they smote him on the head with a reed, and did spit upon him, and bowing *their* knees worshipped him.

LUKE 23:24. And Pilate gave sentence that it should be as they required.

25. And he released unto them him that for sedition and murder was cast into prison, whom they had desired; but he delivered Jesus to their will.

JOHN 19:1. Then Pilate therefore took Jesus, and scourged *him*.

2. And the soldiers platted

a crown of thorns, and put *it* on his head, and they put on him a purple robe,

3. And said, Hail, King of the Jews! and they smote him with their hands.

(l) Pilate Pleads for Jesus but Finally Delivers Him for Crucifixion

Pilate then takes Jesus out again, wearing the crown of thorns and the purple robe, saying he finds no fault in him, "Behold the man"; the chief priests and officers cry, "Crucify him"; Pilate again says he finds no fault in him; Pilate takes Jesus again into the judgment hall, and asks who he is, but Jesus is silent; Pilate points out his power over him; Jesus says Pilate has no power except what he is given from above; Pilate again seeks to release Jesus, until the multitude say that if Pilate lets this man go he is no friend of Caesar; Pilate washes his hands publicly saying he is guiltless of this man's blood; the people cry to let his blood be upon them and their children; Pilate then brings Jesus forth, sits down in the judgment seat in a place called the Pavement; it is about the sixth hour; he says to the Jews, "Behold your King"; the people cry, "Crucify him"; Pilate says, "Shall I crucify your King?"; the priests answer they have no king but Caesar; Pilate then delivers Jesus to them.

Matt. 27:24-25; Mark: No record; Luke: No record; John 19:4-16a.

MATTHEW 27:24. ¶ When Pilate saw that he could prevail nothing, but *that* rather a tumult was made, he took water, and washed *his* hands before the multitude, saying, I am innocent of the blood of this just person: see ye *to it.*

25. Then answered all the people, and said, His blood *be* on us, and on our children.

Mark: No record.

Luke: No record.

JOHN 19:4. Pilate therefore went forth again, and saith unto them, Behold, I bring him forth to you, that ye may know that I find no fault in him.

5. Then came Jesus forth, wearing the crown of thorns, and the purple robe. And *Pilate* saith unto them, Behold the man!

6. When the chief priests therefore and officers saw him, they cried out, saying, Crucify *him*, crucify *him.* Pilate saith unto them, take ye him, and crucify *him*: for I find no fault in him.

7. The Jews answered him, We have a law, and by our law he ought to die, because he made himself the Son of God.

8. ¶ When Pilate therefore heard that saying, he was the more afraid;

9. And went again into the judgment hall, and saith unto Jesus, Whence art thou? But Jesus gave him no answer.

10. Then saith Pilate unto

him, Speakest thou not unto me? knowest thou not that I have power to crucify thee, and have power to release thee?

11. Jesus answered, Thou couldest have no power *at all* against me, except it were given thee from above: therefore he that delivered me unto thee hath the greater sin.

12. And from thenceforth Pilate sought to release him: but the Jews cried out, saying, If thou let this man go, thou art not Cæsar's friend: whosoever maketh himself a king speaketh against Cæsar.

13. ¶ When Pilate therefore heard that saying, he brought Jesus forth, and sat down in the judgment seat in a place that is called the Pavement, but in the Hebrew, Gabbatha.

14. And it was the preparation of the passover, and about the sixth hour: and he saith unto the Jews, Behold your King!

15. But they cried out, Away with *him*, away with *him*, crucify him. Pilate saith unto them, Shall I crucify your King? The chief priests answered, We have no king but Cæsar.

16. Then delivered he him therefore unto them to be crucified . . . .

(m) They Take Him to Be Crucified

After they mock Jesus, they take off the purple from him, put on his own clothes, and lead him away to be crucified, he bearing his own cross, but as they come out they find a man from Cyrene, Simon by name (the father of Alexander and Rufus), and him they compel to bear the cross to Golgotha (Luke calls it Calvary), the place of execution; a great company follow, and they bewail and lament him; Jesus tells them to weep not for him, but for themselves and their children, and he prophesies concerning the ills that are to come; arriving at the place of crucifixion, they offer him a drink of wine mingled with myrrh (Matthew says vinegar and gall), but he refuses it; they crucify him at the third hour, with a thief on each side.

Matt. 27:31-34, 38; Mark 15:20-23, 25, 27-28; Luke 23:26-33; John 19:16b-18.

Time: 9:00 A.M.

MATTHEW 27:31. And after that they had mocked him, they took the robe off from him, and put his own raiment on him, and led him away to crucify *him*.

32. And as they came out, they found a man of Cyrene, Simon by name: him they compelled to bear his cross.

33. And when they were come unto a place called Golgotha, that is to say, a place of a skull,

34. ¶ They gave him vinegar to drink mingled with gall:

and when he had tasted *thereof*, he would not drink . . . .

38. Then were there two thieves crucified with him, one on the right hand, and another on the left.

MARK 15:20. And when they had mocked him, they took off the purple from him, and put his own clothes on him, and led him out to crucify him.

21. And they compel one Simon a Cyrenian, who passed by, coming out of the country, the father of Alexander and Rufus, to bear his cross.

22. And they bring him unto the place Golgotha, which is, being interpreted, The place of a skull.

23. And they gave him to drink wine mingled with myrrh: but he received *it* not . . . .

25. And it was the third hour, and they crucified him . . . .

27. And with him they crucify two thieves; the one on his right hand, and the other on his left.

28. And the scripture was fulfilled, which saith, And he was numbered with the transgressors.

LUKE 23:26. And as they led him away, they laid hold upon one Simon, a Cyrenian, coming out of the country, and on him they laid the cross, that he might bear *it* after Jesus.

27. ¶ And there followed him a great company of people, and of women, which also bewailed and lamented him.

28. But Jesus turning unto them said, Daughters of Jerusalem, weep not for me, but weep for yourselves, and for your children.

29. For, behold, the days are coming, in the which they shall say, Blessed *are* the barren, and the wombs that never bare, and the paps which never gave suck.

30. Then shall they begin to say to the mountains, Fall on us; and to the hills, Cover us.

31. For if they do these things in a green tree, what shall be done in the dry?

32. And there were also two other, malefactors, led with him to be put to death.

33. And when they were come to the place, which is called Calvary, there they crucified him, and the malefactors, one on the right hand, and the other on the left.

JOHN 19:16 . . . And they took Jesus, and led *him* away.

17. And he bearing his cross went forth into a place called *the place* of a skull, which is called in the Hebrew Golgotha:

18. Where they crucified him, and two other with him, on either side one, and Jesus in the midst.

(n) Pilate Places a Superscription on the Cross

Pilate prepares a superscription—in Greek, Latin, and Hebrew—"Jesus of Nazareth the King of the Jews," which is placed on the cross above Jesus' head; the chief priests of the Jews come to Pilate and say: "Write not, The King of the Jews; but that he said, I am King of the Jews. Pilate answered, What I have written I have written."

Matt. 27:37; Mark 15:26; Luke 23:38; John 19:19-22.

MATTHEW 27:37. And set up over his head his accusation written, THIS IS JESUS THE KING OF THE JEWS.

MARK 15:26. And the superscription of his accusation was written over, THE KING OF THE JEWS.

LUKE 23:38. And a superscription also was written over him in letters of Greek, and Latin, and Hebrew, THIS IS THE KING OF THE JEWS.

JOHN 19:19. ¶ And Pilate wrote a title, and put *it* on the cross. And the writing was, JESUS OF NAZARETH THE KING OF THE JEWS.

20. This title then read many of the Jews: for the place where Jesus was crucified was nigh to the city: and it was written in Hebrew, *and* Greek, *and* Latin.

21. Then said the chief priests of the Jews to Pilate, Write not, The King of the Jews; but that he said, I am King of the Jews.

22. Pilate answered, What I have written I have written.

(o) The First Words on the Cross

The first words on the cross: "Father, forgive them; for they know not what they do."

Matt.: No record; Mark: No record; Luke 23:34a; John: No record.

Matthew: No record.

Mark: No record.

LUKE 23:34. ¶ Then said Jesus, Father, forgive them; for they know not what they do . . . .

John: No record.

(p) The Soldiers Divide His Clothes

When the soldiers have crucified him, they take his garments and divide them into four parts and also his coat (woven without a seam) and cast lots for them, what every man shall take; for the coat they cast a special lot so as not to rend it; having done these things, they sit down and watch him there.

Matt. 27:35-36; Mark 15:24; Luke 23:34b; John 19:23-24.

MATTHEW 27:35. And they crucified him, and parted his garments, casting lots: that it might be fulfilled which was spoken by the prophet, They parted my garments among them, and upon my vesture did they cast lots.

36. And sitting down they watched him there; . . .

MARK 15:24. And when they had crucified him, they parted his garments, casting lots upon them, what every man should take.

LUKE 23:34 . . . And they parted his raiment, and cast lots.

JOHN 19:23. ¶ Then the soldiers, when they had crucified Jesus, took his garments, and made four parts, to every soldier a part; and also *his* coat: now the coat was without seam, woven from the top throughout.

24. They said therefore among themselves, Let us not rend it, but cast lots for it, whose it shall be: that the scripture might be fulfilled, which saith, They parted my raiment among them, and for my vesture they did cast lots. These things therefore the soldiers did.

(q) The Mocking and Scoffing of the Rulers and the Multitude

The chief priests and scribes mock among themselves, and call upon Jesus to save himself if he be king of the Jews, if he will descend from the cross they will believe, he has saved others, now let him save himself; those who pass also mock, wagging their heads and taunting him about the destruction of the Temple, the thieves also rail at him in the same way.

Matt. 27:39-44; Mark 15:29-32; Luke 23:35-37; John: No record.

MATTHEW 27:39. ¶ And they that passed by reviled him, wagging their heads,

40. And saying, Thou that destroyest the temple, and buildest *it* in three days, save thyself. If thou be the Son of God, come down from the cross.

41. Likewise also the chief priests mocking *him*, with the scribes and elders, said,

42. He saved others; himself he cannot save. If he be the King of Israel, let him now come down from the cross, and we will believe him.

43. He trusted in God; let him deliver him now, if he will have him: for he said, I am the Son of God.

44. The thieves also, which were crucified with him, cast the same in his teeth.

MARK 15:29. And they that passed by railed on him, wagging their heads, and saying, Ah, thou that destroyest the temple, and buildest *it* in three days,

30. Save thyself, and come down from the cross.

31. Likewise also the chief priests mocking said among themselves with the scribes, He saved others; himself he cannot save.

32. Let Christ the King of Israel descend now from the cross, that we may see and believe. And they that were crucified with him reviled him.

LUKE 23:35. And the people stood beholding. And the rulers also with them derided *him*, saying, He saved others; let him save himself, if he be Christ, the chosen of God.

36. And the soldiers also mocked him, coming to him, and offering him vinegar,

37. And saying, If thou be the king of the Jews, save thyself.

John: No record.

(r) Second Words From the Cross

Second words from the cross: But one of the thieves, when his fellow cries, "If thou be Christ, save thyself and us," rebukes the railer, pointing out that they receive the just reward of their deeds, while Jesus has done nothing amiss; he then says to Jesus, "Lord, remember me when thou comest into thy kingdom," and to him Jesus says, "Verily I say unto thee, To day shalt thou be with me in paradise."

Matt.: No record; Mark: No record; Luke 23:39-43; John: No record.

Matthew: No record.

Mark: No record.

LUKE 23:39. ¶ And one of the malefactors which were hanged railed on him, saying, If thou be Christ, save thyself and us.

40. But the other answering rebuked him, saying, Dost not thou fear God, seeing thou art in the same condemnation?

41. And we indeed justly; for we receive the due reward of our deeds: but this man hath done nothing amiss.

42. And he said unto Jesus, Lord, remember me when thou comest into thy kingdom.

43. And Jesus said unto him, Verily I say unto thee, To day shalt thou be with me in paradise.

John: No record.

(s) Third Words From the Cross

Third words from the cross: By the cross stand the mother of Jesus, her sister Mary, wife of Cleophas, and Mary Magdalene; John stands there also and to his mother Jesus says, "Woman, behold thy son," to his disciple he says, "Behold thy mother," and "from that hour that disciple took her unto his own home."

Matt.: No record; Mark: No record; Luke: No record; John 19:25-27.

Matthew: No record.

Mark: No record.

Luke: No record.

JOHN 19:25. ¶ Now there stood by the cross of Jesus his mother, and his mother's sister, Mary the *wife* of Cleophas, and Mary Magdalene.

26. When Jesus therefore saw his mother, and the disciple standing by, whom he loved, he saith unto his mother, Woman, behold thy son!

27. Then saith he to the disciple, Behold thy mother! And from that hour that disciple took her unto his own *home*.

(t) Darkness Covers the Earth

A darkness comes over "all the earth," from the sixth to the ninth hour.

Matt. 27:45; Mark 15:33; Luke 23:44-45a; John: No record.
Time: 12:00 M.

MATTHEW 27:45. Now from the sixth hour there was darkness over all the land unto the ninth hour.

MARK 15:33. And when the sixth hour was come, there was darkness over the whole land until the ninth hour.

LUKE 23:44. And it was about the sixth hour, and there was a darkness over all the earth until the ninth hour.

45. And the sun was darkened . . . .

John: No record.

(u) Signs in the Western Hemisphere

Great convulsions of nature on the Western Hemisphere; the greatest storm ever known, tempests, thunder, lightning, one city is set on fire, another is sunk in the sea, another is buried under a mountain; in some places the whole face of the land is changed by tempests, storms, and earthquakes; other cities are sunk and buried, others carried away by the whirlwinds; the earth is torn and cracked; the storm lasts for about three hours; then thick darkness comes, so thick its vapors can be felt, and no light will burn; this lasts for the space of three days; the people weep, wail, and howl because of the darkness and great destruction that have come upon them; they vainly cry because they have not repented and listened to the prophets.

3 Nephi 8:5-25.

3 NEPHI 8:5. And it came to pass in the thirty and fourth year, in the first month, on the fourth day of the month, there arose a great storm, such an one as never had been known in all the land.

6. And there was also a great and terrible tempest; and there was terrible thunder, insomuch that it did shake the whole earth as if it was about to divide asunder.

7. And there were exceeding

sharp lightnings, such as never had been known in all the land.

8. And the city of Zarahemla did take fire.

9. And the city of Moroni did sink into the depths of the sea, and the inhabitants thereof were drowned.

10. And the earth was carried up upon the city of Moronihah, that in the place of the city there became a great mountain.

11. And there was a great and terrible destruction in the land southward.

12. But behold, there was a more great and terrible destruction in the land northward; for behold, the whole face of the land was changed, because of the tempest and the whirlwinds, and the thunderings and the lightnings, and the exceeding great quaking of the whole earth;

13. And the highways were broken up, and the level roads were spoiled, and many smooth places became rough.

14. And many great and notable cities were sunk, and many were burned, and many were shaken till the buildings thereof had fallen to the earth, and the inhabitants thereof were slain, and the places were left desolate.

15. And there were some cities which remained; but the damage thereof was exceeding great, and there were many in them who were slain.

16. And there were some who were carried away in the whirlwind; and whither they went no man knoweth, save they know that they were carried away.

17. And thus the face of the whole earth became deformed, because of the tempests, and the thunderings, and the lightnings, and the quaking of the earth.

18. And behold, the rocks were rent in twain; they were broken up upon the face of the whole earth, insomuch that they were found in broken fragments, and in seams and in cracks, upon all the face of the land.

19. And it came to pass that when the thunderings, and the lightnings, and the storm, and the tempest, and the quakings of the earth did cease—for behold, they did last for about the space of three hours; and it was said by some that the time was greater; nevertheless, all these great and terrible things were done in about the space of three hours—and then behold, there was darkness upon the face of the land.

20. And it came to pass that there was thick darkness upon all the face of the land, insomuch that the inhabitants thereof who had not fallen could feel the vapor of darkness;

21. And there could be no light, because of the darkness, neither candles, neither torch-

es; neither could there be fire kindled with their fine and exceedingly dry wood, so that there could not be any light at all;

22. And there was not any light seen, neither fire, nor glimmer, neither the sun, nor the moon, nor the stars, for so great were the mists of darkness which were upon the face of the land.

23. And it came to pass that it did last for the space of three days that there was no light seen; and there was great mourning and howling and weeping among all the people continually; yea, great were the groanings of the people, because of the darkness and the great destruction which had come upon them.

24. And in one place they were heard to cry, saying: O that we had repented before this great and terrible day, and then would our brethren have been spared, and they would not have been burned in that great city Zarahemla.

25. And in another place they were heard to cry and mourn, saying: O that we had repented before this great and terrible day, and had not killed and stoned the prophets, and cast them out; then would our mothers and our fair daughters, and our children have been spared, and not have been buried up in that great city Moronihah. And thus were the howlings of the people great and terrible.

(v) Fourth Words From the Cross

Fourth words from the cross: At the ninth hour Jesus cries: "My God, my God, why hast thou forsaken me?"; some of the bystanders hearing this say, "Behold, he calleth Elias."

Matt. 27:46-47; Mark 15:34-35; Luke: No record; John: No record.

MATTHEW 27:46. And about the ninth hour Jesus cried with a loud voice, saying, Eli, Eli, lama sabachthani? that is to say, My God, my God, why hast thou forsaken me?

47. Some of them that stood there, when they heard *that*, said, This *man* calleth for Elias.

MARK 15:34. And at the ninth hour Jesus cried with a loud voice, saying, Eloi, Eloi, lama sabachthani? which is, being interpreted, My God, my God, why hast thou forsaken me?

35. And some of them that stood by, when they heard *it*, said, Behold, he calleth Elias.

Luke: No record.

John: No record.

(w) Fifth Words From the Cross

Fifth words from the cross: Jesus, "knowing that all things were now accomplished, that the scripture might be fulfilled, saith, I thirst"; they straightway then take a sponge, fill it with vinegar, put it on a reed and give it to him to drink; the rest say: "Let be, let us see whether Elias will come to save him."

Matt. 27:48-49; Mark 15:36; Luke: No record; John 19:28-29.

MATTHEW 27:48. And straightway one of them ran, and took a spunge, and filled *it* with vinegar, and put *it* on a reed, and gave him to drink.

49. The rest said, Let be, let us see whether Elias will come to save him.

MARK 15:36. And one ran and filled a spunge full of vinegar, and put *it* on a reed, and gave him to drink, saying, Let alone; let us see whether Elias will come to take him down.

Luke: No record.

JOHN 19:28. ¶ After this, Jesus knowing that all things were now accomplished, that the scripture might be fulfilled, saith, I thirst.

29. Now there was set a vessel full of vinegar: and they filled a spunge with vinegar, and put *it* upon hyssop, and put *it* to his mouth.

(x) Sixth Words From the Cross

Sixth words from the cross: When Jesus receives the vinegar he says: "It is finished."

Matt.: No record; Mark: No record; Luke: No record; John 19:30a.

Matthew: No record.

Mark: No record.

Luke: No record.

JOHN 19:30. When Jesus therefore had received the vinegar, he said, It is finished....

(y) Seventh Words From the Cross

Seventh words from the cross: Jesus then cries in a loud voice: "Father, into thy hands I commend my spirit," and having said this, "he gave up the ghost."

Matt. 27:50; Mark 15:37; Luke 23:46; John 19:30b.
Time: 3:00 P.M.

MATTHEW 27:50. ¶ Jesus, when he had cried again with a loud voice, yielded up the ghost.

MARK 15:37. And Jesus cried with a loud voice, and gave up the ghost.

LUKE 23:46. ¶ And when Jesus had cried with a loud voice, he said, Father, into thy hands I commend my spirit: and having said thus, he gave up the ghost.

JOHN 19:30 . . . and he bowed his head, and gave up the ghost.

(z) The Centurion's Testimony

The veil of the Temple is rent in twain, the earth quakes, and rocks are rent; the centurion seeing all these things, glorifies God saying, "Certainly this was a righteous man"; many stand afar off, among them Mary Magdalene, Mary the mother of James the less and of Joses, and Salome, and the mother of Zebedee's children, as also many women who, beholding from afar, had followed from Galilee and had come with him to Jerusalem.

Matt. 27:51-56; Mark 15:38-41; Luke 23:45b, 47-49; John: No record.

MATTHEW 27:51. And, behold, the veil of the temple was rent in twain from the top to the bottom; and the earth did quake, and the rocks rent;

52. And the graves were opened; and many bodies of the saints which slept arose,

53. And came out of the graves after his resurrection, and went into the holy city, and appeared unto many.

54. Now when the centurion, and they that were with him, watching Jesus, saw the earthquake, and those things that were done, they feared greatly, saying, Truly this was the Son of God.

55. And many women were there beholding afar off, which followed Jesus from Galilee, ministering unto him:

56. Among which was Mary Magdalene, and Mary the mother of James and Joses, and the mother of Zebedee's children.

MARK 15:38. And the veil of the temple was rent in twain from the top to the bottom.

39. ¶ And when the centurion, which stood over against him, saw that he so cried out, and gave up the ghost, he said, Truly this man was the Son of God.

40. There were also women looking on afar off: among whom was Mary Magdalene, and Mary the mother of James the less and of Joses, and Salome;

41. (Who also, when he was in Galilee, followed him, and ministered unto him;) and many other women which came up with him unto Jerusalem.

LUKE 23:45 . . . and the veil of the temple was rent in the midst . . . .

47. Now when the centurion saw what was done, he glorified God, saying, Certainly this was a righteous man.

48. And all the people that came together to that sight, beholding the things which were done, smote their breasts, and returned.

49. And all his acquaintance, and the women that followed him from Galilee, stood afar off, beholding these things.

John: No record.

(aa) His Side Pierced

The Jews beseech Pilate (in order that the bodies might not be left on the cross on the Sabbath) that the legs of those crucified be broken; the legs of the thieves are broken, but Jesus being already dead, they do not break his legs; but one of the soldiers pierces his side with a spear and there come out blood and water.

Matt.: No record; Mark: No record; Luke: No record; John 19:31-37.

Matthew: No record.

Mark: No record.

Luke: No record.

JOHN 19:31. The Jews therefore, because it was the preparation, that the bodies should not remain upon the cross on the sabbath day, (for that sabbath day was an high day,) besought Pilate that their legs might be broken, and *that* they might be taken away.

32. Then came the soldiers, and brake the legs of the first, and of the other which was crucified with him.

33. But when they came to Jesus, and saw that he was dead already, they brake not his legs:

34. But one of the soldiers with a spear pierced his side, and forthwith came there out blood and water.

35. And he that saw *it* bare record, and his record is true: and he knoweth that he saith true, that ye might believe.

36. For these things were done, that the scripture should be fulfilled, A bone of him shall not be broken.

37. And again another scripture saith, They shall look on him whom they pierced.

(bb) His Burial

When the even was come, Joseph of Arimathaea, an honorable counselor (who had not consented "to the counsel and deed of them"), a secret disciple of Jesus, goes boldly to Pilate and asks for the body of Jesus; Pilate marvels that Jesus is so soon dead, and asks the centurion if Jesus is dead; the centurion saying he is, Pilate gives the body to Joseph, who with Nicodemus, takes the body down, wraps it in fine linen, with an hundred weight of myrrh mixed with aloes, and buries it in his own new tomb, which is in a garden near to the place of crucifixion; a great stone is rolled before the door; Mary Magdalene and Mary the mother of Jesus sit near the sepulchre; the women from Galilee follow, behold the sepulchre, and how the body is laid; then "they returned, and prepared spices and ointments; and rested the sabbath day according to the commandment."

Matt. 27:57-61; Mark 15:42-47; Luke 23:50-56; John 19:38-42.
Time: 3:00—6:00 P.M.

MATTHEW 27:57. When the even was come, there came a rich man of Arimathæa, named Joseph, who also himself was Jesus' disciple:

58. He went to Pilate, and begged the body of Jesus. Then Pilate commanded the body to be delivered.

59. And when Joseph had taken the body, he wrapped it in a clean linen cloth,

60. And laid it in his own new tomb, which he had hewn out in the rock: and he rolled a great stone to the door of the sepulchre, and departed.

61. And there was Mary Magdalene, and the other Mary, sitting over against the sepulchre.

MARK 15:42. ¶ And now when the even was come, because it was the preparation, that is, the day before the sabbath,

43. Joseph of Arimathæa, an honourable counsellor, which also waited for the kingdom of God, came, and went in boldly unto Pilate, and craved the body of Jesus.

44. And Pilate marvelled if he were already dead: and calling *unto him* the centurion, he asked him whether he had been any while dead.

45. And when he knew *it* of the centurion, he gave the body to Joseph.

46. And he bought fine linen, and took him down, and wrapped him in the linen, and laid him in a sepulchre which was hewn out of a rock, and rolled a stone unto the door of the sepulchre.

47. And Mary Magdalene and Mary *the mother* of Joses beheld where he was laid.

LUKE 23:50. ¶ And, behold, *there was* a man named Joseph, a counsellor; *and he was* a good man, and a just:

51. (The same had not consented to the counsel and deed of them:) *he was* of Arimathæa, a city of the Jews: who also himself waited for the kingdom of God.

52. This *man* went unto Pilate, and begged the body of Jesus.

53. And he took it down, and wrapped it in linen, and laid it in a sepulchre that was hewn in stone, wherein never man before was laid.

54. And that day was the preparation, and the sabbath drew on.

55. And the women also, which came with him from Galilee, followed after, and beheld the sepulchre, and how his body was laid.

56. And they returned, and prepared spices and ointments; and rested the sabbath day according to the commandment.

JOHN 19:38. ¶ And after

this Joseph of Arimathæa, being a disciple of Jesus, but secretly for fear of the Jews, besought Pilate that he might take away the body of Jesus: and Pilate gave *him* leave. He came therefore, and took the body of Jesus.

39. And there came also Nicodemus, which at the first came to Jesus by night, and brought a mixture of myrrh and aloes, about an hundred pound *weight*.

40. Then took they the body of Jesus, and wound it in linen clothes with the spices, as the manner of the Jews is to bury.

41. Now in the place where he was crucified there was a garden; and in the garden a new sepulchre, wherein was never man yet laid.

42. There laid they Jesus therefore because of the Jews' preparation *day*; for the sepulchre was nigh at hand.

Seventh Day of the Week

Section 166

THE GUARD PLACED AT THE TOMB AND THE VOICE HEARD IN THE WESTERN HEMISPHERE

Time: A.D. 30, Saturday, April 8, 16th Nisan (ANDREWS).
Place: Jerusalem and the Western Hemisphere

(a) The Placing of the Guard at the Tomb

The chief priests and the Pharisees go to Pilate, and saying that "that deceiver" said while yet alive that he would rise again, asks that the sepulchre be made sure against the third day, lest his disciples come by night and steal him away and then say he is risen from the dead, so that "the last error shall be worse than the first"; Pilate says: "Ye have a watch: go your way, make it as sure as ye can"; so they make the sepulchre sure, sealing the stone, and setting a watch.

Matt. 27:62-66; Mark: No record; Luke: No record; John: No record.

MATTHEW 27:62. ¶ Now the next day, that followed the day of the preparation, the chief priests and Pharisees came together unto Pilate,

63. Saying, Sir, we remember that that deceiver said, while he was yet alive, After three days I will rise again.

64. Command therefore that the sepulchre be made sure until the third day, lest his disciples come by night, and steal him away, and say unto the people, He is risen from the dead: so the last error shall be worse than the first.

65. Pilate said unto them, Ye have a watch: go your way, make *it* as sure as ye can.

66. So they went, and made the sepulchre sure, sealing the stone, and setting a watch.

Mark: No record.
Luke: No record.
John: No record.

(b) In Western Hemisphere, a Voice From Heaven Declares the Woes of the People

A voice comes from heaven, crying wo unto the people, calling them to repentance from their sins; it tells them of the destruction that has come to them because of their iniquities; it names many cities which have been destroyed, because of the wickedness of their people and their abominations; the voice then tells of the mercy and blessings that will be theirs who come to him, and proclaims himself Jesus Christ, the Son of God; the voice tells of the relationship between himself and the Father, gives a discourse upon the peace of those who come unto him; tells his own place, and that the law of Moses is gone, and gives the new sacrifice, and baptism, again speaking of the atonement.

3 Nephi 9:1-22.

3 NEPHI 9:1. And it came to pass that there was a voice heard among all the inhabitants of the earth, upon all the face of this land, crying:

2. Wo, wo, wo unto this people; wo unto the inhabitants of the whole earth except they shall repent; for the devil laugheth, and his angels rejoice, because of the slain of the fair sons and daughters of my people; and it is because of their iniquity and abominations that they are fallen!

3. Behold, that great city Zarahemla have I burned with fire, and the inhabitants thereof.

4. And behold, that great city Moroni have I caused to be sunk in the depths of the sea, and the inhabitants thereof to be drowned.

5. And behold, that great city Moronihah have I covered with earth, and the inhabitants thereof, to hide their iniquities and their abominations from before my face, that the blood of the prophets and the saints shall not come any more unto me against them.

6. And behold, the city of Gilgal have I caused to be sunk, and the inhabitants thereof to be buried up in the depths of the earth;

7. Yea, and the city of Onihah and the inhabitants thereof, and the city of Mocum and the inhabitants thereof, and the city of Jerusalem and the inhabitants thereof; and waters have I caused to come up in the stead thereof, to hide their wickedness and abominations from before my face, that the blood of the prophets and the saints shall not come up any more unto me against them.

8. And behold, the city of Gadiandi, and the city of Gadi-

omnah, and the city of Jacob, and the city of Gimgimno, all these have I caused to be sunk, and made hills and valleys in the places thereof; and the inhabitants thereof have I buried up in the depths of the earth, to hide their wickedness and abominations from before my face, that the blood of the prophets and the saints should not come up any more unto me against them.

9. And behold, that great city Jacobugath, which was inhabited by the people of king Jacob, have I caused to be burned with fire because of their sins and their wickedness, which was above all the wickedness of the whole earth, because of their secret murders and combinations; for it was they that did destroy the peace of my people and the government of the land; therefore I did cause them to be burned, to destroy them from before my face, that the blood of the prophets and the saints should not come up unto me any more against them.

10. And behold, the city of Laman, and the city of Josh, and the city of Gad, and the city of Kishkumen, have I caused to be burned with fire, and the inhabitants thereof, because of their wickedness in casting out the prophets, and stoning those whom I did send to declare unto them concerning their wickedness and their abominations.

11. And because they did cast them all out, that there were none righteous among them, I did send down fire and destroy them, that their wickedness and abominations might be hid from before my face, that the blood of the prophets and the saints whom I sent among them might not cry unto me from the ground against them.

12. And many great destructions have I caused to come upon this land, and upon this people, because of their wickedness and their abominations.

13. O all ye that are spared because ye were more righteous than they, will ye not now return unto me, and repent of your sins, and be converted, that I may heal you?

14. Yea, verily I say unto you, if ye will come unto me ye shall have eternal life. Behold, mine arm of mercy is extended towards you, and whosoever will come, him will I receive; and blessed are those who come unto me.

15. Behold, I am Jesus Christ the Son of God. I created the heavens and the earth, and all things that in them are. I was with the Father from the beginning. I am in the Father, and the Father in me; and in me hath the Father glorified his name.

16. I came unto my own, and my own received me not. And the scriptures concerning my coming are fulfilled.

17. And as many as have received me, to them have I given to become the sons of God; and even so will I to as many as shall believe on my name, for behold, by me redemption cometh, and in me is the law of Moses fulfilled.

18. I am the light and the life of the world. I am Alpha and Omega, the beginning and the end.

19. And ye shall offer up unto me no more the shedding of blood; yea, your sacrifices and your burnt offerings shall be done away, for I will accept none of your sacrifices and your burnt offerings.

20. And ye shall offer for a sacrifice unto me a broken heart and a contrite spirit. And whoso cometh unto me with a broken heart and a contrite spirit, him will I baptize with fire and with the Holy Ghost, even as the Lamanites, because of their faith in me at the time of their conversion, were baptized with fire and with the Holy Ghost, and they knew it not.

21. Behold, I have come unto the world to bring redemption unto the world, to save the world from sin.

22. Therefore, whoso repenteth and cometh unto me as a little child, him will I receive, for of such is the kingdom of God. Behold, for such I have laid down my life, and have taken it up again; therefore repent, and come unto me ye ends of the earth, and be saved.

(c) Silence in the Land of Western Hemisphere

After the voice ceases, there is a silence in the land for many hours, the astonishment of the people being so great that they cease their lamentations.

3 Nephi 10:1-2.

3 NEPHI 10:1. And now behold, it came to pass that all the people of the land did hear these sayings, and did witness of it. And after these sayings there was silence in the land for the space of many hours;

2. For so great was the astonishment of the people that they did cease lamenting and howling for the loss of their kindred which had been slain; therefore there was silence in all the land for the space of many hours.

(d) In Western Hemisphere, Again a Voice From Heaven

Then a voice from heaven comes again to the people, speaking to them as descendants of Jaçob, and so of the house of Israel; the voice tells how often the speaker would have gathered and blessed Israel if they had listened and declared their desolation, "until the time of the fulfilling of the covenant to your fathers"; after they heard these words, they begin anew their lamentations for the loss of their kindred and friends.

3 Nephi 10:3-8.

3 NEPHI 10:3. And it came to pass that there came a voice again unto the people, and all the people did hear, and did witness of it, saying:

4. O ye people of these great cities which have fallen, who are descendants of Jacob, yea, who are of the house of Israel, how oft have I gathered you as a hen gathereth her chickens under her wings, and have nourished you.

5. And again, how oft would I have gathered you as a hen gathereth her chickens under her wings, yea, O ye people of the house of Israel, who have fallen; yea, O ye people of the house of Israel, ye that dwell at Jerusalem, as ye that have fallen; yea, how oft would I have gathered you as a hen gathereth her chickens, and ye would not.

6. O ye house of Israel whom I have spared, how oft will I gather you as a hen gathereth her chickens under her wings, if ye will repent and return unto me with full purpose of heart.

7. But if not, O house of Israel, the places of your dwellings shall become desolate until the time of the fulfilling of the covenant to your fathers.

8. And now it came to pass that after the people had heard these words, behold, they began to weep and howl again because of the loss of their kindred and friends.

First Day of the Week

Section 167

THE RESURRECTION; JERUSALEM AND VICINITY, AND WESTERN HEMISPHERE

Time: A.D. 30, Sunday, April 9; 17th Nisan.
Place: Jerusalem and Vicinity, and Western Hemisphere.

(a) An Angel Opens the Tomb

There is a great earthquake; an angel of the Lord comes down and rolls back the stone from the door and sits upon it; "his countenance was like lightning, and his raiment white as snow"; the keepers of the tomb are smitten and become as dead men.

Matt. 28:2-4; Mark: No record; Luke: No record; John: No record.

MATTHEW 28:2. And, behold, there was a great earthquake: for the angel of the Lord descended from heaven, and came and rolled back the stone from the door, and sat upon it.

3. His countenance was like lightning, and his raiment white as snow:

4. And for fear of him the keepers did shake, and became as dead *men*.

Mark: No record.

Luke: No record.

John: No record.

(b) In Western Hemisphere, Darkness Disappears and Earth Restored

On the morning of the third day darkness disperses off the face of the land, "the earth did cleave together again, that it stood"; the people cease their mournings and become joyful, and give thanks unto Jesus Christ, their Redeemer; the more righteous part of the people have been saved during the great convulsions; the prophets had declared it all beforehand—Zenos and Jacob.

3 Nephi 10:9-17.

3 NEPHI 10:9. And it came to pass that thus did the three days pass away. And it was in the morning, and the darkness dispersed from off the face of the land, and the earth did cease to tremble, and the rocks did cease to rend, and the dreadful groanings did cease, and all the tumultuous noises did pass away.

10. And the earth did cleave together again, that it stood; and the mourning, and the weeping, and the wailing of the people who were spared alive did cease; and their mourning was turned into joy, and their lamentations into the praise and thanksgiving unto the Lord Jesus Christ, their Redeemer.

11. And thus far were the scriptures fulfilled which had been spoken by the prophets.

12. And it was the more righteous part of the people who were saved, and it was they who received the prophets and stoned them not; and it was they who had not shed the blood of the saints, who were spared—

13. And they were spared and were not sunk and buried up in the earth; and they were not drowned in the depths of the sea; and they were not burned by fire, neither were they fallen upon and crushed to death; and they were not carried away in the whirlwind; neither were they overpowered by the vapor of smoke and of darkness.

14. And now, whoso readeth, let him understand; he that hath the scriptures, let him search them, and see and behold if all these deaths and

destructions by fire, and by smoke, and by tempests, and by whirlwinds, and by the opening of the earth to receive them, and all these things are not unto the fulfilling of the prophecies of many of the holy prophets.

15. Behold, I say unto you, Yea, many have testified of these things at the coming of Christ, and were slain because they testified of these things.

16. Yea, the prophet Zenos did testify of these things, and also Zenock spake concerning these things, because they testified particularly concerning us, who are the remnant of their seed.

17. Behold, our father Jacob also testified concerning a remnant of the seed of Joseph. And behold, are not we a remnant of the seed of Joseph? And these things which testify of us, are they not written upon the plates of brass which our father Lehi brought out of Jerusalem?

(c) Mary Magdalene First to the Tomb

On Sunday morning, while it is yet dark, Mary Magdalene comes to the sepulchre and sees the stone taken away.

Matt.: No record; Mark 16:9; Luke: No record; John 20:1.

Matthew: No record.

MARK 16:9. ¶ Now when *Jesus* was risen early the first *day* of the week, he appeared first to Mary Magdalene, out of whom he had cast seven devils.

Luke: No record.

JOHN 20:1. The first *day* of the week cometh Mary Magdalene early, when it was yet dark, unto the sepulchre, and seeth the stone taken away from the sepulchre.

(d) Mary Tells Peter and John

She at once runs to Peter and John, says they have taken the Lord away, "and we know not where they have laid him"; Peter and John run to the sepulchre, John outrunning Peter and arriving first, stoops down and looking in sees the linen clothes lying, but does not go in.

Matt.: No record; Mark: No record; Luke: No record; John 20:2-5.

Matthew: No record.

Mark: No record.

Luke: No record.

JOHN 20:2. Then she runneth, and cometh to Simon Peter, and to the other disciple, whom Jesus loved, and saith unto them, They have taken away the Lord out of the sepulchre, and we know not where they have laid him.

3. Peter therefore went forth, and that other disciple, and came to the sepulchre.

4. So they ran both together: and the other disciple did outrun Peter, and came first to the sepulchre.

5. And he stooping down, *and looking in*, saw the linen clothes lying; yet went he not in.

(e) Peter and John Visit Tomb

Peter arriving, he goes into the sepulchre and sees the grave clothes lying about; John then goes in, who "saw, and believed. For as yet they knew not the scripture, that he must rise again from the dead"; they come out of the sepulchre and go away again to their own home, wondering.

Matt.: No record; Mark: No record; Luke 24:12; John 20:6-10.

Matthew: No record.

Mark: No record.

LUKE 24:12. Then arose Peter, and ran unto the sepulchre; and stooping down, he beheld the linen clothes laid by themselves, and departed, wondering in himself at that which was come to pass.

JOHN 20:6. Then cometh Simon Peter following him, and went into the sepulchre, and seeth the linen clothes lie,

7. And the napkin, that was about his head, not lying with the linen clothes, but wrapped together in a place by itself.

8. Then went in also that other disciple, which came first to the sepulchre, and he saw, and believed.

9. For as yet they knew not the scripture, that he must rise again from the dead.

10. Then the disciples went away again unto their own home.

(f) Jesus Appears to Mary

Mary standing outside the sepulchre, stoops down, looks into the sepulchre, and sees two angels, one sitting at the head and the other at the foot; they ask why she weeps, she says they have taken her Lord away and she does not know where they have laid him; turning back she sees Jesus standing beside her; she does not know him; he asks why she weeps and whom she seeks; she, thinking it is the gardener, says if he has borne her Lord away, tell her where he has laid him and she will take him away; Jesus says, "Mary," she then knows who he is, and would have touched him; but he forbids her, for he has not yet ascended.

Matt.: No record; Mark: No record; Luke: No record; John 20:11-17.

Matthew: No record.
Mark: No record.
Luke: No record.
JOHN 20:11. ¶ But Mary stood without at the sepulchre weeping: and as she wept, she stooped down, *and looked* into the sepulchre,

12. And seeth two angels in white sitting, the one at the head, and the other at the feet, where the body of Jesus had lain.

13. And they say unto her, Woman, why weepest thou? She saith unto them, Because they have taken away my Lord, and I know not where they have laid him.

14. And when she had thus said, she turned herself back, and saw Jesus standing, and knew not that it was Jesus.

15. Jesus saith unto her, Woman, why weepest thou? whom seekest thou? She, supposing him to be the gardener, saith unto him, Sir, if thou have borne him hence, tell me where thou hast laid him, and I will take him away.

16. Jesus saith unto her, Mary. She turned herself, and saith unto him, Rabboni; which is to say, Master.

17. Jesus saith unto her, Touch me not; for I am not yet ascended to my Father: but go to my brethren, and say unto them, I ascend unto my Father, and your Father; and *to* my God, and your God.

(g) Mary Tells Disciples

Mary Magdalene goes and tells the disciples of seeing the Lord and of his words; and they believe her not.

Matt.: No record; Mark 16:10-11; Luke: No record; John 20:18.

Matthew: No record.

MARK 16:10. *And* she went and told them that had been with him, as they mourned and wept.

11. And they, when they had heard that he was alive, and had been seen of her, believed not.

Luke: No record.

JOHN 20:18. Mary Magdalene came and told the disciples that she had seen the Lord, and *that* he had spoken these things unto her.

(h) Other Women Come to the Tomb

Mary the mother of James, and Salome, and Mary Magdalene, and other women come early to the tomb, bringing sweet spices that they may anoint Jesus; they say among themselves who shall roll the stone away from the door of the sepulchre; they find the stone rolled away; they enter but the body of Jesus is not there; as they stand perplexed, two angels are before them; one tells them not to fear, that Jesus whom they seek has risen, as he said, and he asks them to look where the Lord had lain; he tells them to go quickly and tell the disciples, and that Jesus will go before them to Galilee, where they shall see him.

Matt. 28:1, 5-7; Mark 16:1-7; Luke 24:1-8; John: No record.

MATTHEW 28:1. In the end of the sabbath, as it began to dawn toward the first *day* of the week, came Mary Magdalene and the other Mary to see the sepulchre . . . .

5. And the angel answered and said unto the women, Fear not ye: for I know that ye seek Jesus, which was crucified.

6. He is not here: for he is risen, as he said. Come, see the place where the Lord lay.

7. And go quickly, and tell his disciples that he is risen from the dead; and, behold, he goeth before you into Galilee; there shall ye see him: lo, I have told you.

MARK 16:1. And when the sabbath was past, Mary Magdalene, and Mary the *mother* of James, and Salome, had bought sweet spices, that they might come and anoint him.

2. And very early in the morning the first *day* of the week, they came unto the sepulchre at the rising of the sun.

3. And they said among themselves, Who shall roll us away the stone from the door of the sepulchre?

4. And when they looked, they saw that the stone was rolled away: for it was very great.

5. And entering into the sepulchre, they saw a young man sitting on the right side, clothed in a long white garment; and they were affrighted.

6. And he saith unto them, Be not affrighted: Ye seek Jesus of Nazareth, which was crucified: he is risen; he is not here: behold the place where they laid him.

7. But go your way, tell his disciples and Peter that he goeth before you into Galilee: there shall ye see him, as he said unto you.

LUKE 24:1. Now upon the first *day* of the week, very early in the morning, they came unto the sepulchre, bringing the spices which they had prepared, and certain *others* with them.

2. And they found the stone rolled away from the sepulchre.

3. And they entered in, and found not the body of the Lord Jesus.

4. And it came to pass, as they were much perplexed thereabout, behold, two men stood by them in shining garments:

5. And as they were afraid, and bowed down *their* faces to the earth, they said unto them, Why seek ye the living among the dead?

6. He is not here, but is risen: remember how he spake unto you when he was yet in Galilee,

7. Saying, The Son of man must be delivered into the hands of sinful men, and be crucified, and the third day rise again.

8. And they remembered his words, . . .

John: No record.

(i) Christ Appears to the Women

The women go on their way to tell the disciples; Jesus meets them; they come and hold him by the feet and worship him; he tells them not to fear, but to tell "my brethren" that they shall go unto Galilee where he will see them.

Matt. 28:9-10; Mark: No record; Luke: No record; John: No record.

MATTHEW 28:9. ¶ And as they went to tell his disciples, behold, Jesus met them, saying, All hail. And they came and held him by the feet, and worshipped him.

10. Then said Jesus unto them, Be not afraid: go tell my brethren that they go into Galilee, and there shall they see me.

Mark: No record.

Luke: No record.

John: No record.

(j) The Other Women Tell Disciples

The women depart from the sepulchre and having seen Jesus on their way "with fear and great joy" they run to the Eleven and tell all these things; "and their words seemed to them as idle tales, and they believed them not."

Matt. 28:8; Mark 16:8; Luke 24:9-11; John: No record.

MATTHEW 28:8. And they departed quickly from the sepulchre with fear and great joy; and did run to bring his disciples word.

MARK 16:8. And they went out quickly, and fled from the sepulchre; for they trembled and were amazed: neither said they any thing to any *man*; for they were afraid.

LUKE 24:9. And returned from the sepulchre, and told all these things unto the eleven, and to all the rest.

10. It was Mary Magdalene, and Joanna, and Mary *the mother* of James, and other *women that were* with them, which told these things unto the apostles.

11. And their words seemed to them as idle tales, and they believed them not.

John: No record.

(k) Chief Priests Told of Resurrection

While the women were going to tell the disciples of the resurrection, some of the watch go to the city and tell the chief priests all the things that are done; when the elders assemble they give large sums of money to the watch to say that the disciples came by night and stole Jesus; the elders promise that if it comes to the governor's ears "we will persuade him, and secure you"; the soldiers take the money and do as they are taught; "and this saying is commonly reported among the Jews until this day."

Matt. 28:11-15; Mark: No record; Luke: No record; John: No record.

MATTHEW 28:11. ¶ Now when they were going, behold, some of the watch came into the city, and shewed unto the chief priests all the things that were done.

12. And when they were assembled with the elders, and had taken counsel, they gave large money unto the soldiers,

13. Saying, Say ye, His disciples came by night, and stole him *away* while we slept.

14. And if this come to the governor's ears, we will persuade him, and secure you.

15. So they took the money, and did as they were taught: and this saying is commonly reported among the Jews until this day.

Mark: No record.

Luke: No record.

John: No record.

(l) He Appears to Two Disciples On the Road to Emmaus

Two disciples on their way to Emmaus, talking together about events, are overtaken by Jesus, but "their eyes were holden" and they know him not; he asks what they were talking about; one of them, Cleopas, tells Jesus about the happenings; Jesus then upbraids them for not understanding, and, beginning at Moses, goes over the prophecies concerning himself; coming near the village where they are to stop, they urge him to stay with them; when he sits at meat he takes bread and blesses it and breaks and gives to them; their eyes are opened; he vanishes from their sight; they then remember how their hearts burned while he talked with them on the way.

Matt.: No record; Mark 16:12-13; Luke 24:13-32; John: No record.

Matthew: No record.

MARK 16:12. ¶ After that he appeared in another form unto two of them, as they walked, and went into the country.

13. And they went and told *it* unto the residue: neither believed they them.

LUKE 24:13. ¶ And, behold, two of them went that same day to a village called Emmaus, which was from Jerusalem *about* threescore furlongs.

14. And they talked together of all these things which had happened.

15. And it came to pass, that, while they communed *together* and reasoned, Jesus himself drew near, and went with them.

16. But their eyes were holden that they should not know him.

17. And he said unto them, What manner of communications *are* these that ye have one to another, as ye walk, and are sad?

18. And the one of them, whose name was Cleopas, answering said unto him, Art thou only a stranger in Jeru-

salem, and hast not known the things which are come to pass there in these days?
19. And he said unto them, What things? And they said unto him, Concerning Jesus of Nazareth, which was a prophet mighty in deed and word before God and all the people:
20. And how the chief priests and our rulers delivered him to be condemned to death, and have crucified him.
21. But we trusted that it had been he which should have redeemed Israel: and beside all this, to day is the third day since these things were done.
22. Yea, and certain women also of our company made us astonished, which were early at the sepulchre;
23. And when they found not his body, they came, saying, that they had also seen a vision of angels, which said that he was alive.
24. And certain of them which were with us went to the sepulchre, and found *it* even so as the women had said: but him they saw not.
25. Then he said unto them, O fools, and slow of heart to believe all that the prophets have spoken:
26. Ought not Christ to have suffered these things, and to enter into his glory?
27. And beginning at Moses and all the prophets, he expounded unto them in all the scriptures the things concerning himself.
28. And they drew nigh unto the village, whither they went: and he made as though he would have gone further.
29. But they constrained him, saying, Abide with us: for it is toward evening, and the day is far spent. And he went in to tarry with them.
30. And it came to pass, as he sat at meat with them, he took bread, and blessed *it*, and brake, and gave to them.
31. And their eyes were opened, and they knew him; and he vanished out of their sight.
32. And they said one to another, Did not our heart burn within us, while he talked with us by the way, and while he opened to us the scriptures?

John: No record.

(m) Jesus Appears Unto Peter

Matt.: No record; Mark: No record; Luke 24:34; John: No record; 1 Cor. 15:5a.

Matthew: No record.

Mark: No record.

LUKE 24:34. Saying, The Lord is risen indeed, and hath appeared to Simon.

John: No record.

I COR. 15:5. And that he was seen of Cephas . . . .

(n) He Appears to All Disciples Except Thomas

The two return from Emmaus, and meet with the Eleven (Thomas absent), gathered together, the doors shut for fear of the Jews; the two from Emmaus are telling their experience when Jesus stands in their midst, saying: "Peace be unto you"; they are terrified, thinking he is a spirit, he shows his hands and feet; he breathes on them and says, "Receive ye the Holy Ghost"; then asks for something to eat, and he eats fish and honeycomb; he then again goes over the scriptures, and their understandings are opened; he explains somewhat the atonement; tells them what they must preach, and directs them to tarry in Jerusalem till "ye be endued with power from on high."

Matt.: No record; Mark 16:14; Luke 24:33-49; John 20:19-23.

Matthew: No record.

MARK 16:14. ¶ Afterward he appeared unto the eleven as they sat at meat, and upbraided them with their unbelief and hardness of heart, because they believed not them which had seen him after he was risen.

LUKE 24:33. And they rose up the same hour, and returned to Jerusalem, and found the eleven gathered together, and them that were with them,

34. Saying, The Lord is risen indeed, and hath appeared to Simon.

35. And they told what things *were done* in the way, and how he was known of them in breaking of bread.

36. ¶ And as they thus spake, Jesus himself stood in the midst of them, and saith unto them, Peace *be* unto you.

37. But they were terrified and affrighted, and supposed that they had seen a spirit.

38. And he said unto them, Why are ye troubled? and why do thoughts arise in your hearts?

39. Behold my hands and my feet, that it is I myself: handle me, and see; for a spirit hath not flesh and bones, as ye see me have.

40. And when he had thus spoken, he shewed them *his* hands and *his* feet.

41. And while they yet believed not for joy, and wondered, he said unto them, Have ye here any meat?

42. And they gave him a piece of a broiled fish, and of an honeycomb.

43. And he took *it*, and did eat before them.

44. And he said unto them, These *are* the words which I spake unto you, while I was yet with you, that all things must be fulfilled, which were written in the law of Moses, and *in* the prophets, and *in* the psalms, concerning me.

45. Then opened he their understanding, that they might understand the scriptures,

46. And said unto them,

Thus it is written, and thus it behoved Christ to suffer, and to rise from the dead the third day:

47. And that repentance and remission of sins should be preached in his name among all nations, beginning at Jerusalem.

48. And ye are witnesses of these things.

49. ¶ And, behold, I send the promise of my Father upon you: but tarry ye in the city of Jerusalem, until ye be endued with power from on high.

JOHN 20:19. ¶ Then the same day at evening, being the first *day* of the week, when the doors were shut where the disciples were assembled for fear of the Jews, came Jesus and stood in the midst, and saith unto them, Peace *be* unto you.

20. And when he had so said, he shewed unto them *his* hands and his side. Then were the disciples glad, when they saw the Lord.

21. Then said Jesus to them again, Peace *be* unto you: as *my* Father hath sent me, even so send I you.

22. And when he had said this, he breathed on *them*, and saith unto them, Receive ye the Holy Ghost:

23. Whose soever sins ye remit, they are remitted unto them; *and* whose soever *sins* ye retain, they are retained.

Section 168

APPEARANCES SUBSEQUENT TO THOSE OF THE FIRST DAY OF THE WEEK

Time: A.D. 30, April-May.
Place: Jerusalem, Galilee.

(a) He Appears to Disciples, Including Thomas

Thomas, called Didymus, not with the Apostles on the Sunday when Jesus appeared, refuses to believe their testimony and says he must himself see and feel the body of Jesus; eight days later the disciples are all together again; again the doors are shut; Jesus again stands in their midst, saying, "Peace be unto you"; he asks Thomas to verify his identity by touching him; Thomas answers, "My Lord and my God"; Jesus says, "Thomas, because thou hast seen me, thou hast believed: blessed are they that have not seen, and yet have believed."

Matt.: No record; Mark: No record; Luke: No record; John 20:24-29.

Matthew: No record.
Mark: No record.
Luke: No record.
JOHN 20:24. ¶ But Thomas, one of the twelve, called Didymus, was not with them when Jesus came.

25. The other disciples therefore said unto him, We have seen the Lord. But he

said unto them, Except I shall see in his hands the print of the nails, and put my finger into the print of the nails, and thrust my hand into his side, I will not believe.

26. ¶ And after eight days again his disciples were within, and Thomas with them: *then* came Jesus, the doors being shut, and stood in the midst, and said, Peace *be* unto you.

27. Then saith he to Thomas, Reach hither thy finger, and behold my hands; and reach hither thy hand, and thrust *it* into my side: and be not faithless, but believing.

28. And Thomas answered and said unto him, My Lord and my God.

29. Jesus saith unto him, Thomas, because thou hast seen me, thou hast believed: blessed *are* they that have not seen, and *yet* have believed.

(b) He Appears to Disciples at Sea of Tiberias

Seven disciples are at the Sea of Tiberias; Peter takes them fishing; they fish all night and catch nothing; the next morning Jesus (unknown to them) stands on the shore and asks if they have any meat; they answer no; he tells them to cast their net on the right side of the ship; they do so, and are not able to draw for the multitude of fishes; John says to Peter, "It is the Lord"; Peter throws himself into the sea, and the others come in the little ship; when they come to land, they see a fire of coals with fish laid thereon and bread; Jesus tells them to bring of the fish they have caught; Peter draws the net to land full of great fishes, yet the net is not broken; Jesus asks them to come and eat; none durst ask him, "Who art thou? knowing that it was the Lord"; this is the third time he has shown himself to his disciples after he was risen from the dead.

Matt.: No record; Mark: No record; Luke: No record; John 21:1-14.

Matthew: No record.

Mark: No record.

Luke: No record.

JOHN 21:1. After these things Jesus shewed himself again to the disciples at the sea of Tiberias; and on this wise shewed he *himself*.

2. There were together Simon Peter, and Thomas called Didymus, and Nathanael of Cana in Galilee, and the *sons* of Zebedee, and two other of his disciples.

3. Simon Peter saith unto them, I go a fishing. They say unto him, We also go with thee. They went forth, and entered into a ship immediately; and that night they caught nothing.

4. But when the morning was now come, Jesus stood on the shore: but the disciples knew not that it was Jesus.

5. Then Jesus saith unto them, Children, have ye any meat? They answered him, No.

6. And he said unto them, Cast the net on the right side of the ship, and ye shall find. They cast therefore, and now they were not able to draw it for the multitude of fishes.

7. Therefore that disciple whom Jesus loved saith unto Peter, It is the Lord. Now when Simon Peter heard that it was the Lord, he girt *his* fisher's coat *unto him*, (for he was naked,) and did cast himself into the sea.

8. And the other disciples came in a little ship; (for they were not far from land, but as it were two hundred cubits,) dragging the net with fishes.

9. As soon then as they were come to land, they saw a fire of coals there, and fish laid thereon, and bread.

10. Jesus saith unto them, Bring of the fish which ye have now caught.

11. Simon Peter went up, and drew the net to land full of great fishes, an hundred and fifty and three: and for all there were so many, yet was not the net broken.

12. Jesus saith unto them, Come *and* dine. And none of the disciples durst ask him, Who art thou? knowing that it was the Lord.

13. Jesus then cometh, and taketh bread, and giveth them, and fish likewise.

14. This is now the third time that Jesus shewed himself to his disciples, after that he was risen from the dead.

(c) Jesus Asks If Peter Loves Him

Jesus questions Peter—whether Peter loves him; the thrice repeated question and thrice repeated command, "Feed my sheep"; Jesus foretells the manner of Peter's death.

Matt.: No record; Mark: No record; Luke: No record; John 21:15-19.

Matthew: No record.

Mark: No record.

Luke: No record.

JOHN 21:15. ¶ So when they had dined, Jesus saith to Simon Peter, Simon, *son* of Jonas, lovest thou me more than these? He saith unto him, Yea, Lord; thou knowest that I love thee. He saith unto him, Feed my lambs.

16. He saith to him again the second time, Simon, *son* of Jonas, lovest thou me? He saith unto him, Yea, Lord; thou knowest that I love thee. He saith unto him, Feed my sheep.

17. He saith unto him the third time, Simon, *son* of Jonas, lovest thou me? Peter was grieved because he said unto him the third time, Lovest thou me? And he said unto him, Lord, thou knowest all things; thou knowest that I

love thee. Jesus saith unto him, Feed my sheep.

18. Verily, verily, I say unto thee, When thou wast young, thou girdedst thyself, and walkedst whither thou wouldest: but when thou shalt be old, thou shalt stretch forth thy hands, and another shall gird thee, and carry *thee* whither thou wouldest not.

19. This spake he, signifying by what death he should glorify God. And when he had spoken this, he saith unto him, Follow me.

(d) Peter Asks About John

Peter sees John following and asks, "Lord, and what shall this man do?" Jesus saith, "If I will that he tarry till I come, what is that to thee? follow thou me"; from which comes the saying abroad that John should not die; but Jesus did not say this but only, "If I will that he tarry till I come, what is that to thee?"

Matt.: No record; Mark: No record; Luke: No record; John 21:20-23.

Matthew: No record.

Mark: No record.

Luke: No record.

JOHN 21:20. Then Peter, turning about, seeth the disciple whom Jesus loved following; which also leaned on his breast at supper, and said, Lord, which is he that betrayeth thee ?

21. Peter seeing him saith to Jesus, Lord, and what *shall* this man *do?*

22. Jesus saith unto him, If I will that he tarry till I come, what *is that* to thee? follow thou me.

23. Then went this saying abroad among the brethren, that that disciple should not die: yet Jesus said not unto him, He shall not die; but, If I will that he tarry till I come, what *is that* to thee?

(e) Jesus Appears to a Great Multitude, "Above Five Hundred"

Matt.: No record; Mark: No record; Luke: No record; John: No record; 1 Cor. 15:6.

I COR. 15:6. After that, he was seen of above five hundred brethren at once; of whom the greater part remain unto this present, but some are fallen asleep.

(f) Jesus Appears to James

Matt.: No record; Mark: No record; Luke: No record; John: No record; 1 Cor. 15:7a.

I COR. 15:7. After that, he was seen of James . . . .

(g) He Appears to Disciples in Galilee

The eleven disciples go into Galilee, into a mountain where Jesus had appointed them. Here Jesus gives them their final charge. (Luke records in Acts 1:1-8 some matters covered by this charge.)

Matt. 28:16-20; Mark 16:15-18; Luke: No record; John: No record; Acts 1:1-8.

MATTHEW 28:16. ¶ Then the eleven disciples went away into Galilee, into a mountain where Jesus had appointed them.

17. And when they saw him, they worshipped him: but some doubted.

18. And Jesus came and spake unto them, saying, All power is given unto me in heaven and in earth.

19. ¶ Go ye therefore, and teach all nations, baptizing them in the name of the Father, and of the Son, and of the Holy Ghost:

20. Teaching them to observe all things whatsoever I have commanded you: and, lo, I am with you alway, *even* unto the end of the world. Amen.

MARK 16:15. And he said unto them, Go ye into all the world, and preach the gospel to every creature.

16. He that believeth and is baptized shall be saved; but he that believeth not shall be damned.

17. And these signs shall follow them that believe; In my name shall they cast out devils; they shall speak with new tongues;

18. They shall take up serpents; and if they drink any deadly thing, it shall not hurt them; they shall lay hands on the sick, and they shall recover.

Luke: No record.

John: No record.

ACTS 1:1. The former treatise have I made, O Theophilus, of all that Jesus began both to do and teach,

2. Until the day in which he was taken up, after that he through the Holy Ghost had given commandments unto the apostles whom he had chosen:

3. To whom also he shewed himself alive after his passion by many infallible proofs, being seen of them forty days, and speaking of the things pertaining to the kingdom of God:

4. And, being assembled together with *them*, commanded them that they should not depart from Jerusalem, but wait for the promise of the Father, which, *saith he*, ye have heard of me.

5. For John truly baptized with water; but ye shall be baptized with the Holy Ghost not many days hence.

6. When they therefore were come together, they asked of him, saying, Lord, wilt thou at this time restore again the kingdom to Israel?

7. And he said unto them, It is not for you to know the times

or the seasons, which the Father hath put in his own power.

8. But ye shall receive power, after that the Holy Ghost is come upon you: and ye shall be witnesses unto me both in Jerusalem, and in all Judæa, and in Samaria, and unto the uttermost part of the earth.

Section 169

THE ASCENSION

Taking his disciples to Bethany, he lifts his hands and blesses them, and while he yet blesses them, he is parted from them, and ascends into heaven, a cloud receiving him out of their sight, to be received and sit on the right hand of God; Luke records in Acts that while the disciples stood looking towards heaven, two men stood by them in white apparel, asked why they so looked, and said that Jesus would return as he had gone.

Matt.: No record; Mark 16:19; Luke 24:50-51; John: No record; Acts 1:9-11.

Time: A.D. 30, Thursday, May 18 (ANDREWS).

Place: Bethany.

Matthew: No record.

MARK 16:19. ¶ So then after the Lord had spoken unto them, he was received up into heaven, and sat on the right hand of God.

LUKE 24:50. ¶ And he led them out as far as to Bethany, and he lifted up his hands, and blessed them.

51. And it came to pass, while he blessed them, he was parted from them, and carried up into heaven.

John: No record.

ACTS 1:9. And when he had spoken these things, while they beheld, he was taken up; and a cloud received him out of their sight.

10. And while they looked stedfastly toward heaven as he went up, behold, two men stood by them in white apparel;

11. Which also said, Ye men of Galilee, why stand ye gazing up into heaven? this same Jesus, which is taken up from you into heaven, shall so come in like manner as ye have seen him go into heaven.

Section 170

THE DISCIPLES RETURN TO JERUSALEM

They worship and return to Jerusalem, where in an upper room the Eleven with "Mary the mother of Jesus, and with his brethren," continue prayer and supplication, worshipping; they are in the Temple continually, praising and blessing God; they go forth preaching everywhere, the Lord working with them, and confirming the word with signs following; "the number of names together were about an hundred and twenty."

Matt.: No record; Mark 16:20; Luke 24:52-53; John: No record; Acts 1:12-15.
Time: A.D. 30.
Place: Bethany to Jerusalem.

Matthew: No record.

MARK 16:20. And they went forth, and preached every where, the Lord working with *them*, and confirming the word with signs following. Amen.

LUKE 24:52. And they worshipped him, and returned to Jerusalem with great joy:

53. And were continually in the temple, praising and blessing God. Amen.

John: No record.

ACTS 1:12. Then returned they unto Jerusalem from the mount called Olivet, which is from Jerusalem a sabbath day's journey.

13. And when they were come in, they went up into an upper room, where abode both Peter, and James, and John, and Andrew, Philip, and Thomas, Bartholomew, and Matthew, James *the son* of Alphæus, and Simon Zelotes, and Judas *the brother* of James.

14. These all continued with one accord in prayer and supplication, with the women, and Mary the mother of Jesus, and with his brethren.

15. ¶ And in those days Peter stood up in the midst of the disciples, and said, (the number of names together were about an hundred and twenty,) . .

Section 171
JOHN'S CONCLUDING WORDS

Matt.: No record; Mark: No record; Luke: No record; John 20:30-31; 21: 24-25.

Matthew: No record.
Mark: No record.
Luke: No record.

JOHN 20:30. ¶ And many other signs truly did Jesus in the presence of his disciples, which are not written in this book:

31. But these are written, that ye might believe that Jesus is the Christ, the Son of God; and that believing ye might have life through his name. . . .

21:24. This is the disciple which testifieth of these things, and wrote these things: and we know that his testimony is true.

25. And there are also many other things which Jesus did, the which, if they should be written every one, I suppose that even the world itself could not contain the books that should be written. Amen.

EIGHTH PERIOD

THE BENEDICTION UPON OUR LORD'S MINISTRY—HIS VISIT TO THE WESTERN HEMISPHERE AFTER HIS ASCENSION IN PALESTINE—BOOK OF MORMON

Section 172

THE LORD FORETELLS HIS APPEARANCE ON WESTERN HEMISPHERE

Through his prophets (Zenos, Jacob, and others) of the Western Hemisphere, the Lord foretold his appearance on the Western Hemisphere after his life in Palestine and his ascension at Bethany.

3 Nephi 10:18-19.

Time: 125th-126th year of the Reign of the Judges.

3 NEPHI 10:18. And it came to pass that in the ending of the thirty and fourth year, behold, I will show unto you that the people of Nephi who were spared, and also those who had been called Lamanites, who had been spared, did have great favors shown unto them, and great blessings poured out upon their heads, insomuch that soon after the ascension of Christ into heaven he did truly manifest himself unto them—

19. Showing his body unto them, and ministering unto them; and an account of his ministry shall be given hereafter. Therefore for this time I make an end of my sayings.

Section 173

A VOICE OUT OF HEAVEN

A small piercing voice comes out of heaven to the great multitude gathered round about the Temple in the land Bountiful, "and they were marveling and wondering one with another, and were showing one to another the great and marvelous change which had taken place"; they are conversing about Jesus, when they hear a voice as if coming out of heaven, not a harsh voice, nor a loud one, but a small voice that pierces them to their centers and causes their frames to quake.

(a) The First Voice Not Understood

3 Nephi 11:1-3.

3 NEPHI 11:1. And now it came to pass that there were a great multitude gathered together, of the people of Nephi, round about the temple which was in the land Bountiful; and they were marveling and wondering one with another, and were showing one to another the great and marvelous change which had taken place.

2. And they were also conversing about this Jesus Christ, of whom the sign had been given concerning his death.

3. And it came to pass that while they were thus conversing one with another, they heard a voice as if it came out of heaven; and they cast their eyes round about, for they understood not the voice which they heard; and it was not a harsh voice, neither was it a loud voice; nevertheless, and notwithstanding it being a small voice it did pierce them that did hear to the center, insomuch that there was no part of their frame that it did not cause to quake; yea, it did pierce them to the very soul, and did cause their hearts to burn.

(b) The Voice Comes the Second Time, Still Not Understood

3 Nephi 11:4.

3 NEPHI 11:4. And it came to pass that again they heard the voice, and they understood it not.

(c) The Voice Comes a Third Time

The voice is now understood—it is the Father introducing the Son.

3 Nephi 11:5-7.

3 NEPHI 11:5. And again the third time they did hear the voice, and did open their ears to hear it; and their eyes were towards the sound thereof; and they did look steadfastly towards heaven, from whence the sound came.

6. And behold, the third time they did understand the voice which they heard; and it said unto them:

7. Behold my Beloved Son, in whom I am well pleased, in whom I have glorified my name—hear ye him.

Section 174

THE MULTITUDE SEE JESUS DESCENDING

The multitude looking towards heaven, see Jesus descending; they watch in silence; they think him an angel; he comes down and stands in their midst.

3 Nephi 11:8-9.

3 NEPHI 11:8. And it came to pass, as they understood they cast their eyes up again towards heaven; and behold, they saw a Man descending out of heaven; and he was clothed in a white robe; and he came down and stood in the midst of them; and the eyes of the whole multitude were turned upon him, and they durst not open their mouths, even one to another, and wist not what it meant, for they thought it was an angel that had appeared unto them.

9. And it came to pass that he stretched forth his hand and spake unto the people, saying: . . .

Section 175

HE BEGINS HIS MISSION

Jesus beginning his mission, declares who he is, and speaks of his atonement; the multitude fall to the ground, remembering what had been prophesied of the coming of the Christ among them.

3 Nephi 11:10-12.

3 NEPHI 11:10. Behold, I am Jesus Christ, whom the prophets testified shall come into the world.

11. And behold, I am the light and the life of the world; and I have drunk out of that bitter cup which the Father hath given me, and have glorified the Father in taking upon me the sins of the world, in the which I have suffered the will of the Father in all things from the beginning.

12. And it came to pass that when Jesus had spoken these words the whole multitude fell to the earth; for they remembered that it had been prophesied among them that Christ should show himself unto them after his ascension into heaven.

Section 176

THE GREAT OPENING DAY OF CHRIST'S MINISTRY UPON THE WESTERN HEMISPHERE

(a) He Invites Multitude to Handle His Body

Jesus asks the multitude to come forward and handle his body that they may know he is who he claims to be.

3 Nephi 11:13-15.

3 NEPHI 11:13. And it came to pass that the Lord spake unto them saying:

14. Arise and come forth unto me, that ye may thrust your hands into my side, and

also that ye may feel the prints of the nails in my hands and in my feet, that ye may know that I am the God of Israel, and the God of the whole earth, and have been slain for the sins of the world.

15. And it came to pass that the multitude went forth, and thrust their hands into his side, and did feel the prints of the nails in his hands and in his feet; and this they did do, going forth one by one until they had all gone forth, and did see with their eyes and did feel with their hands, and did know of a surety and did bear record, that it was he, of whom it was written by the prophets, that should come.

(b) The People Convinced

The people come forth and test Jesus by their hands, and break forth into hosannas.

3 Nephi 11:16-17.

3 NEPHI 11:16. And when they had all gone forth and had witnessed for themselves, they did cry out with one accord, saying:

17. Hosanna! Blessed be the name of the Most High God! And they did fall down at the feet of Jesus, and did worship him.

(c) Nephi Called Forth, and Others

Jesus first calls forth Nephi, charges him and gives him power; he calls others and makes a like bestowal; instructs them in the manner of baptism; tells them of the relationship of the Trinity.

3 Nephi 11:18-27.

3 NEPHI 11:18. And it came to pass that he spake unto Nephi (for Nephi was among the multitude) and he commanded him that he should come forth.

19. And Nephi arose and went forth, and bowed himself before the Lord and did kiss his feet.

20. And the Lord commanded him that he should arise. And he arose and stood before him.

21. And the Lord said unto him: I give unto you power that ye shall baptize this people when I am again ascended into heaven.

22. And again the Lord called others, and said unto them likewise; and he gave unto them power to baptize. And he said unto them: On this wise shall ye baptize; and there shall be no disputations among you.

23. Verily I say unto you, that whoso repenteth of his sins through your words, and desireth to be baptized in my

name, on this wise shall ye baptize them—Behold, ye shall go down and stand in the water, and in my name shall ye baptize them.

24. And now behold, these are the words which ye shall say, calling them by name, saying:

25. Having authority given me of Jesus Christ, I baptize you in the name of the Father, and of the Son, and of the Holy Ghost. Amen.

26. And then shall ye immerse them in the water, and come forth again out of the water.

27. And after this manner shall ye baptize in my name; for behold, verily I say unto you, that the Father, and the Son, and the Holy Ghost are one; and I am in the Father, and the Father in me, and the Father and I are one.

(d) The Twelve Warned

Jesus warns the Twelve against disputations among themselves, and contentions, especially about doctrine.

3 Nephi 11:28-32.

3 NEPHI 11:28. And according as I have commanded you thus shall ye baptize. And there shall be no disputations among you, as there have hitherto been; neither shall there be disputations among you concerning the points of my doctrine, as there have hitherto been.

29. For verily, verily I say unto you, he that hath the spirit of contention is not of me, but is of the devil, who is the father of contention, and he stirreth up the hearts of men to contend with anger, one with another.

30. Behold, this is not my doctrine, to stir up the hearts of men with anger, one against another; but this is my doctrine, that such things should be done away.

31. Behold, verily, verily, I say unto you, I will declare unto you my doctrine.

32. And this is my doctrine, and it is the doctrine which the Father hath given unto me; and I bear record of the Father, and the Father beareth record of me, and the Holy Ghost beareth record of the Father and me; and I bear record that the Father commandeth all men, everywhere, to repent and believe in me.

(e) Jesus Discourses on Repentance and Baptism and the Necessity Therefor

3 Nephi 11:33-41.

3 NEPHI 11:33. And whoso believeth in me, and is baptized, the same shall be saved; and they are they who shall inherit the kingdom of God.

34. And whoso believeth not in me, and is not baptized, shall be damned.

35. Verily, verily, I say unto you, that this is my doctrine, and I bear record of it from the Father; and whoso believeth in me believeth in the Father also; and unto him will the Father bear record of me, for he will visit him with fire and with the Holy Ghost.

36. And thus will the Father bear record of me, and the Holy Ghost will bear record unto him of the Father and me; for the Father, and I, and the Holy Ghost are one.

37. And again I say unto you, ye must repent, and become as a little child, and be baptized in my name, or ye can in nowise receive these things.

38. And again I say unto you, ye must repent, and be baptized in my name, and become as a little child, or ye can in nowise inherit the kingdom of God.

39. Verily, verily, I say unto you, that this is my doctrine, and whoso buildeth upon this buildeth upon my rock, and the gates of hell shall not prevail against them.

40. And whoso shall declare more or less than this, and establish it for my doctrine, the same cometh of evil, and is not built upon my rock; but he buildeth upon a sandy foundation, and the gates of hell stand open to receive such when the floods come and the winds beat upon them.

41. Therefore, go forth unto this people, and declare the words which I have spoken, unto the ends of the earth.

(f) The Calling of the Twelve Explained

Jesus explains the choosing of the Twelve and their mission to baptize, Jesus saying he would baptize them with the Holy Ghost, after which the testimony of Christ would come to them; tells the multitude how blessed they will be who believe in Jesus because of the testimony of the multitude.

3 Nephi 12:1-2.

3 NEPHI 12:1. And it came to pass that when Jesus had spoken these words unto Nephi, and to those who had been called, (now the number of them who had been called, and received power and authority to baptize, was twelve) and behold, he stretched forth his hand unto the multitude, and cried unto them, saying: Blessed are ye if ye shall give heed unto the words of these twelve whom I have chosen from among you to minister unto you, and to be your servants; and unto them I have given power that they may baptize you with water; and after that ye are baptized with water, behold, I will baptize you with fire and with the Holy Ghost; therefore blessed are ye if ye shall believe in me and be baptized, after that ye have seen me and know that I am.

2. And again, more blessed are they who shall believe in your words because that ye shall testify that ye have seen me, and that ye know that I am. Yea, blessed are they who shall believe in your words, and come down into the depths of humility and be baptized, for they shall be visited with fire and with the Holy Ghost, and shall receive a remission of their sins.

(g) Jesus Repeats the Great Truths Given in the Sermon on the Mount and the Sermon on the Plain

(For the Sermon on the Mount, see Sec. 50 above, and for the Sermon on the Plain, see Sec. 60 above.)

3 Nephi 12:3-48; 13:1-24.

3 NEPHI 12:3. Yea, blessed are the poor in spirit who come unto me, for theirs is the kingdom of heaven.

4. And again, blessed are all they that mourn, for they shall be comforted.

5. And blessed are the meek, for they shall inherit the earth.

6. And blessed are all they who do hunger and thirst after righteousness, for they shall be filled with the Holy Ghost.

7. And blessed are the merciful, for they shall obtain mercy.

8. And blessed are all the pure in heart, for they shall see God.

9. And blessed are all the peacemakers, for they shall be called the children of God.

10. And blessed are all they who are persecuted for my name's sake, for theirs is the kingdom of heaven.

11. And blessed are ye when men shall revile you and persecute, and shall say all manner of evil against you falsely, for my sake;

12. For ye shall have great joy and be exceeding glad, for great shall be your reward in heaven; for so persecuted they the prophets who were before you.

13. Verily, verily, I say unto you, I give unto you to be the salt of the earth; but if the salt shall lose its savor wherewith shall the earth be salted? The salt shall be thenceforth good for nothing, but to be cast out and to be trodden under foot of men.

14. Verily, verily, I say unto you, I give unto you to be the light of this people. A city that is set on a hill cannot be hid.

15. Behold, do men light a candle and put it under a bushel? Nay, but on a candlestick, and it giveth light to all that are in the house;

16. Therefore let your light so shine before this people, that they may see your good works and glorify your Father who is in heaven.

17. Think not that I am come to destroy the law or the prophets. I am not come to destroy but to fulfil;

18. For verily I say unto you, one jot nor one tittle hath not passed away from the law, but in me it hath all been fulfilled.

19. And behold, I have given you the law and the commandments of my Father, that ye shall believe in me, and that ye shall repent of your sins, and come unto me with a broken heart and a contrite spirit. Behold, ye have the commandments before you, and the law is fulfilled.

20. Therefore come unto me and be ye saved; for verily I say unto you, that except ye shall keep my commandments, which I have commanded you at this time, ye shall in no case enter into the kingdom of heaven.

21. Ye have heard that it hath been said by them of old time, and it is also written before you, that thou shalt not kill, and whosoever shall kill shall be in danger of the judgment of God;

22. But I say unto you, that whosoever is angry with his brother shall be in danger of his judgment. And whosoever shall say to his brother, Raca, shall be in danger of the council; and whosoever shall say, Thou fool, shall be in danger of hell fire.

23. Therefore, if ye shall come unto me, or shall desire to come unto me, and rememberest that thy brother hath aught against thee—

24. Go thy way unto thy brother, and first be reconciled to thy brother, and then come unto me with full purpose of heart, and I will receive you.

25. Agree with thine adversary quickly while thou art in the way with him, lest at any time he shall get thee, and thou shalt be cast into prison.

26. Verily, verily, I say unto thee, thou shalt by no means come out thence until thou hast paid the uttermost senine. And while ye are in prison can ye pay even one senine? Verily, verily, I say unto you, Nay.

27. Behold, it is written by them of old time, that thou shalt not commit adultery;

28. But I say unto you, that whosoever looketh on a woman, to lust after her, hath committed adultery already in his heart.

29. Behold, I give unto you a commandment, that ye suffer

none of these things to enter into your heart;

30. For it is better that ye should deny yourselves of these things, wherein ye will take up your cross, than that ye should be cast into hell.

31. It hath been written, that whosoever shall put away his wife, let him give her a writing of divorcement.

32. Verily, verily, I say unto you, that whosoever shall put away his wife, saving for the cause of fornication, causeth her to commit adultery; and whoso shall marry her who is divorced committeth adultery.

33. And again it is written, thou shalt not forswear thyself, but shalt perform unto the Lord thine oaths;

34. But verily, verily, I say unto you, swear not at all; neither by heaven, for it is God's throne;

35. Nor by the earth, for it is his footstool;

36. Neither shalt thou swear by the head, because thou canst not make one hair black or white;

37. But let your communication be Yea, yea; Nay, nay; for whatsoever cometh of more than these is evil.

38. And behold, it is written, an eye for an eye, and a tooth for a tooth;

39. But I say unto you, that ye shall not resist evil, but whosoever shall smite thee on thy right cheek, turn to him the other also;

40. And if any man will sue thee at the law and take away thy coat, let him have thy cloak also;

41. And whosoever shall compel thee to go a mile, go with him twain.

42. Give to him that asketh thee, and from him that would borrow of thee turn thou not away.

43. And behold it is written also, that thou shalt love thy neighbor and hate thine enemy;

44. But behold I say unto you, love your enemies, bless them that curse you, do good to them that hate you, and pray for them who despitefully use you and persecute you;

45. That ye may be the children of your Father who is in heaven; for he maketh his sun to rise on the evil and on the good.

46. Therefore those things which were of old time, which were under the law, in me are all fulfilled.

47. Old things are done away, and all things have become new.

48. Therefore I would that ye should be perfect even as I, or your Father who is in heaven is perfect.

CHAPTER 13

1. Verily, verily, I say that I would that ye should do alms unto the poor; but take heed that ye do not your alms before men to be seen of them;

otherwise ye have no reward of your Father who is in heaven.

2. Therefore, when ye shall do your alms do not sound a trumpet before you, as will hypocrites do in the synagogues and in the streets, that they may have glory of men. Verily I say unto you, they have their reward.

3. But when thou doest alms let not thy left hand know what thy right hand doeth;

4. That thine alms may be in secret; and thy Father who seeth in secret, himself shall reward thee openly.

5. And when thou prayest thou shalt not do as the hypocrites, for they love to pray, standing in the synagogues and in the corners of the streets, that they may be seen of men. Verily I say unto you, they have their reward.

6. But thou, when thou prayest, enter into thy closet, and when thou hast shut thy door, pray to thy Father who is in secret; and thy Father, who seeth in secret, shall reward thee openly.

7. But when ye pray, use not vain repetitions, as the heathen, for they think that they shall be heard for their much speaking.

8. Be not ye therefore like unto them, for your Father knoweth what things ye have need of before ye ask him.

9. After this manner therefore pray ye: Our Father who art in heaven, hallowed be thy name.

10. Thy will be done on earth as it is in heaven.

11. And forgive us our debts, as we forgive our debtors.

12. And lead us not into temptation, but deliver us from evil.

13. For thine is the kingdom, and the power, and the glory, forever. Amen.

14. For, if ye forgive men their trespasses your heavenly Father will also forgive you;

15. But if ye forgive not men their trespasses neither will your Father forgive your trespasses.

16. Moreover, when ye fast be not as the hypocrites, of a sad countenance, for they disfigure their faces that they may appear unto men to fast. Verily I say unto you, they have their reward.

17. But thou, when thou fastest, anoint thy head, and wash thy face;

18. That thou appear not unto men to fast, but unto thy Father, who is in secret; and thy Father, who seeth in secret, shall reward thee openly.

19. Lay not up for yourselves treasures upon earth, where moth and rust doth corrupt, and thieves break through and steal;

20. But lay up for yourselves treasures in heaven, where neither moth nor rust doth corrupt, and where thieves do not break through nor steal.

21. For where your treasure is, there will your heart be also.

22. The light of the body is the eye; if, therefore, thine eye be single, thy whole body shall be full of light.

23. But if thine eye be evil, thy whole body shall be full of darkness. If, therefore, the light that is in thee be darkness, how great is that darkness!

24. No man can serve two masters; for either he will hate the one and love the other, or else he will hold to the one and despise the other. Ye cannot serve God and Mammon.

(h) The Twelve Instructed

Jesus gives special instructions to the Twelve regarding their work; tells them to look after the spiritual things and shows the weakness of the material things; tells them to put their faith and confidence in God.

3 Nephi 13:25-34.

3 NEPHI 13:25. And now it came to pass that when Jesus had spoken these words he looked upon the twelve whom he had chosen, and said unto them: Remember the words which I have spoken. For behold, ye are they whom I have chosen to minister unto this people. Therefore I say unto you, take no thought for your life, what ye shall eat, or what ye shall drink; nor yet for your body, what ye shall put on. Is not the life more than meat, and the body than raiment?

26. Behold the fowls of the air, for they sow not, neither do they reap nor gather into barns; yet your heavenly Father feedeth them. Are ye not much better than they?

27. Which of you by taking thought can add one cubit unto his stature?

28. And why take ye thought for raiment? Consider the lilies of the field how they grow; they toil not, neither do they spin;

29. And yet I say unto you, that even Solomon, in all his glory, was not arrayed like one of these.

30. Wherefore, if God so clothe the grass of the field, which today is, and tomorrow is cast into the oven, even so will he clothe you, if ye are not of little faith.

31. Therefore take no thought, saying, What shall we eat? or, What shall we drink? or, Wherewithal shall we be clothed?

32. For your heavenly Father knoweth that ye have need of all these things.

33. But seek ye first the kingdom of God and his righteousness, and all these things shall be added unto you.

34. Take therefore no thought for the morrow, for

the morrow shall take thought for the things of itself. Sufficient is the day unto the evil thereof.

(i) The Multitude Instructed

Jesus again instructs the multitude on the truths and principles of the Sermons on the Mount and on the Plain.

3 Nephi 14:1-27.

3 NEPHI 14:1. And now it came to pass that when Jesus had spoken these words he turned again to the multitude, and did open his mouth unto them again, saying: Verily, verily, I say unto you, Judge not, that ye be not judged.

2. For with what judgment ye judge, ye shall be judged; and with what measure ye mete, it shall be measured to you again.

3. And why beholdest thou the mote that is in thy brother's eye, but considerest not the beam that is in thine own eye?

4. Or how wilt thou say to thy brother: Let me pull the mote out of thine eye — and behold, a beam is in thine own eye?

5. Thou hypocrite, first cast the beam out of thine own eye; and then shalt thou see clearly to cast the mote out of thy brother's eye.

6. Give not that which is holy unto the dogs, neither cast ye your pearls before swine, lest they trample them under their feet, and turn again and rend you.

7. Ask, and it shall be given unto you; seek, and ye shall find; knock, and it shall be opened unto you.

8. For every one that asketh, receiveth; and he that seeketh, findeth; and to him that knocketh, it shall be opened.

9. Or what man is there of you, who, if his son ask bread, will give him a stone?

10. Or if he ask a fish, will he give him a serpent?

11. If ye then, being evil, know how to give good gifts unto your children, how much more shall your Father who is in heaven give good things to them that ask him?

12. Therefore, all things whatsoever ye would that men should do to you, do ye even so to them, for this is the law and the prophets.

13. Enter ye in at the strait gate; for wide is the gate, and broad is the way, which leadeth to destruction, and many there be who go in thereat;

14. Because strait is the gate, and narrow is the way, which leadeth unto life, and few there be that find it.

15. Beware of false prophets, who come to you in sheep's clothing, but inwardly they are ravening wolves.

16. Ye shall know them by their fruits. Do men gather grapes of thorns, or figs of thistles?

17. Even so every good tree bringeth forth good fruit; but a corrupt tree bringeth forth evil fruit.

18. A good tree cannot bring forth evil fruit, neither a corrupt tree bring forth good fruit.

19. Every tree that bringeth not forth good fruit is hewn down, and cast into the fire.

20. Wherefore, by their fruits ye shall know them.

21. Not every one that saith unto me, Lord, Lord, shall enter into the kingdom of heaven; but he that doeth the will of my Father who is in heaven.

22. Many will say to me in that day: Lord, Lord, have we not prophesied in thy name, and in thy name have cast out devils, and in thy name done many wonderful works?

23. And then will I profess unto them: I never knew you; depart from me, ye that work iniquity.

24. Therefore, whoso heareth these sayings of mine and doeth them, I will liken him unto a wise man, who built his house upon a rock —

25. And the rain descended, and the floods came, and the winds blew, and beat upon that house; and it fell not, for it was founded upon a rock.

26. And every one that heareth these sayings of mine and doeth them not shall be likened unto a foolish man, who built his house upon the sand—

27. And the rain descended, and the floods came, and the winds blew, and beat upon that house; and it fell, and great was the fall of it.

(j) Further Instructions

Jesus tells the multitude that they have heard things which he taught before he ascended to his Father; the blessings of those who remember and do his words.

3 Nephi 15:1.

3 NEPHI 15:1. And now it came to pass that when Jesus had ended these sayings he cast his eyes round about on the multitude, and said unto them: Behold, ye have heard the things which I taught before I ascended to my Father; therefore, whoso remembereth these sayings of mine and doeth them, him will I raise up at the last day.

(k) Jesus Explains His Relationship to the Law of Moses

3 Nephi 15:2-10.

3 NEPHI 15:2. And it came to pass that when Jesus had said these words he perceived that there were some among them who marveled, and wondered what he would concerning the law of Moses; for they understood not the saying that old things had passed away, and that all things had become new.

3. And he said unto them: Marvel not that I said unto you that old things had passed away, and that all things had become new.

4. Behold, I say unto you that the law is fulfilled that was given unto Moses.

5. Behold, I am he that gave the law, and I am he who covenanted with my people Israel; therefore, the law in me is fulfilled, for I have come to fulfil the law; therefore it hath an end.

6. Behold, I do not destroy the prophets, for as many as have not been fulfilled in me, verily I say unto you, shall all be fulfilled.

7. And because I said unto you that old things have passed away, I do not destroy that which hath been spoken concerning things which are to come.

8. For behold, the covenant which I have made with my people is not all fulfilled; but the law which was given unto Moses hath an end in me.

9. Behold, I am the law, and the light. Look unto me, and endure to the end, and ye shall live; for unto him that endureth to the end will I give eternal life.

10. Behold, I have given unto you the commandments; therefore keep my commandments. And this is the law and the prophets, for they truly testified of me.

(l) Special Instructions to Twelve

Jesus speaks again to his disciples—the Twelve—tells them he is giving them instructions and information which the Father did not have him give the people in Palestine; explains how the Gentiles are to know him; tells them they are numbered among those whom the Father has given him.

3 Nephi 15:11-24.

3 NEPHI 15:11. And now it came to pass that when Jesus had spoken these words, he said unto those twelve whom he had chosen:

12. Ye are my disciples; and ye are a light unto this people, who are a remnant of the house of Joseph.

13. And behold, this is the land of your inheritance; and the Father hath given it unto you.

14. And not at any time hath the Father given me commandment that I should tell it unto your brethren at Jerusalem.

15. Neither at any time hath the Father given me commandment that I should tell unto

them concerning the other tribes of the house of Israel, whom the Father hath led away out of the land.

16. This much did the Father command me, that I should tell unto them:

17. That other sheep I have which are not of this fold; them also I must bring, and they shall hear my voice; and there shall be one fold, and one shepherd.

18. And now, because of stiffneckedness and unbelief they understood not my word; therefore I was commanded to say no more of the Father concerning this thing unto them.

19. But, verily, I say unto you that the Father hath commanded me, and I tell it unto you, that ye were separated from among them because of their iniquity; therefore it is because of their iniquity that they know not of you.

20. And verily, I say unto you again that the other tribes hath the Father separated from them; and it is because of their iniquity that they know not of them.

21. And verily I say unto you, that ye are they of whom I said: Other sheep I have which are not of this fold; them also I must bring, and they shall hear my voice; and there shall be one fold, and one shepherd.

22. And they understood me not, for they supposed it had been the Gentiles; for they understood not that the Gentiles should be converted through their preaching.

23. And they understood me not that I said they shall hear my voice; and they understood me not that the Gentiles should not at any time hear my voice—that I should not manifest myself unto them save it were by the Holy Ghost.

24. But behold, ye have both heard my voice, and seen me; and ye are my sheep, and ye are numbered among those whom the Father hath given me.

(m) He Tells of Other Sheep

Jesus tells them he has still other sheep that are not here nor in Jerusalem to whom he has not manifested himself, and who have not heard his voice; that the Father has commanded him to go to them, that all shall be of one fold, and that he goes to show himself to them; they are to write these things so that if those in Jerusalem are not faithful, they may know of him through the Holy Ghost, and that the Gentiles may know of him through these writings, and to the remnant of the seed of the others to whom he goes, all of whom he will gather from the four corners of the earth.

3 Nephi 16:1-5.

3 NEPHI 16:1. And verily, verily, I say unto you that I have other sheep, which are not of this land, neither of the land of Jerusalem, neither in any parts of that land round about whither I have been to minister.

2. For they of whom I speak are they who have not as yet heard my voice; neither have I at any time manifested myself unto them.

3. But I have received a commandment of the Father that I shall go unto them, and that they shall hear my voice, and shall be numbered among my sheep, that there may be one fold and one shepherd; therefore I go to show myself unto them.

4. And I command you that ye shall write these sayings after I am gone, that if it so be that my people at Jerusalem, they who have seen me and been with me in my ministry, do not ask the Father in my name, that they may receive a knowledge of you by the Holy Ghost, and also of the other tribes whom they know not of, that these sayings which ye shall write shall be kept and shall be manifested unto the Gentiles, that through the fulness of the Gentiles, the remnant of their seed, who shall be scattered forth upon the face of the earth because of their unbelief, may be brought in, or may be brought to a knowledge of me, their Redeemer.

5. And then will I gather them in from the four quarters of the earth; and then will I fulfil the covenant which the Father hath made unto all the people of the house of Israel.

(n) The Gentiles Blessed and Warned

Jesus blesses the Gentiles, and says because of Israel's unbelief the truth in the latter days shall come through the Gentiles; but wo unto the unbelieving Gentiles who have scattered his people; foretells how he will bring his Gospel forth among the Gentiles, notwithstanding their wickedness; he will then remember his covenants to his people; tells what will happen if the Gentiles do not serve him; repeats a prophecy of Isaiah.

3 Nephi 16:6-20.

3 NEPHI 16:6. And blessed are the Gentiles, because of their belief in me, in and of the Holy Ghost, which witnesses unto them of me and of the Father.

7. Behold, because of their belief in me, saith the Father, and because of the unbelief of you, O house of Israel, in the latter day shall the truth come unto the Gentiles, that the fulness of these things shall be made known unto them.

8. But wo, saith the Father, unto the unbelieving of the Gentiles—for notwithstanding they have come forth upon the face of this land, and have scattered my people who are of the house of Israel; and my people who are of the house of Israel have been cast out from among them, and have been trodden under feet by them;

9. And because of the mercies of the Father unto the Gentiles, and also the judgments of the Father upon my people who are of the house of Israel, verily, verily, I say unto you, that after all this, and I have caused my people who are of the house of Israel to be smitten, and to be afflicted, and to be slain, and to be cast out from among them, and to become hated by them, and to become a hiss and a byword among them—

10. And thus commandeth the Father that I should say unto you: At that day when the Gentiles shall sin against my gospel, and shall be lifted up in the pride of their hearts above all nations, and above all the people of the whole earth, and shall be filled with all manner of lyings, and of deceits, and of mischiefs, and all manner of hypocrisy, and murders, and priestcrafts, and whoredoms, and of secret abominations; and if they shall do all those things, and shall reject the fulness of my gospel, behold, saith the Father, I will bring the fulness of my gospel from among them.

11. And then will I remember my covenant which I have made unto my people, O house of Israel, and I will bring my gospel unto them.

12. And I will show unto thee, O house of Israel, that the Gentiles shall not have power over you; but I will remember my covenant unto you, O house of Israel, and ye shall come unto the knowledge of the fulness of my gospel.

13. But if the Gentiles will repent and return unto me, saith the Father, behold they shall be numbered among my people, O house of Israel.

14. And I will not suffer my people, who are of the house of Israel, to go through among them, and tread them down, saith the Father.

15. But if they will not turn unto me, and hearken unto my voice, I will suffer them, yea, I will suffer my people, O house of Israel, that they shall go through among them, and shall tread them down, and they shall be as salt that hath lost its savor, which is thenceforth good for nothing but to be cast out, and to be trodden under foot of my people, O house of Israel.

16. Verily, verily, I say unto you, thus hath the Father commanded me—that I should give unto this people this land for their inheritance.

17. And then the words of the prophet Isaiah shall be fulfilled, which say:

18. Thy watchmen shall lift up the voice; with the voice together shall they sing, for they shall see eye to eye when the Lord shall bring again Zion.

19. Break forth into joy, sing together, ye waste places of Jerusalem; for the Lord hath comforted his people, he hath redeemed Jerusalem.

20. The Lord hath made bare his holy arm in the eyes of all the nations; and all the ends of the earth shall see the salvation of God.

(o) He Tells Multitude to Ponder His Words

Jesus, looking round upon the multitude, says his time is at hand; he tells them he sees they are not understanding his words; he sends them to ponder upon the things he has told them, saying he will come again on the morrow; he says he will go to the Father and to the lost tribes, for they are not lost to the Father; the multitude is in tears and look steadfastly upon him as if they wish him to tarry longer with them.

3 Nephi 17:1-5.

3 NEPHI 17:1. Behold, now it came to pass that when Jesus had spoken these words he looked round about again on the multitude, and he said unto them: Behold, my time is at hand.

2. I perceive that ye are weak, that ye cannot understand all my words which I am commanded of the Father to speak unto you at this time.

3. Therefore, go ye unto your homes, and ponder upon the things which I have said, and ask of the Father, in my name, that ye may understand, and prepare your minds for the morrow, and I come unto you again.

4. But now I go unto the Father, and also to show myself unto the lost tribes of Israel, for they are not lost unto the Father, for he knoweth whither he hath taken them.

5. And it came to pass that when Jesus had thus spoken, he cast his eyes round about again on the multitude, and beheld they were in tears, and did look steadfastly upon him as if they would ask him to tarry a little longer with them.

(p) A Feast of Miracles

Jesus tells them he is filled with compassion for them; he asks them to bring to him the lame, blind, halt or maimed, or leprous, or they that are withered, or deaf, or afflicted in any manner; he will heal them and show them what he has done in Jerusalem; then the multitude bring their sick and afflicted, and he heals every one as they are brought to him; all bow down and worship at his feet, kissing his feet and bathing them with tears.

3 Nephi 17:6-10.

3 NEPHI 17:6. And he said unto them: Behold, my bowels are filled with compassion towards you.

7. Have ye any that are sick among you? Bring them hither. Have ye any that are lame, or blind, or halt, or maimed, or leprous, or that are withered, or that are deaf, or that are afflicted in any manner? Bring them hither and I will heal them, for I have compassion upon you; my bowels are filled with mercy.

8. For I perceive that ye desire that I should show unto you what I have done unto your brethren at Jerusalem, for I see that your faith is sufficient that I should heal you.

9. And it came to pass that when he had thus spoken, all the multitude, with one accord, did go forth with their sick and their afflicted, and their lame, and with their blind, and with their dumb, and with all them that were afflicted in any manner; and he did heal them every one as they were brought forth unto him.

10. And they did all, both they who had been healed and they who were whole, bow down at his feet, and did worship him; and as many as could come for the multitude did kiss his feet, insomuch that they did bathe his feet with their tears.

(q) He Blesses the Little Children

Jesus tells them to bring their little children to him; when they have all been brought to him, he has the multitude kneel; he groans within himself over the wickedness of Israel; then kneeling upon the earth he prays a prayer which may not be written, because language cannot express what they saw and heard; when Jesus finishes he arises, but the multitude remain kneeling, overcome; Jesus commands them to arise and he blesses them; he weeps, then takes the children one by one and blesses them; then prays and weeps again.

3 Nephi 17:11-22.

3 NEPHI 17:11. And it came to pass that he commanded that their little children should be brought.

12. So they brought their little children and set them down upon the ground round about him, and Jesus stood in the midst; and the multitude gave way till they had all been brought unto him.

13. And it came to pass that when they had all been brought, and Jesus stood in the midst, he commanded the multitude that they should kneel down upon the ground.

14. And it came to pass that

when they had knelt upon the ground, Jesus groaned within himself, and said: Father, I am troubled because of the wickedness of the people of the house of Israel.

15. And when he had said these words, he himself also knelt upon the earth; and behold he prayed unto the Father, and the things which he prayed cannot be written, and the multitude did bear record who heard him.

16. And after this manner do they bear record: The eye hath never seen, neither hath the ear heard, before, so great and marvelous things as we saw and heard Jesus speak unto the Father;

17. And no tongue can speak, neither can there be written by any man, neither can the hearts of men conceive so great and marvelous things as we both saw and heard Jesus speak; and no one can conceive of the joy which filled our souls at the time we heard him pray for us unto the Father.

18. And it came to pass that when Jesus had made an end of praying unto the Father, he arose; but so great was the joy of the multitude that they were overcome.

19. And it came to pass that Jesus spake unto them, and bade them arise.

20. And they arose from the earth, and he said unto them: Blessed are ye because of your faith. And now behold, my joy is full.

21. And when he had said these words, he wept, and the multitude bare record of it, and he took their little children, one by one, and blessed them, and prayed unto the Father for them.

22. And when he had done this he wept again; . . .

(r) Angels Minister to the Little Ones

Jesus says to the multitude, "Behold your little ones," they look and behold angels descending from heaven as if in the midst of fire; the angels encircle the little ones, who are encircled by fire; the angels minister unto the children; the multitude, about two thousand five hundred souls, bear record of this.

3 Nephi 17:23-25.

3 NEPHI 17:23. And he spake unto the multitude, and said unto them: Behold your little ones.

24. And as they looked to behold they cast their eyes towards heaven, and they saw the heavens open, and they saw angels descending out of heaven as it were in the midst of fire; and they came down and encircled those little ones about, and they were encircled about with fire; and the angels did minister unto them.

25. And the multitude did see and hear and bear record;

and they know that their record is true for they all of them did see and hear, every man for himself; and they were in number about two thousand and five hundred souls; and they did consist of men, women, and children.

(s) The Multitude Fed

Jesus commands his disciples that they shall get bread and wine; they bring it. Jesus blesses it; at his command the disciples first eat, then feed the multitude.

3 Nephi 18:1-4.

3 NEPHI 18:1. And it came to pass that Jesus commanded his disciples that they should bring forth some bread and wine unto him.

2. And while they were gone for bread and wine, he commanded the multitude that they should sit themselves down upon the earth.

3. And when the disciples had come with bread and wine, he took of the bread and brake and blessed it; and he gave unto the disciples and commanded that they should eat.

4. And when they had eaten and were filled, he commanded that they should give unto the multitude.

(t) He Institutes the Sacrament

Jesus tells the multitude that he will ordain one among them who shall break bread and bless it, and give to them in remembrance of his body, which he has shown to them, and remembering him, his spirit shall be with them; he then gives his disciples wine to drink, and tells them to give to the multitude; they and the multitude both drink and are filled; when the disciples have done this he blesses them; he tells them this witnesses unto the Father that they are willing to keep his commandments, and that they do this in remembrance of his blood that was shed for them; those who do these things are built upon a rock, but those who do less are built upon a sandy foundation; blessed are they who keep his commandments; watch and pray as he has prayed; he is the light.

3 Nephi 18:5-16.

3 NEPHI 18:5. And when the multitude had eaten and were filled, he said unto the disciples: Behold there shall one be ordained among you, and to him will I give power that he shall break bread and bless it and give it unto the people of my church, unto all those who shall believe and be baptized in my name.

6. And this shall ye always observe to do, even as I have done, even as I have broken bread and blessed it and given it unto you.

7. And this shall ye do in remembrance of my body, which I have shown unto you. And it shall be a testimony unto the Father that ye do always remember me. And if ye do always remember me ye shall have my Spirit to be with you.

8. And it came to pass that when he said these words, he commanded his disciples that they should take of the wine of the cup and drink of it, and that they should also give unto the multitude that they might drink of it.

9. And it came to pass that they did so, and did drink of it and were filled; and they gave unto the multitude, and they did drink, and they were filled.

10. And when the disciples had done this, Jesus said unto them: Blessed are ye for this thing which ye have done, for this is fulfilling my commandments, and this doth witness unto the Father that ye are willing to do that which I have commanded you.

11. And this shall ye always do to those who repent and are baptized in my name; and ye shall do it in remembrance of my blood, which I have shed for you, that ye may witness unto the Father that ye do always remember me. And if ye do always remember me ye shall have my Spirit to be with you.

12. And I give unto you a commandment that ye shall do these things. And if ye shall always do these things blessed are ye, for ye are built upon my rock.

13. But whoso among you shall do more or less than these are not built upon my rock, but are built upon a sandy foundation; and when the rain descends, and the floods come, and the winds blow, and beat upon them, they shall fall, and the gates of hell are ready open to receive them.

14. Therefore blessed are ye if ye shall keep my commandments, which the Father hath commanded me that I should give unto you.

15. Verily, verily, I say unto you, ye must watch and pray always, lest ye be tempted by the devil, and ye be led away captive by him.

16. And as I have prayed among you even so shall ye pray in my church, among my people who do repent and are baptized in my name. Behold I am the light; I have set an example for you.

(u) He Teaches Prayer

Jesus teaches the multitude that they must pray, he teaches them how to pray, the efficacy of prayer, to pray in their families, and to pray for the wayward; he is the light, they must do as he has done.

3 Nephi 18:17-25.

3 NEPHI 18:17. And it came to pass that when Jesus had spoken these words unto his disciples, he turned again unto the multitude and said unto them:

18. Behold, verily, verily, I say unto you, ye must watch and pray always lest ye enter into temptation; for Satan desireth to have you, that he may sift you as wheat.

19. Therefore ye must always pray unto the Father in my name;

20. And whatsoever ye shall ask the Father in my name, which is right, believing that ye shall receive, behold it shall be given unto you.

21. Pray in your families unto the Father, always in my name, that your wives and your children may be blessed.

22. And behold, ye shall meet together oft; and ye shall not forbid any man from coming unto you when ye shall meet together, but suffer them that they may come unto you and forbid them not;

23. But ye shall pray for them, and shall not cast them out; and if it so be that they come unto you oft ye shall pray for them unto the Father, in my name.

24. Therefore, hold up your light that it may shine unto the world. Behold I am the light which ye shall hold up—that which ye have seen me do. Behold ye see that I have prayed unto the Father, and ye all have witnessed.

25. And ye see that I have commanded that none of you should go away, but rather have commanded that ye should come unto me, that ye might feel and see; even so shall ye do unto the world; and whosoever breaketh this commandment suffereth himself to be led into temptation.

(v) Instructions Regarding the Sacrament

Jesus then turns to his disciples, saying he must give them one further commandment and then go unto his Father; this commandment is that they shall permit no one to partake of the sacrament unworthily, for the unworthy "eateth and drinketh damnation to his soul"; the unworthy are to be forbidden to take of the sacrament, but he shall not be cast out but labored with to bring him back; he gives these commandments because of their disputations.

3 Nephi 18:26-34.

3 NEPHI 18:26. And now it came to pass that when Jesus had spoken these words, he turned his eyes again upon the disciples whom he had chosen, and said unto them:

27. Behold verily, verily, I say unto you, I give unto you another commandment, and then I must go unto my Father that I may fulfil other commandments which he hath given me.

28. And now behold, this is the commandment which I give unto you, that ye shall not suffer any one knowingly to partake of my flesh and blood unworthily, when ye shall minister it;

29. For whoso eateth and drinketh my flesh and blood unworthily eateth and drinketh damnation to his soul; therefore if ye know that a man is unworthy to eat and drink of my flesh and blood ye shall forbid him.

30. Nevertheless, ye shall not cast him out from among you, but ye shall minister unto him and shall pray for him unto the Father, in my name; and if it so be that he repenteth and is baptized in my name, then shall ye receive him, and shall minister unto him of my flesh and blood.

31. But if he repent not he shall not be numbered among my people, that he may not destroy my people, for behold I know my sheep, and they are numbered.

32. Nevertheless, ye shall not cast him out of your synagogues, or your places of worship, for unto such shall ye continue to minister; for ye know not but what they will return and repent, and come unto me with full purpose of heart, and I shall heal them; and ye shall be the means of bringing salvation unto them.

33. Therefore, keep these sayings which I have commanded you that ye come not under condemnation; for wo unto him whom the Father condemneth.

34. And I give you these commandments because of the disputations which have been among you. And blessed are ye if ye have no disputations among you.

(w) The Disciples Given Power to Bestow Holy Ghost; He Ascends Into Heaven

Jesus touches his disciples one by one and speaks unto them; the multitude do not hear but the disciples bear record that he gave them power to give the Holy Ghost; this done, a cloud overshadows them all, so that they can not see Jesus, and while they are overshadowed, he ascends into heaven as the disciples bear record.

3 Nephi 18:35-39.

3 NEPHI 18:35. And now I go unto the Father, because it is expedient that I should go unto the Father for your sakes.

36. And it came to pass that when Jesus had made an end of these sayings, he touched with his hand the disciples whom he had chosen, one by one, even until he had touched them all, and spake unto them as he touched them.

37. And the multitude heard not the words which he spake, therefore they did not bear record; but the disciples bare record that he gave them power to give the Holy Ghost. And I will show unto you hereafter that this record is true.

38. And it came to pass that when Jesus had touched them all, there came a cloud and overshadowed the multitude that they could not see Jesus.

39. And while they were overshadowed he departed from them, and ascended into heaven. And the disciples saw and did bear record that he ascended again into heaven.

Section 177

THE PEOPLE RETURN HOME

After the ascension of Jesus, the people return to their homes, and begin to spread the news of the visit of Jesus and his ministrations, and that he will come on the morrow; great multitudes labor that they may be at the meeting-place on the morrow.

3 Nephi 19:1-3.

3 NEPHI 19:1. And now it came to pass that when Jesus had ascended into heaven, the multitude did disperse, and every man did take his wife and his children and did return to his own home.

2. And it was noised abroad among the people immediately, before it was yet dark, that the multitude had seen Jesus, and that he had ministered unto them, and that he would also show himself on the morrow unto the multitude.

3. Yea, and even all the night it was noised abroad concerning Jesus; and insomuch did they send forth unto the people that there were many, yea, an exceeding great number, did labor exceedingly all that night, that they might be on the morrow in the place where Jesus should show himself unto the multitude.

Section 178

THE SUCCEEDING TWO DAYS OF CHRIST'S MINISTRY ON THE WESTERN HEMISPHERE

(a) The Multitude Gather and Pray

On the morrow when the multitude gather together, the Twelve (named here), go and stand in the midst of them; the Twelve divide the multitude into twelve bodies, and having them kneel, they teach them how to pray; after prayer the Twelve rise and minister unto the people; repeating the words of Jesus, they pray again.

3 Nephi 19:4-8.

3 NEPHI 19:4. And it came to pass that on the morrow, when the multitude was gathered together, behold, Nephi and his brother whom he had raised from the dead, whose name was Timothy, and also his son, whose name was Jonas, and also Mathoni, and Mathonihah, his brother, and Kumen, and Kumenonhi, and Jeremiah, and Shemnon, and Jonas, and Zedekiah, and Isaiah—now these were the names of the disciples whom Jesus had chosen—and it came to pass that they went forth and stood in the midst of the multitude.

5. And behold, the multitude was so great that they did cause that they should be separated into twelve bodies.

6. And the twelve did teach the multitude; and behold, they did cause that the multitude should kneel down upon the face of the earth, and should pray unto the Father in the name of Jesus.

7. And the disciples did pray unto the Father also in the name of Jesus. And it came to pass that they arose and ministered unto the people.

8. And when they had ministered those same words which Jesus had spoken—nothing varying from the words which Jesus had spoken—behold, they knelt again and prayed to the Father in the name of Jesus.

(b) The Twelve Receive the Holy Ghost

They pray for that which they wish for most—that the Holy Ghost shall be given unto them; Nephi being baptized first, baptizes all the Twelve; and the Holy Ghost falls upon them, so that they are filled with it and with fire; they are encircled about with fire as it were, which comes down from heaven; the multitude witness this, and see angels come down from heaven and minister unto the Twelve.

3 Nephi 19:9-14

3 NEPHI 19:9. And they did pray for that which they most desired; and they desired that the Holy Ghost should be given unto them.

10. And when they had thus prayed they went down unto the water's edge, and the multitude followed them.

11. And it came to pass that Nephi went down into the water and was baptized.

12. And he came up out of the water and began to baptize. And he baptized all those whom Jesus had chosen.

13. And it came to pass when they were all baptized and had come up out of the water, the Holy Ghost did fall upon them, and they were filled with the Holy Ghost and with fire.

14. And behold, they were encircled about as if it were by fire; and it came down from heaven, and the multitude did witness it, and did bear record; and angels did come down out of heaven and did minister unto them.

(c) He Comes Again

While the angels minister to the disciples, Jesus comes and stands in their midst and ministers to them; he speaks to the multitude and commands them and his disciples to kneel down; all kneeling, he commands his disciples that they pray.

3 Nephi 19:15-17.

3 NEPHI 19:15. And it came to pass that while the angels were ministering unto the disciples, behold, Jesus came and stood in the midst and ministered unto them.

16. And it came to pass that he spake unto the multitude, and commanded them that they should kneel down again upon the earth, and also that his disciples should kneel down upon the earth.

17. And it came to pass that when they had all knelt down upon the earth, he commanded his disciples that they should pray.

(d) He Prays

As they pray, Jesus moves a little way off and prays; he thanks the Father for the Holy Ghost given unto them; he prays the Father to give the Holy Ghost to all who believe in him; Jesus finishing his prayer returns and finds the disciples still praying; "for it was given unto them what they should pray, and they were filled with desire."

3 Nephi 19:18-24.

3 NEPHI 19:18. And behold, they began to pray; and they did pray unto Jesus, calling him their Lord and their God.

19. And it came to pass that Jesus departed out of the midst

of them, and went a little way off from them and bowed himself to the earth, and he said:

20. Father, I thank thee that thou hast given the Holy Ghost unto these whom I have chosen; and it is because of their belief in me that I have chosen them out of the world.

21. Father, I pray thee that thou wilt give the Holy Ghost unto all them that shall believe in their words.

22. Father, thou hast given them the Holy Ghost because they believe in me; and thou seest that they believe in me because thou hearest them, and they pray unto me; and they pray unto me because I am with them.

23. And now Father, I pray unto thee for them, and also for all those who shall believe on their words, that they may believe in me, that I may be in them as thou, Father, art in me, that we may be one.

24. And it came to pass that when Jesus had thus prayed unto the Father, he came unto his disciples, and behold, they did still continue, without ceasing, to pray unto him; and they did not multiply many words, for it was given unto them what they should pray, and they were filled with desire.

(e) He Again Prays

Jesus smiles upon the disciples praying, and their countenances shine as white as Jesus'; telling them to pray on, he again draws aside and bowing to the earth, again prays to the Father whom he thanks for purifying the disciples, and prays that all who believe on him shall be likewise purified; he prays not for the world, but for those whom the Father has given him out of the world; Jesus again returns and finding the disciples still praying, he again retires and prays what cannot be written, but the multitude understand for their hearts are open; coming back to the disciples, he says he has not seen such great faith among the Jews, and therefore he could not show unto them such great miracles; the Jews had not seen nor heard the things they have seen and heard.

3 Nephi 19:25-36.

3 NEPHI 19:25. And it came to pass that Jesus blessed them as they did pray unto him; and his countenance did smile upon them, and the light of his countenance did shine upon them, and behold they were as white as the countenance and also the garments of Jesus; and behold the whiteness thereof did exceed all the whiteness, yea, even there could be nothing upon earth so white as the whiteness thereof.

26. And Jesus said unto them: Pray on; nevertheless they did not cease to pray.

27. And he turned from them again, and went a little way off and bowed himself to the earth; and he prayed again unto the Father, saying:

28. Father, I thank thee that

thou hast purified those whom I have chosen, because of their faith, and I pray for them, and also for them who shall believe on their words, that they may be purified in me, through faith on their words, even as they are purified in me.

29. Father, I pray not for the world, but for those whom thou hast given me out of the world, because of their faith, that they may be purified in me, that I may be in them as thou, Father, art in me, that we may be one, that I may be glorified in them.

30. And when Jesus had spoken these words he came again unto his disciples; and behold they did pray steadfastly, without ceasing, unto him; and he did smile upon them again; and behold they were white, even as Jesus.

31. And it came to pass that he went again a little way off and prayed unto the Father;

32. And tongue cannot speak the words which he prayed, neither can be written by man the words which he prayed.

33. And the multitude did hear and do bear record; and their hearts were open and they did understand in their hearts the words which he prayed.

34. Nevertheless, so great and marvelous were the words which he prayed that they cannot be written, neither can they be uttered by man.

35. And it came to pass that when Jesus had made an end of praying he came again to the disciples, and said unto them: So great faith have I never seen among all the Jews; wherefore I could not show unto them so great miracles, because of their unbelief.

36. Verily I say unto you, there are none of them that have seen so great things as ye have seen; neither have they heard so great things as ye have heard.

(f) He Tells Them to Cease Their Prayers

Jesus commands the disciples and the multitude to cease praying—though always praying in their hearts—and to arise and stand upon their feet, and they obey.

3 Nephi 20:1-2.

3 NEPHI 20:1. And it came to pass that he commanded the multitude that they should cease to pray, and also his disciples. And he commanded them that they should not cease to pray in their hearts.

2. And he commanded them that they should arise and stand up upon their feet. And they arose up and stood upon their feet.

(g) He Again Administers the Sacrament

Jesus administers the sacrament to the multitude, through the disciples, the bread and wine being miraculously provided; he explains the meaning of the sacrament; when the multitude have partaken of the sacrament they cry with one voice and give glory to Jesus, whom they both see and hear.

3 Nephi 20:3-9.

3 NEPHI 20:3. And it came to pass that he brake bread again and blessed it, and gave to the disciples to eat.

4. And when they had eaten he commanded them that they should break bread, and give unto the multitude.

5. And when they had given unto the multitude he also gave them wine to drink, and commanded them that they should give unto the multitude.

6. Now, there had been no bread, neither wine, brought by the disciples, neither by the multitude;

7. But he truly gave unto them bread to eat, and also wine to drink.

8. And he said unto them: He that eateth this bread eateth of my body to his soul; and he that drinketh of this wine drinketh of my blood to his soul; and his soul shall never hunger nor thirst, but shall be filled.

9. Now, when the multitude had all eaten and drunk, behold, they were filled with the Spirit; and they did cry out with one voice, and gave glory to Jesus, whom they both saw and heard.

Section 179

HE GIVES COMMANDMENTS

Jesus says he must now give them the commandments which the Father has commanded him concerning his people, who are a remnant of the house of Israel.

(a) He Quotes Isaiah

Jesus quotes Isaiah regarding the gathering of the remnants of Israel; declares this land is for the remnant of the house of Jacob; warns the Gentiles; tells of their fate if they do not repent and tells how the remnant will punish them; this shall be a New Jerusalem, and the powers of heaven and Jesus will be in the midst of them.

3 Nephi 20:10-22.

3 NEPHI 20:10. And it came to pass that when they had all given glory unto Jesus, he said unto them: Behold now I finish the commandment which the Father hath commanded me concerning this people, who are a remnant of the house of Israel.

11. Ye remember that I spake unto you, and said that when the words of Isaiah should be fulfilled — behold they are written, ye have them before you, therefore search them—

12. And verily, verily, I say unto you, that when they shall be fulfilled then is the fulfilling of the covenant which the Father hath made unto his people, O house of Israel.

13. And then shall the remnants, which shall be scattered abroad upon the face of the earth, be gathered in from the east and from the west, and from the south and from the north; and they shall be brought to the knowledge of the Lord their God, who hath redeemed them.

14. And the Father hath commanded me that I should give unto you this land, for your inheritance.

15. And I say unto you, that if the Gentiles do not repent after the blessing which they shall receive, after they have scattered my people—

16. Then shall ye, who are a remnant of the house of Jacob, go forth among them; and ye shall be in the midst of them who shall be many; and ye shall be among them as a lion among the beasts of the forest, and as a young lion among the flocks of sheep, who, if he goeth through both treadeth down and teareth in pieces, and none can deliver.

17. Thy hand shall be lifted up upon thine adversaries, and all thine enemies shall be cut off.

18. And I will gather my people together as a man gathereth his sheaves into the floor.

19. For I will make my people with whom the Father hath covenanted, yea, I will make thy horn iron, and I will make thy hoofs brass. And thou shalt beat in pieces many people; and I will consecrate their gain unto the Lord, and their substance unto the Lord of the whole earth. And behold, I am he who doeth it.

20. And it shall come to pass, saith the Father, that the sword of my justice shall hang over them at that day; and except they repent it shall fall upon them, saith the Father, yea, even upon all the nations of the Gentiles.

21. And it shall come to pass that I will establish my people, O house of Israel.

22. And behold, this people will I establish in this land, unto the fulfilling of the covenant which I made with your father Jacob; and it shall be a New Jerusalem. And the powers of heaven shall be in the midst of this people; yea, even I will be in the midst of you.

(b) He Proclaims His Identity

Jesus again declares his identity and refers to the prophecy of Moses and of the prophets since; again tells them who they are, the children of Abraham, the children of the covenant; calls upon them to forsake sin; foretells the curse of the Gentiles, the scattering of the house of Israel, and the returning of their iniquities upon their own heads; he will remember his covenants with his people, their gathering together, the giving to them of the land, which is promised unto them forever.

3 Nephi 20:23-29.

3 NEPHI 20:23. Behold, I am he of whom Moses spake, saying: A prophet shall the Lord your God raise up unto you of your brethren, like unto me; him shall ye hear in all things whatsoever he shall say unto you. And it shall come to pass that every soul who will not hear that prophet shall be cut off from among the people.

24. Verily I say unto you, yea, and all the prophets from Samuel and those that follow after, as many as have spoken, have testified of me.

25. And behold, ye are the children of the prophets; and ye are of the house of Israel; and ye are of the covenant which the Father made with your fathers, saying unto Abraham: And in thy seed shall all the kindreds of the earth be blessed.

26. The Father having raised me up unto you first, and sent me to bless you in turning away every one of you from his iniquities; and this because ye are the children of the covenant—

27. And after that ye were blessed then fulfilleth the Father the covenant which he made with Abraham, saying: In thy seed shall all the kindreds of the earth be blessed—unto the pouring out of the Holy Ghost through me upon the Gentiles, which blessing upon the Gentiles shall make them mighty above all, unto the scattering of my people, O house of Israel.

28. And they shall be a scourge unto the people of this land. Nevertheless, when they shall have received the fulness of my gospel, then if they shall harden their hearts against me I will return their iniquities upon their own heads, saith the Father.

29. And I will remember the covenant which I have made with my people; and I have covenanted with them that I would gather them together in mine own due time, that I would give unto them again the land of their fathers for their inheritance, which is the land of Jerusalem, which is the promised land unto them forever, saith the Father.

(c) Discourse on Glory of Israel

Jesus discourses on the future glory of Israel, quoting from the prophets, and telling when these covenants shall be fulfilled.

3 Nephi 20:30-46.

3 NEPHI 20:30. And it shall come to pass that the time cometh, when the fulness of my gospel shall be preached unto them;

31. And they shall believe in me, that I am Jesus Christ, the Son of God, and shall pray unto the Father in my name.

32. Then shall their watchmen lift up their voice, and with the voice together shall they sing; for they shall see eye to eye.

33. Then will the Father gather them together again, and give unto them Jerusalem for the land of their inheritance.

34. Then shall they break forth into joy—Sing together, ye waste places of Jerusalem; for the Father hath comforted his people, he hath redeemed Jerusalem.

35. The Father hath made bare his holy arm in the eyes of all the nations; and all the ends of the earth shall see the salvation of the Father; and the Father and I are one.

36. And then shall be brought to pass that which is written: Awake, awake again, and put on thy strength, O Zion; put on thy beautiful garments, O Jerusalem, the holy city, for henceforth there shall no more come into thee the uncircumcised and the unclean.

37. Shake thyself from the dust; arise, sit down, O Jerusalem; loose thyself from the bands of thy neck, O captive daughter of Zion.

38. For thus saith the Lord: Ye have sold yourselves for naught, and ye shall be redeemed without money.

39. Verily, verily, I say unto you, that my people shall know my name; yea, in that day they shall know that I am he that doth speak.

40. And then shall they say: How beautiful upon the mountains are the feet of him that bringeth good tidings unto them, that publisheth peace; that bringeth good tidings unto them of good, that publisheth salvation; that saith unto Zion: Thy God reigneth!

41. And then shall a cry go forth: Depart ye, depart ye, go ye out from thence, touch not that which is unclean; go ye out of the midst of her; be ye clean that bear the vessels of the Lord.

42. For ye shall not go out with haste nor go by flight; for the Lord will go before you, and the God of Israel shall be your rearward.

43. Behold, my servant shall deal prudently; he shall be exalted and extolled and be very high.

44. As many were astonished

at thee—his visage was so marred, more than any man, and his form more than the sons of men—

45. So shall he sprinkle many nations; the kings shall shut their mouths at him, for that which had not been told them shall they see; and that which they had not heard shall they consider.

46. Verily, verily, I say unto you, all these things shall surely come, even as the Father hath commanded me. Then shall this covenant which the Father hath covenanted with his people be fulfilled; and then shall Jerusalem be inhabited again with my people, and it shall be the land of their inheritance.

(d) The Signs of the Gathering

Jesus discourses upon the signs which shall tell when all these shall "be about to take place," tells of the great work which the Father shall do for his sake; they who do not receive the word of his servant shall be cut off; the remnant of his people shall be among the Gentiles as a lion among the beasts of the field or a young lion among the sheep, treading down and tearing apart, and "their hand shall be lifted up upon their adversaries, and all their enemies shall be cut off."

3 Nephi 21:1-13.

3 NEPHI 21:1. And verily I say unto you, I give unto you a sign, that ye may know the time when these things shall be about to take place—that I shall gather in, from their long dispersion, my people, O house of Israel, and shall establish again among them my Zion;

2. And behold, this is the thing which I will give unto you for a sign—for verily I say unto you that when these things which I declare unto you, and which I shall declare unto you hereafter of myself, and by the power of the Holy Ghost which shall be given unto you of the Father, shall be made known unto the Gentiles that they may know concerning this people who are a remnant of the house of Jacob, and concerning this my people who shall be scattered by them;

3. Verily, verily, I say unto you, when these things shall be made known unto them of the Father, and shall come forth of the Father, from them unto you;

4. For it is wisdom in the Father that they should be established in this land, and be set up as a free people by the power of the Father, that these things might come forth from them unto a remnant of your seed, that the covenant of the Father may be fulfilled which he hath covenanted with his people, O house of Israel;

5. Therefore, when these works and the works which shall be wrought among you hereafter shall come forth

from the Gentiles, unto your seed which shall dwindle in unbelief because of iniquity;

6. For thus it behooveth the Father that it should come forth from the Gentiles, that he may show forth his power unto the Gentiles, for this cause that the Gentiles, if they will not harden their hearts, that they may repent and come unto me and be baptized in my name and know of the true points of my doctrine, that they may be numbered among my people, O house of Israel;

7. And when these things come to pass that thy seed shall begin to know these things—it shall be a sign unto them, that they may know that the work of the Father hath already commenced unto the fulfilling of the covenant which he hath made unto the people who are of the house of Israel.

8. And when that day shall come, it shall come to pass that kings shall shut their mouths; for that which had not been told them shall they see; and that which they had not heard shall they consider.

9. For in that day, for my sake shall the Father work a work, which shall be a great and a marvelous work among them; and there shall be among them those who will not believe it, although a man shall declare it unto them.

10. But behold, the life of my servant shall be in my hand; therefore they shall not hurt him, although he shall be marred because of them. Yet I will heal him, for I will show unto them that my wisdom is greater than the cunning of the devil.

11. Therefore it shall come to pass that whosoever will not believe in my words, who am Jesus Christ, which the Father shall cause him to bring forth unto the Gentiles, and shall give unto him power that he shall bring them forth unto the Gentiles, (it shall be done even as Moses said) they shall be cut off from among my people who are of the covenant.

12. And my people who are a remnant of Jacob shall be among the Gentiles, yea, in the midst of them as a lion among the beasts of the forest, as a young lion among the flocks of sheep, who, if he go through both treadeth down and teareth in pieces, and none can deliver.

13. Their hand shall be lifted up upon their adversaries, and all their enemies shall be cut off.

(e) The Woes of the Gentiles

Jesus discourses upon the woes which shall come to the Gentiles in those days.

3 Nephi 21:14-21.

3 NEPHI 21:14. Yea, wo be unto the Gentiles except they repent; for it shall come to pass in that day, saith the Father, that I will cut off thy horses out of the midst of thee, and I will destroy thy chariots;

15. And I will cut off the cities of thy land, and throw down all thy strongholds;

16. And I will cut off witchcrafts out of thy land, and thou shalt have no more soothsayers;

17. Thy graven images I will also cut off, and thy standing images out of the midst of thee, and thou shalt no more worship the works of thy hands;

18. And I will pluck up thy groves out of the midst of thee; so will I destroy thy cities.

19. And it shall come to pass that all lyings, and deceivings, and envyings, and strifes, and priestcrafts, and whoredoms, shall be done away.

20. For it shall come to pass, saith the Father, that at that day whosoever will not repent and come unto my Beloved Son, them will I cut off from among my people, O house of Israel;

21. And I will execute vengeance and fury upon them, even as upon the heathen, such as they have not heard.

(f) How Gentiles May Share Glories

Jesus promises that if the Gentiles will repent and assist his people, they shall share in the glories which come to his people; the work shall then commence among all his dispersed peoples, even the tribes which are lost, that they may come unto him and call upon the Father in his name.

3 Nephi 21:22-27.

3 NEPHI 21:22. But if they will repent and hearken unto my words, and harden not their hearts, I will establish my church among them, and they shall come in unto the covenant and be numbered among this the remnant of Jacob, unto whom I have given this land for their inheritance;

23. And they shall assist my people, the remnant of Jacob, and also as many of the house of Israel as shall come, that they may build a city, which shall be called the New Jerusalem.

24. And then shall they assist my people that they may be gathered in, who are scattered upon all the face of the land, in unto the New Jerusalem.

25. And then shall the power of heaven come down among them; and I also will be in the midst.

26. And then shall the work of the Father commence at that day, even when this gospel shall be preached among the remnant of this people. Verily I say unto you, at that day shall the work of the Fa-

ther commence among all the dispersed of my people, yea, even the tribes which have been lost, which the Father hath led away out of Jerusalem.

27. Yea, the work shall commence among all the dispersed of my people, with the Father, to prepare the way whereby they may come unto me, that they may call on the Father in my name.

(g) The Father Will Commence Work

The Father will then commence his work among all the nations for the gathering of his people to the land of their inheritance; they shall go out from all nations, not in haste and not in fright, "and I will be their rearward."

3 Nephi 21:28-29.

3 NEPHI 21:28. Yea, and then shall the work commence, with the Father, among all nations, in preparing the way whereby his people may be gathered home to the land of their inheritance.

29. And they shall go out from all nations; and they shall not go out in haste, nor go by flight, for I will go before them, saith the Father, and I will be their rearward.

(h) He Again Quotes Isaiah

Jesus again repeats from the words of the prophet Isaiah—the rejoicings of God's people, and his rejoicings over his people.

3 Nephi 22:1-17.

3 NEPHI 22:1. And then shall that which is written come to pass: Sing, O barren, thou that didst not bear; break forth into singing, and cry aloud, thou that didst not travail with child; for more are the children of the desolate than the children of the married wife, saith the Lord.

2. Enlarge the place of thy tent, and let them stretch forth the curtains of thy habitations; spare not, lengthen thy cords and strengthen thy stakes;

3. For thou shalt break forth on the right hand and on the left, and thy seed shall inherit the Gentiles and make the desolate cities to be inhabited.

4. Fear not, for thou shalt not be ashamed; neither be thou confounded, for thou shalt not be put to shame; for thou shalt forget the shame of thy youth, and shalt not remember the reproach of thy youth, and shalt not remember the reproach of thy widowhood any more.

5. For thy maker, thy husband, the Lord of Hosts is his name; and thy Redeemer, the

Holy One of Israel—the God of the whole earth shall he be called.

6. For the Lord hath called thee as a woman forsaken and grieved in spirit, and a wife of youth, when thou wast refused, saith thy God.

7. For a small moment have I forsaken thee, but with great mercies will I gather thee.

8. In a little wrath I hid my face from thee for a moment, but with everlasting kindness will I have mercy on thee, saith the Lord thy Redeemer.

9. For this, the waters of Noah unto me, for as I have sworn that the waters of Noah should no more go over the earth, so have I sworn that I would not be wroth with thee.

10. For the mountains shall depart and the hills be removed, but my kindness shall not depart from thee, neither shall the covenant of my people be removed, saith the Lord that hath mercy on thee.

11. O thou afflicted, tossed with tempest, and not comforted! Behold, I will lay thy stones with fair colors, and lay thy foundations with sapphires.

12. And I will make thy windows of agates, and thy gates of carbuncles, and all thy borders of pleasant stones.

13. And all thy children shall be taught of the Lord; and great shall be the peace of thy children.

14. In righteousness shalt thou be established; thou shalt be far from oppression for thou shalt not fear, and from terror for it shall not come near thee.

15. Behold, they shall surely gather together against thee, not by me; whosoever shall gather together against thee shall fall for thy sake.

16. Behold, I have created the smith that bloweth the coals in the fire, and that bringeth forth an instrument for his work; and I have created the waster to destroy.

17. No weapon that is formed against thee shall prosper; and every tongue that shall rise against thee in judgment thou shalt condemn. This is the heritage of the servants of the Lord, and their righteousness is of me, saith the Lord.

(i) The People to Search Scriptures

Jesus commands that they search the words of Isaiah, that they write the things which he has told them and to search the scriptures; he states there are other scriptures they should write which they do not have.

3 Nephi 23:1-6.

3 NEPHI 23:1. And now, behold, I say unto you, that ye ought to search these things. Yea, a commandment I give unto you that ye search these things diligently; for great are the words of Isaiah.

2. For surely he spake as touching all things concerning my people which are of the house of Israel; therefore it must needs be that he must speak also to the Gentiles.

3. And all things that he spake have been and shall be, even according to the words which he spake.

4. Therefore give heed to my words; write the things which I have told you; and according to the time and the will of the Father they shall go forth unto the Gentiles.

5. And whosoever will hearken unto my words and repenteth and is baptized, the same shall be saved. Search the prophets, for many there be that testify of these things.

6. And now it came to pass that when Jesus had said these words he said unto them again, after he had expounded all the scriptures unto them which they had received, he said unto them: Behold, other scriptures I would that ye should write, that ye have not.

(j) Their Records Criticized

Jesus tells Nephi to bring forth the records, and when Nephi brings them, Jesus points out they contain no record of the prophecies of Samuel regarding the resurrection of the Saints, and he tells them to make record of these things; he commands that they shall teach the things he has expounded.

3 Nephi 23:7-14.

3 NEPHI 23:7. And it came to pass that he said unto Nephi: Bring forth the record which ye have kept.

8. And when Nephi had brought forth the records, and laid them before him, he cast his eyes upon them and said:

9. Verily I say unto you, I commanded my servant Samuel, the Lamanite, that he should testify unto this people, that at the day that the Father should glorify his name in me that there were many saints who should arise from the dead, and should appear unto many, and should minister unto them. And he said unto them: Was it not so?

10. And his disciples answered him and said: Yea, Lord, Samuel did prophesy according to thy words, and they were all fulfilled.

11. And Jesus said unto them: How be it that ye have not written this thing, that many saints did arise and appear unto many and did minister unto them?

12. And it came to pass that Nephi remembered that this thing had not been written.

13. And it came to pass that Jesus commanded that it

should be written; therefore it was written according as he commanded.

14. And now it came to pass that when Jesus had expounded all the scriptures in one, which they had written, he commanded them that they should teach the things which he had expounded unto them.

(k) Record to Be Made of Malachi's Words

Jesus commands them to make a record of the words of Malachi, which he gives unto them.

3 Nephi 24:1-18; 25:1-6.

3 NEPHI 24:1. And it came to pass that he commanded them that they should write the words which the Father had given unto Malachi, which he should tell unto them. And it came to pass that after they were written he expounded them. And these are the words which he did tell unto them, saying: Thus said the Father unto Malachi—Behold, I will send my messenger, and he shall prepare the way before me, and the Lord whom ye seek shall suddenly come to his temple, even the messenger of the covenant, whom ye delight in; behold, he shall come, saith the Lord of Hosts.

2. But who may abide the day of his coming, and who shall stand when he appeareth? For he is like a refiner's fire, and like fuller's soap.

3. And he shall sit as a refiner and purifier of silver; and he shall purify the sons of Levi, and purge them as gold and silver, that they may offer unto the Lord an offering in righteousness.

4. Then shall the offering of Judah and Jerusalem be pleasant unto the Lord, as in the days of old, and as in former years.

5. And I will come near to you to judgment; and I will be a swift witness against the sorcerers, and against the adulterers, and against false swearers, and against those that oppress the hireling in his wages, the widow and the fatherless, and that turn aside the stranger, and fear not me, saith the Lord of Hosts.

6. For I am the Lord, I change not; therefore ye sons of Jacob are not consumed.

7. Even from the days of your fathers ye are gone away from mine ordinances, and have not kept them. Return unto me and I will return unto you, saith the Lord of Hosts. But ye say: Wherein shall we return?

8. Will a man rob God? Yet ye have robbed me. But ye say: Wherein have we robbed thee? In tithes and offerings.

9. Ye are cursed with a

curse, for ye have robbed me, even this whole nation.

10. Bring ye all the tithes into the storehouse, that there may be meat in my house; and prove me now herewith, saith the Lord of Hosts, if I will not open you the windows of heaven, and pour you out a blessing that there shall not be room enough to receive it.

11. And I will rebuke the devourer for your sakes, and he shall not destroy the fruits of your ground; neither shall your vine cast her fruit before the time in the fields, saith the Lord of Hosts.

12. And all nations shall call you blessed, for ye shall be a delightsome land, saith the Lord of Hosts.

13. Your words have been stout against me, saith the Lord. Yet ye say: What have we spoken against thee?

14. Ye have said: It is vain to serve God, and what doth it profit that we have kept his ordinances and that we have walked mournfully before the Lord of Hosts?

15. And now we call the proud happy; yea, they that work wickedness are set up; yea, they that tempt God are even delivered.

16. Then they that feared the Lord spake often one to another, and the Lord hearkened and heard; and a book of remembrance was written before him for them that feared the Lord, and that thought upon his name.

17. And they shall be mine, saith the Lord of Hosts, in that day when I make up my jewels; and I will spare them as a man spareth his own son that serveth him.

18. Then shall ye return and discern between the righteous and the wicked, between him that serveth God and him that serveth him not.

CHAPTER 25

1. For behold, the day cometh that shall burn as an oven; and all the proud, yea, and all that do wickedly, shall be stubble; and the day that cometh shall burn them up, saith the Lord of Hosts, that it shall leave them neither root nor branch.

2. But unto you that fear my name, shall the Son of Righteousness arise with healing in his wings; and ye shall go forth and grow up as calves in the stall.

3. And ye shall tread down the wicked; for they shall be ashes under the soles of your feet in the day that I shall do this, saith the Lord of Hosts.

4. Remember ye the law of Moses, my servant, which I commanded unto him in Horeb for all Israel, with the statutes and judgments.

5. Behold, I will send you Elijah the prophet before the

coming of the great and dreadful day of the Lord;

6. And he shall turn the heart of the fathers to the children, and the heart of the children to their fathers, lest I come and smite the earth with a curse.

(l) The Scriptures Expounded

Jesus expounds these scriptures at the direction of the Father, and all things he expounds from the beginning until the end when the heavens and earth should pass away, and the great last day of judgment which shall be given according "to the mercy, and the justice, and the holiness which is in Christ, who was before the world began."

3 Nephi 26:1-5.

3 NEPHI 26:1. And now it came to pass that when Jesus had told these things he expounded them unto the multitude; and he did expound all things unto them, both great and small.

2. And he saith: These scriptures, which ye had not with you, the Father commanded that I should give unto you; for it was wisdom in him that they should be given unto future generations.

3. And he did expound all things, even from the beginning until the time that he should come in his glory—yea, even all things which should come upon the face of the earth, even until the elements should melt with fervent heat, and the earth should be wrapt together as a scroll, and the heavens and the earth should pass away;

4. And even unto the great and last day, when all people, and all kindreds, and all nations and tongues shall stand before God, to be judged of their works, whether they be good or whether they be evil—

5. If they be good, to the resurrection of everlasting life; and if they be evil, to the resurrection of damnation; being on a parallel, the one on the one hand and the other on the other hand, according to the mercy, and the justice, and the holiness which is in Christ, who was before the world began.

(m) Moroni Explains Records

Moroni explains the omissions from these records, and gives the commandment of the Lord touching the matter.

3 Nephi 26:6-12.

3 NEPHI 26:6. And now there cannot be written in this book even a hundredth part of the things which Jesus did truly teach unto the people;

7. But behold the plates of

Nephi do contain the more part of the things which he taught the people.

8. And these things have I written, which are a lesser part of the things which he taught the people; and I have written them to the intent that they may be brought again unto this people, from the Gentiles, according to the words which Jesus hath spoken.

9. And when they shall have received this, which is expedient that they should have first, to try their faith, and if it shall so be that they shall believe these things then shall the greater things be made manifest unto them.

10. And if it so be that they will not believe these things, then shall the greater things be withheld from them, unto their condemnation.

11. Behold, I was about to write them, all which were engraven upon the plates of Nephi, but the Lord forbade it, saying: I will try the faith of my people.

12. Therefore I, Mormon, do write the things which have been commanded me of the Lord. And now I, Mormon, make an end of my sayings, and proceed to write the things which have been commanded me.

Section 180

HE TEACHES THE PEOPLE

Jesus "truly did teach the people, for the space of three days; and after that he did show himself unto them oft, and did break bread oft, and bless it, and give it unto them."

3 Nephi 26:13.

3 NEPHI 26:13. Therefore, I would that ye should behold that the Lord truly did teach the people, for the space of three days; and after that he did show himself unto them oft, and did break bread oft, and bless it, and give it unto them.

Section 181

WORKS OF JESUS AMONG THE PEOPLE

3 Nephi 26:14-16.

3 NEPHI 26:14. And it came to pass that he did teach and minister unto the children of the multitude of whom hath been spoken, and he did loose their tongues, and they did speak unto their fathers great and marvelous things, even greater than he had revealed unto the people; and he loosed their tongues that they could utter.

15. And it came to pass that after he had ascended into heaven—the second time that he showed himself unto them, and had gone unto the Father, after having healed all their sick, and their lame, and opened the eyes of their blind and unstopped the ears of the deaf, and even had done all manner of cures among them, and raised a man from the dead, and had shown forth his power unto them, and had ascended unto the Father—

16. Behold, it came to pass on the morrow that the multitude gathered themselves together, and they both saw and heard these children; yea, even babes did open their mouths and utter marvelous things; and the things which they did utter were forbidden that there should not any man write them.

Section 182

DISCIPLES BEGIN WORK

The disciples begin their work from that time forth, baptizing; those who are baptized are filled with the Holy Ghost and see many unspeakable things not lawful to be written; they teach one another, have all things in common, deal justly one with another, and do all things as Jesus commanded, and those baptized are called the Church of Christ.

3 Nephi 26:17-21.

3 NEPHI 26:17. And it came to pass that the disciples whom Jesus had chosen began from that time forth to baptize and to teach as many as did come unto them; and as many as were baptized in the name of Jesus were filled with the Holy Ghost.

18. And many of them saw and heard unspeakable things, which are not lawful to be written.

19. And they taught, and did minister one to another; and they had all things common among them, every man dealing justly, one with another.

20. And it came to pass that they did do all things even as Jesus had commanded them.

21. And they who were baptized in the name of Jesus were called the church of Christ.

Section 183

ANOTHER WARNING

The disciples, being gathered together and engaged in mighty prayer and fasting, Jesus comes to them and asks what they wish him to give them; he gives them instruction about the name of the Church and why.

3 Nephi 27:1-12.

3 NEPHI 27:1. And it came to pass that as the disciples of Jesus were journeying and were preaching the things which they had both heard and seen, and were baptizing in the name of Jesus, it came to pass that the disciples were gathered together and were united in mighty prayer and fasting.

2. And Jesus again showed himself unto them, for they were praying unto the Father in his name; and Jesus came and stood in the midst of them, and said unto them: What will ye that I shall give unto you?

3. And they said unto him: Lord, we will that thou wouldst tell us the name whereby we shall call this church; for there are disputations among the people concerning this matter.

4. And the Lord said unto them: Verily, verily, I say unto you, why is it that the people should murmur and dispute because of this thing?

5. Have they not read the scriptures, which say ye must take upon you the name of Christ, which is my name? For by this name shall ye be called at the last day;

6. And whoso taketh upon him my name, and endureth to the end, the same shall be saved at the last day.

7. Therefore, whatsoever ye shall do, ye shall do it in my name; therefore ye shall call the church in my name; and ye shall call upon the Father in my name that he will bless the church for my sake.

8. And how be it my church save it be called in my name? For if a church be called in Moses' name then it be Moses' church; or if it be called in the name of a man then it be the church of a man; but if it be called in my name then it is my church, if it so be that they are built upon my gospel.

9. Verily I say unto you, that ye are built upon my gospel; therefore ye shall call whatsoever things ye do call, in my name; therefore if ye call upon the Father, for the church, if it be in my name the Father will hear you;

10. And if it so be that the church is built upon my gospel then will the Father show forth his own works in it.

11. But if it be not built up-

on my gospel, and is built upon the works of men, or upon the works of the devil, verily I say unto you they have joy in their works for a season, and by and by the end cometh, and they are hewn down and cast into the fire, from whence there is no return.

12. For their works do follow them, for it is because of their works that they are hewn down; therefore remember the things that I have told you.

Section 184

JESUS AGAIN DECLARES HIMSELF

Jesus again declares himself and discourses upon his mission and atonement.

3 Nephi 27:13-15.

3 NEPHI 27:13. Behold I have given unto you my gospel, and this is the gospel which I have given unto you—that I came into the world to do the will of my Father, because my Father sent me.

14. And my Father sent me that I might be lifted up upon the cross; and after that I had been lifted up upon the cross, that I might draw all men unto me, that as I have been lifted up by men even so should men be lifted up by the Father, to stand before me, to be judged of their works, whether they be good or whether they be evil—

15. And for this cause have I been lifted up; therefore, according to the power of the Father I will draw all men unto me, that they may be judged according to their works.

Section 185

BAPTISM EXPLAINED

Jesus explains the effect of baptism upon them who endure to the end, and upon them who do not endure; no unclean thing can enter into his kingdom, only they who wash their garments in his blood, and, because of their faith, repent and hold their faithfulness to the end; declares what his Gospel is; the Church must do his works; and if they do these things they are blessed and "shall be lifted up at the last day."

3 Nephi 27:16-22.

3 NEPHI 27:16. And it shall come to pass, that whoso repenteth and is baptized in my name shall be filled; and if he endureth to the end, behold, him will I hold guiltless before my Father at that day when I shall stand to judge the world.

17. And he that endureth not unto the end, the same is he that is also hewn down and cast into the fire, from whence

they can no more return, because of the justice of the Father.

18. And this is the word which he hath given unto the children of men. And for this cause he fulfilleth the words which he hath given, and he lieth not, but fulfilleth all his words.

19. And no unclean thing can enter into his kingdom; therefore nothing entereth into his rest save it be those who have washed their garments in my blood, because of their faith, and the repentance of all their sins, and their faithfulness unto the end.

20. Now this is the commandment: Repent, all ye ends of the earth, and come unto me and be baptized in my name, that ye may be sanctified by the reception of the Holy Ghost, that ye may stand spotless before me at the last day.

21. Verily, verily, I say unto you, this is my gospel; and ye know the things that ye must do in my church; for the works which ye have seen me do that shall ye also do; for that which ye have seen me do even that shall ye do;

22. Therefore, if ye do these things blessed are ye, for ye shall be lifted up at the last day.

Section 186

THE KEEPING OF RECORDS RECOMMENDED

Jesus instructs the disciples to keep record of all things; "out of the books which shall be written shall the world be judged"; all his disciples shall be judged of this people, according to the judgment he shall give them, which shall be just; his disciples ought to be even as Jesus is.

3 Nephi 27:23-27.

3 NEPHI 27:23. Write the things which ye have seen and heard, save it be those which are forbidden.

24. Write the works of this people, which shall be, even as hath been written, of that which hath been.

25. For behold, out of the books which have been written, and which shall be written, shall this people be judged, for by them shall their works be known unto men.

26. And behold, all things are written by the Father; therefore out of the books which shall be written shall the world be judged.

27. And know ye that ye shall be judges of this people, according to the judgment which I shall give unto you, which shall be just. Therefore, what manner of men ought ye to be? Verily I say unto you, even as I am.

Section 187

THE FINAL WORDS TO THE DISCIPLES

(a) He Must Go to the Father

Jesus tells the disciples he must go unto the Father; tells what they ask the Father in his name shall be given.

3 Nephi 27:28.

3 NEPHI 27:28. And now I go unto the Father. And verily I say unto you, whatsoever things ye shall ask the Father in my name shall be given unto you.

(b) None of This Generation to Be Lost

Jesus directs them to ask and they shall receive, declares his joy because of this generation, and the Father rejoiceth also, for none of that generation shall be lost, that is, none of those now alive and in them he has a fulness of joy.

3 Nephi 27:29-31.

3 NEPHI 27:29. Therefore, ask, and ye shall receive; knock, and it shall be opened unto you; for he that asketh, receiveth; and unto him that knocketh, it shall be opened.

30. And now, behold, my joy is great, even unto fulness, because of you, and also this generation; yea, and even the Father rejoiceth, and also all the holy angels, because of you and this generation; for none of them are lost.

31. Behold, I would that ye should understand; for I mean them who are now alive of this generation; and none of them are lost; and in them I have fulness of joy.

(c) Fourth Generation to Be Led Captive

Jesus foretells that the fourth generation from this shall be led away captive, following the son of perdition, and selling Jesus for silver and gold; in that day he will visit them, "turning their works upon their own heads."

3 Nephi 27:32.

3 NEPHI 27:32. But behold, it sorroweth me because of the fourth generation from this generation, for they are led away captive by him even as was the son of perdition; for they will sell me for silver and for gold, and for that which moth doth corrupt and which thieves can break through and steal. And in that day will I visit them, even in turning their works upon their own heads.

(d) Further Instructions

Telling his disciples to enter into the strait gate and narrow way leading to eternal life, he also tells them that wide is the gate and broad the way that leads to death; many travel it; "the night cometh, wherein no man can work."

3 Nephi 27:33.

3 NEPHI 27:33. And it came to pass that when Jesus had ended these sayings he said unto his disciples: Enter ye in at the strait gate; for strait is the gate, and narrow is the way that leads to life, and few there be that find it; but wide is the gate, and broad the way which leads to death, and many there be that travel therein, until the night cometh, wherein no man can work.

(e) Jesus' Gifts to Nine Disciples

Having finished the instructions, Jesus asks them, "What is it that ye desire of me, after that I am gone to the Father"; all speak but three, the others said that when they had finished their normal course they wished they might "speedily come unto thee in thy kingdom"; Jesus said they were blessed because of this desire, and when they were seventy-two years old they should come to him "and with me ye shall find rest."

3 Nephi 28:1-3.

3 NEPHI 28:1. And it came to pass when Jesus had said these words, he spake unto his disciples, one by one, saying unto them: What is it that ye desire of me, after that I am gone to the Father?

2. And they all spake, save it were three, saying: We desire that after we have lived unto the age of man, that our ministry, wherein thou hast called us, may have an end, that we may speedily come unto thee in thy kingdom.

3. And he said unto them: Blessed are ye because ye desired this thing of me; therefore, after that ye are seventy and two years old ye shall come unto me in my kingdom; and with me ye shall find rest.

(f) Jesus' Gifts to Three Disciples

Jesus then asks the three what they wish; they dare not tell their wish; he tells them he knows their thoughts—that they wish what he gave to John; he promises them they shall never taste death, but shall live to behold all of God's dealings with the children of men; when he comes they shall be changed in the twinkling of an eye, never tasting death, nor have pain or sorrow while in the flesh, because they have desired that they might bring the souls of men unto him; he promises them their reward.

3 Nephi 28:4-11.

3 NEPHI 28:4. And when he had spoken unto them, he turned himself unto the three, and said unto them: What will ye that I should do unto you, when I am gone unto the Father?

5. And they sorrowed in their hearts, for they durst not speak unto him the thing which they desired.

6. And he said unto them: Behold, I know your thoughts, and ye have desired the thing which John, my beloved, who was with me in my ministry, before that I was lifted up by the Jews, desired of me.

7. Therefore, more blessed are ye, for ye shall never taste of death; but ye shall live to behold all the doings of the Father unto the children of men, even until all things shall be fulfilled according to the will of the Father, when I shall come in my glory with the powers of heaven.

8. And ye shall never endure the pains of death; but when I shall come in my glory ye shall be changed in the twinkling of an eye from mortality to immortality; and then shall ye be blessed in the kingdom of my Father.

9. And again, ye shall not have pain while ye shall dwell in the flesh, neither sorrow save it be for the sins of the world; and all this will I do because of the thing which ye have desired of me, for ye have desired that ye might bring the souls of men unto me, while the world shall stand.

10. And for this cause ye shall have fulness of joy; and ye shall sit down in the kingdom of my Father; yea, your joy shall be full, even as the Father hath given me fulness of joy; and ye shall be even as I am, and I am even as the Father; and the Father and I are one;

11. And the Holy Ghost beareth record of the Father and me; and the Father giveth the Holy Ghost unto the children of men, because of me.

Section 188

JESUS ASCENDS; THE THREE AS IF TRANSFIGURED

Having finished his instructions, he touches all but the three with his finger, and then he departs. The heavens are opened and the three are caught up into heaven and hear unspeakable things, and whether they were in the body or out, they knew not, but it seemed like a transfiguration, that they were changed from a body of flesh into an immortal state that they could behold the things of God.

3 Nephi 28:12-15.

3 NEPHI 28:12. And it came to pass that when Jesus had spoken these words, he touched every one of them with his finger save it were the three who were to tarry, and then he departed.

13. And behold, the heavens were opened, and they were caught up into heaven, and saw and heard unspeakable things.

14. And it was forbidden them that they should utter; neither was it given unto them power that they could utter the things which they saw and heard;

15. And whether they were in the body or out of the body, they could not tell; for it did seem unto them like a transfiguration of them, that they were changed from this body of flesh into an immortal state, that they could behold the things of God.

Section 189

MINISTRY OF THE THREE

The ministry of the Three Nephites among the people, their mighty works and miracles, and miraculous deliveries; they teach and convert the people.

3 Nephi 28:16-23.

3 NEPHI 28:16. But it came to pass that they did again minister upon the face of the earth; nevertheless they did not minister of the things which they had heard and seen, because of the commandment which was given them in heaven.

17. And now, whether they were mortal or immortal, from the day of their transfiguration, I know not;

18. But this much I know, according to the record which hath been given—they did go forth upon the face of the land, and did minister unto all the people, uniting as many to the church as would believe in their preaching; baptizing them, and as many as were baptized did receive the Holy Ghost.

19. And they were cast into prison by them who did not belong to the church. And the prisons could not hold them, for they were rent in twain.

20. And they were cast down into the earth; but they did smite the earth with the word of God, insomuch that by his power they were delivered out of the depths of the earth; and therefore they could not dig pits sufficient to hold them.

21. And thrice they were cast into a furnace and received no harm.

22. And twice were they cast into a den of wild beasts; and behold they did play with the

beasts as a child with a suckling lamb, and received no harm.

23. And it came to pass that thus they did go forth among all the people of Nephi, and did preach the gospel of Christ unto all people upon the face of the land; and they were converted unto the Lord, and were united unto the church of Christ, and thus the people of that generation were blessed, according to the word of Jesus.

Section 190

MORONI FINISHES RECORD

Moroni finishes his record of the Three Nephites, he does not tell their names; they will work among the Jews and Gentiles, and go unto the scattered tribes of Israel; they are the angels of God, and will do a mighty and marvelous work; Moroni tells of the woes of those who do not listen to their message and speaks more of the condition of the bodies of the Three Nephites and their final reward.

3 Nephi 28:24-40.

3 NEPHI 28:24. And now I, Mormon, make an end of speaking concerning these things for a time.

25. Behold, I was about to write the names of those who were never to taste of death, but the Lord forbade; therefore I write them not, for they are hid from the world.

26. But behold, I have seen them, and they have ministered unto me.

27. And behold they will be among the Gentiles, and the Gentiles shall know them not.

28. They will also be among the Jews, and the Jews shall know them not.

29. And it shall come to pass, when the Lord seeth fit in his wisdom that they shall minister unto all the scattered tribes of Israel, and unto all nations, kindreds, tongues and people, and shall bring out of them unto Jesus many souls, that their desire may be fulfilled, and also because of the convincing power of God which is in them.

30. And they are as the angels of God, and if they shall pray unto the Father in the name of Jesus they can show themselves unto whatsoever man it seemeth them good.

31. Therefore, great and marvelous works shall be wrought by them, before the great and coming day when all people must surely stand before the judgment-seat of Christ;

32. Yea even among the Gentiles shall there be a great and marvelous work wrought by them, before that judgment day.

33. And if ye had all the scriptures which give an account of all the marvelous

works of Christ, ye would, according to the words of Christ, know that these things must surely come.

34. And wo be unto him that will not hearken unto the words of Jesus, and also to them whom he hath chosen and sent among them; for whoso receiveth not the words of Jesus and the words of those whom he hath sent receiveth not him; and therefore he will not receive them at the last day;

35. And it would be better for them if they had not been born. For do ye suppose that ye can get rid of the justice of an offended God, who hath been trampled under feet of men, that thereby salvation might come?

36. And now behold, as I spake concerning those whom the Lord hath chosen, yea, even three who were caught up into the heavens, that I knew not whether they were cleansed from mortality to immortality—

37. But behold, since I wrote, I have inquired of the Lord, and he hath made it manifest unto me that there must needs be a change wrought upon their bodies, or else it needs be that they must taste of death;

38. Therefore, that they might not taste of death there was a change wrought upon their bodies, that they might not suffer pain nor sorrow save it were for the sins of the world.

39. Now this change was not equal to that which shall take place at the last day; but there was a change wrought upon them, insomuch that Satan could have no power over them, that he could not tempt them; and they were sanctified in the flesh, that they were holy, and that the powers of the earth could not hold them.

40. And in this state they were to remain until the judgment day of Christ; and at that day they were to receive a greater change, and to be received into the kingdom of the Father to go no more out, but to dwell with God eternally in the heavens.

Section 191

MORONI'S CLOSING WORDS TO THE GENTILES

3 Nephi Chapters 29-30.

3 NEPHI 29:1. And now behold, I say unto you that when the Lord shall see fit, in his wisdom, that these sayings shall come unto the Gentiles according to his word, then ye may know that the covenant which the Father hath made with the children of Israel, concerning their restoration to the lands of their inheritance, is already beginning to be fulfilled.

2. And ye may know that the words of the Lord, which have been spoken by the holy prophets, shall all be fulfilled; and ye need not say that the Lord delays his coming unto the children of Israel.

3. And ye need not imagine in your hearts that the words which have been spoken are vain, for behold, the Lord will remember his covenant which he hath made unto his people of the house of Israel.

4. And when ye shall see these sayings coming forth among you, then ye need not any longer spurn at the doings of the Lord, for the sword of his justice is in his right hand; and behold, at that day, if ye shall spurn at his doings he will cause that it shall soon overtake you.

5. Wo unto him that spurneth at the doings of the Lord; yea, wo unto him that shall deny the Christ and his works!

6. Yea, wo unto him that shall deny the revelations of the Lord, and that shall say the Lord no longer worketh by revelation, or by prophecy, or by gifts, or by tongues, or by healings, or by the power of the Holy Ghost!

7. Yea, and wo unto him that shall say at that day, to get gain, that there can be no miracle wrought by Jesus Christ; for he that doeth this shall become like unto the son of perdition, for whom there was no mercy, according to the word of Christ!

8. Yea, and ye need not any longer hiss, nor spurn, nor make game of the Jews, nor any of the remnant of the house of Israel; for behold, the Lord remembereth his covenant unto them, and he will do unto them according to that which he hath sworn.

9. Therefore ye need not suppose that ye can turn the right hand of the Lord unto the left, that he may not execute judgment unto the fulfilling of the covenant which he hath made unto the house of Israel.

CHAPTER 30

1. Hearken, O ye Gentiles, and hear the words of Jesus Christ, the Son of the living God, which he hath commanded me that I should speak concerning you, for, behold he commandeth me that I should write, saying:

2. Turn, all ye Gentiles, from your wicked ways; and repent of your evil doings, of your lyings and deceivings, and of your whoredoms, and of your secret abominations, and your idolatries, and of your murders, and your priestcrafts, and your envyings, and your strifes, and from all your wick-

edness and abominations, and come unto me, and be baptized in my name, that ye may receive a remission of your sins, and be filled with the Holy Ghost, that ye may be numbered with my people who are of the house of Israel.

Division Four

Tables, Charts, and Maps

SOME OLD TESTAMENT PROPHECIES CONCERNING THE COMING, LIFE, AND MISSION OF JESUS THE CHRIST, AS LISTED BY COMMENTATORS

Genesis

1:1	The Word of God. (With Ps. 33:6.)
3:15	Advent; lineage; the seed of the woman; his sufferings or passion.
9:18, 27	Descendant of Shem.
9:26-27	Lineage; descendant of Shem.
12:3	Lineage; descendant of Abraham.
17:19	Descendant of Isaac.
18:18	Descendant of Abraham.
21:12	Descendant of Isaac.
22:18	The promised seed of Abraham.
26:4	Lineage; descendant of Isaac.
28:4-14	Lineage; descendant of Jacob.
49:9-10	Lineage; of the tribe of Judah; sent of God.

Exodus

12:1-14	The Lamb of God.
12:46	His bones not broken.

Leviticus

16:7-22	Sin offering in behalf of the people.

Numbers

24:17, 19	Descendant of Israel or Jacob; time and place of birth.

Deuteronomy

18:15-19	Advent; prophet.
32:21	Jews reluctant to admit the Gentiles.
32:43	Gentiles included in the summons.

I Samuel

7:12-15	Of the house of David.
23:1-5	Of the house of David.

II Samuel

7:12	King of Israel.
7:13	Messianic Kingdom built in Jehovah's name.
7:14-16	Lineage; heir of David; Son of God; relation to God.
23:4	Time of advent.

I Chronicles

5:2	Of the tribe of Judah.
17:10-14	Of the house of David.
17:13	Son of God.

Job

19:25	Coming to judgment.
19:25-27	Our Redeemer.

Psalms

2:1-12	Characteristics of his life and work.
2:1-2	His death procured by Jews and Gentiles combined.
2:2, 6	Anointed One, King of Israel.
2:6-8	Exaltation.
2:7	The Father acknowledges him to be his Son; our Lord, the Son of God.
2:7, 12	Relation to God; Son of Jehovah.
2:8	To draw all nations; Messianic Kingdom universal.
2:12	Citizens of Messianic Kingdom protected.
8:2	Entry into Jerusalem.

Psalms, Cont'd

8:4-6	Our Lord, the son of man; ascension into heaven.
16:8-10	As to his resurrection and enthronement.
16:10	Embalmed and entombed; raised on the third day; Holy One.
16:11	Ascension.
17:15	Raised on the third day.
18:49	The Gentiles included in the summons.
18:50	His anointed.
19:4	Universal diffusion of the Gospel.
22:1-21	His sufferings or passion.
22:1	Cries from the cross; his exclamation on the cross.
22:6	Persecuted.
22:7,8,16	Mocked.
22:12	Rejected of men.
22:14-17	Crucified, cut off.
22:15	His hands and feet are pierced.
22:16	His hands and feet pierced; death on the cross.
22:18	Lots cast for his vesture.
22:22	Our Lord, man.
31:5	Cries from the cross; his commendation of his spirit to his Father.
33:6	The Word of God.
34:20	No bone broken.
35:11	He is condemned on the evidence of false witnesses.
40:6-8	His sacrifice supersedes all others.
41:9	His betrayal by a friend and disciple.
45:1-17	Characteristics of his life and work.
45:4	Warrior for truth.
45:6-7	Our Lord, a King; our Lord, God.

Psalms, Cont'd

45:7	Hating iniquity.
45:17	Messianic Kingdom everlasting.
56:5	His enemies try to catch him in his words.
68:18	His ascension.
69:8	His brethren do not believe on him; rejected of men.
69:9	The desecration of the temple, and his cleansing of it; his bearing undeserved of reproach.
69:21	Sufferings on the cross; thirst; they give him vinegar to drink.
71:10	A plot formed against him.
72:1-20	Characteristics of his life and work.
72:1	King of Israel.
72:2	Messianic Kingdom founded in Zion.
72:2-4	Citizens of Messianic Kingdom poor and afflicted; Judge.
72:8	Messianic Kingdom universal; relation to God; Son of Jehovah.
72:9,10,15	Magi.
72:17	Messianic Kingdom everlasting.
78:2	Method of teaching, parables.
89:4, 36	Of the house of David.
89:26	He appeals to God as his Father.
89:27	King.
102:25-27	Our Lord, the Everlasting, the Creator.
109:25	Mocked.
110:1-7	Characteristics of his life and work.
110:1	As to his resurrection and ascension, exaltation and enthrone-

Psalms, Cont'd

	ment; our Lord sits on the Father's throne; relation to God; Son of Jehovah; King.
110:1-3	Exaltation; Messianic Kingdom universal.
110:4	Our Lord, a High Priest.
110:6	Coming to judgment; Judge.
117:1	The Gentiles included in the summons.
118:17	Resurrection.
118:19	Ascension.
118:22	Cornerstone; Messianic Kingdom founded in Zion.
118:22-23	Rejected of men; his teaching rejected.
118:25-26	The acclamations at his triumphal entry; entry to Jerusalem.
132:10-17	Of the house of David.

Proverbs

8:22-31	Wisdom of God.

Ecclesiastes

12:14	Coming to judgment.

Isaiah

2:2-4	Messianic Kingdom, peaceful; its citizens instructed.
2:3	To draw all nations.
4:3	Messianic Kingdom, its citizens holy.
4:6	Messianic Kingdom, its citizens protected.
6:9, 10	His teaching rejected.
7:14	Born of a virgin.
8:12-13	Our Lord, the Lord Jehovah.
8:14	Rejected of men; to the Jews a stumbling stone.
8:18	Our Lord, man.
8:23to9:6	Characteristics of his life and work.

Isaiah, Cont'd

9:1	The place of his ministry, Galilee.
9:1-2	In Galilee.
9:1-6	Place of birth.
9:6	Counsellor; Wonderful; Everlasting Father; Prince of Peace; relation to God; birth; Mighty God.
9:7	Messianic Kingdom ever-increasing; exaltation; of the house of David.
11:1-9	Characteristics of his life and work.
11:1	Lineage.
11:1, 10	Of the house of David.
11:2	Full of spirit of Jehovah; supreme in knowledge.
11:2-3	Relation to God.
11:3-4	Judge; Messianic Kingdom, founded on equity and righteousness.
11:4	Just.
11:10	Ensign; the Gentiles included in the summons.
28:16	Cornerstone; Messianic Kingdom, founded in Zion.
29:13-14	Their heartless lip-service rejected.
29:18	To restore wholeness.
32:1	Advent.
33:22	Lawgiver.
35:3-6	To restore wholeness.
35:5	His miracles of healing.
35:5-6	To relieve the suffering.
40:3	A special herald, messenger, or forerunner.
40:9-11	Time of advent.
40:10	Second advent.
42:1-7	Characteristics of his life and work.
42:1	Servant.
42:1-3	His teaching, its manner.
42:1, 6	To save Gentiles.

Isaiah, Cont'd

42:1-7	Servant of the Lord.
42:6	Advent; Christ, the light of the Gentiles; messenger of the covenant.
42:7	To relieve the suffering.
45:23	Universal worship paid to God.
49:1-9	Characteristics of his life and work; servant of the Lord.
49:1	Advent; born of a virgin.
49:3,5,6	Descendant of Israel or Jacob.
49:6	Servant; Christ, the light of the Gentiles; to restore Israel.
49:7	Persecuted.
49:8	Mediator.
50:4-9	Characteristics of his life and work.
50:6	His sufferings or passion; they spit in his face; they scourge him.
52:13-15	Characteristics of his life and work; servant of the Lord.
52:13	Servant.
53:1-12	Characteristics of his life and work; his sufferings or passion; servant of the Lord.
53:1	His rejection.
53:3	Man of sorrows; persecuted.
53:4	To relieve the suffering; his miracles of healing.
53:4-6	Our Savior, or Redeemer.
53:4-6,12	Vicarious sacrifice.
53:5	His sufferings, vicarious and expiratory.
53:7	The Lamb of God; silent under abuse; he bears in silence.
53:7-8	His innocence and meekness.
53:8-12	Death on the cross.

Isaiah, Cont'd

53:9	His sinlessness; he is buried as a rich man.
53:11	Servant.
53:12	Intercessor; his treatment as a criminal; death with transgressors.
55:3-4	Of the house of David.
55:4	Commander; advent.
56:7	The desecration of the temple, and his cleansing of it. (With Jer. 7:11.)
57:18	To relieve the suffering.
59:16	Intercessor.
59:20	Redeemer.
60:3, 6, 9	Magi.
61:1	Characteristics of his life and work; the Messiah, Christ, Anointed One, King of Israel; mediator, advocate, intercessor.
61:1-2	His teaching, its character and subject matter.
61:1-3	To relieve the suffering.
61:3	To restore wholeness.
61:11	To draw all nations.
62:11	Our Savior, or Redeemer; his triumphal entry; second advent.
63:1	Our Savior, or Redeemer.
65:2	His rejection.

Jeremiah

7:11	The desecration of the temple and his cleansing of it. (With Isa. 56:7.)
23:5	The characteristics of his life and work; righteous one; just one.
23:5-6	Of the house of David; lineage.
23:6	Relation to God; righteous.
31:15	Massacre of the innocents.

Jeremiah, Cont'd

31:31	The new covenant foretold.
33:15	Lineage.

Ezekiel

34:23	One shepherd.

Daniel

2:44	Advent.
3:25	Son of God.
7:13	Son of man.
7:13-14	Coming to judgment; Priest and King.
7:14	Exaltation; Messianic Kingdom, everlasting.
9:24	Time of advent; most holy.
9:26	Crucified, cut off; vicarious sacrifice.
12:2-3	Coming to judgment.

Hosea

1:10	The Gentiles included in the summons.
2:23	The Gentiles included in the summons.
11:1	Taken for refuge into Egypt.
13:4	No Savior beside me.
13:14	The Redeemer and Ransomer.

Joel

2:28-32	Messianic Kingdom; filled with the spirit.
2:32	To save the Gentiles; Jews and Gentiles equally invited.

Amos

9:11	Of the house of Judah.

Jonah

1:17	Raised on the third day.

Micah

4:1-4	Messianic Kingdom, peaceful.

Micah, Cont'd

4:2	To draw all nations.
5:2	Relation to God; of the Tribe of Judah; born in Bethlehem; King.
5:3	Birth; born of a virgin.

Haggai

2:7, 9	I will give peace.

Zechariah

3:8	Advent.
9:9	His triumphal entry into Jerusalem; just one.
9:10	Messianic Kingdom, universal.
11:12	Betrayed.
11:12-13	His betrayal by a friend and disciple; for 30 pieces of silver.
12:10	Pierced; wounds, hands, feet, and side.
13:1	To restore Israel.
13:6	Betrayed; pierced.
13:6-7	His hands and feet pierced.
13:7	His sufferings or passion; abandonment by his disciples; sheep (disciples) scattered.
14:4-6	Darkness and earthquake.
14:9	King.

Malachi

3:1	Time of birth; relation to God; messenger of the covenant.
4:1-3	Characteristics of his life and work.
4:1-2	Coming to judgment.
4:5	The herald.
4:5-6	A forerunner (a second Elijah) to immediately precede Messiah's coming.

THE TWELVE APOSTLES

MATTHEW 10:2-4	MARK 3:13-21	LUKE 6:12-16
Simon, who is called Peter	Simon, he surnamed Peter	Simon, whom he also named Peter
Andrew, his brother	James, the son of Zebedee	Andrew, his brother
James, the son of Zebedee	John, the brother of James, and he surnamed them Boanerges, which is, The sons of thunder.	James
John, his brother	Andrew	John
Philip	Philip	Philip
Bartholomew	Bartholomew	Bartholomew
Thomas	Matthew	Matthew
Matthew, the publican	Thomas	Thomas
James, the son of Alphæus	James, the son of Alphæus	James, the son of Alphæus
Lebbæus, whose surname was Thaddæus	Thaddæus	Simon, called Zelotes
Simon, the Canaanite	Simon, the Canaanite	Judas, the brother of James
Judas Iscariot, who also betrayed him	Judas Iscariot, which also betrayed him	Judas Iscariot, which also was the traitor

SOME NAMES, TITLES, AND CHARACTERIZATIONS OF JESUS THE CHRIST, AS LISTED BY COMMENTATORS

Adam, the last .... I Cor. 15:45
Advocate .... I John 2:1
Almighty .... Rev. 1:8
Alpha and Omega .... Rev. 1:8; 22:13
Amen .... Rev. 3:14
Ancient of days .... Dan. 7:22
Angel who redeemed ...... Gen. 48:16
Anointed .... Ps. 45:7
Apostle and High Priest of our profession .... Heb. 3:1
Author and finisher of our faith .... Heb. 12:2
Author of eternal salvation .... Heb. 5:9
Balm of Gilead .... Jer. 8:22
Beginning and the ending .... Rev. 1:8; 22:13
Beginning of the creation of God .... Rev. 3:14
Beloved .... Matt. 12:18; Eph. 1:6
Bishop of your souls .... I Pet. 2:25
Blessed and only Potentate .... I Tim. 6:15
Branch .... Zech. 3:8; 6:12
Branch, a righteous .... Jer. 23:5
Branch of righteousness .. Jer. 33:15
Branch of the root of Jesse .... Isa. 11:1
Bread .... John 6:41
Bread of God .... John 6:33
Bread of life .... John 6:35, 48
Bread, the living .... John 6:51
Bright and morning star .... Rev. 22:16
Captain of salvation .... Heb. 2:10
Carpenter .... Mark 6:3
Carpenter's son .... Matt. 13:55
Chief corner stone .... Eph. 2:20; I Pet. 2:6
Chief Shepherd .... I Pet. 5:4
Child .... Isa. 9:6
Child Jesus .... Luke 2:27, 43
Child, young .... Matt. 2:8, 13
Chosen of God .... I Pet. 2:4
Christ .... Matt. 16:16; Mark 8:29; John 4:29
Christ a King .... Luke 23:2
Christ Jesus our Lord .... I Tim. 1:12
Christ of God ...... Luke 9:20; 23:35
Christ the Lord .... Luke 2:11
Christ, the Lord's .... Luke 2:26
Christ, the Son of the Blessed .... Mark 14:61
Commander .... Isa. 55:4
Consolation of Israel .... Luke 2:25
Corner stone .... Isa. 28:16; I Pet. 2:6
Counsellor .... Isa. 9:6
Covenant .... Isa. 42:6
Covert from the tempest .... Isa. 32:2
Creator .... Eph. 3:9; Col. 1:16; Rev. 4:11
David .... Ezek. 34:23; 37:24
David, son of .... Matt. 9:27; 21:9
David their king .... Jer. 30:9; Hos. 3:5
Daysman .... Job 9:33
Dayspring .... Luke 1:78
Day star .... II Pet. 1:19
Deliverer .... Rom. 11:26
Desire of all nations .... Hag. 2:7
Dew unto Israel .... Hos. 14:5
Door .... John 10:9
Door of the sheep .... John 10:7
Elect .... Isa. 42:1; I Pet. 2:6
Emmanuel .... Matt. 1:23
Everlasting Father .... Isa. 9:6
Faithful and True .... Rev. 19:11
Faithful witness .... Rev. 1:5
Fellow, my .... Zech. 13:7
Finisher of our faith .... Heb. 12:2
First and the last .... Rev. 1:17; 22:13
Firstbegotten .... Heb. 1:6
First begotten of the dead .. Rev. 1:5
Firstborn among many brethren .... Rom. 8:29
Firstborn of every creature .... Col. 1:15
Firstfruits of them that slept .... I Cor. 15:20
Forerunner .... Heb. 6:20
Foundation .... Isa. 28:16; I Cor. 3:11

Fountain ......Zech. 13:1; Rev. 21:6
Friend of publicans and sinners ....Matt. 11:19
Gift of God ....John 4:10
Glory of the Lord..................Isa. 40:5
Glory of thy people Israel..Luke 2:32
God ....John 1:1; 20:28
God blessed for ever ....Rom. 9:5
God of the Jews and of the Gentiles ....Rom. 3:29
God our Saviour I Tim. 2:3; Jude 25
God, the only wise ....Jude 25
God, the true ....I John 5:20
Good shepherd ....John 10:14
Governor ....Matt. 2:6
Great high priest...............Heb. 4:14
Head of every man ....I Cor. 11:3
Head of the body, the church...Col. 1:18
Head of the corner ....Matt. 21:42
Heir of all things ....Heb. 1:2
Hiding place ....Isa. 32:2
High Priest ....Heb. 3:1; 5:10
High priest of good things to come ....Heb. 9:11
Holy child Jesus ....Acts 4:30
Holy, he that is......................Rev. 3:7
Holy One ....Isa. 41:14; Acts 2:27; 3:14
Holy One of God ....Mark 1:24; Luke 4:34
Holy, the most ....Dan. 9:24
Holy thing ....Luke 1:35
Hope, our ....I Tim. 1:1
Horn of salvation ....Luke 1:69
I Am ....Ex. 3:14; John 8:58
Image of God......................II Cor. 4:4
Image of his person ....Heb. 1:3
Immanuel ....Isa. 7:14
Intercessor ....Rom. 8:34
Jehovah ....Isa. 26:4
Jesus ....Matt. 1:21; I Thess. 1:10
Jesus Christ our Saviour....Tit. 3:6
Jesus of Nazareth ....Mark 1:24; John 19:19
Jesus the King of the Jews.................................. Matt. 27:37
Jesus the Son of God........Heb. 4:14
Judge of quick and dead ....Acts 10:42
Judge, the righteous ....II Tim. 4:8

Just One ....Acts 3:14; 7:52
Justified in the Spirit....I Tim. 3:16
King ....
Zech. 9:9; Matt. 21:5; Luke 19:38
King of Israel ....John 1:49
King of Kings ....
....I Tim. 6:15; Rev. 17:14; 19:16
King of the Jews.................Matt. 2:2
King over all the earth....Zech. 14:9
Lamb ....Rev. 5:6, 8
Lamb of God ....John 1:29, 36
Lamb that was slain ....Rev. 5:12
Lawgiver ....Isa. 33:22
Leader ....Isa. 55:4; Rev. 7:17
Life ....John 14:6
Life, bread of ....John 6:35
Life, our ....Col. 3:4
Light ....John 12:35
Light of the Gentiles ....Isa. 42:6; Luke 2:32
Light of the world....John 8:12; 9:5
Light, true ....John 1:9
Lion of the tribe of Juda ....Rev. 5:5
Lord....Matt. 3:3; 22:43; Mark 11:3
Lord and Saviour Jesus Christ ....II Pet. 2:20
Lord both of the dead and living ....Rom. 14:9
Lord Christ ....Col. 3:24
Lord Jesus ....Acts 1:21
Lord Jesus Christ ....Rom. 1:7; Eph. 6:24
Lord of all ....Acts 10:36
Lord of glory......I Cor. 2:8; Jas. 2:1
Lord of heaven and earth...Acts 17:24
Lord of hosts ....Isa. 54:5
Lord of lords ....
....I Tim. 6:15; Rev. 17:14; 19:16
Lord of the sabbath ....
..Matt. 12:8; Mark 2:28; Luke 6:5
Lord our Righteousness..Jer. 23:6; 33:16
Lord over all ....Rom. 10:12
Maker of all things ....
............John 1:3, 10; Heb. 1:2, 10
Man Christ Jesus ....I Tim. 2:5
Man of sorrows ....Isa. 53:3
Man of thy right hand......Ps. 80:17
Man, the ....John 19:5
Man, the second ....I Cor. 15:47
Manifested in the flesh..I Tim. 3:16

Master ....Matt. 19:16; 23:10; John 11:28
Mediator ....I Tim. 2:5; Heb. 9:15
Mediator of the new covenant .... Heb. 12:24
Messenger of the covenant..Mal. 3:1
Messiah the Prince ....Dan. 9:25
Messias ....John 1:41; 4:25
Mighty God ....Isa. 9:6; Eph. 1:21
Mighty One of Jacob ....Isa. 49:26; 60:16
Mighty to save ....Isa. 63:1
Morning star ....Rev. 22:16
Nazarene ....Matt. 2:23
Offspring of David ....Rev. 22:16
Only begotten of the Father........John 1:14
Our peace ....Eph. 2:14
Over all ....Rom. 9:5
Passover, our ....I Cor. 5:7
Plant of renown ....Ezek. 34:29
Potentate, blessed and only ....I Tim. 6:15
Power of God ....I Cor. 1:24; Rom. 1:16
Priest for ever after the order of Melchisedec ....Ps. 110:4; Heb. 5:6; 7:17
Prince ....Acts 5:31
Prince of Life ....Acts 3:15
Prince of Peace ....Isa. 9:6
Prince of the kings of the earth ....Rev. 1:5
Prophet ....Deut. 18:18; Luke 24:19; John 6:14
Propitiation ....Rom. 3:25; I John 4:10
Purifier ....Mal. 3:3; Tit. 2:14
Rabbi ....John 1:38; 3:2
Rabboni ....John 20:16
Redeemer ....Job 19:25; Isa. 59:20; 60:16; Tit. 2:14
Redemption ....I Cor. 1:30
Refiner ....Mal. 3:3
Refuge ....Ps. 46:1; Heb. 6:18
Resurrection, and the life........John 11:25
Righteous ....I John 2:1
Righteousness ....I Cor. 1:30
Rock ....I Cor. 10:4
Rock of offence ....Isa. 8:14; I Pet. 2:8
Rod out of the stem of Jesse, and a Branch ....Isa. 11:1
Root of David ....Rev. 5:5; 22:16
Root of Jesse ....Isa. 11:10; Rom. 15:12
Rose of Sharon ....S. of Sol. 2:1
Ruler in Israel ....Mic. 5:2
Same yesterday, and to day, and for ever ....Heb. 13:8
Sanctification ....I Cor. 1:30
Sanctuary ....Isa. 8:14; Heb. 9:1
Saviour ....Isa. 19:20; 60:16; Jer. 14:8; Luke 2:11; John 4:42; Acts 5:31; 13:23; I Tim. 4:10; II Pet. 2:20
Saviour, Jesus the........Matt. 1:21; 2:1; 8:22
Saviour of the body ....Eph. 5:23
Saviour of the world ....I John 4:14
Scepter ....Gen. 49:10; Num. 24:17; Heb. 1:8
Seed of David ....II Tim. 2:8
Servant, my ....Isa. 42:1; 52:13; Matt. 12:18
Sharp sword ....Isa. 49:2
Shepherd and Bishop of your souls ....I Pet. 2:25
Shepherd, chief ....I Pet. 5:4
Shepherd, good ....John 10:11, 14
Shepherd, my ....Ps. 23:1
Shepherd of the sheep, the great..............................Heb. 13:20
Shiloh ....Gen. 49:10
Son, my beloved ....Matt. 3:17; Luke 9:35
Son of David ......Matt. 9:27; 12:23; 15:22; 20:30; 21:9; Mark 10:48; Luke 18:38
Son of God....Dan. 3:25; Matt. 3:17; 4:3; 8:29; 27:40; Mark 15:39; Luke 1:35; 4:3; 4:41; John 1:49; I John 5:10; Rev. 2:18
Son of man ....Matt. 8:20; 9:6; 11:19; 12:8; 13:41; 16:27, 28; Mark 8:31; 9:9, 31; 14:21; Luke 12:8; 18:8; 24:7; John 1:51; 3:14; 5:27; 6:27; 13:31; Acts 7:56; Rev. 1:13; 14:14
Son of Mary ....Mark 6:3
Son of the Blessed ....Mark 14:61

Son of the Father ....I John 1:3; II John 3
Son of the Highest (most high) ....Mark 5:7; Luke 1:32
Son of the living God....Matt. 16:16
Son of the most high God........................Mark 5:7; Luke 8:28
Son, only begotten ..John 1:18; 3:16
Son over his own house ....Heb. 3:6
Star and Sceptre ....Num. 24:17
Star out of Jacob ....Num. 24:17
Star, the bright and morning ....Rev. 22:16
Stone ....Matt. 21:42
Stone, a living.....................I Pet. 2:4
Stone, chief corner ....Eph. 2:20; I Pet. 2:6
Stone of stumbling...Isa. 8:14; I Pet. 2:8
Stone, tried and precious..Isa. 28:16
Sun of righteousness ....Mal. 4:2
Surety of a better testament ....Heb. 7:22
Sword ....Rev. 1:16; 2:16
Teacher ....John 3:2
True, Faithful and ....Rev. 19:11
Truth ....John 14:6
Vine, the true ....John 15:1, 5
Wall of fire ....Zech. 2:5
Way ....Isa. 35:8; John 14:6
Way, the truth, and the life, the ....John 14:6
Well of living water.............................S. of Sol. 4:15; John 4:10
Wisdom ....I Cor. 1:30
Wisdom of God ....I Cor. 1:24
Witness, faithful and true..Rev. 3:14
Wonderful ....Isa. 9:6
Word ....John 1:1
Word of God ....Rev. 19:13
Word of life ....I John 1:1

SOME REFERENCES BY JESUS IN THE FOUR GOSPELS TO SAYINGS AND PASSAGES IN THE OLD TESTAMENT, AS LISTED BY COMMENTATORS

Matthew

4:4	Man shall not live by bread alone	Deut. 8:3
4:7	Thou shalt not tempt . . . God	Deut. 6:16
4:10	Thou shalt worship . . . God . . . only	Ex. 20:3
5:3, 4	Blessed are the poor . . . they that mourn	Isa. 61:1, 2
5:5	The meek . . . shall inherit the earth	Ps. 37:11
5:8	Blessed are the pure in heart	Ps. 24:4
5:21	Thou shalt not kill	Ex. 20:13; Deut. 5:17
5:27	Thou shalt not commit adultery	Ex. 20:14; Deut. 5:18
5:31	A writing of divorcement	Deut. 24:1
5:33	Thou shalt not forswear thyself	Num. 30:2; Deut. 23:21
5:34, 35	Heaven . . . is God's throne . . . the earth is his footstool	Isa. 66:1
5:35	The city of the great King	Ps. 48:2
5:38	An eye for an eye	Deut. 19:21
5:43	Love thy neighbour	Lev. 19:18
5:48	Be ye therefore perfect	Gen. 17:1; Deut. 18:13
6:6	Enter into thy closet . . . shut thy door, pray	Isa. 26:20; II Kings 4:33
7:22	Have we not prophesied in thy name	Jer. 14:14
7:23	Depart . . . ye that work iniquity	Ps. 6:8
8:4	Shew thyself to the priest	Lev. 13:49
8:11	From the east and west	Mal. 1:11; Isa. 59:19
9:13	Will have mercy (see also ch. 12:7)	Hos. 6:6
10:35	I am come to set a man at variance	Mic. 7:6
11:5	The blind receive their sight, &c.	Isa. 61:1
11:10	Behold, I send my messenger	Mal. 3:1
11:23	Exalted unto heaven . . . brought down to hell	Isa. 14:13, 15, 29; Jer. 6:16 (Heb.)
12:3	Have ye not read what David did	I Sam. 21:6
12:18	My servant, whom I have chosen	Isa. 41:9; 42:1-4
12:40	Jonas . . . three days . . . in the whale's belly	Jonah 1:17
13:14	Ye shall hear . . . and shall not understand	Isa. 6:9
13:32	The birds of the air . . . lodge in the branches	Dan. 4:12, 21 (Chald.)
13:35	I will open my mouth in parables	Ps. 78:2
13:41	Things that offend . . . do iniquity	Zeph. 1:3 (Heb.)
13:43	Then shall the righteous shine forth	Dan. 12:3
15:4	Honour thy father and mother	Ex. 20:12; Deut. 5:16
15:4	He that curseth father or mother	Ex. 21:17
15:8	This people draweth nigh . . . lips	Isa. 29:13
15:9	Teaching for doctrines . . . commandments of men	Isa. 29:13
16:4	The sign of the prophet Jonas	Jonah 1:17
16:27	He shall reward every man according to his works	Ps. 62:12; Prov. 24:12
18:16	Mouth of two or three witnesses	Deut. 19:15

Matthew, Cont'd

19:4	Made them male and female	Gen. 1:27
19:5	They twain shall be one flesh	Gen. 2:24
19:18	Thou shalt do no murder	Ex. 20:13-16; Deut. 5:17-20
19:19	Love thy neighbour as thyself	Ex. 20:13-16; Lev. 19:18; Deut. 5:17-20
19:26	With God all things are possible	Gen. 18:14; Job 42:2; Zech. 8:6 (LXX.)
21:13	My house . . . called . . . house of prayer	Isa. 56:7
21:13	But ye . . . made it . . . den of thieves	Jer. 7:11
21:16	Out of the mouth of babes	Ps. 8:2
21:33	Planted a vineyard, &c.	Isa. 5:1
21:42	Stone which the builders rejected	Ps. 118:22
22:32	I am the God of Abraham	Ex. 3:6
22:37	Thou shalt love the Lord thy God	Deut. 6:5
22:39	And . . . thy neighbour as thyself	Lev. 19:18
22:44	The Lord said unto my Lord	Ps. 110:1
23:38	Your house is left unto you desolate	Ps. 69:25; Jer. 12:7; 22:5
24:6	These things must come to pass	Dan. 2:28
24:7	Nation shall rise against nation, &c.	Isa. 19:2
24:10	Then shall many be offended	Dan. 11:41 (LXX.)
24:21	Great tribulation, such as was not since, &c.	Dan. 12:1
24:24	False prophets . . . shall shew great signs and wonders	Deut. 13:1
24:29	Shall the sun be darkened	Isa. 13:10; 34:4; Ezek. 32:7; Joel 2:10; 3:15
24:30	Then shall all the tribes of the earth mourn	Zech. 12:12
24:30	The Son of man coming in the clouds of heaven	Dan. 7:13
24:31	With a great [sound of a] trumpet	Isa. 27:13
24:31	They shall gather together . . . from the four winds, &c.	Deut. 30:4; Zech. 2:6
24:37	But as the days of Noe were	Gen. 6:13
24:38	Noe entered into the ark	Gen. 7:7
25:41	Depart from me, ye cursed	Ps. 6:8
25:46	The righteous into life eternal	Dan. 12:3
26:24	Son of man goeth as it is written	Ps. 22
26:28	Blood of the . . . testament	Ex. 24:8; Zech. 9:11
26:31	I will smite the shepherd	Zech. 13:7
26:38	My soul is exceeding sorrowful	Ps. 42:5
26:64	The Son of man sitting . . . coming, &c.	Ps. 110:1; Dan. 7:13
27:46	My God, why hast thou forsaken me	Ps. 22:1

Mark

1:44	Shew thyself to the priest	Lev. 13:49
2:25-26	David . . . did eat the shewbread	I Sam. 21:6
4:12	May see, and not perceive	Isa. 6:9
4:29	He putteth in the sickle, because, &c.	Joel 3:13
4:32	The fowls of the air may lodge under the shadow	Dan. 4:12, 21 (Chald.); Ezek. 17:23
7:6	This people honoureth me . . . lips	Isa. 29:13
7:10	Honour thy father and thy mother	Ex. 20:12

Mark, Cont'd

7:10	Whoso curseth father or mother	Ex. 21:17; Lev. 20:9; Prov. 20:20
8:18	Having eyes, see ye not, &c.	Jer. 5:21; Ezek. 12:2
9:44	Where their worm dieth not	Isa. 66:24
10:6	God made . . . male and female	Gen. 1:27
10:7	A man leave his father and mother	Gen. 2:24
10:19	Do not commit adultery	Ex. 20:14; Deut. 5:18
11:17	Of all nations the house of prayer	Isa. 56:7
11:17	Ye have made it a den of thieves	Jer. 7:11
12:1	A certain man planted a vineyard	Isa. 5:1
12:10	Stone which the builders rejected	Ps. 118:22
12:26	I am the God of Abraham	Ex.3:6
12:29	The Lord our God is one Lord	Deut. 6:4
12:31	Love thy neighbour as thyself	Lev. 19:18
12:36	Sit thou on my right hand	Ps. 110:1
13:7	Such things must needs be	Dan. 2:28
13:8	Nation shall rise against nation	Isa. 19:2
13:14	Abomination of desolation	Dan. 9:27; 12:11
13:19	Affliction, such as was not	Dan. 12:1
13:22	False prophets . . . shall shew signs	Deut. 13:1
13:24	The sun shall be darkened	Isa. 13:10
13:25	The stars of heaven shall fall	Isa. 34:4
13:26	The Son of man coming in the clouds	Dan. 7:13
13:27	He . . . shall gather together his elect from the four winds	Zech. 2:6; Deut. 30:4
13:31	My words shall not pass away	Isa. 40:8
14:18	One . . . which eateth with me	Ps. 41:9
14:24	Blood of the . . . testament	Ex. 24:8; Zech. 9:11
14:27	I will smite the shepherd	Zech. 13:7
14:34	My soul is exceeding sorrowful	Ps. 42:6
14:62	Ye shall see the Son of man sitting . . . coming	Ps. 110:1; Dan. 7:13
15:34	My God, why hast thou forsaken me	Ps. 22:1

Luke

4:4	Man shall not live by bread alone	Deut. 8:3
4:8	Thou shalt worship the Lord thy	Deut. 6:13; 10:20
4:12	Thou shalt not tempt the Lord thy	Deut. 6:16
4:18, 19	To preach the gospel to the poor	Isa. 61:1, 2
5:14	Shew thyself to the priest	Lev. 13:49
6:3,4	What David did . . . when . . . an hungred	I Sam. 21:6
7:22	The blind see, the lame walk, &c.	Isa. 35:5
7:27	Behold, I send my messenger	Mal. 3:1
8:10	That seeing they might not see	Isa. 6:9
10:15	Exalted to heaven . . . thrust down to hell	Isa. 14:13, 15
10:19	Power to tread on serpents	Ps. 91:13
10:28	This do, and thou shalt live	Lev. 18:5
12:53	The father . . . against the son, &c.	Mic. 7:6
13:19	The fowls of the air lodged in the branches	Dan. 4:12, 21
13:27	Depart . . . ye workers of iniquity	Ps. 6:8
13:29	From the east, and from the west	Isa. 59:19; Mal. 1:11
13:35	House is left unto you desolate	Jer. 12:7; 22:5

Luke, Cont'd

13:35	Blessed is he that cometh, &c.	Ps. 118:26
17:14	Shew yourselves unto the priests	Lev. 13:49
17:26	As it was in the days of Noe	Gen. 7
17:29	Lot went out of Sodom	Gen. 19:16
17:32	Remember Lot's wife	Gen. 19:26
18:20	The commandments	Ex. 20:12-16; Deut. 5:16-20
18:20	Do not commit adultery, &c.	Ex. 20:14; Deut. 5:16-20
19:10	To seek and to save that which was lost	Ezek. 34:16
19:44	Shall lay thee even with the ground, &c.	Ps. 137:9
19:46	My house is the house of prayer	Isa. 56:7
19:46	Ye have made it a den of thieves	Jer. 7:11
20:9	A certain man planted a vineyard	Isa. 5:1
20:17	Stone which the builders rejected	Ps. 118:22
20:37	Even Moses shewed at the bush	Ex. 3:6
20:42	The Lord said unto my Lord	Ps. 110:1
21:10	Nation shall rise against nation	Isa. 19:2
21:22	These be the days of vengeance	Hos. 9:7
21:24	Jerusalem shall be trodden down, &c.	Ps. 79:1; Isa. 63:18
21:26	The powers of heaven shall be shaken	Isa. 34:4
21:27	The Son of man coming in a cloud	Dan. 7:13
22:20	Testament . . . in . . . blood	Ex. 24:8; Zech. 9:11
22:37	Reckoned among the transgressors	Isa. 53:12
22:69	The Son of man sit on the right hand	Ps. 110:1; Dan. 7:13
23:29	Blessed are the barren	Isa. 54:1
23:30	Say to the mountains, Fall on us	Hos. 10:8
23:46	Father, into thy hands . . . my spirit	Ps. 31:5
24:46	It behoved Christ to suffer	Isa. 53:5

John

1:51	Ye shall see heaven open	Gen. 28:12
6:45	They shall be all taught of God	Isa. 54:13
8:17	The testimony of two men is true	Deut. 19:15
10:16	One shepherd	Ezek. 34:23; 37:24
10:34	I said, Ye are gods	Ps. 82:6
12:15	King cometh, sitting on an ass's colt	Zech. 9:9
12:27	Now is my soul troubled	Ps. 6:3; 42:6
12:49	Commandment, what I should say	Deut. 18:18
13:18	He that eateth bread with me	Ps. 41:9
15:25	They hated me without a cause	Ps. 35:19; 69:4; 109:3
16:22	Your heart shall rejoice	Isa. 66:14

THE MIRACLES OF JESUS

SEC. & PG.	MIRACLE	WHEN AND WHERE	WHERE RECORDED
§32 p. 191	The first miracle, water converted into wine.	A.D. 27, March, Cana of Galilee.	John 2:1-11
§43 p. 201	Healing nobleman's son.	A.D. 27-28, Winter, Cana and Capernaum.	John 4:46-54
§44 p. 202	Jesus passes unseen through the crowd.	A.D. 28, Winter, Nazareth.	Luke 4:28-30
§46 p. 204	The draught of fishes.	A.D. 28, Winter, Sea of Galilee.	Luke 5:1-11
§47 p. 206	An unclean spirit cast out.	A.D. 28, Winter, Capernaum.	Mark 1:21-28 Luke 4:31-37
§48 p. 207	Peter's wife's mother healed.	A.D. 28, Winter, Capernaum.	Matt. 8:14-15 Mark 1:29-31 Luke 4:38-39
§48 p. 207	A multitude healed.	A.D. 28, Winter, Capernaum.	Matt. 8:16-17 Mark 1:32-34 Luke 4:40-41
§51 p. 215	The leper healed.	A.D. 28, March, Galilee.	Matt. 8:1-4 Mark 1:40-45 Luke 5:12-15
§52 p. 216	One sick with palsy healed.	A.D. 28, March, Capernaum.	Matt. 9:2-8 Mark 2:1-12 Luke 5:17-26
§55 p. 221	A man with an infirmity of thirty-eight years' standing healed.	A.D. 28, April, Pool of Bethesda.	John 5:1-16
§57 p. 225	Man with withered hand healed.	A.D. 28, April, Synagogue in Galilee.	Matt. 12:9-13 Mark 3:1-5 Luke 6:6-10
§61 p. 231	Centurion's servant healed of palsy.	A.D. 28, Summer, Capernaum.	Matt. 8:5-13 Luke 7:2-10
§62 p. 232	The son of a widow of Nain raised.	A.D. 28, Summer, Nain.	Luke 7:7-17
§66 p. 238	Blind and dumb demoniac healed.	A.D. 28, Autumn, Capernaum.	Matt. 12:22-23
§71 p. 249	The storm stilled.	A.D. 28, Autumn, Sea of Galilee.	Matt. 8:23-27 Mark 4:35-41 Luke 8:22-25
§72 p. 250	The two Gadarene demoniacs healed.	A.D. 28, Autumn, Gadara.	Matt. 8:28-34 Mark 5:1-20 Luke 8:26-39
§72 p. 250	The swine rush down into the sea and perish.	A.D. 28, Autumn, Gadara.	Matt. 8:32-34 Mark 5:13-20 Luke 8:33-39

Sec. & Pg.	Miracle	When and Where	Where Recorded
§74 p. 253	The daughter of Jairus raised.	A.D. 28, Autumn, Capernaum.	Matt. 9:18-26 Mark 5:22-43 Luke 8:41-56
§75 p. 255	The woman with the issue of blood healed.	A.D. 28, Autumn, Capernaum.	Matt. 9:20-22 Mark 5:25-34 Luke 8:43-48
§76 p.257	Two blind men healed.	A.D. 28, Autumn, Capernaum.	Matt. 9:27-31
§77 p.257	The dumb demoniac healed.	A.D. 28, Autumn, Capernaum.	Matt. 9:32-34
§86 p. 265	The five thousand fed.	A.D. 29, April, Near Bethsaida.	Matt. 14:14-21 Mark 6:33-34 Luke 9:11-17 John 6:1-14
§88 p. 268	Jesus walks on the sea.	A.D. 29, April, Sea of Galilee.	Matt. 14:24-33 Mark 6:47-52 John 6:16-21
§88 p. 268	Peter saved.	A.D. 29, April, Sea of Galilee.	Matt. 14:28-33
§88 p. 268	The wind ceases, and the ship is immediately at the land.	A.D. 29, April, Sea of Galilee.	Matt. 14:24-33 Mark 6:47-52 John 6:16-21
§90 p.273	People healed by touch of his garment.	A.D. 29, April, Gennesaret.	Matt. 14:34-36 Mark 6:53-56
§93 p. 277	Daughter of the Greek woman healed.	A.D. 29, Summer, Region of Tyre and Sidon.	Matt. 15:22-28 Mark 7:25-30
§95 p. 278	Deaf man with impediment in speech healed.	A.D. 29, Summer, Decapolis.	Mark 7:32-37
§96 p. 279	The four thousand fed.	A.D. 29, Summer, Decapolis.	Matt. 15:29-38 Mark 8:1-9
§99 p. 282	A blind man healed.	A.D. 29, Summer, Bethsaida.	Mark 8:22-26
§103 p. 288	A demoniac boy healed after failure of disciples.	A.D. 29, Summer-Autumn, Mt. Hermon.	Matt. 17:14-21 Mark 9:14-29 Luke 9:37-43
§105 p. 291	The tribute money in the fish.	A.D. 29, Summer-Autumn, Capernaum.	Matt. 17:24-27
§117 p. 306	Jesus passes through crowd unseen.	A.D. 29, Oct. 11-18, Temple, Jerusalem.	John 8:59
§122 p. 312	Jesus casts out a dumb devil.	A.D. 29, Oct.-Dec., Judea.	Luke 11:14-26
§126 p. 320	Jesus heals a man born blind.	A.D. 29, Oct.-Dec., Pool of Siloam.	John 9:1-7
§130 p. 327	The woman long ill healed on Sabbath.	A.D. 30, Perea.	Luke 13:11-17

Sec. & Pg.	Miracle	When and Where	Where Recorded
§135 p. 331	The man with dropsy healed on Sabbath.	A.D. 30, Winter ?, Perea.	Luke 14:1-6
§141 p. 340	The raising of Lazarus from the dead.	A.D. 30, Winter ?, Bethany.	John 11:17-46
§144 p. 343	The ten lepers healed.	A.D. 30, Feb.-Mar., Galilee, Samaria.	Luke 17:11-19
§154 p. 355	Sight restored to Bartimaeus and another blind beggar.	A.D. 30, March, near Jericho.	Matt. 20:29-34 Mark 10:46-52 Luke 18:35-43
§162a p. 365 §163a p. 367	Barren fig tree cursed.	A.D. 30, Apr. 3, near Bethany.	Matt. 21:18-21 Mark 11:12-21
§164r p. 413	They who were sent to take Jesus fall to the ground.	A.D. 30, Apr. 6, Jerusalem, Garden of Gethsemane.	John 18:3-6
§164s p. 415	The ear of Malchus, the high priest's servant, healed.	A.D. 30, Apr. 6, Jerusalem, Garden of Gethsemane.	Luke 22:50-51
§168b p. 456	The great haul of fishes.	A.D. 30, Apr.-May, Sea of Tiberias.	John 21:6-14

THE PARABLES OF JESUS

Sec. & Pg.	Parable	When and Where	Where Recorded
§34 p. 193	Temple, if destroyed, to be raised in three days.	A.D. 27, Apr. 11-18, Temple, Jerusalem.	John 2:19-22
§50 p. 209	Candle under bushel.	A.D. 28, Sermon on the Mount, Galilee.	Matt. 5:14-16
§50 p. 214	House on rock, and on sand.	A.D. 28, Sermon on the Mount, Galilee.	Matt. 7:24-27
§54 p. 220	Children of the bridechamber.	A.D. 28, March, Sea of Galilee.	Matt. 9:14-15 Mark 2:18-20 Luke 5:33-35
§54 p. 220	Piece of new cloth in an old garment.	A.D. 28, March, Sea of Galilee.	Matt. 9:16 Mark 2:21 Luke 5:36
§54 p. 220	New wine in old bottles.	A.D. 28, March, Sea of Galilee.	Matt. 9:17 Mark 2:22 Luke 5:37-38
§54 p. 220	New wine as against old wine.	A.D. 28, March, Sea of Galilee.	Luke 5:39
§60 p. 229	The beam and the mote.	A.D. 28, Midsummer, Sermon on the Plain, near Capernaum.	Luke 6:37-42
§64 p. 236	The two debtors.	A.D. 28, Autumn, Galilee.	Luke 7:36-50
§70a p. 242	The sower.	A.D. 28, Autumn, Sea of Galilee.	Matt. 13:3-23 Mark 4:3-25 Luke 8:5-18
§70b p. 246	The seed growing by itself.	A.D. 28, Autumn, Sea of Galilee.	Mark 4:26-29
§70c p. 246	The tares.	A.D. 28, Autumn, Sea of Galilee.	Matt. 13:24-30
§70d p. 247	The mustard seed and the leaven.	A.D. 28, Autumn, Sea of Galilee.	Matt. 13:31-35 Mark 4:30-34
§70e p. 247	Parable of the tares explained.	A.D. 28, Autumn, Sea of Galilee.	Matt. 13:36-43
§70f p. 248	Treasure hid in a field.	A.D. 28, Autumn, Sea of Galilee.	Matt. 13:44
§70f p. 248	Pearl of great price.	A.D. 28, Autumn, Sea of Galilee.	Matt. 13:45-46
§70f p. 248	The dragnet.	A.D. 28, Autumn, Sea of Galilee.	Matt. 13:47-48
§106 p. 291	The lost sheep, and the ninety and nine.	A.D. 29, Summer-Autumn, Capernaum.	Matt. 18:12-14

Sec. & Pg.	Parable	When and Where	Where Recorded
§108 p. 294	The harsh servant and the debt.	A.D. 29, Summer-Autumn, Capernaum.	Matt. 18:23-35
§119 p. 309	The good Samaritan.	A.D. 29, October-December, Judea.	Luke 10:25-37
§121 p. 310	The friend at midnight.	A.D. 29, October-December, Judea.	Luke 11:5-13
§122 p. 312	The unclean spirit.	A.D. 29, October-December, Judea.	Luke 11:24-26
§124 p. 315	The foolish rich man.	A.D. 29, October-December, Judea.	Luke 12:13-21
§124 p. 315	The watchful servants.	A.D. 29, October-December, Judea.	Luke 12:35-40
§124 p. 315	The faithful and wise steward.	A.D. 29, October-December, Judea.	Luke 12:41-48
§125 p. 319	The unfruitful fig tree.	A.D. 29, October-December, Judea.	Luke 13:6-9
§127 p. 322	The good shepherd.	A.D. 29, October-December, Jerusalem.	John 10:1-18
§131 p. 328	The mustard seed and the leaven.	A.D. 30, Perea.	Luke 13:18-21
§132 p. 328	The shut door.	A.D. 30, Perea.	Luke 13:23-30
§135 p. 331	The wedding feast.	A.D. 30, Winter ?, Perea.	Luke 14:7-11
§135 p. 331	The great supper.	A.D. 30, Winter ?, Perea.	Luke 14:16-24
§136 p. 333	The building of the tower.	A.D. 30, Winter ?, Perea.	Luke 14:25-30
§136 p. 333	The king going to make war.	A.D. 30, Winter ?, Perea.	Luke 14:31-33
§137a p. 334	The lost sheep.	A.D. 30, Winter ?, Perea.	Luke 15:3-7
§137b p. 334	The ten pieces of silver.	A.D. 30, Winter ?, Perea.	Luke 15:8-10
§137c p. 335	The return of the prodigal son.	A.D. 30, Winter ?, Perea.	Luke 15:11-32
§137d p. 336	The unjust steward.	A.D. 30, Winter ?, Perea.	Luke 16:1-13
§139 p. 338	The rich man and Lazarus.	A.D. 30, Winter ?, Perea.	Luke 16:19-31
§140 p. 339	Servant and master supping.	A.D. 30, Winter ?, Perea.	Luke 17:7-10
§146a p. 345	The importunate widow.	A.D. 30, Feb.-Mar., Galilee.	Luke 18:1-8
§146b p. 345	The Pharisee and the publican.	A.D. 30, Feb.-Mar., Galilee.	Luke 18:9-14

Sec. & Pg.	Parable	When and Where	Where Recorded
§151 p. 352	The labourers in the vineyard.	A.D. 30, February-March, Perea.	Matt. 20:1-16
§156 p. 358	The ten pounds.	A.D. 30, March, in or near Jericho.	Luke 19:11-27
§163c p. 369	The two sons.	A.D. 30, Apr. 4, Jerusalem.	Matt. 21:28-32
§163d p. 369	The wicked husbandman.	A.D. 30, Apr. 4, Jerusalem.	Matt. 21:33-46 Mark 12:1-12 Luke 20:9-18
§163e p. 372	The king's son.	A.D. 30, Apr. 4, Jerusalem.	Matt. 22:1-14
§163o p. 383	The fig tree leaves.	A.D. 30, Apr. 4, Jerusalem.	Matt. 24:32-33 Mark 13:28-29 Luke 21:29-33
§163o p. 383	The man taking a long journey.	A.D. 30, Apr. 4, Jerusalem.	Mark 13:34-37
§163o p. 383	The faithful and the evil servant.	A.D. 30, Apr. 4, Jerusalem.	Matt. 24:42-51
§163p p. 390	The ten virgins.	A.D. 30, Apr. 4, Jerusalem.	Matt. 25:1-13
§163q p. 390	The talents.	A.D. 30, Apr. 4, Jerusalem.	Matt. 25:14-30
§163r p. 392	The sheep and the goats.	A.D. 30, Apr. 4, Jerusalem.	Matt. 25:31-46

THE HEBREW CALENDAR

Jewish Month	English Month	Festival	Season
Abib or Nisan (Ex. 12:2; 13:4; 23:15; Neh. 2:1)	March April	First Sabbath of this month, "second sabbath after the first." (Luke 6:1) 14. Passover. (Ex. 12:18, 19; 13:3-10) 15-21. Feast of Unleavened Bread. (Lev. 23:6) 16. Sheaf of firstfruits of harvest waved before the Lord. (Lev. 23:10-14)	Harvest begins. Barley ripe in lowlands; wheat partly in ear. Dry, hot wind from deserts; fall of latter or spring rains. (Deut. 11:14) Jordan overflows banks. (Josh. 3:15)
Zif (Ijar) (I Kings 6:1, 37)	April May	14. Passover for those who could not observe the first. (Num. 9:10-11)	General harvest in lower districts. Summer; cloudless; rain and thunderstorms rare. (I Sam. 12:17-18) Hot winds in Jordan Valley.
Sivan (Esth. 8:9)	May June	6. Pentecost, or Feast of Weeks, or of Harvest, or Firstfruits. (Ex. 23:16; 34:22; Lev. 23:17, 20; Num. 28:26; Deut. 16:9, 10)	Harvest in upland. Summer. Air motionless and clear.
(Tammuz)	June July		Wheat in highlands; various fruits ripen. Hot, dry season.
(Ab)	July August		Vintage time. (Lev. 26:5) Hot and dry.
Elul (Neh. 6:15)	August September		Vintage time. Intense heat.
Ethanim (Tisri) (I Kings 8:2)	September October	1. Feast of Trumpets; New Year's Day. (Num. 29:1) 10. Day of Atonement. (Lev. 16:29) 15-21. Feast of Harvest Home, or of Ingathering; or of Tabernacles. (Ex. 23:16; Lev. 23:34, 39, 43; Deut. 16:13) 22. Great Day of the Feast. (Lev. 23:36; Num. 29:35; Neh. 8:18; John 7:37)	Sowing begins. Early rains and frosty nights. (Gen. 31:40; Deut. 11:14; Joel 2:23)
Bul (Marchesvan) (I Kings 6:38)	October November		Winter figs; grain sowing. Rains.

JEWISH MONTH	ENGLISH MONTH	FESTIVAL	SEASON
Chisleu (Neh. 1:1)	November December	25. Feast of Dedication, or of Lights. (John 10:22.)	Plains and deserts become green. Winter. (John 10:22) Stormy, snows and rains.
Tebeth (Esth. 2:16)	December January		Jordan Valley cultivation begins. Mid-winter. Rain, hail, snow on highlands. (Josh. 10:11)
Sebat (Zech. 1:7)	January February		Trees in warmer places in blossom. Winter; "cool season" begins.
Adar (Esth. 3:7)	February March	The first Sabbath of this month, is "The First Sabbath." 14-15. Feast of Purim, or of Lots. (Esth. 9:21-28)	Cultivation in Jordan Valley draws to end. Spring, or rainy season.

THE HEBREW METHOD OF RECKONING HOURS OF DAY AND NIGHT

OLD TESTAMENT

Morning: sunrise until about 10:00 a.m.

Noon, or Heat of the Day: until about 2:00 p.m.

Evening, or Cool of the Day: until sunset, or about 6:00 p.m.

First, or Beginning of the Watches: sunset to about midnight.

Second, or Middle Watch: midnight until about 3:00 a.m.

Third, or Morning Watch: until sunrise, or about 6:00 a.m.

NEW TESTAMENT

First Hour of the Day: sunrise, about 6:00 a.m., to about 7:00 a.m.

Second Hour of the Day: until about 8:00 a.m.

Third Hour of the Day: until about 9:00 a.m.

Fourth Hour of the Day: until about 10:00 a.m.

Fifth Hour of the Day: until about 11:00 a.m.

Sixth Hour of the Day: until about 12:00 noon.

Seventh Hour of the Day: until about 1:00 p.m.

Eighth Hour of the Day: until about 2:00 p.m.

Ninth Hour of the Day: until about 3:00 p.m.

Tenth Hour of the Day: until about 4:00 p.m.

Eleventh Hour of the Day: until about 5:00 p.m.

Twelfth Hour of the Day: until twilight, or about 6:00 p.m.

First, or Evening Watch: until about 9:00 p.m.

Second, or Midnight Watch: until about 12:00 midnight.

Third Watch (or Cockcrowing): until about 3:00 a.m.

Fourth, or Morning Watch: until day-break, or about 6:00 a.m.

THE FAMILY OF HEROD

ANTIPAS (Idumean; General of Idumea)

ANTIPATER
Made Procurator of Judea by Julius Caesar; m. Kypros (Cypros), Arabian; Poisoned, B.C. 43

JOSEPH
m. Salome; Executed

PHASAEL
(Phasaelus)
Suicide

HEROD I (Called "the Great")
Governor of Coele-Syria; Governor, Syria; Tetrarch; King; builds Temple in Samaria; rebuilds Temple in Jerusalem; builds Temple to Caesar; d. B.C. 4; Married

JOSEPH
Defeated and slain

PHERORAS
Out of favor with Herod

SALOME
m. (1) Joseph (2) Costobar

BERNICE
m. Aristobulus

DORIS
Cast out of Court by Herod

ANTIPATER
Put to death by his father, B.C. 4

MARIAMNE
d. of Alexandra, d. of Hyrcanus; put to death by Herod

MARIAMNE, d. of Simon, the High Priest

HEROD PHILIP I
m. Herodias, who caused execution of John the Baptist

SALOME
m. (1) Herod Philip II (2) Aristobulus, King of Chalcis

MALTHACE
a Samaritan

CLEOPATRA
of Jerusalem

HEROD PHILIP II
Tetrarch of Iturea and Trachonitis
m. Salome, d. Herodias
d. A.D. 33

ALEXANDER
Put to death (strangled) by his father, B.C. 6

ARISTOBULUS
m. Bernice, d. Salome, sister of Herod I
Put to death (strangled) by his father, B.C. 6

HEROD ANTIPAS
Tetrarch of Galilee
m. (1) d. Aretas, Arab King;
(2) Herodias, divorcee of H. Philip I, who caused execution of John the Baptist; Banished, A.D. 40

ARCHELAUS
Ethnarch of Idumea, Judea, and Samaria
Banished, A.D. 6

HEROD, King of Chalcis
m. (1) Mariamne (2) Bernice
d. A.D. 48

ARISTOBULUS
m. Salome
d. of Herodias
by H. Philip I

HEROD AGRIPPA I
Successor (1) to Tetrarchy of Herod Philip II, A.D. 37; and (2) to Tetrarchy of Herod Antipas, A.D. 40; Judea and Samaria added, A.D. 41; m. Cypros, granddaughter of Phasael; d. A.D. 44

HERODIAS
m. (1) H. Philip I
(2) H. Antipas

HEROD AGRIPPA II
King of Chalcis; successor to Tetrarchy of Philip II; and of Lysanias; "the last prince of the line"; heard Paul's defense; d. A.D. 100

DRUSILLA
m. (1) Aziz (2) Felix

AGRIPPA
d. A.D. 79

BERNICE

REFERENCES IN THE NEW TESTAMENT TO HEROD'S FAMILY

Matthew

2:1-22	Herod I ("the Great")
2:22	Archelaus, Ethnarch of Idumea, Judea, and Samaria
14:1-10	Herod Antipas, Tetrarch of Galilee
14:3	Herod Philip I
14:3-11	Herodias, wife of Herod Philip I; later, wife of Herod Antipas
14:6-11	Salome, daughter of Herodias and Herod Philip I

Mark

6:14-27	Herod Antipas, Tetrarch of Galilee
6:17	Herod Philip I
6:17-28	Herodias, wife of Herod Philip I; later, wife of Herod Antipas
6:22-28	Salome, daughter of Herodias and Herod Philip I
8:15	Herod Antipas, Tetrarch of Galilee

Luke

1:5	Herod I ("the Great")
3:1	Herod Philip II, Tetrarch of Iturea and Trachonitis
3:1	Herod Antipas, Tetrarch of Galilee
3:19	Herod Antipas, Tetrarch of Galilee
3:19	Herod Philip I
3:19	Herodias, wife of Herod Philip I; later, wife of Herod Antipas
8:3	Herod Antipas, Tetrarch of Galilee
9:7-9	Herod Antipas, Tetrarch of Galilee
13:31	Herod Antipas, Tetrarch of Galilee
23:7-15	Herod Antipas, Tetrarch of Galilee

Acts

4:27	Herod Antipas, Tetrarch of Galilee
12:1-23	Herod Agrippa I
13:1	Herod Antipas, Tetrarch of Galilee
23:35	Herod Agrippa II
24:24	Drusilla, sister of Herod Agrippa II; wife of Felix
25:13-27	Herod Agrippa II
25:13, 23	Bernice, sister of Herod Agrippa II, daughter of Herod Agrippa I
26:1-32	Herod Agrippa II
26:30	Bernice, sister of Herod Agrippa II, daughter of Herod Agrippa I

HEROD'S TEMPLE

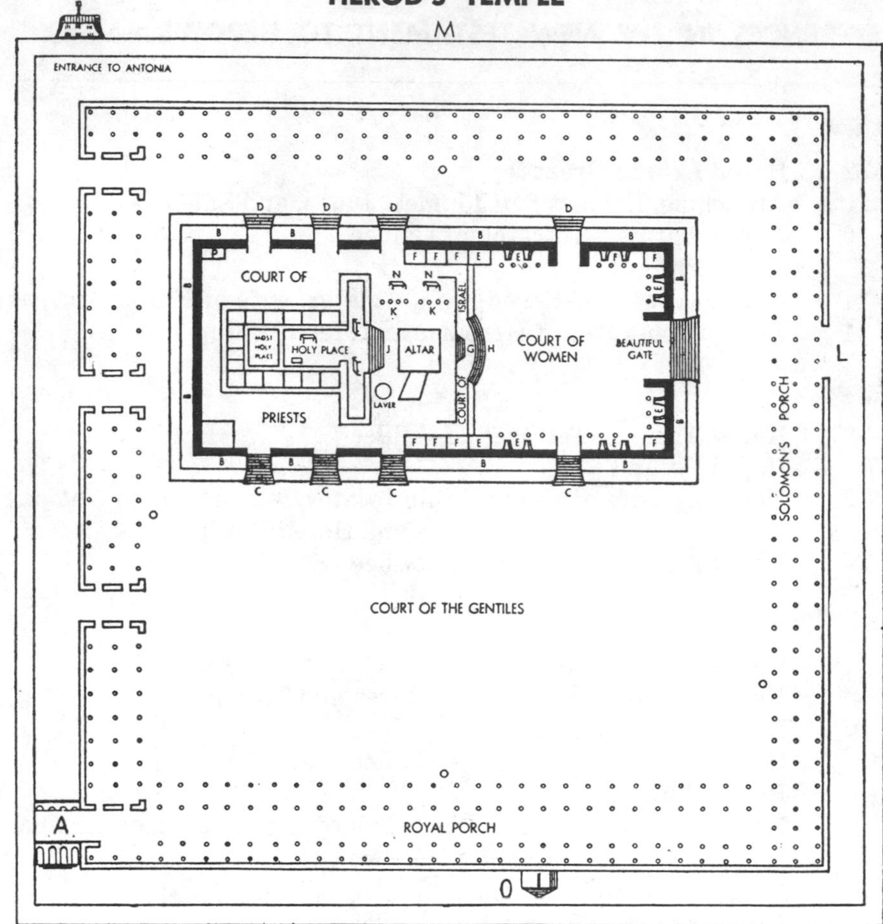

HEROD'S TEMPLE, DESTROYED A.D. 70

- A Royal Tyropœon Bridge
- B's Terrace or Chel—some authorities say outside of this was a low enclosure called the Soreg
- C's South Side Gates, the second on the right hand being the ancient Water Gate
- D's North Side Gates
- E's Money Chests
- F's Courts and Chambers
- G Nicanor Gate
- H Fifteen Steps of the Levites
- J Steps of the Priests
- K Rings for tying sacrificial animals
- L Shushan Gate (traditional) with arched roadway to Mount of Olives
- M To Bezetha
- N Marble Tables for cutting up sacrificial animals
- O Ophel Gate
- P Beth-Moked

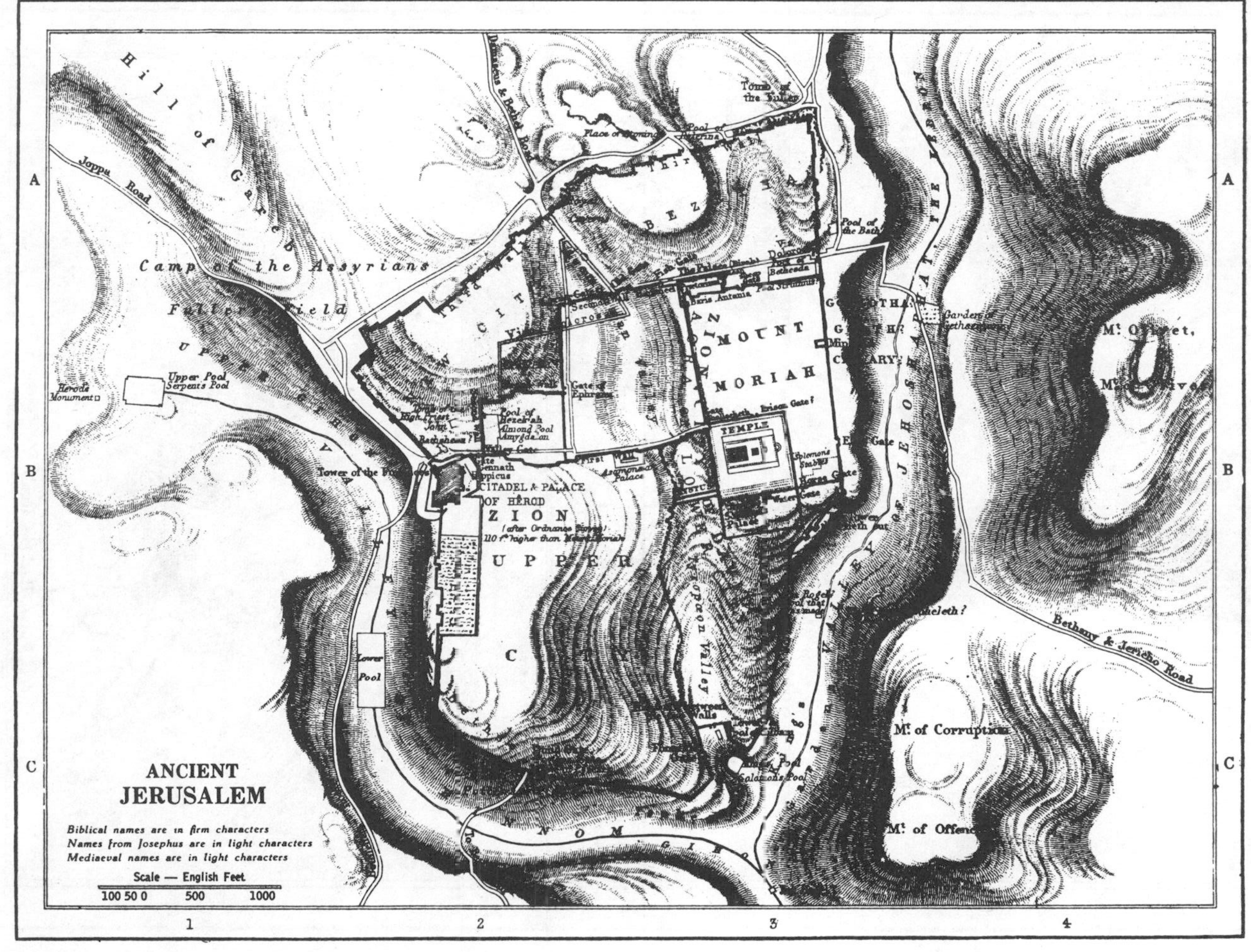
ANCIENT
JERUSALEM
Biblical names are in firm characters
Names from Josephus are in light characters
Mediaeval names are in light characters
Scale — English Feet
100 50 0 500 1000
Hill of Gareb
Camp of the Assyrians
Fuller's Field
Joppa Road
Damascus & Bethel Road
Bethany & Jericho Road
Upper Pool
Serpent's Pool
Herod's Monument
Tower of the Furnaces
CITADEL & PALACE OF HEROD
ZION
(after Ordnance Survey)
110 ft. higher than Mount Moriah
UPPER
Pool of Hezekiah
Almond Pool
Amygdalon
Valley Gate
Gate of Ephraim
Asmonean Palace
MOUNT
MORIAH
TEMPLE
Solomon's Stables
Pool of the Bath
Pool of Bethesda
GOLGOTHA?
CALVARY?
Garden of Gethsemane
Mt. Olivet,
Mt. of Olives
Tyropœon Valley
Lower Pool
Solomon's Pool
Mt. of Corruption
Mt. of Offence
A
B
C
1
2
3
4

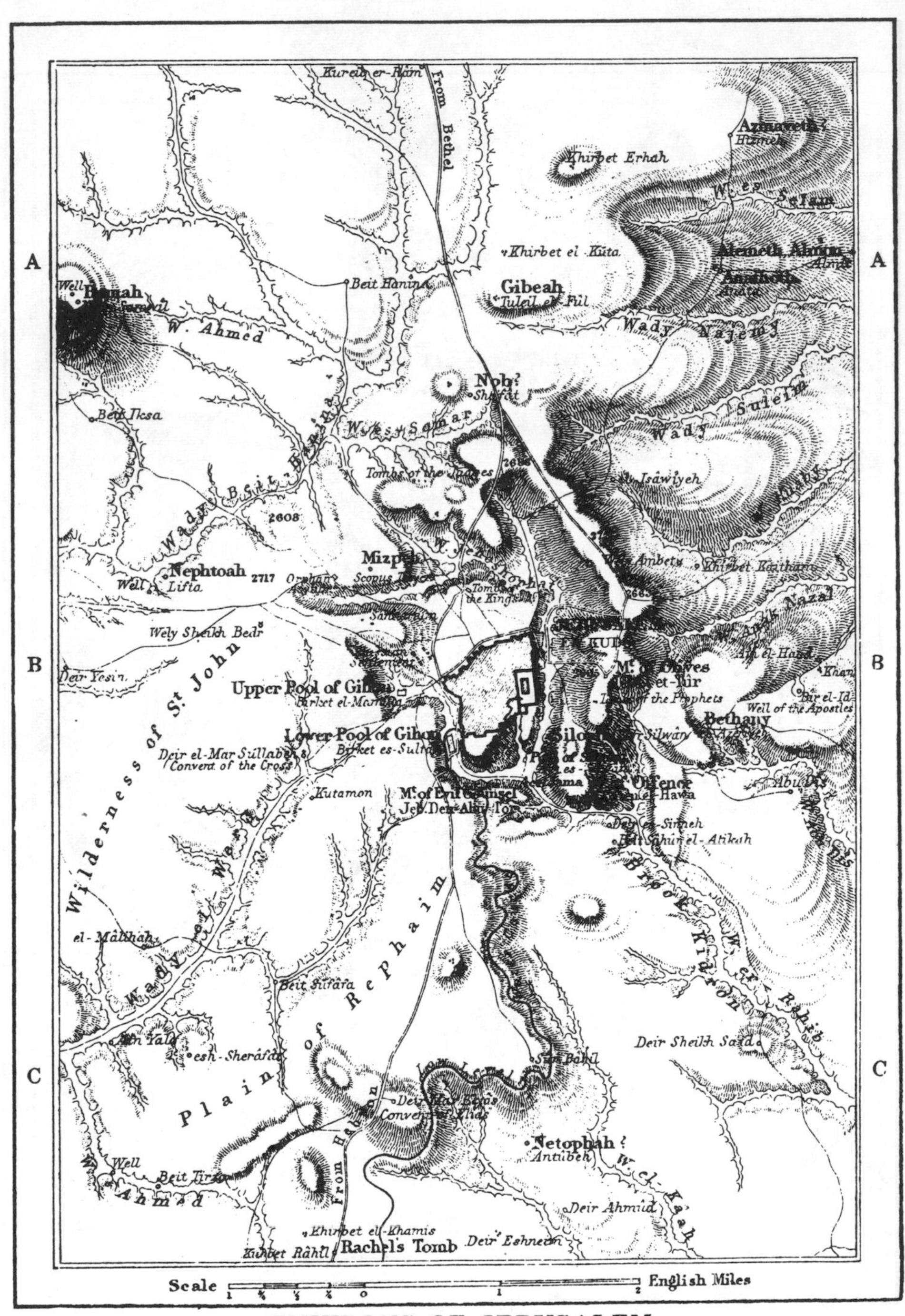

ENVIRONS OF JERUSALEM

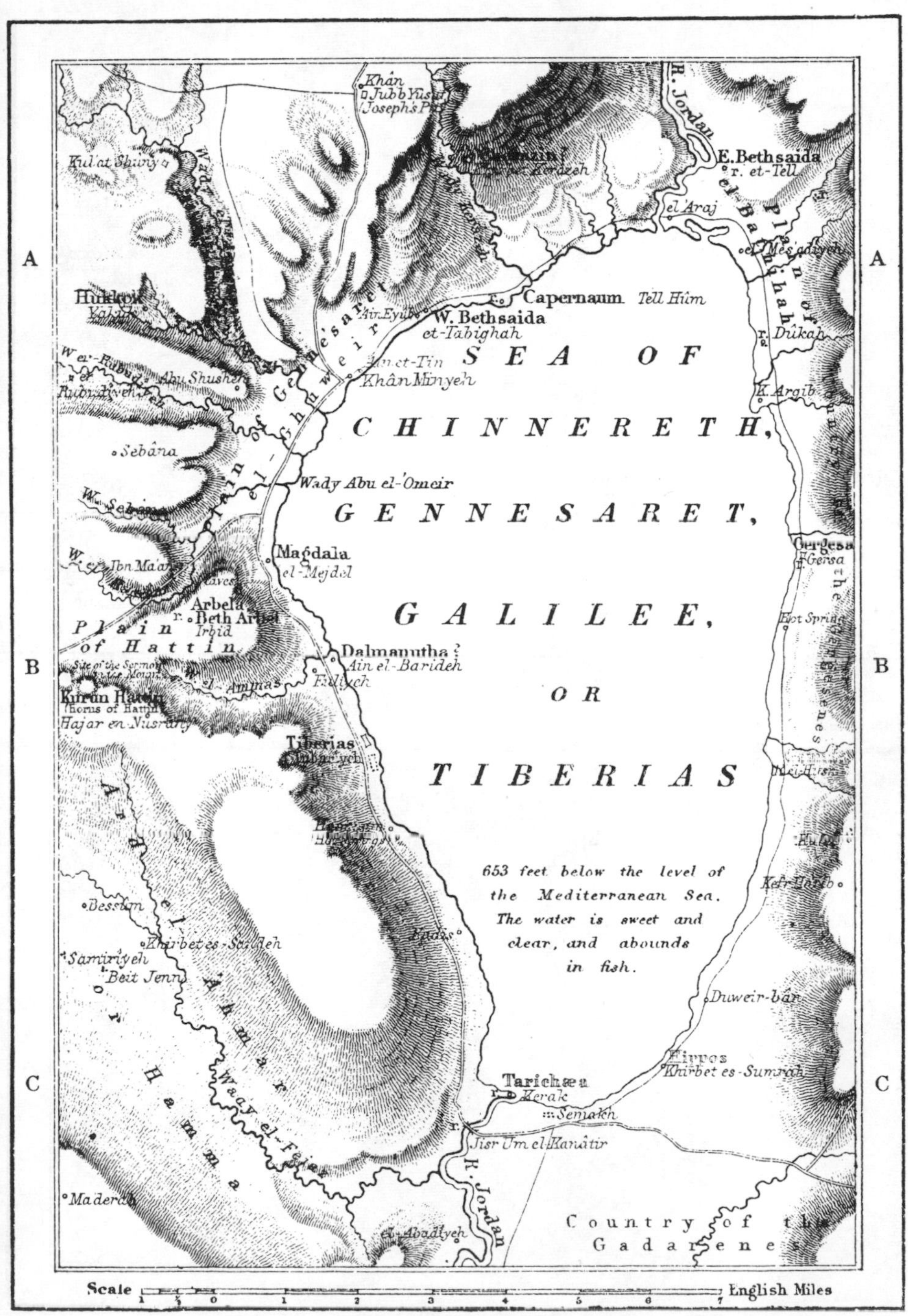

SEA OF GALILEE

Bibliography

American Tract Society, *Bible Atlas and Gazetteer,* New York, 1862.

Andrews, Samuel J., *The Life of Our Lord Upon the Earth,* rev. ed. New York, Charles Scribner's Sons, 1891.

Broadus, John A., *A Harmony of the Gospels in the Revised Version,* A. T. Robertson, rev. ed. New York, George H. Doran Company, 1920.

Case, O. D., & Company, *Case's Bible Atlas,* Hartford, 1880.

Clark, George W., *A New Harmony of the Four Gospels in English (According to the Common Version)*, rev. ed. Philadelphia, American Baptist Publication Society, 1893.

Croscup, George E., *Historical Charts of the Life and Ministry of Christ, with an Outline Harmony of the Gospels.* Philadelphia, The Sunday School Times Company, 1912.

Dickson, John A., Publishing Company, *The New Indexed Bible,* rev. ed. Chicago, 1923.

Edersheim, Alfred, *The Temple, Its Ministry and Services as They Were at the Time of Jesus Christ.* New York, Fleming H. Revell Company, 1874.

Eyre and Spottiswoode, *The E. & S. Teacher's Edition, The Holy Bible (Authorized Version)*. London, 1894.

Eyre and Spottiswoode, *The Sunday School Centenary Bible, The Holy Bible (Authorized Version)*, Variorum Teacher's Edition. London, 1880.

Eyre and Spottiswoode, *The Variorum Teacher's Edition, of The Holy Bible (Authorized Version)*, Variorum Reference Edition. London, 1893.

Farrar, Frederick W., *The Herods.* New York, Thomas Whittaker.

Josephus, *Antiquities of the Jews,* trans. by Havercamp, rev. ed. New York, Bigelow, Brown & Co., Inc.

Nelson, Thomas, & Sons, *A Combined Concordance to the Bible, Dictionary of Proper Names, and Subject Index, to The Holy Bible (King James Version)*. New York.

Robertson, A. T., *A Harmony of the Gospels for Students of the Life of Christ* (Based on the Broadus Harmony in the Revised Version). New York, Richard R. Smith, Inc., 1922.

Robinson, Edward, *A Harmony of the Four Gospels in English (According to the Common Version)*, 11th ed. rev. Boston, Crocker & Brewster 1846.

Robinson, Edward, *A Harmony of the Four Gospels in English (According to the Common Version)*, M. B. Riddle, rev. ed. Boston, Houghton, Mifflin and Company, 1886.

Smith, Hyrum M., and Sjodahl, Janne M., *Doctrine and Covenants Commentary,* Salt Lake City, The Deseret News Press, 1919.

Stevens, William Arnold, and Burton, Ernest DeWitt, *A Harmony of the Gospels for Historical Study,* 12th ed. rev. New York, Charles Scribner's Sons, 1904.

Talmage, James E., *Jesus the Christ,* Salt Lake City, The Deseret News Press, 1915.

Bibliography